Freedom on My Mind

The Columbia Documentary History of the African American Experience

Manning Marable
General Editor

Nishani Frazier and John McMillian
Assistant Editors

Columbia University Press
New York

Columbia University Press
Publishers Since 1893
New York Chichester, West Sussex

ISBN 0-231-10890-7

The Library of Congress Cataloging-in-Publication data is available under LCCN 2003051605.

Columbia University Press books are printed on permanent and durable acid-free paper.

Printed in the United States of America

c 10 9 8 7 6 5 4 3 2 1

Contents

Introduction

Let America be America again.
Let it be the dream it used to be. . . .

(America never was America to me.). . . .

O, yes,
I say it plain,
America never was America to me,
And yet I swear this oath—
America will be!

Langston Hughes,
"Let America Be America Again"

The central idea behind the long history of people of African descent in the Americas is the constant struggle for freedom. In the British colonies that later became the United States, enslaved Africans almost immediately encountered an existence that denied the legality not only of their citizenship but of their reality as human beings as well. Consequently, over the course of many generations, the Africans who gradually became African Americans forged their own culture, rituals, and traditions, which provided a sense of purpose and existential meaning for themselves and for their children yet to be born. The quest for freedom was expressed culturally in thousands of complex and sometimes even contradictory ways.

It is, however, crucial to understand that black and white Americans did not understand "freedom" in the same ways. Eventually, blacks and whites would come to speak the same language and one day would be governed theoretically by the same sets of laws, but we would continue to perceive the meaning and content of "freedom" in fundamentally different ways. For European immigrants, the freedom of the New World primarily meant an escape from the rigid social class hierarchies and cultural restrictions of Europe. Freedom in the context of the American frontier meant individual freedom of choice about religious beliefs, unrestricted movement from place to place, and the right to own private property. For white Americans in a wilderness that was often brutal and filled with physical hardships, freedom came to mean the exploitation of the land's natural resources. Freedom was essentially a deeply personal and individualistic sense of liberty and entitlement, the power to determine one's destiny without unnecessary interference by governmental authorities. It was perhaps inevitable, therefore, that European colonists convinced themselves that the Africans who had been involuntarily imported to labor in their fields and homes were not fully human, that their color and physical features provided a handy justification for defining them as property for life.

Freedom on My Mind is an anthology that was constructed primarily to present the subaltern view of American freedom, a narrative of struggle and sacrifice not from the top down but from the bottom up. The inspiration for producing this work, however, came nearly two decades ago in a conversation with the famous West Indian intellectual C.L.R. James. In the summer of 1985, I spent a better part of a day in a private dialogue with James in his small, third-floor flat in Brixton. I asked James what he regretted most about the body of his massive published works—from the novel *Minty Alley* to the *Black Jacobins*, a brilliant history of the black slave revolution in Haiti, to his foundational work of cultural studies, *Beyond a Boundary*. James replied that, with some notable exceptions, too much of his earlier work reflected a narrowly partisan, ideological character, which he now regretted. At first, I took James's remarks to mean that his ideological adherence to Trotskyist Marxism in the 1930s and 1940s had tainted his writing style with a polemical or dogmatic character. But over the years, I began to acquire a deeper understanding of what James had meant.

In James's *Beyond a Boundary*, he presents the question "What do men live by?" James wrote a detailed study of the sport of cricket as a way of unearthing the West Indian people's cultural materiality and consciousness of resistance under the hegemony of British colonialism. It is here in what could be termed the "living space" the various realms of daily life and interaction, that politics first takes shape. James suggests that politics is much more than the realization of specific interests expressed in the calculated actions of constituencies or well-defined groups. Rather, for oppressed people, it is usually expressed through their imagination as creative possibilities. When the real world presents itself to the oppressed as a series of almost impenetrable barriers, hierarchies of authority and power that cannot be overcome, all that is left is the dream of an alternative existence. In the context of enslavement, therefore, African Americans were forced to dream of a freedom that did not yet exist but could one day only through their collective actions.

This subaltern approach to the reconstruction of American freedom from the vantage point of enslaved Africans admitted has certain limitations. As Amiri Baraka has critically observed, the mainstream versions of the American experience are anchored to "the hopeless hypothesis that no one is supposed to remember that for almost three centuries there was slavery in America"—and that whites were the masters and blacks, the slaves.[1] We lack a vivid account of the day that a Dutch ship brought the first "twenty and odd negroes" to the shores of Jamestown, Virginia, in 1619. Although their fate was largely tied to that of white indentured servants, their black skins tarnished them with an added badge of exploitation and subordination from the very beginning. And we all know what happened next; the contours of African American history include the nightmarish ordeal of the Middle Passage, the institutionalization of slavery, the trying adjustment to North American life as a "despised minority," and the battle for freedom that has in many different ways been fought, each in a variety of fashions. "The history of the American Negro," the great W.E.B. Du Bois remarked, "is the history of . . . strife."[2]

Du Bois's insight also helps to illustrate how African Americans endeavored to illustrate through their examples of resistance what a higher, richer interpretation of American freedom and democracy could be. Especially since the Black Power struggles of the 1960s, from which sprang an unprecedented demand for attention to African American history, scholars have lined the shelves with books that document the sundry ways that blacks have tried to force white Americans to live up to their own highest ideals (and the ways that whites, mostly for venal reasons, have failed to do so). But as Ralph Ellison once asked, "Can a people live and develop for over three hundred years simply by *reacting*?" Or, rather, have African Americans "at least helped to create themselves out of what they found around them?"[3] Of course, the respective answers are no and yes. However much themes of struggle and protest have informed black history, it would be absurd to suggest they have encompassed black life itself! Such a claim would deny the fullness of the humanity that African Americans share with all other human societies. Therefore, *Freedom on My Mind* endeavors to illustrate and document the innumerable connections between culture and resistance—between humor and anguish, comedy and tragedy, as African Americans made themselves as a people.There is a long and very rich black intellectual tradition in the United States dating back over two centuries. Consequently, it should not be surprising that two black anthologies were published as early as the nineteenth century.[4] A few collections showcasing the earliest representations of black literature appeared in the 1920s and 1930s, and Alain Locke's landmark anthology, *The New Negro* (1925), captured the flowering of what became known as the Harlem Renaissance. But the first comprehensive, multigenre collection of black writing, *The Negro Caravan*, did not appear until 1941. Edited by Sterling A. Brown, Arthur P. Davis, and Ulysses Lee, this tribute to black literary achievement helped to pioneer the study of Negro folk literature and probably did more to establish the African American canon than any other single work. But not even this was enough to countermand the prevailing racist assumptions, exaggerations, and stereotypes that relegated the study of black history and life to a backwater of white academia—a sad state of affairs that remained in place until the 1960s and early 1970s.

When "We Shall Overcome" rapidly evolved into demands for black empowerment on white campuses "by any means necessary," white scholars and students scrambled to gain new clarity and insights into a "Negro problem" that they had mistakenly thought they already knew. Black Studies programs mushroomed at universities across the country, and books on black history became a minor cottage industry. Although the Black Power movement inspired several classic works in African American Studies, it also opened the floodgates to a welter of African American anthologies that clearly reflect the haste with which they were produced, and which generally ignored the contributions of black women writers. All of which is to say, simply, that inclusive, multigenre collections of African American writing—anthologies that reflect the diversity of black history, the various stages in racial consciousness, and the expansion of the African American canon—represent a new and long overdue trend. Along with such recent milestones as *The Norton Anthology of American Literature* (1997), *The Oxford Companion to African-American Literature* (1997), *Africana Encarta* (2000), and *Let Nobody Turn Us Around: Voices of Resistance, Reform and Renewal* (2000), *Freedom on My Mind* is part of a larger effort to create a shared platform of knowledge and information about black culture. In collecting over one hundred speeches, autobiographies, academic essays, interviews, letters, editorials, political documents, poems, lyrics, sermons, folk tales (and more), this volume attempts to provide a broad outline of the historical and cultural currents of African American history and collective consciousness.

The criteria for inclusion were manifold, and some have already been suggested. First and foremost, we wanted *Freedom on My Mind* to illustrate that the politics of resistance was embedded in all aspects of what men and women lived by, to paraphrase C.L.R. James. How the politics of resistance was reflected through gender and sexuality, kinship and community, work and leisure, faith and spirituality—these were some of the topics of primary interest. Our anthology suggests that *all* black literature is political, insofar as it expresses black humanity and rebukes the tired shibboleths of African American inferiority.

Second, we agree with the criticisms of black feminists who have insisted that African American Studies must reflect a complete range of women's experiences. Although this book opens with a chapter on "Women and Gender," the contributions that women have made to African American identity, history, and consciousness have been woven into the book's fabric.

Esthetic considerations played a role in our selection of documents, but not an overriding one. To proceed otherwise would have shackled our ability to illustrate the guiding currents of thought within African American history. Literary merit has its place, and there can be no mistaking that this volume contains some of the finest stylists in the African American canon, from Phillis Wheatley to James Baldwin. But this book is not about canon formation. Decisions on which documents to include rested primarily upon their significance as cultural artifacts. To cite just one example: few readers will have heard of Nimrod Rowley, whose 1864 letter to Abraham Lincoln is so rife with grammatical errors that readers might find it difficult to comprehend; but who could tell us more about the sacrifices of black soldiers in the Civil War? However magnificent some of these documents are, they're not intended to seduce readers with their prose or to sweep them away with their narratives; rather, they are to be scrutinized, interrogated, and grappled with. Those who are patient enough to explore these primary *texts* in their social *con*texts will find that they often reveal much more than even their authors ever intended.

***

Part One of this book, "Gender, Kinship, and Community," demonstrates the incredible capacity for endurance and survival that African Americans have shown, throughout slavery and beyond. The struggles for family, the quest for identity and community, the importance of loyalty, the passing of values, and solidarity with African-descended persons across the globe—all of these have been recurring themes of the black experience. The first chapter, "Women and Gender," examines the dual burdens that black women have faced in a society that is obsessed not only with color but with gendered identities as well. Sojourner Truth speaks to the agony that slavery caused black families. More recent essays, from Frances Beal, Audre Lorde, and Barbara Smith, contend that battles against racism need to be conjoined with the fight against patriarchy. Also included are several documents that highlight the contributions and resilience of black women. So famous has been their ability to endure that Du Bois wrote a tribute "to their memory and inspiration" in his famous essay "The Damnation of Women," included herein. According to Du Bois, "No other women on earth could have emerged from the hell of force and temptation which once engulfed and still surrounds black women in America with half the modesty and womanliness that they retain."

Chapter Two, "Kinship and Community," stands as a sharp rebuke to sociological characterizations of the black family that have historically emphasized disorganization, pathology, and a "culture of poverty." There can be no doubt that the brutal weight of structural racism has for hundreds of years had disastrous consequences on the family life of black folk. But those in search of a more sociologically holistic approach to the black family, which emphasizes love and strength over victimization and damage, need look no further than, say, Lewis Williamson's account of the night his wife and children were kidnapped in the dead of night, savagely beaten, and carried off to slavery. On a tip from a sympathetic riverboat captain, Williamson wandered about the South "in the forlorn hope of lighting upon them" and ended up giving away his farm to a white neighbor in return for his assistance. It was six years before the family was reunited. Or one might turn to Henry Louis Gates's humorous, nostalgic reminiscences of the family support that anchored his Virginia childhood or Maya Angelou's inspirational poem, "From a Black Woman to a Black Man," where—once again—hardiness and stoicism emerge as themes. Writes Angelou: "The hells we have lived through and live through still / Have sharpened our senses and toughened our will."

The ways that African Americans have considered their relationship to other black persons are considered in Chapter Three, "Imagining the Black World." In the antebellum period, some African Americans argued that white Americans were so hopelessly racist that the only solution was a voluntary migration to Africa; John Russwurm and Henry McNeal Turner each make this case here. Others, such as Marcus Garvey and Paul Robeson, express their determination to fight for black liberation, not just on the U.S. mainland but also in a global context. Still others, with Audre Lorde, have questioned and redefined "what . . . Africanness could mean, within our particular communities." Countee Cullen's poem "Heritage," is in this vein. Some "three centuries removed" from "the scenes his fathers loved," the yearning, reflective narrator sits alone in a grove and wonders, "What is Africa to me?"

***

This book's middle section, "Political, Economic, and Social Justice," highlights the ways that African Americans have always been the active agents of their own liberation. African Americans have resisted oppression from the very moment of their arrival upon New World shores. Sometimes the rebellions were violent and dramatic; more often they grew out of daily struggles. What remains clear is that everyday people understood the reality of oppression that defined their existence and actively sought ways to overcome it.

Chapter Four, "Political Leadership and Social Protest," illustrates strategies of racial uplift as articulated by black elites. In the colonial era, African Americans typically couched their appeals in a language and style that would be most persuasive to colonial whites. They emphasized their religious virtue and exhorted the ideals of the American Revolution. This book reprints several formal petitions for freedom that exemplify these qualities, as well as Benjamin Banneker's famous letter to Thomas Jefferson. The antebellum period saw increased levels of militance from black abolitionists, as well as calls for African Americans to fight for the Union cause in the Civil War, here represented by Frederick Douglass's stirring essay "Men of Color, To Arms!" The debates over accommodation versus protest, which have been recurrent in African American history, are twice expressed in this chapter: first in the well-known debate between Du Bois and Booker T. Washington and then again in the twentieth century (in more nuanced form) in the dialogue between the political pragmatist Bayard Rustin and the nonviolent moralist Martin Luther King Jr. The chapter concludes with some of the stirring voices of the modern civil rights era. King's "Letter from a Birmingham Jail" outlines the case for nonviolent civil disobedience; Shirley Chisholm charges that U.S. military priorities have come at the expense of black human and civil rights; and Jesse Jackson trumpets the possibilities—still unfulfilled—of a Democratic-left coalition that would promote a restructuring of U.S. government and society and make justice a reality. "Our suffering," Jackson proclaims, "will not be in vain."

The oppressive structural racism of the modern U.S. criminal justice system is the topic of Chapter Five, "In Pursuit of Justice." During slavery, the formal power that owners had over their slaves was nearly absolute; in the immediate aftermath of slavery came the notorious "black codes," designed to anchor African Americans in peonage, along with rampant lynching and arbitrary violence. In the Jim Crow system, black defendants were routinely denied bail and tried before all-white juries without legal counsel, whereas whites who committed crimes against blacks were rarely prosecuted. Despite the legal reforms and constitutional rights achieved through civil rights struggles, African Americans are still afflicted by racism in the criminal justice system. Racial profiling and police brutality are hot-button issues in most urban centers, and a small mountain of social science literature has demonstrated the persistence of racial bias in court processing and sentencing. The historical antecedents of this oppressive situation are here described in a variety of fashions. Samuel Rinngold Ward denounces the Fugitive Slave Act of 1850, which did so much to propel the United States into a sectional crisis that preceded the Civil War. Ida B. Wells-Barnett's gripping essay "Lynch Law in All Its Phases" captures the grotesquery of lynching in the South, which cost 3,400 black lives between 1892–1930. Although the United States has long proclaimed itself to be the "land of the free and home of the brave," Wells-Barnett reminds us that from a black perspective, it has too often been a "land of lawlessness, murder, and outrage."

Given that the purpose of bringing Africans to America was to exploit their labor power, it is scarcely surprising that work, labor, and economic development have been important themes in black history. These make up the subject of Chapter Six, which reflects the misery that dawn-to-dusk work schedules inflicted upon so many slaves as well as the hardscrabble situations that blacks have had to overcome in order to earn their livings. The chapter opens with several field holler and work songs of the slave plantation that express the drudgery that marked so many millions of black lives: "Lawdy, nobody feels sorry / for the lifetime man," goes one song. Given this legacy, one might be surprised to find African Americans extolling the virtues of Calvinism as a moral system, but as Thomas McCants Stewart suggests in his essay "Industrial Education for the Negro," many ex-slaves believed that technical training, disciplined hard work, and menial labor were propitious to black advancement. Those who graduated from the Hampton Institute, he wrote, were ready to engage in the "battle of life." In "Song to a Negro Wash-Woman," Langston Hughes pays tribute to the otherwise unheralded work of so many black women, whose daily toils were so poignant that even he was at a loss to describe them: "Oh, wash-woman / Arms elbow-deep in white suds / Soul washed clean / I have many songs to sing you / Could I but find the words." The exploitation of black laborers in the Jim Crow South is chronicled here in the reminiscences of Richard Wright and Ned Cobb; Wright describes how the torment he received from redneck whites caused him to flee the region. Cobb tells how unscrupulous landowners denied sharecroppers a chance to succeed, regardless of their effort or productivity. Recalling one transaction, Cobb says, "I had the brains to see how [it] was runnin over me, but I had no voice on account of my color."

Several other documents showcase the ways that black workers have organized against labor market discrimination. A. Philip Randolph's "Why Should We March?" was a response to racism in the defense industries during World War Two and helped spur President Franklin Roosevelt into issuing the historic Executive Order 8802, which barred antiblack discrimination and created the Fair Employment Practices Commission. In the late 1960s and early 1970s groups like the Dodge Revolutionary Union Movement and the Coalition of Black Trade Unionists relied heavily on Marxist critiques in their attempts to revitalize the labor movement and to stir the black masses into action. Although they met with mixed success, they were among the most advanced black workers' organizations to emerge from the Black Power movement.

***

The ways that African Americans have addressed the existential imperatives of everyday life in the realms of religion and popular culture form the subject of Part Three, "Culture, Faith, and Celebration." Chapter Eight, "Popular Culture," celebrates the ways that music, sports, folklore, humor, literature, and film have been sustaining resources for black Americans. The triumphs of African Americans have always had a special place in black pop culture. Harlem's elation when Joe Louis knocked out the German Max Schmeling at Yankee Stadium in 1938 is vividly described by Richard Wright in his essay "High Tide in Harlem." At the announcement of Louis's victory, over a hundred thousand African Americans "surged out of taprooms, flats, restaurants, and filled the streets and sidewalks, like the Mississippi River overflowing in flood-time," Wright reports. "In their joy they were feeling an impulse which only the oppressed can feel to the full. They wanted to fling the heavy burden out of their hearts and embrace the world." A famous folktale, "All God's

Chillen Had Wings," tells of black slaves who literally flew away from their vicious drivers, laughing, clapping, and singing as they made their escape. But other vehicles of cultural expression in this chapter articulate black sorrow. For instance, blues lyrics from W. C. Handy and Bessie Smith express a very personal suffering. Still other documents here suggest something of what is at stake when we talk about black popular culture. James Weldon Johnson's essay "The Dilemmas of the Negro Author" argues that black writers ought to "rise above race" to explore the universal in the human condition. Responding to the sensationalist "blaxploitation" films of the mid-1970s, Ellen Holly calls for black auteurs to present "the full spectrum of Black life in all its remarkable variety."

The book's final chapter centers upon faith and spirituality—two qualities that have always flourished in the African American community, for reasons that should be fairly obvious. During slavery, religion helped black people to endure. It gave depth and meaning to lives that might have otherwise seemed absurd and promised redemption in the afterlife. Meanwhile, free African Americans in the North founded their own churches as part of a larger effort to foster independence and empowerment. And, of course, in the postslavery era, the black church has continued to be a site of social action. But at the same time, it is important to recognize the complex diversity of spiritual experiences in the African American community.

African Americans commonly saw their own ordeals of suffering in the Old Testament stories, as evinced here by Absalom Jones's "A Thanksgiving Sermon." More recently, faith-based institutions have been fundamental to the struggle for black equality—a point that is inescapable in Martin Luther King Jr.'s sermon "The Most Durable Power." In the thick of the civil rights movement, King proclaimed, "Always be sure that you struggle with Christian methods and Christian weapons. . . . I still believe that standing up for the truth of God is the greatest thing in the world." Although Christianity has not been the only religion to resonate with African Americans, its appeal to black activists has been profound. For instance, James Cones's essay, "Black Theology and Black Power," finds Christian validation for the radical expressions of the black freedom struggle. Cornel West contends that although the black church is the "major source of political leadership" in the African American community, it must make a greater effort to address black poverty as well as the "rapacious hedonism and narcissism in late U.S. capitalist culture." Closing the chapter is a sermon by the Nation of Islam leader Louis Farrakhan. The "greatest of all religious principles," he says, "is to follow the Golden Rule: Do unto others as you would have them do unto you, and love for your brother what you love yourself."

***

Freedom on My Mind, like all other anthologies and edited volumes of this type, has a number of limitations. Perhaps chief among them are its underrepresentation of women's voices and its relative lack of contemporary sources reflecting the dynamic culture of the hip-hop generation. Many of the works we had originally selected, which addressed these concerns, were unfortunately deleted in the process of editorial revision, or the cost of permissions to reprint them in this volume was too prohibitive. The strengths of this anthology, hopefully, will outweigh its deficiencies and will hopefully provide a solid introduction to the culture and consciousness of African Americans as they struggled to find freedom for themselves and for the totality of American society.

Manning Marable, general editor
April 8, 2003

Notes

1. Leroi Jones (Amiri Baraka), *Blues People: Negro Music in America* (New York: William Morrow, 1963), 136.
2. W.E.B. Du Bois, *Souls of Black Folk* (New York: New American Library, 1969), 45.
3. Ralph Ellison, *Shadow and Act* (New York: Random House, 1963), 315.
4. The first, *Les Cenelles* (1845), was a collection of poems by New Orleans Creoles, and it completely ignored the pressing issues in contemporary black culture. The second, *Autographs for Freedom* (1853), had a different agenda; a product of the antislavery movement, its entire raison d'être was to expose its readers to the evils of slavery and proselytize for its abolition. In this context, African Americans were a people to be pitied; their interior lives were scarcely a consideration.

part 1

Gender, Kinship, and Community

chapter one

Women and Gender

one

Selected Speeches by Sojourner Truth

An antislavery and women's rights advocate, Sojourner Truth (c. 1799–1883) was among the most widely known black women of the nineteenth century. Truth commonly authenticated her remarks by recalling her experience in slavery (although she sometimes claimed her mother's experiences as her own). Her "Proceedings of the Annual Meeting of the Friends of Human Progress in Michigan" speech, delivered in Battle Creek, Michigan, on October 5, 1856, laments how female slaves had husbands and children yet no right to possess their husbands or the very children they bore.[1] Truth's second speech delivered to the Church of the Puritans in New York City on May 10, 1867, scrutinizes the rights of men and women and argues that liberty for women brings liberty for all.[2]

Born with the name Isabella in Ulster County, New York, Truth was separated form her parents as a small child, and she lived as a slave until she was emancipated by New York state law in 1827. In 1843, Truth had a powerful religious experience that convinced her to adopt her new name and work as an itinerant preacher. In Massachusetts, she met fellow abolitionists William Lloyd Garrison and Frederick Douglass, and she earned a reputation as a folksy, witty, insightful, and fiery lecturer. She continued her activism throughout the 1860s and early 1870s, and she died in Battle Creek, Michigan, in 1883.

Proceedings of the Annual Meeting of the Friends of Human Progress in Michigan

As you were speakin this mornin of little children, I was lookin round and thinkin it was most beautiful. But I have had children and yet never owned one, no never owned one; and of such ther's millions—who goes to teach dem? who goes to teach dem? You have teachers for your children, but who will teach de poor slave children?

I want to know what has become of the love I ought to have for my children? I did have love for them but what has become of it. I cannot tell you. I have had two husbands yet I never possessed one of my own. I have had five children and never could take any one of dem up and say, "my child" or "my children," unless it was when no one could see me.

I believe in Jesus, and I was forty years a slave, but I did not know how dear to me was my posterity, I was so beclouded and crushed. But how good and wise is God, for if the slaves knowed what that true condition was, it would be more than de mine could bear. While de race is sold of all dere rights—what is dare on God's footstool to bring dem up? Has not God given to all his creatures the same rights? How could I trable and live and speak? If I ha'nt got something to bear me up, when I'se been robbed of all my affection for my husband and my children.

My mother said when we were sold, we must ask God to make our masters good, and I asked who he was. She told me He sit up in the sky. When I was sol I had a severe, hard master, and I was tied up in de barn and whipped. Oh! 'till de blood run down on de floor; and I asked God, why don't you come 'nd 'leave me—if I was you, and you'se tied up so, I'd do it for you.

First Annual Meeting of the American Equal Rights Association (Second Speech)

Well, children—I know it is hard for men to give up entirely. They must run in the old track. I was amused how men speaks up for one another. They cannot bear that a woman should say anything about the man, but they will stand here and take up the time in man's cause. But we are going, tremble or no tremble. Men is trying to help us. I know that all—the spirit they have got; and they cannot help us much until some of the spirit is taken out of them that belongs among the women. Men have got their rights, and women has not got their rights. That is the trouble. When woman gets her rights man will be right. How beautiful that will be. Then it will be peace on earth and good will to men. But it cannot be that until it be right. I am glad that men got here. They have to do it. I know why they edge off, for there is a power they cannot gainsay or resist. It will come. A woman said to me, "Do you think it will come in ten or twenty years?" Yes, it will come quickly. It must come. And now then the waters is troubled, and now is the time to step into the pool. There is a great deal now with the minds, and now is the time to start forth. I was going to say that it was said to me some time ago that "a woman was not fit to have any rule. Do you want women to rule? They ain't fit. Don't you know that a woman had seven devils in her, and do you suppose that a man should put her to rule in the government?" "Seven devils is of no account" said I, "just behold, the man had a legion." They never thought about that. A man had a legion and the devils didn't know where to go. That was the trouble. They asked if they might get among the swine; they thought it was about as good a place as where they came from. Why didn't the devils ask to go among the sheep? But no. But that may have been selfish of the devils and certainly a man has a little touch of that selfishness that don't want to give the women their right. I have been twitted many times about this, and I thought how queer it is that men don't think of that. Never mind. Look at the woman after all, the woman when they were cast out, and see how much she loved Jesus, and how she followed, and stood and waited for him. That was the faithfulness of a woman. You cannot find any faith of man like that, go where you will. After those devils had gone out of the man he wanted to follow Jesus. But what did Jesus say? He said: "Better go back and tell what had been done for you!" He didn't seem as he wanted him to come along right away. He was to be clean after that. Look at that and look at the woman; what a mighty courage. When Mary stood and looked for Jesus, the man looked and didn't stop long enough to find out whether He was there or not; but when the woman stood there (blessed be God, I think I can see her!) she staid until she knew where He was, and said: "I will carry Him away!" Was woman true? She guarded it. The truth will reign triumphant. I want to see, before I leave here—I want to see equality. I want to see women have their rights, and then there will be no more war. All the fighting has been for selfishness. They wanted something more than their own, or to hold something that was not their own; but when we have woman's rights, there is nothing to fight for. I have got all I want, and you have got all you want, and what do you fight for? All the battles that have even been was for selfishness—for a right that belonged to some one else, or fighting for his own right. The great fight was to keep the rights of the poor colored people. That made a great battle. And now I hope that this will be the last battle that will be in the world. Fighting for rights. And there never will be a fight without it is a fight for rights. See how beautiful it is! It covers the whole ground. We ought to have it all finished up now. Let us finish it up so that there be no more fighting. I have faith in God, and there is truth in humanity. Be strong women! blush not! tremble not! I know men will get up and brat, brat, brat, brat about something which does not amount to anything except talk. We want to carry the point to one particular thing, and that is woman's rights, for nobody has any business with a right that belongs to her. I can make use of my own right. I want the same use of the same right. Do you want it? Then get it. If men had not taken something that did not belong to them they would not fear. But they tremble! They dodge! We will have nothing owned by anybody. That is the time you will be a man, if you don't get scared before it goes to parties. I want you to look at it and be men and women. Men speak great lies, and it has made a great sore, but it will soon heal up. For I know when men, good men, discuss sometimes, that they say something or other and then take it half back. You must make a little allowance. I hear them say good enough at first, but then there was a going back a little more like the old times. It is hard for them to get out of it. Now we will help you out, if you want to get out. I want you to keep a good faith and good courage. And I am going round after I get my business settled and get more equality. People in the North, I am going round to lecture on human rights. I will shake every place I go to.

Notes

1. First appeared in the Salem, Ohio, *Anti-Slavery Bugle* (November 8, 1856), p. 4.
2. This version of "First Annual Meeting of the American Equal Rights Association (Second Speech)" first appeared in the *National Anti-Slavery Standard* (June 1, 1867), p. 3.

Source

Sojourner Truth, "Proceedings of the Annual Meeting of the Friends of Human Progress in Michigan" and "First Annual Meeting of the American Equal Rights Association (Second Speech)," in Suzanne Pullon Fitch and Roseann M. Mandziuk, eds., *Sojourner Truth as Orator* (Westport, Conn.: Greenwood Press, 1997), 117–18 and 127–28.

Selected Bibliography

Bernard, Jacqueline. *Journey Toward Freedom: The Story of Sojourner Truth.* New York: Feminist Press at City University of New York, 1990.

Gilbert, Oliver. *Narrative of Sojourner Truth: A Bondswoman of Olden Time, with a History of Her Labors and Correspondence Drawn from Her Book of Life.* New York: Penguin, 1988.

Mabee, Carlton (with Susan Mabee-Newhouse). *Sojourner Truth: Slave, Prophet, Legend.* New York: New York University Press, 1993.

Oritz, Victoria. *Sojourner Truth, A Self-Made Woman.* Philadelphia: Lippincot, 1974.

Painter, Nell Irvin. *Sojourner Truth, A Life, A Symbol.* New York: W. W. Norton, 1996.

Yellin, Jean Fagan. *Women and Sisters: The Antislavery Feminists in American Culture.* New Haven, Conn.: Yale University Press, 1989.

two

The Jealous Mistress

Harriet Ann Jacobs (1813–1897) wrote one of the most important slave narratives in American history. Her memoir marked the first occasion in which a slave narrator offered firsthand testimony on the sexual abuse of women slaves—a topic so scandalous that other writers were too timid to bring it up. Its publication made Jacobs a minor celebrity, and along with Frederick Douglass, she is thought to be among the most accomplished prose stylists of all the antebellum slave narrators.

Born a slave in Edenton, North Carolina, Jacobs was orphaned as a child, and in 1825 she was placed in the custody of Dr. James Norcom, an abusive sexual predator. Jacobs later became involved with a white attorney, Samuel Tredwell Sawyer, with whom she had two children. In 1835, Jacobs went into hiding for seven years, and in 1842 she finally escaped slavery and moved to New York. Her memoir, *Incidents in the Life of a Slave Girl,* was edited by Lydia Maria Child, an abolitionist who was thought by many to be the book's primary author. Historians have since proved that Jacobs did indeed write the book herself, with only minimal assistance from Child. She died in Washington, D.C., in 1897.

I would ten thousand times rather that my children should be the half-starved paupers of Ireland than to be the most pampered among the slaves of America. I would rather drudge out my life on a cotton plantation, till the grave opened to give me rest, than to live with an unprincipled master and a jealous mistress. The felon's home in a penitentiary is preferable. He may repent, and turn from the error of his ways, and so find peace; but it is not so with a favorite slave. She is not allowed to have any pride of character. It is deemed a crime in her to wish to be virtuous.

Mrs. Flint possessed the key to her husband's character before I was born.[1] She might have used this knowledge to counsel and to screen the young and the innocent among her slaves; but for them she had no sympathy. They were the objects of her constant suspicion and malevolence. She watched her husband with unceasing vigilance; but he was well practised in means to evade it. What he could not find opportunity to say in words he manifested in signs. He invented more than were ever thought of in a deaf and dumb asylum. I let them pass, as if I did not understand what he meant; and many were the curses and threats bestowed on my for my stupidity. One day he caught me teaching myself to write. He frowned, as if he was not well pleased; but I suppose he came to the conclusion that such an accomplishment might help to advance his favorite scheme. Before long, notes were often slipped into my hand. I would return them, saying "I can't read them, sir." "Can't you?" he replied; "then I must read them to you." He always finished the reading by asking, "Do you understand?" Sometimes he would complain of the heat of the tea room, and order his supper to be placed on a small table in the piazza. He would seat himself there with a well-satisfied smile, and tell me to stand by and brush away the flies. He would eat very slowly, pausing between the mouthfuls. These intervals were employed in describing the happiness I was so foolishly throwing away, and in threatening me with the penalty that finally awaited my stubborn disobedience. He boasted much of the forbearance he had exercised towards me, and reminded me that there was a limit to his patience. When I succeeded in avoiding opportunities for him to talk to me at home, I was ordered to come to his office, to do some errand. When there, I was obliged to stand and listen to such language as he saw fit to address to me. Sometimes I so openly expressed my contempt for him that he would become violently enraged, and I wondered why he did not strike me. Circumstanced as he was, he probably thought it was better policy to be forbearing. But the state of things grew worse and worse daily. In desperation I told him that I must and would apply to my grandmother for protection. He threatened me with death, and worse than death, if I made any complaint to her. Strange to say, I did not despair. I was naturally of a buoyant disposition, and always I had a hope of somehow getting out of his clutches. Like many a poor simple slave before me, I trusted that some threads of joy would yet be woven into my dark destiny.

I had entered my sixteenth year, and every day it became more apparent that my presence was intolerable to Mrs. Flint. Angry words frequently passed between her and her husband. He had never punished me himself, and he would not allow any body else to punish me. In that respect, she was never satisfied; but, in her angry moods, no terms were too vile for her to bestow upon me. Yet I, whom she detested so bitterly, had far more pity for her than he had, whose duty it was to make her life happy. I never wronged her, or wished to wrong her; and one word of kindness from her would have brought me to her feet.

After repeated quarrels between the doctor and his wife, he announced his intention to take his youngest daughter, then four years old, to sleep in his apartment. It was necessary that a servant should sleep in the same room, to be on hand if the child stirred. I was selected for that office, and informed for what purpose that arrangement had been made. By managing to keep within sight of people, as much as possible, during the day time, I had hitherto succeeded in eluding my master, though a razor was often held to my throat to force me to change this line of policy. At night I slept by the side of my great aunt, where I felt safe. He was too prudent to come into her room. She was an old woman, and had been in the family many years. Moreover, as a married man, and a professional man, he deemed it necessary to save appearances in some degree. But he resolved to remove the obstacle in the way of his scheme; and he thought he had planned it so that he should evade suspicion. He was well aware how much I prized my refuge by the side of my old aunt, and he determined to dispossess me of it. The first night the doctor had the little child in his room alone. The next morning, I was ordered to take my station as nurse the following night. A kind Providence interposed in my favor. During the day Mrs. Flint heard of his new arrangement and a storm followed. I rejoiced to hear it rage.

After a while my mistress sent for me to come to her room. Her first question was, "Did you know you were to sleep in the doctor's room?"

"Yes, ma'am."

"Who told you?"

"My master."

"Will you answer truly all the questions I ask?"

"Yes, ma'am."

"Tell me, then, as you hope to be forgiven, are you innocent of what I have accused you?"

"I am."

She handed me a Bible, and said, "Lay your hand on your heart, kiss this holy book, and swear before God that you tell me the truth."

I took the oath she required, and I did it with a clear conscience.

"You have taken God's holy word to testify your innocence," she said. "If you have deceived me, beware! Now take this stool, sit down, look me directly in the face, and tell me all that has passed between your master and you."

I did as she ordered. As I went on with my account her color changed frequently, she wept, and sometimes groaned. She spoke in tones so sad, that I was touched by her grief. The tears came to my eyes; but I was soon convinced that her emotions arose from anger and wounded pride. She felt that her marriage vows were desecrated, her dignity insulted; but she had no compassion for the poor victim of her husband's perfidy. She pitied herself as a martyr; but she was incapable of feeling for the condition of shame and misery in which her unfortunate, helpless slave was placed.

Yet perhaps she had some touch of feeling for me; for when the conference was ended, she spoke kindly, and promised to protect me. I should have been much comforted by this assurance if I could have had confidence in it; but my experiences in slavery had filled me with distrust. She was not a very refined woman, and had not much control over her passions. I was an object of her jealousy, and consequently, of her hatred; and I knew I could not expect kindness or confidence from her under the circumstances in which I was placed. I could not blame her. Slaveholders' wives feel as other women would under similar circumstances. The fire of her temper kindled from small sparks, and now the flame became so intense that the doctor was obliged to give up his intended arrangement.

I knew I had ignited the torch, and I expected to suffer for it afterwards; but I felt too thankful to my mistress for the timely aid she rendered me to care much about that. She now took me to sleep in a room adjoining her own. There I was an object of her especial care, though not of her especial comfort, for she spent many a sleepless night to watch over me. Sometimes I woke up, and found her bending over me. At other times she whispered in my ear, as though it was her husband who was speaking to me, and listened to hear what I would answer. If she startled me, on such occasions, she would glide stealthily away; and the next morning she would tell me I had been talking in my sleep, and ask who I was talking to. At last, I began to be fearful for my life. It had been often threatened; and you can imagine, better than I can describe, what an unpleasant sensation it must produce to wake up in the dead of the night and find a jealous woman bending over you. Terrible as this experience was, I had fears that it would give place to one more terrible.

My mistress grew weary of her vigils; they did not prove satisfactory. She changed her tactics. She now tried the trick of accusing my master of crime, in my presence, and gave my name as the author of the accusation. To my utter astonishment, he replied, "I don't believe it; but if she did acknowledge it, you tortured her into exposing me." Tortured into exposing him! Truly, Satan had no difficulty in distinguishing the color of his soul! I understood his object in making this false representation. It was to show me that I gained nothing by seeking the protection of my mistress; that the power was still all in his own hands. I pitied Mrs. Flint. She was a second wife, many years the junior of her husband; and the hoary-headed miscreant was enough to try the patience of a wiser and better woman. She was completely foiled, and knew not how to proceed. She would gladly have had me flogged for my supposed false oath; but, as I have already stated, the doctor never allowed any one to whip me. The old sinner was politic. The application of the lash might have led to remarks that would have exposed him in the eyes of his children and grandchildren. How often did I rejoice that I lived in a town where all the inhabitants knew each other! If I had been on a remote plantation, or lost among the multitude of a crowded city, I should not be a living woman at this day.

The secrets of slavery are concealed like those of the Inquisition. My master was, to my knowledge, the father of eleven slaves. But did the mothers dare to tell who was the father of their children? Did the other slaves dare to allude to it, except in whispers among themselves? No, indeed! They knew too well the terrible consequences.

My grandmother could not avoid seeing things which excited her suspicions. She was uneasy about me, and tried various ways to buy me; but the never-changing answer was always repeated: "Linda does not belong to *me*. She is my daughter's property, and I have no legal right to sell her."[2] The conscientious man! He was too scrupulous to *sell* me; but he had no scruples whatever about committing a much greater wrong against the helpless young girl placed under his guardianship, as his daughter's property. Sometimes my persecutor would ask me whether I would like to be sold, I told him I would rather be sold to any body than to lead such a life as I did. On such occasions he would assume the air of a very injured individual, and reproach me for my ingratitude. "Did I not take you into the house, and make you the companion of my own children?" he would say. "Have I ever treated you like a negro? I have never allowed you to be punished, not even to please your mistress. And this is the recompense I get, you ungrateful girl!" I answered that he had reasons of his own for screening me from punishment, and that the course he pursued made my mistress hate me and persecute me. If I wept, he would say. "Poor child! Don't cry! don't cry! I will make peace for you with your mistress. Only let me arrange matters in my own way. Poor, foolish girl! you don't know what is for your own good. I would cherish you. I would make a lady of you. Now go, and think of all I have promised you."

I did think of it.

Reader, I draw no imaginary pictures of southern homes. I am telling you the plain truth. Yet when victims make their escape from this wild beast of Slavery, northerners consent to act the part of bloodhounds, and hunt the poor fugitive back into his den, "full of dead men's bones, and all uncleanness." Nay, more, they are not only willing, but proud, to give their daughters in marriage to slaveholders. The poor girls have romantic notions of a sunny clime, and of the flowering vines that all the year round shade a happy home. To what disappointments are they destined! The young wife soon learns that the husband in whose hands she has placed her happiness pays no regard to his marriage vows. Children of every shade of complexion play with her own fair babies, and too well she knows that they are born unto him of his own household. Jealousy and hatred enter the flowery home, and it is ravaged of its loveliness.

Southern women often marry a man knowing that he is the father of many little slaves. They do not trouble themselves about it. They regard such children as property, as marketable as the pigs on the plantation; and it is seldom that they do not make them aware of this by passing them into the slave-trader's hands as soon as possible, and thus getting them out of their sight. I am glad to say there are some honorable exceptions.

I have myself known two southern wives who exhorted their husbands to free those slaves towards whom they stood in a "parental relation": and their request was granted. These husbands blushed before the superior nobleness of their wives' natures. Though they had only counselled them to do that which it was their duty to do, it commanded their respect, and rendered their conduct more exemplary. Concealment was at an end, and confidence took the place of distrust.

Though this bad institution deadens the moral sense, even in white women, to a fearful extent, it is not altogether extinct. I have heard southern ladies say of Mr. Such a one, "He not only thinks it no disgrace to be the father of those little niggers, but he is not ashamed to call himself their master. I declare, such things ought not to be tolerated in any decent society."

Notes

1. A pseudonym for the real-life wife of Dr. James Norcum, who owned Jacobs and attempted to sexually abuse her.
2. "Linda Brent" was the pseudonym that Jacobs used when she wrote her memoir.

Source

Harriet Jacobs, "The Jealous Mistress" (1861; reprinted in Deirdre Mullane, ed., *Three Hundred Years of African-American Writing,* 162–67 [New York: Anchor Books, 1993]).

Selected Bibliography

Andrews, William L. *To Tell a Free Story: The First Century of African-American Autobiography.* Urbana: University of Illinois Press, 1986.

Braxton, Joanne M. *Black Women Writing Autobiography: A Tradition Within a Tradition.* Philadelphia: Temple University Press, 1989.

Fox-Genovese, Elizabeth. *Within the Plantation Household: Black and White Women of the Old South.* Chapel Hill: University of North Carolina Press, 1988.

Jacobs, Harriet A. *Incidents in the Life of a Slave Girl: Written by Herself.* Edited by Maria L. Child. Cambridge, Mass.: Harvard University Press, 1987.

Peterson, Carla L. *"Doers of the Word": African American Women and Speakers in the North (1830–1880).* New York: Oxford University Press, 1995.

Smith, Valerie. *Self-Discovery and Authority in Afro-American Narrative.* Cambridge, Mass.: Harvard University Press, 1987.

three

Womanhood: A Vital Element in the Regeneration and Progress of a Race

Anna Julia Cooper (c. 1858–1964) was a well-known feminist, writer, scholar, and educator. Her speech "Womanhood, A Vital Element in the Regeneration and Progress of a Race" was read before a group of African American clergy at the Protestant Episcopal Church in Washington, D.C., in 1886. In her elegant and erudite style for which she was known, Cooper cited the important roles that women have played in history and appealed to ministers, teachers, and enlightened men to help elevate the condition of women in postbellum America.

Born Annie Julia Haywood in Raleigh, North Carolina, Cooper did her undergraduate work at Oberlin College and earned an M.A. there in 1887. Cooper's finest work, *A Voice From the South*, appeared in 1892. Subsequently, she served as principal of Washington, D.C.'s famous M Street (now Paul Laurence Dunbar) High School. In 1897 she became the only woman elected to membership in the American Negro Academy, a prestigious black think tank, and in 1925 (at the age of sixty-six) she became only the fourth black American woman

Read before the convocations of colored clergy of the Protestant Episcopal Church at Washington. D.C., 1886 [Cooper's note].

to earn a Ph.D., receiving her degree in French from the Sorbonne, in Paris, France. She died in Washington, D.C., at the age of 105.

The two sources from which, perhaps, modern civilization has derived its noble and ennobling ideal of woman are Christianity and the Feudal System.

In Oriental countries, woman has been uniformly devoted to a life of ignorance, infamy, and complete stagnation. The Chinese shoe of today does not more entirely dwarf, cramp, and destroy her physical powers, than have the customs, laws, and social instincts, which from remotest ages have governed our sister of the East, enervated and blighted her mental and moral life.

Mahomet makes no account of woman whatever in his polity. The Koran, which, unlike our Bible, was a product and not a growth, tried to address itself to the needs of Arabian civilization as Mahomet with his circumscribed powers saw them. The Arab was a nomad. Home to him meant his present camping place. That deity who, according to our western ideals, makes and sanctifies the home, was to him a transient bauble to be toyed with so long as it gave pleasure and then to be thrown aside for a new one. As a personality, an individual soul, capable of eternal growth and unlimited development, and destined to mould and shape the civilization of the future to an incalculable extent, Mahomet did not know woman.

There was no hereafter, no paradise for her. The heaven of the Mussulman is peopled and made gladsome not by the departed wife, or sister, or mother, but by *houri*—a figment of Mahomet's brain, partaking of the ethereal qualities of angels, yet imbued with all the vices and inanity of Oriental women. The harem here, and—"dust to dust" hereafter, this was the hope, the inspiration, the *summum bonum* of the Eastern woman's life! With what result on the life of the nation, the "Unspeakable Turk," the "sick man" of modern Europe can to-day exemplify.

Says a certain writer: "The private life of the Turk is vilest of the vile, unprogressive, unambitious, and inconceivably low." And yet Turkey is not without her great men. She has produced most brilliant minds; men skilled in all the intricacies of diplomacy and statesmanship; men whose intellects could grapple with the deep problems of empire and manipulate the subtle agencies which check-mate kings. But these minds were not the normal outgrowth of a healthy trunk. They seemed rather ephemeral excrescencies which shoot far out with all the vigor and promise, apparently, of strong branches; but soon alas fall into decay and ugliness because there is no soundness in the root, no life-giving sap, permeating, strengthening, and perpetuating the whole. There is a worm at the core! The home-life is impure! and when we look for fruit, like apples of Sodom, it crumbles within our grasp into dust and ashes.

It is pleasing to turn from this effete and immobile civilization to a society still fresh and vigorous, whose seed is in itself, and whose very name is synonymous with all that is progressive, elevating and inspiring, viz., the European bud and the American flower of modern civilization.

And here let me say parenthetically that our satisfaction in American institutions rests not on the fruition we now enjoy, but springs rather from the possibilities and promise that are inherent in the system, though as yet, perhaps, far in the future.

"Happiness," says Madame de Stael, "consists not in perfections attained, but in a sense of progress, the result of our own endeavor under conspiring circumstances *toward* a goal which continually advances and broadens and deepens till it is swallowed up in the Infinite." Such conditions in embryo are all that we claim for the land of the West. We have not yet reached our ideal in American civilization. The pessimists even declare that we are not marching in that direction. But there can be no doubt that here in America is the arena in which the next triumph of civilization is to be won; and here too we find promise abundant and possibilities infinite.

Now let us see on what basis this hope for our country primarily and fundamentally rests. Can any one doubt that it is chiefly on the homelife and on the influence of good women in those homes? Says Macaulay: "You may judge a nation's rank in the scale of civilization from the way they treat their women." And Emerson, "I have thought that a sufficient measure of civilization is the influence of good women." Now this high regard for woman, this germ of a prolific idea which in our own day is bearing such rich and varied fruit, was ingrafted into European civilization, we have said, from two sources, the Christian Church and the Feudal System. For although the Feudal System can in no sense be said to have originated the idea, yet there can be no doubt that the habits of life and modes of thought to which Feudalism gave rise, materially fostered and developed it; for they gave us chivalry, than which no institution has more sensibly magnified and elevated woman's position in society.

Tacitus dwells on the tender regard for woman entertained by these rugged barbarians before they left their northern homes to overrun Europe. Old Norse legends too, and primitive poems, all breathe the same spirit of love of home and veneration for the pure and noble influence there presiding—the wife, the sister, the mother.

And when later on we see the settled life of the Middle Ages "oozing out," as M. Guizot expresses it, from the plundering and pillaging life of barbarism and crystallizing into the Feudal System, the tiger of the field is brought once more within the charmed circle of the goddesses of his castle, and his imagination weaves around them a halo whose reflection possibly has not yet altogether vanished.

It is true the spirit of Christianity had not yet put the seal of catholicity on this sentiment. Chivalry, according to Bascom, was but the toning down and softening of a rough and lawless period. It gave a roseate glow to a bitter winter's day. Those who looked out from castle windows revelled in its "amethyst tints." But God's poor, the weak, the unlovely, the common-place were still freezing and starving none the less in unpitied, unrelieved loneliness.

Respect for woman, the much lauded chivalry of the Middle Ages, meant what I fear it still means to some men in our own day—respect for the elect few among whom they expect to consort.

The idea of the radical amelioration of womankind, reverence for woman as woman regardless of rank, wealth, or culture, was to come from that rich and bounteous fountain from which flow all our liberal and universal ideas—the Gospel of Jesus Christ.

And yet the Christian Church at the time of which we have been speaking would seem to have been doing even less to protect and elevate woman than the little done by secular society. The Church as an organization committed a double offense against woman in the Middle Ages. Making of marriage a sacrament and at the same time insisting on the celibacy of the clergy and other religious orders, she gave an inferior if not an impure character to the marriage relation, especially fitted to reflect discredit on woman. Would this were all or the worst! but the Church by the licentiousness of its chosen servants invaded the household and established too often as vicious connections those relations which it forbade to assume openly and in good faith. "Thus," to use the words of our authority, "the religious corps became as numerous, as searching, and as unclean as the frogs of Egypt, which penetrated into all quarters, into the ovens and kneading troughs, leaving their filthy trail wherever they went." Says Chaucer with characteristic satire, speaking of the Friars:

> Women may now go safely up and doun,
> In every bush, and under every tree,
> Ther is non other incubus but he,
> And he ne will don hem no dishonour.

Henry, Bishop of Liege, could unblushingly boast the birth of twenty-two children in fourteen years.

It may help us under some of the perplexities which beset our way in "the one Catholic and Apostolic Church" today, to recall some of the corruptions and incongruities against which the Bride of Christ has had to struggle in her past history and in spite of which she has kept, through many vicissitudes, the faith once delivered to the saints. Individuals, organizations, whole sections of the Church militant may outrage the Christ whom they profess, may ruthlessly trample under foot both the spirit and the letter of his precepts, yet not till we hear the voices audibly saying "Come let us depart hence," shall we cease to believe and cling to the promise, *"I am with you to the end of the world."*

Yet saints their watch are keeping,
The cry goes up 'How long!'
And soon the night of weeping
Shall be the morn of song.

However much then the facts of any particular period of history may seem to deny it, I for one do not doubt that the source of the vitalizing principle of woman's development and amelioration is the Christian Church, so far as that church is coincident with Christianity.

Christ gave ideals not formulae. The Gospel is a germ requiring millennia for its growth and ripening. It needs and at the same time helps to form around itself a soil enriched in civilization, and perfected in culture and insight without which the embryo can neither be unfolded or comprehended. With all the strides our civilization has made from the first to the nineteenth century, we can boast not an idea, not a principle of action, not a progressive social force but was already mutely foreshadowed, or directly enjoined in that simple tale of a meek and lowly life. The quiet face of the Nazarene is ever seen a little way ahead, never too far to come down to and touch the life of the lowest in days the darkest, yet ever leading onward, still onward, the tottering childish feet of our strangely boastful civilization.

By laying down for woman the same code of morality, the same standard of purity, as for man; by refusing to countenance the shameless and equally guilty monsters who were gloating over her fall,—graciously stooping in all the majesty of his own spotlessness to wipe away the filth and grime of her guilty past and bid her go in peace and sin no more; and again in the moments of his own careworn and footsore dejection, turning trustfully and lovingly, away from the heartless snubbing and sneers, away from the cruel malignity of mobs and prelates in the dusty marts of Jerusalem to the ready sympathy, loving appreciation and unfaltering friendship of that quiet home at Bethany; and even at the last, by his dying bequest to the disciple whom he loved, signifying the protection and tender regard to be extended to that sorrowing mother and ever afterward to the sex she represented;—throughout his life and in his death he has given to men a rule and guide for the estimation of woman as an equal, as a helper, as a friend, and as a sacred charge to be sheltered and cared for with a brother's love and sympathy, lessons which nineteen centuries' gigantic strides in knowledge, arts, and sciences, in social and ethical principles have not been able to probe to their depth or to exhaust in practice.

It seems not too much to say then of the vitalizing, regenerating, and progressive influence of womanhood on the civilization of today, that, while it was foreshadowed among Germanic nations in the far away dawn of their history as a narrow, sickly and stunted growth, it yet owes its catholicity and power, the deepening of its roots and broadening of its branches to Christianity.

The union of these two forces, the Barbaric and the Christian, was not long delayed after the Fall of the Empire. The church, which fell with Rome, finding herself in danger of being swallowed up by barbarism, with characteristic vigor and fertility of resources, addressed herself immediately to the task of conquering her conquerers. The means chosen does credit to her power of penetration and adaptability, as well as to her profound, unerring, all-compassing diplomacy; and makes us even now wonder if aught human can successfully and ultimately withstand her far-seeing designs and brilliant policy, or gainsay her well-earned claim to the word *Catholic.*

She saw the barbarian, little more developed than a wild beast. She forbore to antagonize and mystify his warlike nature by a full blaze of the heart-searching and humanizing tenets of her great Head. She said little of the rule "If thy brother smite thee on one check, turn to him the other also;" but thought it sufficient for the needs of those times, to establish the so-called "Truce of God" under which men were bound to abstain from butchering one another for three days of each week and on Church festivals. In other words, she respected their individuality; non-resistance pure and simple being for them an utter impossibility, she contented herself with less radical measures calculated to lead up finally to the full measure of the benevolence of Christ.

Next she took advantage of the barbarian's sensuous love of gaudy display and put all her magnificent garments on. She could not capture him by physical force, she would dazzle him by gorgeous spectacles. It is said that Romanism gained more in pomp and ritual during this trying period of the Dark Ages than throughout all her former history.

The result was she carried her point. Once more Rome laid her ambitious hand on the temporal power, and allied with Charlemagne, aspired to rule the world through a civilization dominated by Christianity and permeated by the traditions and instincts of those sturdy barbarians.

Here was the confluence of the two streams we have been tracing, which, united now, stretch before us as a broad majestic river. In regard to woman it was the meeting of two noble and ennobling forces, two kindred ideas the resultant of which, we doubt not, is destined to be a potent force in the betterment of the world.

Now after our appeal to history comparing nations destitute of this force and so destitute also of the principle of progress, with other nations among whom the influence of woman is prominent coupled with a brisk, progressive, satisfying civilization,—if in addition we find this strong presumptive evidence corroborated by reason and experience, we may conclude that these two equally varying concomitants are linked as cause and effect; in other words, that the position of woman in society determines the vital elements of its regeneration and progress.

Now that this is so on a *priori* grounds all must admit. And this not because woman is better or stronger or wiser than man, but from the nature of the case, because it is she who must first form the man by directing the earliest impulses of his character.

Byron and Wordsworth were both geniuses and would have stamped themselves on the thought of their age under any circumstances; and yet we find the one a savor of life unto life, the other of death unto death. "Byron, like a rocket, shot his way upward with scorn and repulsion, flamed out in wild, explosive, brilliant excesses and disappeared in darkness made all the more palpable."

Wordsworth lent of his gifts to reinforce that "power in the Universe which makes for righteousness" by taking the harp handed him from Heaven and using it to swell the strains of angelic choirs. Two locomotives equally mighty stand facing opposite tracks; the one to rush headlong to destruction with all its precious freight, the other to toil grandly and gloriously up the steep embattlements to Heaven and to God. Who—who can lay what a world of consequences hung on the first placing and starting of these enormous forces!

Woman, Mother,—your responsibility is one that might make angels tremble and fear to take hold! To trifle with it, to ignore or misuse it, is to treat lightly the most sacred and solemn trust ever confided by God to human kind. The training of children is a task on which an infinity of weal[1] or woe depends. Who does not covet it? Yet who does not stand awestruck before its momentous issues! It is a matter of small moment, it seems to me, whether that lovely girl in whose accomplishments you take such pride and delight, can enter the gay and crowded salon with the ease and elegance of this or that French or English gentlewoman, compared with the decision as to whether her individuality is going to reinforce the good or the evil elements of the world. The lace and the diamonds, the dance and the theater, gain a new significance when scanned in their bearings on such issues. Their influence on the individual personality, and through her on the society and civilization which she vitalizes and inspires—all this and more must be weighed in the balance before the jury can return a just and intelligent verdict as to the innocence or banefulness of these apparently simple amusements.

Now the fact of woman's influence on society being granted, what are its practical bearings on the work which brought together this conference of colored clergy and laymen in Washington? "We come not here to talk." Life is too busy, too pregnant with meaning and far reaching consequences to allow you to come this far for mere intellectual entertainment.

The vital agency of womanhood in the regeneration and progress of a race, as a general question, is conceded almost before it is fairly stated. I confess one of the difficulties for me in the subject assigned lay in its obviousness. The plea is taken away by the opposite attorney's granting the whole question.

"Woman's influence on social progress"—who in Christendom doubts or questions it? One may as well be called on to prove that the sun is the source of light and heat and energy to this many-sided little world.

Nor, on the other hand, could it have been intended that I should apply the position when taken and proven, to the needs and responsibilities of the women of our race in the South. For is it not written, "Cursed is he that cometh after the king?" and has not the King already preceded me in "The Black Woman of the South"?[2]

They have had both Moses and the Prophets in Dr. Crummell and if they hear not him, neither would they be persuaded though one came up from the South.

I would beg, however, with the Doctor's permission, to add my plea for the *Colored Girls* of the South:—that large, bright, promising fatally beautiful class that stand shivering like a delicate plantlet before the fury of tempestuous elements, so full of promise and possibilities, yet so sure of destruction; often without a father to whom they dare apply the loving term, often without a stronger brother to espouse their cause and defend their honor with his life's blood; in the midst of pitfalls and snares, waylaid by the lower classes of white men, with no shelter, no protection nearer than the great blue vault above, which half conceals and half reveals the one Care-Taker they know so little of. Oh, save them, help them, shield, train, develop, teach, inspire them! Snatch them, in God's name, as brands from the burning! There is material in them well worth your while, the hope in germ of a staunch, helpful, regenerating womanhood on which, primarily, rests the foundation stones of our future as a race.

It is absurd to quote statistics showing the Negro's bank account and rent rolls, to point to the hundreds of newspapers edited by colored men and lists of lawyers, doctors, professors, D. D.'s, LL. D.'s, etc., etc., etc., while the source from which the life-blood of the race is to flow is subject to taint and corruption in the enemy's camp.

True progress is never made by spasms. Real progress is growth. It must begin in the seed. Then, "first the blade, then the car, after that the full corn in the ear." There is something to encourage and inspire us in the advancement of individuals since their emancipation from slavery. It at least proves that there is nothing irretrievably wrong in the shape of the black man's skull, and that under given circumstances his development, downward or upward, will be similar to that of other average human beings.

But there is no time to be wasted in mere felicitation. That the Negro has his niche in the infinite purposes of the Eternal, no one who has studied the history of the last fifty years in America will deny. That much depends on his own right comprehension of his responsibility and rising to the demands of the hour, it will be good for him to see; and how best to use his present so that the structure of the future shall be stronger and higher and brighter and nobler and holier than that of the past, is a question to be decided each day by every one of us.

The race is just twenty-one years removed from the conception and experience of a chattel, just at the age of ruddy manhood. It is well enough to pause a moment for retrospection, introspection, and prospection. We look back, not to become inflated with conceit because of the depths from which we have arisen, but that we may learn wisdom from experience. We look within that we may gather together once more our forces, and, by improved and more practical methods, address ourselves to the tasks before us. We look forward with hope and trust that the same God whose guiding hand led our fathers through and out of the gall and bitterness of oppression, will still lead and direct their children, to the honor of His name, and for their ultimate salvation.

But this survey of the failures or achievements of the past, the difficulties and embarrassments of the present, and the mingled hopes and fears for the future, must not degenerate into mere dreaming nor consume the time which belongs to the practical and effective handling of the crucial questions of the hour: and there can be no issue more vital and momentous than this of the womanhood of the race.

Here is the vulnerable point, not in the heel, but at the heart of the young Achilles;[3] and here must the defenses be strengthened and the watch redoubled.

We are the heirs of a past which was not our fathers' moulding. "Every man the arbiter of his own destiny" was not true for the American Negro of the past: and it is no fault of his that he finds himself today the inheritor of a manhood and womanhood impoverished and debased by two centuries and more of compression and degradation.

But weaknesses and malformations, which today are attributable to a vicious schoolmaster and a pernicious system, will a century hence be rightly regarded as proofs of innate corruptness and radical incurability.

Now the fundamental agency under God in the regeneration, the retraining of the race, as well as the ground work and starting point of its progress upward, must be the *black woman.*

With all the wrongs and neglects of her past, with all the weakness, the debasement, the moral thralldom of her present, the black woman of today stands mute and wondering at the Herculean task devolving upon her. But the cycles wait for her. No other hand can move the lever. She must be loosed from her bands and set to work.

Our meager and superficial results from past efforts prove their futility; and every attempt to elevate the Negro, whether undertaken by himself or through the philanthropy of others, cannot but prove abortive unless so directed as to utilize the indispensable agency of an elevated and trained womanhood.

A race cannot be purified from without. Preachers and teachers are helps, and stimulants and conditions as necessary as the gracious rain and sunshine are to plant growth. But what are rain and dew and sunshine and cloud if there be no life in the plant germ? We must go to the root and see that that is sound and healthy and vigorous; and not deceive ourselves with waxen flowers and painted leaves of mock chlorophyll.

We too often mistake individuals' honor for race development and so are ready to substitute pretty accomplishments for sound sense and earnest purpose.

A stream cannot rise higher than its source. The atmosphere of homes is no rarer and purer and sweeter than are the mothers in those homes. A race is but a total of families. The nation is the aggregate of its homes. As the whole is sum of all its parts, so the character of the parts will determine the characteristics of the whole. These are all axioms and so evident that it seems gratuitous to remark it; and yet, unless I am greatly mistaken, most of the unsatisfaction from our past results arises from just such a radical and palpable error, as much almost on our own part as on that of our benevolent white friends.

The Negro is constitutionally hopeful and proverbially irrepressible; and naturally stands in danger of being dazzled by the shimmer and tinsel of superficials. We often mistake foliage for fruit and overestimate or wrongly estimate brilliant results.

The late Martin R. Delany,[4] who was an unadulterated black man, used to say when honors of state fell upon him, that when he entered the council of kings the black race entered with him; meaning, I suppose, that there was no discounting his race identity and attributing his achievements to some admixture of Saxon blood. But our present record of eminent men, when placed beside the actual status of the race in America today, proves that no man can represent the race. Whatever the attainments of the individual may be, unless his home has moved on *pari passu,* he can never be regarded as identical with or representative of the whole.

Not by pointing to sun-bathed mountain tops do we prove that Phoebus[5] warms the valleys. We must point to homes, average homes, homes of the rank and file of horny handed toiling men and women of the South (where the masses are) lighted and cheered by the good, the beautiful, and the true,—then and not till then will the whole plateau be lifted into the sunlight.

Only the Black Woman can say "when and where I enter, in the quiet, undisputed dignity of my womanhood, without violence and without suing or special patronage, then and there the whole *Negro race enters with me.*" Is it not evident then that as individual workers for this race we must address ourselves with no half-hearted zeal to this feature of our mission. The need is felt and must be recognized by all. There is a call for workers, for missionaries, for men and women with the double consecration of a fundamental love of humanity and a desire for its melioration through the Gospel; but superadded to this we demand an intelligent and sympathetic comprehension of the interests and special needs of the Negro.

I see not why there should not be an organized effort for the protection and elevation of our girls such as the White Cross League[6] in England. English women are strengthened and protected by more than twelve centuries of Christian influences, freedom, and civilization: English girls are dispirited and crushed down by no such all-levelling prejudice as that supercilious caste spirit in America which cynically assumes "A Negro woman cannot be a lady." English womanhood is beset by no such snares and traps as betray the unprotected, untrained colored girl of the South, whose only crime and dire destruction often is her unconscious and marvelous beauty. Surely then if English indignation is aroused and English manhood thrilled under the leadership of a Bishop of the English church to build up bulwarks around their wronged sisters. Negro sentiment cannot remain callous and Negro effort nerveless in view of the imminent peril of the mothers of the next generation. *"I am my Sister's keeper!"* should be the hearty response of every man and woman of the race, and this conviction should purify and exalt the narrow, selfish and petty personal aims of life into a noble and sacred purpose.

We need men who can let their interest and gallantry extend outside the circle of their aesthetic appreciation; men who can be a father, a brother, a friend to every weak, struggling unshielded girl. We need women who are so sure of their own social footing that they need not fear learning to lend a hand to a fallen or falling sister. We need men and women who do not exhaust their genius splitting hairs on aristocratic distinctions and thanking God they are not as others: but earnest, unselfish souls, who can go into the highways and byways, lifting up and leading, advising and encouraging with the truly catholic benevolence of the Gospel of Christ.

As Church workers we must confess our path of duty is less obvious: or rather our ability to adapt our machinery to our conception of the peculiar exigencies of this work as taught by experience and our own consciousness of the needs of the Negro, is as yet not demonstrable. Flexibility and aggressiveness are not such strong characteristics of the Church today as in the Dark Ages.

As a Mission field for the Church the Southern Negro is in some aspects most promising; in others, perplexing. Aliens neither in language and customs, nor in associations and sympathies, naturally of deeply rooted religious instincts and taking most readily and kindly to the worship and teachings of the Church, surely the task of proselytizing the American Negro is infinitely less formidable than that which confronted the Church in the Barbarians of Europe. Besides, this people already look to the Church as the hope of their race. Thinking colored men almost uniformly admit that the Protestant Episcopal Church with its quiet, chaste dignity and decorous solemnity, its instructive and elevating ritual, its bright chanting and joyous hymning, is eminently fitted to correct the peculiar faults of worship—the rank exuberance and often ludicrous demonstrativeness of their people. Yet, strange to say, the Church, claiming to be missionary and Catholic, urging that schism is sin and denominationalism inexcusable, has made in all these years almost no inroads upon this semi-civilized religionism.

Harvests from this over ripe field of home missions have been gathered in by Methodists, Baptists, and not least by Congregationalists, who were unknown to the Freedmen before their emancipation.

Our clergy numbers less than two dozen priests of Negro blood and we have hardly more than one self-supporting colored congregation in the entire Southland. While the organization known as the A.M.E. Church has 14,063 ministers, itinerant and local, 4,069 self-supporting churches, 4,275 Sunday-schools, with property valued at $7,772,284, raising yearly for church purposes $1,427,000.

Stranger and more significant than all, the leading men of this race (I do not mean demagogues and politicians, but men of intellect, heart, and race devotion, men to whom the elevation of their people means more than personal ambition and sordid gain—and the men of that stamp have not all died yet) the Christian workers for the race, of younger and more cultured growth, are noticeably drifting into sectarian churches, many of them declaring all the time that they acknowledge the historic claims of the Church, believe her apostolicity, and would experience greater personal comfort, spiritual and intellectual, in her revered communion. It is a fact which any one may verify for himself, that representative colored men, professing that in their heart of hearts they are Episcopalians, are actually working in Methodist and Baptist pulpits, while the ranks of the Episcopal clergy are left to be filled largely by men who certainly suggest the propriety of a "*perpetual* Diaconate" if they cannot be said to have created the necessity for it.

Now where is the trouble? Something must be wrong. What is it?

A certain Southern Bishop of our Church reviewing the situation, whether in Godly anxiety or in "Gothic antipathy" I know not, deprecales the fact that the colored people do not seem *drawn* to the Episcopal Church, and comes to the sage conclusion that the Church is not adapted to the rude untutored minds of the Freedmen, and that they may be left to go to the Methodists and Baptists whither their racial proclivities undeniably tend. How the good Bishop can agree that all-foreseeing Wisdom, and Catholic Love would have framed his Church as typified in his seamless garment and unbroken body, and yet not leave it broad enough and deep enough and loving enough to seek and save and hold seven millions of God's poor, I cannot see.

But the doctors while discussing their scientifically conclusive diagnosis of the disease, will perhaps not think it presumptuous in the patient if he dares to suggest where at least the pain is. If this be allowed, a *Black woman of the South* would beg to point out two possible oversights in this southern work which may indicate in part both a cause and a remedy for some failure. The first is *not calculating for the Black man's personality*: not having respect, if I may so express it, to his manhood or deferring at all to his conceptions of the needs of his people. When colored persons have been employed it was too often as machines or as manikins. There has been no disposition, generally, to get the black man's ideal or to let his individuality work by its own gravity, as it were. A conference of earnest Christian men have met at regular intervals for some years past to discuss the best methods of promoting the welfare and development of colored people in this country. Yet, strange as it may seem, they have never invited a colored man or even intimated that one would be welcome to take part in their deliberations. Their remedial contrivances are purely theoretical or empirical, therefore, and the whole machinery devoid of soul.

The second important oversight in my judgment is closely allied to this and probably grows out of it, and that is not developing Negro womanhood as an essential fundamental for the elevation of the race, and utilizing this agency in extending the work of the Church.

Of the first I have possibly already presumed to say too much since it does not strictly come within the province of my subject. However, Macaulay somewhere criticises the Church of England as not knowing how to use fanatics, and declares that had Ignatius Loyola been in the Anglican instead of the Roman communion, the Jesuits would have been schismatics instead of Catholics; and if the religious awakenings of the Wesleys had been in Rome, she would have shaven their heads, tied ropes around their waists, and sent them out under her own banner and blessing. Whether this be true or not, there is certainly a vast amount of force potential for Negro evangelization rendered latent, or worse, antagonistic by the halting, uncertain, I had almost said, *trimming* policy of the Church in the South. This may sound both presumptuous and ungrateful. It is mortifying, I know, to benevolent wisdom, after having spent itself in the execution of well conned theories for the ideal development of a particular work, to hear perhaps the weakest and humblest element of that work asking "what doest thou?"

Yet so it will be in life. The "thus far and no farther" pattern cannot be fitted to any growth in God's kingdom. The universal law of development is "onward and upward." It is God-given and inviolable. From the unfolding of the germ in the acorn to reach the sturdy oak, to the growth of a human soul into the full knowledge and likeness of its Creator, the breadth and scope of the movement in each and all are too grand, too mysterious, too like God himself, to be encompassed and locked down in human molds.

After all the Southern slave owners were right: either the very alphabet of intellectual growth must be forbidden and the Negro dealt with absolutely as a chattel having neither rights nor sensibilities; or else the clamps and irons of mental and moral, as well as civil compression must be riven asunder and the truly enfranchised soul led to the entrance of that boundless vista through which it is to toil upwards to its beckoning God as the buried seed germ to meet the sun.

A perpetual colored diaconate, carefully and kindly superintended by the white clergy; congregations of shiny faced peasants with their clean white aprons and sunbonnets catechised at regular intervals and taught to recite the creed, the Lord's prayer and the ten commandments—duty towards God and duty towards neighbor, surely such well tended sheep ought to be grateful to their shepherds and content in that station of life to which it pleased God to call them. True, like the old professor lecturing to his solitary student, we make no provision here for irregularities. "Questions must be kept till after class," or dispensed with altogether. That some do ask questions and insist on answers, in class too, must be both impertinent and annoying. Let not our spiritual pastors and masters however be grieved at such self-assertion as merely signifies we have a destiny to fulfill and as men and women we must *be about our Father's business.*

It is a mistake to suppose that the Negro is prejudiced against a white ministry. Naturally there is not a more kindly and implicit follower of a white man's guidance than the average colored peasant. What would to others be an ordinary act of friendly or pastoral interest he would be more inclined to regard gratefully as a condescension. And he never forgets such kindness. Could the Negro be brought near to his white priest or bishop, he is not suspicious. He is not only willing but often longs to unburden his soul to this intelligent guide. There are no reservations when he is convinced that you are his friend. It is a saddening satire on American history and manners that it takes something to convince him.

That our people are not "drawn" to a church whose chief dignitaries they see only in the chancel, and whom they reverence as they would a painting or an angel, whose life never comes down to and touches theirs with the inspiration of an objective reality, may be "perplexing" truly (American caste and American Christianity both being facts) but it need not be surprising. There must be something of human nature in it, the same as that which brought about that "the Word was made flesh and dwelt among us" that He might "draw" us towards God.

Men are not "drawn" by abstractions. Only sympathy and love can draw, and until our Church in America realizes this and provides a clergy that can come in touch with our life and have a fellow feeling for our woes, without being imbedded and frozen up in their "Gothic antipathies," the good bishops are likely to continue "perplexed" by the sparsity of colored Episcopalians.

A colored priest of my acquaintance recently related to me, with tears in his eyes, how his reverend Father in God, the Bishop who had ordained him, had met him on the cars on his way to the diocesan convention and warned him, not unkindly, not to take a seat in the body of the convention with the white clergy. To avoid disturbance of their godly placidity he would of course please sit back and somewhat apart. I do not imagine that that clergyman had very much heart for the Christly (!) deliberations of that convention.

To return, however, it is not on this broader view of Church work, which I mentioned as a primary cause of its halting progress with the colored people, that I am to speak. My proper theme is the second oversight of which in my judgment our Christian propagandists have been guilty; or, the necessity of church training, protecting and uplifting our colored womanhood as indispensable to the evangelization of the race.

Apelles did not disdain even that criticism of his lofty art which came from an uncouth cobbler; and may I not hope that the writer's oneness with her subject both in feeling and in being may palliate undue obtrusiveness of opinions here. That the race cannot be effectually lifted up till its women are truly elevated we take as proven. It is not for us to dwell on the needs, the neglects, and the ways of succor, pertaining to the black woman of the South. The ground has been ably discussed and an admirable and practical plan proposed by the oldest Negro priest in America, advising and urging that special organizations such as Church Sisterhoods and industrial school be devised to meet her pressing needs in the Southland. That some such movements are vital to the life of this people and the extension of the Church among them, is not hard to see. Yet the pamphlet fell stillborn from the press. So far as I am informed the Church has made no motion towards carrying out Dr. Crummell's suggestion.

The denomination which comes next our own in opposing the proverbial emotionalism of Negro worship in the South, and which in consequence like ours receives the cold shoulder from the old heads, resting as we do under the charge of not "having religion" and not believing in conversion—the Congregationalists—have quietly gone to work on the young, have established industrial and training schools, and now almost every community in the South is yearly enriched by a fresh infusion of vigorous young hearts, cultivated heads, and helpful hands that have been trained at Fisk, at Hampton, in Atlanta University, and in Tuskegee, Alabama.

These young people are missionaries actual or virtual both here and in Africa. They have learned to love the methods and doctrines of the Church which trained and educated them; and so Congregationalism surely and steadily progresses.

Need I compare these well known facts with results shown by the Church in the same field and during the same or even a longer time.

The institution of the Church in the South to which she mainly looks for the training of her colored clergy and for the help of the "Black Woman" and "Colored Girl" of the South, has graduated since the year 1868, when the school was founded, *five young women*; and while yearly numerous young men have been kept and trained for the ministry by the charities of the Church, the number of indigent females who have here been supported, sheltered and trained, is phenomenally small. Indeed, to my mind, the attitude of the Church toward this feature of her work is as if the solution of the problem of Negro missions depended solely on sending a quota of deacons and priests into the field, girls being a sort of *tertium quid* whose development may be promoted if they can pay their way and fall in with the plans mapped out for the training of the other sex. Now I would ask in all earnestness, does not this force potential deserve by education and stimulus to be made dynamic? Is it not a solemn duty incumbent on all colored churchmen to make it so? Will not the aid of the Church be given to prepare our girls in head, heart, and hand for the duties and responsibilities that await the intelligent wife, the Christian mother, the earnest, virtuous, helpful woman, at once both the lever and the fulcrum for uplifting the race.

As Negroes and churchmen we cannot be indifferent to these questions. They touch us most vitally on both sides. We believe in the Holy Catholic Church. We believe that however gigantic and apparently remote the consummation, the Church will go on conquering and to conquer till the kingdoms of this world, not excepting the black man and the black woman of the South, shall have become the kingdoms of the Lord and of his Christ.

That past work in this direction has been unsatisfactory we must admit. That without a change of policy results in the future will be as meagre, we greatly fear. Our life as a race is at stake. The dearest interests of our hearts are in the scales. We must either break away from dear old landmarks and plunge out in any line and every line that enables us to meet the pressing need of our people, or we must ask the Church to allow and help us, untrammelled by the prejudices and theories of individuals, to work aggressively under her direction as we alone can, with God's help, for the salvation of our people.

The time is ripe for action. Self-seeking and ambition must be laid on the altar. The battle is one of sacrifice and hardship, but our duty is plain. We have been recipients of missionary bounty in some sort for twenty-one years. Not even the senseless vegetable is content to be a mere reservoir. Receiving without giving is an anomaly in nature. Nature's cells are all little workshops for manufacturing sunbeams, the product to be *given out* to earth's inhabitants in warmth, energy, thought, action. Inanimate creation always pays back an equivalent.

Now, *How much owest thou my* Lord? Will his account be overdrawn if he call for singleness of purpose and self-sacrificing labor for your brethren? Having passed through your drill school, will you refuse a general's commission even if it entail responsibility, risk and anxiety, with possibly some adverse criticism? Is it too much to ask you to step forward and direct the work for your race along those lines which you know to be of first and vital importance?

Will you allow these words of Ralph Waldo Emerson? "In ordinary," says he, "we have a snappish criticism which watches and contradicts the opposite party. We want the will which advances and dictates [acts]. Nature has made up her mind that what cannot defend itself, shall not be defended. Complaining never so loud and with never so much reason, is of no use. What cannot stand must fall; *and the measure of our sincerity and therefore of the respect of men is the amount of health and wealth we will hazard in the defense of our right.*"

Notes

1. Synonym for *happiness.*
2. Pamphlet published by Alexander Crummell (1819–1895), African American writer, theologian, and activist.

3. In Greek mythology, Achilles was the foremost hero of the Trojan War. He was most vulnerable in his heel, the spot on his body that his mother held onto when she dipped him into the river Styx to immortalize him.
4. Martin Delany (1812–1885), African American doctor, abolitionist, and writer.
5. God of the sun.
6. An organization of men, founded in England in the early nineteenth century, that aimed to uphold female chastity and purity.

Source

Anna J. Cooper, "Womanhood: A Vital Element in the Regeneration and Progress of a Race" (1892; reprinted in Henry Louis Gates and Nellie Y. McKay, eds., *The Norton Anthology of African-American Literature,* 559–63 [New York and London: W. W. Norton, 1997]).

Selected Bibliography

Baker-Fletcher, Karen. *A Singing Something: Womanist Reflections on Anna Julia Cooper.* New York: Crossroad, 1994.

Cooper, Anna Julia. *A Voice from the South.* 1892. Reprint, New York: Oxford University Press, 1969.

Giddings, Paula. *When and Where I Enter: The Impact of Black Women on Race and Sex in America.* New York: Morrow, 1984.

Lowenberg, Bert and Ruth Bogin, eds. *Black Women in Nineteenth Century American Life: Their Words, Their Thoughts, Their Feelings.* University Park: Pennsylvania State University Press, 1976.

four

The Damnation of Women

A historian, sociologist, novelist, editor, activist, and educator, W.E.B. Du Bois (1868–1963) was among the foremost intellectuals in American history. Black women in the early twentieth century had few allies as committed to their cause as Du Bois, who favored birth control, women's suffrage, and women's liberation in the workplace. In "The Damnation of Women," an essay that appeared in his book *Darkwater,* Du Bois drew on his command of history and sociology to put forth a race/class/gender analysis of women's oppression that was shared by some of his female contemporaries, such as Anna Julia Cooper and Mary Church Terrell.

Du Bois was born in Great Barrington, Massachusetts, and received his Ph.D. in history from Harvard in 1895. In 1903 he published his best known work, *The Souls of Black Folk*, a collection of essays on African American history, sociology, religion, politics, and music that contained his famous prediction: "The problem of the twentieth century will be the problem of the color line." Du Bois was a key organizer of the National Association for the Advancement of Colored People (NAACP), and in 1910 he launched *Crisis* magazine, the official organ of the NAACP. During the 1930s, DuBois moved leftward politically, embracing Marxian socialism and anticolonialism. As a result, DuBois was ostracized from mainstream civil rights organizations, and in 1961 he moved to Ghana. He died in 1963.

I remember four women of my boyhood: my mother, cousin Inez, Emma, and Ide Fuller. They represented the problem of the widow, the wife, the maiden, and the outcast. They were, in color, brown and light brown, yellow with brown freckles, and white. They existed not for themselves, but for men; they were named after the men to whom they were related and not after the fashion of their own souls.

They were not beings, they were relations and these relations were enfilmed with mystery and secrecy. We did not know the truth or believe it when we heard it. Motherhood! What was it? We did not know or greatly care. My mother and I were good chums. I liked her. After she was dead I loved her with a fierce sense of personal loss.

Inez was a pretty, brown cousin who married. What a marriage! We did not know, neither did she, poor thing! It came to mean for her a litter of children, poverty, a drunken, cruel companion, sickness, and death. Why?

There was no sweeter sight than Emma,—slim, straight, and dainty, darkly flushed with the passion of youth; but her life was a wild, awful struggle to crush her natural, fierce joy of love. She crushed it and became a cold, calculating mockery.

Last there was that awful outcast of the town, the white woman, Ide Fuller. What she was, we did not know. She stood to us as embodied filth and wrong,—but whose filth, whose wrong?

Grown up I see the problem of these women transfused; I hear all about me the unanswered call of youthful love, none the less glorious because of its clean, honest, physical passion. Why unanswered? Because the youth are too poor to marry or if they marry, too poor to have children. They turn aside, then, in three directions; to marry for support, to what men call shame, or to that which is more evil than nothing. It is an unendurable paradox; it must be changed or the bases of culture will totter and fall.

The world wants healthy babies and intelligent workers. Today we refuse to allow the combination and force thousands of intelligent workers to go childless at a horrible expenditure of moral force, or we damn them if they break our idiotic conventions. Only at the sacrifice of intelligence and the chance to do their best work can the majority of modern women bear children. This is the damnation of women.

All womanhood is hampered today because the world on which it is emerging is a world that tries to worship both virgins and mothers and in the end despises motherhood and despoils virgins.

The future woman must have a life work and economic independence. She must have knowledge. She must have the right of motherhood at her own discretion. The present mincing horror at free womanhood must pass if we are ever to be rid of the bestiality of free manhood; not by guarding the weak in weakness do we gain strength, but by making weakness free and strong.

The world must choose the free woman or the white wraith of the prostitute. Today it wavers between the prostitute and the nun. Civilization must show two things: the glory and beauty of creating life and the need and duty of power and intelligence. This and this only will make the perfect marriage of love and work.

> God is Love,
> Love is God,
> There is no God but Love
> And Work is His Prophet!

All this of woman,—but what of black women?

The world that wills to worship womankind studiously forgets its darker sisters. They seem in a sense to typify that veiled Melancholy:

> Whose saintly visage is too bright
> To hit the sense of human sight,
> And, therefore, to our weaker view
> O'er-laid with black.

Yet the world must heed these daughters of sorrow, from the primal black All-Mother of men down through the ghostly throng of mighty womanhood, who walked in the mysterious dawn of Asia and Africa; from Neith, the primal mother of all, whose feet rest on hell, and whose almighty hands uphold the heavens; all religion, from beauty to beast, lies on her eager breasts; her body bears the stars, while her shoulders are necklaced by the dragon; from black Neith down to

> That starr'd Ethiop queen who strove
> To set her beauty's praise above
> The sea-nymphs,

through dusky Cleopatras, dark Candaces, and darker, fiercer Zinghas, to our own day and our own land,—in gentle Phillis; Harriet, the crude Moses; the sybil, Sojourner Truth; and the martyr, Louise De Mortie.

The father and his worship is Asia; Europe is the precocious, self-centered, forward-striving child; but the land of the mother is and was Africa. In subtle and mysterious way, despite her curious history, her slavery, polygamy, and toil, the spell of the African mother pervades her land. Isis, the mother, is still titular goddess, in thought if not in name, of the dark continent. Nor does this all seem to be solely a survival of the historic matriarchate through which all nations pass,—it appears to be more than this,—as if the great black race in passing up the steps of human culture gave the world, not only the Iron Age, the cultivation of the soil, and the domestication of animals, but also, in peculiar emphasis, the mother-idea.

"No mother can love more tenderly and none is more tenderly loved than the Negro mother," writes Schneider. Robin tells of the slave who bought his mother's freedom instead of his own. Mungo Park writes: "Everywhere in Africa, I have noticed that no greater affront can be offered a Negro than insulting his mother. 'Strike me,' cries a Mandingo to his enemy, 'but revile not my mother!' " And the Krus and Fantis say the same. The peoples on the Zambezi and the great lakes cry in sudden fear or joy: "O, my mother!" And the Herero swears (endless oath) "By my mother's tears!" "As the mist in the swamps," cries the Angola Negro, "so lives the love of father and mother."

A student of the present Gold Coast life describes the work of the village headman, and adds: "It is a difficult task that he is set to, but in this matter he has all-powerful helpers in the female members of the family, who will be either the aunts or the sisters or the cousins or the nieces of the headman, and as their interests are identical with his in every particular, the good women spontaneously train up their children to implicit obedience to the headman, whose rule in the family thus becomes a simple and an easy matter. 'The hand that rocks the cradle rules the world.' What a power for good in the native state system would the mothers of the Gold Coast and Ashanti become by judicious training upon native lines!"

Schweinfurth declares of one tribe: "A bond between mother and child which lasts for life is the measure of affection shown among the Dyoor" and Ratzel adds:

"Agreeable to the natural relation the mother stands first among the chief influences affecting the children. From the Zulus to the Waganda, we find the mother the most influential counsellor at the court of ferocious sovereigns, like Chaka or Mtesa; sometimes sisters take her place. Thus even with chiefs who possess wives by hundreds the bonds of blood are the strongest and that the woman, though often heavily burdened, is in herself held in no small esteem among the Negroes is clear from the numerous Negro queens, from the medicine women, from the participation in public meetings permitted to women by many Negro peoples."

As I remember through memories of others, backward among my own family, it is the mother I ever recall,—the little, far-off mother of my grand mothers, who sobbed her life away in song, longing for her lost palm-trees and scented waters; the tall and bronzen grandmother, with beaked nose and shrewish eyes, who loved and scolded her black and laughing husband as he smoked lazily in his high oak chair; above all, my own mother, with all her soft brownness,—the brown velvet of her skin, the sorrowful black-brown of her eyes, and the tiny brown-capped waves of her midnight hair as it lay new parted on her forehead. All the way back in these dim distances it is mothers and mothers of mothers who seem to count, while fathers are shadowy memories.

Upon this African mother-idea, the westward slave trade and American slavery struck like doom. In the cruel exigencies of the traffic in men and in the sudden, unprepared emancipation the great pendulum of social equilibrium swung from a time, in 1800,—when America had but eight or less black women to every ten black men,—all too swiftly to a day, in 1870,—when there were nearly eleven women to ten men in our Negro population. This was but the outward numerical fact of social dislocation; within lay polygamy, polyandry, concubinage, and moral degradation. They fought against all this desperately, did these black slaves in the West Indies, especially among the half-free artisans; they set up their ancient household gods, and when Toussaint and Cristophe founded their kingdom in Haiti, it was based on old African tribal ties and beneath it was the mother-idea.

The crushing weight of slavery fell on black women. Under it there was no legal marriage, no legal family, no legal control over children. To be sure, custom and religion replaced here and there what the law denied, yet one has but to read advertisements like the following to see the hell beneath the system:

> One hundred dollars reward will be given for my two fellows, Abram and Frank. Abram has a wife at Colonel Stewart's, in Liberty County, and a mother at Thunder-bolt, and a sister in Savannah.
>
> *WILLIAM ROBERTS.*

> Fifty dollars reward—Ran away from the subscriber a Negro girl named Maria. She is of a copper color, between thirteen and fourteen years of age—bareheaded and barefooted. She is small for her age—very sprightly and very likely. She stated she was going to see her mother at Maysville.
>
> *SANFORD THOMSON.*

> Fifty dollars reward—Ran away from the subscriber his Negro man Pauladore, commonly called Paul. I understand General R. Y. Hayne has purchased his wife and children from H. L. Pinkney, Esq., and has them now on his plantation at Goose Creek, where, no doubt, the fellow is frequently lurking.
>
> *T. DAVIS.*

The Presbyterian synod of Kentucky said to the churches under its care in 1835: "Brothers and sisters, parents and children, husbands and wives, are torn asunder and permitted to see each other no more. These acts are daily occurring in the midst of us. The shrieks and agony often witnessed on such occasions proclaim, with a trumpet tongue, the iniquity of our system. There is not a neighborhood where these heartrending scenes are not displayed. There is not a village or road that does not behold the sad procession of manacled outcasts whose mournful countenances tell that they are exiled by force from all that their hearts hold dear."

A sister of a president of the United States declared: "We Southern ladies are complimented with the names of wives, but we are only the mistresses of seraglios."

Out of this, what sort of black women could be born into the world of today? There are those who hasten to answer this query in scathing terms and who say lightly and repeatedly that out of black slavery came nothing decent in womanhood; that adultery and uncleanness were their heritage and are their continued portion.

Fortunately so exaggerated a charge is humanly impossible of truth. The half-million women of Negro descent who lived at the beginning of the 19th century had become the mothers of two and one-fourth million daughters at the time of the Civil War and five million granddaughters in 1910. Can all these women be vile and the hunted race continue to grow in wealth and character? Impossible. Yet to save from the past the shreds and vestiges of self-respect has been a terrible task. I most sincerely doubt if any other race of women could have brought its fineness up through so devilish a fire.

Alexander Crummell[1] once said of his sister in the blood: "In her girlhood all the delicate tenderness of her sex has been rudely outraged. In the field, in the rude cabin, in the press-room, in the factory she was thrown into the companionship of coarse and ignorant men. No chance was given her for delicate reserve or tender modesty. From her childhood she was the doomed victim of the grossest passion. All the virtues of her sex were utterly ignored. If the instinct of chastity asserted itself, then she had to fight like a tiger for the ownership and possession of her own person and ofttimes had to suffer pain and lacerations for her virtuous self-assertion. When she reached maturity, all the tender instincts of her womanhood were ruthlessly violated. At the age of marriage,—always prematurely anticipated under slavery—she was mated as the stock of the plantation were mated, not to be the companion of a loved and chosen husband, but to be the breeder of human cattle for the field or the auction block."

Down in such mire has the black motherhood of this race struggled,—starving its own wailing off-spring to nurse to the world their swaggering masters; welding for its children chains which affronted even the moral sense of an unmoral world. Many a man and woman in the South have lived in wedlock as holy as Adam and Eve[2] and brought forth their brown and golden children, but because the darker woman was helpless, her chivalrous and whiter mate could cast her off at his pleasure and publicly sneer at the body he had privately blasphemed.

I shall forgive the white South much in its final judgment day: I shall forgive its slavery, for slavery is a world-old habit; I shall forgive its fighting for a well-lost cause, and for remembering that struggle with tender tears; I shall forgive its so-called "pride of race," the passion of its hot blood, and even its dear, old, laughable strutting and posing; but one thing I shall never forgive, neither in this world nor the world to come: its wanton and continued and persistent insulting of the black womanhood which it sought and seeks to prostitute to its lust. I cannot forget that it is such Southern gentlemen into whose hands smug Northern hypocrites of today are seeking to place our women's eternal destiny,—men who insist upon withholding from my mother and wife and daughter those signs and appellations of courtesy and respect which elsewhere he withholds only from bawds and courtesans.

The result of this history of insult and degradation has been both fearful and glorious. It has birthed the haunting prostitute, the brawler, and the beast of burden; but it has also given the world an efficient womanhood, whose strength lies in its freedom and whose chastity was won in the teeth of temptation and not in prison and swaddling clothes.

To no modern race does its women mean so much as to the Negro nor come so near to the fulfilment of its meaning. As one of our women writes: "Only the black woman can say 'when and where I enter, in the quiet, undisputed dignity of my womanhood, without violence and without suing or special patronage, then and there the whole Negro race enters with me.'"[3]

They came first, in earlier days, like foam flashing on dark, silent waters,—bits of stern, dark womanhood here and there tossed almost carelessly aloft to the world's notice. First and naturally they assumed the panoply of the ancient African mother of men, strong and black, whose very nature beat back the wilderness of oppression and contempt. Such a one was that cousin of my grandmother, whom western Massachusetts remembers as "Mum Bett." Scarred for life by a blow received in defense of a sister, she ran away to Great Barrington and was the first slave, or one of the first, to be declared free under the Bill of Rights of 1780. The son of the judge who freed her, writes:

> Even in her humble station, she had, when occasion required it, an air of command which conferred a degree of dignity and gave her an ascendancy over those of her rank, which is very unusual in persons of any rank or color. Her determined and resolute character, which enabled her to limit the ravages of Shay's mob, was manifested in her conduct and deportment during her whole life. She claimed no distinction, but it was yielded to her from her superior experience, energy, skill, and sagacity. Having known this woman as familiarly as I knew either of my parents, I cannot believe in the moral or physical inferiority of the race to which she belonged. The degradation of the African must have been otherwise caused than by natural inferiority.

It was such strong women that laid the foundations of the great Negro church of today, with its five million members and ninety millions of dollars in property. One of the early mothers of the church, Mary Still, writes thus quaintly, in the forties:

> When we were as castouts and spurned from the large churches, driven from our knees, pointed at by the proud, neglected by the careless, without a place of worship, Allen, faithful to the heavenly calling, came forward and laid the foundation of this connection. The women, like the women at the sepulcher, were early to aid in laying the foundation of the temple and in helping to carry up the noble structure and in the name of their God set up their banner; most of our aged mothers are gone from this to a better state of things. Yet some linger still on their slaves, watching with intense interest the ark as it moves over the tempestuous waves of opposition and ignorance. . . .
>
> But the labors of these women stopped not here, for they knew well that they were subject to affliction and death. For the purpose of mutual aid, they banded themselves together in society capacity, that they might be better able to administer to each others' sufferings and to soften their own pillows. So we find the females in the early history of the church abounding in good works and in acts of true benevolence.

From such spiritual ancestry came two striking figures of war-time,—Harriet Tubman[4] and Sojourner Truth.[5]

For eight or ten years previous to the breaking out of the Civil War, Harriet Tubman was a constant attendant at anti-slavery conventions, lectures, and other meetings; she was a black woman of medium size, smiling countenance, with her upper front teeth gone, attired in coarse but neat clothes, and carrying always an old-fashioned reticule at her side. Usually as soon as she sat down she would drop off in sound sleep.

She was born a slave in Maryland, in 1820, bore the marks of the lash on her flesh; and had been made partially deaf, and perhaps to some degree mentally unbalanced by a blow on the head in childhood. Yet she was one of the most important agents of the Underground Railroad and a leader of fugitive slaves. She ran away in 1849 and went to Boston in 1854, where she was welcomed into the homes of the leading abolitionists and where every one listened with tense interest to her strange stories. She was absolutely illiterate, with no knowledge of geography, and yet year after year she penetrated the slave states and personally led North over three hundred fugitives without losing a single one. A standing reward of $10,000 was offered for her, but as she said: "The whites cannot catch us, for I was born with the charm, and the Lord has given me the power." She was one of John Brown's[6] closest advisers and only severe sickness prevented her presence at Harper's Ferry.[7]

When the war cloud broke, she hastened to the front, flitting down along her own mysterious paths, haunting the armies in the field, and serving as guide and nurse and spy. She followed Sherman[8] in his great march to the sea and was with Grant[9] at Petersburg, and always in the camps the Union officers silently saluted her.

The other woman belonged to a different type,—a tall, gaunt, black, unsmiling sibyl,[10] weighted with the woe of the world. She ran away from slavery and giving up her own name took the name of Sojourner Truth. She says: "I can remember when I was a little, young girl, how my old mammy would sit out of doors in the evenings and look up at the stars and groan, and I would say, 'Mammy, what makes you groan so?' And she would say, 'I am groaning to think of my poor children; they do not know where I be and I don't know where they be. I look up at the stars and they look up at the stars!' "

Her determination was founded on unwavering faith in ultimate good. Wendell Phillips[11] says that he was once in Faneuil Hall, when Frederick Douglass[12] was one of the chief speakers. Douglass had been describing the wrongs of the Negro race and as he proceeded he grew more and more excited and finally ended by saying that they had no hope of justice from the whites, no possible hope except in their own right arms. It must come to blood! They must fight for themselves. Sojourner Truth was sitting, tall and dark, on the very front seat facing the platform, and in the hush of feeling when Douglass sat down she spoke out in her deep, peculiar voice, heard all over the hall:

"Frederick, is God dead?"

Such strong, primitive types of Negro womanhood in America seem to some to exhaust its capabilities. They know less of a not more worthy, but a finer type of black woman wherein trembles all of that delicate sense of beauty and striving for self-realization, which is as characteristic of the Negro soul as is its quaint strength and sweet laughter. George Washington[13] wrote in grave and gentle courtesy to a Negro woman, in 1776, that he would "be happy to see" at his headquarters at any time, a person "to whom nature has been so liberal and beneficial in her dispensations." This child, Phillis Wheatley,[14] sang her trite and halting strain to a world that wondered and could not produce her like. Measured today her muse was slight and yet, feeling her striving spirit, we call to her still in her own words:

Through thickest glooms look back, immortal shade.

Perhaps even higher than strength and art loom human sympathy and sacrifice as characteristic of Negro womanhood. Long years ago, before the Declaration of Independence, Kate Ferguson[15] was born in New York. Freed, widowed, and bereaved of her children before she was twenty, she took the children of the streets of New York, white and black, to her empty arms, taught them, found them homes, and with Dr. Mason of Murray Street Church established the first modern Sunday School in Manhattan.

Sixty years later came Mary Shadd[16] up out of Delaware. She was tall and slim, of that ravishing dream-born beauty,—that twilight of the races which we call mulatto. Well-educated, vivacious, with determination shining from her sharp eyes, she threw herself singlehanded into the great Canadian pilgrimage when thousands of hunted black men hurried northward and crept beneath the protection of the lion's paw. She became teacher, editor, and lecturer; tramping afoot through winter snows, pushing without blot or blemish through crowd and turmoil to conventions and meetings, and finally becoming recruiting agent for the United States government in gathering Negro soldiers in the West.

After the war the sacrifice of Negro women for freedom and uplift is one of the finest chapters in their history. Let one life typify all: Louise De Mortie,[17] a free-born Virginia girl, had lived most of her life in Boston. Her high forehead, swelling lips, and dark eyes marked her for a woman of feeling and intellect. She began a successful career as a public reader. Then came the War and the Call. She went to the orphaned colored children of New Orleans,—out of freedom into insult and oppression and into the teeth of the yellow fever. She toiled and dreamed. In 1887 she had raised money and built an orphan home and that same year, in the thirty-fourth of her young life, she died, saying simply: "I belong to God."

As I look about me today in this veiled world of mine, despite the noisier and more spectacular advance of my brothers, I instinctively feel and know that it is the five million women of my race who really count. Black women (and women whose grandmothers were black) are today furnishing our teachers; they are the main pillars of those social settlements which we call churches; and they have with small doubt raised three-fourths of our church property. If we have today, as seems likely, over a billion dollars of accumulated goods, who shall say how much of it has been wrung from the hearts of servant girls and washer women and women toilers in the fields? As makers of two million homes these women are today seeking in marvelous ways to show forth our strength and beauty and our conception of the truth.

In the United States in 1910 there were 4,931,882 women of Negro descent; over twelve hundred thousand of these were children, another million were girls and young women under twenty, and two and a half-million were adults. As a mass these women were unlettered,—a fourth of those from fifteen to twenty-five years of age were unable to write. These women are passing through, not only a moral, but an economic revolution. Their grandmothers married at twelve and fifteen, but twenty-seven per cent of these women today who have passed fifteen are still single.

Yet these black women toil and toil hard. There were in 1910 two and a half million Negro homes in the United States. Out of these homes walked daily to work two million women and girls over ten years of age,—over half of the colored female population as against a fifth in the case of white women. These, then, are a group of workers, fighting for their daily bread like men; independent and approaching economic freedom! They furnished a million farm laborers, 80,000 farmers, 22,000 teachers, 600,000 servants and washerwomen, and 50,000 in trades and merchandizing.

The family group, however, which is the ideal of the culture with which these folk have been born, is not based on the idea of an economically independent working mother. Rather its ideal harks back to the sheltered harem with the mother emerging at first as nurse and homemaker, while the man remains the sole breadwinner. What is the inevitable result of the clash of such ideals and such facts in the colored group? Broken families.

Among native white women one in ten is separated from her husband by death, divorce, or desertion. Among Negroes the ratio is one in seven. Is the cause racial? No, it is economic, because there is the same high ratio among the white foreign-born. The breaking up of the present family is the result of modern working and sex conditions and it hits the laborers with terrible force. The Negroes are put in a peculiarly difficult position, because the wage of the male breadwinner is below the standard, while the openings for colored women in certain lines of domestic work, and now in industries, are many. Thus while toil holds the father and brother in country and town at low wages, the sisters and mothers are called to the city. As a result the Negro women outnumber the men nine or ten to eight in many cities, making what Charlotte Gilman bluntly calls "cheap women."

What shall we say to this new economic equality in a great laboring class? Some people within and without the race deplore it. "Back to the homes with the women," they cry, "and higher wage for the men." But how impossible this is has been shown by war conditions. Cessation of foreign migration has raised Negro men's wages, to be sure—but it has not only raised Negro women's wages, it has opened to them a score of new avenues of earning a living. Indeed, here, in microcosm and with differences emphasizing sex equality, is the industrial history of labor in the 19th and 20th centuries. We cannot abolish the new economic freedom of women. We cannot imprison women again in a home or require them all on pain of death to be nurses and housekeepers.

What is today the message of these black women to America and to the world? The uplift of women is, next to the problem of the color line and the peace movement, our greatest modern cause. When, now, two of these movements—woman and color—combine in one, the combination has deep meaning.

In other years women's way was clear: to be beautiful, to be petted, to bear children. Such has been their theoretic destiny and if perchance they have been ugly, hurt, and barren, that has been forgotten with studied silence. In partial compensation for this narrowed destiny the white world has lavished its politeness on its womankind,—its chivalry and bows, its uncoverings and courtesies—all the accumulated homage disused for courts and kings and craving exercise. The revolt of white women against this preordained destiny has in these latter days reached splendid proportions, but it is the revolt of an aristocracy of brains and ability,—the middle class and rank and file still plod on in the appointed path, paid by the homage, the almost mocking homage, of men.

From black women of America, however, (and from some others, too, but chiefly from black women and their daughters' daughters) this gauze has been withheld and without semblance of such apology they have been frankly trodden under the feet of men. They are and have been objected to, apparently for reasons peculiarly exasperating to reasoning human beings. When in this world a man comes forward with a thought, a deed, a vision, we ask not, how does he look,—but what is his message? It is of but passing interest whether or not the messenger is beautiful or ugly,—the *message* is the thing. This, which is axiomatic among men, has been in past ages but partially true if the messenger was a woman. The world still wants to ask that a woman primarily be pretty and if she is not, the mob pouts and asks querulously, "What else are women for?" Beauty "is its own excuse for being," but there are other excuses, as most men know, and when the white world objects to black women because it does not consider them beautiful, the black world of right asks two questions: "What is beauty?" and, "Suppose you think them ugly, what then? If ugliness and unconventionality and eccentricity of face and deed do not hinder men from doing the world's work and reaping the world's reward, why should it hinder women?"

Other things being equal, all of us, black and white, would prefer to be beautiful in face and form and suitably clothed; but most of us are not so, and one of the mightiest revolts of the century is against the devilish decree that no woman is a woman who is not by present standards a beautiful woman. This decree the black women of America have in large measure escaped from the first. Not being expected to be merely ornamental, they have girded themselves for work, instead of adorning their bodies only for play. Their sturdier minds have concluded that if a woman be clean, healthy, and educated, she is as pleasing as God wills and far more useful than most of her sisters. If in addition to this she is pink and white and straight-haired, and some of her fellow-men prefer this, well and good; but if she is black or brown and crowned in curled mists (and this to us is the most beautiful thing on earth), this is surely the flimsiest excuse for spiritual incarceration or banishment.

The very attempt to do this in the case of Negro Americans has strangely over-reached itself. By so much as the defective eyesight of the white world rejects black women as beauties, by so much the more it needs them as human beings—an enviable alternative, as many a white woman knows. Consequently, for black women alone, as a group, "handsome is that handsome does" and they are asked to be no more beautiful than God made them, but they are asked to be efficient, to be strong, fertile, muscled, and able to work. If they marry, they must as independent workers be able to help support their children, for their men are paid on a scale which makes sole support of the family often impossible.

On the whole, colored women are paid as well as white working women for similar work, save in some higher grades, while colored men get from one-fourth to three-fourths less than white men. The result is curious and threefold: the economic independence of black women is increased, the breaking up of Negro families must be more frequent, and the number of illegitimate children is decreased more slowly among them than other evidences of culture are increased, just as was once true in Scotland and Bavaria.

What does this mean? It forecasts a mighty dilemma which the whole world of civilization, despite its will, must one time frankly face: the unhusbanded mother or the childless wife. God send us a world with woman's freedom and married motherhood inextricably wed, but until He sends it, I see more of future promise in the betrayed girl-mothers of the black belt than in the childless wives of the white North, and I have more respect for the colored servant who yields to her frank longing for motherhood than for her white sister who offers up children for clothes. Out of a sex freedom that today makes us shudder will come in time a day when we will no longer pay men for work they do not do, for the sake of their harem; we will pay women what they earn and insist on their working and earning it; we will allow those persons to vote who know enough to vote, whether they be black or female, white or male; and we will ward race suicide, not by further burdening the over-burdened, but by honoring motherhood, even when the sneaking father shirks his duty.

"Wait till the lady passes," said a Nashville white boy.

"She's no lady; she's a nigger," answered another.

So some few women are born free, and some amid insult and scarlet letters achieve freedom; but our women in black had freedom thrust contemptuously upon them. With that freedom they are buying an untrammeled independence and dear as is the price they pay for it, it will in the end be worth every taunt and groan. Today the dreams of the mothers are coming true. We have still our poverty and degradation, our lewdness and our cruel toil; but we have, too, a vast group of women of Negro blood who for strength of character, cleanness of soul, and unselfish devotion of purpose, is today easily the peer of any group of women in the civilized world. And more than that, in the great rank and file of our five million women we have the up-working of new revolutionary ideals, which must in time have vast influence on the thought and action of this land.

For this, their promise, and for their hard past, I honor the women of my race. Their beauty,—their dark and mysterious beauty of midnight eyes, crumpled hair, and soft, full-featured faces—is perhaps more to me than to you, because I was born to its warm and subtle spell; but their worth is yours as well as mine. No other women on earth could have emerged from the hell of force and temptation which once engulfed and still surrounds black women in America with half the modesty and womanliness that they retain. I have always felt like bowing myself before them in all abasement, searching to bring some tribute to these long-suffering victims, these burdened sisters of mine, whom the world, the wise, white world, loves to affront and ridicule and wantonly to insult. I have known the women of many lands and nations,—I have known and seen and lived beside them, but none have I known more sweetly feminine, more unswervingly loyal, more desperately earnest, and more instinctively pure in body and in soul than the daughters of my black mothers. This, then,—a little thing—to their memory and inspiration.

Notes

1. Alexander Crummell (1819–1895), African American writer, theologian, and activist.
2. In the book of Genesis of the Bible, Adam and Eve were the first man and woman, created by God in his image.
3. The quote comes from Anna Julia Cooper's *A Voice from the South* (1894).
4. Harriet Tubman (c. 1820–1913), slave, reformer, abolitionist, and lecturer.
5. Sojourner Truth (c. 1799–1883), slave, abolitionist, lecturer, and religious worker.
6. John Brown (1800–1859), abolitionist, insurrectionist, and entrepreneur.
7. On October 16, 1859, John Brown and a party of twenty-one followers raided a U.S. arsenal at Harper's Ferry, Virginia (now West Virginia), in an attempt to start a slave revolt. The plan failed, and Brown was hanged at Charles Town in December 1859.
8. Gen. William Tecumseh Sherman (1820–1891), Union general in the American Civil War.
9. Ulysses Simpson Grant (1822–1885), commander in chief of the Union army in the American Civil War and eighteenth president of the United States (1869–1877).
10. In classical mythology, the sibyl was a prophetic woman.
11. Wendell Phillips (1811–1894), American reformer, abolitionist, and editor
12. Frederick Douglass (1818–1895), abolitionist, orator, reformer, editor, humanitarian, and statesman.
13. George Washington (1732–1799), first president of the United States (1789–1797), commander in chief of the Continental Army in the American Revolution, called "The Father of His Country."
14. Phillis Wheatley (c. 1753–1784), slave and poet.
15. Catherine Ferguson (1749–1854), religious worker, slave, reformer, and educator.
16. Mary Ann Shadd Cary (1823–1893), educator, lecturer, agriculturalist, journalist, author, and abolitionist.

17. Louise De Mortie (1833–1867), lecturer, reformer, performing artist, and missionary.

Source

W. E. B. Du Bois, "The Damnation of Women," in *Darkwater: Voices from Within the Veil,* 163–86 (New York: Harcourt, Brace & Howe, 1920; Millwood, N.Y.: Kraus-Thomson Organization Limited, 1975).

Selected Bibliography

Andrews, William L., ed. *Critical Essays on W. E. B. Du Bois*. Boston: G. K. Hall, 1985.

Du Bois, W. E. B. *Black Reconstruction in America* (New York: Harcourt, Brace and Co., 1935; New York: Atheneum, 1992).

—— *Souls of Black Folk*. New York: Modern Library, 1996.

—— *W. E. B. Du Bois: A Reader*. Edited by David Levering Lewis. New York: H. Holt, 1995.

Lewis, David Levering. *W. E. B. Du Bois: Biography of a Race, 1868–1919*. New York: H. Holt, 1993.

—— *W.E.B. Du Bois: The Fight for Equality and the American Century, 1919–1963*. New York: H. Holt, 2000.

five

Women's Most Serious Problem

Alice Moore Dunbar-Nelson (1875–1935) was an activist and an author who was proficient in a wide variety of genres, including poetry, short fiction, drama, scholarly literature, and journalism. In her essay "Woman's Most Serious Problem," Dunbar-Nelson drew attention to declining African American birth rates in the early twentieth century. Although this particular issue ceased to be a concern among black activists, the essay is significant because it revealed the social costs that were entailed when women, out of economic desperation, had to forsake some of their family responsibilities in order to enter the work force.

Born Alice Ruth Moore in New Orleans, Louisiana, Dunbar-Nelson graduated from a teacher's program at Straight College (now Dillard University) in 1892 and studied at Cornell University, Columbia University, and the University of Pennsylvania. In March 1898, she married the famous poet Paul Laurence Dunbar. In 1910, she edited the landmark anthology *Masterpieces of Negro Eloquence* (1914). Her diary, which was discovered and published in 1984, is one of only two known, full-length diaries of nineteenth-century African American women and revealed that she was secretly a lesbian and that there was, in this period, an active black lesbian network. She died at the University of Pennsylvania hospital in 1935.

E. B. Reuter, in his latest book, "The American Race Problem," makes this comment, "During the past decade there has been a somewhat marked improvement in the economic conditions of the Negroes. This is reflected in the decline of the number of women employed, and in the shift in numbers in different occupations." This statement is followed by a table showing the shift in occupational employment.

From one elevator operator in 1910, the number jumped to 3,073 in 1920. Those engaged in lumber and furniture industries in 1910 were 1,456. In 1920, 4,066. Textile industries jumped from 2,234 to 7,257. On the other hand, chambermaids in 1910 were numbered 14,071, but in 1920 they had declined to 10,443. Untrained nurses from 17,874 to 13,888; cooks from 205,584 to 168,710; laundresses, not in public laundries, from 361,551 to 283,557. On the other hand, cigar and tobacco workers jumped from 10,746 to 21,829, and the teaching profession showed a normal increase from 22,528 to 29,244.

Just what do these figures indicate? That the Negro woman is leaving the industries of home life, cooking, domestic service generally, child nursing, laundry work and going into mills, factories, operation of elevators, clerking, stenography (for in these latter occupations there is an almost 400 percent increase). She is doing a higher grade of work, getting better money, commanding better respect from the community because of her higher economic value, and less menial occupation. Domestic service claims her race no longer as its inalienable right. She is earning a salary, not wages.

This sounds fine. For sixty-three years the Negro woman has been a coworker with the Negro man. Now that she is more than ever working by his side, she feels a thrill of pride in her new economic status.

But—"the ratio of children to women has declined from census to census for both races. The declines has in general been more rapid for the Negro than for the white elements in the population."[1] In 1850 the number of children under five years of age per 1,100 women from 15 to 44 years of age for Negro women was 741, for white women, 659. In 1920 the Negro birth had decreased to 439, the white to 471. While the percentage of children under five years of age had decreased in the case of Negro women from 13.8 in Negro families to 10.9, and in white families from 11.9 to 10.9!

"In spite of the considerable increase in the Negro population and in the increase of the marriage rate, the actual number of Negro children under five years of age was less in 1920 than at any of the previous enumerations."[2] In 1900 the number of Negro children under five years of age was 1,215,655; in 1910, the number was 1,263,288; in 1920 it was 1,143,699!

And this sharp decline in the face of increased knowledge of the care and feeding of infants; the work of the insurance companies in health, Negro Health Week, public health nurses, clinics, dispensaries, and all the active agencies for the conservation and preservation of health.

One startling fact is apparent. Negro women are exercising birth control in order to preserve their new economic independence. Or, because of poverty of the family, they are compelled to limit their offspring.

The same author, Dr. Reuter, tells us that a recent study showed that fifty-five Negro professors at Howard University[3] had come from families averaging 6.5 children, while the professors themselves had an average of 0.7 children. Some were unmarried, but for each family formed, the average number of children was 1.6. "The birth rate of the cultured classes is apparently only one-third of the masses."

The race is here faced with a startling fact. Our birth rate is declining; our infant mortality is increasing; our normal rate of increase must necessarily be slowing up; our educated and intelligent classes are refusing to have children; our women are going into the kind of work that taxes both physical and mental capacities, which of itself, limits fecundity. While white women are beginning to work more away from home, at present, even with the rush of all women into the wage earners class, in New York City alone, seven times as many colored as white women work away from home.

The inevitable disruption of family life necessitated by the woman being a co-wage earner with the man has discouraged the Negro woman from child-bearing. Juvenile delinquents are recruited largely from the motherless home. That is the home that is without the constant care of the mother or head of the house. For a child to arise in the morning after both parents are gone, get itself an indifferent breakfast, go to school uncared for, lunch on a penny's worth of sweets, and return to a cold and cheerless house or apartment to await the return of a jaded and fatigued mother to get supper, is not conducive to sweetness and light in its behavior. Truancy, street walking, petty thievery and gang rowdyism are the natural results of this lack of family life. The Negro woman is awakening to the fact that the contribution she makes to the economic life of the race is too often made at the expense of the lives of the boys and girls of the race—so she is refusing to bring into the world any more potential delinquents.

This is the bald and ungarnished statement of a startling series of facts. The decline in the birth rate of the Negro. The rise in the economic life of the Negro woman. The sharpest peak of the decline—if a decline can be said to have a peak—is in the birth rate of the more cultured and more nearly leisure classes. The slow increase in the national family life, caused by the women workers not having time to make homes in the strictest sense of homemaking. The sharp rise in juvenile delinquency—in the cities, of course, and among the children of women workers. And worst of all because more subtle and insinuating in its flattering connotation of economic freedom, handsome salaries and social prestige—the growing use of married women of the child-bearing age as public school teachers, with the consequent temptation to refrain from child-bearing in order not to interfere with the independent life in the school room.

This is the situation. I would not suggest any remedy, make any criticism, raise any question, nor berate the men and women who are responsible for this crisis. For it is a serious crisis. I would only ask the young and intelligent women to give pause.

The new Negro is the topic most dwelt upon these days by the young folks, whom some call, frequently in derisive envy, the "Intelligentsia." In every race, in every nation and in every clime in every period of history there is always an eager-eyed group of youthful patriots who seriously set themselves to right the wrongs done to their race, or nation or sect or sometimes to art of self-expression. No race or nation can advance without them. Thomas Jefferson was an ardent leader of youthful patriots of his day, and Alexander Hamilton would have been dubbed a leader of the intelligentsia were he living now. They do big things, these young people.

Perhaps they may turn their attention, these race-loving slips of girls and slim ardent youths who make hot-eyed speeches about the freedom of the individual and the rights of the Negro, to the fact that at the rate we are going the Negro will become more and more negligible in the life of the nation. For we must remember that while the Negro constituted 19.3 percent of the population in 1790, and 18.9 in 1800, he constitutes only 9.9 percent today, and his percentage of increase has steadily dropped from 37.5 in 1810 to 6.3 in 1920.

No race can rise higher that its women is an aphorism that is so trite that it has ceased to be tiresome from its very monotony. If it might be phrased otherwise to catch the attention of the Negro woman, it would be worth while making the effort. No race can be said to be a growing race, whose birth rate is declining, and whose natural rate of increase is dropping sharply. No race will amount to anything economically, no matter how high the wages it collects nor how many commercial enterprises it supports, whose ownership of homes has not kept proportionate pace with its business holdings. Churches, social agencies, schools and Sunday schools cannot do the work of mothers and heads of families. Their best efforts are as cheering and comforting to the soul of a child in comparison with the welcoming smile of the mother when it comes from school as the machine-like warmth of an incubator is to the chick after the downy comfort of a clucking hen. Incubators are an essential for the mass production of chickens, but the training of human souls needs to begin at home in the old-fashioned family life, augmented later, if necessary, in the expensive schools and settlements of the great cities.

Notes

1. E. B. Reuter.
2. E. B. Reuter.
3. Howard University, in Washington, D.C., is a predominantly black university with federal support. It was founded in 1867 by Gen. Oliver O. Howard of the Freedman's Bureau to provide education for newly emancipated slaves.

Source

Alice Dunbar-Nelson, "Women's Most Serious Problem," *The Messenger* 9, no. 3 (1927): 73; reprinted in *The Messenger Reader: Stories, Poetry and Essays* (New York: Modern Library 2000).

Selected Bibliography

Dunbar-Nelson, Alice. *An Alice Dunbar-Nelson Reader*. Edited by Ora Williams. Washington, D.C.: University Press of America, 1979.

—— *Give Us Each Day: The Diary of Alice Dunbar Nelson*. Edited by Gloria T. Hull. New York: W. W. Norton, 1984.

—— *The Work of Alice Dunbar Nelson*. 3 vols. Edited by Gloria T. Hull. New York: Oxford University Press, 1988.

—— ed. *The Dunbar-Speaker and Entertainer, Containing the Best Prose and Poetic Selections by and About the Negro Race, with Programs Arranged for Special Entertainments*. Naperville, Ill.: J. L. Nichols, 1920.

—— ed. *Masterpieces of Negro Eloquence: The Best Speeches Delivered by the Negro from the Days of Slavery to the Present Time*. New York: G. K. Hall, 1997.

six

On Being Young—A Woman—and Colored

Marita Bonner's (1899–1971) first essay, "On Being Young—A Woman—and Colored" appeared in 1925 and remains her most famous piece. Like much of her writing, it is an overtly poetic and highly introspective essay, which explores the double oppressions of race and gender. Bonner urged women to concentrate on raising their own self-esteem and to learn to outwit those who would oppress them.

An essayist, playwright, and short story writer, Bonner was born in Boston and educated at Brookline High School and Radcliffe College, where she studied English and comparative literature. Throughout the interwar period, she published in some of the leading magazines of her day, including *Opportunity* and *Crisis*. Between 1922 and 1930, she was also associated with the "S" Salon, a circle of important writers who met weekly in the home of Georgia Douglas Johnson. In 1930, Bonner married and moved to Chicago, where she devoted most of the rest of her life to writing fiction. She also taught periodically, raised four children, and worked with persons with disabilities. She died from injuries sustained in a fire in her Chicago apartment in 1971.

You start out after you have gone from kindergarten to sheepskin covered with sundry Latin phrases.

At least you know what you want life to give you. A career as fixed and as calmly brilliant as the North Star. The one real thing that money buys. Time. Time to do things. A house that can be as delectably out of order and as easily put in order as the doll-house of "playing-house" days. And of course, a husband you can look up to without looking down on yourself.

Somehow you feel like a kitten in a sunny catnip field that sees sleek, plump brown field mice and yellow baby chicks sitting coyly, side by side, under each leaf. A desire to dash three or four ways seizes you.

That's Youth.

But you know that things learned need testing—acid testing—to see if they are really after all, an interwoven part of you. All your life you have heard of the debt you owe "Your People" because you have managed to have the things they have not largely had.

So you find a spot where there are hordes of them—of course below the Line—to be your catnip field while you close your eyes to mice and chickens alike.

If you have never lived among your own, you feel prodigal. Some warm untouched current flows through them—through you—and drags you out into the deep waters of a new sea of human foibles and mannerisms; of a peculiar psychology and prejudices. And one day you find yourself entangled—enmeshed—pinioned in the seaweed of a Black Ghetto.

Not a Ghetto, placid like the Strasse[1] that flows, outwardly unperturbed and calm in a stream of religious belief, but a peculiar group. Cut off, flung together, shoved aside in a bundle because of color and with no more in common.

Unless color is, after all, the real bond.

Milling around like live fish in a basket. Those at the bottom crushed into a sort of stupid apathy by the weight of those on top. Those on top leaping, leaping; leaping to scale the sides; to get out.

There are two "colored" movies, innumerable parties—and cards. Cards played so intensely that it fascinates and repulses at once.

Movies.

Movies worthy and worthless—but not even a low-caste spoken stage

Parties, plentiful. Music and dancing and much that is wit and color and gaiety. But they are like the richest chocolate; stuffed costly chocolates that make the taste go stale if you have too many of them. That make plain whole bread taste like ashes.

There are all the earmarks of a group within a group. Cut off all around from ingress from or egress to other groups. A sameness of type. The smug self-satisfaction of an inner measurement; a measurement by standards known within a limited group and not those of an unlimited, seeing, world. . . . Like the blind, blind mice. Mice whose eyes have been blinded.

Strange longing seizes hold of you. You wish yourself back where you can lay your dollar down and sit in a dollar seat to hear voices, strings, reeds that have lifted the World out, up, beyond things that have bodies and walls. Where you can marvel at new marbles and bronzes and flat colors that will make men forget that things exist in a flesh more often than in spirit. Where you can sink your body in a cushioned seat and sink your soul at the same time into a section of life set before you on the boards for a few hours.

You hear that up at New York this is to be seen; that, to be heard.

You decide the next train will take you there.

You decide the next second that that train will not take you, nor the next—nor the next for some time to come.

For you know that—being a woman—you cannot twice a month or twice a year, for that matter, break away to see or hear anything in a city that is supposed to see and hear too much.

That's being a woman. A woman of any color.

You decide that something is wrong with a world that stifles and chokes; that cuts off and stunts; hedging in, pressing down on eyes, ears and throat. Somehow all wrong.

You wonder how it happens there that—say five hundred miles from the Bay State[2]—Anglo Saxon intelligence is so warped and stunted.

How judgment and discernment are bred out of the race. And what has become of discrimination? Discrimination of the right sort. Discrimination that the best minds have told you weighs shadows and nuances and spiritual differences before it catalogues. The kind they have taught you all of your life was best: that looks clearly past generalization and past appearance to dissect, to dig down to the real heart of matters. That casts aside rapid summary conclusions, drawn from primary inference, as Daniel did the spiced meats.[3]

Why can't they then perceive that there is a difference in the glance from a pair of eyes that look, mildly docile, at "white ladies" and those that, impersonally and perceptively—aware of distinctions—see only women who happen to be white?

Why do they see colored woman only as a gross collection of desires, all uncontrolled, reaching out for their Apollos and the Quasimodos[4] with avid indiscrimination?

Why unless you talk in staccato squawks—brittle as seashells—unless you "champ" gum—unless you cover two yards square when you laugh—unless your taste runs to violent colors—impossible perfumes and more impossible clothes—are you a feminine Caliban craving to pass for Ariel?[5]

An empty imitation of an empty invitation. A mime; a sham; a copy-cat. A hollow re-echo. A froth, a foam. A fleck of the ashes of superficiality?

Everything you touch or taste now is like the flesh of an unripe persimmon.

. . . Do you need to be told what that is being . . . ?

Old ideas, old fundamentals seem worm-eaten, out-grown, worthless, bitter; fit for the scrap-heap of Wisdom.

What you had thought tangible and practical has turned out to be a collection of "blue-flower" theories.

If they have not discovered how to use their accumulation of facts, they are useless to you in Their world.

Every part of you becomes bitter.

But—"In Heaven's name, do not grow bitter. Be bigger than they are"—exhort white friends who have never had to draw breath in a Jim-Crow train. Who have never had petty putrid insult dragged over them—drawing blood—like pebbled sand on your body where the skin is tenderest. On your body where the skin is thinnest and tenderest.

You long to explode and hut everything white unfriendly. But you know that you cannot live with a chip on your shoulder even if you can manage a smile around your eyes—without getting steely and brittle and losing the softness that makes you a woman.

For chips make you bend your body to balance them. And once you bend, you lose your poise, your balance, and the chip gets into you. The real you. You get hard.

. . . And many things in you can ossify . . .

And you know, being a woman, you have to go about it gently and quietly, to find out and to discover just what is wrong. Just what can be done.

You see clearly that they have acquired things.

Money; money. Money to build with, money to destroy. Money to swim in. Money to drown in. Money.

An ascendancy of wisdom. An incalculable hoard of wisdom in all fields, in all things collected from all quarters of humanity.

A stupendous mass of things.

Things.

So, too, the Greeks . . . Things.

And the Romans. . . .

And you wonder and wonder why they have not discovered how to handle deftly and skillfully, Wisdom, stored up for them—like the honey for the Gods on Olympus—since time unknown.

You wonder and you wonder until you wander out into Infinity, where—if it is to be found anywhere—Truth really exists.

The Greeks had possessions, culture. They were lost because they did not understand.

The Romans owned more than anyone else. Trampled under the heel of Vandals and Civilization, because they would not understand.

Greeks. Did not understand.

Romans. Would not understand.

"They." Will not understand.

So you find they have shut Wisdom up and have forgotten to find the key that will let her out. They have trapped, trammeled, lashed her to themselves with thews and thongs and theories. They have ransacked sea and earth and air to bring every treasure to her. But she sulks and will not work for a world with a whitish hue because it has snubbed her twin sister, Understanding.

You see clearly—off there is Infinity—Understanding Standing alone, waiting for someone to really want her.

But she is so far out there is not way to snatch at her and really drag her in.

So—being a woman—you can wait.

You must sit quietly without a chip. Not sodden—and weighted as if your feet were cast in the iron of your soul. Not wasting strength in enervating gestures as if two hundred years of bonds and whips had really tricked you into nervous uncertainty.

But quiet; quiet. Like Buddha—who brown like I am—sat entirely at case, entirely sure of himself; motionless and knowing, a thousand years before the white man knew there was so very much difference between feet and hands.

Motionless on the outside. But on the inside?

Silent.

Still . . . "Perhaps Buddha is a woman."

So you too. Still; quiet; with a smile, ever so slight, at the eyes so that Life will flow into and not by you. And you can gather, as it passes, the essences, the overtones, the tints, the shadows; draw understanding to yourself.

And then you can, when Time is ripe, swoop to your feet—at your full height—at a single gesture.

Ready to go where?

Why . . . Wherever God motions.

Notes

1. German for "street."
2. Massachusetts.
3. Refers to Daniel 1:8–16, where Daniel would not "defile himself with the portion of the King's meat."
4. Quasimodo is the grotesque, hunchbacked character in Victor Hugo's novel, *Notre-Dame de Paris* (1831).
5. Base and ugly pretending to be lofty and beautiful. Caliban and Ariel are characters in Shakespeare's play *The Tempest*.

Source

Marita Bonner, "On Being Young—a Woman—and Colored," in Joyce Flynn and Joyce Occomy Stricklin, eds., *Frye Street and Environs: The Collected Works of Marita Bonner*, 87 (Boston: Beacon Press, 1987).

Selected Bibliography

Allen, Carol. *Black Women Intellectuals: Strategies of Nation, Family, and Neighborhood in the Works of Pauline Hopkins, Jessie Fauset, and Marita Bonner.* New York: Garland, 1998.

Bonner, Marita. *Frye Street and Environs: The Collected Works of Marita Bonner.* Edited by Joyce Flynn and Joyce Occomy Stricklin. Boston: Beacon Press, 1987.

Brown-Guillory, Elizabeth, ed. *Wines in the Wilderness: Plays by African-American Women from the Harlem Renaissance to the Present.* New York: Greenwood Press, 1990.

seven

A Century of Progress of Negro Women

Throughout most of her life, Mary McLeod Bethune (1875–1955) was a visible advocate of racial justice and an active helper of others. In her speech "A Century of Progress of Negro Women," delivered in 1933 to the Chicago Women's Federation, Bethune follows a long tradition of female activists who have highlighted the agency, achievements, and contributions of African American women in the face of extraordinary adversity.

Bethune was born near Mayesville, South Carolina, in 1875, the fifteenth of seventeen children, to parents who were ex-slaves. After building an impressive résumé as a missionary, educator, and activist, Bethune came to national attention when she was appointed director of the Negro Division of the National Youth Administration in 1939, then the highest federal appointment held by a black woman. In this capacity, she successfully used federal funds to aid black high school and college students with education, job training, and job placement. Bethune had a warm relationship with Eleanor Roosevelt, and she was closely involved with most federal issues relative to the status of black Americans. She died of a heart attack in 1955.

To Frederick Douglass[1] is credited the plea that, "the Negro by not judged by the heights to which he is risen, but by the depths from which he has climbed." Judged on that basis, the Negro woman embodies one of the modern miracles of the New World.

One hundred years ago she was the most pathetic figure on the American continent. She was not a person, in the opinion of many, but a thing—a thing whose personality had no claim to the respect of mankind. She was a household drudge,—a means for getting distasteful work done; she was an animated agricultural implement to augment the service of moles and plows in cultivating and harvesting the cotton crop. Then she was an automatic incubator, a producer of human live stock, beneath whose heart and lungs more potential laborers could be bred and nurtured and brought to the light of toilsome day.

Today she stands side by side with the finest manhood the race has been able to produce. Whatever the achievements of the Negro man in letters, business, art, pulpit, civic progress and moral reform, he cannot but share them with his sister of darker hue. Whatever glory belongs to the race for a development unprecedented in history for the given length of time, a full share belongs to the womanhood of the race. . . .

By the very force of circumstances, the part she has played in the progress of the race has been of necessity, to a certain extent, subtle and indirect. She has not always been permitted a place in the front ranks where she could show her face and make her voice heard with effect. . . . [But] she has been quick to seize every opportunity which presented itself to come more and more into the open and strive directly for the uplift of the race and nation. In that direction, her achievements have been amazing. . . .

Negro women have made outstanding contributions in the arts. Meta V. W. Fuller and May Howard Jackson are significant figures in Fine Arts development. Angelina Grimké,[1] Georgia Douglass Johnson and Alice Dunbar Nelson are poets of note. Jessie Fausett has become famous as a novelist. In the field of Music Anita Patti Brown, Lillian Evanti, Elizabeth Greenfield. Florence Cole-Talbert. Marian Anderson and Marie Selika stand out pre-eminently.

Very early in the post-emancipation period women began to show signs of ability to contribute to the business progress of the Race Maggie L. Walker, who is outstanding as the guiding spirit of the Order of Saint Luke in 1902 . . . went before her Grand Council with a plan for a Saint Luke Penny Savings

1. Angelina Weld Grimké (1880–1958), poet and teacher, was the daughter of Archibald Henry Grimké, a lawyer and distinguished race leader. Her father was the son of slaveholder Henry Grimké and his slave, Nancy Weston. Angelina Weld Grimké was named after her white great-aunt, the abolitionist Angelina Grimké Weld, who after the Civil War learned of the existence of her three mulatto nephews, accepted them as family members, and paid for their education.

Bank. This organization started with a deposit of about eight thousand dollars and twenty-five thousand in paid-up capital, with Maggie L. Walker as the first Woman Bank President in America. For twenty-seven years she has held this place. Her bank has paid dividends to its stockholders; has served as a depository for gas and water accounts of the city of Richmond and has given employment to hundreds of Negro clerks, bookkeepers and office workers. . . .

With America's great emphasis on the physical appearance, a Negro woman left her wash-tub and ventured into the field of facial beautification. From a humble beginning Madame C. J. Walker built a substantial institution that is a credit to American business in every way.

Mrs. Annie M. Malone is another pioneer in this field of successful business. The C. J. Walker Manufacturing Company and the Poro College do not confine their activities in the field of beautification, to race. They serve both races and give employment to both. . . .

When the ballot was made available to the Womanhood of America, the sister of darker hue was not slow to seize the advantage. In sections where the Negro could gain access to the voting booth, the intelligent, forward-looking element of the Race's women have taken hold of political issues with an enthusiasm and mental acumen that might well set worthy examples for other groups. Oftimes she has led the struggle toward moral improvement and political record, and has compelled her reluctant brother to follow her determined lead. . . .

In time of war as in time of peace, the Negro woman has ever been ready to . . . [serve] . . . for her people's and the nation's good. . . . During the recent World War . . . she . . . pleaded to go in the uniform of the Red Cross nurse and was denied the opportunity only on the basis of racial distinction.

Addie W. Hunton and Kathryn M. Johnson gave yeoman service with the American Expeditionary Forces . . . with the YMCA group. . . .

Negro women have thrown themselves whole-heartedly into the organization of groups to direct the social uplift of their fellowmen . . . one of the greatest achievements of the race.

Perhaps the most outstanding individual social worker of our group today is Jane E. Hunter, founder and executive secretary of the Phillis Wheatley Association, Cleveland, Ohio.

In November, 1911, Miss Hunter, who had been a nurse in Cleveland for only a short time, recognizing the need for a Working Girls' Home, organized the Association and prepared to establish the work. Today the Association is housed in a magnificent structure of nine stories, containing one hundred thirty-five rooms, offices, parlours, a cafeteria and beauty parlour. It is not only a home for working girls but a recreational center and ideal hospice for the Young Negro woman who is living away from home. It maintains an employment department and a fine, up-to-date camp. Branches of the activities of the main Phillis Wheatley are located in other sections of Cleveland, special emphasis being given to the recreational facilities for children and young women of the vicinities in which the branches are located.

In no field of modern social relationship has the hand of service and the influence of the Negro woman been felt more distinctly than in the Negro orthodox church. . . . It may be safely said that the chief sustaining force in support of the pulpit and the various phases of missionary enterprise has been the feminine element of the membership. The development of the Negro church since the Civil War has been another of the modern miracles. Throughout its growth the untiring effort, the unflagging enthusiasm, the sacrificial contribution of time, effort and cash earnings of the black woman have been the most significant factors, without which the modern Negro church would have no history worth the writing. . . .

Both before and since emancipation, by some rare gift, she has been able . . . to hold onto the fibres of family unity and keep the home one unimpaired whole. In recent years it has become increasingly the case where in many instances, the mother is the sole dependence of the home, and single-handed, fights the wolf from the door, while the father submits unwillingly to enforced idleness and unavoidable unemployment. Yet in myriads of instances she controls home discipline with a tight rein and exerts a unifying influence that is the miracle of the century. . . .

The true worth of a race must be measured by the character of its womanhood. . . .

As the years have gone on the Negro woman has touched the most vital fields in the civilization of today. Wherever she has contributed she has left the mark of a strong character. The educational institutions she has established and directed have met the needs of her young people; her cultural development has concentrated itself into artistic presentation accepted and acclaimed by meritorious critics; she is successful as a poet and novelist; she is shrewd in business and capable in politics; she recognizes the importance of uplifting her people through social, civic and religious activities; starting at the time when as a "mammy" she nursed the infants of the other race and taught [them] her meagre store of truth, she has been a contributing factor of note to interracial relations. Finally, through the past century she has made and kept her home intact—humble though it may have been in many instances. She has made and is making history.

Note

1. Frederick Douglass (1817–1895), abolitionist, orator, reformer, editor, humanitarian, statesman.

Source

Mary McLeod Bethune, "A Century of Progress of Negro Women," in Gerda Lerner, ed., *Black Women in America*, 579–84 (New York: Pantheon Books, 1972).

Selected Bibliography

Bethune, Mary McLeod. "My Last Will and Testament." *Ebony* 10 (August 1955): 105–11.

Hanson, Joyce Ann. "The Ties That Bind: Mary McLeod Bethune and the Political Mobilization of African-American Women." Ph.D. diss., University of Connecticut, 1997.

McCulskey, Audrey Thomas. "Mary McLeod Bethune and the Education of Black Girls in the South, 1904–1923." Ph.D. diss., Indiana University, 1991.

Smith, Elaine M. "Mary McLeod Bethune and the National Youth Administration." In Mabel E. Deutrich and Virginia C. Purdy, eds., *Clio Was a Woman: Studies in the History of American Women.* Washington, D.C.: Howard University Press, 1980.

eight

To All Black Women, from All Black Men

The writer, Black Panther, and revolutionary celebrity of the 1960s Eldridge Cleaver's (1935–1998) disturbing, provocative essay "To All Black Women, from All Black Men" demonstrated some of the macho chauvinism of the Black Power movement, which African American women were forced to struggle against.

Cleaver was born in Wabbeseka, Arkansas, in 1935. In 1954 he was convicted of drug possession, and over the course of the next twelve years he served time at Soledad, Folsom, and San Quentin prisons. While incarcerated, Cleaver studied the Black Muslim faith and devoted his time to self-education. Upon his release, he began writing for the left-wing *Ramparts* magazine, and in 1967 he became minister of information of the Black Panther Party. In 1968 he published *Soul on Ice*, a best-selling collection of essays that is now commonly regarded as a classic of revolutionary black literature. Following a shoot-out with police in Oakland, California, Cleaver fled the United States, living for brief periods in Cuba, France, and Algeria, where he established an international branch of the Black Panther Party (BPP) with his wife, Kathleen Cleaver. In 1975 he finally returned to the United States, surrendering to authorities and announcing his rebirth as a fundamentalist Christian.

Queen-Mother-Daughter of Africa
Sister of My Soul
Black Bride of My Passion
My Eternal Love

I greet you, my Queen, not in the obsequious whine of a cringing Slave to which you have become accustomed, neither do I greet you in the new voice, the unctuous supplications of the sleek Black Bourgeoise, nor the bullying bellow of the rude Free Slave—but in my own voice do I greet you, the voice of the Black Man. And although I greet you *anew*, my greeting is not *new*, but as old as the Sun, Moon, and Stars. And rather than mark a new beginning, my greeting signifies only my Return.

I have Returned from the dead. I speak to you now from the Here And Now. I was dead for four hundred years. For four hundred years you have been a woman alone, bereft of her man, a manless woman. For four hundred years I was neither your man nor my own man. The white man stood between us, over us, around us. The white man was your man and my man. Do not pass lightly over this truth, my Queen, for even though the fact of it has burned into the marrow of our bones and diluted our blood, we must bring it to the surface of the mind, into the realm of knowing, glue our gaze upon it and stare at it as at a coiled serpent in a baby's playpen or the fresh flowers on a mother's grave. It is to be pondered and realized in the heart, for the heel of the white man's boot is our point of departure, our point of Resolve and Return—the bloodstained pivot of our future. (But I would ask you to recall, that before we could come up from slavery, we had to be pulled down from our throne.)

Across the naked abyss of negated masculinity, of four hundred years minus my Balls, we face each other today, my Queen. I feel a deep, terrifying hurt, the pain of humiliation of the vanquished warrior. The shame of the fleet-footed sprinter who stumbles at the start of the race. I feel unjustified. I can't bear to look into your eyes. Don't you know (surely you must have noticed by now: four hundred years!) that for four hundred years I have been unable to look squarely into your eyes? I tremble inside each time you look at me. I can feel . . . in the ray of your eye, from a deep hiding place, a long-kept secret you harbor. That is the unadorned truth. Not that I would have felt justified, under the circumstances, in taking such liberties with you, but I want you to know that I feared to look into your eyes because I knew I would find reflected there a merciless Indictment of my impotence and a compelling challenge to redeem my conquered manhood.

My Queen, it is hard for me to tell you what is in my heart for you today—what is in the heart of all my black brothers for you and all your black sisters—and I fear I will fail unless you reach out to me, tune in on me with the antenna of your love, the sacred love in ultimate degree which you were unable to give me because I, being dead, was unworthy to receive it; that perfect, radical love of black on which our Fathers thrived. Let me drink from the river of your love at its source, let the lines of force of your love seize my soul by its core and heal the wound of my Castration, let my convex exile end its haunted Odyssey in your concave essence which receives that it may give. Flower of Africa, it is only through the liberating power of your *re*-love that my manhood can be redeemed. For it is in your eyes, before you, that my need is to be justified, Only, only, only you and only you can condemn or set me free.

Be convinced, Sable Sister, that the past is no forbidden vista upon which we dare not look, out of a phantom fear of being, as the wife of Lot, turned into pillars of salt. Rather the past is an omniscient mirror: we gaze and see reflected there ourselves and each other—what we used to be, what we are today, how we got this way, and what we are becoming. To decline to look into the Mirror of Then, my heart, is to refuse to view the face of Now.

> I have died the ninth death of the cat, have seen Satan face to face and turned my back on God, have dined in the Swine's Trough, and descended to the uttermost echelon of the Pit, have entered the Den and seized my Balls from the teeth of a roaring lion!

Black Beauty, in impotent silence I listened, as if to a symphony of sorrows, to your screams for help, anguished pleas of terror that echo still throughout the Universe and through the mind, a million scattered screams across the painful years that merged into a single sound of pain to haunt and bleed the soul, a white-hot sound to char the brain and blow the fuse of thought, a sound of fangs and teeth sharp to eat the heart, a sound of moving fire, a sound of frozen heat, a sound of licking flames, a fiery-fiery sound, a sound of fire to burn the steel out of my Balls, a sound of Blue fire, a Bluesy sound, the sound of dying, the sound of my woman in pain, *the sound of my woman's pain*, THE SOUND OF MY WOMAN CALLING ME, ME, I HEARD HER CALL FOR HELP, I HEARD THAT MOURNFUL SOUND BUT HUNG MY HEAD AND FAILED TO HEED IT, I HEARD MY WOMAN'S CRY, I HEARD MY WOMAN'S SCREAM, I HEARD MY WOMAN BEG THE BEAST FOR MERCY, I HEARD HER BEG FOR ME, I HEARD MY WOMAN BEG THE BEAST FOR MERCY FOR ME, I HEARD MY WOMAN DIE, I HEARD THE SOUND OF HER DEATH, A SNAPPING SOUND, A BREAKING SOUND, A SOUND THAT SOUNDED FINAL, THE LAST SOUND, THE ULTIMATE SOUND, THE SOUND OF DEATH, ME, I HEARD, I HEAR IT EVERY DAY, I HEAR HER NOW . . . I HEAR YOU NOW . . . I HEAR YOU. . . . I heard you then . . . your scream came like a searing bolt of lightning that blazed a white streak down my black back. In a cowardly stupor, with a palpitating heart and quivering knees, I watched the Slaver's lash of death slash through the opposing air and bite with teeth of fire into your delicate flesh, the black and tender flesh of African Motherhood, forcing the startled Life untimely from your torn and outraged womb, the sacred womb that cradled primal man, the womb that incubated Ethiopia and populated Nubia and gave forth Pharaohs unto Egypt, the womb that painted the Congo black and mothered Zulu, the womb of Mero, the womb of the Nile, of the Niger, the womb of Songhay, of Mali, of Ghana, the womb that felt the might of Chaka[1] before he saw the Sun, the Holy Womb, the womb that knew the future form of Jomo Kenyatta,[2] the womb of Mau Mau,[3] the womb of the blacks, the womb that nurtured Toussaint L'Ouverture,[4] that warmed Nat Turner,[5] and Gabriel Prosser,[6] and Denmark Vesey,[7] the black womb that surrendered up in tears that nameless and endless chain of Africa's Cream, the Black Cream of the Earth, that nameless and endless black chain that sank in heavy groans into oblivion in the great abyss, the womb that received and nourished and held firm the seed and gave back Sojourner Truth,[8] and Sister Tubman,[9] and Rosa Parks,[10] and Bird,[11] and Richard Wright,[12] and your other works of art who wore and wear such names as Marcus Garvey[13] and DuBois[14] and Kwame Nkrumah[15] and Paul Robeson[16] and Malcolm X[17] and Robert Williams,[18] and the one you bore in pain and called Elijah Muhammad,[19] but most of all that nameless one they tore out of your womb in a flood of murdered blood that splashed upon and seeped into the mud. And Patrice Lumumba,[20] and Emmett Till,[21] and Mack Parker.

O, My Soul! I became a sniveling craven, a funky punk, a vile, groveling bootlicker, with my will to oppose petrified by a cosmic fear of the Slavemaster. Instead of inciting the Slaves to rebellion with eloquent oratory, I soothed their hurt and eloquently sang the Blues! Instead of hurling my life with contempt into the face of my Tormentor, *I shed your precious blood!* When Nat Turner sought to free me from my Fear, my Fear delivered him up unto the Butcher—a martyred monument to my Emasculation. My spirit was unwilling and my flesh was weak. Ah, eternal ignominy!

I, the Black Eunuch, divested of my Balls, walked the earth with my mind locked in Cold Storage. I would kill a black man or woman quicker than I'd smash a fly, while for the white man I would pick a thousand pounds of cotton a day. What profit is there in the blind, frenzied efforts of the (Guilty!) Black Eunuchs (Justifiers!) who hide their wounds and scorn the truth to mitigate their culpability through the pallid sophistry of postulating a Universal Democracy of Cowards, pointing out that in history no one can hide, that if not at one time then surely at another the iron heel of the Conqueror has ground into the mud the Balls of Everyman? Memories of yesterday will not assuage the torrents of blood that flow today from my crotch. Yes, History could pass for a scarlet text, its jot and tittle graven red in human blood. More armies than shown in the books have planted flags on foreign soil leaving Castration in their wake. But no Slave should die a natural death. There is a point where Caution ends and Cowardice begins. Give me a bullet through the brain from the gun of the beleaguered oppressor on the night of seige. Why is there dancing and singing in the Slave Quarters? A Slave who dies of natural causes cannot balance two dead flies in the Scales of Eternity. Such a one deserves rather to be pitied than mourned.

Black woman, without asking how, just say that we survived our forced march and travail through the Valley of Slavery, Suffering, and Death—there, that Valley there beneath us hidden by that drifting mist. Ah, what sights and sounds and pain lie beneath that mist! And we had thought that our hard climb out of that cruel valley led to some cool, green and peaceful, sunlit place—but it's all jungle here, a wild and savage wilderness that's overrun with ruins.

But put on your crown, my Queen, and we will build a New City on these ruins.

Notes

1. Chaka (or Shaka), paramount chief of the Zulus, 1818–1828.
2. Jomo Kenyatta (c. 1893–1978), African political leader and the first president of Kenya, 1964–1978.
3. Secret insurgent organization in Kenya, mainly made up of Kikuyu tribesmen. In 1952 the Mau Mau began reprisals against white Europeans who occupied Kikuyu lands.
4. Toussaint L' Overture (c.1745–1803), slave, reformer, military person, and insurrectionist.
5. Nat Turner (1800–1831), slave, liberation theologian, and insurrectionist.
6. Gabriel Prosser (c. 1775–1800), slave and insurrectionist.
7. Denmark Vesey (1767–1822), carpenter, liberation theologian, and slave insurrectionist.
8. Sojourner Truth (1799–1883), abolitionist, lecturer, slave, and religious worker.
9. Harriet Tubman (c. 1820–1913), slave, reformer, abolitionist, and lecturer.
10. Rosa Parks (1913–), American civil rights activist who provided the impetus for the Montgomery Bus Boycott of 1955 that launched the modern civil rights movement.
11. Charlie Parker (1920–1955), jazz musician.
12. Richard Wright (1906–1960), novelist, poet, dramatist, and screenwriter.
13. Marcus Garvey (1887–1940), organization founder, Pan-Africanist leader, newspaper publisher, writer, and entrepreneur.
14. W. E. B. Du Bois (1868–1963), writer, scholar, educator, Pan-Africanist, and editor.
15. Kwame Nkrumah (1909–1972), African political leader and president of Ghana (1960–1966).
16. Paul Robeson (1897–1976), singer, activist, lawyer, and college athlete.
17. Malcolm X (1925–1965), human rights activist, lecturer, organizer for the Nation of Islam (NOI), and black nationalist.
18. Robert F. Williams (1925–1996), editor, writer, grassroots leader, and radio disc jockey.
19. Elijah Muhammad (1897–1975), religious leader of the Nation of Islam (NOI) and black nationalist.
20. Patrice Lumumba (1925–1961), prime minister (1960) of the Republic of Congo (now Zaire).
21. Emmett Till (1941–1955), African American teenager who was murdered by white racists.

Source

Eldridge Cleaver, "To All Black Women, from All Black Men," in *Soul On Ice,* 205–10 (New York: McGraw Hill, 1968).

Selected Bibliography

Cleaver, Eldridge. *Soul on Ice*. New York: Dell Publishing Company, 1968.

Jones, Charles E., ed. *The Black Panther Party (Reconsidered)*. Baltimore: Black Classic Press, 1998.

Lockwood, Lee. *Conversations with Eldridge Cleaver; Algiers*. New York: McGraw-Hill, 1970.

Rout, Kathleen. *Eldridge Cleaver.* Boston: Twayne, 1991.

nine

Double Jeopardy: To Be Black and Female

Frances Beal's (n.d.) essay "Double Jeopardy: To Be Black and Female" is a landmark text of the black feminist movement and has been widely reprinted since it first appeared in Robin Morgan's classic anthology *Sisterhood Is Powerful: An Anthology of Writings from the Women's Liberation Movement* (1970). Beal captured some of the revolutionary zeal that the black feminist movement later became known for, attacking not simply racism and sexism but also capitalism, which, according to Beal, had drastically circumscribed the economic, social, and psychological lives of black women.

Beal cut her political teeth in the 1960s, when she was a member of the Student Nonviolent Coordinating Committee (SNCC) and led the New York chapter of SNCC's Black Women's Liberation Committee. She has since worked as a journalist, served as associate editor of the *Black Scholar,* and has been active in the Black Radical Congress (BRC).

In attempting to analyze the situation of the black woman in America, one crashes abruptly into a solid wall of grave misconceptions, outright distortions of fact, and defensive attitudes on the part of many. The System of capitalism (and its afterbirth—racism) under which we all live, has attempted by many devious ways and means to destroy the humanity of all people, and particularly the humanity of black people. This has meant an outrageous assault on every black man, woman, and child who resides in the United States.

In keeping with its goal of destroying the black race's will to resist its subjugation, capitalism found it necessary to create a situation where the black man found it impossible to find meaningful or productive employment. More often than not, he couldn't find work of any kind. And the black woman, likewise, was manipulated by the System, economically exploited and physically assaulted. She could often find work in the white man's kitchen, however, and sometimes became the sole breadwinner of the family. This predicament has led to many psychological problems on the part of both man and woman and has contributed to the turmoil in the black family structure.

Unfortunately, neither the black man nor the black woman understood the true nature of the forces working upon them. Many black women tended to accept the capitalist evaluation of manhood and womanhood and believed, in fact, that black men were shiftless and lazy; otherwise they would get a job and support their families as they ought to. Personal relationships between black men and women were thus torn asunder and one result has been the separation of man from wife, mother from child, etc.

America has defined the roles to which each individual should subscribe. It has defined "manhood" in terms of its own interests and "femininity" likewise. Therefore, an individual who has a good job, makes a lot of money, and drives a Cadillac is a real "man," and conversely, an individual who is lacking in these "qualities" is less of a man. The advertising media in this country continuously informs the American male of his need for indispensable signs of his virility—the brand of cigarettes that cowboys prefer, the whisky that has a masculine tang, or the label of the jock strap that athletes wear.

The ideal model that is projected for a woman is to be surrounded by hypocritical homage and estranged from all real work, spending idle hours primping and preening, obsessed with conspicuous consumption, and limiting life's functions to simply a sex role. We unqualitatively reject these respective models. A woman who stays at home, caring for children and the house, leads an extremely sterile existence. She must lead her entire life as a satellite to her mate. He goes out into society and brings back a little piece of the world for her. His interests and his understanding of the world become her own and she cannot develop herself as an individual, having been reduced to only a biological function. This kind of woman leads a parasitic existence that can aptly be described as "legalized prostitution."

Furthermore, it is idle dreaming to think of black women simply caring for their homes and children like the middle-class white model. Most black women have to work to help house, feed, and clothe their families. Black women make up a substantial percentage of the black working force and this is true for the poorest black family as well as the so-called "middle-class" family.

Black women were never afforded any such phony luxuries. Though we have been browbeaten with this white image, the reality of the degrading and dehumanizing jobs that were relegated to us quickly dissipated this mirage of womanhood. The following excerpts from a speech that Sojourner Truth[1] made at a Women's Rights Convention in the nineteenth century show us how misleading and incomplete a life this model represents for us:

> . . . Well, children whar dar is so much racket dar must be something out o'kilter. I tink dat 'twixt de niggers of de Souf and de women at de Norf all a talkin' 'bout rights, de white men will be in a fix pretty soon. But what's all dis here talkin' 'bout? Dat man ober dar say dat women needs to be helped into carriages, and lifted ober ditches, and to have de best place every whar. Nobody ever help me into carriages, or ober mud puddles, or gives me any best places . . . and ar'nt I a woman? Look at me! Look at my arm! . . . I have plowed, and planted, and gathered into barns, and no man could head me—and ar'nt I a woman? I could work as much as a man (when I could get it), and bear de lash as well—and ar'nt I a woman? I have borne five chilern and I seen 'em mos' all sold off into slavery, and when I cried out with a mother's grief, none but Jesus heard—and ar'nt I a woman?

Unfortunately, there seems to be some confusion in the Movement today as to who has been oppressing whom. Since the advent of Black Power, the black male has exerted a more prominent leadership role in our struggle for justice in this country. He sees the System for what it really is, for the most part, but where he rejects its values and mores on many issues, when it comes to women, he seems to take his guidelines from the pages of the *Ladies' Home Journal*. Certain black men are maintaining that they have been castrated by society but that black women somehow escaped this persecution and even contributed to this emasculation.

Let me state here and now that the black woman in America can justly be described as a "slave of a slave." When the black man in America was reduced to such an abject state, the black woman had no protector and was used and is still being used in some cases as the scapegoat for the evils that this horrendous System has perpetrated on black men. Her physical image has been maliciously maligned; she has been sexually assaulted and abused by the white colonizer; she has suffered the worst kind of economic exploitation, having been forced to serve as the white woman's maid and wet nurse for white offspring while her own children were starving and neglected. It is the depth of degradation to be socially manipulated, physically raped, used to undermine your own household—and to be powerless to reverse this syndrome.

It is true that our husbands, fathers, brothers, and sons have been emasculated, lynched, and brutalized. They have suffered from the cruellest assault of mankind that the world has ever known. However, it is a gross distortion of fact to state that black women have oppressed black men. The capitalist System found it expedient to oppress them and proceeded to do so without consultation or the signing of any agreements with black women.

It must also be pointed out at this time, that black women are not resentful of the rise to power of black men. We welcome it. We see in it the eventual liberation of all black people from this oppressive System of capitalism. Nevertheless, this does not mean that you have to negate one for the other. This kind of thinking is a product of miseducation; that it's either *X* or it's *Y*. It is fallacious reasoning that in order for the black man to be strong, the black woman has to be weak.

Those who are exerting their "manhood" by telling black women to step back into a submissive role are assuming a counterrevolutionary position. Black women likewise have been abused by the System and we must begin talking about the elimination of all kinds of oppression. If we are talking about building a strong nation, capable of throwing off the yoke of capitalist oppression, then we are talking about the total involvement of every man, woman, and child, each with a highly developed political consciousness. We need our whole army out there dealing with the enemy, and not half an army.

There are also some black women who feel that there is no more productive role in life than having and raising children. This attitude often reflects the conditioning of the society in which we live and is adopted from a bourgeois white model. Some young sisters who have never had to maintain a household and accept the confining role which this entails, tend to romanticize (along with the help of a number of brothers) this role of housewife and mother. Black women who have had to endure this kind of function are less apt to have these utopian visions. Those who project in an intellectual manner how great and rewarding this role will be and who feel that the most important thing that they can contribute to the black nation is children, are doing themselves a great injustice. This line of reasoning completely negates the contributions that black women have historically made to our struggle for liberation. These black women include Sojourner Truth, Harriet Tubman,[2] Mary McLeod Bethune,[3] and Fannie Lou Hamer,[4] to name but a few.

We live in a highly industrialized society and every member of the black nation must be as academically and technologically developed as possible. To wage a revolution, we need competent teachers, doctors, nurses, electronics experts, chemists, biologists, physicists, political scientists, and so on and so forth. Black women sitting at home reading bedtime stories to their children are just not going to make it.

Economic Exploitation of Black Women

The economic System of capitalism finds it expedient to reduce women to a state of enslavement. They oftentimes serve as a scapegoat for the evils of this system. Much in the same way that the poor white cracker of the South, who is equally victimized, looks down upon blacks and contributes to the oppression of blacks—so, by giving to men a false feeling of superiority (at least in their own home or in their relationships with women)—the oppression of women acts as an escape valve for capitalism. Men may be cruelly exploited and subjected to all sorts of dehumanizing tactics on the part of the ruling class, but they have someone who is below them—at least they're not women.

Women also represent a surplus labor supply, the control of which is absolutely necessary to the profitable functioning of capitalism. Women are consistently exploited by the System. They are often paid less for the same work that men do and jobs that are specifically relegated to women are lowpaying and without the possibility of advancement. Statistics from the Women's Bureau of the United States Department of Labor show that in 1967, the wage scale for white women was even below that of black men; and the wage scale for nonwhite women was the lowest of all:

White Males	$6704
Non-White Males	4277
White Females	3991
Non-White Females	2861

Those industries that employ mainly black women are the most exploitative in the country. The hospital workers are a good example of this oppression; the garment workers in New York City provide us with another view of this economic slavery. The International Ladies Garment Workers Union (ILGWU), whose overwhelming membership consists of black and Puerto Rican women, has a leadership that is nearly all lily-white and male. This leadership has been working in collusion with the ruling class and has completely sold its soul to the corporate structure.

To add insult to injury, ILGWU has invested heavily in business enterprises in racist, apartheid South Africa—with union funds. Not only does this bought-off leadership contribute to our continued exploitation in this country by not truly representing the best interests of its membership, but it audaciously uses funds that black and Puerto Rican women have provided to support the economy of a vicious government that is engaged in the exploitation and murder of our black brothers and sisters in our motherland, Africa.

The entire labor movement in the United States has suffered as a result of the superexploitation of black workers and women. The unions have historically been racist and male chauvinistic. They have upheld racism in this country and have failed to fight the white-skin privileges of white workers. They have failed to struggle against inequities in the hiring and pay of women workers. There has been virtually no struggle against either the racism of the white worker or the economic exploitation of the working woman, two factors which have consistently impeded the advancement of the real struggle against the ruling class.

The racist, chauvinistic, and manipulative use of black workers and women, especially black women, has been a severe cancer on the American labor scene. It therefore becomes essential for those who understand the workings of capitalism and imperialism to realize that the exploitation of black people and women works to everyone's disadvantage and that the liberation of these two minority groups is a stepping stone to the liberation of all oppressed people in this country and around the world.

Bedroom Politics

I have briefly discussed the economic and psychological manipulation of black women, but perhaps the most outlandish act of oppression in modern times is the current campaign to promote sterilization of nonwhite women, in an attempt to maintain the population and power imbalance between the white "haves" and the non-white "have nots."

These tactics are but another example of the many devious schemes that the ruling class elite attempts to perpetrate on the black population in order to keep itself in control. It has recently come to our attention that a massive campaign for so-called "birth control" is presently being prompted not only in the underdeveloped non-white areas of the world, but also in black communities here in the United States. However, what the authorities in charge of these programs refer to as "birth control" is in fact nothing but a method of outright surgical genocide.

The United States has been sponsoring sterilization clinics in nonwhite countries, especially in India where already some three million young men and boys in and around New Delhi have been sterilized in makeshift operating rooms set up by the American Peace Corps workers. Under these circumstances, it is understandable why certain countries view the Peace Corps not as a benevolent project, not as evidence of America's concern for underdeveloped areas, but rather as a threat to their very existence. This program could more aptly be named the "Death Corps."

The vasectomy, which is performed on males and takes only six or seven minutes, is a relatively simple operation. The sterilization of a woman, on the other hand, is admittedly major surgery. This operation (salpingectomy) must be performed in a hospital under general anesthesia. This method of "birth control" is a common procedure in Puerto Rico. Puerto Rico has long been used by the colonialist exploiter, the United States, as a huge experimental laboratory for medical research before allowing certain practices to be imported and used here. When the birth-control pill was first being perfected, it was tried out on Puerto Rican women and selected black women (poor), as if they were guinea pigs to see what its effect would be and how efficient the Pill was.

The salpingectomy has now become the commonest operation in Puerto Rico, commoner than an appendectomy or a tonsilectomy. It is so widespread that it is referred to simply as *la operación. On the Island, 20 percent of the women between the ages of fifteen and forty-five have already been sterilized.*

And now, as previously occurred with the Pill, this method has been imported into the United States. These sterilization clinics are cropping up around the country in the black and Puerto Rican communities. These so-called "Maternity Clinics," specifically outfitted to purge black women or men of their reproductive possibilities, are appearing more and more in hospitals and clinics across the country.

A number of organizations have recently been formed to popularize the idea of sterilization, such as The Association for Voluntary Sterilization, and the Human Betterment (!!!?) Association for Voluntary Sterilization, Inc., which has its headquarters in New York City. Front Royal, Virginia, has one such "Maternity Clinic" in Warren Memorial Hospital. The tactics used in the clinic in Fauquier County, Virginia, where poor and helpless black mothers and young girls are pressured into undergoing sterilization, are certainly not confined to that clinic alone.

Threatened with the cut-off of relief funds, some black welfare women have been forced to undergo this sterilization procedure in exchange for a continuation of welfare benefits. Mt. Sinai Hospital in New York City performs these operations on its ward patients whenever it can convince the women to undergo this surgery. Mississippi and some of the other Southern states are notorious for this act. Black women are often afraid to permit any kind of necessary surgery because they know from bitter experience that they are more likely than not to come out without their insides. (Both salpingectomies and hysterectomies are performed.)

We condemn this use of the black woman as a medical testing ground for the white middle class. Reports of the ill effects, including deaths, from the use of the birth-control pill only started to come to light when the white privileged class began to be affected. These outrageous Nazi-like procedures on the part of medical researchers are but another manifestation of the totally amoral and brutal behavior that the capitalist System perpetrates on black women. The sterilization experiments carried on in concentration camps some twenty-five years ago have been denounced the world over, but no one seems to get upset by the repetition of these same racist practices today in the United States of America—the land of the free and home of the brave.

The rigid laws concerning abortions in this country are another means of subjugation and, indirectly, of outright murder. Rich white women somehow manage to obtain these operations with little or no difficulty. It is the poor black and Puerto Rican woman who is at the mercy of the local butcher. Statistics show us that the non-white death rate at the hands of the unqualified abortionist is substantially higher than for white women. Nearly half of the child-bearing deaths in New York City are attributed to abortion alone and out of these, 79 percent are among non-whites and Puerto Rican women.

We are not saying that black women should not practice birth control. Black women have the right and the responsibility to determine when it is in *the interest of the struggle to have children or not to have them and this right must not be relinquished to anyone.* It is also her right and responsibility to determine when it is in *her own best interests* to have children, how many she will have, and how far apart. The lack of the availability of safe birth-control methods, the forced sterilization practices, and the inability to obtain legal abortions are all symptoms of a sick society that jeopardizes the health of black women (and thereby the entire black race) in its attempt to control the very life processes of human beings. This is a symptom of a society that is attempting to bring economic and political factors into the privacy of the bedchamber. The elimination of these horrendous conditions will free black women for full participation in the revolution, and thereafter in the building of the new society.

Relationship to White Movement

Much has been written recently about the white women's liberation movement in the United States and the question arises whether there are any parallels between this struggle and the movement on the part of black women for total emancipation. While there are certain comparisons that one can make because we both live under the same exploitative System, there are certain differences, some of which are quite basic.

The white woman's movement is far from being monolithic. Any white woman's group that does not have an anti-imperialist and antiracist ideology has absolutely nothing in common with the black woman's struggle. In fact, some groups come to the incorrect conclusion that their oppression is due simply to male chauvinism. They therefore have an extremely antimale tone to their dissertations. Black people are engaged in a life-and-death struggle and the main emphasis of black women must be to combat the capitalist, racist exploitation of black people. While it is true that male chauvinism has become institutionalized in American society, one must always look for the main enemy—the fundamental cause of the female condition.

Another major differentiation is that the white woman's movement is basically middle class. Very few of these women suffer the extreme economic exploitation that most black women are subjected to day by day. This is the factor that is most crucial for us. It is not an intellectual persecution alone; it is not an intellectual outburst for us; it is quite real. We as black women have got to deal with the problems that the black masses deal with, for our problems in reality are one and the same.

If the white groups do not realize that they are in fact fighting capitalism and racism, we do not have common bonds. If they do not realize that the reasons for their condition lie in the System and not simply that men get a vicarious pleasure out of "consuming their bodies for exploitative reasons" (this kind of reasoning seems to be quite prevalent in certain white women's groups), then we cannot unite with them around common grievances or even discuss these groups in a serious manner because they're completely irrelevant to the black struggle.

The New World

The black community and black women especially must begin raising questions about the kind of society we wish to see established. We must note the ways in which capitalism oppresses us and then move to create institutions that will eliminate these destructive influences.

The new world that we are attempting to create must destroy oppression of any type. The value of this new system will be determined by the status of the person who was low man on the totem pole. Unless women in any enslaved nation are completely liberated, the change cannot really be called a revolution. If the black woman has to retreat to the position she occupied before the armed struggle, the whole movement and the whole struggle will have retreated in terms of truly freeing the colonized population.

A people's revolution that engages the participation of every member of the community, including man, woman, and child, brings about a certain transformation in the participants as a result of this participation. Once you have caught a glimpse of freedom or experienced a bit of self-determination, you can't go back to old routines that were established under the racist, capitalist regime. We must begin to understand that a revolution entails not only the willingness to lay our lives on the firing line and get killed. In some ways, this is an easy commitment to make. To die for the revolution is a one-shot deal; to live for the revolution means taking on the more difficult commitment of changing our day-to-day life patterns.

This will mean changing the routines that we have established as a result of living in a totally corrupting society. It means changing how you relate to your wife, your husband, your parents, and your co-workers. If we are going to liberate ourselves as a people, it must be recognized that black women have very specific problems that have to be spoken to. We must be liberated along with the rest of the population. We cannot wait to start working on those problems until that great day in the future when the revolution, somehow, miraculously, is accomplished.

To assign women the role of housekeeper and mother while men go forth into battle is a highly questionable doctrine for a revolutionary to maintain. Each individual must develop a high political consciousness in order to understand how this System enslaves us all and what actions we must take to bring about its total destruction. Those who consider themselves revolutionary must begin to deal with other revolutionaries as equals. And, so far as I know, revolutionaries are not determined by sex.

Old people, young people, men, and women must take part in the struggle. To relegate women to purely supportive roles or purely cultural consideration is dangerous doctrine to project. Unless black men who are preparing themselves for armed struggle understand that the society which we are trying to create is one in which the oppression of *all* members of that society is eliminated, then the revolution will have failed in its avowed purpose.

Given the mutual commitment of black men and black women alike to the liberation of our people and other oppressed peoples around the world, the total involvement of each individual is necessary. A revolutionary has the responsibility of not only toppling those who are now in a position of power, but creating new institutions that will eliminate all forms of oppression. We must begin to rewrite our understanding of traditional personal relationships between man and woman.

All the resources that the black community can muster up must be channeled into the struggle. Black women must take an active part in bringing about the kind of society where our children, our loved ones, and each citizen can grow up and live as decent human beings, free from the pressures of racism and capitalist exploitation.

Notes

1. Sojourner Truth (c. 1799–1883), abolitionist, lecturer, slave, and religious worker.
2. Harriet Tubman (c. 1820–1913), slave, reformer, and abolitionist, lecturer.
3. (c. 1875–1955), American educator and special advisor on minority affairs to President Franklin Delano Roosevelt.
4. Fannie Lou Hamer (1917–1977), civil rights activist.

Source

Frances Beal, "Double Jeopardy: To Be Black and Female," in Robin Morgan, ed., *Sisterhood is Powerful: An Anthology of Writings from the Women's Liberation Movement,* 340–53 (New York: Random House, 1970).

Selected Bibliography

Collins, Patricia Hill. *Black Feminist Thought: Knowledge, Consciousness, and the Politics of Empowerment.* New York: Routledge, 2000.

hooks, bell. *Ain't I a Woman: Black Women and Feminism.* Boston: South End Press, 1981.

ten

Feminism and Black Liberation

Audre (Geraldine) Lorde was born in 1934 to West Indian parents in Harlem. She was educated in Catholic schools and took an interest in poetry at an early age. In high school, she published her first poem in *Seventeen* magazine; the poem was rejected from her school's publication for being "too romantic." She was so immersed in poetry she would occasionally find herself speaking in verse.

She received her B.A. from Hunter College in 1959 and her M.A. in library science from Columbia University in 1961. In 1962 she married attorney Edwin Ashley Rollins, had two children, and soon divorced. She established herself as a poet as a member of the Black Arts movement in the late 1960s and early 1970s and published *The First Cities,* her first book of poetry, in 1968. She helped establish Kitchen Table: Women of Color Press and founded Sisterhood in Support of Sisters in South Africa to address the struggles of black women under apartheid.

An unyielding writer, Lorde condemned the way in which "lesbians" and "black women" were categorized and marginalized. Working as an associate professor at John Jay College, Audre Lorde wrote "Feminism & Black Liberation," a critical reaction to Robert Staples's essay "The Myth of Black Macho: A Response to Angry Black Feminists."[1]

Lorde published her first major prose work, *The Cancer Journals,* in 1980 while fighting breast cancer. In 1988, four years after being diagnosed with liver cancer, she wrote *A Burst of Light,* chronicling her battle with both the illness and the callousness of traditional medicine. She died in St. Croix in 1992.

The Great American Disease

In Robert Staples' attack upon black feminists, there are saddening and obvious fallacies and errors.

Despite the economic gains made by black women recently, we are still the lowest paid group in the nation by sex and race. This should give the reader some idea of the inequality from which we started. In Staples' own words, black women now only "threaten to overtake black men" by the "next century" in education, occupation, and income. In other words, the inequality is self-evident; but how is it justifiable?

Furthermore, if Shange and Wallace are, as Staples suggests, unqualified to speak for black women merely because of their middle-class backgrounds, how does that reflect upon Staples' qualifications to speak for black men?

Black feminists speak as women because we are women, and do not need others to speak for us. It is for black men to speak up and tell us why their manhood is so threatened, and by what, that we should be the prime targets of their justifiable rage.

Staples pleads his cause by saying capitalism has left the black man only his penis for fulfillment, and a "curious rage." Is this rage any more legitimate than the rage of black women? And why are black women supposed to absorb that male rage in silence? Why isn't that male rage turned upon our oppressors? Staples sees in Shange's play a "collective appetite for black male blood." But my female children and my black sisters lie bleeding all around me, victims of the appetites of their brothers.

Into what theoretical analysis would Staples fit Pat Cowan? She was a young black actress in Detroit, 22 years old and a mother. She answered an ad last spring for a black actress to audition in a play called "Hammer." As she acted out an argument scene, watched by the playwright's brother and her son, the black male playwright picked up a sledgehammer and bludgeoned her to death from behind. Will Staples' "compassion for misguided black men" bring this young mother back, or make her senseless death more acceptable?

1. Staples's article appeared in the March–April 1979 issue of *The Black Scholar.* Staples has written a number of works on black families and male/female relations.

Black men's feelings of nobodiness and their fear of vulnerability must indeed be talked about, but not by black women any more, at the expense of our own "curious rage."

If society ascribes roles to black men which they are not allowed to fulfill, is it black women who must bend and alter our lives to compensate or is it society that needs changing? And what about the blanket acceptance on the part of black men that these roles are correct ones, or anything other than a narcotic promise extended to them to encourage them to accept other facets of their own oppression?

One aspect of the Great American Disease has been always to blame the victim for the oppressor's victimization: black people are said to invite lynching by not knowing their place; black women are said to invite rape and murder and abuse by not being submissive enough, or by being too seductive, or too etc.

Staples "fact" that black women get their sense of fulfillment from having children is only a "fact" stated out of the mouth of black men, and any black person in this country, even "happily married women" who "have no pent-up frustrations that need release"(!) is either a fool or insane. This smacks of the oldest sexist canard of all time, that all a woman needs to "keep her quiet" is a "good man."

Instead of beginning the much-needed dialogue between black men and black women, Staples retreats to a passive and defensive stance, sadly mirroring the fallacy of white liberals of the '60s, who saw any statement of black pride and self-assertion as an automatic threat to their own identity, as an attempt to wipe them out. Here we have an intelligent black man believing—or at least saying—that a call to black women to love ourselves (and no one said 'only') is a denial of, or threat to, his male identity!

In this country, black women traditionally have had compassion for everybody else except ourselves. We cared for whites because we had to for pay or survival; we cared for our children and our fathers and our brothers and our lovers. We need to also learn to care for ourselves. Our history and popular culture, as well as our personal lives, are full of tales of black women who had "compassion for misguided black men." Our scarred, broken, battered and dead daughters and sisters are a mute testament to that.

Shange's exhortation to black women at the end of her play is for us to extend that compassion and love at last to ourselves. In the light of what black women sacrifice for their children and their men, this is a much needed exhortation, no matter in what illegitimate manner the white media sees fit to use it. And this call for self-value, self-love, is quite different from narcissism, as Staples must certainly realize. The black man's well-documented narcissism comes, not out of self-love, but out of self-hatred.

The lack of a reasonable and articulate male viewpoint on these questions is not the responsibility of black women. We have too often been expected to be all things to all people, and speak everyone else's position but our very own. But black men do not need to be so passive under their veneer of macho, that they must have black women to speak for them. Even my 14 year old son knows that. It is for black men themselves to examine and articulate their own position, and to stand by the conclusions thereof. Unfortunately, the Staples article does not do this. It merely whines at the absence of his viewpoint in women's work. But oppressors have always expected the oppressed to extend to them the understanding and moral forebearance so lacking in themselves.

For Staples to suggest for instance, that black men leave their families as a form of male protest against female decision-making in the home is in direct contradiction to his own observations in "The Myth of The Black Matriarchy."

Now it is quite true that many black men with middle-class aspirations frequently turn to white women, who they feel better fit the model of "femininity" set forth in this country. But for Staples to justify the act in terms of the reason is not only another error in reasoning, it also is akin to justifying the actions of a lemming who follows its companions over the cliff to sure death. Because it happens does not mean it should happen, nor that it is functional for the well-being of the individual or the group.

As I have said elsewhere, it is not the destiny of black America to repeat white America's mistakes. But we will, if we mistake the trappings of success in a sick society for the signs of a meaningful life. If black men continue to do so, defining 'femininity' in its archaic European terms, this augurs ill for our survival as a people, let alone our survival as individuals. Freedom and future for blacks does not mean absorbing the dominant white male disease.

As black people, we cannot begin our dialogue by denying the oppressive nature of male privilege. And if black males choose to assume that privilege, for whatever reason, raping, brutalizing, and killing women, then we cannot ignore black male oppression. One oppression does not justify another.

Staples states that black men cannot be denied their personal choice of the woman who meets their need to dominate. In that case, black women also cannot be denied our personal choices, and those choices are increasingly self-assertive ones, and female-oriented. "Personal choice" and "ontological" reasoning are knives that cut both ways.

As a people, we should most certainly work together to end our common oppression, and toward a future which is viable for us all. In that context, it is short-sighted to believe that black men alone are to blame for the above situations, in a society dominated by white male privilege. But the black male consciousness must be raised so that he realizes that sexiam and woman-hating are critically dysfunctinal to his liberation as a black man, because they arise out of the same constellation that engenders racism and homophobia, a constellation of intolerance for difference serving a profit motivation. And until this is done, black men like Staples will view sexism and the destruction of black women only as tangential to the cause of black liberation, rather than as central to that struggle. So long as this occurs, we will never be able to embark upon that dialogue between black women and black men that is so essential to our survival as a people. And this continued blindness between us can only serve the oppressive system within which we live.

Men avoid women's observations by accusing us of not being 'global', or of being too 'visceral'. But no amount of understanding the roots of black sexism and woman-hating will bring back Patricia Cowans, nor mute her family's loss. Pain is never global, it is very visceral, particularly to the people who are hurting. And as the poet McAnally said, "pain teaches us to take our hands *out* the fucking fire!"

If the problems of black women are derivatives only of a larger contradiction between capital and labor, then so is racism, and both must be equally fought against by all of us, since the capitalist structure is a many-headed monster. I might add here that in no socialist country that I have visited have I found absence of racism nor of sexism, so the eradication of both of these diseases seems to involve more than the abolition of capitalism as an institution.

No reasonable black man can possibly condone or excuse the rape and slaughter of black women by black men as any fitting response to capitalist oppression. And that destruction of black women by black men clearly cuts across all class lines at this point.

Whatever the "structural underpinnings" for sexism in the black community may be, it is obviously black women who are bearing the brunt of that sexism, and so it is in our vested interest to abolish it. We invite our black brothers to join us, since ultimately that destruction is in their best interests also. But since it is black women who are being abused, and our female blood that is being shed, it is for black women to decide whether or not sexism in the black community is pathological, not Staples. And we do not approach that question theoretically, as Staples does, who evidently cannot recognize how he himself is diminished by that sexism. Those "creative relationships" of which he speaks within the community are almost invariably to the benefit of black males, given the sex ratio of males to females and the implied power balance therein within a supply and demand situation. This is much the same as how "creative relationships" between master and slave were to the benefit of the master.

The occurrence of woman-hating in the black community is a tragedy which diminishes all black people. It must be seen in the context of the systematic devaluation of black women by this total society, for it is within this context that we become an acceptable target for black male rage, so acceptable that even a man of Staples' stature does not even question the depersonalizing abuse.

What black women are saying is that this abuse is no longer acceptable in the name of solidarity nor of black liberation. Any dialogue between black women and black men must begin there, no matter where it ends.

Source

Audre Lorde, "Feminism & Black Liberation, The Great American Disease," *The Black Scholar* 10 (May–June 1979): 17–20.

Selected Bibliography

Lorde, Audre. *The Black Unicorn: Poems.* New York: Norton, 1978.
—— *A Burst of Light: Essays.* Ithaca, N.Y.: Firebrand Books, 1988.
—— *The Cancer Journals.* Argyle, N.Y.: Spinsters, Ink, 1980.
—— *The Collected Poems of Audre Lorde.* New York: Norton, 1997.
—— *Sister Outsider: Essays and Speeches.* Trumansburg, N.Y.: Crossing Press, 1984.
—— *Zami, A New Spelling of My Name.* Trumansburg, N.Y.: Crossing Press, 1982.
Staples, Robert. *The Black Family: Essays and Studies.* Belmont, Calif.: Wadsworth, 1971.

eleven

The Approaching Obsolescence of Housework

A well-known professor at the University of California at Santa Cruz, Angela Yvonne Davis (1944–) was a revolutionary activist during the Black Power Movement. Her treatise "The Approaching Obsolescence of Housework" is significant as a socialist/feminist critique of domestic gender politics. Davis pointed out that women have generally been held responsible for so-called "housework," and that this has fueled the sexual and psychological oppression of women. Accordingly, she argued that the prevailing notions of housework should be reordered in such a fashion that it is no longer thought of as the private responsibility of individual women.

Davis entered Brandeis University in 1961, studied abroad at the Sorbonne, took courses with the famous philosopher Herbert Marcuse, and graduated magna cum laude in 1965. At then California Governor Ronald Reagan's request, she was fired from a teaching position at the University of California, Los Angeles, for being a communist. Through her work with the Black Panthers, Davis became involved with the case of George Jackson, an imprisoned activist. In 1970, she was charged with conspiracy, kidnapping, and murder for her alleged connection with a poorly orchestrated plot to rescue Jackson from a San Rafael courtroom, in which a Black Panther and a judge were killed. Davis's trial quickly became a cause célèbre, and she was acquitted on all charges in 1972. Subsequently, she has worked as an activist, lecturer, and writer.

The Approaching Obsolescence of Housework: A Working-Class Perspective

The countless chores collectively known as "housework"—cooking, washing dishes, doing laundry, making beds, sweeping, shopping, etc.—apparently consume some three to four thousand hours of the average housewife's year.[1] As startling as this statistic may be, it does not even account for the constant and unquantifiable attention mothers must give to their children. Just as a woman's maternal duties are always taken for granted, her neverending toil as a housewife rarely occasions expressions of appreciation within her family. Housework, after all, is virtually invisible: "No one notices it until it isn't done—we notice the unmade bed, not the scrubbed and polished floor."[2] Invisible, repetitive, exhausting, unproductive, uncreative—these are the adjectives which most perfectly capture the nature of housework.

The new consciousness associated with the contemporary women's movement has encouraged increasing numbers of women to demand that their men provide some relief from this drudgery. Already, more men have begun to assist their partners around the house, some of them even devoting equal time to household chores. But how many of these men have liberated themselves from the assumption that housework is "women's work"? How many of them would not characterize their housecleaning activities as "helping" their women partners?

If it were at all possible simultaneously to liquidate the idea that housework is women's work and to redistribute it equally to men and women alike, would this constitute a satisfactory solution? Freed from its exclusive affiliation with the female sex, would housework thereby cease to be oppressive? While most women would joyously hail the advent of the "househusband," the desexualization of domestic labor would not really alter the oppressive nature of the work itself. In the final analysis, neither women nor men should waste precious hours of their lives on work that is neither stimulating, creative nor productive.

One of the most closely guarded secrets of advanced capitalist societies involves the possibility—the real possibility—of radically transforming the nature of housework. A substantial portion of the housewife's domestic tasks can actually be incorporated into the industrial economy. In other words, house-

1. Oakley, *op. cit.*, p. 6.

2. Barbara Ehrenreich and Deirdre English, "The Manufacture of Housework," in *Socialist Revolution*, No. 26, Vol. 5, No. 4 (October–December 1975), p. 6.

work need no longer be considered necessarily and unalterably private in character. Teams of trained and well-paid workers, moving from dwelling to dwelling, engineering technologically advanced cleaning machinery, could swiftly and efficiently accomplish what the present-day housewife does so arduously and primitively. Why the shroud of silence surrounding this potential of radically redefining the nature of domestic labor? Because the capitalist economy is structurally hostile to the industrialization of housework. Socialized housework implies large government subsidies in order to guarantee accessibility to the working-class families whose need for such services is most obvious. Since little in the way of profits would result, industrialized housework—like all unprofitable enterprises—is anathema to the capitalist economy. Nonetheless, the rapid expansion of the female labor force means that more and more women are finding it increasingly difficult to excel as housewives according to the traditional standards. In other words, the industrialization of housework, along with the socialization of housework, is becoming an objective social need. Housework as individual women's private responsibility and as female labor performed under primitive technical conditions, may finally be approaching historical obsolescence.

Although housework as we know it today may eventually become a bygone relic of history, prevailing social attitudes continue to associate the eternal female condition with images of brooms and dustpans, mops and pails, aprons and stoves, pots and pans. And it is true that women's work, from one historical era to another, has been associated in general with the homestead. Yet female domestic labor has not always been what it is today, for like all social phenomena, housework is a fluid product of human history. As economic systems have arisen and faded away, the scope and quality of housework have undergone radical transformations.

As Frederick Engels[1] argued in his classic work on the *Origin of the Family, Private Property and the State,*[3] sexual inequality as we know it today did not exist before the advent of private property. During early eras of human history the sexual division of labor within the system of economic production was complementary as opposed to hierarchical. In societies where men may have been responsible for hunting wild animals and women, in turn, for gathering wild vegetables and fruits, both sexes performed economic tasks that were equally essential to their community's survival. Because the community, during those eras, was essentially an extended family, women's central role in domestic affairs meant that they were accordingly valued and respected as productive members of the community.

---

3. Friedrich Engels, *Origin of the Family, Private Property and the State,* edited, with an introduction, by Eleanor Burke Leacock (New York: International Publishers, 1973). See Chapter II. Leacock's introduction to this edition contains numerous enlightening observations on Engels' theory of the historical emergence of male supremacy.

The centrality of women's domestic tasks in pre-capitalist cultures was dramatized by a personal experience during a jeep trip I took in 1973 across the Masai Plains. On an isolated dirt road in Tanzania, I noticed six Masai women enigmatically balancing an enormous board on their heads. As my Tanzanian friends explained, these women were probably transporting a house roof to a new village which they were in the process of constructing. Among the Masai, as I learned, women are responsible for all domestic activities, thus also for the construction of their nomadic people's frequently relocated houses. Housework, as far as Masai women are concerned, entails not only cooking, cleaning, child-rearing, sewing, etc., but house-building as well. As important as their men's cattle-raising duties may be, the women's "housework" is no less productive and no less essential than the economic contributions of Masai men.

Within the pre-capitalist, nomadic economy of the Masai, women's domestic labor is as essential to the economy as the cattle-raising jobs performed by their men. As producers, they enjoy a correspondingly important social status. In advanced capitalist societies, on the other hand, the service-oriented domestic labor of housewives, who can seldom produce tangible evidence of their work, diminishes the social status of women in general. When all is said and done, the housewife, according to bourgeois ideology, is, quite simply, her husband's lifelong servant.

The source of the bourgeois notion of woman as man's eternal servant is itself a revealing story. Within the relatively short history of the United States, the "housewife" as a finished historical product is just a little more than a century old. Housework, during the colonial era, was entirely different from the daily work routine of the housewife in the United States today.

> A woman's work began at sunup and continued by firelight as long as she could hold her eyes open. For two centuries, almost everything that the family used or ate was produced at home under her direction. She spun and dyed the yarn that she wove into cloth and cut and hand-stitched into garments. She grew much of the food her family ate, and preserved enough to last the winter months. She made butter, cheese, bread, candles, and soap and knitted her family's stockings.[4]

In the agrarian economy of pre-industrial North America, a woman performing her household chores was thus a spinner, weaver and seamstress as well as a baker, butter-churner, candlemaker and soap-maker. And et cetera, et cetera, et cetera. As a matter of fact,

> . . . the pressures of home production left very little time for the tasks that we would recognize today as housework. By all accounts, pre-

4. Wertheimer, *op. cit.*, p. 12.

> industrial revolution women were sloppy housekeepers by today's standards. Instead of the daily cleaning or the weekly cleaning, there was the *spring* cleaning. Meals were simple and repetitive; clothes were changed infrequently; and the household wash was allowed to accumulate, and the washing done once a month, or in some households once in three months. And, of course, since each wash required the carting and heating of many buckets of water, higher standards of cleanliness were easily discouraged.[5]

Colonial women were not "house-cleaners" or "housekeepers" but rather full-fledged and accomplished workers within the home-based economy. Not only did they manufacture most of the products required by their families, they were also the guardians of their families' and their communities' health.

> It was [the colonial woman's] responsibility to gather and dry wild herbs used ... as medicines; she also served as doctor, nurse, and midwife within her own family and in the community.[6]

Included in the *United States Practical Receipt Book*—a popular colonial recipe book—are recipes for foods as well as for household chemicals and medicines. To cure ringworm, for example, "obtain some blood-root ... slice it in vinegar, and afterwards wash the place affected with the liquid."[7]

The economic importance of women's domestic functions in colonial America was complemented by their visible roles in economic activity outside the home. It was entirely acceptable, for example, for a woman to become a tavern keeper.

> Women also ran sawmills and gristmills, caned chairs and built furniture, operated slaughterhouses, printed cotton and other cloth, made lace, and owned and ran dry-goods and clothing stores. They worked in tobacco shops, drug shops (where they sold concoctions they made themselves), and general stores that sold everything from pins to meat scales. Women ground eyeglasses, made netting and rope, cut and stitched leather goods, made cards for wool carding, and even were housepainters. Often they were the town undertakers ... [8]

The postrevolutionary surge of industrialization resulted in a proliferation of factories in the northeastern section of the new country. New England's textile mills were the factory system's successful pioneers. Since spinning and

5. Ehrenreich and English, "The Manufacture of Housework," p. 9.
6. Wertheimer, *op. cit.,* p. 12.
7. Quoted in Baxandall *et al., op. cit.,* p. 17.
8. Wertheimer, *op. cit.,* p. 13.

weaving were traditional female domestic occupations, women were the first workers recruited by the mill-owners to operate the new power looms. Considering the subsequent exclusion of women from industrial production in general, it is one of the great ironies of this country's economic history that the first industrial workers were women.

As industrialization advanced, shifting economic production from the home to the factory, the importance of women's domestic work suffered a systematic erosion. Women were the losers in a double sense: as their traditional jobs were usurped by the burgeoning factories, the entire economy moved away from the home, leaving many women largely bereft of significant economic roles. By the middle of the nineteenth century the factory provided textiles, candles and soap. Even butter, bread and other food products began to be mass-produced.

> By the end of the century, hardly anyone made their own starch or boiled their laundry in a kettle. In the cities, women bought their bread and at least their underwear ready-made, sent their children out to school and probably some clothes out to be laundered, and were debating the merits of canned foods . . . The flow of industry had passed on and had left idle the loom in the attic and the soap kettle in the shed."[9]

As industrial capitalism approached consolidation, the cleavage between the new economic sphere and the old home economy became ever more rigorous. The physical relocation of economic production caused by the spread of the factory system was undoubtedly a drastic transformation. But even more radical was the generalized revaluation of production necessitated by the new economic system. While home-manufactured goods were valuable primarily because they fulfilled basic family needs, the importance of factory-produced commodities resided overwhelmingly in their exchange value—in their ability to fulfill employers' demands for profit. This revaluation of economic production revealed—beyond the physical separation of home and factory—a fundamental *structural* separation between the domestic home economy and the profit-oriented economy of capitalism. Since housework does not generate profit, domestic labor was naturally defined as an inferior form of work as compared to capitalist wage labor.

An important ideological by-product of this radical economic transformation was the birth of the "housewife." Women began to be ideologically redefined as the guardians of a devalued domestic life. As ideology, however, this redefinition of women's place was boldly contradicted by the vast numbers of immigrant women flooding the ranks of the working class in the Northeast.

---

9. Ehrenreich and English, "The Manufacture of Housework," p. 10.

These white immigrant women were wage earners first and only secondarily housewives. And there were other women—millions of women—who toiled away from home as the unwilling producers of the slave economy in the South. The reality of women's place in nineteenth-century U.S. society involved white women, whose days were spent operating factory machines for wages that were a pittance, as surely as it involved Black women, who labored under the coercion of slavery. The "housewife" reflected a partial reality, for she was really a symbol of the economic prosperity enjoyed by the emerging middle classes.

Although the "housewife" was rooted in the social conditions of the bourgeoisie and the middle classes, nineteenth-century ideology established the housewife and the mother as universal models of womanhood. Since popular propaganda represented the vocation of *all* women as a function of their roles in the home, women compelled to work for wages came to be treated as alien visitors within the masculine world of the public economy. Having stepped outside their "natural" sphere, women were not to be treated as full-fledged wage workers. The price they paid involved long hours, substandard working conditions and grossly inadequate wages. Their exploitation was even more intense than the exploitation suffered by their male counterparts. Needless to say, sexism emerged as a source of outrageous super-profits for the capitalists.

The structural separation of the public economy of capitalism and the private economy of the home has been continually reinforced by the obstinate primitiveness of household labor. Despite the proliferation of gadgets for the home, domestic work has remained qualitatively unaffected by the technological advances brought on by industrial capitalism. Housework still consumes thousands of hours of the average housewife's year. In 1903 Charlotte Perkins Gilman proposed a definition of domestic labor which reflected the upheavals which had changed the structure and content of housework in the United States:

> ... The phrase "domestic work" does not apply to a special kind of work, but to a certain grade of work, a state of development through which all kinds pass. All industries were once "domestic," that is, were performed at home and in the interests of the family. All industries have since that remote period risen to higher stages, except one or two which have never left their primal stage.[10]

"The home," Gilman maintains, "has not developed in proportion to our other institutions." The home economy reveals

10. Charlotte Perkins Gilman, *The Home: Its Work and Its Influence* (Urbana, Chicago, London: University of Illinois Press, 1972. Reprint of the 1903 edition), pp. 30–31.

> . . . the maintenance of primitive industries in a modern industrial community and the confinement of women to these industries and their limited area of expression.[11]

Housework, Gilman insists, vitiates women's humanity:

> She is feminine, more than enough, as man is masculine, more than enough; but she is not human as he is human. The house-life does not bring out our humanness, for all the distinctive lines of human progress lie outside.[12]

The truth of Gilman's statement is corroborated by the historical experience of Black women in the United States. Throughout this country's history, the majority of Black women have worked outside their homes. During slavery, women toiled alongside their men in the cotton and tobacco fields, and when industry moved into the South, they could be seen in tobacco factories, sugar refineries and even in lumber mills and on crews pounding steel for the railroads. In labor, slave women were the equals of their men. Because they suffered a grueling sexual equality at work, they enjoyed a greater sexual equality at home in the slave quarters than did their white sisters who were "housewifes."

As a direct consequence of their outside work—as "free" women no less than as slaves—housework has never been the central focus of Black women's lives. They have largely escaped the psychological damage industrial capitalism inflicted on white middle-class housewives, whose alleged virtues were feminine weakness and wifely submissiveness. Black women could hardly strive for weakness; they had to become strong, for their families and their communities needed their strength to survive. Evidence of the accumulated strengths Black women have forged through work, work and more work can be discovered in the contributions of the many outstanding female leaders who have emerged within the Black community. Harriet Tubman, Sojourner Truth, Ida Wells and Rosa Parks are not exceptional Black women as much as they are epitomes of Black womanhood.

Black women, however, have paid a heavy price for the strengths they have acquired and the relative independence they have enjoyed. While they have seldom been "just housewives," they have always done their housework. They have thus carried the double burden of wage labor and housework—a double burden which always demands that working women possess the persevering powers of Sisyphus. As W. E. B. DuBois observed in 1920:

---

11. *Ibid.*, p. 10.
12. *Ibid.*, p. 217.

> ... some few women are born free, and some amid insult and scarlet letters achieve freedom; but our women in black had freedom thrust contemptuously upon them. With that freedom they are buying an untrammeled independence and dear as is the price they pay for it, it will in the end be worth every taunt and groan.[13]

Like their men, Black women have worked until they could work no more. Like their men, they have assumed the responsibilities of family providers. The unorthodox feminine qualities of assertiveness and self-reliance—for which Black women have been frequently praised but more often rebuked—are reflections of their labor and their struggles outside the home. But like their white sisters called "housewives," they have cooked and cleaned and have nurtured and reared untold numbers of children. But unlike the white housewives, who learned to lean on their husbands for economic security, Black wives and mothers, usually workers as well, have rarely been offered the time and energy to become experts at domesticity. Like their white working-class sisters, who also carry the double burden of working for a living and servicing husbands and children, Black women have needed relief from this oppressive predicament for a long, long time.

For Black women today and for all their working-class sisters, the notion that the burden of housework and child care can be shifted from their shoulders to the society contains one of the radical secrets of women's liberation. Child care should be socialized, meal preparation should be socialized, housework should be industrialized—and all these services should be readily accessible to working-class people.

The shortage, if not absence, of public discussion about the feasibility of transforming housework into a social possibility bears witness to the blinding powers of bourgeois ideology. It is not even the case that women's domestic role has received no attention at all. On the contrary, the contemporary women's movement has represented housework as an essential ingredient of women's oppression. There is even a movement in a number of capitalist countries, whose main concern is the plight of the housewife. Having reached the conclusion that housework is degrading and oppressive primarily because it is *unpaid* labor, this movement has raised the demand for wages. A weekly government paycheck, its activists argue, is the key to improving the housewife's status and the social position of women in general.

The Wages for Housework Movement originated in Italy, where its first public demonstration took place in March, 1974. Addressing the crowd assembled in the city of Mestre, one of the speakers proclaimed:

> Half the world's population is unpaid—this is the biggest class contradiction of all! And this is our struggle for wages for housework. It is *the* strate-

13. DuBois, *Darkwater,* p. 185.

> gic demand; at this moment it is the most revolutionary demand for the whole working class. If we win, the class wins, if we lose, the class loses.[14]

According to this movement's strategy, wages contain the key to the emancipation of housewives, and the demand itself is represented as the central focus of the campaign for women's liberation in general. Moreover, the housewife's struggle for wages is projected as the pivotal issue of the entire working-class movement.

The theoretical origins of the Wages for Housework Movement can be found in an essay by Mariarosa Dalla Costa[2] entitled "Women and the Subversion of the Community."[15] In this paper, Dalla Costa argues for a redefinition of housework based on her thesis that the private character of household services is actually an illusion. The housewife, she insists, only appears to be ministering to the private needs of her husband and children, for the real beneficiaries of her services are her husband's present employer and the future employers of her children.

> (The woman) has been isolated in the home, forced to carry out work that is considered unskilled, the work of giving birth to, raising, disciplining, and servicing the worker for production. Her role in the cycle of production remained invisible because only the product of her labor, the *laborer,* was visible.[16]

The demand that housewives be paid is based on the assumption that they produce a commodity as important and as valuable as the commodities their husbands produce on the job Adopting Dalla Costa's logic, the Wages for Housework Movement defines housewives as creators of the labor-power sold by their family members as commodities on the capitalist market.

Dalla Costa was not the first theorist to propose such an analysis of women's oppression. Both Mary Inman's *In Woman's Defense* (1940)[17] and Margaret Benston's "The Political Economy of Women's Liberation" (1969)[18] define

---

14. Speech by Polga Fortunata. Quoted in Wendy Edmond and Suzie Fleming, editors, *All Work and No Pay: Women, Housework and the Wages Due!* (Bristol, England: Falling Wall Press, 1975), p. 18.
15. Mariarosa Dalla Costa and Selma James, *The Power of Women and the Subversion of the Community* (Bristol, England: Falling Wall Press, 1973).
16. *Ibid.,* p. 28.
17. Mary Inman, *In Women's Defense* (Los Angeles:; Committee to Organize the Advancement of Women, 1940). See also Inman, *The Two Forms of Production Under Capitalism* (Long Beach, Cal.): Published by the Author, 1964.
18. Margaret Benston, "The Political Economy of Women's Liberation," *Monthly Review,* Vol. XXI, No. 4 (September, 1969).

housework in such a way as to establish women as a special class of workers exploited by capitalism called "housewives." That women's procreative, child-rearing and housekeeping roles make it possible for their family members to work—to exchange their labor-power for wages—can hardly be denied. But does it automatically follow that women in general, regardless of their class and race, can be fundamentally defined by their domestic functions? Does it automatically follow that the housewife is actually a secret worker inside the capitalist production process?

If the industrial revolution resulted in the structural separation of the home economy from the public economy, then housework cannot be defined as an integral component of capitalist production. It is, rather, related to production as a *precondition.* The employer is not concerned in the least about the way labor-power is produced and sustained, he is only concerned about its availability and its ability to generate profit. In other words, the capitalist production process presupposes the existence of a body of exploitable workers.

> The replenishment of (workers') labor-power is not a part of the process of social production but a prerequisite to it. It occurs *outside* of the labor process. Its function is the maintenance of human existence which is the ultimate purpose of production in all societies.[19]

In South African society, where racism has led economic exploitation to its most brutal limits, the capitalist economy betrays its structural separation from domestic life in a characteristically violent fashion. The social architects of Apartheid have simply determined that Black labor yields higher profits when domestic life is all but entirely discarded. Black men are viewed as labor units whose productive potential renders them valuable to the capitalist class. But their wives and children

> ... are superfluous appendages—non-productive, the women being nothing more than adjuncts to the procreative capacity of the black male labor unit.[20]

This characterization of African women as "superfluous appendages" is hardly a metaphor. In accordance with South African law, unemployed Black women are banned from the white areas (87 percent of the country!), even, in most cases, from the cities where their husbands live and work.

19. "On the Economic Status of the Housewife." Editorial Comment in *Political Affairs,* Vol. LIII, No. 3 (March, 1974), p. 4.
20. Hilda Bernstein, *For Their Triumphs and For Their Tears: Women in Apartheid South Africa* (London: International Defense and Aid Fund, 1975), p. 13.

Black domestic life in South Africa's industrial centers is viewed by Apartheid supporters as superfluous and unprofitable. But it is also seen as a threat.

> Government officials recognize the homemaking role of the women and fear their presence in the cities will lead to the establishment of a stable black population.[21]

The consolidation of African families in the industrialized cities is perceived as a menace because domestic life might become a base for a heightened level of resistance to Apartheid. This is undoubtedly the reason why large numbers of women holding residence permits for white areas are assigned to live in sex-segregated hostels. Married as well as single women end up living in these projects. In such hostels, family life is rigorously prohibited—husbands and wives are unable to visit one another and neither mother nor father can receive visits from their children.[22]

This intense assault on Black women in South Africa has already taken its toll, for only 28.2 percent are currently opting for marriage.[23] For reasons of economic expediency and political security, Apartheid is eroding—with the apparent goal of destroying—the very fabric of Black domestic life. South African capitalism thus blatantly demonstrates the extent to which the capitalist economy is utterly dependent on domestic labor.

The deliberate dissolution of family life in South Africa could not have been undertaken by the government if it were truly the case that the services performed by women in the home are an essential constituent of wage labor under capitalism. That domestic life can be dispensed with by the South African version of capitalism is a consequence of the separation of the private home economy and the public production process which characterizes capitalist society in general. It seems futile to argue that on the basis of capitalism's internal logic, women ought to be paid wages for housework.

Assuming that the theory underlying the demand for wages is hopelessly flawed, might it not be nonetheless politically desirable to insist that housewives be paid. Couldn't one invoke a moral imperative for women's right to be paid for the hours they devote to housework? The idea of a paycheck for housewives would probably sound quite attractive to many women. But the attraction would probably be short-lived. For how many of those women would actually be willing to reconcile themselves to deadening, never-ending household tasks, all for the sake of a wage? Would a wage alter the fact, as Lenin said, that

---

21. Elizabeth Landis, "Apartheid and the Disabilities of Black Women in South Africa," *Objective: Justice,* Vol. VII, No. 1 (January–March, 1975), p. 6. Excerpts from this paper were published in *Freedomways,* Vol. XV, No. 4, 1975.
22. Bernstein, *op. cit.,* p. 33.
23. Landis, *op. cit.,* p. 6.

> . . . petty housework crushes, strangles, stultifies and degrades (the woman), chains her to the kitchen and to the nursery, and wastes her labor on barbarously unproductive, petty, nerve-racking, stultifying and crushing drudgery.[24]

It would seem that government paychecks for housewives would further legitimize this domestic slavery.

Is it not an implicit critique of the Wages for Housework Movement that women on welfare have rarely demanded compensation for keeping house. Not "wages for housework" but rather "a guaranteed annual income for all" is the slogan articulating the immediate alternative they have most frequently proposed to the dehumanizing welfare system. What they want in the long run, however, is jobs and affordable public child care. The guaranteed annual income functions, therefore, as unemployment insurance pending the creation of more jobs with adequate wages along with a subsidized system of child care.

The experiences of yet another group of women reveal the problematic nature of the "wages for housework" strategy. Cleaning women, domestic workers, maids—these are the women who know better than anyone else what it means to receive wages for housework. Their tragic predicament is brilliantly captured in the film by Ousmane Sembene entitled *La Noire de . . .* [25] The main character is a young Senegalese woman who, after a search for work, becomes a governess for a French family living in Dakar. When the family returns to France, she enthusiastically accompanies them. Once in France, however, she discovers she is responsible not only for the children, but for cooking, cleaning, washing and all the other household chores. It is not long before her initial enthusiasm gives way to depression—a depression so profound that she refuses the pay offered her by her employers. Wages cannot compensate for her slavelike situation. Lacking the means to return to Senegal, she is so overwhelmed by her despair that she chooses suicide over an indefinite destiny of cooking, sweeping, dusting, scrubbing . . .

In the United States, women of color—and especially Black women—have been receiving wages for housework for untold decades. In 1910, when over half of all Black females were working outside their homes, one-third of them were employed as paid domestic workers. By 1920 over one-half were domestic servants, and in 1930 the proportion had risen to three out of five.[26] One of the consequences of the enormous female employment shifts during World War II was a much-welcomed decline in the number of Black domes-

24. V. I. Lenin, "A Great Beginning," pamphlet published in July, 1919. Quoted in *Collected Works,* Vol. 29 (Moscow: Progress Publishers, 1966), p. 429.
25. Released in the United States under the title *Black Girl.*
26. Jackson, *op. cit.,* pp. 236–237.

tic workers. Yet in 1960 one-third of all Black women holding jobs were still confined to their traditional occupations.[27] It was not until clerical jobs became more accessible to Black women that the proportion of Black women domestics headed in a definitely downward direction. Today the figure hovers around 13 percent.[28]

The enervating domestic obligations of women in general provide flagrant evidence of the power of sexism. Because of the added intrusion of racism, vast numbers of Black women have had to do their own housekeeping and other women's home chores as well. And frequently, the demands of the job in a white woman's home have forced the domestic worker to neglect her own home and even her own children. As paid housekeepers, they have been called upon to be surrogate wives and mothers in millions of white homes.

During their more than fifty years of organizing efforts, domestic workers have tried to redefine their work by rejecting the role of the surrogate housewife. The housewife's chores are unending and undefined. Household workers have demanded in the first place a clear delineation of the jobs they are expected to perform. The name itself of one of the houseworkers' major unions today—Household Technicians of America—emphasizes their refusal to function as surrogate housewives whose job is "just housework." As long as household workers stand in the shadow of the housewife, they will continue to receive wages which are more closely related to a housewife's "allowance" than to a worker's paycheck. According to the National Committee on Household Employment, the average, full-time household technician earned only $2,732 in 1976, two-thirds of them earning under $2,000.[29] Although household workers had been extended the protection of the minimum wage law several years previously, in 1976 an astounding 40 percent still received grossly substandard wages. The Wages for Housework Movement assumes that if women were paid for being housewives, they would accordingly enjoy a higher social status. Quite a different story is told by the age-old struggles of the paid household worker, whose condition is more miserable than any other group of workers under capitalism.

Over 50 percent of all U.S. women work for a living today, and they constitute 41 percent of the country's labor force. Yet countless numbers of women are currently unable to find decent jobs. Like racism, sexism is one of the great justifications for high female unemployment rates. Many women are "just housewives" because in reality they are unemployed workers. Cannot, therefore, the "just housewife" role be most effectively challenged by demanding jobs for women on a level of equality with men and by pressing for the social

27. Victor Perlo, *Economics of Racism U.S.A., Roots of Black Inequality* (New York: International Publishers, 1975), p. 24.
28. Staples, *The Black Woman in America,* p. 27.
29. *Daily World,* July 26, 1977, p. 9.

services (child care, for example) and job benefits (maternity leaves, etc.) which will allow more women to work outside the home?

The Wages for Housework Movement discourages women from seeking outside jobs, arguing that "slavery to an assembly line is not liberation from slavery to the kitchen sink."[30] The campaign's spokeswomen insist, nonetheless, that they don't advocate the continued imprisonment of women within the isolated environment of their homes. They claim that while they refuse to work on the capitalist market per se, they do not wish to assign to women the permanent responsibility for housework. As a U.S. representative of this movement says:

> . . . we are not interested in making our work more efficient or more productive for capital. We are interested in reducing our work, and ultimately refusing it altogether. But as long as we work in the home for nothing, no one really cares how long or how hard we work. For capital only introduces advanced technology to cut the costs of production after wage gains by the working class. Only if we make our work cost (i.e., only if we make it uneconomical) will capital "discover" the technology to reduce it. At present, We often have to go out for a second shift of work to afford the dishwasher that should cut down our housework.[31]

Once women have achieved the right to be paid for their work, they can raise demands for higher wages, thus compelling the capitalists to undertake the industrialization of housework. Is this a concrete strategy for women's liberation or is it an unrealizable dream?

How are women supposed to conduct the initial struggle for wages? Dalla Costa advocates the *housewives' strike:*

> We must reject the home, because we want to unite with other women, to struggle against all situations which presume that women will stay at home . . . To abandon the home is already a form of struggle, since the social services we perform there would then cease to be carried out in those conditions.[32]

But if women are to leave the home, where are they to go? How will they unite with other women? Will they really leave their homes motivated by no other desire than to protest their housework? Is it not much more realistic to call upon women to "leave home" in search of outside jobs—or at least to participate in a massive campaign for decent jobs for women? Granted, work

30. Dalla Costa and James, *op. cit.,* p. 40.
3. Pat Sweeney, "Wages for Housework: The Strategy for Women's Liberation," *Heresies,* January, 1977, p. 104.
32. Dalla Costa and James, *op. cit.,* p. 41.

under the conditions of capitalism is brutalizing work. Granted, it is uncreative and alienating. Yet with all this, the fact remains that on the job, women can unite with their sisters—and indeed with their brothers—in order to challenge the capitalists at the point of production. As workers, as militant activists in the labor movement, women can generate the real power to fight the mainstay and beneficiary of sexism which is the monopoly capitalist system.

If the wages-for-housework strategy does little in the way of providing a long-range solution to the problem of women's oppression, neither does it substantively address the profound discontent of contemporary housewives. Recent sociological studies have revealed that housewives today are more frustrated by their lives than ever before. When Ann Oakley conducted interviews for her book *The Sociology of Housework,*[33] she discovered that even the housewives who initially seemed unbothered by their housework eventually expressed a very deep dissatisfaction. These comments came from a woman who held an outside factory job:

> (Do you like housework?) I don't mind it . . . I suppose I don't mind housework because I'm not at it all day. I go to work and I'm only on housework half a day. If I did it all day I wouldn't like it—woman's work is never done, she's on the go all the time—even before you go to bed, you've still got something to do—emptying ashtrays, wash a few cups up. You're still working. It's the same thing every day; you can't sort of say you're not going to do it, because you've got to do it—like preparing a meal: it's got to be done because if you don't do it, the children wouldn't eat . . . I suppose you get used to it, you just do it automatically. . . . I'm happier at work than I am at home.
>
> (What would you say are the worst things about being a housewife?) I suppose you get days when you feel you get up and you've got to do the same old things—you get bored, you're stuck in the same routine. I think if you ask any housewife, if they're honest, they'll turn around and say they feel like a drudge half the time—everybody thinks when they get up in the morning "Oh no, I've got the same old things to do today, till I go to bed tonight." It's doing the same things—boredom.[34]

Would wages diminish this boredom? This woman would certainly say no. A full-time housewife told Oakley about the compulsive nature of housework:

> The worst thing is I suppose that you've got to do the work because you *are* at home. Even though I've got the option of not doing it, I don't really feel I *could* not do it because I feel I *ought* to do it.[35]

---

33. Ann Oakley, *The Sociology of Housework* (New York: Pantheon Books, 1974).
34. *Ibid.,* p. 65.
35. *Ibid.,* p. 44.

In all likelihood, receiving wages for doing this work would aggravate this woman's obsession.

Oakley reached the conclusion that housework—particularly when it is a full-time job—so thoroughly invades the female personality that the housewife becomes indistinguishable from her job.

> The housewife, in an important sense, *is* her job: separation between subjective and objective elements in the situation is therefore intrinsically more difficult.[36]

The psychological consequence is frequently a tragically stunted personality haunted by feelings of inferiority. Psychological liberation can hardly be achieved simply by paying the housewife a wage.

Other sociological studies have confirmed the acute disillusionment suffered by contemporary housewives. When Myra Ferree[37] interviewed over a hundred women in a working community near Boston, "almost twice as many housewives as employed wives said they were dissatisfied with their lives." Needless to say, most of the working women did not have inherently fulfilling jobs: they were waitresses, factory workers, typists, supermarket and department store clerks, etc. Yet their ability to leave the isolation of their homes, "getting out and seeing other people," was as important to them as their earnings. Would the housewives who felt they were "going crazy staying at home" welcome the idea of being paid for driving themselves crazy? One woman complained that "staying at home all day is like being in jail"—would wages tear down the walls of her jail? The only realistic escape path from this jail is the search for work outside the home.

Each one of the more than 50 percent of all U.S. women who work today is a powerful argument for the alleviation of the burden of housework. As a matter of fact, enterprising capitalists have already begun to exploit women's new historical need to emancipate themselves from their roles as housewives. Endless profit-making fast-food chains like McDonald's and Kentucky Fried Chicken bear witness to the fact that more women at work means fewer daily meals prepared at home. However unsavory and unnutritious the food, however exploitative of their workers, these fast-food operations call attention to the approaching obsolescence of the housewife. What is needed, of course, are new social institutions to assume a good portion of the housewife's old duties. This is the challenge emanating from the swelling ranks of women in the working class. The demand for universal and subsidized child care is a direct consequence of the rising number of working mothers. And as more women organize around the demand for more jobs—for jobs on the basis of full equality

36. *Ibid.*, p. 53.
37. *Psychology Today,* Vol. X, No. 4 (September, 1976), p. 76.

with men—serious questions will increasingly be raised about the future viability of women's housewife duties. It may well be true that "slavery to an assembly line" is not in itself "liberation from the kitchen sink," but the assembly line is doubtlessly the most powerful incentive for women to press for the elimination of their age-old domestic slavery.

The abolition of housework as the private responsibility of individual women is clearly a strategic goal of women's liberation. But the socialization of housework—including meal preparation and child care—presupposes an end to the profit-motive's reign over the economy. The only significant steps toward ending domestic slavery have in fact been taken in the existing socialist countries. Working women, therefore, have a special and vital interest in the struggle for socialism. Moreover, under capitalism, campaigns for jobs on an equal basis with men, combined with movements for institutions such as subsidized public child care, contain an explosive revolutionary potential. This strategy calls into question the validity of monopoly capitalism and must ultimately point in the direction of socialism.

Notes

1. Frederick Engels (1820–1895), German socialist; with Karl Marx, one of the founders of radical communism.
2. Mariarosa Dalla Costa is a political historian at the University of Padua (Italy).

Source

Angela Davis, "The Approaching Obsolescence of Housework: A Working-Class Perspective," in *Women, Race and Class,* 222–44 (New York: Vintage Books, 1983).

Selected Bibliography

Aptheker, Bettina. *The Morning Breaks: The Trial of Angela Davis.* New York: International Publishers, 1975.

Davis, Angela. *Angela Davis: An Autobiography.* New York: International Publishers, 1988.

—— *The Angela Y. Davis Reader.* Edited by Joy James. Malden, Mass.: Blackwell, 1998.

—— *Women, Culture and Politics.* New York: Random House, 1989.

—— *Women, Race, and Class.* New York: Vintage Books, 1983.

twelve

Statement of Anita Hill to the Senate Judiciary Committee, October 11, 1991

Anita Hill (1956–) is the law professor who rose to national attention when she charged Clarence Thomas with sexual harassment in the midst of his Senate confirmation hearings to become a justice of the Supreme Court in October 1991. Hill's statement to the Senate Judiciary Committee polarized much of the nation, although it also helped to bring the issue of workplace harassment into the national dialogue and, according to some, contributed to the numerous gains that women made in state elections in 1992. However, Hill also faced serious repercussions for coming forward with her charges: in addition to being savaged by conservative politicians on the Judiciary Committee, she was hounded by the press and had to contend with lawmakers who asked that she be fired from her professorship at the University of Oklahoma Law School.

Hill was born in Morns, Oklahoma, and educated at Oklahoma State University and Yale Law School. From 1982 to 1983, she worked for the U.S. Department of Education as a special assistant to Clarence Thomas. During this period, she alleged that Thomas had pressured

---

The ellipses indicate repetitions and/or restatements that have been deleted to facilitate reading fluency. Otherwise, this is as exact transcription of Professor Anita F. Hill's statement to the Senate Judiciary Committee.—Ed.

her to date him, described the details of pornographic movies, and bragged about his sexual prowess. Thomas was narrowly confirmed anyway. In 1997, Hill published her memoir, *Speaking Truth to Power.*

Mr. Chairman. Senator Thurmond,[1] members of the committee, my name is Anita F. Hill, and I am a professor of law at the University of Oklahoma. I was born on a farm in Okmulgee County, Oklahoma, in 1956. I am the youngest of thirteen children. I had my early education in Okmulgee County. My father, Albert Hill, is a farmer in that area. My mother's name is Irma Hill. She is also a farmer and a housewife.

My childhood was one of a lot of hard work and not much money, but it was one of solid family affection, as represented by my parents. I was reared in a religious atmosphere in the Baptist faith, and I have been a member of the Antioch Baptist Church in Tulsa, Oklahoma, since 1983. It is a very warm part of my life at the present time.

For my undergraduate work, I went to Oklahoma State University and graduated from there in 1977. I am attaching to this statement a copy of my résumé for further details of my education.

I graduated from the university with academic honors and proceeded to the Yale Law School where I received my J. D. degree in 1980. Upon graduation from law school, I became a practicing lawyer with the Washington, D.C., firm of Wald, Hardraker, and Ross.

In 1981, I was introduced to now-Judge Thomas by a mutual friend.[2] Judge Thomas told me that he was anticipating a political appointment, and he asked if I would be interested in working with him. He was, in fact, appointed as assistant secretary of Education for civil rights. After he had taken that post, he asked if I would become his assistant, and I accepted that position.

In my early period there, I had two major projects. The first was an article I wrote for Judge Thomas's signature on the education of minority students. The second was the organization of a seminar on high-risk students which was abandoned because Judge Thomas transferred to the EEOC,[3] where he became the chairman of that office.

During this period at the Department of Education, my working relationship with Judge Thomas was positive. I had a good deal of responsibility and independence. I thought he respected my work and that he trusted my judgment. After approximately three months of working there, he asked me to go out socially with him.

What happened next and telling the world about it are the two most difficult . . . experiences of my life. It is only after a great deal of agonizing consideration . . . and a great number of sleepless nights that I am able to talk of these unpleasant matters to anyone but my close friends.

I declined the invitation to go out socially with him and explained to him that I thought it would jeopardize what at the time I considered to be a very good working relationship. I had a normal social life with other men outside of the office. I believed then, as now, that having a social relationship with a person who was supervising my work would be ill advised. I was very uncomfortable with the idea and told him so.

I thought that by saying no and explaining my reasons, my employer would abandon his social suggestions. However, to my regret, in the following few weeks, he continued to ask me out on several occasions. He pressed me to justify my reasons for saying no to him. These incidents took place in his office or mine. They were in the form of private conversations which would not have been overheard by anyone else.

My working relationship became even more strained when Judge Thomas began to use work situations to discuss sex. On these occasions, he would call me into his office for reports on education issues and projects, or he might suggest that because of the time pressures of his schedule, we go to lunch to a government cafeteria. After a brief discussion of work, he would turn the conversation to a discussion of sexual matters.

His conversations were very vivid. He spoke about acts that he had seen in pornographic films involving such matters as women having sex with animals and films showing group sex or rape scenes. He talked about pornographic materials depicting individuals with large penises or large breasts involved in various sex acts. On several occasions, Thomas told me graphically of his own sexual prowess.

Because I was extremely uncomfortable talking about sex with him at all and particularly in such a graphic way, I told him that I did not want to talk about these subjects. I would also try to change the subject to education matters or to nonsexual personal matters such as his background or his beliefs. My efforts to change the subject were rarely successful.

Throughout the period of these conversations, he also, from time to time, asked me for social engagements. My reaction to these conversations was to avoid them by eliminating opportunities for us to engage in extended conversations. This was difficult because at the time I was his only assistant at the Office of Education . . . Civil Rights.

During the latter part of my time at the Department of Education, the social pressures and his conversation of offensive behavior ended. I began both to believe and hope that our working relationship could be a proper, cordial, and professional one.

When Judge Thomas was made chair of the EEOC, I needed to face the question of whether to go with him. I was asked to do so, and I did. The work itself was interesting, and at that time it appeared that the sexual overtures, which had so troubled me, had ended. I also faced the realistic fact that I had no alternative job. While I might have gone back to private practice, perhaps in my old firm or at another, I was dedicated to civil rights work, and my first choice was to be in that field. Moreover, the Department of Education itself was a dubious venture. President Reagan was seeking to abolish the entire department.[4]

For my first months at the EEOC, where I continued to be an assistant to Judge Thomas, there were no sexual conversations or overtures. However, during the fall and winter of 1982, these began again. The comments were random and ranged from pressing me about why I didn't go out with him to remarks about my personal appearance. I remember his saying that someday I would have to tell him the real reason that I wouldn't go out with him.

He began to show displeasure in his tone and voice and his demeanor and his continued pressure for an explanation. He commented on what I was wearing in terms of whether it made me more or less sexually attractive. The incidents occurred in his inner office at the EEOC.

One of the oddest episodes I remember was an occasion in which Thomas was drinking a Coke in his office. He got up from the table at which we were working, went over to his desk to get the Coke, looked at the can, and asked, "Who has put pubic hair on my Coke?" On other occasions, he referred to the size of his own penis as being larger than normal, and he also spoke on some occasions of the pleasures he had given to women with oral sex.

At this point, late 1982, I began to feel severe stress on the job. I began to be concerned that Clarence Thomas might take out his anger with me by degrading me or not giving me important assignments. I also thought that he might find an excuse for dismissing me.

In January of 1983, I began looking for another job. I was handicapped because I feared that, if he found out, he might make it difficult for me to find other employment, and I might be dismissed from the job I had. Another factor that made my search more difficult was that . . . this was during a period of a hiring freeze in the government. In February of 1983, I was hospitalized for five days on an emergency basis for acute stomach pains, which I attributed to stress on the job.

Once out of the hospital, I became more committed to finding other employment and sought further to minimize my contact with Thomas. This became easier when Allison Duncan became office director, because most of my work was then funneled through her, and I had contact with Clarence Thomas mostly in staff meetings.

In the spring of 1983, an opportunity to teach at Oral Roberts University opened up. I . . . taught an afternoon session and seminar at Oral Roberts University. The dean of the university saw me teaching and inquired as to whether I would be interested in . . . pursuing a career in teaching, beginning at Oral Roberts University. I agreed to take the job in large part because of my desire to escape the pressures I felt at the EEOC due to Judge Thomas.

When I informed him that I was leaving in July. I recall that his response was that now I would no longer have an excuse for not going out with him. I told him that I still preferred not to do so. At some time after that meeting, he asked if he could take me to dinner at the end of the term. When I declined, he assured me that the dinner was a professional courtesy only, and not a social invitation.

I reluctantly agreed to accept that invitation, but only if it was at the very end of a working day.

On, as I recall, the last day of my employment at the EEOC in the summer of 1983. I did have dinner with Clarence Thomas. We went directly from work to a restaurant near the office. We talked about the work I had done, both at Education and at the EEOC. He told me that he was pleased with all of it except for an article and speech that I had done for him while we were at the Office for Civil Rights. Finally, he made a comment that I will vividly remember. He said that if I ever told anyone of his behavior that it would ruin his career. This was not an apology, nor was it an explanation. That was his last remark about the possibility of our going out or reference to his behavior.

In July of 1983, I left the Washington, D.C., area and have had minimal contact with Judge Clarence Thomas since. I am, of course, aware from the press that some questions have been raised about conversations I had with Judge Clarence Thomas after I left the EEOC. From 1983 until today, I have seen Judge Thomas only twice. On one occasion, I needed to get a reference from him, and on another, he made a public appearance in Tulsa.

On one occasion, he called me at home, and we had an inconsequential conversation. On one occasion, he called me without reaching me, and I returned the call without reaching him, and nothing came of it. I have, on at least three occasions, been asked to act as a conduit to him for others.

I knew his secretary, Diane Holt. We had worked together at both EEOC and Education. There were occasions on which I spoke to her, and on some of these occasions, undoubtedly, I passed on some casual comment to then-Chairman Thomas. There were a series of calls in the first three months of 1985, occasioned by a group in Tulsa which wished to have a civil rights conference. They wanted Judge Thomas to be the speaker and enlisted my assistance for this purpose.

I did call in January and February to no effect, and finally suggested to the person directly involved, Susan Cahall, that she put the matter into her own hands and call directly. She did so in March of 1985. In connection with that March invitation. Ms. Cahall wanted conference materials for the seminar, and some research was needed. I was asked to try to get the information and did attempt to do so.

There was another call about a possible conference in July of 1985. In August of 1987. I was in Washington, D.C., and I did call Diane Holt. In the course of this conversation, she asked me how long I was going to be in town, and I told her. It is recorded in the message as August 15. It was, in fact, August 20. She told me about Judge Thomas's marriage, and I did say congratulate him.

It is only after a great deal of agonizing consideration that I am able to talk of these unpleasant matters to anyone except my closest friends. As I've said before, these last few days have been very trying and very hard for me, and it hasn't just been the last few days this week. It has actually been over a month now that I have been under the strain of this issue.

Telling the world is the most difficult experience of my life, but it is very close to having to live through the experience that occasioned this meeting. I may have used poor judgment early on in my relationship with this issue. I was aware, however, that telling at any point in my career could adversely affect my future career. And I did not want early on to burn all the bridges to the EEOC.

As I said, I may have used poor judgment. Perhaps I should have taken angry or even militant steps, both when I was in the agency, or after I left it. But I must confess to the world that the course that I took seemed the better, as well as the easier approach.

I declined any comment to newspapers, but later when Senate staff asked me about these matters, I felt I had a duty to report. I have no personal vendetta against Clarence Thomas. I seek only to provide the committee with information which it may regard as relevant.

It would have been more comfortable to remain silent. I took no initiative to inform anyone. But when I was asked by a representative of this committee to report my experience, I felt that I had to tell the truth. I could not keep silent.

Notes

1. Senator James Strom Thurmond (1902–), conservative U.S. senator from South Carolina.
2. Clarence Thomas (1948–), U.S. Supreme Court justice, lawyer, administrator, jurist.
3. U.S. Equal Employment Opportunity Commission.
4. Ronald Wilson Reagan (1911–), fortieth president of the United States (1981–1988).

Source

Anita Hill, "Statement of Anita Hill to the Senate Judiciary Committee, October 11, 1991," in Geneva Smitherman, ed., *African American Women Speak Out on Anita Hill*, 19–24 (Detroit: Wayne State University Press, 1995).

Selected Bibliography

Hill, Anita. *Speaking Truth to Power.* New York: Doubleday, 1997.

Hill, Anita and Emma Coleman Jordan, eds. *Race, Gender, and Power in America: The Legacy of the Hill-Thomas Hearings.* New York: Oxford University Press, 1995.

Mayer, Jane and Jill Abramson. *Strange Justice: The Selling of Clarence Thomas*. Boston: Houghton Mifflin, 1994.

Morrison, Toni, ed. *Race-ing Justice, En-Gendering Power: Essays on Anita Hill, Clarence Thomas, and the Construction of Social Reality*. New York: Pantheon Books, 1992.

Phelps, Timothy M. and Helen Winternitz. *Capitol Games: Clarence Thomas, Anita Hill, and the Story of a Supreme Court Nomination*. New York: Hyperion, 1992.

thirteen

Establishing Black Feminism

Barbara Smith is one of the first and still few black female writers who identifies as a lesbian in her writing. Smith presented her most innovative and controversial work in 1977 at the National Conference of Afro-American Writers. There she read "Toward a Black Feminist Criticism," the first essay to examine black lesbian relationships in classic black novels and as a fundamental part of black literature. It also argued that all black and Third World women should have a greater presence in literature. Smith has taught in a number of different colleges and universities and frequently contributes to popular and scholarly publications.

Smith was born in 1946 and was raised in a predominantly female family in a poor neighborhood in Cleveland, Ohio. Her mother died when she was nine years old. Smith went on to receive her B.A. from Mount Holyoke College in 1969 and her M.A. from the University of Pittsburgh in 1971. She began teaching at the University of Massachusetts in 1976.

Smith is a self-identified feminist and socialist and is also a committed social activist. She is a cofounder of Kitchen Table: Women of Color Press and the Combahee River Collective (1974–1981) which sponsored a number of retreats for black women writers who saw the interconnectedness of racism, sexism, homophobia, and class oppression in establishing strategies for social change.

The following essay is a reprint of the preface for the second edition of *Home Girls: A Black Feminist Anthology,* which was presented at Columbia University's Black Feminism 2000 Symposium.

More than twenty years after some of the work in *Home Girls* was written, the primary question I want to examine is how effective have Black women been in establishing Black feminism. The answer depends on where one looks. Black feminism has probably been most successful in its impact on the academy, in its opening a space for courses, research, and publications about Black women. Although Black women's studies continues to be challenged by racism, misogyny, and general disrespect, scholarship in the field has flourished in the decades since *Home Girls* was published.

Not only is it possible to teach both graduate and undergraduate courses focusing on Black and other women of color, but it is also possible to write dissertations in a variety of disciplines that focus on Black women. Academic conferences about Black and other women of color regularly occur all over the country, and sessions about Black women are also presented at annual meetings of professional organizations. Hundreds if not thousands of books have been published that document Black women's experience using the methodologies of history, the social sciences, and psychology. In the academy, at least, Black women are not nearly as invisible as we were when *Home Girls* first appeared. It is important to keep in mind, however, that discrimination continues to affect Black women academics' salaries, opportunities for promotion, and daily working conditions.

When we search for Black feminism outside the academy and ask how successful have we been in building a visible Black feminist movement, the answer is not as clear. In reading my original introduction, I was struck by how many examples of organizing by women of color I could cite. When *Home Girls* was published in 1983 the feminist movement as a whole was still vital and widespread. Although the media loved to announce that feminism was dead, they had not yet concocted the 1990s myth of a "postfeminist" era in which all women's demands have supposedly been met and an organized movement is irrelevant. Reaganism was only a few years old, and it had not yet, in collaboration with an ever more powerful right wing, turned back the clock to eradicate many of the gains that had been made in the 1960s and 1970s toward racial, sexual, and economic justice. Now, much as in the beginning of this century, the end of the twentieth century is a time of lynchings, whether motivated by racism as in Jasper, Texas; by homophobia as in Laramie, Wyoming; by misogyny as in Yosemite, California; or by a lethal mix of hatreds as in Oklahoma City and Littleton, Colorado. Twenty years of conservative federal administrations and the U.S. populace's increasing move to the right have been detrimental to all progressive and leftist organizing, including the building of Black feminism.

There are specific factors that make Black feminist organizing even more difficult to accomplish than activism focused on other political concerns. Raising issues of oppression within already oppressed communities is as likely to be met with attacks and ostracism as with comprehension and readiness to change. To this day most Black women are unwilling to jeopardize their racial credibility (as defined by Black men) to address the reality of sexism. Even fewer are willing to bring up homophobia and heterosexism, which are of course inextricably linked to gender oppression.

Black feminist author Jill Nelson pointedly challenges the Black community's reluctance to deal with sexual politics in her book *Straight, No Chaser: How I Became a Grown-up Black Woman.* She writes:

> As a group, Black men and, heartbreakingly, many Black women, refuse to acknowledge and confront violence toward women, or, truth be told, any other issue that specifically affects Black women. To be concerned with any gender issue is, by and large, still dismissed as a "white woman's thing," as if Black men in America, or anywhere else in the world, for that matter, have managed to avoid the contempt for women that is a fundamental element of living in a patriarchy. Even when lip service is given to sexism as a valid concern, it is at best a secondary issue. First and foremost is racism and the ways in which it impacts Black men. It is the naïve belief that once racism is eradicated, sexism, and its unnatural outgrowth, violence toward women, will miraculously melt away, as if the abuse of women is solely an outgrowth of racism and racial oppression.[1]

Since *Home Girls* was published there has actually been an increase of overt sexism in some Black circles as manifested by responses to the Anita Hill—Clarence Thomas Senate Hearings, Mike Tyson's record of violence against women (and men), the O. J. Simpson trial, and the Million Man March. Some regressive elements of Black popular culture are blatantly misogynist. Both Black men and women have used the term "endangered species" to describe Black men because of the verifiable rise in racism over the last two decades; yet despite simultaneous attacks on women, including Black women who are also subjected to racism, Black women are often portrayed as being virtually exempt from oppression and much better off than their male counterparts. It is mistaken to view Black feminism as Black "male bashing" or as a battle between Black women and men for victim status, but as Nelson points out it has been extremely difficult to convince most in the Black community to take Black women's oppression seriously.

Twenty years ago I would have expected there to be at least a handful of nationally visible Black feminist organizations and institutions by now. The cutbacks, right-wing repression, and virulent racism of this period have been devastating for the growth of our movement, but we must also look at our own practice. What if more of us had decided to build multi-issued grass-roots organizations in our own communities that dealt with Black women's basic survival issues and at the same time did not back away from raising issues of sexual politics? Some of the things I think of today as Black feminist issues are universal access to quality health care; universal accessibility for people with disabilities; quality public education for all; a humane and nonpunitive system of support for poor women and children, i.e., genuine welfare reform; job training and placement in real jobs that have a future; decent, affordable housing; and the eradication of violence of all kinds including police brutality. Of course, violence against women; reproductive freedom; equal employment opportunity; and lesbian, gay, bisexual, and transgender liberation still belong on any Black feminist agenda.

Since the 1980s few groups have been willing to do the kind of Black feminist organizing that the Combahee River Collective took on in Boston in the 1970s, which was to carry out an antiracist, feminist *practice* with a radical, anticapitalist analysis. It is not surprising that Black feminism has seemed to be more successful in the more hospitable environment on campuses than on the streets of Black communities, where besides all the other challenges, we would also need to deal with the class difference among us. To me Black feminism has always encompassed basic bread-and-butter issues which affect women of *all* economic groups. It is a mistake to characterize Black feminism as only relevant to middle-class, educated women, simply because Black women who are currently middle class have been committed to building the contemporary movement. From my own organizing experience I know that there are working-class and poor Black women who not only relate to the basic principles of Black feminism but who live them. I believe our movement will be very much stronger when we develop a variety of ways to bring Black feminism home to the Black communities from which it comes.[2]

In the present women of color of all races, nationalities, and ethnicity's are leaders in labor organizing, immigration struggles, dismantling the prison industrial complex, challenging environmental racism, sovereignty struggles, and opposition to militarism and imperialism. Black feminists mobilized a remarkable national response to the Anita Hill—Clarence Thomas Senate Hearings in 1991. Naming their effort "African American Women in Defense of Ourselves," they gathered more than sixteen hundred signatures for an incisive statement that appeared in the *New York Times* and in a number of Black newspapers shortly after the hearings occurred.

Black feminists were centrally involved in organizing the highly successful Black Radical Congress (BRC) which took place in Chicago in June 1998. This gathering of two thousand activists marked the first time in the history of the African American liberation movement that Black feminist and Black lesbian, gay, bisexual, and transgender issues were on the agenda from the outset. A Black feminist caucus formed within the BRC before last June's meeting and is continuing its work.

Black feminists have also been active in the international struggle to free the political prisoner Mumia Abu-Jamal, who is currently on death row in Pennsylvania. The Millions for Mumia mobilization, which took place in Philadelphia on April 24, 1999, included a huge Rainbow Flags for Mumia contingent. This effort marked a first for significant, planned participation by the lesbian, gay, bisexual, and transgender community in a militant antiracist campaign. This participation in both the Black Radical Congress and the Millions for Mumia March did not occur without struggle. Not all the participants were on the same page in recognizing the necessity to challenge sexism and homophobia, and some did not even understand these to be critical political issues. But twenty years ago we most likely would not have been present, let alone part of the leadership of these two events. The success of these coalitions and others also indicates that there are some Black men who work as committed allies to Black feminists.

Within the lesbian, gay, bisexual, and transgender movement itself Black lesbian feminists have been extremely active in the Ad Hoc Committee for an Open Process, the grass-roots group that has successfully questioned the undemocratic, corporate, and tokenistic tactics of the proposed gay millennium rally in Washington in 2000. The Ad Hoc Committee has also been instrumental in initiating a dynamic national dialogue about the direction of the lesbian, gay, bisexual, and transgender movement, whose national leadership has distanced itself more and more from a commitment to economic and social justice.

Although the Black feminist movement is not where I envisioned it might be during those first exciting days, it is obvious that our work has made a difference. Radical political change most often happens by increments rather than through dramatically swift events. Indeed, dramatic changes are made possible by the daily, unpublicized work of countless activists working on the ground. The fact that there is an audience for the writing in this collection, as a new century begins, indicates that *Home Girls* has made a difference as well, and that in itself is a sign of progress and hope.

Notes

1. Jill Nelson, *Straight, No Chaser: How I Became a Grown-up Black Woman* (New York: G. P. Putnam's Sons, 1997), p. 156.
2. A new anthology, *Still Lifting, Still Climbing: African American Women's Contemporary Activism,* edited by Kimberly Springer (New York: New York University Press, 1999), provides an excellent overview of Black women's activism since the Civil Rights era.

Source

Barbara Smith, "Establishing Black Feminism," *Souls: A Critical Journal of Black Politics, Culture and Society* 2 (fall 2000): 50–55.

Selected Bibliography

Hull, Gloria T., Patricia Bell-Scott, and Barbara Smith. *All the Women Are White, All the Blacks Are Men, but Some of Us Are Brave.* Old Westbury, N.Y.: Feminist Press, 1982.

Smith, Barbara. *Home Girls: A Black Feminist Anthology.* New York: Kitchen Table—Women of Color Press, 1983.

—— *The Truth That Never Hurts: Writings on Race, Gender, and Freedom.* New Brunswick, N.J.: Rutgers University Press, 1998.

fourteen

Toward a Black Feminist Liberation Agenda: Race Gender and Violence

Kristen Clarke is a trial attorney in the Civil Rights Division of the U.S. Department of Justice. Her primary area of focus is voting rights, where she has a worked on a range of issues including felon disenfranchisement, city–county consolidations, challenges to at-large electoral systems, expanding voter registration opportunities through the National Voter Registration Act and ensuring minority electoral opportunity in city, county and state redistricting efforts. Clarke is a graduate of Harvard University, where she received a B.A. cum laude in government and African American studies. She received her law degree from the Columbia University School of Law. Between 1999 and 2000, Clarke served as an assistant editor for *Souls: A Critical Journal of Black Politics, Culture and Society*. Prior to joining the U.S. Department of Justice, Clarke served as a freelance photographer and writer. Her work has appeared in a broad range of publications including *VIBE, The Source, Souls,* and *Rap Pages*.

What do the federal sentencing guidelines mean with respect to freedom in a nation where family plays a critical social and political function and where the struggle for racial equality persists? The following essay attempts to provide an answer to this question by exploring the intersections between race, gender, and justice. The impact that the federal sentencing guidelines have had on women on color is directly connected to issues of racial equality, family, and freedom. As an increasing number of women of color have become entangled in the web of mandatory minimums, growing numbers of children are being raised without mothers, and the black family unit is being further torn apart. Indeed, the prospects for achieving real freedom and racial equality are seriously threatened by mandatory minimums and other criminal sentencing laws that bear a disparate impact on African Americans.

There are a series of social, cultural, and political institutions that reproduce, support, or perpetuate dangerous stereotypes about Black women. Many of these stereotypes and labels are informed by both historical and contemporary understandings of Black women. Indeed, the persistent myth of the Black woman as masculine, fiercely independent, hostile, aggressive, and domineering[1] works to frustrate the use of legal strategies generally available for Black women who come into contact with the criminal justice system. It also works to strip them of their womanhood, a central aspect of their identity. In addition, this stereotyping of Black women works to further subordinate and marginalize them, thus forcing them to contend with the challenges brought by the intersection of race, gender, and violence in social and political life. Indeed, the current expansion of the prison industrial complex and growing incarceration rates among women of color call for the development of a Black feminist liberation agenda that transforms the social and political identities of Black women while offering new strategies to slow escalating incarceration rates among Black mothers.

Expansion of the Prison Industrial Complex: The Place of Black Women

Over the past few years, there has been increased emphasis on the expansion of the prison industrial complex. In many states, prison construction outpaces the development of new public schools, parks, and community centers. Increasing percentages of state budgets are committed to the development of prisons, jails, and detention centers, and police departments have watched their annual budget allocations grow. The current boom in the prison industry coincides with the largest incarceration rate that this country has ever witnessed. With the current prison population standing at more than 2 million, the United States now has one of the largest incarcerated populations of any country. In fact, the United States houses over a quarter of the world's prison population despite having less than 5 percent of the world's overall population.

The current expansion of the prison industrial complex brings with it a series of troubling consequences, particularly for women of color. The current number of women in prisons and jails throughout the United States is increasing at a faster rate than that of men.[2] Seventy-five percent of women in prison are mothers. Two-thirds of these women have children under the age of eighteen. Seventy-eight percent of women in prison report that they have been physically or sexually abused. Finally, Black women are incarcerated at a rate eight times that of women generally.[3] Vigorous enforcement of drug laws and the incarceration of persons in possession of small quantities of drugs provide some explanation for the current crisis. But increased racism and sexism among law enforcement agencies and officials provides a fuller explanation for rising incarceration rates among women of color. These alarming rates call for a new understanding of the social construction of Black women within the criminal context. They also call for an exploration of issues surrounding the intersection of race, gender, and violence[4] and an examination of the impact that incarceration bears on the Black family unit.

Black women have become new targets in our incarceration-obsessed world. Increasingly, Black women are the victims of racial profiling by police officers, store managers, and airline security. Black women are viewed as providing shields for Black men, who are already presumed to be engaged in some form of criminal activity. When Black women come in contact with the criminal justice system, they are often denied the benefit of defense strategies that are readily employed by their white counterparts. One such strategy, the battered women's defense, helps illustrate this dual crisis of racism and sexism in the justice system.

The battered woman's defense (originally referred to as the battered women's syndrome) is a legal strategy generally invoked when an individual, usually a woman, is continuously subjected to a pattern of domestic violence and forced to submit to the dictates of an abusive partner. The concept of battered women was first introduced by Lenore Walker, a forensic psychologist, who observed that women in these situations suffer from "learned helplessness" whereby the psychological stresses of living in a constant state of fear inhibits [a woman's] ability to perceive the possibility of escape." According to research, battered women become submissive, compliant, passive, and meek. All their energies are "focused on avoiding the next attack, and when that has failed, living through it." Many critics have challenged Walker's conception of battered women as essentially stigmatizing them as "sick" or "mentally ill." To better reflect concerns about background gender inequality, the battered women's defense has undergone some theoretical transformation over the decades, expanding to include more feminist understandings of abusive relationships.

The domestic violence that results in abusive contexts can manifest in the form of physical, emotional, sexual, or economic abuse and is largely aimed at controlling or dominating the other partner. Generally, women in these situations find that the abuse and violence escalate over a period of time. A single abusive event such as a slap, unwanted sex, or vicious taunting steadily degenerates into a systematic and pervasive cycle of abuse. Experts who have studied and monitored women in these situations note that there is a tremendous feeling of entrapment, a learned helplessness, among women in these situations. Women rarely feel that they are able to turn away from an abusive partner and start their lives over. In addition to some of these emotional responses of entrapment, there are more objective, gender-based reasons that provide an explanation for the sense of entrapment that battered women feel. Indeed, the greatest contribution that feminists have lent to the construction of the battered women's defense is an alternative rationale as to why women tend to feel trapped in abusive situations. A feminist understanding of the battered woman recognizes that women tend to respond to abuse "with help-seeking methods that are largely unmet and that women increase their help-seeking as the danger to themselves and their children increases."[5] A Black feminist liberation ideology can be applied to these situations to help unpack the influence of coercive state power, inaccessible social service delivery, and racism on the experiences of Black women in abusive situations.

Given pervasive gender inequality, women are less likely to find jobs that pay salaries commensurate with those obtainable by their male counterparts. Women are more likely to experience gender-based discrimination in the workplace that impacts the prospects of promotions, benefit packages, and wage increases. Black women, who contend with the challenges associated with both race and gender, have an even more difficult time in the workplace. Black women are among the lowest wage earners and are the primary group likely to experience some form of dual gender- and race-based discrimination during their working lives. In addition, Black women are unemployed at rates much higher than their white counterparts.[6] As a result, Black women are more likely to be in positions where there is reliance or dependence on the joint income provided by their spouse. Thus, the economics of family maintenance suggests that Black working-class women tend to be more reliant on the supplemental income of their spouses to help provide basic life necessities for them and their children.

In addition to general workplace inequality, divorce laws in many states are constructed in ways that might impact a woman's decision to walk away from an abusive male. Women who are more reluctant to divorce a spouse in the hopes of repairing the relationship are unlikely to receive child support or alimony during periods of separation. In some states, women's organizations are petitioning their state legislatures for laws that would mandate prosecution for domestic violence. It is believed that if the abusers are in jail, women would have a safer and more meaningful opportunity to consider joining a shelter that could provide the necessary therapy and economic independence.

State coercive power also impacts Black women's decisions about the level of interaction that they seek to have with the criminal justice system. The tremendous levels of distrust and fear that exist in Black communities as a result of escalating police brutality and misconduct discourage many Black women from seeking refuge with local police departments. Where women feel that their claims are unlikely to be followed through on and investigated or where there is a sense that immediate intervention is unlikely, they are less likely to turn to police officers. The full range of this background inequality is worth considering in deconstructing the choices that women make in battering situations. Social and political forces, predominant stereotypes and myths, and the lurking threat of coercive state power are all factors that influence and shape the decisions of women in abusive situations.

Certainly, the battered women's defense has been met with a fair share of emotion from policymakers, politicians, feminists and activists. Some find that the defense pathologizes women by suggesting that they lack the reason and free will to walk away from abusive and negative situations. Others feel that the defense is disempowering in that it discourages women from leaving abusive partners where they are aware of the safety valve within the law. Finally, some hold that the defense stigmatizes women as vulnerable children in need of special protection under the law.

Despite these varied criticisms, the situation of battered women is deemed one of the nation's most studied and critical public health problems. The battered women's defense is raised frequently in trials involving a battered spouse and is often used as evidence to explain the actions of the battered individual. The defense can be offered during a trial for women who were trapped in abusive situations and are seeking to provide evidence of a mitigating factor that will encourage the judge or jury to be lenient. In some instances, women who have killed a spouse or partner are acquitted on expert testimony and evidence about the effects that the battering has had on the women.

For a number of reasons, Black women have been far less successful than white women in raising the battered women's defense during trial. I would argue that the social construction and media depictions of Black women as independent, domineering, aggressive, and hostile individuals helps explain, in part, why some judges and juries are far less likely to apply the defense in examining these women's experiences with violent men. In addition, racism works to create inequity in the way in which strategies such as the battered women's defense are applied. Because white women historically enjoy a reputation of innocence, honor, and virtue,[7] they are deemed worthy of greater protection and immunity as compared with other racial minorities.

Kemba Smith and the Battered Women's Defense

The story of Kemba Smith, a twenty-six-year-old Black woman currently incarcerated at a medium-security prison, is a case worth serious examination in this context. Kemba grew up in a middle-class family in a small suburban town and attended Hampton University, a historically Black college located in Virgina. During her first year at Hampton, Kemba began dating a young man, Peter Michael Hall. Hall was about eight years her senior and the ringleader of a massive drug-trafficking scheme operating throughout the northeastern part of the United States. During their relationship, Peter kept his drug activity somewhat separate from his relationship. Thus, Kemba never physically handled or sold drugs during the course of her relationship with him.

Given the extent of illegal activity that Peter was involved with, one would think that Kemba would have chosen to turn her back on the situation and walk away. Kemba was later contacted by FBI agents after Peter was placed on their Most Wanted list. For a number of reasons, Kemba initially chose to not cooperate with officials. Today, Black women don't enjoy second chances. Where Black women acquiesce in Black men's illicit activity, they are stigmatized and branded just the same. There is rarely opportunity to look into the circumstances surrounding Black women's situations to unravel the layers of complexity that define those situations.

Careful analysis of Kemba's story, reveals that she suffered a pattern of violent abuse at the hands of her boyfriend. This pattern of physical abuse greatly influenced Kemba's initial decision to not cooperate with the FBI. She was often beaten badly by Peter and was forced to seek emergency room medical treatment on one occasion for her injuries. She experienced a miscarriage after another particularly violent incident. Kemba witnessed Peter murder his best friend when he believed that the friend had become a police informant. He also made an implicit threat against her father, who he had believed might be cooperating with federal law enforcement. Kemba had dropped out of school on Peter's urging and was forced to travel with him around the country as he attempted to evade police authorities. Before he could be brought to trial and before Kemba had an opportunity to inform authorities of his whereabouts, Peter was murdered by an unknown assailant at a hotel room in Texas.

During trial, Kemba was held accountable for the entire 225 kilograms of crack cocaine that was trafficked under Peter Michael Hall's leadership. Under the stiff penalties of the federal sentencing guidelines, Kemba received a sentence of twenty-four years in prison with no possibility of parole. Under the guidelines, a judge is forbidden to consider any other facts in a case, as punishment is based solely on the amount of drugs involved in the offense. Thus, the particularities of Kemba's case were not a factor in the judge's decision-making. Neither the violent beatings that Kemba suffered, the systematic abuse, nor her miscarriage were issues that could be weighed in determining the extent of Kemba's guilt. Despite the inflexibility of the sentencing scheme established by the guidelines, it is Black women who have suffered the greatest under these laws. For whatever reason, white women who are brought in under similar circumstances rarely make it that far along in the system. Prosecutors might exercise their discretion not to take action in their case or white women found in actual possession are more likely to receive the benefit of treatment centers and rehabilitation programs. Black women are stigmatized as guilty and as criminals worthy of the greatest criminal sanction and punishment that the criminal system has to offer.

In many ways, Kemba's case merely exemplifies the reassignment of guilt and punishment. Where Black men become inaccessible or less reachable, Black women serve as a proxy on which the system can carry out its harsh enforcement policy. Black women are viewed as unworthy of exemption or defense, as they are perceived as always having the means to turn away. Although this social construction of Black women assumes a false and overstated sense of independence, it does help explain why they rarely enjoy the opportunity to exercise legal defenses and strategies that their white peers benefit from.

Toward a Black Feminist Liberation Understanding of Battered Women

As Joy James notes, Black feminist liberation ideology should be constructed in a way that challenges state power by addressing class exploitation, racism, and sexual violence. Indeed, the sexual stereotyping of Black women as domineering, aggressive, hostile individualists is an image reinforced through social structures and reproduced by institutions such as the media. Deconstructing the mythology surrounding the hostile Black woman is a necessary first step in creating an environment in which the particular needs of abused Black women can be addressed. Indeed, Black women have been denied the privileges of femininity and protection from physical and discursive violence that is generally granted to white women.[8] Breaking down these stereotypes calls for a delicate balancing of a woman's need to be protected from violence and misogyny with a desire to eradicate patriarchy and paternalism.

Historically, the notion of the empowered Black woman has been regarded as an emasculating Black matriarchy in which women seek complete and absolute independence from men.[9] This antiquated notion of Black feminist theory has worked to create tension and conflict between the sexes. The typecasting of Black women has had tremendous consequences for those women who come into contact with the criminal justice system, however. This typecasting makes it more difficult for judges and juries to sympathize with Black women who are trapped in abusive relationships. This racial typecasting also creates obstacles that prevent judges and juries from understanding why some Black women fail to seek intervention or outside help.

Given increased tensions between the Black community and police officers, there is a general reluctance in minority communities to report crime incidents to the police or to work in cooperation with the police to investigate these incidents. This reluctance, distrust, and fear have tremendous influence on Black women's decisions to report abusive spouses or partners to the police. In the case of Kemba Smith, the decision to postpone cooperation with FBI officials worked to her detriment, as officials read this choice as an indication of complicity or participation in the illegal activity of her partner.

In addition, race, gender, and class also converge to create a unique set of circumstances experienced largely by Black women. When domestic violence erupts in urban communities, the stresses of poverty and unemployment create a situation where the woman is more likely to feel trapped in the home. Given the recent cuts in social spending, decreases in social service delivery, increasing unemployment among the urban poor, and reform of welfare policy, Black women are more likely to feel trapped and unable to turn to peers or family members for refuge or support. Although many of these concerns are shared equally by poor white women, these issues become compounded when race is factored into the equation.

Redefining Black Womanhood

Two-thirds of mothers in prison today have children who are under the age of eighteen. Many women of color who come into contact with the criminal justice system leave behind children who are generally institutionalized, placed in the foster care systems, or taken in by relatives. Because women tend to be children's primary caregivers, there is rarely complete assurance that children will receive proper care and guidance once separated from their mother. Because most single-parent families are headed by women, the absence of the mother carries with it tremendous social stigma for the child. For Black women, parental status is rarely a characteristic given any kind of assessment or consideration in determining whether incarceration is the best option in a given situation. Black mothers are rarely given access to alternative incarceration programs that help sustain relationships between mothers and their children. For Black mothers in prison, such as Kemba Smith, parental status is a personal characteristic that is seldom dignified or granted substantial consideration in the criminal justice system. The fact that Kemba Smith was a new first-time mother was not a factor taken into consideration when she was sentenced to a stiff penalty of twenty-five years for her relationship with Peter Michael Hall. The lack of consideration for a Black woman's parental status compounds the current stereo-typing that Black women experience in the criminal justice system, thus stripping them of their womanhood—a central aspect of their identity. A range of historical and contemporary factors contribute to the current devaluation of Black womanhood.

The legacy of enslaved Africans, in part, informs current conceptions of Black womanhood. Thus, any liberation agenda aimed at deconstructing the dual influence of gender and race on contemporary understandings of Black women's experiences must be based, in part, on the conditions that Black women endured during slavery. Indeed, analysis of the female slave's experiences provides two possible theories for the current application of drug laws that disproportionately work to strip Black mothers from their children. First of all, female slaves were largely classified as "breeders" as opposed to "mothers";[10] thus their children could be sold away from them at the will of their white male owners. One way of interpreting state coercion or force as a means of stripping apart the Black family unit is by tracing the historical legacy of "breeding" that has persisted the slave period. Historically, Black women were expected to give up their children where the law dictated that they do so. Numerous laws were established in this system that stripped female slaves of their parental rights, as both mother and child were deemed property of their owners. Today, the parental rights of Black women, such as Kemba Smith, are of little consequence when they come into conflict with the criminal justice system. Indeed, we are continuing to overcome the legacy of "breeding," as Black women's parental rights have yet to be accorded full dignity. Given the inequities in the system, particularly racial sentencing disparities, Black mothers bear a heavier burden as compared with white mothers.

Second, many of the persisting stereotypes of Black women are based on notions of the female slave as resistant, unruly, and disruptive. Today, many Black women continue to be similarly stereotyped as aggressive and defiant. Like Black men, Black women are also deemed to have a greater propensity for crime on the basis of their racial status. Although the majority of studies and analyses of racism in the criminal justice system have focused on the stereotyping of Black men, Black women experience comparable levels of abuse and mistreatment in the criminal justice system. The typecasting of Black women is compounded by some of the gender stereotypes that have carried over since the slave era, however. Thus, a liberation agenda must also support strategies aimed at breaking down these stigmatizing stereotypes while simultaneously redefining Black womanhood. Indeed, "collective actions, . . . must be directed at changing the social conditions that both allow the dominant group to control the manufacture and dissemination of ideological constructions and lend strength and credibility to stereotypes."[11] This new conception of Black womanhood can help judges, juries, the media, and political institutions better understand, sympathize with, and interpret the experiences of Black women. This new conception can also help generate greater sympathy for the plight of Black battered women and restore the dignity and humanity of Black women while providing a new focus on the importance of maintaining the Black family unit.

Conclusion

As the prison population continues to expand, there is growing need to focus on the impact that incarceration has on women of color and Black women in particular. Indeed, incarceration has a tremendous impact on the stability of the Black family unit that works to further dehumanize and demoralize Black women. Kemba Smith's case provides an illustration of current disregard for the Black family unit and of the disparate treatment of Black and white women who come into contact with the criminal justice system. The current social and political construction of Black women's identities are shaped in large part by persisting stereotypes that label women as aggressive, violent, and domineering individuals. It is also influenced by a historical legacy of Black women as "breeders" that impacts ideas of Black motherhood and parental rights. For Black feminists and others concerned with the development of a liberation ideology, a political praxis must be developed that accounts for intersections that exist across lines of race, gender, and violence. This political praxis must also incorporate advocacy models and litigation strategies that can be used on behalf of the growing numbers of Black women who come into contact with the criminal justice system.

Notes

1. May King, "The Politics of Sexual Stereotypes," *Black Scholar,* Vol. 12, no. 4; Sharon Angella Allard, "Rethinking Battered Woman Syndrome: A Black Feminist Perspective," *UCLA Women's Law Journal,* Vol. 191, no. 1 (1991).
2. U.S. Department of Justice Office of Justice Programs, Bureau of Justice Statistics Bulletin, August 1998.
3. U.S. Department of Justice Office of Justice Programs, Bureau of Justice Statistics Bulletin, August 1998.
4. Kimberlé Crenshaw, Neil Gotanda, Gary Peller, and Kendall Thomas, "Mapping the Margins: Intersectionality, Identity Politics, and Violence Against Women of Color," in *Critical Race Theory: The Key Writings That Formed the Movement* (New York: The New Press, 1995).
5. Allard, "Rethinking Battered Woman Syndrome."
6. Claudette E. Bennett, *The Black Population in the United States: March 1994 and 1993,* U.S. Bureau of Census, Current Population Reports (Washington, D.C.: Government Printing Office, 1995).
7. Maxine Atkinson and Jacqueline Boles, "The Shaky Pedestal: Southern Ladies Yesterday and Today," *Southern Studies,* Vol. 34, no. 4 (1985), pp. 398–406.
8. Farrah Griffin,
9. Michelle Wallace, *Black Macho and the Myth of the Superwoman* (London: Verso, 1978).
10. Angela Davis, *Women, Race and Class,* 7 (Vintage Press, 1981).
11. Leith Mullings, "Images, Ideology and Women of Color," in *On Our Own Terms: Race, Class and Gender in the Lives of African American Women* (New York: Routledge Press, 1997), p. 125.

Source

Kristen Clarke, "Toward a Black Feminist Liberation Agenda, Race Gender and Violence," *Souls: A Critical Journal of Black Politics, Culture, and Society* 2 (fall 2000) 80–88.

Selected Bibliography

Mullings, Leith. "Images, Ideology and Women of Color," in *In Our Own Terms: Race, Class and Gender in the Lives of African American Women,* 125. New York: Routledge Press, 1997.

Wallace, Michelle. *Black Macho and the Myth of the Superwoman.* London: Verso, 1978.

chapter two

Kinship and Community

one

Kidnappers!

Throughout slavery, in both the North and the South, free blacks faced the possibility that they could be kidnapped and sold as slaves. Although it is impossible to know how often kidnapping occurred, Thomas P. Cope and other abolitionists said it was a daily occurrence. Because African Americans often lacked any effective legal protections, there was little they could do to redress this violation. In this article from *The Liberator*, an Ohio farmer named Lewis Williamson describes the kidnapping and subsequent return of his children.

Three miles below Gallipolis [Ohio] I once possessed a farm of rich soil, that yielded seventy-five bushels to the acre. I lived in comfort with my family and there I might have been living now, had not my prosperity raised the envy of a neighbor whose land joined mine. He employed me to assist in rebuilding a corn crib that had fallen five miles below. We could easily have done the work and returned home the same day, but [the other workmen] loitered and I, with one or two others, were sent to stay at his brother's.

At dead of night they entered my little habitation and dragged my wife and three small children from their beds. With savage brutality, they were driven over frozen ground to the river and thrown into a canoe. Two hundred and forty miles below, my wife was set ashore. With a heart burning with anguish she got on board of a steamboat and returned home.

But to return to myself. I arose early. I set about finishing the work. When the business was accomplished, we set out for home. On the way a neighbor came running to tell me the state in which he had seen my house. The horrible conviction flashed on my mind. I turned to my employer and said, "Did you get me away to sell my wife and children?"

He swore he knew nothing of it, but he looked like a monster to me. If a weapon had been at hand, I fear I should have taken his life.

But I had no time to lose. The thought that I might overtake and regain my dearest earthly treasures spurred me on. I took passage on a steamboat for Louisville, but could hear nothing of them. I then procured handbills and had them distributed in every steamboat. My name was called by a Capt. Buckner, who had one of my handbills. I soon found that he had conveyed my children to Natchez, whither I pursued with all possible speed. On my arrival, I learned they had been resold and taken three days before, no one, alas! knew whither.

I now wandered about in Mississippi, Alabama, Georgia, Tennessee, and Louisiana in the forlorn hope of lighting upon them. I then learned the name of the second purchaser. I found that he resided in Louisiana, about 80 miles from Natchez. I immediately went to his plantation and saw my children, but did not make myself known to them or their master, for it might have prevented forever their return to liberty.

I returned home to procure one of my white neighbors for evidence. As compensation, I gave him my farm, besides handsome suit of broadcloth, traveling expenses, &c. When we arrived [in Louisiana] the master was from home and the mistress, who heard of our coming, had sent the children 100 miles farther into the country.

But when the master came home, he sent for them. About midnight, I heard voices approaching. The people began to arouse and said, "Wake up, Williamson." Ah! they thought a father could sleep.

I fell back from the light of the door and saw them enter. Tears ran down my cheeks to see their famished and miserable appearance. The man whom I had brought as witness kept his face from them for a time. When he turned around the boy rushed to him, exclaiming, "Oh, Mr. Gibson. Where's my father—my mother?"

I approached the door and said, "Beck, are you here?"

My daughter dashed through the crowd crying, "That's my father—Oh, father, where's mother?" and sunk into my arms.

After this the owner said, "Old man, come in. These children are yours and you must have them." Thus joyfully ended my six years' search.

The Liberator, December 10, 1841

Source

Lewis Williamson, "Kidnappers!" (1841; reprinted in Dorothy Sterling, ed., *Speak Out in Thunder Tones: Letters and Other Writings by Black Northerners, 1787–1865,* 145–47 [New York: Da Capo Press, 1973]).

Selected Bibliography

Harding, Vincent. *There Is a River: The Black Struggle for Freedom in America.* San Diego: Harcourt Brace Jovanovich, 1992.

Hopper, Isaac T. *Kidnappers in Philadelphia: Isaac Hooper's Tales of Oppression, 1780–1843.* Edited by Daniel E. Meaders. New York: Garland, 1994.

Von Frank, Albert. *The Trials of Anthony Burns: Freedom and Slavery in Emerson's Boston.* Cambridge, Mass.: Harvard University Press, 1998.

Wilson, Carol. *Freedom at Risk: The Kidnapping of Free Blacks in America, 1780–1865.* Lexington: University Press of Kentucky, 1994.

two

William J. Walker, To His Son, 2/2/1850

As a result of the social exigencies that African Americans faced in the antebellum period—including rampant discrimination, dire poverty, and slavery or the threat of slavery—blacks often had to struggle simply to maintain close family ties. In this poignant letter, William J. Walker wrote his son to relay some family hardships but also to impart his love, to recommend that he look to the Bible as a source for spiritual sustenance, and to encourage him to marry.

Fredericksburg
February 2, 1850

Dear John

With pen in hand I seate myself to write you in ancer to your very kind letter which came to hand on the first of this present month—It found us well thank God—and we are in hope's when these lines reaches you They will find you injoyin all the blessings of a kind and benevolent Redeemer—Dear John you stated in yours that it was the secont letter you had writen—well it is the secont one we have received—and this is the secont one I have written in ancer to yours your grand Mother Departed this life on the 20th of November and

Harry Hulet Dido Just about one month before your grand Mother and Brother A Daniel Dide on the 22 of January 1850 and one of the largest possession I ever saw in this place turn out on such a cation boath societys turned out with their bages which seen was monefull But pretty—I think I have gaven you all the News of Interest there fore I will turn my thoughts to sumthin elce—I will make none your request to the Brethren Askin of them to pray for you and Dear John dont you forget to approach a throne of grace often and I pray God that you may grow in grace and in the knolege of the truth as is in our lord and Saviour Jesus Christ and read you Bible at every Idle moment you will find It a grate strenght in your Christian Warfare in this world yes and in the world to come I pray God that you and Brother Brook may be preserved unto the secont comming of our lord and Saviour—Jesus Christ—Ever Be foun washing in the blood of the lamb I will see Mr. J Chew and ask of him when Mr. Minor's Brother will leave and will have your Shirts Ready if God be willing—Dear John I have one more thing to say Before I close and it is this of all the pretty Spanish girls you have seen I do hope you will not Come Clare Back home to pick up nothing let your old song Be true get you a wife from old Virginia old Virginia Shore—John for the sake of your happyness here after take the advice which I gave I am now about to close and my last wish is that you may hold out faithfull to the end—old fredericksburg is in the same place. let me here from you often farewell if we never meet on erth I hop to mee you in heaven where parting is noe more Davy H sends his love to you your Mother and Sister all join In love to you I Close good by John good by

Yours untell Death
William J. Walker

Source

William J. Walker, "To His Son, 2/2/1850," in Carter G. Woodson, ed., *The Mind of the Negro as Reflected in Letters Written During the Crisis, 1800–1860,* 522 (New York: Negro Universities Press, 1926).

Selected Bibliography

Ball, Edward. *Slaves in the Family.* New York: Farrar, Straus and Giroux, 1998.

Berlin, Ira and Leslie S. Rowland, eds. *Families and Freedom: A Documentary History of African-American Kinship in the Civil War Era.* New York: New Press, 1997.

Bogger, Tommy. *Free Blacks in Norfolk, Virginia, 1790–1860: The Darker Side of Freedom.* Charlottesville: University Press of Virginia, 1997.

At this time this young man John was away with the navy. The letter is found in the collection of manuscripts of the Association for the Study of Negro Life and History.

Gutman, Herbert. *The Black Family in Slavery and Freedom, 1750–1925*. New York: Pantheon Books, 1976.

Jones, Jacqueline. *Labor of Love: Black Women, Work, and the Family from Slavery to the Present*. New York: Basic Books, 1985.

Stevenson, Brenda E. *Life in Black and White: Family and Community and the Slave South*. New York: Oxford University Press, 1996.

three

Childhood

Harriet Jacobs was born into slavery in Edenton, North Carolina, in 1813. Her mother, Delilah, was the slave of Margaret and John Horniblow. Her father, Daniel Jacobs, was a skilled slave carpenter. After her mother's death, Jacobs was sent to live at the Horniblow estate, where she learned to read, spell, and sew.

Under the pseudonym Linda Brent, Jacobs authored *Incidents of the Life of a Slave Girl: Written by Herself* (1861), regarded as the most important female slave narrative. It first appeared in Horace Greeley's *New York Tribune* in 1855 under the heading "Letter from a Fugitive Slave." Publishing the work was a task of great difficulty. The following is an excerpt from the first chapter, "Childhood." In it, Jacobs begins her narrative with the conventional opening, "I was born a slave," but breaks new ground with her harrowing account of the sexual violence that female slaves endured at the hands of their white owners. Jacobs details the hardships she encountered after escaping such abuse, hiding as a fugitive slave. She also recalls her heroic efforts to reunite her family, illustrating how slaves used their families as a bulwark against a system that was designed to dehumanize *African Americans*.

Jacobs worked as a nurse during the Civil War and as a teacher in the relief effort in Alexandria, Virginia. She spent the latter part of her life with her daughter in Washington, D.C. She died on March 7, 1897.

I. Childhood

I was born a slave; but I never knew it till six years of happy childhood had passed away. My father was a carpenter, and considered so intelligent and skillful in his trade, that, when buildings out of the common line were to be erected, he was sent for from long distances, to be head workman. On condition of paying his mistress two hundred dollars a year, and supporting himself, he was allowed to work at his trade, and manage his own affairs. His strongest wish was to purchase his children; but, though he several times offered his hard earnings for that purpose, he never succeeded. In complexion my parents were a light shade of brownish yellow, and were termed mulattoes. They lived together in a comfortable home; and, though we were all slaves, I was so fondly shielded that I never dreamed I was a piece of merchandise, trusted to them for safe keeping, and liable to be demanded of them at any moment. I had one brother, William, who was two years younger than myself—a bright, affectionate child. I had also a great treasure in my maternal grandmother, who was a remarkable woman in many respects. She was the daughter of a planter in South Carolina, who, at his death, left her mother and his three children free, with money to go to St. Augustine, where they had relatives. It was during the Revolutionary War; and they were captured on their passage, carried back, and sold to different purchasers. Such was the story my grandmother used to tell me; but I do not remember all the particulars. She was a little girl when she was captured and sold to the keeper of a large hotel. I have often heard her tell how hard she fared during childhood. But as she grew older she evinced so much intelligence, and was so faithful, that her master and mistress could not help seeing it was for their interest to take care of such a valuable piece of property. She became an indispensable personage in the household, officiating in all capacities, from cook and wet nurse to seamstress. She was much praised for her cooking; and her nice cackers became so famous in the neighborhood that many people were desirous of obtaining them. In consequence of numerous requests of this kind, she asked permission of her mistress to bake crackers at night, after all the household work was done; and she obtained leave to do it, provided she would clothe herself and her children from the profits. Upon these terms, after working hard all day for her mistress, she began her midnight bakings, assisted by her two oldest children. The business proved profitable; and each year she laid by a little, which was saved for a fund to purchase her children. Her master died, and the property was divided among his heirs. The widow had her dower in the hotel, which she continued to keep open. My grandmother remained in her service as a slave; but her children were divided among her master's children. As she had five, Benjamin, the youngest one, was sold, in order that each heir might have an equal portion of dollars and cents. There was so little difference in our ages that he seemed more like my brother than my uncle. He was a bright, handsome lad, nearly white; for he inherited the complexion my grandmother had derived from Anglo-Saxon ancestors. Though only ten years old, seven hundred and twenty dollars were paid for him. His sale was a terrible blow to my grandmother; but she was naturally hopeful, and she went to work with renewed energy, trusting in time to be able to purchase some of her children. She had laid up three hundred dollars, which her mistress one day begged as a loan, promising to pay her soon. The reader probably knows that no promise or writing given to a slave is legally binding; for, according to Southern laws, a slave, being property, can hold no property. When my grandmother lent her hard earnings to her mistress, she trusted solely to her honor. The honor of a slaveholder to a slave!

To this good grandmother I was indebted for many comforts. My brother Willie and I often received portions of the crackers, cakes, and preserves, she made to sell; and after we ceased to be children we were indebted to her for many more important services.

Such were the unusually fortunate circumstances of my early childhood. When I was six years old, my mother died; and then, for the first time, I learned, by the talk around me, that I was a slave. My mother's mistress was the daughter of my grandmother's mistress. She was the foster sister of my mother; they were both nourished at my grandmother's breast. In fact, my mother had been weaned at three months old, that the babe of the mistress might obtain sufficient food. They played together as children; and, when they became women, my mother was a most faithful servant to her whiter foster sister. On her death-bed her mistress promised that her children should never suffer for any thing; and during her lifetime she kept her word. They all spoke kindly of my dead mother, who had been a slave merely in name, but in nature was noble and womanly. I grieved for her, and my young mind was troubled with the thought who would now take care of me and my little brother. I was told that my home was now to be with her mistress; and I found it a happy one. No toilsome or disagreeable duties were imposed upon me. My mistress was so kind to me that I was always glad to do her bidding, and proud to labor for her as much as my young years would permit. I would sit by her side for hours, sewing diligently, with a heart as free from care as that of any free-born white child. When she thought I was tired, she would send me out to run and jump; and away I bounded, to gather berries or flowers to decorate her room. Those were happy days—too happy to last. The slave child had no thought for the morrow; but there came that blight, which too surely waits on every human being born to be a chattel.

When I was nearly twelve years old, my kind mistress sickened and died. As I saw the cheek grow paler, and the eye more glassy, how earnestly I prayed in my heart that she might live! I loved her; for she had been almost like a mother to me. My prayers were not answered. She died, and they buried her in the little churchyard, where, day after day, my tears fell upon her grave.

I was sent to spend a week with my grandmother. I was now old enough to begin to think of the future; and again and again I asked myself what they would do with me. I felt sure I should never find another mistress so kind as the one who was gone. She had promised my dying mother that her children should never suffer for any thing; and when I remembered that, and recalled her many proofs of attachment to me, I could not help having some hopes that she had left me free. My friends were almost certain it would be so. They thought she would be sure to do it, on account of my mother's love and faithful service. But, alas! we all know that the memory of a faithful slave does not avail much to save her children from the auction block.

After a brief period of suspense, the will of my mistress was read, and we learned that she had bequeathed me to her sister's daughter, a child of five years old. So vanished our hopes. My mistress had taught me the precepts of God's Word: "Thou shalt love thy neighbor as thyself."[1] "Whatsoever ye would that men should do unto you, do ye even so unto them."[2] But I was her slave, and I suppose she did not recognize me as her neighbor. I would give much to blot out from my memory that one great wrong. As a child, I loved my mistress; and, looking back on the happy days I spent with her, I try to think with less bitterness of this act of injustice. While I was with her, she taught me to read and spell; and for this privilege, which so rarely falls to the lot of a slave, I bless her memory.

She possessed but few slaves; and at her death those were all distributed among her relatives. Five of them were my grandmother's children, and had shared the same milk that nourished her mother's children. Notwithstanding my grandmother's long and faithful service to her owners, not one of her children escaped the auction block. These God-breathing machines are no more, in the sight of their masters, than the cotton they plant, or the horses they tend.

II. The New Master and Mistress

Dr. Flint, a physician in the neighborhood, had married the sister of my mistress, and I was now the property of their little daughter. It was not without murmuring that I prepared for my new home; and what added to my unhappiness, was the fact that my brother William was purchased by the same family. My father, by his nature, as well as by the habit of transacting business as a skillful mechanic, had more of the feelings of a freeman than is common among slaves. My brother was a spirited boy; and being brought up under such influences, he early detested the name of master and mistress. One day, when his father and his mistress had happened to call him at the same time, he hesitated between the two; being perplexed to know which had the strongest claim upon his obedience. He finally concluded to go to his mistress. When my father reproved him for it, he said, "You both called me, and I didn't know which I ought to go to first."

"You are *my* child," replied our father, "and when I call you, you should come immediately, if you have to pass through fire and water."

Poor Willie! He was now to learn his first lesson of obedience to a master. Grandmother tried to cheer us with hopeful words, and they found an echo in the credulous hearts of youth.

When we entered our new home we encountered cold looks, cold words, and cold treatment. We were glad when the night came. On my narrow bed I moaned and wept, I felt so desolate and alone.

I had been there nearly a year, when a dear little friend of mine was buried. I heard her mother sob, as the clods fell on the coffin of her only child, and I turned away from the grave, feeling thankful that I still had something left to love. I met my grandmother, who said, "Come with me, Linda;" and from her tone I knew that something sad had happened. She led me apart from the people, and then said, "My child, your father is dead." Dead! How could I believe it? He had died so suddenly I had not even heard that he was sick. I went home with my grandmother. My heart rebelled against God, who had taken from me mother, father, mistress, and friend. The good grandmother tried to comfort me. "Who knows the ways of God?" said she. "Perhaps they have been kindly taken from the evil days to come." Years afterwards I often thought of this. She promised to be a mother to her grandchildren, so far as she might be permitted to do so; and strengthened by her love, I returned to my master's. I thought I should be allowed to go to my father's house the next morning: but I was ordered to go for flowers, that my mistress's house might be decorated for an evening party. I spent the day gathering flowers and weaving them into festoons, while the dead body of my father was lying within a mile of me. What cared my owners for that? He was merely a piece of property. Moreover, they thought he had spoiled his children, by teaching them to feel that they were human beings. This was blasphemous doctrine for a slave to teach; presumptuous in him, and dangerous to the masters.

The next day I followed his remains to a humble grave beside that of my dear mother. There were those who knew my father's worth, and respected his memory.

My home now seemed more dreary than ever. The laugh of the little slave-children sounded harsh and cruel. It was selfish to feel so about the joy of others. My brother moved about with a very grave face. I tried to comfort him, by saying, "Take courage, Willie; brighter days will come by and by."

"You don't know any thing about it, Linda," he replied. "We shall have to stay here all our days; we shall never be free."

I argued that we were growing older and stronger, and that perhaps we might, before long, be allowed to hire our own time, and then we could earn money to buy our freedom. William declared this was much easier to say than to do; moreover, he did not intend to *buy* his freedom. We held daily controversies upon this subject.

Little attention was paid to the slaves' meals in Dr. Flint's house. If they could catch a bit of food while it was going, well and good. I gave myself no trouble on that score, for on my various errands I passed my grandmother's house, where there was always something to spare for me. I was frequently threatened with punishment if I stopped there; and my grandmother, to avoid detaining me, often stood at the gate with something for my breakfast or dinner. I was indebted to *her* for all my comforts, spiritual or temporal. It was *her* labor that supplied my scanty wardrobe. I have a vivid recollection of the linsey-woolsey dress given me every winter by Mrs. Flint. How I hated it! It was one of the badges of slavery.

While my grandmother was thus helping to support me from her hard earnings, the three hundred dollars she had lent her mistress were never repaid. When her mistress died, her son-in-law, Dr. Flint, was appointed executor. When grandmother applied to him for payment, he said the estate was insolvent, and the law prohibited payment. It did not, however, prohibit him from retaining the silver candelabra, which had been purchased with that money. I presume they will be handed down in the family, from generation to generation.

My grandmother's mistress had always promised her that, at her death, she should be free; and it was said that in her will she made good the promise. But when the estate was settled, Dr. Flint told the faithful old servant that, under existing circumstances, it was necessary she should be sold.

On the appointed day, the customary advertisement was posted up, proclaiming that there would be a "public sale of negroes, horses, &c." Dr. Flint called to tell my grandmother that he was unwilling to wound her feelings by putting her up at auction, and that he would prefer to dispose of her at private sale. My grandmother saw through his hypocrisy she understood very well that he was ashamed of the job. She was a very spirited woman, and if he was base enough to sell her, when her mistress intended she should be free, she was determined the public should know it. She had for a long time supplied many families with crackers and preserves; consequently, "Aunt Marthy," as she was called, was generally known, and every body who knew her respected her intelligence and good character. Her long and faithful service in the family was also well known, and the intention of her mistress to leave her free. When the day of sale came, she took her place among the chattels, and at the first call she sprang upon the auction-block. Many voices called out, "Shame! Shame! Who is going to sell you, aunt Marthy? Don't stand there! That is no place for you." Without saying a word, she quietly awaited her fate. No one bid for her. At last, a feeble voice said, "Fifty dollars." It came from a maiden lady, seventy years old, the sister of my grandmother's deceased mistress. She had lived forty years under the same roof with my grandmother; she knew how faithfully she had served her owners, and how cruelly she had been defrauded of her rights; and she resolved to protect her. The auctioneer waited for a higher bid; but her wishes were respected; no one bid above her. She could neither read nor write; and when the bill of sale was made out, she signed it with a cross. But what consequence was that, when she had a big heart overflowing with human kindness? She gave the old servant her freedom.

At that time, my grandmother was just fifty years old. Laborious years had passed since then; and now my brother and I were slaves to the man who had defrauded her of her money, and tried to defraud her of her freedom. One of my mother's sisters, called Aunt Nancy, was also a slave in his family. She was a kind, good aunt to me; and supplied the place of both housekeeper and waiting maid to her mistress. She was, in fact, at the beginning and end of every thing.

Mrs. Flint, like many southern women, was totally deficient in energy. She had not strength to superintend her household affairs; but her nerves were so strong, that she could sit in her easy chair and see a woman whipped, till the blood trickled from every stroke of the lash. She was a member of the church; but partaking of the Lord's supper did not seem to put her in a Christian frame of mind. If dinner was not served at the exact time on that particular Sunday, she would station herself in the kitchen, and wait till it was dished, and then spit in all the kettles and pans that had been used for cooking. She did this to prevent the cook and her children from eking out their meagre fare with the remains of the gravy and other scrapings. The slaves could get nothing to eat except what she chose to give them. Provisions were weighed out by the pound and ounce, three times a day. I can assure you she gave them no chance to eat wheat bread from her flour barrel. She knew how many biscuits a quart of flour would make, and exactly what size they ought to be.

Dr. Flint was an epicure. The cook never sent a dinner to his table without fear and trembling; for if there happened to be a dish not to his liking, he would either order her to be whipped, or compel her to eat every mouthful of it in his presence. The poor, hungry creature might not have objected to eating it; but she did object to having her master cram it down her throat till she choked.

They had a pet dog, that was a nuisance in the house.

The cook was ordered to make some Indian mush for him. He refused to eat, and when his head was held over it, the froth flowed from his mouth into the basin. He died a few minutes after. When Dr. Flint came in, he said the mush had not been well cooked, and that was the reason the animal would not eat it. He sent for the cook, and compelled her to eat it. He thought that the woman's stomach was stronger than the dog's; but her sufferings afterwards proved that he was mistaken. This poor woman endured many cruelties from her master and mistress; sometimes she was locked up, away from her nursing baby, for a whole day and night.

When I had been in the family a few weeks, one of the plantation slaves was brought to town, by order of his master. It was near night when he arrived, and Dr. Flint ordered him to be taken to the work house, and tied up to the joist, so that his feet would just escape the ground. In that situation he was to wait till the doctor had taken his tea. I shall never forget that night. Never before, in my life, had I heard hundreds of blows fall, in succession, on a human being. His piteous groans, and his "O, pray don't, massa," rang in my ear for months afterwards. There were many conjectures as to the cause of this terrible punishment. Some said master accused him of stealing corn; others said the slave had quarrelled with his wife, in presence of the overseer, and had accused his master of being the father of her child. They were both black, and the child was very fair.

I went into the work house next morning, and saw the cowhide still wet with blood, and the boards all covered with gore. The poor man lived, and continued to quarrel with his wife. A few months afterwards Dr. Flint handed them both over to a slave-trader. The guilty man put their value into his pocket, and had the satisfaction of knowing that they were out of sight and hearing. When the mother was delivered into the trader's hands, she said, "You promised to treat me well." To which he replied, "You have let your tongue run too far; damn you!" She had forgotten that it was a crime for a slave to tell who was the father of her child.

From others than the master persecution also comes in such cases. I once saw a young slave girl dying soon after the birth of a child nearly white. In her agony she cried out, "O Lord, come and take me!" Her mistress stood by, and mocked at her like an incarnate fiend. "You suffer, do you?" she exclaimed. "I am glad of it. You deserve it all, and more too."

The girl's mother said, "The baby is dead, thank God; and I hope my poor child will soon be in heaven, too."

"Heaven!" retorted the mistress. "There is no such place for the like of her and her bastard."

The poor mother turned away, sobbing. Her dying daughter called her, feebly, and as she bent over her, I heard her say, "Don't grieve so, mother; God knows all about it; and HE will have mercy upon me."

Her sufferings, afterwards, became so intense, that her mistress felt unable to stay; but when she left the room, the scornful smile was still on her lips. Seven children called her mother. The poor black woman had but the one child, whose eyes she saw closing in death, while she thanked God for taking her away from the greater bitterness of life.

Notes

1. Mark 12:31.
2. Matthew 7:12.

Source

Harriet A. Jacobs, *Incidents in the Life of a Slave Girl* (New York: Penquin Books, 2000).

Selected Bibliography

Ball, Edward. *Slaves in the Family.* New York: Farrar, Straus, and Giroux, 1988.

Hauss, Jon. "Masquerades in Black: A Cultural Encounter in Late Antebellum American Literature." Ph.D. diss., University of Washington, 1990.

King, Wilma. *Stolen Childhood: Slave Youth in Nineteenth Century America.* Bloomington: Indiana University Press, 1995.

Zafar, Rafia and Deborah Garfield, eds. *Harriet Jacobs and Incidents in the Life of a Slave Girl: New Critical Essays.* Cambridge, U.K., and New York: Cambridge University Press, 1996.

four

For My People

Margaret Walker's (1915–1998) important career spanned from the Harlem Renaissance through the Black Power movement. The poem "For My People" is probably her single most important work, and it won the Yale University Younger Poet's Award in 1942. Here, Walker conveyed a rhythmic series of images that spoke to the hardship, beauty, pathos, strength, and resilience that characterize the African American experience.

Born into a comfortable, well-educated family in Birmingham, Alabama, Walker showed an early love of writing, studied at Northwestern University, and worked for the W.P.A. Federal Writers' Project, where she met and became friends with Richard Wright. Walker later attended the prestigious Iowa Writers' Workshop, where she finished her most famous collection of poems, *For My People* (1942). She didn't publish again, however, until 1966, when she released the acclaimed novel *Jubilee*. She published several other collections of poems, and in 1985 she released *Richard Wright, a Daemonic Genius: A Portrait of the Man, a Critical Look at His Work.*

For my people everywhere singing their slave songs repeatedly: their dirges and their ditties and their blues and jubilees, praying their prayers nightly to an unknown god, bending their knees humbly to an unseen power;

For my people lending their strength to the years, to the gone years and the now years and the maybe years, washing ironing cooking scrubbing sewing mending hoeing plowing digging planting pruning patching dragging along never gaining never reaping never knowing and never understanding.

For my playmates in the clay and dust and sand of Alabama backyards playing baptizing and preaching and doctor and jail and soldier and school and mama and cooking and playhouse and concert and store and hair and Miss Choomby and company;

For the cramped bewildered years we went to school to learn to know the reasons why and the answers to and the people who and the places where and the days when, in memory of the bitter hours when we discovered we were black and poor and small and different and nobody cared and nobody wondered and nobody understood;

For the boys and girls who grew in spite of these things to be Man and Woman, to laugh and dance and sing and play and drink their wine and religion and success, to marry their playmates and bear children and then die of consumption and anemia and lynching;

For my people thronging 47th Street in Chicago and Lenox Avenue in New York and Rampart Street in New Orleans, lost disinherited dispossessed and happy people filling the cabarets and taverns and other people's pockets needing bread and shoes and milk and land and money and something—something all our own;

For my people walking blindly spreading joy, losing time being lazy, sleeping when hungry, shouting when burdened, drinking when hopeless, tied and shackled and tangled among ourselves by the unseen creatures who tower over us omnisciently and laugh;

For my people blundering and groping and floundering in the dark of churches and schools and clubs and societies, associations and councils and committees and conventions, distressed and disturbed and deceived and devoured by money-hungry glory-craving leeches, preyed on by facile force of state and fad and novelty, by false prophet and holy believer;

For my people standing staring trying to fashion a better way from confusion, from hypocrisy and misunderstanding, trying to fashion a world that will hold all the people all the faces, all the adams and eves and their countless generations;

Let a new earth rise. Let another world be born. Let a bloody peace be written in the sky. Let a second generation full of courage issue forth; let a people loving freedom come to growth. Let a beauty full of healing and a strength of final clenching be the pulsing in our spirits and out blood. Let the martial songs be written, let the dirges disappear. Let a race of men now rise and take control.

1937, 1942

Source

Margaret Walker, "For My People," in *This Is My Century: New and Collected Poems,* 6–7 (Athens: The University of Georgia Press, 1980).

Selected Bibliography

Collier, Eugina. "Fields and Watered Blood: Myth and Ritual in the Poetry of Margaret Walker." In Mari Evans, ed., *Black Women Writers (1950–1980): A Critical Evaluation.* Garden City, N.Y.: Anchor Press/Doubleday, 1984.

Jones, John Griffin, ed. *Mississippi Writers Talking.* Vol. 2. Jackson: University Press of Mississippi, 1983.

Walker, Margaret. *On Being Female, Black, and Free: Essays by Margaret Walker, 1932–1992.* Edited by Maryemme Graham. Knoxville: University of Tennessee Press, 1997.

—— *A Poetic Equation: Conversations Between Nikki Giovanni and Margaret Walker.* Washington, D.C.: Howard University Press, 1974.

—— *This Is My Century: New and Collected Poems.* Athens: University of Georgia Press, 1989.

five

Ella Baker

In this passage, Ella Baker (1903–1986) describes the deep sense of community that she felt as a child growing up in rural Virginia, which informed her subsequent civil rights activism. Baker spent much of her life immersed in behind-the-scenes political activity.

Baker was born in Norfolk, Virginia, and later lived in Littleton, North Carolina, and New York City. In 1958 she began working for the Southern Christian Leadership Conference (SCLC), although she was always somewhat critical of the organization's top-down leadership style. In April 1960, she called a conference of young civil rights leaders, and this meeting led to the creation of the Student Nonviolent Coordinating Committee (SNCC), one of the premier civil rights organizations of the 1960s. Although Baker was never a member of SNCC, many students regarded her as a wise and trusted counsel, and SNCC embraced the grassroots, decentralized organizing strategy of which she was an advocate. She died in 1986.

Where we lived there was no sense of hierarchy, in terms of those who have, having a right to look down upon, or to evaluate as a lesser breed, those who didn't have. Part of that could have resulted, I think, from two factors. One was the proximity of my maternal grandparents to slavery. They had known what it was to not have. Plus, my grandfather had gone into the Baptist ministry, and that was past of the quote, unquote, Christian concept of sharing with others. I went to a school that went in for Christian training. Then, there were people who "stood for something," as I call it. Your relationship to human beings was more important than your relationship to the amount of money that you made.

There was a deep sense of community that prevalled in this little neck of the woods. It wasn't a town, it was just people. And each of them had their twenty-thirty-forty-fifty acre farms, and if there were emergencies, the farmer next to you would share in something to meet that emergency. For Instance, when you thresh wheat. If there was a thresher around, you didn't have each person having his own. So you came to my farm and threshed, then you went to the next one and the next one and the next one. You joined in. Part of the land was on a riverbank, the Roanoke River, and now it has been made into a lake through a dam process. But the river would overflow at times and certain crops might be ruined. So if that took place, and it wrecked havoc with the food supply, I am told that my grandfather would take his horse and wagon and go up to the county seat, which was the only town at that point, and mortgage, if necessary, his land, to see that people ate.

The sense of community was pervasive in the black community as a whole, I mean especially the community that had a sense of roots. This community had been composed to a large extent by relatives. Over the hill was my grandfather's sister who was married to my Uncle Carter, and up the grove was another relative who had a place. So it was a deep sense of community. I think these are the things that helped to strengthen my concept about the need for people to have a sense of their own value, and *their* strengths, and it became accentuated when I began to travel in the forties for the National Association for the Advancement of Colored People.[1] Because during that period, in the forties, racial segregation and discrimination were very harsh. As people moved to towns and cities, the sense of community diminished. A given area was made up of people from various and sundry other areas. They didn't come from the same place. So they had to *learn* each other, and they came into patterns of living that they had not been accustomed to. And so whatever deep sense of community that may have been developed in that little place that I spoke of, didn't always carry over to the city when they migrated. They lost their roots. When you lose that, what will you do next. You *hope* that you begin to think in terms of the *wider* brotherhood.

Note

1. A civil rights organization formed in 1910, the NAACP is composed mainly of African Americans but has some white members.

Source

Ella Baker, as quoted in Ella Cantarow, ed., *Moving the Mountain: Women Working for Social Change,* 60–61 (New York: The Feminist Press, 1980).

Selected Bibliography

Baker, Ella Jo. "Developing Community Leadership." In Gerda Lerner, ed., *Black Women in White America*. New York: Vintage Books, 1992.

Carson, Clayborne. *In Struggle: SNCC and the Black Awakening of the 1960s*. Cambridge, Mass.: Harvard University Press, 1981.

Grant, Joanne. *Ella Baker: Freedom Bound*. New York: Wiley, 1988.

Morris, Aldon D. *The Origins of the Civil Rights Movement: Black Communities Organizing for Change*. New York: Free Press; London: Collier MacMillan, 1984.

Ransby, Barbara. "Ella J. Baker and the Black Radical Tradition." Ph.D. diss., University of Michigan, 1996.

six

Notes of a Native Son

James Baldwin (1924–1987) is among the most renowned writers of the twentieth century, and his urgent, angry, prophetic voice was enormously influential to both black and white Americans during the heady days of the civil rights movement. Baldwin had a trying relationship with his father, a strict evangelical preacher. In the following excerpt from his classic essay *Notes of a Native Son,* Baldwin described his father's funeral and the ways that social tensions in Harlem greatly complicated his family life.

Always a precocious intellect, Baldwin excelled in his classes at De Witt Clinton High School, where he graduated in 1942. Richard Wright helped him win a fellowship to support work on his first novel, *Go Tell It on the Mountain,* which he finished in Paris in 1948. Baldwin wrote six more novels over the course of his career; however, most critics agree that his various essays—including *Notes of a Native Son* (1955), *Nobody Knows My Name* (1961), and *The Fire Next Time* (1963)—were his most significant contributions to American literature. Baldwin died in France in 1987.

On the 29th of July, in 1943, my father died. On the same day, a few hours later, his last child was born. Over a month before this, while all our energies were concentrated in waiting for these events, there had been, in Detroit, one of the bloodiest race riots of the century. A few hours after my father's funeral, while he lay in state in the undertaker's chapel, a race riot broke out in Harlem. On the morning of the 3rd of August, we drove my father to the graveyard through a wilderness of smashed plate glass.

The day of my father's funeral had also been my nineteenth birthday. As we drove him to the graveyard, the spoils of injustice, anarchy, discontent, and hatred were all around us. It seemed to me that God himself had devised, to mark my father's end, the most sustained and brutally dissonant of codas. And it seemed to me, too, that the violence which rose all about us as my father left the world had been devised as a corrective for the pride of his eldest son. I had declined to believe in that apocalypse which had been central to my father's vision; very well, life seemed to be saying, here is something that will certainly pass for an apocalypse until the real thing comes along. I had inclined to be contemptuous of my father for the conditions of his life, for the conditions of our lives. When his life had ended I began to wonder about that life and also, in a new way, to be apprehensive about my own.

I had not known my father very well. We had got on badly, partly because we shared, in our different fashions, the vice of stubborn pride. When he was dead I realized that I had hardly ever spoken to him. When he had been dead a long time I began to wish I had. It seems to be typical of life in America, where opportunities, real and fancied are thicker than anywhere else on the globe, that the second generation has no time to talk to the first. No one, including my father, seems to have known exactly how old he was, but his mother had been born during slavery. He was of the first generation of free men. He, along with thousands of other Negroes, came North after 1919, and I was part of that generation which had never seen the landscape of what Negroes sometimes call the Old Country.

He had been born in New Orleans and had been a quiet young man there during the time that Louis Armstrong, a boy, was running errands for the dives and honky-tonks of what was always presented to me as one of the most wicked of cities—to this day, whenever I think of New Orleans, I also helplessly think of Sodom and Gomorrah. My father never mentioned Louis Armstrong, except to forbid us to play his records; but there was a picture of him on our wall for a long time. One of my father's strong-willed female relatives had placed it there and forbade my father to take it down. He never did, but he eventually maneuvered her out of the house and when, some years later, she was in trouble and near death, he refused to do anything to help her.

He was, I think, very handsome. I gather this from photographs and from my own memories of him, dressed in his Sunday best and on his way to preach a sermon somewhere, when I was little. Handsome, proud, and ingrown, "like a toe-nail," somebody said. But he looked to me, as I grew older, like pictures I had seen of African tribal chieftains: he really should have been naked, with war-paint on and barbaric mementos, standing among spears. He could be chilling in the pulpit and indescribably cruel in his personal life and he was certainly the most bitter man I have ever met; yet it must be said that there was something else in him, buried in him, which lent him his tremendous power and, even, a rather crushing charm. It had something to do with his blackness, I think—he was very black—with his blackness and his beauty, and with the fact that he knew that he was black but did not know that he was beautiful. He claimed to be proud of his blackness but it had also been the cause of much humiliation and it had fixed bleak boundaries to his life. He was not a young man when we were growing up and he had already suffered many kinds of ruin; in his outrageously demanding and protective way he loved his children, who were black like him and menaced, like him; and all these things sometimes showed in his face when he tried, never to my knowledge with any success, to establish contact with any of us. When he took one of his children on his knee to play, the child always became fretful and began to cry; when he tried to help one of us with our homework the absolutely unabating tension which emanated from him caused our minds and our tongues to become paralyzed, so that he, scarcely knowing why, flew into a rage and the child, not knowing why, was punished. If it ever entered his head to bring a surprise home for his children, it was almost unfailingly, the wrong surprise and even the big watermelons he often brought home on his back in the summertime led to the most appalling scenes. I do not remember, in all those years, that one of his children was ever glad to see him come home. From what I was able to gather of his early life, it seemed that this inability to establish contact with other people had always marked him and had been one of the things which had driven him out of New Orleans. There was something in him, therefore, groping and tentative, which was never expressed and which was buried with him. One saw it most clearly when he was facing new people and hoping to impress them. But he never did, not for long. We went from church to smaller and more improbable church, he found himself in less and less demand as a minister, and by the time he died none of his friends had come to see him for a long time. He had lived and died in an intolerable bitterness of spirit and it frightened me, as we drove him to the graveyard through those unquiet, ruined streets, to see how powerful and overflowing this bitterness could be and to realize that his bitterness now was mine.

When he died I had been away from home for a little over a year. In that year I had had time to become aware of the meaning of all my father's bitter warnings, had discovered the secret of his proudly pursed lips and rigid carriage: I had discovered the weight of white people in the world. I saw that this had been for my ancestors and now would be for me an awful thing to live with and that the bitterness which had helped to kill my father could also kill me.

He had been ill a long time—in the mind, as we now realized, reliving instances of his fantastic intransigence in the new light of his affliction and endeavoring to feel a sorrow for him which never, quite, came true. We had not known that he was being eaten up by paranoia, and the discovery that his cruelty, to our bodies and our minds, had been one of the symptoms of his illness was not, then, enough to enable us to forgive him. The younger children felt, quite simply, relief that he would not be coming home anymore. My mother's observation that it was he, after all, who had kept them alive all these years meant nothing because the problems of keeping children alive are not real for children. The older children felt, with my father gone, that they could invite their friends to the house without fear that their friends would be insulted or, as had sometimes happened with me, being told that their friends were in league with the devil and intended to rob our family of everything we owned. (I didn't fail to wonder, and it made me hate him, what on earth we owned that anybody else would want.)

His illness was beyond all hope of healing before anyone realized that he was ill. He had always been so strange and had lived, like a prophet, in such unimaginably close communion with the Lord that his long silences which were punctuated by moans and hallelujahs and snatches of old songs while he sat at the living-room window never seemed odd to us. It was not until he refused to eat because, he said, his family was trying to poison him that my mother was forced to accept as a fact what had, until then, been only an unwilling suspicion. When he was committed, it was discovered that he had tuberculosis and, as it turned out, the disease of his mind allowed the disease of his body to destroy him. For the doctors could not force him to eat, either, and, though he was fed intravenously, it was clear from the beginning that there was no hope for him.

In my mind's eye I could see him, sitting at the window, locked up in his terrors; hating and fearing every living soul including his children who had betrayed him, too, by reaching toward the world which had despised him. There were nine of us. I began to wonder what it could have felt like for such a man to have had nine children whom he could barely feed. He used to make little jokes about our poverty, which never, of course, seemed very funny to us; they could not have seemed very funny to him, either, or else our all too feeble response to them would never have caused such rages. He spent great energy and achieved, to our chagrin, no small amount of success in keeping us away from the people who surrounded us, people who had all-night rent parties to which we listened when we should have been sleeping, people who cursed and drank and flashed razor blades on Lenox Avenue. He could not understand why, if they had so much energy to spare, they could not use it to make their lives better. He treated almost everybody on our block with a most uncharitable asperity and neither they, nor, of course, their children were slow to reciprocate.

The only white people who came to our house were welfare workers and bill collectors. It was almost always my mother who dealt with them, for my father's temper, which was at the mercy of his pride, was never to be trusted. It was clear that he felt their very presence in his home to be a violation: this was conveyed by his carriage, almost ludicrously stiff, and by his voice, harsh and vindictively polite. When I was around nine or ten I wrote a play which was directed by a young, white schoolteacher, a woman, who then took an interest in me, and gave me books to read and, in order to corroborate my theatrical bent, decided to take me to see what she somewhat tactlessly referred to as "real" plays. Theater-going was forbidden in our house, but, with the really cruel intuitiveness of a child, I suspected that the color of this woman's skin would carry the day for me. When, at school, she suggested taking me to the theater, I did not, as I might have done if she had been a Negro, find a way of discouraging her, but agreed that she should pick me up at my house one evening. I then, very cleverly, left all the rest to my mother, who suggested to my father, as I knew she would, that it would not be very nice to let such a kind woman make the trip for nothing. Also, since it was a schoolteacher, I imagine that my mother countered the idea of sin with the idea of "education," which word, even with my father, carried a kind of bitter weight.

Before the teacher came my father took me aside to ask *why she was coming, what* interest she could possibly have in our house, in a boy like me. I said I didn't know but I, too, suggested that it had something to do with education. And I understood that my father was waiting for me to say something—I didn't quite know what; perhaps that I wanted his protection against this teacher and her "education." I said none of these things and the teacher came and we went out. It was clear, during the brief interview in our living room, that my father was agreeing very much against his will and that he would have refused permission if he had dared. The fact that he did not dare caused me to despise him: I had no way of knowing that he was facing in that living room a wholly unprecedented and frightening situation.

Later, when my father had been laid off from his job, this woman became very important to us. She was really a very sweet and generous woman and went to a great deal of trouble to be of help to us, particularly during one awful winter. My mother called her by the highest name she knew: she said she was a "christian." My father could scarcely disagree but during the four or five years of our relatively close association he never trusted her and was always trying to surprise in her open, Midwestern face the genuine, cunningly hidden, and hideous motivation. In later years, particularly when it began to be clear that this "education" of mine was going to lead me to perdition, he became more explicit and warned me that my white friends in high school were not really my friends and that I would see, when I was older, how white people would do anything to keep a Negro down. Some of them could be nice, he admitted, but none of them were to be trusted and most of them were not even nice. The best thing was to have as little to do with them as possible. I did not feel this way and I was certain, in my innocence, that I never would.

But the year which preceded my father's death had made a great change in my life. I had been living in New Jersey, working in defense plants, working and living among southerners, white and black. I knew about the south, of course, and about how southerners treated Negroes and how they expected them to behave, but it had never entered my mind that anyone would look at me and expect *me* to behave that way. I learned in New Jersey that to be a Negro meant, precisely, that one was never looked at but was simply at the mercy of the reflexes the color of one's skin caused in other people. I acted in New Jersey as I had always acted, that is as though I thought a great deal of myself—I had to *act* that way—with results that were, simply, unbelievable. I had scarcely arrived before I had earned the enmity, which was extraordinarily ingenious, of all my superiors and nearly all my co-workers. In the beginning, to make matters worse, I simply did not know what was happening. I did not know what I had done, and I shortly began to wonder what *anyone* could possibly do, to bring about such unanimous, active, and unbearably vocal hostility. I knew about jim-crow but I had never experienced it. I went to the same self-service restaurant three times and stood with all the Princeton boys before the counter, waiting for a hamburger and coffee; it was always an extraordinarily long time before anything was set before me; but it was not until the fourth visit that I learned that, in fact, nothing had ever been set before me: I had simply picked something up. Negroes were not served there, I was told, and they had been waiting for me to realize that I was always the only Negro present. Once I was told this, I determined to go there all the time. But now they were ready for me and, though some dreadful scenes were subsequently enacted in that restaurant, I never ate there again.

It was the same story all over New Jersey, in bars, bowling alleys, diners, places to live. I was always being forced to leave, silently, or with mutual imprecations. I very shortly became notorious and children giggled behind me when I passed and their elders whispered or shouted—they really believed that I was mad. And it did begin to work on my mind, of course; I began to be afraid to go anywhere and to compensate for this I went places to which I really should not have gone and where, God knows, I had no desire to be. My reputation in town naturally enhanced my reputation at work and my working day became one long series of acrobatics designed to keep me out of trouble. I cannot say that these acrobatics succeeded. It began to seem that the machinery of the organization I worked for was turning over, day and night, with but one aim: to eject me. I was fired once, and contrived, with the aid of a friend from New York, to get back on the payroll; was fired again, and bounced back again. It took a while to fire me for the third time, but the third time took. There were no loopholes anywhere. There was not even any way of getting back inside the gates.

That year in New Jersey lives in my mind as though it were the year during which, having an unsuspected predilection for it, I first contracted some dread, chronic disease, the unfailing symptom of which is a kind of blind fever, a pounding in the skull and fire in the bowels. Once this disease is contracted, one can never be really carefree again, for the fever, without an instant's warning, can recur at any moment. It can wreck more important things than race relations. There is not a Negro alive who does not have this rage in his blood—one has the choice, merely, of living with it consciously or surrendering to it. As for me, this fever has recurred in me, and does, and will until the day I die.

My last night in New Jersey, a white friend from New York took me to the nearest big town, Trenton, to go to the movies and have a few drinks. As it turned out, he also saved me from, at the very least, a violent whipping. Almost every detail of that night stands out very clearly in my memory. I even remember the name of the movie we saw because its title impressed me as being so patly ironical. It was a movie about the German occupation of France, starring Maureen O'Hara and Charles Laughton and called *This Land Is Mine*. I remember the name of the diner we walked into when the movie ended: it was the "American Diner." When we walked in the counterman asked what we wanted and I remember answering with the casual sharpness which had become my habit: "We want a hamburger and a cup of coffee, what do you think we want?" I do not know why, after a year of such rebuffs, I so completely failed to anticipate his answer, which was, of course, "We don't serve Negroes here." This reply failed to discompose me, at least for the moment. I made some sardonic comment about the name of the diner and we walked out into the streets.

This was the time of what was called the "brown-out," when the lights in all American cities were very dim. When we re-entered the streets something happened to me which had the force of an optical illusion, or a nightmare. The streets were very crowded and I was facing north. People were moving in every direction but it seemed to me, in that instant, that all of the people I could see, and many more than that, were moving toward me, against me, and that everyone was white. I remember how their faces gleamed. And I felt, like a physical sensation, a *click* at the nape of my neck as though some interior string connecting my head to my body had been cut. I began to walk. I heard my friend call after me, but I ignored him. Heaven only knows what was going on in his mind, but he had the good sense not to touch me—I don't know what would have happened if he had—and to keep me in sight. I don't know what was going on in my mind, either; I certainly had no conscious plan. I wanted to do something to crush these white faces, which were crushing me. I walked for perhaps a block or two until I came to an enormous, glittering, and fashionable restaurant in which I knew not even the intercession of the Virgin would cause me to be served. I pushed through the doors and took the first vacant seat I saw, at a table for two, and waited.

I do not know how long I waited and I rather wonder, until today, what I could possibly have looked like. Whatever I looked like, I frightened the waitress who shortly appeared, and the moment she appeared all of my fury flowed towards her. I hated her for her white face, and for her great, astounded, frightened eyes. I felt that if she found a black man so frightening I would make her fright worth-while.

She did not ask me what I wanted, but repeated, as though she had learned it somewhere, "We don't serve Negroes here." She did not say it with the blunt, derisive hostility to which I had grown so accustomed, but, rather, with a note of apology in her voice, and fear. This made me colder and more murderous than ever. I felt I had to do something with my hands. I wanted her to come close enough for me to get her neck between my hands.

So I pretended not to have understood her, hoping to draw her closer. And she did step a very short step closer, with her pencil poised incongruously over her pad, and repeated the formula: ". . . don't serve Negroes here."

Somehow, with the repetition of that phrase, which was already ringing in my head like a thousand bells of a nightmare, I realized that she would never come any closer and that I would have to strike from a distance. There was nothing on the table but an ordinary water-mug half full of water, and I picked this up and hurled it with all my strength at her. She ducked and it missed her and shattered against the mirror behind the bar. And, with that sound, my frozen blood abruptly thawed, I returned from wherever I had been, I *saw,* for the first time, the restaurant, the people with their mouths open, already, as it seemed to me, rising as one man, and I realized what I had done, and where I was, and I was frightened. I rose and began running for the door. A round, pot-bellied man grabbed me by the nape of the neck just as I reached the doors and began to beat me about the face. I kicked him and got loose and ran into the streets. My friend whispered, *"Run!"* and I ran.

My friend stayed outside the restaurant long enough to misdirect my pursuers and the police, who arrived, he told me, at once. I do not know what I said to him when he came to my room that night. I could not have said much. I felt, in the oddest, most awful way, that I had somehow betrayed him. I lived it over and over and over again, the way one relives an automobile accident after it has happened and one finds oneself alone and safe. I could not get over two facts, both equally difficult for the imagination to grasp, and one was that I could have been murdered. But the other was that I had been ready to commit murder. I saw nothing very clearly but I did see this: that my life, my *real* life, was in danger, and not from anything other people might do but from the hatred I carried in my own heart.

II

I had returned home around the second week in June—in great haste because it seemed that my father's death and my mother's confinement were both but a matter of hours. In the case of my mother, it soon became clear that she had simply made a miscalculation. This had always been her tendency and I don't believe that a single one of us arrived in the world, or has since arrived anywhere else, on time. But none of us dawdled so intolerably about the business of being born as did my baby sister. We sometimes amused ourselves, during those endless, stifling weeks, by picturing the baby sitting within in the safe, warm dark, bitterly regretting the necessity of becoming a part of our chaos and stubbornly putting it off as long as possible. I understood her perfectly and congratulated her on showing such good sense so soon. Death, however, sat as purposefully at my father's bedside as life stirred within my mother's womb and it was harder to understand why he so lingered in that long shadow. It seemed that he had bent, and for a long time, too, all of his energies towards dying. Now death was ready for him but my father held back.

All of Harlem, indeed, seemed to be infected by waiting. I had never before known it to be so violently still. Racial tensions throughout this country were exacerbated during the early years of the war, partly because the labor market brought together hundreds of thousands of ill-prepared people and partly because Negro soldiers, regardless of where they were born, received their military training in the south. What happened in defense plants and army camps had repercussions, naturally, in every Negro ghetto. The situation in Harlem had grown bad enough for clergymen, policemen, educators, politicians, and social workers to assert in one breath that there was no "crime wave" and to offer, in the very next breath, suggestions as to how to combat it. These suggestions always seemed to involve playgrounds, despite the fact that racial skirmishes were occurring in the playgrounds, too. Playground or not, crime wave or not, the Harlem police force had been augmented in March, and the unrest grew—perhaps, in fact, partly as a result of the ghetto's instinctive hatred of policemen. Perhaps the most revealing news item, out of the steady parade of reports of muggings, stabbings, shootings, assaults, gang wars, and accusations of police brutality, is the item concerning six Negro girls who set upon a white girl in the subway because, as they all too accurately put it, she was stepping on their toes. Indeed she was, all over the nation.

I had never before been so aware of policemen, on foot, on horseback, on corners, everywhere, always two by two. Nor had I ever been so aware of small knots of people. They were on stoops and on corners and in doorways, and what was striking about them, I think, was that they did not seem to be talking. Never, when I passed these groups, did the usual sound of a curse or a laugh ring out and neither did there seem to be any hum of gossip. There was certainly, on the other hand, occurring between them communication extraordinarily intense. Another thing that was striking was the unexpected diversity of the people who made up these groups. Usually, for example, one would see a group of sharpies standing on the street corner, jiving the passing chicks; or a group of older men, usually, for some reason, in the vicinity of a barber shop, discussing baseball scores, or the numbers, or making rather chilling observations about women they had known. Women, in a general way, tended to be seen less often together—unless they were church women, or very young girls, or prostitutes met together for an unprofessional instant. But that summer I saw the strangest combinations: large, respectable, churchly matrons standing on the stoops or the corners with their hair tied up, together with a girl in sleazy satin whose face bore the marks of gin and the razor, or heavy-set, abrupt, no-nonsense older men, in company with the most disreputable and fanatical "race" men, or these same "race" men with the sharpies, or these sharpies with the churchly women. Seventh Day Adventists and Methodists and Spiritualists seemed to be hobnobbing with Holyrollers and they were all, alike, entangled with the most flagrant disbelievers; something heavy in their stance seemed to indicate that they had all, incredibly, seen a common vision, and on each face there seemed to be the same strange, bitter shadow.

The churchly women and the matter-of-fact, no-nonsense men had children in the Army. The sleazy girls they talked to had lovers there, the sharpies and the "race" men had friends and brothers there. It would have demanded an unquestioning patriotism, happily as uncommon in this country as it is undesirable, for these people not to have been disturbed by the bitter letters they received, by the newspaper stories they read, not to have been enraged by the posters, then to be found all over New York, which described the Japanese as "yellow-bellied Japs." It was only the "race" men, to be sure, who spoke ceaselessly of being revenged—how this vengeance was to be exacted was not clear—for the indignities and dangers suffered by Negro boys in uniform; but everybody felt a directionless, hopeless bitterness, as well as that panic which can scarcely be suppressed when one knows that a human being one loves is beyond one's reach, and in danger. This helplessness and this gnawing uneasiness does something, at length, to even the toughest mind. Perhaps the best way to sum all this up is to say that the people I knew felt, mainly, a peculiar kind of relief when they knew that their boys were being shipped out of the south, to do battle overseas. It was, perhaps, like feeling that the most dangerous part of a dangerous journey had been passed and that now, even if death should come, it would come with honor and without the complicity of their countrymen. Such a death would be, in short, a fact with which one could hope to live.

It was on the 28th of July, which I believe was a Wednesday, that I visited my father for the first time during his illness and for the last time in his life. The moment I saw him I knew why I had put off this visit so long. I had told my mother that I did not want to see him because I hated him. But this was not true. It was only that I *had* hated him and I wanted to hold on to this hatred. I did not want to look on him as a ruin: it was not a ruin I had hated. I imagine that one of the reasons people cling to their hates so stubbornly is because they sense, once hate is gone, that they will be forced to deal with pain.

We traveled out to him, his older sister and myself, to what seemed to be the very end of a very Long Island. It was hot and dusty and we wrangled, my aunt and I, all the way out, over the fact that I had recently begun to smoke and, as she said, to give myself airs. But I knew that she wrangled with me because she could not bear to face the fact of her brother's dying. Neither could I endure the reality of her despair, her unstated bafflement as to what had happened to her brother's life, and her own. So we wrangled and I smoked and from time to time she fell into a heavy reverie. Covertly, I watched her face, which was the face of an old woman; it had fallen in, the eyes were sunken and lightless; soon she would be dying, too.

In my childhood—it had not been so long ago—I had thought her beautiful. She had been quick-witted and quick-moving and very generous with all the children and each of her visits had been an event. At one time one of my brothers and myself had thought of running away to live with her. Now she could no longer produce out of her handbag some unexpected and yet familiar delight. She made me feel pity and revulsion and fear. It was awful to realize that she no longer caused me to feel affection. The closer we came to the hospital the more querulous she became and at the same time, naturally, grew more dependent on me. Between pity and guilt and fear I began to feel that there was another me trapped in my skull like a jack-in-the-box who might escape my control at any moment and fill the air with screaming.

She began to cry the moment we entered the room and she saw him lying there, all shriveled and still, like a little black monkey. The great, gleaming apparatus which fed him and would have compelled him to be still even if he had been able to move brought to mind, not beneficence, but torture; the tubes entering his arm made me think of pictures I had seen when a child, of Gulliver, tied down by the pygmies on that island. My aunt wept and wept, there was a whistling sound in my father's throat; nothing was said; he could not speak. I wanted to take his hand, to say something. But I do not know what I could have said, even if he could have heard me. He was not really in that room with us, he had at last really embarked on his journey; and though my aunt told me that he said he was going to meet Jesus, I did not hear anything except that whistling in his throat. The doctor came back and we left, into that unbearable train again, and home. In the morning came the telegram saying that he was dead. Then the house was suddenly full of relatives, friends, hysteria, and confusion and I quickly left my mother and the children to the care of those impressive women, who, in Negro communities at least, automatically appear at times of bereavement armed with lotions, proverbs, and patience, and an ability to cook. I went downtown. By the time I returned, later the same day, my mother had been carried to the hospital and the baby had been born.

Source

James Baldwin, *Notes of a Native Son,* 85–114 (Boston: Beacon Press, 1984).

Selected Bibliography

Baldwin, James. *Giovanni's Room*. New York: Dell, 1988.
—— *Go Tell It on the Mountain*. New York: Knopf, 1985.
—— *The Price of the Ticket: Collected Nonfiction, 1948–1955*. New York: St. Martin's Press, 1985.
Campbell, James. *Talking at the Gates: A Life of James Baldwin*. London and Boston: Faber and Faber, 1991.
Leeming, David. *James Baldwin: A Biography*. New York: Knopf, 1994.
Porter, Horace A. *Stealing the Fire: The Art and Protest of James Baldwin*. Middletown, Conn.: Wesleyan University Press, 1989.

seven

Playing Hardball

A W.E.B. Du Bois Professor of Humanities at Harvard University, Henry Louis Gates (1950–) is among the most visible intellectuals in the United States. In the following piece, Gates recalls his childhood relationship with his father, which illustrates some of the conflicts and difficulties that African American parents face while raising children in a racist environment.

Gates was born in Piedmont, West Virginia, and he studied at Yale University during the Black Power movement. He earned a prestigious Macarthur Fellowship in 1981, and in 1983 he rediscovered Harriet Wilson's 1859 novel *Our Nig*. He has written many books, which have been well received by both scholarly and popular audiences alike, and he is a frequent contributor to the *New Yorker*. He has also overseen the development of several landmark research projects, including the *Norton Anthology of African-American Literature* (1997) and the *Encarta Africana* (1999), a massive encyclopedia of Pan Africa that was originally envisioned by W. E. B. Du Bois.

From Colored People

Playing Hardball

Daddy worked all the time, every day but Sunday. Two jobs—twice a day, in and out, eat and work, work and eat. Evenings, we watched television together, all of us, after I'd done my homework and Daddy had devoured the newspaper or a book. He was always reading, it seemed, especially detective stories. He was a charter subscriber to *Alfred Hitchcock's Magazine* and loved detective movies on TV.

My brother Rocky was the one he was close to. Rocky worshiped sports, while I worshiped Rocky. I chased after him like a lapdog. I wanted to be just like him. But the five years between us loomed like Kilimanjaro. We were always out of phase. And he felt crowded by my adoring gaze.

Rocky and I didn't exactly start off on the right foot. When I was born, my parents moved my brother to Big Mom's house, to live with her and Little Jim, who was our first cousin and Nemo's son and the firstborn male of our generation in the Coleman family. It was not an uncommon arrangement to shift an older child to his or her grandparents', because of crowding. Since we had only three rooms, plus a tiny room with a toilet, my parents thought the move was for the best. And Big Mom's house was only a couple hundred yards straight up the hill. Still, it's difficult to gauge the trauma of that displacement, all these years later. Five years of bliss, ended by my big head popping out.

But Rocky was compensated: he was Daddy's boy. Like the rest of Piedmont, they were baseball fanatics. They knew who had done what and when, how much everyone had hit, in what inning, who had scored the most runs in 1922, who the most rbi's. They could sit in front of a TV for hours at a time, watching inning after tedious inning of baseball, baseball, baseball. Or sit at Forbes Field in Pittsburgh through a doubleheader without getting tired or longing to go home. One night, when I was seven, we saw Sandy Koufax of the Dodgers pitch one game, then his teammate Don Drysdale pitch another. It was the most boring night of my life, though later I came to realize what a feat I had witnessed, two of baseball's greatest pitchers back-to-back.

I enjoyed *going* to the games in Pittsburgh because even then I loved to travel. One of Daddy's friends would drive me. I was fascinated with geography. And since I was even more fascinated with food, a keen and abiding interest of mine, I liked the games for the reason, too. We would stop to eat at Howard Johnson's, going and coming. And there'd be hot dogs and sodas at the games, as well as popcorn and candy, to pass the eternity of successive innings in the July heat. Howard Johnson's was a five-star restaurant in Piedmont.

I used to get up early to have breakfast with Daddy, eating from his plate. I'll still spear a heavily peppered fried potato or a bit of egg off his plate today. My food didn't taste as good as his. Still doesn't. I used to drink coffee, too, in order to be just like Daddy. "Coffee will make you black," he'd tell me, with the intention of putting me off. From the beginning, I used a lot of pepper, because he did, and he did because his father did. I remember reading James Agee's[1] *A Death in the Family* and being moved by a description of the extra pepper that the father's wife put on his eggs the very morning that he is killed in a car. Why are you frying eggs *this* time of day, Mama asked me that evening. Have you seen the pepper, Mama? I replied.

An unathletic child with too great an interest in food—no wonder I was fat, and therefore compelled to wear "husky" clothes.

My Skippy's not *fat,* Mama would lie. He's husky.

But I *was* fat, and felt fatter every time Mama repeated her lie. My mama loved me like life itself. Maybe she didn't see me as fat. But I was. And whoever thought of the euphemism "husky" should be shot. I was short and round—not obese, mind you, but *fat.* Still, I was clean and energetic, and most of the time I was cheerful. And I liked to play with other kids, not so much because I enjoyed the things we did together but because I could watch them be happy.

But sports created a bond between Rocky and my father that excluded me, and, though my father had no known athletic talent himself, my own unathletic bearing compounded my problems. For not only was I overweight; I had been born with flat feet and wore "corrective shoes." They were the bane of my existence, those shoes. While Rocky would be wearing long, pointy-toed, cool leather gentlemen, I'd be shod in blunt-ended, round-toed, fat-footed shoes that nobody but your mother could love.

And Mama *did* love those shoes. Elegant, she'd say. They're Stride-Rite. Stride-wrong, I'd think. Mama, I want some nice shoes, I'd beg, like Rocky's.

Still, I guess they did what they were meant to do, because I have good arches now. Even today, I look at the imprint of my wet foot at a swimming pool, just to make certain that my arch is still arched. I don't ever again want to wear those dull brown or black corrective shoes.

What made it all the more poignant was that Rocky—tall, lean, and handsome, blessed with my father's metabolism—was a true athlete. He would be the first Negro captain of the basketball team in high school and receive "the watch" at graduation. (He was the first colored to do that, too.)

Maybe Mama thought I was husky, but Daddy knew better, and he made no secret of it. "Two-Ton Tony Galento," he and Rocky would say, or they'd call me Chicken Flintserwall or Fletcher Bissett, Milton Berle's or Jack Benny's character in a made-for-TV movie about two complete cowards. I hated Daddy for doing that and yielded him as unconquerable terrain to my brother, clinging desperately to my mother for protection.

Ironically, I had Daddy's athletic ability, or lack thereof, just as I have his body. (We wear the same size ring, gloves, shoes, shirt, suits, and hat.) And like him, I love to hear a good story. But during my first twelve or so years we were alienated from each other. I despised sports because I was overweight and scared to death. Especially of baseball—hardball, we called it. Yet I felt I had no choice but to try out for Little League. Everyone my age did Little League, after all. They made me a Giant, decided I was a catcher because I was "stout, like Roy Campanella," dressed me in a chest protector and a mask, and squatted me behind a batter.

It's hard to catch a baseball with your eyes closed. Each time a ball came over the plate, I thanked the Good Lord that the batter hadn't confused my nappy head with the baseball that had popped its way into my mitt. My one time at bat was an experience in blindness; miraculously, I wasn't hit in the head. With a 3 and 2 count, I got a ball, so I walked. They put in a runner for me. Everybody patted me on the back like I had just won the World Series. And everybody said nice things about my "eye." Yeah, I thought. My tightly closed eye.

Afterward, Pop and I stopped at the Cut-Rate to get a caramel ice cream cone, then began the long walk up the hill to Pearl Street. I was exhausted, so we walked easy. He was biding his time, taking smaller steps than usual so that I could keep up. "You know that you don't have to play baseball, don't you, boy?" All of a sudden I knew how Moses had felt on Mount Sinai.[2] His voice was a bolt out of the blue. Oh I want to play, I responded in a squeaky voice. "But you know that you don't *have* to play. I never was a good player. Always afraid of the ball. Uncoordinated, too. I can't even run straight." We laughed. "I became the manager of the team," he said. That caramel ice cream sure tasted good. I held Daddy's hand almost all the way home.

In my one time at bat, I had got on base. I had confronted the dragon and he was mine. I had, I had . . . been absurdly lucky . . . and I couldn't *wait* to give them back their baseball suit. It was about that time that Daddy stopped teasing me about being fat. That day he knew me, and he seemed to care.

Yes, Pop and I had some hard times. He thought that I didn't love him, and I thought he didn't love me. At times, we both were right. I didn't think you wanted me around, he told me much later. I thought that I embarrassed you. He did embarrass me, but not like you might think, not the usual way parents embarrass children in front of their friends, for example. He had a habit of correcting me in front of strangers or white people, especially if they were settling an argument between me and Pop by something they had just said, by a question they had answered. See, I *told* you so, he'd say loudly, embarrassing the hell out of me with a deliberateness that puzzled and vexed me. I hated him when he did that.

And despite my efforts to keep up, he and my brother had somehow made me feel as if I were an android, something not quite a person. I used to dream about going away to military school, and wrote to our congressman, Harley Staggers, for a list of names. I used to devour *McKeever and the Colonel*[3] on Sunday nights and dream about the freedom of starting over, at a high powered, regimented school away from home. Daddy and Rocky would make heavy handed jokes about queers and sissies. I wasn't their direct target, but I guess it was another form of masculine camaraderie that marked me as less manly than my brother.

And while I didn't fantasize about boys, I did love the companionship of boys and men, loved hearing them talk and watching their rituals, loved the warmth that their company could bring. I even loved being with the Coleman boys, at one of their shrimp or squirrel feeds, when they would play cards. Generally, though, I just enjoyed being on the edge of the circle, watching and listening and laughing, basking in the warmth, memorizing the stories, trying to strip away illusions, getting at what was really coming down.

I made my peace with sports, by and by, and was comfortable watching Rock and Daddy watch sports. But I could never experience it with the absorption they were capable of, could never live and breathe sports as they did. Oh I loved to watch all the tournaments, the finals, the Olympics—the ritual events. But my relation to sports was never as visceral and direct as theirs.

After I returned my Little League uniform, I became the team's batboy and then the league's official scorekeeper, publishing our results in a column in the *Piedmont Herald,* our weekly newspaper.

Much more than for sports, I had early on developed an avidity for information about The Negro. I'm not sure why, since Daddy was not exactly a race man. Niggers are crabs in a barrel: if he said that once, he said it to us a thousand times. My father was hard on colored people—and funny about it, too.

Aside from the brief stint as a student in New Jersey, Daddy's major contact with Negro culture from Elsewhere had been in the army, at Camp Lee, Virginia. He used to tell us all kinds of stories about the colored troops at Camp Lee, especially blacks from the rural South. It was clear that the army in World War II had been a great cauldron, mixing the New Negro culture, which had developed in the cities since the great migration of the twenties and thirties, and the Old Negro culture, the remnants of traditional rural black culture in the South.

Camp Lee was where colored soldiers were sent to learn how to be quartermasters—butlers, chefs, and service people, generally. Because the Army replicates the social structure of the larger society it defends, almost all black draftees were taught to cook and clean. Of course, it was usually women who cooked and cleaned outside the Army, but *someone* had to do the work, so it would be black men. Gender and race conflate in a crisis. Even educated black people were put in the quartermasters.

Well, Camp Lee was a circus and my daddy its scribe. He told us stories about how he beat the system, or damn well tried to. The first day, he had raised his hand when an officer asked who knew accounting. How hard could it be? he responded when I laughed. Hell, all you had to be able to do was add and subtract. The one thing I knew, he said, was that an accountant had an office and everybody else had to do basic training. Now, which one would you have picked? For two years, he stayed at Camp Lee and avoided being shipped to the front. Everybody else would be processed, then shipped out to Europe. But Daddy became a staff sergeant, serving as secretary and accountant to the commanding officer, who liked him a lot. He sent for Mama, who took a room in a colored home in town. Daddy slept there, too, Mama got a job in a dry cleaners. The pictures that I carry of them in my wallet are from this time, 1942.

The war wouldn't take Pop any farther than Camp Lee, but even that was an experience that stayed with him. There he encountered the customs and sayings, the myths and folklore, of all sorts of black people he had never even heard about. The war did more to recement black American culture, which migration had fragmented, than did any other single event or experience. "War? What is it good for? You tell 'em: absolutely nothing."[4] Nothing for the Negro but the transfer of cultures, the merging of the old black cultures with the new. And the transfer of skills. Daddy was no "race man," but for all his sardonicism, he respected race men and women, the people who were articulate and well educated, who comported themselves with dignity and who "achieved." Being at Camp Lee, an all-colored world, he'd say a decade later, was like watching episodes of *Amos and Andy*.[5]

Hard as Daddy could be on colored people, he was Marcus Garvey[6] compared to *his* father. Pop Gates used to claim that the government should lock up all the niggers in a big reservation in Kansas or Oklahoma or somewhere, feed them, clothe them, and give them two names: John or Mary. Nobody would hurt them, he'd add plaintively when his children would either protest or burst into howls of laughter. Pop Gates *hated* to see black people in loud clothes, and he hated just as much our traditional poetic names, such as Arbadella or Ethelretta. Made-up names, he'd say. Shouldn't be allowed, he'd say.

I was more aggressive around white people than Daddy, and it didn't go down well with him—or anybody else. Especially my Coleman uncles. Daddy, as noted, would almost never take my side in front of others. And if he felt I had violated a boundary, he would name it publicly and side with the boundary. He would do so loudly, even with what struck my child's ears as a certain malice. It tore me up.

He was not always this way with me. At a Little League game when I was ten, I told off a white man, Mr. Frank Price, not for anything he'd done to me, but for the rude way he treated Mr. Stanley Fisher, a black man in his sixties, who was maybe twenty years Price's senior. The details are murky, but Price had been rude to the older man in a way that crossed a line, that made the colored people feel he was a racist.

I do remember that I was unable to control myself, unable to contain my anger. I found myself acting without thinking. I felt the blood rushing to my face, and a flood of nasty words poured out of my mouth, just this side of profanity. Everybody on the first-base side of the Little League field over in Westernport looked up and froze in silence as I stood in front of that big-bellied man's fat red face and told him to leave Mr. Stanley alone. Then I turned to Mr. Stanley and told him not to waste his dignity on that trash: "Don't sweat the small stuff," I said. The colored held their breaths, and Daddy looked like a cat caught between two fighting dogs and not knowing which way to turn. Even Mr. Stanley's face showed surprise at this snot-nosed kid talking right up in some redneck's face. Mr. Stanley must have been more embarrassed by me than reassured.

Daddy stepped in finally, put his arm around my shoulder, and started woofing at Frank Price and giving him those dirty glares of his, all the while pushing me gently up the field toward Stanley and the colored men who always sat together on their lawn chairs out in right field. And we then all walked together up the dusty back road that bordered the Little League field like the rim of a crater, passing the new filtration plant, which made the whole place stink worse than the sulfurous chemicals that it had been built to remove, and all the old colored men were saying what an asshole Frank Price was and always had been, and how he had been rude to Stanley, and how nobody liked or respected him (not even white people), and how nobody within earshot should pay that motherfucker no mind.

Now, you know you are supposed to respect your elders, don't you? Daddy said to me much later, after we had bought a caramel ice cream cone, to go, at the Cut-Rate. And you know you are not supposed to talk back to older people, now don't you? And you know that Stanley Fisher can take care of himself? And you know that you can get in trouble talking back to white people, don't you? Don't you, boy? Boy, you crazy sometimes. That ice cream is dripping down your fingers. Don't let it go to waste.

Notes

1. James Agee (1909–1955), American writer.
2. In the book of Exodus in the Bible, Moses spent forty days fasting on Mount Sinai, where God presented him with The Ten Commandments. Moses' experience on Mt. Sinai was a time of great devotion, sacrifice, and almost ecstatic communion with God.
3. Television situation comedy, 1962–1963.
4. Lyric from the protest song "War" by Edwin Starr.
5. "The Amos n' Andy Show," radio series (1926–1960) and CBS television comedy (syndicated, 1952–1966); withdrawn from syndication in 1966 due to pressure from civil rights groups, who protested the program's crude racial stereotypes.
6. Marcus Garvey (1887–1940), organization founder, Pan-Africanist leader, newspaper publisher, writer, and entrepreneur.

Source

Henry Louis Gates, "Playing Hardball," in *Colored People: A Memoir,* 78–88 (New York: Knopf, 1994).

Selected Bibliography

Banks, William. *Black Intellectuals: Race and Responsibility in American Life.* New York: W. W. Norton, 1996.

Gates, Henry Louis. *Loose Canons: Notes on the Culture Wars.* New York: Oxford University Press, 1992.

—— *The Signifying Monkey: A Theory of African-American Literary Criticism.* New York: Oxford University Press, 1989.

—— *Thirteen Ways of Looking at a Black Man.* New York: Random House, 1997.

Gates, Henry Louis and Cornel West. *The Future of the Race.* New York: Knopf, 1996.

eight

From a Black Woman to a Black Man

Maya Angelou (1928–) is a noted poet and memoirist. The following poem was read by Angelou at the Million Man March on October 16, 1995. The march brought together hundreds of thousands of black men to Washington, D.C., to promote personal responsibility and community involvement. Angelou's poem spoke to these themes.

Born Marguerite Johnson in St. Louis, Missouri, she grew up in Arkansas and San Francisco. Angelou originally aimed for a career in show business, working for a time as a professional dancer, actress, and a nightclub singer. In the early 1960s she lived in Cairo and Ghana, were she honed her craft as a writer and taught briefly. Her first autobiography, *I Know Why the Caged Bird Sings* (1970), became a best-seller and was nominated for the National Book Award. She has continued to publish her life story in four subsequent volumes. She has also published many volumes of poetry, including *Just Give Me a Cool Drink of Water 'for I Die* (1971), which was nominated for a Pulitzer Prize. When Angelou was chosen to read a poem at Bill Clinton's presidential inauguration on January 21, 1993, she became the first African American and the first woman to be so honored.

The night has been long,
The wound has been deep,
The pit has been dark,
And the walls have been steep.

Under a dead blue sky on a distant beach,
I was dragged by my braids just beyond your reach.
Your hands were tied, your mouth was bound,
You couldn't even call out my name.
You were helpless and so was I,
But unfortunately throughout history
You've worn a badge of shame.

I say, the night has been long,
The wound has been deep,
The pit has been dark
And the walls have been steep.

But today, voices of old spirit sound
Speak to us in words profound,
Across the years, across the centuries,
Across the oceans, and across the seas.
They say, draw near to one another,
Save your race.
You have been paid for in a distant place,
The old ones remind us that slavery's chains
Have paid for our freedom again and again.

The night has been long,
The pit has been deep,
The night has been dark,
And the walls have been steep.

The hells we have lived through and live through still,
Have sharpened our senses and toughened our will.
The night has been long.
This morning I look through your anguish
Right down to your soul.
I know that with each other we can make ourselves whole.
I look through the posture and past your disguise,
And see your love for family in your big brown eyes.

I say, clap hands and let's come together in this meeting ground,
I say, clap hands and let's deal with each other with love,
I say, clap hands and let us get from the low road of indifference,
Clap hands, let us come together and reveal our hearts,
Let us come together and revise our spirits,
Let us come together and cleanse our souls,

Clap hands, let's leave the preening
And stop impostering our own history.
Clap hands, call the spirits back from the ledge,
Clap hands, let us invite joy into our conversation,
Courtesy into our bedrooms,
Gentleness into our kitchen,
Care into our nursery.

The ancestors remind us, despite the history of pain
We are a going-on people who will rise again.

And still we rise.

Source

Maya Angelou, "From a Black Woman to a Black Man," in Haki R. Madhubuti and Maulana Karenga, eds., *Million Man March/Day of Absence: A Commemorative Anthology,* 30–31 (Chicago: Third World Press; Los Angeles: University of Sankore Press, 1996).

Selected Bibliography

Angelou, Maya. *The Complete Collected Poems of Maya Angelou.* New York: Random House, 1994.

—— *Conversations with Maya Angelou.* Edited by Jeffrey M. Elliot. Jackson: University of Mississippi Press, 1989.

Lupton, Mary Jane. *Maya Angelou: A Critical Companion.* Westport, Conn.: Greenwood Press, 1998.

McPherson, Dolly Aimee. *Order out of Chaos: The Autobiographical Works of Maya Angelou.* London: Virago Press, 1991.

nine

In My Father's House

Manning Marable (1950–) is a professor of history and the founding director of the Institute for Research in African-American Studies at Columbia University. His essay "In My Father's House" describes the hardships his father faced while coming of age in rural Alabama as well as the opportunities he capitalized on to improve his station in life. By paying careful attention to the personal histories of other family members, Marable suggests that one can find selfhood, affirmation, and sense of purpose.

Marable received his doctorate in American history at the University of Maryland, College Park, in 1976, and has taught at Colgate University, Ohio State University, and the University of Colorado. He is the author of thirteen books, including *Black Leadership*, *Beyond Black and White*, and *Race, Reform and Rebellion*. He is also the editor of *Souls: A Critical Journal of Black Politics, Culture, and Society;* an author of "Along the Color Line," a popular newspaper column; and an activist in the Black Radical Congress (BRC).

I.

James Palmer Marable was born November 16, 1921, in a wooden cabin deep in the piney woods of east-central Alabama near the small town of Wedowee. He was the third child and second son of Manning Marable and Fannie Heard Marable. Manning and Fannie would eventually have thirteen children in all, the last child born in 1944. Manning was essentially a rural entrepreneur. Although he was the son of slaves and had attended school less than six years, Manning was determined to make something of his life. With his growing family as his primary labor force, he cultivated several hundred acres of land, mostly planting cotton and corn. On the side, Manning constructed a whiskey still and peddled corn liquor to rural farmers, Black and white, during Prohibition. With the extra cash from selling moonshine, Manning purchased more land, farm animals, cattle, and timber. My father recalls that even during the depression, Manning had boundless confidence in his ability to make money. Manning would "buy anything!" my father still exclaims. "He'd buy a mule, whether we needed or not. He'd see an old mule and say, 'We'll buy it! How much you want for it?' . . . He was always successful in negotiating, in buying and selling."

Life in rural Alabama was fairly predictable. Work began well before dawn, milking the cows and feeding the livestock. The boys were assigned various outside chores, from sawing timber to ploughing. At home, Fannie was the dominant presence: cooking meals, sewing, mending and washing clothes, supervising a rapidly expanding number of children, cousins, nieces, and nephews, and managing the household budget. The older girls helped with the cooking, cleaning, and supervising the younger children. "We'd all work in the field," my father remembers. On weekends, Manning and his sons went fishing or hunting. On Sundays, the entire family attended church services in the morning, and often invited the preacher and his family to their home for Sunday dinner.

White people usually seemed peripheral to the daily routine. "We were usually just around Black people," my father explains. "We rarely came out of those hills. We went to a Black school close by." Of course, direct contact with whites was inevitable. Several times each year, my father traveled with Manning carrying a load of raw cotton or fresh produce from their farm to Wedowee. "When we'd go there, when I was a kid, I soon learned that white people were 'white people.' These were the bosses and the people you bought groceries from."

It was during these visits to Wedowee and the larger neighboring town of Roanoke that James first encountered the harsh reality of racism. "White people were pretty much in control of everything," my father observes. "When you walked down the street, you'd hear Black people say, 'Those little white girls are coming down the street, and you have to get out of the way!' And I'd see other Black people move over. . . . Everybody just moved to the right or to the left. You didn't get in their way." Whites were a privileged caste, and demanded to be treated deferentially.

You had to learn at an early age to avoid situations where confrontations with whites might develop. About once each year, the Marable family would go to Roanoke's department store to purchase shoes and clothing. My father states, "I remember the white clerks would say, 'You can't try that hat on!' You'd buy a shirt or a pair of trousers and you'd have to guess at your size." Once my father was taken by his parents to the local white dentist to have a tooth removed. Walking into the dentist's office, he was immediately forbidden to sit down. "And they said, 'You go over in this room. We take you all over here in this room.' And *that* was where they pulled the teeth of Black people." The room was dirty and poorly lighted, and the dental equipment had been used. Blacks came to expect inferior treatment and second-class service. Sometimes the humiliations were public and vulgar. "I never remember any whites calling me 'nigger,' " my father says. "They'd just refer to me and my brothers as 'boys.' But I'd see other white men walk up to Black people in the street and kick them." For whites it was humorous just giving "niggers a boot in the butt." In the classroom, the conditions for Black learning were always substandard. "It was just common knowledge that we would get used textbooks," my father states. "But nobody ever questioned or challenged racial segregation. I don't remember anyone protesting it. I don't remember any of my teachers or my parents' friends talking about it. It was just sort of the rule of doing business for everyone: whites were in charge." This was the omnipresent reality that Manning Marable could never forget, not for a single moment. In private, my grandfather's constant was "*never* to be under the white man's thumb."

Coming of age in a racially segregated environment, opportunities were limited for my father. But on the Marable farm even as a boy, James excelled at fixing household appliances and farm implements. "I was always tinkering with things, tinkering with cars, tinkering with machines," my father explains. "I was always building something." With his younger brothers, my father would construct wagons for hauling farm machinery and produce. "You'd cut off a log that's round—maybe twelve inches in diameter—knock a hole in it and you got your wheels." James watched and learned how every piece of machinery around the farm worked. By the age of thirteen, he could repair and service the family model A Ford and drive the tractor.

My father's experience operating and maintaining vehicles led to what he now describes as his "glorious opportunity." As a high school student, James would walk one mile each way down a dirt country road, where the school bus stopped for Negro children. The bus slowly meandered about twenty miles each way between the village of Malone and Roanoke every morning, taking more than one hour for the journey. At the beginning of James's tenth grade, the owner of the school bus asked my father if he would be interested in driving the vehicle every day. "I'd been driving everything else," my father thought, and replied quickly "Yeah, I'd like to take a shot at it." The pay was twenty-five cents per day, about five dollars a month. Throughout his tenth-grade year, my father got up early before dawn every morning, walked several miles to pick up the bus, and drove twenty miles each way to and from Roanoke.

Since the school bus was never completely filled with students, my father would pick up additional passengers, who would simply wave the bus to a halt. "They gave me a nickel or a dime to ride the bus," my father explains. "You'd really be surprised how that added up. I didn't spend it. I didn't have to because I carried my lunch from home." Soon James was earning more than five dollars each month from the extra passengers on his bus route.

"This was the beginning of really being an entrepreneur, understanding what money was all about," my father reflects. By his final year in high school, "I basically hit the jackpot. By that time I was the senior driver. I had a perfect record driving without any accidents." When the high school football team scheduled its games away from Roanoke, James was asked to drive the bus for several extra dollars. He earned a reputation for being reliable and trustworthy. Soon the high school principal's wife asked James to be her regular driver: "A lot of times she'd go to the high school and would ask me to come to the principal's office. The principal would hand me his keys and say, 'My wife wants you to take her downtown.' I'd say, 'Yes, sir.' And I'd get tips like that. I'd drive her. She'd want to go home or shopping. It was quite an honor to drive the principal's car." James's financial independence directly influenced his relationships with other students. "I was rather shy, as I recall, and not all that aggressive," my father relates. "But I had money, and everybody knew it. I would loan money to people even then because I had money. And they would pay me back."

James's new privileged status also had a direct impact upon his social life. "I sort of fancied and played around with some of the girls in high school," my father admits. "They chased me because I had money, you know, and because I drove the school bus." James and his older brother Morris often accompanied each other on "dates" with young women from church or high school.

"In those days you actually sat in the living room with the girls on one side and you sat on the other," my father explains. "No hanky-panky stuff, not in that living room! You'd go over there and sit until about nine or ten o'clock, when the old man (of the house) would either start coughing or he'd say, 'BEDTIME!' Either way, you got the message loud and clear, to get ready and go home."

II.

James graduated from high school in the spring of 1942 and briefly began working full-time on his father's farm. During his senior year, Pearl Harbor was attacked by the Japanese, and the United States entered World War II. So it was not surprising when on July 20, 1942, my father received his draft notification. After basic training, my father was part of a racially segregated unit in the army air corps. Because he had graduated from high school, he was assigned to a special training school for mechanics and engineers. Throughout the remainder of the war, my father was a staff sergeant and head mechanic of a flight crew which repaired and serviced airplanes. The routine of army life was easy for the farm boy. "I was sort of gifted with having worked with tools and cars and trucks in my background," James recounts. Checking the fuselage of an airplane or making sure that the nuts and bolts were properly tightened "was very easy to do." The biggest adjustment my father had to make was in the context of race relations. The U.S. military was racially segregated, and would remain so until 1948. But within the military bases and during wartime, African Americans were often treated better than they had ever been before. For nearly two years, my father was stationed just outside Detroit, where he had the opportunity to experience a large urban environment without legal Jim Crow.[1] During the war years, my father's expectations and attitudes concerning segregation subtly but fundamentally changed.

By 1946, when James was discharged from the military, it was difficult to relearn the social etiquette of Jim Crow. Leaving Detroit, my father traveled south, headed home to Alabama. James recalls that as the train passed through Cincinnati and crossed the Ohio River, the conductor walked down the aisles of each car, shouting: "The Mason-Dixon line,[2] all of you people must move to the rear." "No one said 'Negroes,' but everyone knew what he meant," my father comments. When the train arrived in Birmingham, James walked up to a lunch counter in the station. He failed to notice the sign which read "whites only." "When I went in to get a sandwich, the white girl said to me, 'You have to go to that window.' She thought I was just ignorant." But my father bristled silently inside himself. "I'd been up above the Mason-Dixon line, in places where they didn't pay too much attention to race," my father observed. But despite his sergeant's uniform, plus his good conduct medal, flight wings, "and all that good stuff," he was still treated as a second-class citizen. It was this realization that prompted James finally to decide to leave the South.

Back in Roanoke, James once again began working full-time for his father. But some of his high school friends who had also served in the military were already talking about enrolling in college, either at nearby Tuskegee Institute or in the North. One of his buddies mentioned that there was an all-Negro college "up there in Ohio, Wilberforce University, a fine school where there's no segregation." My father thought about attending Tuskegee Institute, but decided against it, largely because it was in the South. "Anyway," my father reasoned at the time, "all they do down there is teach you about farming. You could teach agriculture maybe with a Tuskegee degree,[3] but if you wanted to be a schoolteacher or doctor of something like that, you ought to go to that Negro school in Ohio." By the time James and three of his high school classmates finally decided to apply for admission to Wilberforce, it was almost Labor Day: "Somebody must of told us to call the dean of men at Wilberforce

College.[4] We got him on the phone. We said, 'We've got four veterans down here and we'd like to come to your school. We want to know if you'll admit us?' " My father remembers: "I got my bag and collected my other personal items together in a paper sack. With my buddies, we caught a bus and headed for Ohio. Somehow we figured out how to get from Dayton to Wilberforce." They arrived only one day before classes began for the fall semester.

The segregated curriculum of the all-Negro high school in Roanoke had not prepared James adequately for a northern college. In math and the sciences, my father continued to excel. But in English, he struggled below a C average. "I should have asked for help, but I didn't," he says. "It was very difficult to write and it always bugged the heck out of me." James could answer questions in class, and was able to discuss ideas with confidence. But in his written assignments he was completely unsure of himself. He began spending more time in the library, asking other students to help him.

It was in the library at the beginning of his sophomore year that James began to notice an attractive young woman who always seemed to be studying. Occasionally she would assist him in locating books and reference materials. She was a minister's daughter, very pleasant and somewhat talkative. "But I could see she could write and do all that kind of stuff," my father observed. One Saturday evening James attended one of the college dances, and he recognized the young woman from the library. Ten months later, they were married. Within a year James, Jr., was born.

In an old automobile he had purchased, James drove thirty miles each way to go to work. He obtained a job in a tool and die industrial company, but it was anything but pleasant. "I was called a 'utility man.' In the plant, there were machines that were grinding the tools out—where you poke iron through the machines to make bolts or screws or whatever." The waste from the tool machines, irregular chips of metal, grease, and oil fell to the factory floor. "My job was to shovel it up, put it in a wheelbarrow, roll it, and dump it someplace." Here, as elsewhere, racial segregation was the general pattern of employment. Whites held the higher-paying jobs as managers, machinists, and technicians. All of the utility men "were Black people," James recalled.

By my father's senior year in college, June was again pregnant (this time with me). My father was deeply concerned about his future after graduation: "I wanted a better job and I was going all around (to find work). My highest hope at that time was to get on as an airplane mechanic or even to become an airplane pilot. I still loved planes and I knew that I would enjoy working on them. I knew we were coming into an age of commercial flying, the airlines at that time were expanding, and that there was money to be made." But getting an equal opportunity for employment for Negroes was rare in the late 1940s. My father explains, "Every time I went out to Wright Patterson airbase (near Dayton) to apply for the job, I was always told that I was a finalist. Sometimes they'd say, 'It's down to three of you.' But they always picked one of the whites." After applying for different positions and being turned down a half dozen times, my father's dream of being a pilot or a flight mechanic finally died.

It was about this time that my mother, who had graduated from college in 1948 and was now working full-time, had the idea for her husband's future. James had one year's eligibility remaining of his GI educational benefits. Why not enroll in the master's program at Ohio State University, in nearby Columbus? My father resisted the suggestion, telling his young wife: "I didn't really feel I could hack it. I knew I could talk in class, but I never felt comfortable putting it on paper. Never did." June replied: "You take your notes in class, bring them home to me, and I'll fix them up." So James reluctantly agreed to enroll in the M.A. program in education at Ohio State. Throughout the next year, my father attended classes during the day and held down a job after school. June revised his rough drafts and lecture notes into excellent essays. But successfully completing homework assignments was only part of the challenge. "In those days, there were very few Blacks in graduate school," my father states. The white professors "would constantly watch me and they would ask me questions. But I always read their books, and knew what to say." My father's basic strategy was to read carefully the books written by his instructors, and to ask specific questions based on their own publications: "I'd read their old books. And I usually would say, 'Doctor So-And-So, in your chapter on so-and-so, what did you mean? Now sometimes I really knew the answer. But they were always impressed, and they loved that." By the summer of 1951, at the age of twenty-nine, James Marable received his M.A. degree in school administration with a minor in counseling.

III.

June and James moved to Kansas City for several years, both working as teachers in the public school system. As before, my father held down a second job at night, and they saved that salary to purchase a home. They moved to Dayton, Ohio, with two growing boys in 1955, the year my brother went to the first grade. James continued working sixteen-hour days for years, teaching at predominantly Black Dunbar High School during the day, and working as a laborer at Dayton Tire factory, on the second shift every evening. Finally at the age of forty, my father collapsed from exhaustion in a suburban department store. It was my most traumatic experience as a boy, watching my father, who had always been so strong, being taken away in an ambulance. After a short time in the hospital, my father recovered. But somehow I could never look at him in quite the same way. Now I appreciated just how hard he worked, and had always worked. As an adult years later, I would search to find the words to tell my father just what he had meant to me. But the words did not come.

Do we ever really comprehend the world of our Black fathers, the factors which made them who they are? Do we hear their personal stories, understanding their hardships and mistakes, difficulties and triumphs? There are many Black men who bore the weight of racial oppression without surrendering to bitterness and alienation. They worked at multiple jobs to care for and to support their families. They quietly sacrificed their own chances for upward mobility to improve the material conditions for their daughters and sons. No one mentions their sacrifices in the pages of African-American history books. Their names are largely unknown and their voices rarely heard. But it is in our fathers' houses, in the world they courageously helped to build with our mothers and sisters, that we are able to affirm ourselves.

In their personal stories, we can listen to the quiet dignity of our men. We can bear witness to the simple sacrifices and day-to-day experiences of our fathers, which create new possibilities and new visions. Through their voices, we begin to learn about and to find ourselves.

Notes

1. So-called Jim Crow statutes were enacted in Southern states and cities in the 1880s, legalizing segregation.
2. Boundary between Pennsylvania and Maryland, surveyed by the English astronomers Charles Mason and Jeremiah Dixon from 1763–1767. Before the Civil War, the term "Mason-Dixon line" popularly designated the boundary dividing slave states from free states, and it is still used to distinguish the North from the South.
3. Tuskegee Institute, at Tuskegee, Alabama; chartered and opened in 1881 by Booker T. Washington as Tuskegee Normal Institute. Tuskegee Institute stressed the practical applications of learning and was one of the first important schools to provide adequate education for African Americans.
4. In Wilberforce, Ohio; chartered and opened in 1865, African Methodist Episcopal. Wilberforce provided one of the first opportunities for African Americans to pursue advanced academic training.

Source

Manning Marable, "In My Father's House," in Gloria Wade Gayles, ed., *Father Songs: Testimonials by African-American Sons and Daughters,* 177–85 (Boston: Beacon Press, 1997).

Selected Bibliography

Banks, William M. *Black Intellectuals: Race and Responsibility in American Life.* New York: W. W. Norton, 1996.

Marable, Manning. *Beyond Black and White.* London: Verso, 1995.

—— *Black Leadership.* New York: Columbia University Press, 1998.

—— *Race, Reform, and Rebellion: The Second Reconstruction in Black America.* Jackson: University of Mississippi Press, 1991.

—— ed. *Dispatches from the Ebony Tower: Intellectuals Confront the African-American Experience.* New York: Columbia University Press, 2000.

t e n

Kwanzaa and the Ethics of Sharing

Forging our Future in a New Era

Maulana Karenga (1941–) was the leading light of the Black Arts movement. Karenga founded the African American holiday Kwanzaa in 1966 in an effort to reaffirm African culture during the Black Power movement. Since 1994, he has made an annual address to Kwanzaa followers to explain the holiday's origins and meanings. The address below was posted on the Official Kwanzaa Web site in 1999.

Born Ronald Everett in Parsonburg, Maryland, Karenga earned both his B.A. and M.A. at the University of California at Los Angeles and his Ph.D. from International University in 1977. During the 1960s he served as chair of Us (United Slaves), a revolutionary organization that promoted black cultural nationalism. Karenga has also been a vocal advocate of Black Studies programs and authored several books. He is currently a professor of Black Studies at California State University, Long Beach.

The African American Holiday of Kwanzaa: A Celebration of Family, Community, and Culture

It is out of the common values and practices of Continental African first fruit celebrations, that I began to conceive and develop Kwanzaa. But it was in and through the context of African American life and struggle that I completed its creation. Kwanzaa was created in 1966 to serve several functions in the African American community. First, Kwanzaa was created to reaffirm and restore our African heritage and culture. The encouragement for its creation as an expression of recovery and reconstruction of African culture occurred in the *general* context of the Black liberation movement of the 60s and in the *specific* context of Us organization.[1]

In the 60s the Black Movement after 1965 was defined by its thrust to "return to the source," to go "back to Black." It stressed the rescue and reconstruction of African history and culture, redefinition of ourselves and our culture and a restructuring of the goals and purpose of our struggle for liberation and a higher level of human life based on an Afrocentric model.[2] This stress on restoration was evidenced in cultural practices such as renaming of oneself and one's children with African names, wearing the Natural of Afro hair style and African clothes, relearning African languages, especially Swahili, and reviving African life-cycle ceremonies such as naming, nationalization, i.e., initiation or rites of passage [Akika]; wedding [Arusi] and funeral [Maziko].

This restorative thrust also involved the struggle for and establishment of Black Studies [i.e., African and African American Studies] in academia and the building of community institutions which restored and reintroduced African culture, i.e., cultural centers, theatres, art galleries, independent schools, etc. Moreover, there was an emphasis on returning to the Continent permanently or temporarily for cultural revitalization, to reestablish links and build ongoing mutually beneficial and reinforcing relationships. And finally, there was the attempt to recover and begin to live—even relive—African values in the family and community as a way to rebuild and reinforce family, community and culture.

Us, under the leadership of this writer, was and remains a vanguard organization in this process of cultural restoration. In fact upon its founding, it declared itself dedicated to "the creation, recreation and circulation of Black culture." This, Us maintained, would be accomplished by self-conscious construction, institution-building and social struggle which shaped the culture and the people and aided in the creation of a society in which they could live and develop freely. Thus, Us argued, that key to the improvement and enrichment of African American life was the rescue and reconstruction of their culture.

---

1. Maulana Karenga, *Kwanzaa: Origin, Concepts, Practice*. Los Angeles: Kawaida Publications, 1977, p. 1B.
2. Afrocentric essentially means African centered or having a quality, character or approach rooted in the cultural image and human interest of African people. See Molefi Asante, *The Afro-Centric Idea*. Philadelphia: Temple University Press, 1987. See also Maulana Karenga, "Black Studies and the Problematic of Paradigm: The Philosophical Dimension," *Journal of Black Studies*, 18.4 (June 1988), pp. 103–104.

Us defined culture in its fullest sense as the totality of thought and practice by which a people creates itself, celebrates, sustains and develops itself, and introduces itself to history and humanity. Culture for Us, then, is not simply fine art, but the totality of thought and practice of a people which occurs in at least seven fundamental areas: history, religion [spirituality]; social organization: economic organization; political organization: creative production [art, music, literature, dance]; and ethos [the collective psychology which results from activity in the other six areas]. Us further defined culture in terms of its view and value dimensions and the quality of practice that proceeds from these. It maintains that the quality of social practice is directly related to the quality of cultural vision and values. Values here are defined as categories of commitment and priorities which enhance or diminish human possibilities. In a word, what a person determines as important and puts first in his/her life determines the human quality and direction of that life. And as it is with a person, so it is with a people.

Secondly, then, Kwanzaa was created to introduce and reinforce the *Nguzo Saba* [the Seven Principles]. These values were and are a self-conscious contribution to the general Movement call and the specific Us call and struggle for an African [African American] value system. These seven communitarian African values are: Umoja [Unity]; Kujichagulia [Self-determination]; Ujima [Collective Work and Responsibility]; Ujamaa [Cooperative Economics]; Nia [Purpose]: Kuumba [Creativity]; and Imani [Faith]. Their communitarian character was viewed as especially important because of their collective emphasis, positive composition and their rootedness and prevalence in African culture. The Nguzo Saba were thus projected as the moral minimum set of African values that African Americans needed in order to rebuild and strengthen family, community and culture and become a self-conscious social force in the struggle to control their destiny and daily life.

Thirdly, Kwanzaa was created to address the absence of non-heroic holidays in the national African American community. With the possible exception of African American History Month, which itself is essentially organized around heroes and heroines, there was no national holiday to celebrate a communal event of great historic and cultural significance before the creation of Kwanzaa. Even African American History Month, as suggested above, focuses not so much on communal events and issues as on heroic achievement of persons who serve as models. This is clearly important, but it is not a substitute for holidays which call for and cultivate communal rituals around major events and issues in communal history and culture. Thus, Kwanzaa serves an important function as the only nationally celebrated non-heroic African American holiday.

Fourthly, then, Kwanzaa was created to serve as a regular communal celebration which reaffirmed and reinforced the bonds between us as a people. It was designed to be an ingathering to strengthen community and reaffirm common identity, national purpose and ultimate common direction. And finally,

Kwanzaa was created as an act of cultural self-determination, as a self-conscious statement of our cultural truth as an African people. That is to say, it was an important way and expression of being African in a European-dominated context. The first act of a self-conscious, self-determining people, Us contended, is to redefine and reshape their world in their own image and interest. This, as stated above, is a cultural project in the full sense of the word, i.e., a total project involving restructuring thought and practice on every level. Moreover, it is a project which requires *recovering lost models and memory suppressed principles and practices of African culture,* and putting these in their struggle to free themselves and realize their highest aspirations.

The First Fruit Model

The choice of African first fruit celebrations as the focal point and foundation of a new African American holiday was based on several considerations. First, these celebrations were prevalent throughout Africa and thus had the Pan-African character necessary to be defined as African in general as distinct from simply ethnically specific. This was important to Us given its policy of making, whenever possible, a creative and useful synthesis from various African cultural sources rather than choosing only one culture for emulation. Secondly, the core common aspects of these festivals which were discussed above, i.e., ingathering, reverence, commemoration, recommitment and celebration were seen as very relevant to building family, community and culture. This is especially true in terms of their stress on bonding, reaffirmation, restoration, remembrance, spirituality and recommitment to ever higher levels of human life as well as celebration of the Good in general.

Thirdly, the length of the festivals was between seven and nine days for their core celebrations. In Southeastern Africa the festivals are essentially seven days. In West Africa celebrations are sometimes longer and vary from seven to nine days.[3] Among the Yoruba, however, one New Yam Festival, Odun Ijesu, lasts only three days, while the Odwira festival of the Ashanti lasts "a period of one week or more."[4] The Zulu first fruit celebration, Umkhosi, which played an important part in the conceptualization of Kwanzaa, is a seven-day holiday. This seven-day holiday framework was of value because it complemented and reinforced the decision to make Kwanzaa a seven-day holiday in which each day is dedicated to and representative of one of the Nguzo Saba [The

3. D. G. Coursey, "The New Yam Festival Among the Ewe." *Ghana Notes and Queries,* 10 (December 1968).

4. J. B. Danquah, *Gold Coast: Akan Laws and Customs and the Abuakwa Constitution.* London: George Routledge and Sons, Ltd., 1928, p. 129.

Ibid. Danquah notes that Odwira generally falls in December or January also. But he sees Odwira as a thanksgiving festival rather than a harvest festival although it is celebrated in some places during the harvest season in July and August. According to him, the real New Yam festival is Ohum, which occurs in July and August.

Seven Principles]. Finally, the first fruit celebrations of Southeastern Africa occurred at the end of one year and at the beginning of the next, i.e., in late December and early January.[5] In fact, the Zulu first fruit celebration. Umkhosi, is celebrated roughly about the same time as Kwanzaa and again is seven days. Thus, the first fruit festivals and the time of their celebration, especially in Southeastern Africa, became a model for Kwanzaa. And the dates for its celebrations were established as *26 December–1 January*.

This year-end time period became the choice for the time of celebrating Kwanzaa for several reasons. First, it would answer the concern for cultural authenticity in terms of time correspondence between Continental celebrations and Kwanzaa. Secondly, this time of celebration of Kwanzaa fits into the existing pattern of year-end celebrations in the U.S. and thus allowed us to build on the holiday spirit and orientation already present. Not only were there Christmas and Hanukkah celebrations, there was also the New Year celebration which is an essential feature of African first fruit celebrations. Therefore, celebrants of Kwanzaa, living in a multicultural context, remained participants in the general season of celebration of newness, remembrance and recommitment with the decided advantage of being able to celebrate in their own culturally specific way.

Moreover, this time period was chosen to establish Kwanzaa because the dates, 26 December–1 January, marked the end of the high-priced hustle and bustle of Christmas buying and selling. This allowed for avoidance of the crass commercialism usually associated with this period and for savings on any modest gifts one might want to purchase in the context of Kwanzaa gift-giving guidelines. Finally, the time for Kwanzaa celebration was chosen to give those who wished it a culturally specific holiday alternative to the existing ones. In a word, it was to give African Americans an opportunity to celebrate themselves, their culture and history rather than simply imitate the dominant culture. And placing it in the context of the general celebrations of the season offered a definite chance for a proactive choice at a time when one could clearly be made.

It is important here to make several observations. First, the above opportunity was specifically offered for those who wanted such an alternative either before or after becoming aware of Kwanzaa. It was not meant to deny choice but to allow it. For one can't choose if s/he doesn't have a choice and cultural choice is fundamental to the principle of Self-determination [Kujichagulia]. Secondly, "alternative" here clearly refers to opportunity, option and chance to make a proactive choice as distinct from substitute or reactive choice or pos-

5. W. C. Willoughby, *The Soul of the Bantu.* Garden City, NY: Doubleday, Doran Co., 1928, pp. 235, 237 Max Gluckman, "Social Aspects of First Fruit Celebrations and the South Eastern Bantu," *Africa,* 11 (January, 1938), p. 25; O. F. Raum, "The Interpretation of the Ngoni First Fruit Ceremony," *Paideuma,* Vol. 13, 1967.

ture. Thus, Kwanzaa is not a reaction to or substitute for anything. It is the outgrowth of a normal need of a people to shape its world in its own cultural image and interests.

Thirdly, Kwanzaa is above all a cultural choice as distinct from a religious one. This point is important because when the question arises as to the relation between choosing Kwanzaa or/and Christmas, this distinction is not always made. This failure to make this distinction causes confusion, for it appears to suggest one must give up one's religion to practice one's culture. Whereas this might be true in other cases, it is not so in this case. For here, one can and should make a distinction between one's specific religion and one's general culture in which that religion is practiced. On one hand, Christmas is a religious holiday for Christians, but it is also a cultural holiday for Europeans. Thus, one can accept and revere the religious message and meaning but reject its European cultural accretions of Santa Claus, reindeer, mistletoe, frantic shopping, alienated gift-giving, etc.

This point can be made by citing two of the most frequent reasons Christian celebrants of Kwanzaa give for turning to Kwanzaa. The first reason is that it provides them with cultural grounding and reaffirmation as African Americans. The other reason is that it gives them a spiritual alternative to the commercialization of Christmas and the concurrent move away from its original spiritual values and message. Here it is of value also to note that there is a real and important difference between spirituality as a general appreciation for and commitment to the transcendent and religion which suggests formal structures and doctrines. Kwanzaa is not a religious holiday, but a cultural one with an inherent spiritual quality as with all major African celebrations. Thus, *Africans of all faiths* can and do celebrate Kwanzaa, i.e., Muslims, Christians, Black Hebrews, Jews, Buddhists, and Hindus as well as those who follow the ancient traditions of Maat, Yoruba, Dogon, etc. For what Kwanzaa offers is not an alternative to their religion or faith but *a common ground of African culture* which they all share and cherish. It is this common ground of culture on which they all meet, find ancient and enduring meaning, and by which they are thus reaffirmed and reinforced.

Nguzo Saba

(The Seven Principles)

1. UMOJA (Unity)
   To strive for and maintain unity in the family, community, nation and race.
2. KUJICHAGULIA (Self-determination)
   To define ourselves, name ourselves, create for ourselves and speak for ourselves instead of being defined, named, created for and spoken for by others.

3. UJIMA (Collective Work and Responsibility)
   To build and maintain our community together and make our sister's and brother's problems our problems and to solve them together.
4. UJAMMA (Cooperative Economics)
   To build and maintain our own stores, shops and other businesses and to profit from them together.
5. NIA (Purpose)
   To make our collective vocation the building and developing of our community in order to restore our people to their traditional greatness.
6. KUUMBA (Creativity)
   To do always as much as we can, in the way we can, in order to leave our community more beautiful and beneficial than we inherited it.
7. IMANI (Faith)
   To believe with all our heart in our people, our parents, our teachers, our leaders and the righteousness and victory of our struggle.

Black Cultural Nationalism

There is no such thing as individualism, we're all Black. The only thing that saved us from being lynched like Emmett Till or shot down like Medger Evers was not our economics or social status, but our absence.

Values are not abstract. Values are superior to reason.

The white boy engaged in the worship of technology; we must not sell our souls for money and machines.

A Nationalist has a love of the people and values of his nation.

A Man without values is a Man that is unpredictable.

Cultural background transcends education. Having a scope is different from having a content.

We must address ourselves to needs not desires. When we fill our concrete need then we will talk about desires.

Membership in the Black community requires more than just physical presence.

We don't believe what we have is better than others. We believe it is better for Blacks than others.

A value system has three functions. It gives some predictability of behavior, it is an ultimate authority and it serves as a means of security.

Everyone in the Black World has been so concerned with humanity that they have forgotten about themselves. Until Blacks develop themselves, they can do nothing for humanity.

If we could get a nigger to see how worthless, unimportant, ignorant and weak he is by himself, then we will have made a contribution.

I reject individualism for I am of all Black men. I am Joe the sharecropper, John the janitor and Mose the miner. When they catch hell. I catch hell!

Individualism means being yourself at the expense of others.

A Nationalist should be a man who saves his brother from a leaking boat. But he should also teach them how to save themselves by being a good swimmer.

Socially speaking, we want our effects to be collective or more clearly communal rather than collective. For, to be communalistic is to share willingly, but to be collectivistic is to force to share, which is a European concept.

The purpose of a Nationalist should be to build and make the Black Nation eternal.

We want unity to get a collective effort; otherwise there is no need for unity.

Thinking Black is thinking collective minded. You must put the Nation first and yourself last.

We don't need anymore street corner philosophers. We don't need any individualist that work out of contributing in their own way. You've had 450 years to get your own way and it hasn't worked yet. It's about time we had a collective effort and moved on that.

The seven-fold path of the Blackness is to Think Black, Talk Black, Act Black, Create Black, Buy Black, Vote Black, and Live Black.

Individualism is a white desire; co-operation is a Black need.

We belong first to the Black community, second to the American society. The community is a group of people who share values; a society takes care of goods and services.

To talk Black is to start talking "we" instead of "me."

Source

Maulana Karenga, "Kwanzaa and the Ethics of Sharing: Forging Our Future in a New Era," http://www.OfficialKwanzaaWebsite.org/message99.html, accessed June 10, 2002; and *The Quotable Karenga,* ed. Clyde Halisi (Los Angeles: Temple of Kawaida, California, 1967).

Selected Bibliography

Karenga, Maulana. *Introduction to Black Studies.* Los Angeles: University of Sankore Press, 1993.

Paley, Vivian Gussin. *Kwanzaa and Me: A Teacher's Story.* Cambridge, Mass.: Harvard University Press, 1995.

Van Deburg, William. *New Day in Babylon: The Black Power Movement and American Culture, 1965–1975.* Chicago: University of California Press, 1992.

chapter three

Imagining the Black World

one

Poems by Phillis Wheatley

Phillis Wheatley (c. 1753–1784) was the first African American to publish a book and only the second woman of any race to publish a collection of poems. At the time, poetry was widely considered to be the highest form of creative expression, and many prejudiced whites were surprised by Wheatley's erudition and her mastery of eighteenth-century poetic forms. (Others, even less charitable, doubted that the poems were truly hers.)

Despite the loyalist proclivities of her owners Wheatley was an adherent patriot. Although patriot themes were often prominent in her poetry, the two selections below exemplify Wheatley's connection to Africa. She also demonstrated a great concern for liberation. According to John C. Shields, "Wheatley would not have required anyone to teach her the meaning of freedom. As a slave until mid-October of 1773, she chose the American quest for independence. Indeed American patriot rhetoric must have held and inexorable attraction for one who in her poetry struggled so determinedly for freedom."[1]

1. John C. Shields, "Phillis Wheatley," in Jessie Carney Smith, ed. *Notable Black American Women* (Detroit: Gale Research Inc., 1992) 1246.

Phillis Wheatley got her name from the slave ship *Philis,* which carried her from Gambia, Africa, in 1761, when she was about seven or eight years old. She grew up in Boston and was taught both English and Latin by her well-to-do owners. Her book, *Poems on Various Subjects, Religious and Moral,* appeared in London in 1773, and she was emancipated shortly afterward. She died in Boston of complications arising from the birth to her third child.

On Being Brought from Africa to America

"Twas mercy brought me from my *Pagan* land,
Taught my benighted soul to understand
That there's a God, that there's a *Saviour* too:
Once I redemption neither sought nor knew.
Some view our sable[1] race with scornful eye,
"Their colour is a diabolic die."
Remember, *Christians, Negros.* black as *Cain.*[2]
May be refin'd, and join th' angelic train.

1773

To S. M.,[3] a Young African *Painter, on Seeing His Works*

To show the lab'ring bosom's deep intent,
And thought in living characters to paint.
When first thy pencil did those beauties give.
And breathing figures learnt from thee to live.
How did those prospects give my soul delight.
A new creation rushing on my sight?
Still, wond'rous youth! each noble path pursue.
On deathless glories fix thine ardent view:
Still may the painter's and the poet's fire
To aid thy pencil, and thy verse conspire!
And may the charms of each seraphic[4] theme
Conduct thy footsteps to immortal fame!
High to the blissful wonders of the skies
Elate thy soul, and raise thy wishful eyes.
Thrice happy, when exalted to survey
That splendid city, crown'd with endless day,
Whose twice six gates on radiant hinges ring:
Celestial *Salem*[5] blooms in endless spring.

Calm and serene thy moments glide along,
And may the muse inspire each future song!
Still, with the sweets of contemplation bless'd,
May peace with balmy wings your soul invest!
But when these shades of time are chas'd away.
And darkness ends in everlasting day,
On what seraphic pinions shall we move.
And view the landscapes in the realms above?
There shall thy tongue in heav'nly murmurs flow.
And there my muse with heav'nly transport glow:
No more to tell of *Damon's* tender sighs.
Or rising radiance of *Aurora's*[6] eyes.
For nobler themes demand a nobler strain.
And purer language on th' ethereal plain.
Cease, gentle muse! the solemn gloom of night
Now seals the fair creation from my sight.

Notes

1. Black.
2. Described as "marked" by God in Genesis 4:1–15 and therefore thought by some to be the first black man.
3. "S. M." refers to Scipio Moorhead, slave of Reverend John Moorhead of Boston.
4. Angelic.
5. Heavenly Jerusalem, described in Revelation 21:12.
6. In classical mythology, the goddess of the dawn.

Source

Phillis Wheatley, "On Being Brought from Africa to America" and "To S.M., a Young *African* Painter, on Seeing His Works" (1733; reprinted in John Shields, ed., *The Collected Works of Phillis Wheatley,* 171, 175 [New York: Oxford University Press, 1988].

Selected Bibliography

Foster, Frances Smith. *Written by Herself: Literary Productions of Early African American Women Writers, 1746–1892.* Bloomington: Indiana University Press, 1993.

Login, Vernon. *The Negro Author, His Development in America.* New York: Columbia University Press, 1931.

Richmond, Merle A. *Bid the Vassal Soar: Interpretive Essays on the Life and Poetry of Phillis Wheatley and George Moses Horton.* Washington, D.C.: Howard University Press, 1974.

Robinson, William H. *Phillis Wheatley and Her Writings.* New York: Garland, 1984.

Wheatley, Phillis. *The Collected Works of Phillis Wheatley.* Edited by John C. Shields. New York: Oxford University Press, 1988.

two

Argument for Colonization

John Russwurm (1799–1851) was the editor of the first African American newspaper, *Freedom's Journal,* which he founded in 1827. *Freedom's Journal* was a profoundly important paper that won the support of many abolitionists because of its opposition to colonization programs that would have relocated African Americans to Africa. But as the following document illustrates, Russwurm changed his position on this issue in 1829, proclaiming "our rightful place is in Africa." This ideological shift caused a storm of controversy that forced Russwurm to resign.

Russwurm was born in Port Antonio, Jamaica, to a slave woman and a white American merchant, who raised him as if he were white. Later, he became only the third African American to graduate from a college in the United States. After launching *Freedom's Journal,* Russwurm moved to Africa, where he established another newspaper, and in 1836 he became governor of Maryland Colony, which—thanks to Russwurm's efforts—was eventually incorporated into Liberia. After his death in Liberia in 1851, a monument was erected at Cape Palmas in his honor, and a nearby island bears his name.

The Argument For

We feel proud in announcing to our distant readers, that many of our brethren in this city,[1] who have lately taken this subject into consideration, have like ourselves, come out from the examination warm advocates of the Colony,[2] and ready to embrace the first convenient opportunity to embark for the shores of Africa. This we may say looks like coming to the point—as if they had examined for themselves and satisfied of the practicability of the plan, are not afraid the world should know it.

The subject of Colonization is certainly important, as having a great bearing on that of slavery: for it must be evident that the universal emancipation so ardently desired by *us* by all our friends can never take place unless some door is opened whereby the emancipated may be removed, as fast as they drop their galling chains, to some other land beside the free states for it is a fact, that prejudices now in our part of the country, are so high, that it is often the remark of liberal men from the south, that their free people are treated better than we are, in the boasted free states of the north. If the free states have passed no law as yet forbidding the emigration of free persons of colour into their limits; it is no reason that they will not, as soon as they find themselves a little more burdened. We will suppose that a general law of emancipation should be promulgated in the state of Virginia, under the existing statutes which require every emancipated slave to leave the state, would not the other states, in order to shield themselves from the evils of having so many thousands of ignorant beings thrown upon them be obliged in self-defense to pass prohibitory laws? Much as we may deplore the evils of slavery—much as we *may* desire the freedom of the enslaved; who could reproach the free states for enacting such laws? so, that if no good whatever arose from the establishment of colonies, the fact that they remove all obstacles in the way of emancipation should gain for them the support and good wishes of every friend of humanity, & of every enlightened man of colour. It is true, that no such laws at present are in force to our knowledge, but who can foretell how soon before they may, without waiting for the period of a general emancipation in any of the slaveholding states.

Our wiseacres may talk as much as they please upon amalgamations, and our future standing in society, but it does not alter the case in the least; it does not improve our situation in the least; but it is calculated rather to stay the exertions of those who are really willing to make some efforts to improve their own present conditions. We are considered a distinct people, in the midst of the millions around us, and in the most favorable parts of the country; and it matters not from what cause this sentence has been passed upon us; the fiat has gone forth and should each of us live to the age of Methuselah, at the end of the thousand years, we should be exactly in our present situation: a proscribed race, however unjustly—a degraded people, deprived of all the rights of freemen and in the eyes of the community, a race who had no lot nor portion with them.

We hope none of our readers will from our remarks think that we approve in the least of the present prejudices in the way of the man of colour; far from it, we deplore them as much as any man; but they are not of our creating, and they are not in our power to remove. They at present exist against us—and from the length of their existence—from the degraded light in which we have ever been held—we are bold in saying, that it will never be in our power to remove or overcome them. So easily are these prejudices imbibed that we have often noticed the effects on young children who could hardly speak plainly, and were we a believer in dreams, charms, etc., we should believe they imbibed them with their mothers' milk.

Sensible then, as all are of the disadvantages under which we at present labour, can any consider it a mark of folly, for us to cast our eyes upon some other portion of the globe where all these inconveniences are removed—where the Man of Colour freed from the fetters and prejudice and degradation, under which he labours in this land, may walk forth in all the majesty of his creation—a new born creature—a Free Man! It was, we believe, the remark of Sir James Yeo, while on the African coast, that the natives whom he saw were a fine athletic race, walking fearlessly as if sensible of their important station as men, and quite different from the thousands of their brethren whom he had seen in the West Indies and the United States; and never was truer remark made, if we are to credit all other travellers on that Continent, who have likewise born testimony to the same fact.

While some of our friends have wondered at our change, others have been bold enough to call them in question and to accuse us of improper motive; of such, we ask, who has made half the sacrifice we have to oppose the Colonization society? who has labored half so much by night and by day for the same end? who has had to bear the brunt of the battle while those who led us into action were sitting quietly at home? who has suffered much for conscience sake? Let none consider these as vain boastings. We merely insert them to refresh the memories of those who are now loud in denouncing our change. . . .

Freedom's Journal, *March 14, 1829*

Notes

1. New York City.
2. Supporters of an African American emigration to Liberia.

Source

John Russwurm, "Argument for Colonization" (1829; reprinted in Deirdre Mullane, ed., *Crossing the Danger Water: Three Hundred Years of African-American Writing,* 70–71 [New York: Anchor Books, 1993]).

Select Bibliography

Brewer, William M. "John B. Russwurm." *Journal of Negro History* 13 (October 1928): 413–22.

Goodman, Paul. *Of One Blood: Abolitionism and the Origins of Racial Equality*. Berkeley: University of California Press, 1998.

Gros, Bella. "Freedom's Journal and the Rights of All," *Journal of Negro History* 17 (July 1932): 241–86.

Jacobs, Donald M. *Antebellum Black Newspapers: Indiced to New York Freedom's Journal (1827–1829), Rights of All (1829), The Weekly Advocate (1837), and The Colored American (1837–1841)*. Westport, Conn.: Greenwood Press, 1976.

three

Ethiopia

Frances Ellen Watkins Harper (1825–1911) was an internationally known journalist, novelist, and poet. She also harbored runaway slaves, delivered abolitionist lectures, and founded the Women's Christian Temperance Union (WCTU). She is best known for her *Poems on Miscellaneous Subjects* (1857), a pioneering volume of African American protest poetry that saw twenty reprints in her life alone. In the poem reprinted below, Watkins Harper championed the cause of Ethiopia, which in the nineteenth century was commonly understood to mean "black Africa."

By the standards of her day, Watkins Harper led a privileged life, and she received an outstanding education at the William Watkins Academy for Negro Youth. Later, she moved to Ohio and then to Philadelphia, where she became a committed abolitionist. She was a popular lecturer, and she furthered her fame with the publication *Eliza Harris,* a response to Harriet Beecher Stowe's novel *Uncle Tom's Cabin.* She married in 1860 but continued teaching, writing, and speaking and was involved with numerous organizations. She died in Philadelphia in 1911.

Yes! Ethiopia yet shall stretch
Her bleeding hands abroad;
Her cry of agony shall reach

The burning throne of God.

The tyrant's yoke from off her neck,
His fetters from her soul,
The mighty hand of God shall break,
And spurn the base control.

Redeemed from dust and freed from chains,
Her sons shall lift their eyes;
From cloud-capt hills and verdant plains
Shall shouts of triumph rise.

Upon her dark, despairing brow,
Shall play a smile of peace;
For God shall bend unto her wo,
And bid her sorrows cease.

'Neath sheltering vines and stately palms
Shall laughing children play,
And aged sires with joyous psalms
Shall gladden every day.

Secure by night, and blest by day,
Shall pass her happy hours;
Nor human tigers hunt for prey
Within her peaceful bowers.

Then, Ethiopia! stretch, oh! stretch
Thy bleeding hands abroad;
Thy cry of agony shall reach
And find redress from God.

Source

Frances Ellen Watkins Harper, "Ethiopia"(1854; reprinted in Henry Louis Gates, and Nellie Y. McKay, eds., *Norton Anthology of African-American Literature,* 412 [New York: W. W. Norton, 1997]).

Selected Bibliography

Boyd, Melba. *Discarded Legacy: Politics and Poetics in the Life of Frances E. W. Harper, 1825–1911*. Detroit: Wayne State University Press, 1994.

Carby, Hazel V. *Reconstructing Womanhood: The Emergence of the Afro-American Woman Novelist.* New York: Oxford University Press, 1987.

Foster, Frances Smith. *Written by Herself: Literary Production of Early African-American Women, 1746–1892*. Bloomington: Indiana University Press, 1993.

Harper, Frances Ellen Watkins. *A Brighter Coming Day: A Francis E. W. Harper Reader.* Edited by Frances Smith Foster. New York: Feminist Press at the University of New York, 1990.

Saunders, Redding J. *To Make a Poet Black*. Ithaca, N.Y.: Cornell University Press, 1986.

four

West India Emancipation

Frederick Douglass (c. 1817–1895) was the most famous abolitionist of the antebellum era and the first African American leader of national stature in the United States. The following excerpt is from a lengthy speech that Frederick Douglass made in commemoration of the emancipation of the British West Indies on August 1, 1834. In this address, Douglass signaled his support for oppressed blacks across the globe, but he also drew attention to the ongoing struggle for freedom that blacks were facing in the United States.

He was born in Maryland around 1817, and in 1825 his master sent him to Baltimore, where he gained a rudimentary education (although he was largely self-taught). In 1838 he borrowed a black sailor's protection papers and escaped from slavery. Once free, he quickly became involved in abolitionism, lecturing for the Massachusetts Antislavery Society and writing his first autobiography, *The Narrative of the Life of Frederick Douglass,* in 1845.

Douglass lived in England from 1845 to 1847, where he earned enough money to legally purchase his freedom, and he subsequently settled in Rochester, New York, where he published his newspaper, *North Star* (which he continued to publish under various names until 1863). During the Civil War, Douglass met with President Lincoln to lobby on behalf of black soldiers. In 1870 he began publishing the *New National Era* newspaper in Washington, D.C., and he was appointed to several small offices, such as recorder of deeds for the District of Columbia and consul general to the Republic of Haiti. He died in Washington, D.C., on February 20, 1895.

Mr. Chairman, Friends, and Fellow Citizens:

In coming before you to speak a few words, bearing on the great question of human freedom, and having some relation to the sublime event which has brought us together, I am cheered by your numbers, and deeply gratified by the cordial, generous, and earnest reception with which you have been pleased to greet me. I sincerely thank you for this manifestation of your kindly feeling, and if I had as many voices and hearts as you have, I would give as many evidences of my pleasure in meeting you as you have given me, of your pleasure at my appearance before you to-day. As it is I can only say, I sincerely rejoice to be here, and am exceedingly glad to meet you. No man who loves the cause of human freedom, can be other than happy when beholding a multitude of freedom-loving, human faces like that I now see before me.

Sir, it is just ten years and three days ago, when it was my high privilege to address a vast concourse of the friends of Liberty in this same beautiful town, on an oceasion similar to the one which now brings us here. I look back to that meeting—I may say, that great meeting—with most frateful emotions. That meeting was great in its numbers, great in the spirit that pervaded it, and great in the truths enunciated by some of the speakers on that occasion.

Sir, that meeting seems to me a thing a yesterday. The time between then and now seems but a speek, and it is hard to realize that ten long years, crowded with striking events, have rolled away: yet such is the solemn fact. Mighty changes, great transactions, have taken place since the first of August, 1647. Territory has been acquired from Mexico; political parties in the country have assumed a more open and shameless subserviency to slavery; the fugitive slave bill has been passed; ancient landmarks of freedom have been overthrown; the government has entered upon a new and dreadful career in favor of slavery; the slave power has become more aggressive; freedom of speech has been beaten down by ruffian and murderous blows; innocent and freedom-loving men have been murdered by scores on the soil of Kansas, and the end is not yet. Of these things, however, I will not speak now; indeed I may leave them entirely to others who are to follow me.

Mr. President, I am deeply affected by the thought that many who were with us ten years ago, and who bore an honorable part in the joyous exercises of that occasion, are now numbered with the silent dead. Sir, I miss one such from this platform. Soon after that memorable meeting, our well beloved friend, Chas, Van Loon, was cut down, in the midst of his years and his usefulness, and transfered to that undiscovered country, from whose bourne no traveler returns. Many who now hear me, will remember how nobly he bore himself on the occasion of our celebration. You remember how he despised, disregarded and trampled upon the mean spirit of color caste, which was then so rampant and bitter in the country, and his cordial and peratical recognition of the great truths of human brotherhood. Some of you will never forget, as I shall nevre forget, his glorious, towering, spontaneous, copious, truthful, and fountain-like outgushing eloquence. I never think of that meeting without thinking of Chas, Van Loon. He was a true man, a genuine friend of liberty, and of liberty for all men, without the least regard for any of the wicked distinctions, arbitrarily set up by the pride and depravity of the wealthy and strong, against the right of the humble and weak. My friends, we should cherish the members of Chas, Van Loon as a precious treasure, for it is not often that a people like once, has such a memory to cherish. The poor have but few friends, and we, the colored people, are emphatienlly and peculiary, the poor of this land.

Sir, I believe Chas, Van Loon is the only one of those who addressed us at that time, who has been removed from us by the hand of death. Many of the five thousand of the rank and file, have doubtless gone the way of all the earth. We shall see their faces and hear their voices no more, save as we recall them to the mind's eye and ear, by the aid of memory. Some of the marshalls who ordered our procession on that occasion, are no more, and very few of the glorious choir, which filled your grove with songs of joyous freedom, are with us to-day. What death, the common destroyer of all, has not done towards thinning our ranks, the fugitive slave bill has done, and done with terrible effect. It came upon us like a wolf upon the fold, and left our ranks thinned and trembling. The first six months after this whrlwind and pestilence set in, were six of the gloomiest months I ever experienced. It did seem that the infernal regions were broken up, and that devils, not men, had taken possession of our government and our church. The most shocking feature of those times was, that the infernal business of hunting men and women went on under the sanction of heaven as well as earth. Kidnapping proclamations, and kidnapping sermons, the one backed up by the terrors of the gallows, and the others by the terrors of hell, were promulgated at the same time. Our leading divines, had no higher law for the poor, the needy, the hunted, and helpless; their God was with the slaveholder, and the brutal and savage man hunter, carried his warrant from Millard Fillmore, in one pocket, and a sermon from Doctor Lord in the other. I say, sir, these were gloomy days for me. Our people fled in darkening trains from this country, to Canada. There seemed no place for the free black man, in this Republic. It appeared that we were to be driven out of the country by a system of cruelty and violence as murderous and as bellish as that which snatched us from our homes in our fatherland, and planted us here, as the white man's slaves.

Sir, the many changes, vicissitudes, and deaths, which have occurred within the range of our knowledge, during this decade, afford matter for serious thought. I cannot now dwell upon them. Perhaps the occasion does not require that I should dwell upon them, yet I must say, what we all more or less feel, and that is that the flight of the last ten years, with its experience of trial and death, admonish us that we are all hastening down the tide of time, and that our places in the world's activities are soon to be occupied by other generations. They remind us that the present only is ours, and that what our hands now find to do, we should do quickly, and with all our might.

Sir, I have thought much on this subject of the present, and the future, the seen, and the unseen, and about what things should engage our thoughts, and energies while here, and I have come to the conclusion that from no work would I rather go to meet my Eternal Father, than from the work of breaking the fetters from the limbs of his suffering children.

Mr. President, [Austin Steward] I am happy to see here to-day many faces that were here ten years ago. I am especially glad to see you here, and to hear your voice. Sir, you have grown venerable in the service of your enslaved people, and I am glad to find that you are not weary in this department of well doing. Time has dealt gently with you this last ten years, and you seem as vigorous now as when I saw you then. You presided on that occasion, you preside now; and notwithstanding the gloomy aspect of the times, I am not without hope, that you will live to preside over a grander celebration than this; a celebration of the American jubilee, in which four millions of our countrymen shall rejoice in freedom. That jubilee will come. You and I may, or we may not live to see it; but whether we do, or do not, God regins, and Slavery must yet fall; unless the devil is more potent than the Almighty; unless sin is stronger than righteousness, Slavery must perish, and that not very long hence.

Here, too, I am most happy to meet again my loved and honored and much respected friend, HENRY HIGHLAND GARNET. He was here with us, and spoke to us ten years ago. He has traveled much and labored much since that time. England, Ireland, Scotland, and Wales, have listened to his eloquent advocacy of our cause since then. While in the old world, it was his privilege to associate with refined and cultivated people; and I venture to say that no man from among us, visiting the old country, has left in his pathway a better impression for himself and people than H. H. GARNET. We need a thousand such representative men at home and abroad, to meet and repel the floods of slander of our race, which two thousand millions of dollars invested in our people, as property, constantly provoke. The American government dose not need a minister at the court of St. James to look after American interests, more than we need in England a representative of our people against whom all manner of lies are told.

Happy am I too, to meet here to-day, as ten years ago, J. W. LOOUEN, the interpid and faithful conductor of the Underground Railroad, who has, during the interval of our former celebrations, conveyed from Republican slavery to Monarchieal Liberty, not fewer than a thousand souls.

Mr. President, you miss, and we all miss, our old friend, SAML. R. WARD. He was with us ten years ago, and if he were now in the country, he would doubtless be with us here to-day. I will say for Mr. Ward what he can not say for himself. Though absent in body he is with us in spirit. Mr. Ward is now in Jamaica, and I am told is soon to be joined in his new home by his dear family, of whom we have often heard him lovingly speak. They are now in Canada, and he has sent for them to come out to him. I will say another word of Mr. Ward, and that is, he was, in many respects, a head and shoulders above us all. No colored man who has yet attracted public observation in this country, was ever capable of rendering his people greater service than he. And while we all deeply regret that he has seen fit to leave us for other fields of usefulness, we will here and now tender him our best wishes while he may remain abroad, and pledge him an earnest welcome should he ever return to the Empire State.

My friends, you will also miss, as I do, the eloquent Chas. L. Remond. He was on this platform ten years ago. I should have been glad to have met him here to-day, for though he differs from us in his mode of serving our cause, he doubtless fully sympathises with us in the sentiment which brings us together on this occasion.

Mr. President, you will pardon those homely but grateful references to individuals. The great poet has told us that one touch of nature makes all the world skin, and the cause of freedom, I think makes friends of all its friends. At any rate, I can say that I can love an enemy, if he loves the slave, for I know that if he loves the slave, he loves him intelligently, and if he hates me, he does it ignorantly. I can easily forgive such. Sir, there are other names I might well refer to, as worthy as those already mentioned, but the time would fail. I hasten, therefore, to the consideration of those topics naturally suggested by this occasion.

Friends and fellow-citizens: We have met here today to celebrate with all fitting demonstrations of joy and gladness, this the twenty-third anniversary of the inauguration of freedom as the ruling law of the British West India. The day and the deed are both greatly distinguished. They are as a city set upon a hill. All civilized men at least, have looked with wonder and admiration upon the great deed of justice and humanity which has made the first of August illustrious among all the days of the year. But to no people on the globe, leaving out the emancipated men and women of the West Indies themselves, does this day address itself with so much force and significance, as to the people of the United States. It has made the name of England known and loved in every Slave Cabin, from the Potomac to the Rio Grande, and has spread alarm, hatred, and dread in all the accursed slave markets of our boasted Republic from Baltimore to New Orleans.

Slavery in America, and slavery everywhere, never received a more stunning and killing condemnation.

The event we celebrate is the finding and the restoration to the broken ranks of human brotherhood eight hundred thousand lost members of the human family. It is the resurrection of a mighty multitude, from the grave of moral, mental, social, and spiritual death, where ages of slavery and oppression, and lust and pride, and cruelty had bound them. Here they were instantly clothed with all the rights, responsibilities, powers, and duties, of free men and women.

Up to the morning of the first of August, 1834,[1] these people were slaves, numbered with the beasts of the field, marked, branded, priced valued, and ranged as articles of property. The gates of human brotherhood were bolted and barred against them. They were outside of both law and gospel. The love taught in the Bible, and the justice recorded in the Statute Book did not embrace them: they were outside. Their fellow men had written their names with horses, sheep, and swine, and with horned cattle. They were not governed by the law, but the lash, they were not paid for their work, but whipped on to toil as the American slave now is. Their degradation was complete. They were slaves; and when I have said that, I have said all. The essence of wickedness, the intensified sum of all iniquity, the realization of the idea of a burning hell upon the earth, in which every passion is an unchained devil, let loose to deal out ten thousand pains, and horrors start up to view at the very mention of slavery!—It comprehends all that is foul, shocking, and dreadful. Human nature shudders, and turns pale at its presence, and flies from it as from a den of lions, a nest of scorpions, or an army of rattlesnakes. The very soul sickens, and the mind revolts at the thought of slavery, and the true man welcomes instant death in preference to being reduced to its degradation and ruin.

Yet such was the condition of our brothers and sisters in the British West Indies, up to the morning of the first of August, 1834. The wicked love of dominion by man over man, had made strong their fetters and multiplied their chains. But on the memorable morning which we are met to celebrate, one bolt from the moral sky of Britain left these blood stained irons all scattered and broken throughout the West Indies, and the limbs they had bruised, outstretched in praise and thanksgiving to God for deliverance. No man of any sensibility can read the account of that great transaction without emotions too great for utterance. There was something Godlike in this decree of the British nation. It was the spirit of the Son of God commanding the devil of slavery to go out of the British West Indies.

It said tyrant slave-driver, fling away your blood-stained whip, and bury out of sight your broken fetters and chains. Your accursed occupation is gone. It said to the slave, with wounds, bruises, and scars yet fresh upon him, you are emancipated—set free—enfranchised—no longer slaves, but British subjects, and henceforth equal before the British law!

Such my friends, was the change—the revolution—the wondrous transformation which took place in the condition of the colored people in the British West Indies, twenty-three years ago. With the history of the causes, which led to this great consummation, you are perhaps already sufficiently acquainted. I do not intend in my present remarks to enter into the tedious details of this history, although it might prove quite instructive to some in this assembly. It might prove especially interesting to point out various steps in the progress of the British Anti-Slavery movement, and to dwell upon some of the more striking analogies between that and our movement in this country. The materials at this point are ample, did the limits of the hour permit me to bring them forward.

One remark in this connection I will make. The abolition movement in America, like many other institutions of this country, was largely derived from England. The defenders of American slavery often excuse their villainy on the ground that they inherited the system from England. Abolitionism may be traced to the same source, yet I don't see that it is any more popular on that account. Mr. Garrison applied British abolitionism to American slavery. He did that and nothing more. He found its principles here plainly scared and defined; its truths glowingly enunciated, and the whole subject illustrated, and elaborated in a masterly manner. The sin—the crime—the curse of slavery, were all demonstrated in the light of reason, religion, and morality, and by a startling array of facts. We owe Mr. Garrison our grateful homage in that he was among the first of his countrymen who zealously applied the British argument for abolition, against American slavery. Even the doctrine of immediate emancipation as against gradualism, is of English, not American origin. It was expounded and enforced by Elizabeth Herrick, and adopted by all the earnest abolitionists in England. It came upon the British nation like Uncle Tom's Cabin upon our land after the passing of the fugitive slave law, and it is remarkable that the highest services rendered the anti-slavery cause in both countries, were rendered by women. Elizabeth Herrick, who wrote only a pamphlet, will be remembered as long as the West India Emancipation is remembered, and the name of Harriet Beecher Stowe can never die while the love of freedom lives in the world.

But my friends, it is not with these analogies and minute references that I mean in my present talk, to deal.

I wish you to look at West India Emancipation as one complete transaction of vast and sublime significance, surpassing all power of exaggeration. We hear and read much of the achievements of this nineteenth century, and much can be said, and truthfully said of them. The world has literally shot forward with the speed of steam and lightning. It has probably made more progress during the last fifty years, than in any five hundred years to which we can refer in the history of the race. Knowledge has been greatly increased, and its blessing, widely diffused. Locomotion has been marvelously improved, so that the very ends of the earth are being rapidly brought together. Time to the traveler has been annihilated.

Deep down beneath the stormy surface of the wide, wide waste of waters, a pathway has been formed for human thought. Machinery of almost every conceivable description, and for almost every conceivable purpose, has been invented and applied; ten thousand discoveries and combinations have been made during these last fifty years, till the world has ceased to ask in astonishment "what next?" for there seems scarcely any margin left for a next. We have made hands of iron and brass, and copper and wood, and though we have not been able to endow them with life and soul, yet we have found the means of endowing them with intelligent motion, and of making them do our work, and to do it more easily, quickly and more abundantly than the hands in their palmiest days were able to perform it. I am not here to disparage or underrate this physical and intellectual progress of the race. I thank my God for every advance which is made in this direction.

I fully appreciate the beautiful sentiment which you farmers, now before me, so highly regard, "that he who makes two blades of grass grow where only one grew before," is a benefactor. I recognize and honor, as you do, all such benefactors. There is not the slightest danger that those who contribute directly to the world's wealth and case will ever be forgotten by the world. The world loves its own. A hungry man will not forget the hand that feeds him, though he may forget that Providence which caused the bread to grow. Arkwright,[2] Watt,[3] Fulton,[4] Franklin,[5] Morse,[6] and Daguerre,[7] are names which will not fade from the memories of men. They are grand civilizers, but civilizers after their kind—and great as are their achievements, they sink to nothingness when compared with that great achievement which has given us the first day of August as a sacred day, "What shall it profit a man if he gain the whole world and lose his own soul!" We are to view this grand event in the light of this sublime enquiry.

"Men do not live by bread alone," said the great Redeemer. What is true of individual men, is also true of societies, and nations of men. Nations are not held in their spheres, and perpetuated in health by cunning machinery. Railroads, steamships, electric wires, tons of gold and silver, and precious stones cannot save them. A nation may perish in the midst of them all, or in the absence of them all. The true life principle is not in them.

Egypt died in the sight of all her imposing wealth and her everlasting Pyramids. The polished stone is there, but Egypt is gone. Greece has vanished, her life disappeared as it were, in a trance of artistic beauty, and architectural splendor. Great Babylon, the mother of harlots and the abominations of the earth, fell in the midst of barbaric wealth and glory. The lesson taught by the history of nations is that the preservation or destruction of communities does not depend upon external prosperity. Men do not live by bread alone, so with nations. They are not saved by art, but by honesty. Not by the gilded splendors of wealth, but by the hidden treasure of manly virtue. Not by the multitudinous gratification of the flesh, but by the celestial guidance of the spirit.

It is in this view that West India Emancipation becomes the most interesting and sublime event of the nineteenth century. It was the triumph of a great moral principle, a decisive victory, after a severe and protracted struggle, of freedom over slavery; of justice and mercy against a grim and bloody system of devilish brutality. It was an acknowledgment by a great nation of the sacredness of humanity, as against the claims of power and cupidity.

As such, it stands out as a large and glorious contribution to the moral and spiritual growth of mankind, and just such a contribution as the world needed, and needs now to have repeated a thousand times over, in our own land especially. Look at New York city; beautiful without to be sure. She has great churches, great hotels, great wealth, great commerce, but you all know that she is the victim of a dreadful disease, and that her best friends regard her as a cage of unclean bird in danger at any moment of being swallowed up by a social earthquake. Look at Philadelphia, Baltimore, Louisville, New Orleans. Look where you will, and you will see that while all without is covered and studded with the evidences of prosperity, there is yet no real sense of that stability which conscious rectitude imparts. All the great acts of the nation of late have looked away from the right path. Our very Temple of Justice has inverted and outraged all the principles of justice which it was professedly established to maintain. The government at Washington is mostly exercised in schemes by which it can cheat one section of the country for the benefit of another, and yet, seem honest to all. Where this will end, Heaven only knows.

But I was calling attention to this great example of British justice not in anger, but in sorrow. Great Britian bowing down, confessing and forsaking her sins—her sins against the weak and despised—is a spectacle which nations present but seldom. No achievement in arts or arms, in letters or laws, can equal this. And the world owes Britian more for this example of humility and honest repentance than for all her other contributions to the world's progress.

I know, and you know, it is easy enough for a nation to assume the outward and hollow seemings of humility and repentance. The world is full of such tongue-wise demonstrations. Our own country can show a long list of them. We have thanksgivings and fasts, and are unrivalled in this department of religious observances. On our fast days and fourth of Julys, we seem unto men to fast, but the sequal shows that our confessions and prayers have only come from men whose hearts are crammed with arrogancy, pride and hate.

We have bowed down our heads as a bulrush, and have spread sack-cloth and ashes under us, and like the stiff-necked Jews, whose bad practices we imitate more closely than we do their religion, we have exacted all our labors.

I am not here to make invidious and insulting comparisons; but all must allow, that the example of England, in respect to the great act before us, differs widely from our manifestations of sorrow for great national sin. Here we have, indeed, a chosen fast of the Living God, an acceptable day unto the Lord, a day in which the burdens of wickedness were loosed; the heavy burdens undone; the oppressed let go free; every yoke broken; the poor that were cast out of the house brought in; and men no longer hiding themselves from their own flesh.

It has been said that corporations have no souls, that with nations might is the standard of right, and that self interest governs the world.

The abolition of slavery in the West Indies is a shining evidence of the reverse of all this profanity. Nobler ideas and principles of action are here brought to view. The vital, animating, and all-controlling power of the British Abolition movement was religion. Its philosophy was not educated and enlightened selfishness, (such as some are relying upon now to do away with slavery in this country.) but the pure, single eyed spirit of benevolence. It was not impelled or guided by the fine-spun reasonings of political expediency, but by the unmistakable and imperative demands of principle. It was not commerce, but conscience; not considerations of climate and productions of the earth, but the heavenly teachings of Christianity, which every where teaches that God is our Father, and man, however degraded, is our brother.

The men who were most distinguished in carrying forward the movement, from the great Willberforce downward, were eminent for genuine piety. They worked for the slave as if they had been working for the Son of God. They believed that righteousness exalteth a nation and that sin is a reproach to any people. Hence they united religions with patriotism, and pressed home the claims of both upon the national heart with the tremendous energy of truth and love, till all England cried out with one accord, through Exeter Hall, through the press, through the pulpit, through parliament, and through the very throne itself, *slavery must and shall be destroyed.*

Herein is the true significance of West India Emancipation. It stands out before all the world as a mighty, moral, and spiritual triumph. It is a product of the soul, not of the body. It is a contribution to common honesty without which nations as well as individuals sink to ruin. It is one of those words of life that proceedeth out of the mouth of God, by which nations are established, and kept alive and in moral health.

Now, my friends, how has this great act of freedom and benevolence been received in the United States. How has our American Christian Church and our American Democratic Government received this glorious new birth of National Righteousness.

From our professions as a nation, it might have been expected that a shout of joy and gladness would have shook the hollow sky, that loud hallelujahs would have rolled up to heaven from all our borders, saying, "Glory to God, in the highest, on earth peace and good will toward man. Let the earth be glad." "The Lord God omnipotent reigneth."

Alas, no such responsive note of rejoicing has reached my ear, except from a part of the colored people and their few white friends. As a nation, we are deaf, dumb, and blind to the moral beauty, and transcendent sublimity of West India Emancipation. We have passed it by with averted eyes, regarding it rather as a reflection to be resented than as an example to be imitated. First, we looked for means of impeaching England's motives for abolishing Slavery, and not being able to find any such, we have made ourselves hoarse in denouncing emancipation as a failure.

We have not viewed the great fact in the light of a liberal philosophy, but have applied to it rules of judgment which were not intended to reveal its true character and make known its actual worth. We have taken a microscope to view the stars, and a fish line to measure the ocean's depths.

We have approached it as though it were a railroad, a canal, a steamship, or a newly invented mowing machine, and out of the fullness of our dollar-loving hearts, we have asked with owl-like wisdom, Will it pay! Will it increase the growth of sugar! Will it cheapen tobacco! Will it increase the imports and exports of the Islands! Will it enrich or ruin the planters! How will it effect Jamaica spirits! Can the West Indies be successfully cultivated by free labor! These and sundry other questions, springing out of the gross materialism of our age and nation, have been characteristically put respecting West India Emancipation. All our tests of the grand measure have been such as we might look for from slave-holders themselves. They all proceed from the slave-holders side, and never from the side, of the emancipated slaves.

The effect of freedom upon the emancipated people of the West Indies passes for nothing. It is nothing that the plundered slave is now a freeman; it is nothing with our sagacious, economical philosophers, that the family now takes the place of concubinage; it is nothing that marriage is now respected where before it was a mockery; it is nothing that moral purity has now a chance to spring up, where before pollution was only possible; it is nothing that education is now spreading among the emancipated men and women, bearing its precious fruits, where only ignorance, darkness, superstition and idolatry prevailed before; it is nothing that the whipping post has given way to the school house; it is nothing that the church stands now where the salve prison stood before; all these are nothing, I say, in the eyes of our slavery-cursed country.

But the first and last question, and the only question which we Americans have to press in the premises, is the great American question (viz.) *will it pay?*

Sir, If such a people as ours had heard the beloved disciple of the Lord, exclaiming in the rapture of the apocalyptic vision, "And I saw another angel fly in the midst of heaven, having the everlasting gospel to preach to them that dwell on the earth, and to every nation, kindred, tongue, and people," they, instead of answering, Amen Glory to God in the Highest, would have responded,—But brother John, *will it pay?* Can money be made out of it? Will it make the rich richer, and the strong stronger? How will it effect property? In the eyes of such people, there is no God but wealth; no right and wrong but profit and loss.

Sir, our national morality and religion have reached a depth of baseness than which there is no lower deep. They both allow that if men can make money by stealing men and women, and by working, them up into sugar, rice, and tobacco, they may innocently continue the practice, and that he who condemns it is an unworthy citizen, and a disturber of the church. Money is the measure of morality, and the success or failure of slavery, as a money-making system, determines with many whether the thing is virtuous, or villainous, and whether it should be maintained or abolished. They are for Slavery where climate and soil are said to be for it, and are really not opposed to it any where, though as a nation we have made a show of opposition to it where the system does not exist. With our geographical ethics, and climatic religion, we have naturally sided with the slave-holders and women-whippers of the West Indies, in denouncing the abolition of slavery in the West Indies a failure.

Sir: As to what has been the effect of West India freedom upon the material condition of the people of these Islands, I am happy that there is one on this platform, who can speak with the authority of positive knowledge. Henry Highland Garnet, has lived and labored among those emancipated people. He has enjoyed ample opportunity for forming an intelligent judgment in respect to all that pertains to the subject. I therefore most willingly leave this branch of the subject to him.

One remark, however, I will venture to make—and that is this: I take it that both the friends and the enemies of the emancipated have been too impatient for results. They seem to forget that although a nation can be born in a day, it can mature only in centuries—that though the fetters on the limbs can be broken in an instant, the fetters on the soul can wear off only in the ages.

Degradation, mental, moral, and physical, ground into the very bones of a people by ages of unremitting bondage, will not depart from that people in the course, even of many generations.

West India freedom, though more than twenty-one years old, is yet but an infant. And to predicate its future on its present weakness, awkwardness, and improvidence now, is about as wise as to apply the same rule to your little toothless children. It has taken at least a thousand years to bring some of the leading nations of the earth from the point where the Negroes of the West Indies started twenty-three years ago, to their present position. Let considerations like these be duly weighed, and black man though I am, I do not fear the world's judgment.

Now, sir, I like these annual celebrations. I like them because they call us to the contemplation of great interests, and afford an opportunity of presenting salutary truths before the American people. They bring our people together, and enable us to see and commence with each other to mutual profit. If these occasions are conducted wisely, decorously, and orderly, they increase our respectability in the eyes of the world, and silence the slanders of prejudice. If they are otherwise conducted they cover us with shame and confusion. But, sir, these celebrations have been objected to by our slaveholding democracy; they do not think it in good taste. Slaveholders are models of taste. With them, propriety is every thing; honesty, nothing. For a long time they have taught our Congress, and Senate, and Pulpits, what subjects should be discussed, and what objects should command our attention. Senator Sumner, fails to observe the prescribed rules and he falls upon the Senate floor, stunned and bleeding beneath the ruffian blows of one of our southern models of propriety. By such as these, and by their timid followers this is called a *British* celebration.

From the inmost core of my soul I pity the mean spirits, who can see in these celebrations nothing but British feeling. The man who limits his admiration of good actions to the country in which he happens to he born, (if he ever was born,) or to the nation or community of which he forms a small part, is a most pitiable object. With him to be one of a nation is more than to be one of the human family. He don't live in the world, but he lives in the United States. Into his little soul the thought of God as our common Father, and of man our common Brother has never entered. To such a soul as that, this celebration cannot but be exceedingly distasteful.

But sarcasm aside, I hold it to be eminently fit that we keep up these celebrations from year to year, at least until we shall have an American celebration to take its place. That the event we thus commemorate transpired in another country, and was wrought out by the labors and sacrifices of the people of another nation, forms no valid objection to its grateful, warm, hearty, and enthusiastic celebration by us. In a very high sense, we may claim that great deed as our own. It belongs not exclusively to England and the English people, but to the lovers of Liberty and of mankind the world over. It is one of those glorious emanations of Christianity, which, like the sun in the Heavens, takes no cognizance of national lines or geographical boundaries, but pours its golden floods of living light upon all. In the great Drama of Emancipation, England was the theatre but universal and everywhere applying principles of Righteousness, Liberty, and Justice were the actors. The great Ruler of the Universe, the God and Father of all men, to whom be honor, glory, and praise for evermore, roused the British conscience by his truth moved the British heart, and West India Emancipation was the result. But if only Englishmen may properly celebrate this great concession to justice and liberty, then, sir, we may claim to be Englishmen, Englishmen in the love of Justice and Liberty. Englishmen in magnanimous efforts to protect the weak against the strong, and the slave against the slaveholder. Surely in this sense, it ought to be no disgrace to be an Englishman, even on the soil of the freest people on the globe.

But, Mr. Chairman, we celebrate this day on the broad platform of Philanthropy—whose country is the world, and whose countrymen are all mankind. On this platform we are neither Jews nor Greeks, strangers nor foreigners, but fellow citizens of the household of faith. We are the brothers and friends of Clarkson, Wilberforce,[8] Granville, Sharpe, Richard Baxter, John Wesley, Thomas Day, Bishop Portius and George Fox, and the glorious company of those who first wrought to turn the moral sense of mankind in active opposition to slavery. They labored for freedom not as Englishmen, but as men, and as brothers to men—the world over—and it is meet and right to commemorate and imitate their noble example. So much for the Anti-British objection.

I will now notice a special objection. It is said that we, the colored people, should do something ourselves worthy of celebration, and not be everlastingly celebrating the deeds of a race by which we are despised.

This objection, strange as it may seem, comes from no enemy of our people, but from a friend. He is himself a colored man, a high spirited and patriotic man, eminent for learning and ability, and to my mind, he has few equals, and no superior among us. I thank Dr. J. M'Cune Smith for this objection, since in the answer I may make to it, I shall be able to give a few of my thoughts on the relation subsisting between the white and colored people of this country, a subject which it well becomes us to consider whenever and wherever we congregate.

In so far as this objection to our celebrating the first of August has a tendency to awaken in us a higher ambition than has hitherto distinguished us, and to raise our aims and activities above the dull level of our present physical wants, and so far as it shall tend to stimulate us to the execution of great deeds of heroism worthy to be held in admiration and perpetual remembrance, for one, sir, I say amen to the whole of it. I am free to say, that nothing is more humiliating than the insignificant part we, the colored people, are taking in the great contest now going on with the powers of oppression in this land. I can stand the insults, assaults, misrepresentations, and slanders of the known haters of my race, and brave them all. I look for such opposition. It is a natural incident of the war, and I trust I am to a certain degree prepared for it; but the stolid contentment, the listless indifference, the moral death which reigns over many of our people, we who should be all on fire, beats down my little flame of enthusiasm and leaves me to labor, half robbed of my natural force. This indifference, in us, is outrageous. It is giving aid and comfort to the men who are warring against our very manhood. The highest satisfaction of our oppressors, is to see the Negro degraded, divested of public spirit, insensible to patriotism, and to all concern for the freedom, elevation, and respectability of the race.

Senator Toombs with a show of truth, lyingly said in Boston a year or two ago in defence of the slavery of the black race, they are mentally and morally inferior, and that if the whole colored population were swept from this country, there would be nothing in twenty years to tell that such a people had ever existed. He exulted over our assumed ignorance and over our destitution of valuable achievements. Of course the slaveholder uttered a falsehood, but to many it seemed to be a truth, and vast numbers of the American people receive it as a truth today, and shape their action accordingly.

The general sentiment of mankind is, that a man who will not fight for himself, when he has the means of doing so, is not worth being fought for by others, and this sentiment is just. For a man who does not value freedom for himself will never value it for others, nor put himself to any inconvenience to gain it for others. Such a man, the world says, may lay down until he has sense enough to stand up. It is useless and cruel to put a man on his legs, if the next moment his head is to be brought against a curb-stone.

A man of that type will never lay the world under any obligation to him, but will be a moral pauper, a drag on the wheels of society, and if he, too, be identified with a peculiar variety of the race he will entail disgrace upon his race as well as upon himself. The world in which we live is very accommodating to all sorts of people. It will co-operate with them in any measure which they propose; it will help those who earnestly help themselves, and will hinder those who hinder themselves. It is very polite, and never offers its services unasked.—Its favors to individuals are measured by an unerring principle in this: viz—respect those who respect themselves, and despise those who despise themselves. It is not within the power of unaided human nature to persevere in pitying a people who are insensible to their own wrongs, and indifferent to the attainment of their own rights. The poet was as true to common sense as to poetry when he said,

"Who would be free, themselves must strike the blow."

When O'Connel, with all Ireland at his back, was supposed to be contending for the just rights and liberties of Ireland, the sympathies of mankind were with him, and even his enemies were compelled to respect his patriotism. Kossuth, fighting for Hungary with his pen long after she had fallen by the sword, commanded the sympathy and support of the liberal world till his own hopes died out. The Turks while they fought bravely for themselves and scourged and drove back the invading legions of Russia, shared the admiration of mankind. They were standing up for their own rights against an arrogant and powerful enemy; but as soon as they let out their fighting to the Allies, admiration gave way to contempt. These are not the maxims and teachings of a cold-hearted world. Christianity itself teaches that a man shall provide for his own house. This covers the whole ground of nations as well as individuals. Nations no more than individuals can innocently be improvident. They should provide for all wants mental, moral, and religious, and against all evils to which they are liable as nations. In the great struggle now progressing for the freedom and elevation of our people, we should be found at work with all our might, resolved that no man or set of men shall be more abundant in labors, according to the measure of our ability, than ourselves.

I know, my friends, that in some quarters the efforts of colored people meet with very little encouragement. We may fight, but we must fight like the Seapoys of India, under white officers. This class of Abolitionists don't like colored celebrations, they don't like colored conventions, they don't like colored Anti-Slavery fairs for the support of colored newspapers. They don't like any demonstrations whatever in which colored men take a leading part. They talk of the proud Anglo-Saxon blood, as flippantly as those who profess to believe in the natural inferiority of races. Your humble speaker has been branded as an ingrate, because he has ventured to stand up on his own rights and to plead our common cause as a colored man, rather than as a Garrisonian. I hold it to be no part of gratitude to allow our white friends to do all the work, while we merely hold their coats. Opposition of the sort now referred to, is partisan opposition, and we need not mind it. The white people at large will not largely be influenced by it. They will see and appreciate all honest efforts on our part to improve our condition as a people.

Let me give you a word of the philosophy of reform. The whole history of the progress of human liberty shows that all concessions yet made to her august claims, have been born of earnest struggle. The conflict has been exciting, agitating, all-absorbing, and for the time being putting all other tumults to silence. It must do this or it does nothing. If there is no struggle there is no progress. Those who profess to favor freedom and yet depreciate agitation, are men who want crops without plowing up the ground, they want rain without thunder and lightning. They want the ocean without the awful roar of its many waters.

This struggle may be a moral one, or it may be a physical one, and it may be both moral and physical, but it must be a struggle. Power concedes nothing without a demand. It never did and it never will. Find out just what any people will quietly submit to and you have found out the exact measure of injustice and wrong which will be imposed upon them, and these will continue till they are resisted with either words or blows, or with both. The limits of tyrants are prescribed by the endurance of those whom they oppress. In the light of these ideas, Negroes will be hunted at the North, and held and flogged at the South so long as they submit to those devilish cut rages, and make no resistance, either moral or physical. Men may not get all they pay for in this world, but they must certainly pay for all they get. If we ever get free from the oppressions and wrongs heaped up on us, we must pay for their removal. We must do this by labor, by suffering, by sacrifice, and if needs be, by our lives and the lives of others.

Hence, my friends, every mother who, like Margaret Garner, plunges a knife into the bosom of her infant to save it from the bell of our Christian Slavery, should be held and honored as a benefactress. Every fugitive from slavery who like the noble William Thomas at Wilksbarre, prefers to perish in a river made red by his own blood, to submission to the bell bounds who were bunting and shooting ban, should be esteemed as a glorious martyr, worthy to be held in grateful memory by our people. The fugitive Horace, at Mechanicsburgh, Ohio, the other day, who taught the slave catchers from Kentucky that it was safer to arrest white men than to arrest him, did a most excellent service to our cause. Parker and his noble band of fifteen at Christiana, who defended themselves from the kidnappers with prayers and pistols, are entitled to the honor of making the first successful resistance to the Fugitive Slave Bill. But for that resistance, and the rescue of Jerry, and Shadrack, the man-hunters would have hunted our hills and valleys, here with the same freedom with which they now hunt their own dismal swamps.

There was an important lesson in the conduct of that noble Krooman in New York, the other day, who, supposing that the American Christians were about to enslave him, betook himself to the mast head, and with knife in hand, said he would cut his throat before he would be made a slave. Joseph Cinque on the deck of the Amistad, did that which should make his name dear to us. He bore nature's burning protest against slavery. Madison Washington who struck down his oppressor on the deck of the Creole, is more worthy to be remembered than the colored man who shot Pitcairn at Bunker Hill.

My friends, you will observe that I have taken a wide range, and you think it is about time that I should answer the special objection to this celebration. I think so too. This, then, is the truth concerning the inauguration of freedom in the British West Indies. Abolition was the act of the British Government. The motive which led the Government to act, no doubt was mainly a philanthropic one, entitled to our highest admiration and gratitude. The National Religion, the justice, and humanity, cried out in thunderous indignation against the foul abomination, and the government yielded to the storm. Nevertheless a share of the credit of the result falls justly to the slaves themselves. "Though slaves, they were rebellious slaves." They bore themselves well. They did not hug their chains, but according to their opportunities, swelled the general protest against oppression. What Wilberforce was endeavoring to win from the British Senate by his magic eloquence, the Slaves themselves were endeavoring to gain by outbreaks and violence. The combined action of one and the other wrought out the final result. While one showed that slavery was wrong, the other showed that it was dangerous as well as wrong. Mr. Wilberforce, peace man though he was, and a model of piety, availed himself of this element to strengthen his case before the British Parliament, and warned the British government of the danger of continuing slavery in the West Indies. There is no doubt that the fear of the consequences, acting with a sense of the moral evil of slavery led to its abolition. The spirit of freedom was abroad in the Islands. Insurrection for freedom kept the planters in a constant state of alarm and trepidation. A standing army was necessary to keep the slaves in their chains. This state of facts could not be without weight in deciding the question of freedom in these countries.

I am aware that the rebellious disposition of the slaves was said to arise out of the discussions which the abolitionists were carrying on at home, and it is not necessary to refute this alleged explanation. All that I contend for is this: that the slaves of the West Indies did fight for their freedom, and that the fact of their discontent was known in England, and that it assisted in bringing about that state of public opinion which finally resulted in their emancipation. And if this be true, the objection is answered.

Again, I am aware that the insurrectionary movements of the slaves were held by many to be prejudicial to their cause. This is said now of such movements at the South. The answer is that abolition followed close on the heels of insurrection in the West Indies, and Virginia, was never nearer emancipation than when General Turner kindled the fires of insurrection at Southampton.

Sir, I have now more than filled up the measure of my time. I thank you for the patient attention given to what I have had to say. I have aimed, as I said at the beginning, to express a few thoughts having some relation to the great interests of freedom both in this country and in the British West Indies, and I have said all that I meant to say, and the time will not permit me to say more.

Notes

1. The date that slavery was eradicated in the British West Indies.
2. Sir Richard Arkwright (1732–1792), English inventor.
3. James Watt (1736–1819), Scottish inventor.
4. Robert Fulton (1765–1814), American inventor.
5. Benjamin Franklin (1706–1790), American statesman, printer, scientist, and writer.
6. Samuel Finley Breece Morse (1840–1937), American inventor and artist.
7. Louis Jacques Monde Daguerre (1789–1851), French scene painter and physicist.
8. William Wilberforce (1759–1833), British politician, abolitionist, and humanitarian.

Source

Frederick Douglass, "West India Emancipation," in *Two Speeches By Frederick Douglass,* 4–24 (Rochester, N.Y.: C. P. Dewey, 1857).

Selected Bibliography

Douglass, Frederick. *Life and Times of Frederick Douglass.* New York: Canal, 1984.

—— *My Bondage, My Freedom.* Urbana: University of Illinois Press, 1988.

Duberman, Martin. *The Antislavery Vanguard: New Essays on the Abolitionists.* Princeton, N.J.: Princeton University Press, 1965.

Lampe, Gregory P. *Frederick Douglass: Freedom's Voice, 1818–1845.* East Lansing: Michigan State University Press, 1998.

Levine, Robert S. *Martin Delany, Frederick Douglass, and the Politics of Representative Identity.* Chapel Hill: University of North Carolina Press, 1997.

Martin, Waldo. *The Mind of Frederick Douglass.* Chapel Hill: University of North Carolina Press, 1986.

five

The American Negro and His Fatherland

Henry McNeal Turner (1834–1915) was a clergyman, activist, and author. In his famous speech, "The American Negro and His Fatherland," Turner articulated his support for colonization, which he believed was the only way African Americans could escape the racist oppression they faced in the United States. The speech solidified Turner's reputation as an ardent black nationalist, and in the early 1890s he actually took two shiploads of black Americans to Liberia. However, his relocation plan fared badly, and Turner's role as a spokesperson was further eclipsed in the wake of Booker T. Washington's 1895 Atlanta Exposition speech.

Turner was born to a family of free blacks in South Carolina in 1834, and as a teenager he became an itinerant minister. During the 1850s, he preached to African Americans all across the deep South, and in 1858 he joined the African Methodist Episcopal Church (AME). He studied several languages and was trained in theology at Trinity College. He then became a pastor of the Union Bethel Church in Washington, D.C., and during the Civil War he was a chaplain for black soldiers, whom he often accompanied into battle. After the war, he was elected to the Georgia state legislature, but white lawmakers quickly passed a bill that made it illegal for African Americans to hold elective office. In 1876 he was elected president of the American Colonization Society. In 1880, Turner became a bishop in the AME. When he died in 1915, his funeral was attended by some 25,000 mourners.

It would be a waste of time to expend much labor, the few moments I have to devote to this subject, upon the present status of the Negroid race in the United States. It is too well-known already. However, I believe that the Negro was brought to this country in the providence of God to a heaven-permitted if not a divine-sanctioned manual laboring school, that he might have direct contact with the mightiest race that ever trod the face of the globe.

The heathen Africans, to my certain knowledge, I care not what others may say, eagerly yearn for that civilization which they believe will elevate them and make them potential for good. The African was not sent and brought to this country by chance, or by the avarice of the white man, single and alone. The white slave-purchaser went to the shores of that continent and bought our ancestors from their African masters. The bulk who were brought to this country were the children of parents who had been in slavery a thousand years. Yet hereditary slavery is not universal among the African slaveholders. So that the argument often advanced, that the white man went to Africa and stole us, is not true. They bought us out of a slavery that still exists over a large portion of that continent. For there are millions and millions of slaves in Africa today. Thus the superior African sent us, and the white man brought us, and we remained in slavery as long as it was necessary to learn that a God, who is a spirit, made the world and controls it, and that that Supreme Being could be sought and found by the exercise of faith in His only begotten Son. Slavery then went down, and the colored man was thrown upon his own responsibility, and here he is today, in the providence of God, cultivating self-reliance and imbibing a knowledge of civil law in contradistinction to the dictum of one man, which was the law of the black man until slavery was overthrown. I believe that the Negroid race has been free long enough now to begin to think for himself and plan for better conditions than he can lay claim to in this country or ever will. *There is no manhood future in the United States for the Negro.* He may eke out an existence for generations to come, but he can never be a *man*—full, symmetrical and undwarfed. Upon this point I know thousands who make pretensions to scholarship, white and colored, will differ and may charge me with folly, while I in turn pity their ignorance of history and political and civil sociology. We beg here to itemize and give a cursory glance at a few facts calculated to convince any man who is not biased or lamentably ignorant. Let us note a few of them.

1. There is a great chasm between the white and black, not only in this country, but in the West India Islands, South America, and as much as has been said to the contrary, I have seen inklings of it in Ireland, in England, in

France, in Germany, and even away down in southern Spain in sight of Morocco in Africa. We will not, however, deal with foreign nations, but let us note a few facts connected with the United States.

I repeat that a great chasm exists between the two race varieties in this country. The white people, neither North or South, will have social contact as a mass between themselves and any portion of the Negroid race. Although they may be as white in appearance as themselves, yet a drop of African blood imparts a taint, and the talk about two races remaining in the same country with mutual interest and responsibility in its institutions and progress, with no social contact, is the jargon of folly, and no man who has read the history of nations and the development of countries, and the agencies which have culminated in the homogeneity of racial variations, will proclaim such a doctrine. Senator Morgan,[1] of Alabama, tells the truth when he says that the Negro has nothing to expect without social equality with the whites, and that the whites will never grant it.

This question must be examined and opinions reached in the light of history and sociological philosophy, and not by a mere think-so on the part of men devoid of learning. When I use the term learning, I do not refer to men who have graduated from some college and have a smattering knowledge of Greek, Latin, mathematics and a few school books, and have done nothing since but read the trashy articles of newspapers. That is not scholarship. Scholarship consists in wading through dusty volumes for forty and fifty years. That class of men would not dare to predict symmetrical manhood for the Negroid race in this or any other country, without social equality. The colored man who will stand up and in one breath say that the Negroid race does not want social equality and in the next predict a great future in the face of all the proscription of which the colored man is the victim, is either an ignoramus, or is an advocate of the perpetual servility and degradation of his race variety. I know, as Senator Morgan says, and as every white man in the land will say, that the whites will not grant social equality to the Negroid race, nor am I certain that God wants them to do it. And as such, I believe that two or three millions of us should return to the land of our ancestors, and establish our own nation, civilization, laws, customs, style of manufacture, and not only give the world, like other race varieties, the benefit of our individuality, but build up social conditions peculiarly our own, and cease to be grumblers, chronic complainers and a menace to the white man's country, or the country he claims and is bound to dominate.

The civil status of the Negro is simply what the white man grants of his own free will and accord. The black man can demand nothing. He is deposed from the jury and tried, convicted and sentenced by men who do not claim to be his peers. On the railroads, where the colored race is found in the largest numbers, he is the victim of proscription, and he must ride in the Jim Crow car or walk. The Supreme Court of the United States decided, October 15th,

1883, that the colored man had no civil rights under the general government, and the several States, from then until now, have been enacting laws which limit, curtail and deprive him of his civil rights, immunities and privileges, until he is now being disfranchised, and where it will end no one can divine.

They told me in the Geographical Institute in Paris, France, that according to their calculation there are not less than 400,000,000 of Africans and their descendants on the globe, so that we are not lacking in numbers to form a nationality of our own.

2. The environments of the Negroid race variety in this country tend to the inferiority of them, even if the argument can be established that we are equals with the white man in the aggregate, notwithstanding the same opportunities may be enjoyed in the schools. Let us note a few facts.

The discriminating laws, all will concede, are degrading to those against whom they operate, and the degrader will be degraded also. "For all acts are reactionary, and will return in curses upon those who curse," said Stephen A. Douglass,[2] the great competitor of President Lincoln.[3] Neither does it require a philosopher to inform you that degradation begets degradation. Any people oppressed, proscribed, belied, slandered, burned, flayed and lynched will not only become cowardly and servile, but will transmit that same servility to their posterity, and continue to do so *ad infinitum,* and as such will never make a bold and courageous people. The condition of the Negro in the United States is so repugnant to the instincts of respected manhood that thousands, yea hundreds of thousands, of miscegenated will pass for white, and snub the people with whom they are identified at every opportunity, thus destroying themselves, or at least *unracing* themselves. They do not want to be black because of its ignoble condition, and they cannot be white, thus they become monstrosities. Thousands of young men who are even educated by white teachers never have any respect for people of their own color and spend their days as devotees of white gods. Hundreds, if not thousands, of the terms employed by the white race in the English language are also degrading to the black man. Everything that is satanic, corrupt, base and infamous is denominated *black,* and all that constitutes virtue, purity, innocence, religion, and that which is divine and heavenly, is represented as *white.* Our Sabbath-school children, by the time they reach proper consciousness, are taught to sing to the laudation of white and to the contempt of black. Can any one with an ounce of common sense expect that these children, when they reach maturity, will ever have any respect for their black or colored faces, or the faces of their associates? But, without multiplying words, the terms used in our religious experience, and the hymns we sing in many instances, are degrading, and will be as long as the black man is surrounded by the idea that *white* represents God and black represents the devil. The Negro should, therefore, build up a nation of his own, and create a language in keeping with his color, as the whites have done. Nor will he ever respect himself until he does it.

3. In this country the colored man, with a few honorable exceptions, folds his arms and waits for the white man to propose, project, erect, invent, discover, combine, plan and execute everything connected with civilization, including machinery, finance, and indeed everything. This, in the nature of things, dwarfs the colored man and allows his great faculties to slumber from the cradle to the grave. Yet he possesses mechanical and inventive genius, I believe, equal to any race on earth. Much has been said about the natural inability of the colored race to engage in the professions of skilled labor. Yet before the war, right here in this Southland he erected and completed all of the fine edifices in which the lords of the land luxuriated. It is idle talk to speak of a colored man not being a success in skilled labor or the fine arts. What the black man needs is a country and surroundings in harmony with his color and with respect for his manhood. Upon this point I would delight to dwell longer if I had time. Thousands of white people in this country are ever and anon advising the colored people to keep out of politics, but they do not advise themselves. If the Negro is a man in keeping with other men, why should he be less concerned about politics than any one else? Strange, too, that a number of would-be colored leaders are ignorant and debased enough to proclaim the same foolish jargon. For the Negro to stay out of politics is to level himself with a horse or a cow, which is no politician, and the Negro who does it proclaims his inability to take part in political affairs. If the Negro is to be a man, full and complete, he must take part in everything that belongs to manhood. If he omits a single duty, responsibility or privilege, to that extent he is limited and incomplete.

Time, however, forbids my continuing the discussion of this subject, roughly and hastily as these thoughts have been thrown together. Not being able to present a dozen or two more phases, which I would cheerfully and gladly do if opportunity permitted, I conclude by saying the argument that it would be impossible to transport the colored people of the United States back to Africa is an advertisement of folly. Two hundred millions of dollars would rid this country of the last member of the Negroid race, if such a thing was desirable, and two hundred and fifty millions would give every man, woman and child excellent fare, and the general government could furnish that amount and never miss it, and that would only be the pitiful sum of a million dollars a year for the time we labored for nothing, and for which somebody or some power is responsible. The emigrant agents at New York, Boston, Philadelphia, St. John, N.B., and Halifax, N.S., with whom I have talked, establish beyond contradiction, that over a million, and from that to twelve hundred thousand persons, come to this country every year, and yet there is no public stir about it. But in the case of African emigration, two or three millions only of self-reliant men and women would be necessary to establish the conditions we are advocating in Africa.

Notes

1. John Tyler Morgan (1824–1907), senator of Alabama.
2. Stephen A. Douglass (1813–1861), American statesman.
3. Abraham Lincoln (1809–1865), fifteenth president of the United States (1861–1865).

Source

Henry McNeal Turner, "The American Negro and his Fatherland" (1856; reprinted in William Jeremiah Moses, *Classical Black Nationalism: From the American Revolution to Marcus Garvey,* 221–27 [New York: New York University Press, 1990]).

Selected Bibliography

Angell, Stephen W. *Bishop Henry McNeal Turner and African-American Religion in the South.* Knoxville: University of Tennessee Press, 1992.

Drago, Edmund L. *Black Politicians and Reconstruction in Georgia: A Splendid Future.* Baton Rouge: Louisiana State University Press, 1982.

Wilmore, Gayraud S. *Black Religion and Black Radicalism: An Interpretation of the Religious History of Afro-American People.* Maryknoll, N.Y.: Orbis Books, 1998.

six

Declaration of the Rights of Negro Peoples of the World

A committed black nationalist, Marcus Garvey (1887–1940) was one of the most influential black leaders of the twentieth century. Garvey's "Declaration of the Rights of Negro Peoples of the World" is a classic Pan-Africanist document that suggested that all blacks have a common cultural and political identification with Africa and should be united as a result. As the Black Power movement took hold during the 1960s, these notions were revived, and today Garvey is widely recognized as a forefather of Pan-Africanism.

Garvey was born in St. Ann's Bay, Jamaica, in 1887. In London, he wrote for a militant publication called *African Times and Orient Review,* and in 1914 he founded the United Negro Improvement Association (UNIA) in Jamaica, adopting the motto of "One God! One Aim! One Destiny!" In 1920 he led a massive parade down Lenox Avenue in Harlem, and he drew 25,000 African Americans to Madison Square Garden for the first UNIA convention. He was involved in several business ventures, including the Black Star Shipping Line, which was poorly managed and was investigated by the federal government. After being imprisoned for fraud in 1923, he was deported to Jamaica in 1927. Although the UNIA continued, it never again amassed a substantial membership. Many of his subsequent political efforts were ineffectual, and he died of a stroke in 1940.

Be it resolved. That the negro people of the world, through their chosen representatives in convention assembled in Liberty Hall, in the City of New York and United States of America, from August 1 to August 31, in the year of our Lord, one thousand nine hundred and twenty, protest against the wrongs and injustices they are suffering at the hands of their white brethren, and state what they deem their fair and just rights, as well as the treatment they propose to demand of all men in the future.

We complain:

I. That nowhere in the world, with few exceptions, are black men accorded equal treatment with white men, although in the same situation and circumstances, but on the contrary, are discriminated against and denied the common rights due to human beings for no other reason than their race and color.

We are not willingly accepted as guests in the public hotels and inns of the world for no other reason than our race and color.

II. In certain parts of the United States of America our race is denied the right of public trial accorded to other races when accused of crime, but are lynched and burned by mobs, and such brutal and inhuman treatment is even practised upon our women.

III. That European nations have parcelled out among them and taken possession of nearly all of the continent of Africa, and the natives are compelled to surrender their lands to aliens and are treated in most instances like slaves.

IV. In the southern portion of the United States of America, although citizens under the Federal Constitution, and in some states almost equal to the whites in population and are qualified land owners and taxpayers, we are, nevertheless, denied all voice in the making and administration of the laws and are taxed without representation by the state governments, and at the same time compelled to do military service in defense of the country.

V. On the public conveyances and common carriers in the Southern portion of the United States we are jim-crowed and compelled to accept separate and inferior accommodations, and made to pay the same fare charged for first-class accommodations, and our families are often humiliated and insulted by drunken white men who habitually pass through the jim-crow cars going to the smoking car.

VI. The physicians of our race are denied the right to attend their patients while in the public hospitals of the cities and states where they reside in certain parts of the United States.

Our children are forced to attend inferior separate schools for shorter terms than white children and the public school funds are unequally divided between the white and colored schools.

VII. We are discriminated against and denied an equal chance to earn wages for the support of our families, and in many instances are refused admission into labor unions, and nearly everywhere are paid smaller wages than white men.

VIII. In Civil Service and departmental offices we are everywhere discriminated against and made to feel that to be a black man in Europe, America, and the West Indies is equivalent to being an outcast and a leper among the races of men, no matter what the character and attainments of the black man may be.

IX. In the British and other West Indian Islands and colonies, Negroes are secretly and cunningly discriminated against, and denied those fuller rights of government to which white citizens are appointed, nominated and elected.

X. That our people in those parts are forced to work for lower wages than the average standard of white men and are kept in conditions repugnant to good civilized tastes and customs.

XI. That the many acts of injustice against members of our race before the courts of law in the respective islands and colonies are of such nature as to create disgust and disrespect for the white man's sense of justice.

XII. Against all such inhuman, unchristian and uncivilized treatment we here and now emphatically protest, and invoke the condemnation of all mankind.

In order to encourage our race all over the world and to stimulate it to a higher and grander destiny, we demand and insist on the following Declaration of Rights:

1. Be it known to all men that whereas, all men are created equal and entitled to the rights of life, liberty and the pursuit of happiness, and because of this we, the duly elected representatives of the Negro peoples of the world, invoking the aid of the just and Almighty God do declare all men, women and children of our blood throughout the world free citizens, and do claim them as free citizens of Africa, the Motherland of all Negroes.
2. That we believe in the supreme authority of our race in all things racial; that all things are created and given to man as a common possession; that there should be an equitable distribution and apportionment of all such things, and in consideration of the fact that as a race we are now deprived of those things that are morally and legally ours, we believe it right that all such things should be acquired and held by whatsoever means possible.
3. That we believe the Negro, like any other race, should be governed by the ethics of civilization, and therefore, should not be deprived of any of those rights or privileges common to other human beings.
4. We declare that Negroes, wheresoever they form a community among themselves, should be given the right to elect their own representatives to represent them in legislatures, courts of law, or such institutions as may exercise control over the particular community.
5. We assert that the Negro is entitled to even-handed justice before all courts of law and equity in whatever country he may be found, and when this

is denied him on account of his race or color such denial is an insult to the race as a whole and should be resented by the entire body of Negroes.

6. We declare it unfair and prejudicial to the rights of Negroes in communities where they exist in considerable numbers to be tried by a judge and jury composed entirely of an alien race, but in all such cases members of our race are entitled to representation on the jury.
7. We believe that any law or practice that tends to deprive any African of his land or the privileges of free citizenship within his country is unjust and immoral, and no native should respect any such law or practice.
8. We declare taxation without representation unjust and tyrannous, and there should be no obligation on the part of the Negro to obey the levy of a tax by any law-making body from which he is excluded and denied representation on account of his race and color.
9. We believe that any law especially directed against the Negro to his detriment and singling him out because of his race or color is unfair and immoral, and should not be respected.
10. We believe all men entitled to common human respect, and that our race should in no way tolerate any insults that may be interpreted to mean disrespect to our color.
11. We deprecate the use of the term "nigger" as applied to Negroes, and demand that the word "Negro" be written with a capital "N."
12. We believe that the Negro should adopt every means to protect himself against barbarous practices inflicted upon him because of color.
13. We believe in the freedom of Africa for the Negro people of the world, and by the principle of Europe for the Europeans and Asia for the Asiatics, we also demand Africa for the Africans at home and abroad.
14. We believe in the inherent right of the Negro to possess himself of Africa, and that his possession of same shall not be regarded as an infringement on any claim or purchase made by any race or nation.
15. We strongly condemn the cupidity of those nations of the world who, by open aggression or secret schemes, have seized the territories and inexhaustible natural wealth of Africa, and we place on record our most solemn determination to reclaim the treasures and possession of the vast continent of our forefathers.
16. We believe all men should live in peace one with the other, but when races and nations provoke the ire of other races and nations by attempting to infringe upon their rights, war becomes inevitable, and the attempt in any way to free one's self or protect one's rights or heritage becomes justifiable.
17. Whereas, the lynching, by burning, hanging or any other means, of human beings is a barbarous practice, and a shame and disgrace to civilization, and we therefore declare any country guilty of such atrocities outside the pale of civilization.

18. We protest against the atrocious crime of whipping, flogging and overworking the native tribes of Africa and Negroes everywhere. These are methods that should be abolished, and all means should be taken to prevent a continuance of such brutal practices.
19. We protest against the atrocious practice of shaving the heads of Africans, especially of African women or individuals of Negro blood, when placed in prison as a punishment for crime by an alien race.
20. We protest against segregated districts, separate public conveyances, industrial discrimination, lynchings and limitations of political privileges of any Negro citizen in any part of the world on account of race, color or creed, and will exert our full influence and power against all such.
21. We protest against any punishment, inflicted upon a Negro with severity, as against lighter punishment inflicted upon another of an alien race for like offense, as an act of prejudice and injustice, and should be resented by the entire race.
22. We protest against the system of education in any country where Negroes are denied the same privileges and advantages as other races.
23. We declare it inhuman and unfair to boycott Negroes from industries and labor in any part of the world.
24. We believe in the doctrine of the freedom of the press, and we therefore emphatically protest against the suppression of Negro newspapers and periodicals in various parts of the world, and call upon Negroes everywhere to employ all available means to prevent such suppression.
25. We further demand free speech universally for all men.
26. We hereby protest against the publication of scandalous and inflammatory articles by an alien press tending to create racial strife and the exhibition of picture films showing the Negro as a cannibal.
27. We believe in the self-determination of all peoples.
28. We declare for the freedom of religious worship.
29. With the help of Almighty God, we declare ourselves the sworn protectors of the honor and virtue of our women and children, and pledge our lives for their protection and defense everywhere, and under all circumstances from wrongs and outrages.
30. We demand the right of unlimited and unprejudiced education for ourselves and our posterity forever.
31. We declare that the teaching in any school by alien teachers to our boys and girls, that the alien race is superior to the Negro race, is an insult to the Negro people of the world.
32. Where Negroes form a part of the citizenry of any country, and pass the civil service examination of such country, we declare them entitled to the same consideration as other citizens as to appointments in such civil service.

33. We vigorously protest against the increasingly unfair and unjust treatment accorded Negro travellers on land and sea by the agents and employees of railroad and steamship companies and insist that for equal fare we receive equal privileges with travellers of other races.
34. We declare it unjust for any country, state or nation to enact laws tending to hinder and obstruct the free immigration of Negroes on account of their race and color.
35. That the right of the Negro to travel unmolested throughout the world be not abridged by any person or persons, and all Negroes are called upon to give aid to fellow Negro when thus molested.
36. We declare that all Negroes are entitled to the same right to travel over the world as other men.
37. We hereby demand that the governments of the world recognize our leader and his representatives chosen by the race to look after the welfare of our people under such governments.
38. We demand complete control of our social institutions without interference by any alien race or races.
39. That the colors, Red, Black and Green, be the colors of the Negro race.
40. Resolved, that the anthem "Ethiopia, Thou Land of Our Fathers," etc., shall be the anthem of the Negro race.

The Universal Ethiopian Anthem

(poem by Burrell and Ford)

Ethiopia, thou land of our fathers,
Thou land where the gods loved to be,
As storm cloud at night suddenly gathers
Our armies come rushing to thee.
We must in the fight be victorious
When swords are thrust outward to gleam;
For us will the vict'ry be glorious
When led by the red, black and green.

Chorus:
Advance, advance to victory,
Let Africa be free;
Advance to meet the foe
With the might
Of the red, the black and the green.

II

Ethiopia, the tyrant's falling,
Who smote thee upon thy knees,
And thy children are lustily calling
From over the distant seas.
Jehovah, the Great One has heard us,
Has noted our sighs and our tears,
With His spirit of Love He has stirred us
To be One through the coming years.

CHORUS: Advance, advance, etc.

III

O Jehovah, thou God of the Ages
Grant unto our sons that lead
The wisdom Thou gave to Thy sages
When Israel was sore in need.
Thy voice thro' the dim past has spoken,
Ethiopia shall stretch forth her hand,
By Thee shall all fetters be broken,
And Heav'n bless our dear fatherland.

CHORUS: Advance, advance, etc.

41. We believe that any limited liberty which deprives one of the complete rights and prerogatives of full citizenship is but a modified form of slavery.
42. We declare it an injustice to our people and a serious impediment to the health of the race to deny to competent licensed Negro physicians the right to practice in the public hospitals of the communities in which they reside for no other reason than their race and color.
43. We call upon the various governments of the world to accept and acknowledge Negro representatives who shall be sent to the said governments to represent the general welfare of the Negro peoples of the world.
44. We deplore and protest against the practice of confining juvenile prisoners in prisons with adults, and we recommend that such youthful prisons be taught gainful trades under humane supervision.
45. Be it further resolved, that we as a race of people declare the League of Nations null and void as far as the Negro is concerned, in that it seeks to deprive Negroes of their liberty.

46. We demand of all men to do unto us as we would do unto them, in the name of justice; and we cheerfully accord to all men all the rights we claim herein for ourselves.
47. We declare that no Negro shall engage himself in battle for an alien race without first obtaining the consent of the leader of the Negro people of the world, except in a matter of national self-defense.
48. We protest against the practice of drafting Negroes and sending them to war with alien forces without proper training, and demand in all cases that Negro soldiers be given the same training as the aliens.
49. We demand that instructions given Negro children in schools include the subject of "Negro History," to their benefit.
50. We demand a free and unfettered commercial intercourse with all the Negro people of the world.
51. We declare for the absolute freedom of the seas for all peoples.
52. We demand that our daily accredited representatives be given proper recognition in all leagues, conferences, conventions or courts of international arbitration wherever human rights are discussed.
53. We proclaim the 31st day of August of each year to be an international holiday to be observed by all Negroes.
54. We want all men to know we shall maintain and contend for the freedom and equality of every man, woman and child of our race, with our lives, our fortunes and our sacred honor.

These rights we believe to be justly ours and proper for the protection of the Negro race at large, and because of this belief, we, on behalf of the four hundred million Negroes of the world, do pledge herein the sacred blood of the race in defense, and we hereby subscribe our names as a guarantee of the truthfulness and faithfulness hereof in the presence of Almighty God, on the 13th day of August, in the year of our Lord one thousand nine hundred and twenty.

—Issued at the First International Convention of the Universal Negro Improvement Association, New York City, 1920

Note

1. In the nineteenth century, Ethiopia was commonly understood as a synonym for "black Africa."

Source

Marcus Garvey, "Declaration of the Rights of Negro Peoples of the World" (1925; reprinted in Deirdre Mullane, ed., *Crossing the Danger Water: Three Hundred Years of African-American Writing,* 128–31 [New York: Anchor Books, 1993]).

Selected Bibliography

Cronon, Edmund David. *Black Moses: The Story of Marcus Garvey and the Universal Negro Improvement Association.* Madison: University of Wisconsin Press, 1969.

Irvin, Jeannette Smith. *Footsoldiers of the United Negro Improvement Association.* Trentonville, N.J.: African World Press, 1989.

Lewis, Rupert. *Marcus Garvey: Anti-Colonial Champion.* Lawrenceville: African World Press, 1988.

Martin, Tony. *Race First: The Ideological and Organizational Struggles of Marcus Garvey and the United Negro Improvement Association.* Dover, Mass.: Majority Press, 1986.

Stein, Judith. *The World of Marcus Garvey: Race and Class in Modern Society.* Baton Rouge: Louisiana State University Press, 1986.

seven

Heritage

In the 1920s, Countee Cullen (1903–1946) was perhaps the most famous black writer in America. Unlike many of the Harlem Renaissance poets, who utilized the rhythms of jazz or modern free verse style, Cullen was greatly influenced by European forms, the works of classical antiquity, and Biblical imagery—all of which are on display in his 1925 poem "Heritage," reprinted here. But even though Cullen generally tried to transcend the boundaries of race, this poem reveals that like many other African American writers, he still grappled with the meaning of his African heritage.

Cullen was born Countee Leroy Porter, probably in Louisville, Kentucky. He attended the prestigious DeWitt Clinton High School, and after graduating in 1922 he attended New York University. In college, he began a distinguished career as a poet, publishing in the leading periodicals of his time. His first collection of poems, *Color* (1925), was widely acclaimed, and later that year he entered Harvard University, where he earned an M.A. in 1926. He was briefly married to Yolanda Du Bois (W. E. B. Du Bois's daughter), and he studied French literature at the Sorbonne. Subsequent works, such as *The Black Christ and Other Poems* (1930) and the novel *One Way to Heaven* (1932), were less well received. Cullen died in New York City in 1946.

What is Africa to me:
Copper sun or scarlet sea,
Jungle star or jungle track,
Strong bronzed men, or regal black
Women from whose loins I sprang
When the birds of Eden sang?
One three centuries removed
From the scenes his fathers loved,
Spicy grove, cinnamon tree,
What is Africa to me?

So I lie, who all day long
Want no sound except the song
Sung by wild barbaric birds
Goading massive jungle herds,
Juggernauts of flesh that pass
Trampling tall defiant grass
Where young forest lovers lie
Plighting troth beneath the sky.
So I lie, who always hear
Though I cram against my ear
Both my thumbs, and keep them there,
Great drums throbbing through the air.
So I lie, whose fount of pride,
Dear distress, and joy allied,
Is my somber flesh and skin,
With the dark blood dammed within
Like great pulsing tides of wine
That, I fear, must burst the fine
Channels of the chafing net
Where they surge and foam and fret.

Africa? A book one thumbs
Listlessly, till slumber comes.
Unremembered are her bats
Circling through the night, her cats
Crouching in the river reeds,
Stalking gentle flesh that feeds
By the river brink; no more
Does the bugle-throated roar
Cry that monarch claws have leapt
From the scabbards where they slept.

Silver snakes that once a year
Doff the lovely coats you wear,
Seek no covert in your fear.
Lest a mortal eye should see;
What's your nakedness to me?
Here no leprous flowers rear
Fierce corollas in the air;
Here no bodies sleek and wet,
Dripping mingled rain and sweat,
Tread the savage measures of
Jungle boys and girls in love.
What is last year's snow to me,
Last year's anything? The tree
Budding yearly must forget
How its past arose or set—
Bough and blossom, flower, fruit,
Even what shy bird with mute
Wonder at her travail there,
Meekly labored in its hair.
One three centuries removed
From the scenes his fathers loved,
Spicy grove, cinnamon tree,
What is Africa to me?

So I lie, who find no peace
Night or day, no slight release
From the unremittant beat
Made by cruel padded feet
Walking through my body's street.
Up and down they go, and back,
Treading out a jungle track.
So I lie, who never quite
Safely sleep from rain at night—
I can never rest at all
When the rain begins to fall;
Like a soul gone mad with pain
I must match its weird refrain;
Ever must I twist and squirm,
Writhing like a baited worm,
While its primal measures drip
Through my body, crying, "Strip!
Doff this new exuberance.

Come and dance the Lover's Dance!"
In an old remembered way
Rain works on me night and day.

Quaint, outlandish heathen gods.
Black men fashion out of rods,
Clay, and brittle bits of stone,
In a likeness like their own,
My conversion came high-priced;
I belong to Jesus Christ,
Preacher of humility;
Heathen gods are naught to me.

Father, Son, and Holy Ghost,
So I make an idle boast;
Jesus of the twice-turned cheek,
Lamb of God, although I speak
With my mouth thus, in my heart
Do I play a double part.
Ever at Thy glowing altar
Must my heart grow sick and falter,
Wishing He I served were black,
Thinking then it would not lack
Precedent of pain to guide it.
Let who would or might deride it;
Surely then this flesh would know
Yours had borne a kindred woe.
Lord, I fashion dark gods, too,
Daring even to give You
Dark despairing features where,
Crowned with dark rebellious hair,
Patience wavers just so much as
Mortal grief compels, while touches
Quick and hot, of anger, rise
To Smitten check and weary eyes.
Lord, forgive me if my need
Sometimes shapes a human creed.

All day long and all night though.
One thing only must I do:
Quench my pride and cool my blood,
Lest I perish in the flood.

Lest a hidden ember set
Timber that I thought was wet
Burning like the dryest flax,
Melting like the merest wax,
Lest the grave restore its dead.
Not yet has my heart or head
In the least way realized
They and I are civilized.

Source

Countee Cullen, *Color* (New York: Harper & Brothers, 1925), 222–26.

Selected Bibliography

Baker, Houston. *Afro-American Poetics: Revisions of Harlem and the Black Aesthetic.* Madison: University of Wisconsin Press, 1988.

Cullen, Countee, ed. *Caroling Dusk: An Anthology of Verse by Negro Poets.* New York: Carol, 1993.

—— *Color.* New York: Harper & Brothers, 1925.

Ferguson, Blanche E. *Countee Cullen and the Negro Renaissance.* New York: Dodd, 1966.

Lewis, David Levering. *When Harlem Was in Vogue.* New York: Oxford University Press, 1981.

Redding, Saunders J. *To Make a Poet Black.* Ithaca, N.Y.: Cornell University Press, 1986.

eight

Writings by Paul Robeson

Paul Robeson (1898–1976) was one of the most talented and highly celebrated African Americans in history. His editorial "Africa Calls—Will You Help?" demonstrated his commitment to anticolonialism as well as his awareness that the struggle for black liberation in Africa was closely related to the campaign for civil rights in the United States. However, Robeson's praise for the U.S.S.R.'s attempts to redress racial discrimination and prejudice—on display in the speech "The Negro People and the Soviet Union"—caused him to be branded as un-American in the media, to have his concerts boycotted, to be denounced by the NAACP, and to be harassed by the federal government. (However, "Africa Calls—Will You Help?" shows that Robeson's interest in world affairs transcended his identification with the Soviet Union.)

Born in Princeton, New Jersey, in 1898, Robeson was an All-American running back at Rutgers University, where he graduated at the top of his class in 1919. He then attended Columbia Law School and briefly became a lawyer before he pursued his real loves of singing and acting in the early 1920s. In 1930 he earned his reputation as one of the great Shakespearean actors when he played the part of the Moor in Shakespeare's *Othello*. Although he was well paid and praised by critics, Robeson also experienced a great deal of racism during his career as a performer. In the 1930s, he began to move toward political activism. Although Robeson championed such causes as South African Famine Relief and an antilynching law in the United States, he is best known for his statements in support of the Soviet Union, a nation that he believed was far ahead of the United States in its support of equality and democracy. In retaliation, the U.S. government helped to destroy his career by denying him permission to travel abroad. He died in 1976.

Africa Calls—Will You Help?

"Here's My Story," Freedom, *May 1953*

It must be tough to be a believer in "white supremacy" these days. As never before the ruling forces have to deal with the longings, aspirations and the struggle of the colored peoples of the earth for freedom; for their complete liberation and self-determination, the assuming of full control over their own destinies. Some folks still try to blink their eyes, run away from the facts and convince themselves that things are just as they were in the days of Kipling's "white man's burden."[1] But, to paraphrase Joe Louis,[1] "They may run, but they can't hide." The area of conflict stretches wide—Asia, the West Indies, Latin America; and, high in the headlines are Indo-China and Africa. It includes—and not the least important—Alabama, Georgia, Mississippi, Arkansas, and fanning out from Washington, North, East and West in these United States of ours.

The signs have long been clear that so-called "colonial" peoples, mostly colored, were moving toward some measure of freedom.

Of all developments, the change in China has been the most significant. The overlords have gone, and forever. These are about 500 million people. Bound to them in centuries-old ties are 400 million in India; and some day as of yore the Japanese must make their common future with the Chinese.

These lands are going forward under their own leaders, allying themselves with those who are their real friends; the states where the working masses have taken over their own destiny in the East European and European world.

And what about our responsibilities to Africa? I move about in many cities among many sections of our folk, and they're deeply interested—to put it mildly—in Africa.

---

1. Rudyard Kipling (1865–1936), British novelist, short-story writer, and poet. His major works celebrated British imperialism, which he hailed as bringing civilization to the backward peoples of Africa and Asia thereby carrying the "white man's burden."

Kenyatta's[2] name is on everyone's tongue, and what's going on in South Africa is of immediate concern. And of course the advancements made in Gold Coast and Nigeria are closely watched.

Tomorrow we'll know more about French West Africa where the urge for a freer life moves on at a fast pace. We'll know of Gabriel D'Arboussier[2] and the organization he heads of roughly a million members, influencing millions more. They work in close alliance with the strong working class of France, a working class of differing political faiths.

As for South Africa, I see it's gradually becoming clear that Malan[3] is not doing all that evil by himself. In the barber shop the other day I heard some fellows remarking that the *Wall Street Journal* had said: "Not moral, but investment, interests concern America in South Africa."

My barber shop acquaintance went on to say, "Man, these folks here have a lot of dough sunk over there in gold, copper, uranium. They want to protect it—that's the reason you don't hear any real squawk coming from here about Malan." And of course the man was right. Even in the United Nations our delegation has avoided this South African issue like poison.

And now comes Max Yergan[4] with an article in *U.S. News and World Report.*[3] If one did not know that Yergan was a Negro (no insult intended to my folk—I'm just stating the hard fact of life!) he would have to assume that the article was written by a white State Department mouthpiece assigned to working out a formula for maintaining white rule throughout Africa.

Yergan says: "The issue is: How can the whites in Africa be relieved of their fear? How can they have a sense of security living on a little island in the midst of this *great black sea?"* (My emphasis.)

Can you imagine! Now, we know how the British used the Indian princes against the Indian people, and others like Aga Khan (father of Ali Khan) in Persia. It's that old technique of pitting the Big House servants against the folks in the hard-labor fields.

---

2. Gabriel D'Arboussier was the Marxist leader of the Réassemblement Démocratique Africain in the Ivory Coast. He was displaced by the conservative pro-French Felix Houghouet Boigny.

3. The article was actually an interview with Dr. Max Yergan who was described by the *U.S. News & World Report* as "America's Foremost Authority on Africa." It was entitled, "Africa: Next Goal of Communists," and it was an apology for the South African government's Apartheid policies, defending the repression in that country on the ground that it was needed to eliminate Communist influence. "I think the Government is completely justified in its policy of suppressing Communist influence," Yergan told the interviewer. He added that "it is easy enough to criticize white South Africa . . . but any person in Europe or America who levels criticism against white South Africa has to ask himself what he would do under similar circumstances. The white population there is dominated by fear. . . ." Yergan ventured the prediction "that when all the other European powers are out of Africa, the Portuguese would still be there," and praised the Portuguese for drawing "no social lines." (May 1, 1953, pp. 52–63.)

Well, maybe the British, French, and now the American ruling groups, the officialdom, have an idea they can do that to Africans? And do it to the Africans through American Negroes like Yergan and a few others of his ilk.

When Yergan was in South Africa an African paper pointed out that he stayed at a very special hotel ("for Europeans only") and conferenced only with the Malan forces. Of course the article in *U.S. News and World Report* makes his role clear. I imagine he'd better be mighty careful where he lights on African soil again.

American Negroes have a real duty to our African brothers and sisters, a sacred duty. Yergan calls it merely a "sentimental interest" but Negroes who have not lost all pride and dignity know that if we are at all serious about our full freedom here in American we must understand what the future of Africa means.

The Indian people understand it. One of the leaders of the Kikuyu, a close associate of Kenyatta, is now in India and Nehru[5] himself has spoken out about the necessity of supporting the African and Indian people in South and East Africa.

Can we here in America fail to bring pressure upon the corporations involved, not to sabotage the African struggle? Can we fail to point the finger at Malan? Should we not do all in our power to help the people there, speaking out in their behalf, raising funds to send them, letting them know that we are on their side?

Now I know that, being a people like any other, many of us approach problems in different ways. So, in whatever way various groups or leaders see fit, should we not all come at once to the side of the African people?

Should we not arouse the youth in the universities? Should we not swing our churches, fraternal bodies, professional groups, women's organizations and civic clubs into action. Who will go before the great labor organizations (CIO,[6] AFL[7] and independent) and call for actions of solidarity with the terribly exploited African workers? Will the NAACP[8] leap into the struggle with all its resources?

Not only is this a struggle in the interests of the African people. Their freedom and dignity will be of immeasurable assistance in our final break-through here in these United States. New Africa will mean in the end a new Alabama, a new Mississippi, Arkansas, Georgia, a new Washington, D.C. for us.

African liberation calls for assistance. Our leadership is weighed in the balance. I'm confident it will not be found wanting.

The Negro People and the Soviet Union

I am deeply grateful for this opportunity to join more than half the people of the world in celebrating a great anniversary.[1] Yes, with fully half of human-

---

In the notice "About the Author," New Century Publishers, which published Robeson's speech as a pamphlet, wrote: "Paul Robeson is one of the foremost leaders of the Negro people and a concert artist of great renown. He has been chairman of the Council on African Affairs since the formation of that vital organization 12 years ago. In the summer

ity—and even this is an underestimation. For it would be a mistake to assume that this 32nd anniversary of the Union of Soviet Socialist Republics is an occasion of joy and pride and thanks-giving only for the eight hundred million people who live in the Soviet Union and the People's Democracies of Eastern Europe and China.

True, these eight hundred million, as *direct* beneficiaries of the establishment of the Soviet Union and of its policies of struggle for peace and democracy, are rejoicing because of the new economic security and political liberty, the new promise of a fuller and richer life for all, which they enjoy because they live in the Soviet land or in countries of the People's Democracies. The feelings of all these people must be very like those of the President of the Chinese People's Republic, Mao Tse-tung.[2]

"If the Soviet Union did not exist," Mao wrote, "if there had been no victory in the anti-fascist second World War, if . . . Japanese imperialism had not been defeated, if the various new democracies of Europe had not come into being, if there were no rising struggle of the masses of the people in the United States, Britain, France, Germany, Italy, Japan and other capitalist countries against the reactionary cliques ruling over them, if this sum-total of factors did not exist, then the pressure of the international-reactionary forces upon us would surely be far greater than at present. Could we have been victorious under such circumstances? Certainly not."

That is the way Mao explains how much the liberation of China is indebted to the decisive influence of the Soviet Union in international affairs. And so with the Romanians and Bulgarians, the Hungarians and Albanians, the Czechs and the Polish people. It is because of this sum-total of factors that they today are the masters of their own lands—a sum-total which means that the world balance of power has shifted in favor of the forces of peace and democracy. And this portentous transformation, which has occurred within three decades, stems mainly from the mighty impact of the events of November 7, 1917.

I traveled recently in Western Europe and Scandinavia, and I know from what I saw and heard in those countries, that there, too, the peoples are able to struggle against the total colonization of their countries by Wall Street prin-

of 1949 he returned from a four-month speaking and concert tour which took this beloved spokesman of the Negro people to eight countries of Europe, including the Soviet Union. While in Europe he participated as an honored guest in the celebration of the Pushkin centennial anniversary in Moscow, and in the World Peace Congress in Paris. A world-wide storm of indignation greeted the storm-troop attacks upon him in Peeskill, N.Y."

The speech was translated into Spanish and published in Cuba in the magazine *Fundamentos,* Año X, No. 102, pp. 901–7. This was the journal of the Communist Party in Cuba.

2. Mao Tse-tung (1893–1976), principal Chinese Communist leader, who led his nation's revolution that defeated the forces of Chiang Kai-Shek and established the People's Republic of China in October 1949.

cipally because of this new balance of power. And if the Viet Namese and the Indonesians, if the Burmese and Malay people, indeed, if the people of long-suffering India have advanced to a higher stage of struggle for their independence, it is because of this sum-total of factors and the decisive influence of the Soviet Union.

We of the Council on African Affairs know well, also, that the people of Africa and the West Indies understand who are their real friends in the council of nations. Yes, the Nigerians who only yesterday were told by Creech-Jones of the British Empire that their demand for full self-rule could not be granted because they were not ready—these Nigerians know very well that the peoples in the Asian republics of the Soviet Union less than three decades ago stood on the same cultural and political level as they; yet, in a single generation these so-called "backward" peoples have been able to take their place as free, independent peoples with their own industries and their own culture.

Yes, all Africa remembers that it was Litvinov who stood alone beside Haile Selassie in Geneva,[3] when Mussolini's sons flew with the blessings of the Pope to drop bombs on Ethiopian women and children. Africa remembers that it was the Soviet Union which fought the attempt of Smuts to annex Southwest Africa to the slave reservations of the Union of South Africa. Africa knows it was the Soviet Union who demanded at San Francisco that the Charter of the United Nations contain a guarantee of self-government for the peoples of so-called "trust" territories. And is it not the struggle of the Soviet Union today which prevents the former Italian colonies from being slave-warrens and military bases for Britain and the United States?

Certainly, the changed balance of power in the world today favors the liberation struggles of the African and West Indian peoples. And if the people of Tanganyika and Kenya are not content with the benevolent schemes for turning their land into mass peanut plantations; if the Africans of Rhodesia rebel against the theft of their copper and the exploitation of their labor; if the Bantus and the slave-pens of the Union of South Africa grow more defiant of the pass laws and the forced-labor system; if the peoples of the Congo refuse to mine the uranium for the atom bombs made in Jim-Crow factories in the United States; if all these peoples demand an end to floggings, an end to the farce of "trusteeship" in the former Italian colonies and all other colonies, an end to colonial exploitation schemes hidden beneath humanitarian pretenses; and if the people of the West Indies press for some move leading to independence—to federation in the interests of the West Indian people and not of absentee landlords—as in Truman's

3. Haile Selassie (1892–1975), emperor of Ethiopia who led the resistance to the invading Italian fascist forces but was forced into exile in 1936. He was reinstated as emperor in 1941.

Maxim Litvinov (1876–1951), first Soviet Ambassador to the United States and leader of the Soviet delegation to the League of Nations.

"Point Four"[4] program—if, in a word, the peoples of Africa and the West Indies now shout their demands for self-determination to the entire world, is it not because they have a mighty friend and champion who by example and repeated challenge has proved this friendship?

No, despite all the censorship and repression, the word has gotten around.

The Soviet Union is the friend of the African and West Indian peoples. And no imperialist wolf disguised as a benevolent watchdog, and not Tito[9] disguised as a revolutionary, can convince them that Moscow oppresses the small nations. Africa knows the Soviet Union is the defender and champion of the rights of all nations—large and small—to control their own destinies.

The Soviet Socialist program of ethnic and national democracy is precisely the opposite of the Nazi, fascist, South African and Dixiecrat programs of racial superiority. One of Africa's foremost leaders, Gabriel D'Arboussier, Vice-President of the African Democratic Union in France's African colonies below the Sahara, leader of an organization, millions strong—representing 21,000,000 Africans, has said this:

"All the anger of the reactionaries directed against the Soviet Union is also directed in other forms against the colonial peoples. The latter have learned, thanks to these reactionaries, that there is a natural alliance between the country of socialism and the oppressed people the world over."

But I have a deeply personal reason for speaking here tonight. And it is more than the fact that as an artist I know what Soviet culture means for the young artists of today, what great horizons of imagination and creativeness are being pushed back in the Soviet land. And it is more than the fact that I have many dear friends in the Soviet Union whom I met and grew to know during my visits there. I think the real reason I love the Soviet Union and why I can speak personally about it is because I am a Negro and an American.

Let me explain.

In America today the Negro people are the core of the struggle against war and fascism. Three hundred years of oppression and terror have brought my people to the forefront in this struggle.

There is no democracy for the masses of my people. The achievements of a few are no answer—in fact this is being used in reverse—to cover up the in-

4. The Point Four program was the U.S. policy of technical assistance and economic aid to underdeveloped countries, so named because it was the fourth point of President Harry F. Truman's 1949 inaugural address.

9. The Ober Law provided for fines and prison sentences for membership in "subversive organizations," and required a loyalty oath for public employment. It was held unconstitutional by the Maryland State Circuit Court on August 16, 1949. The law was again declared "unconstitutional and invalid" in September 1949, but the Maryland Court of Appeals reinstated the law in February 1950, and it was upheld by the U.S. Supreme Court in April 1951. The law was drawn up by Frank Ober, a Baltimore corporation lawyer and chairman of the state commission on subversive activities.

justices to our millions. The millions of Negroes who are denied the right to vote are mountainous testimony.

Unemployment is a constant specter. Thirty-one percent of the heads of Negro families in America earn less than $500 per year. An additional 44 percent earn between $500 and $1000 annually. This 75 percent of my people earn less than one-third of what is necessary to support a family of four.

We are the last hired and the first fired.

Seven-tenths of our farm people are landless, with cotton planted right up to their very doorstep. The overwhelming mass live in houses where the sky, the earth and the trees may be seen without going outside.

Five thousand Negroes have been lynched. Not one lyncher has been brought to justice. Not one lyncher has been made to pay for this horrible crime.

Maceo Snipes, a World War II veteran, went to vote in Taylor County, Alabama. One hour later he was killed on the doorstep of his home, within sight of his wife and children. His murderers walked away saying, "We told you not to vote." But the widow of Maceo Snipes told her children, "When you grow up, you'll vote too."[5]

Ninety Negroes have been lynched since President Truman began occupying the White House with promises of civil rights. The most horrible of the blood-lettings took place in Greenville, South Carolina, where 28 men stood in an American courtroom and admitted killing Willie Earle. Several owned to tying him up. Several others to pouring gasoline over his body. Still others to firing sixty shells into him from six feet away. Even others admitted setting matches to the gasoline, making a flaming pyre.[6]

They were all freed by the jury. And the federal government never intervened. The reason is clear. Tom Clark was the Attorney-General then, the same Attorney-General who later prosecuted any number of liberal thinkers and resorted to the worst kind of persecution and the most despicable use of our courts in indicting the 12 leaders of the Communist Party.

5. Maceo Snipes was dragged from his home in Taylor County, Georgia, and killed by four men on July 17, 1946, the night after he had voted (the only Negro to vote in that district) in the state primaries.

6. More brutal than even that of the lynching of Willie Earle was the torture-killing of John C. Jones, a 28-year-old war veteran and former Army corporal, near Minden, Louisiana, August 8, 1946. Jones, an oil refinery worker, was beaten by a mob, his hands were cut off, and a blow-torch was held to his face. He died in the arms of Albert Harris, his 17-year-old companion, who had also been beaten and left for dead. The U.S. Department of Justice ordered a federal grand jury inquiry and six men—the Minden police chief, two deputy sheriffs and three others—were indicted for the lynching. One of the sheriffs was later released. Despite the testimony of Albert Harris, the other five were acquitted by an all-white jury on March 1, 1947.

The Negro people know that they can expect no answer from American imperialism. American imperialism cannot relinquish its Jim-Crow terror while it pursues its Marshall Plans[10] and Atlantic Pacts[11] and its drive toward war.

But there is another side to this miserable picture. A hopeful side. It is the rising militancy of the Negro people's struggle for land, equality and freedom. In meetings that I have had throughout the country with tens of thousands, this rising militancy has shown itself under a new leadership, a leadership made up of Negro trade unionists, veterans, working women and youth, ministers of our churches, fraternal leaders and others. This rising militancy has emerged as the core of unity with many groups, with the Jewish people, with trade unions and the foreign born.

On my southern tour for Henry Wallace,[12] I recall our stops in Memphis, Tennessee, where the fighting organization of the Mine, Mill and Smelter Workers joined hands with my people to guarantee that progressive thought and action could find a channel for expression.[7]

In Winston-Salem, North Carolina, I saw the tobacco workers.[8] I saw progressives and liberals like Larkin Marshall in Georgia, Mrs. Andrew Simkins of South Carolina, and Velma Hopkins—all fighters who are leading a valiant struggle for liberation.

It was during Peekskill that this unity was most sharply set forward. There, in Peekskill, trade unionists, Jewish people, foreign born, Negro and white, stood side by side, fighting off the fascist attack of gangs led by Dewey and Dulles,[13] the real source of force and violence.

I see this rising fighting temper of the Negro people as one of the important reasons for the granting of bail for the "eleven," for the defeat of the Ober Bill in Maryland.[9] Yes, it even forces Supreme Court Justice Jackson to proclaim the trial of Eugene Dennis as a "political" trial.

I have heard some honest and sincere people say to me, "Yes, Paul, we agree with you on everything you say about Jim Crow and persecution. We're with you one hundred percent on these things. But what has Russia ever done for us Negroes?" And in answering this question I feel that I go beyond my own personal feelings and put my finger on the very crux of what the Soviet Union means to me—a Negro and an American. For the answer is very simple and very clear: "Russia," I say, "the Soviet Union's very existence, its example before the world of abolishing all discrimination based on color or nationality,

7. The Mine, Mill and Smelter Workers, originally the Western Federation of Miners, was one of the eleven progressive unions expelled by the CIO.

8. The Food and Tobacco Workers were also one of the unions expelled by the CIO. For the role of the union among the black tobacco workers in Winston-Salem, North Carolina, and Robeson's contributions, see Philip S. Foner, Organized Labor and the Black Worker, 1619–1973, New York, 1974, reprinted in paperback, New York, 1976, pp. 282–83, 296.

its fight in every arena of world conflict for genuine democracy and for peace, this has given us Negroes the chance of achieving our complete liberation within our own time, within this generation."

For where, indeed, would the Negro people's struggle for freedom be today, if world imperialism had not been critically wounded and its forces weakened throughout the world? Where would the fight to vote in the South be today if this new balance of power in the world did not exist?

And I know that the growing unity of these great sections of the American people with the Negro people, the growing power of their struggle to save America from fascism, the very principle of solidarity in the teeth of the enemy owes its endurance and its force in the last analysis to that sum-total of factors which have transformed the world, that sum-total in which the example and might of the Soviet Union is decisive.

To every Negro mother who has her sons to comfort her, to every young Negro girl who looks forward to marriage, to every Negro youth who enters upon the threshold of this struggle with confidence, I say: "Where would your son be, where would your sweetheart be, where would YOU be, but for Stalingrad?" For in speaking of Stalingrad,[14] it was Roosevelt[15] who in a letter to Stalin spoke of how civilization had been saved by the battle of Stalingrad. And it was the Soviet people and the children who said, "Carry back my love to the Negro people, to the American people for we want peace and honest cooperation."

No one need be or can allow himself to be afraid of declaring himself for real friendship with the Soviet Union Republics and the People's Democracies. Today the real patriots of every nation are exactly those who work for friendship with these great nations.

Must we go back over the last three decades to document this fact? Has not the history of every country shown that it was precisely those who sowed hatred against the Soviet Union who proved to be the real traitors to their country? Was it not those who advocated and worked for friendship with the Soviet Union who proved to be the genuine patriots?

To those who dare to question my patriotism, who have the unmitigated insolence to question my love for the true America and my right to be an American—to question me, whose father and forefathers fertilized the very soil of this country with their toil and with their bodies—to such people I answer that those and *only* those who work for a policy of friendship with the Soviet Union are genuine American patriots. And all others who move toward a war that would destroy civilization, whether consciously or unconsciously, are betraying the interests of this country and the American people.

Finally, my friends, I want to say that I believe the great majority of the American people will come to realize their identity of interests with the people of the Soviet Union and the growing People's Democracies. In this era of change, normal trade relations and peaceful cooperation can be the only answer.

I am and always will be an anti-fascist and a fighter for the freedom and dignity of all men. We anti-fascists—the true lovers of American democracy—have a tremendous responsibility. We are not a small band—we are millions who believe in peace and friendship. If we mobilize with courage, the forces of world fascism can and will be defeated—in Europe, in Africa and in the United States.

Because of this, I am and always will be, a firm and true friend of the Soviet Union and of the beloved Soviet people.

Notes

1. Joe Louis (1914–1981), Heavyweight boxing champion.
2. Jomo Kenyatta (c. 1893–1978), African political leader and the first president of Kenya (1864–1978).
3. Daniel Francois Malan (1874–1959), South African political leader.
4. Max Yergan (1896–1975), U.S. educator and civil rights leader.
5. Jawaharlal Nehru (1889–1964), Indian statesman and the first prime minister of India (1947–1964).
6. Congress of Industrial Organizations. A labor organization, founded as the Committee for Industrial Organizations in 1935 by John L. Lewis, it organized workers in basic, mass-production industries.
7. American Federation of Labor. A labor organization, formed in 1886, that emphasized the organization of skilled workers into craft unions.
8. National Association for the Advancement of Colored People. A civil rights organization formed in 1910.
9. Joseph Broz Tito, Yugoslav Communist leader and marshal of Yugoslavia.
10. Also known as the European Recovery Program, the Marshall Plan was a project instituted at the Paris Economic Conference (July 1974) to foster economic recovery in certain European countries after World War II; named after Secretary of State George C. Marshall.
11. North Atlantic Treaty Organization (NATO). A military alliance established in 1949 by Belgium, Canada, Denmark, France, Great Britain, Iceland, Italy, Luxembourg, the Netherlands, Norway, Portugal, and the United States. Its aim was to safeguard member nations from the threat of Soviet aggression.
12. Henry Wallace (1888–1965), vice president of the United States (1941–1945) and U.S. presidential candidate in 1948 for the Progressive Party.
13. Thomas Edmund Dewey (1902–1971), U.S. politician, governor of New York (1943–1955), and twice a Republican presidential candidate; John Foster Dulles (1888–1959), U.S. secretary of state (1953–1959).
14. Now Volgograd, city in southeastern Russia.
15. Franklin Delano Roosevelt (1882–1945), thirty-second president of the United States (1933–1945).

Source

Paul Robeson, "Africa Calls—Will You Help?" in *Freedom,* ed. Paul Robeson (New York, NY: Freedom Associates), reprinted in Philip S. Foner, ed., *Paul Robeson*

Speaks: Writings, Speeches, Interviews, 1918–1974, 349–51(Larchmont, N.Y.: Brunner/Mazel, 1978); and "The Negro People and the Soviet Union," in Foner, ed., *Paul Robeson Speaks*, 219–21.

Selected Bibliography

Boyle, Shelia T. *Paul Robeson: The Years of Promise and Achievement.* Amherst: University of Massachusetts Press, 1998.

Duberman, Martin. *Paul Robeson.* New York: Knopf, 1988.

Robeson, Paul. *Here I Stand.* Boston: Beacon Press, 1998.

—— *Paul Robeson Speaks: Writings, Speeches, Interviews, 1918–1974.* Edited by Philip S. Foner. New York: Carol, 1982.

n i n e

Letters from Abroad

Malcolm X (1925–1965) was one of the most influential African American leaders of the twentieth century. Following his split with the Nation of Islam (NOI), Malcolm formed his own groups (the Muslim Mosque, Inc., and the Organization of Afro-American Unity) and changed his name to El-Hajj Malik El Shabazz. In 1964 he made a widely reported pilgrimage to the holy land of Mecca. Each of the letters below were written while Malcolm was abroad, and they show that his ideological orientation was shifting at the time of his assassination. One of his plans was to carry the cause of African Americans before the United Nations, thereby internationalizing the struggle for black freedom. The letters also show that Malcolm was beginning to champion orthodox Islam and displaying a measure of openness toward progressive whites that had been missing from his earlier statements.

Malcolm X was born Malcolm Little in Omaha, Nebraska. His father, a Baptist minister who was an ardent follower of Marcus Garvey, was murdered in 1931, probably by the Ku Klux Klan. As a young adult, Little engaged in an array of sordid criminal activity in Boston, Massachusetts, and in 1946 he was convicted of burglary and handed a harsh, ten-year prison sentence. While serving time, Malcolm had a profound religious conversion to the teachings of Elijah Muhammad and the NOI. Upon his emergence from prison, he took "X" as his surname and worked as a minister for the NOI. A gifted, charismatic, and sharp-witted orator, he soon became a national spokesperson for Muhammad's organization, advocating black self-defense, self-respect, and self-determination. In 1963, he had a headline-making conflict with Elijah Muhammad, and on February 14, 1965, three members of the NOI shot and killed him at the Audubon Ballroom in Harlem, New York.

From Letters from Abroad

Jedda, Saudi Arabia

April 20, 1964

Never have I witnessed such sincere hospitality and the overwhelming spirit of true brotherhood as is practiced by people *of all colors and races* here in this ancient holy land, the home of Abraham, Muhammad and all the other prophets of the Holy Scriptures. For the past week I have been utterly speechless and spellbound by the graciousness I see displayed all around me by people *of all colors.*

Last night, April 19, I was blessed to visit the Holy City of Mecca, and complete the "Omra" part of my pilgrimage. Allah willing, I shall leave for Mina tomorrow, April 21, and be back in Mecca to say my prayers from Mt. Arafat on Tuesday, April 22. Mina is about twenty miles from Mecca.

Last night I made my seven circuits around the Kaaba, led by a young Mutawlf named Muhammad. I drank water from the well of Zem Zem, and then ran back and forth seven times between the hills of Mt. Al-Safa and Al-Marwah.

There were tens of thousands of pilgrims from all over the world. They were *of all colors,* from blue-eyed blonds to black-skinned Africans, but were all participating in the same ritual, displaying a spirit of unity and brotherhood that my experiences in America had led me to believe could never exist between the white and non-white.

America needs to understand Islam, because this is the one religion that erases the race problem from its society. Throughout my travels in the Muslim world. I have met, talked to, and even eaten with, people who would have been considered "white" in America, but the religion of Islam in their hearts has removed the "white" from their minds. They practice sincere and true brotherhood with other people irrespective of their color.

Before America allows herself to be destroyed by the "cancer of racism" she should become better acquainted with the religious philosophy of Islam, a religion that has already molded people of all colors into one vast family, a nation or brotherhood of Islam that leaps over all "obstacles" and stretches itself into almost all the Eastern countries of this earth."

The whites as well as the non-whites who accept true Islam become a changed people. I have eaten from the same plate with people whose eyes were the bluest of blue, whose hair was the blondest of blond, and whose skin was the whitest of white—all the way from Cairo to Jedda and even in the Holy City of Mecca itself—and I felt the same sincerity in the words and deeds of these "white" Muslims that I felt among the African Muslims of Nigeria, Sudan and Ghana.

True Islam removes racism, because people of all colors and races who accept its religious principles and bow down to the one God, Allah, also automatically accept each other as brothers and sisters, regardless of differences in complexion.

You may be shocked by these words coming from me, but I have always been a man who tries to face facts, and to accept the reality of life as new experiences and knowledge unfold it. The experiences of this pilgrimage have taught me much, and each hour here in the Holy Land opens my eyes even more. If Islam can place the spirit of true brotherhood in the hearts of the "whites" whom I have met here in the Land of the Prophets, then surely it can also remove the "cancer of racism" from the heart of the white American, and perhaps in time to save America from imminent racial disaster the same destruction brought upon Hitler by his racism that eventually destroyed the Germans themselves.

Lagos, Nigeria

May 10, 1964

Each place I have visited, they have insisted that I don't leave. Thus I have been forced to stay longer than I originally intended in each country. In the Muslim world they loved me once they learned I was an American Muslim, and here in Africa they love me as soon as they learn that I am Malcolm X of the militant American Muslims. Africans in general and Muslims in particular love militancy.

I hope that my Hajj to the Holy City of Mecca will officially establish the religious affiliation of the Muslim Mosque, Inc., with the 750 million Muslims of the world of Islam once and for all—and that my warm reception here in Africa will forever repudiate the American white man's propaganda that the black man in Africa is not interested in the plight of the black man in America.

The Muslim world is forced to concern itself, from the moral point of view in its own religious concepts, with the fact that our plight clearly involves the violation of our *human rights.*

The Koran compels the Muslim world to take a stand on the side of those whose humanrights are being violated, no matter what the religious persuasion of the victims is. Islam is a religion which concerns itself with the human rights of all mankind, despite race, color, or creed. It recognizes all (everyone) as part of one human family.

Here in Africa, the 22 million American blacks are looked upon as the long-lost brothers of Africa. Our people here are interested in every aspect of our plight, and they study our struggle for freedom from every angle. Despite Western propaganda to the contrary, our African brothers and sisters love us, and are happy to learn that we also are awakening from our long "sleep" and are developing strong love for them.

Accra, Ghana

May 11, 1964

I arrived in Accra yesterday from Lagos, Nigeria. The natural beauty and wealth of Nigeria and its people are indescribable. It is full of Americans and other whites who are well aware of its untapped natural resources. The same whites, who spit in the faces of blacks in America and sic their police dogs upon us to keep us from "Integrating" with them, are seen throughout Africa, bowing, grinning and smiling in an effort to "integrate" with the Africans—they want to "Integrate" into Africa's wealth and beauty. This is ironical.

This continent has such great fertility and the soil is so profusely vegetated that with modern agricultural methods it could easily become the "bread-basket" of the world.

I spoke at Ibadan University in Nigeria, Friday night, and gave the *true* picture of our plight in America, and of the necessity of the independent African nations helping us bring our case before the United Nations. The reception of the students was tremendous. They made me an honorary member of the "Muslim Students Society of Nigeria," and renamed me "Omowale," which means "the child has come home" in the Yoruba language.

The people of Nigeria are strongly concerned with the problems of their African brothers in America, but the U.S. information agencies in Africa create the impression that progress is being made and the problem is being solved. Upon close study, one can easily see a gigantic design to keep Africans here and the African-Americans from getting together. An African official told me, "When one combines the number of peoples of *African descent* in South, Central and North America, they total well over 80 million. One can easily understand the attempts to keep the Africans from ever uniting with the Africans-Americans." Unity between the Africans of the West and the Africans of the father land will well change the course of history.

Being in Ghana now, the fountainhead of Pan-Africanism, the last days of my tour should be intensely interesting and enlightening.[1]

Just as the American Jew is in harmony (politically, economically and culturally) with world Jewry, it is time for all African-Americans to become an integral part of the world's Pan-Africanists, and even though we might remain in America physically while fighting for the benefits the Constitution guarantees us, we must "return" to Africa philosophically and culturally and develop a working unity in the framework of Pan-Africanism.

Note

1. An ideology that suggests that all blacks have a common social and political bond with Africa and that seeks to unite blacks across the globe.

Source

El-Shabazz, El Hajj Malik [Malcolm X], "Letter from Jedda, Saudi Arabia, April 20, 1964" and "Letter from Accra, Ghana, May 11, 1964," in George Breitman, ed., *Malcolm X Speaks: Selected Speeches and Statements,* 58–63 (New York: Merit Publishers, 1965).

Selected Bibliography

Cone, James H. *Martin and Malcolm and America: A Dream or a Nightmare?* Maryknoll, N.Y.: Orbis Books, 1992.

Decaro, Louis A. *On the Side of My People: A Religious Life of Malcolm X.* New York: New York University Press, 1995.

Dyson, Michael Eric. *Making Malcolm: The Myth and Meaning of Malcolm X.* New York: Oxford University Press, 1996.

Goldman, Peter L. *The Death and Life of Malcolm X.* Urbana: University of Illinois Press, 1979.

X, Malcolm, with Alex Haley. *The Autobiography of Malcolm X.* New York: Ballantine Books, 1964.

ten

Selected Essays by Audre Lorde

Audre (Geraldine) Lorde once described herself as a "black, lesbian, mother, warrior, poet,"[1] As a poetic warrior she protested issues such as the imposition of white culture on black Americans, the oppression of black women by black men, and the insensitivity of the health care system. As a healer she focused on love, sexuality, parenthood, and the African diaspora.

The following two essays were inspired by Lorde's concern for the diaspora and her familial connection to Grenada. Her father was originally from Barbados, and her mother, from Grenada. Prior to the Great Depression, her parents moved from Grenada to Harlem, where Lorde was born in 1934. They intended to escape the poor economic conditions of their home country.

In December 1983, two months after the U.S. invasion of the black Caribbean island, Lorde visited Grenada, her second trip in five years. "Grenada Revisited" was written as her work *Sister Outsider* was being published. Lorde traveled widely between 1983 and 1986, thus inspiring "Sisterhood and Survival."

Sisterhood and Survival

I am truly happy to be here to see your faces, to be a part of the Black Women Writers of the Diaspora. I would like to say a few words of what sisterhood and survival mean to me. For myself personally, survival means working for the future, and if I am to use all of my self power in the service of what I believe—that all people across the earth must be free—then I must also identify that self and the sources from which that power springs.

I am a black feminist lesbian poet, and I identify myself as such because if there is one other black feminist lesbian poet in isolation somewhere within the reach of my voice, I want her to know she is not alone. I have been teaching the poems of Angelina Weld Grimke recently, another black lesbian poet of the Harlem Renaissance. And I often think of her dying alone in an apartment in New York City in 1958, while I was a young black lesbian, in isolation not too far away, and I think of what it could have meant in terms of sisterhood and survival for each one of us to have known of the other's existence, for me to have had her words, and for her to have known I needed them! That we were not alone.

In the last two years I have been traveling around a lot and learning what an enormous amount I don't know as a black American woman. And wherever I went it was so heartening to see black women doing—reclaiming our lands, reclaiming our heritage, reclaiming our selves, even in the face of enormous odds. And we are everywhere, those of us who define black as a political position, and those of us who define black as of African heritage. And I recognize the inherent differences between those positions.

All over the world I found black women coming together around their identities, questioning and re-defining what that Africanness could mean, within our particular communities, and upon the world stage. And I don't mean in the abstract. I mean, for example, in the lives of the Afro-German women examining the strengths it took to survive literally being scrubbed white as children, or to Katerina Birchenwald, the Afro-German poet who in her work is refashioning the German language through her poetry of blackness. I mean in the lives of the Afro-Dutch women fighting racism in Holland while also actively engaged in the anti-apartheid struggle.

For me as an African-American woman writer, sisterhood and survival mean it is not enough to say we are for peace when our sisters' children are dying in the streets of Soweto. There are no stones in Johannesberg, Ellen Kuzwayo told me last week. The little chaps who were gunned down throwing stones at policemen must have filled their pockets with those stones and carried them all the way from Soweto. What does it mean, our wars being fought by our children?

Sisterhood and survival demands that I ask myself as an African-American woman, What does it mean to be a citizen of the most powerful country on earth? And we are that. What does it mean to be a citizen of a country that stands upon the wrong side of every liberation struggle on this earth? Let that sink in for a moment.

We cannot join the children in kneepants and jumpers throwing stones at army hippos in Capetown, but we can refuse to support companies that do business in South Africa. And we can persuade others to refuse to support companies that do business in South Africa.

Even closer to home, what are we saying to our sons and nephews and students as they are herded into the U.S. Army by unemployment and despair, to become meat in battles to occupy the lands of other people of color? How can we ever forget the faces of young black American soldiers, bayonets drawn, in front of a shack in Grenville, Grenada?

What is our work for sisterhood and survival as black women writers of the Diaspora? Our responsibilities to other black women and their children across the globe we share, struggling for futures?

What if our sons are ordered into Namibia, and South West Africa, and Angola?

Where does our power lie and how do we use it in the service of what we believe?

And where do our lives intersect with the lives of other women of color and where do they diverge?

In traveling I came into contact with black women all over the earth. Pacific Island women, the Kanak women in struggle in New Caledonia, Maori women of Aotearoa, New Zealand. I marched with black Australians, the Koori women of Melbourne, in a land rights march, the women of Angola, and South Africa, out of their countries, and still in battle. And what I found, besides the particular differences of our struggles, was also a great similarity—the origins of our oppressions are the same. It was very affirming to see all over the world women of color rising up and demanding—"You took our land, you didn't pay for it, you messed it up, polluted it, misused it, now give it back!"

It made me think a lot about what it means to be indigenous, and what my relationship as a black woman is to the land struggles of the indigenous peoples of this land, to Native American women, and how can we translate that consciousness into a new level of working together; how do we use each other's differences in our common battles?

In Melbourne, Australia, I attended a play by an urban Aboriginal woman, the very first play written and produced in Australia by a black woman playwright. The play was entitled, "Tjindarela," by Eva Johnson. It speaks from the pain of children stolen from us in body and mind, a pain well known to indigenous women of color the world over. All of our children are prey. How do we raise them not to prey upon themselves and each other? This is why we cannot be silent, because our silences will come to testify against us in the mouths of our children.

So long as we believe ourselves to be powerless we will never be able to use the power we have. We are black women writers of the diaspora. I think I can say for each of us that we believe in speaking the truth as we know it, and making those truths work within our lives and the lives of our children.

Yes, black children are being killed on the streets of every city in this country, and black neighborhoods incinerated, and our black elders are being evicted with shotguns. And these are not isolated events upon the world stage; they are directly related to apartheid in South Africa: Genocide is genocide.

So while we are fighting for survival in our schools and in the streets of Detroit and New York and Austin, sisterhood requires us to also remember that black Americans still control over $200 million a year in this country. As long as we think of ourselves as powerless we will waste the power we have. $200 million. That's one kind of power. Where do you bank? Buy gasoline? What position does your congressman hold on sanctions against South Africa?

Each of us is called upon to take a stand. So in these days ahead, as we examine ourselves and each other, our works, our hopes, our fears, our differences, our sisterhood and survivals, I urge you to tackle what is most difficult for us all, self-scrutiny of our complacencies, that idea that since each one of us believes she is on the side of right, she need not examine her position.

We are sisters, and our survivals are mutual.

Grenada Revisited: An Interim Report

The first time I came to Grenada I came seeking "home," for this was my mother's birthplace and she had always defined it so for me. Vivid images remained of what I saw there and of what I knew it could become.

- Grand Anse Beach was a busy thoroughfare in the early, direct morning. Children in proper school uniforms carrying shoes, trying to decide between the lure of a coco palm adventure to one side and the delicious morning sea on the other, while they are bound straightforward to well-worn chalky desks.
- The mended hem of the print dress the skinny old woman wore, swinging along down the beach, cutlass in hand. Oversized, high rubber boots never once interfering with her determined step. Her soft shapeless hat. Underneath, sharp, unhurried eyes snapped out from chocolate skin dusted grey with age. . . .
- The Fat-Woman-Who-Fries-Fish-In-The-Market actually did, and it was delicious, served on the counterboards with her fragrant chocolate-tea in mugs fashioned from Campbell's Pork 'n Beans cans with metal handles attached.
- The full moon turning the night beach flash green.

I came to Grenada for the first time eleven months before the March 13, 1979, bloodless coup of the New Jewel Movement which ushered in the People's Revolutionary Government (PRG) of Grenada under Prime Minister Maurice Bishop. This brought an end to twenty-nine years of Sir Eric Gairy's regime—wasteful, corrupt, and United States sanctioned. . . .

In 1978 there was only one paved road in Grenada. During the People's Revolutionary Government, all roads were widened and reworked, and a functioning bus service was established that did more than ferry tourists back and forth to the cruise ships lying at anchor in the creenage. Wild banana fronds, *baligey,* in clumps below the road's slope. Stands of particular trees within the bush—red cocoa fruit, golden apple, mango, breadfruit, peach-ripe nutmeg, banana. Girls on the road to Annandale, baskets of laundry balanced on their heads, hands on hips, swaying, reminiscent of 100 roads through Africa.

Grenada, tiny spice island, is the second largest producer of nutmeg in the world. Its cocoa has a 45 percent fat content and sells for premium prices on the world market. But Grenadians pay eight times more than that price if they wish to drink processed hot chocolate, all of which is imported.

The second time I came to Grenada I came in mourning and fear that this land which I was learning had been savaged, invaded, its people maneuvered into saying thank you to their invaders. I knew the lies and distortions of secrecy surrounding the invasion of Grenada by the United States on October 25, 1983; the rationalizations which collapse under the weight of facts; the facts that are readily available, even now, from the back pages of the *New York Times.*

1. *That the St. Georges Medical School students were in danger.* Officials of the school deny this.[1] Students deny this.[2] The U.S. government had received assurances from General Hudson Austin of the Revolutionary Military Council guaranteeing the students' safety. These assurances were ignored.[3]

2. *That the U.S. was invited to intervene by the signers of an Organization of Eastern Caribbean States Treaty.* This would only have been internationally legal had *Grenada* invaded another island.[4] The decision to invade was made by four of the seven signatories. The invitation itself was actually drafted by the U.S. State Department and sent down to the Eastern Caribbean nations.[5]

3. *That Grenada threatened U.S. security because of the construction of a military airport and the stockpiling of an arsenal of modern weapons.* Grenada's new airport is a civilian airport built to accommodate tourists. It has been in planning for over twenty-five years, half financed by several Western European coun-

* Slogan of the Grenadian Revolution.

1. P. Tyler, *Washington Post,* October 10, 1983, p. A14.

2. A. Cockburn, *Village Voice,* November 8, 1983, p. 11.

3. B.D. Ayers, *New York Times,* October 22, 1983, p. A5 and J. McQuiston, *New York Times,* October 26, 1983, p. A20.

4. Text of Treaty, *New York Times,* October 26, 1983, p. A19.

tries and Canada. According to Plessey, the British firm which underwrote the project the airport was being built to civil, not military, standards.[6] All U.S. reports on Grenada now stress the necessity of this airport for a Grenadian tourist industry.[7] The "stockpile" of weapons was less than two warehouses. Of 6,300 rifles, about 400 were fairly modern; the rest were very old, and some antique.[8]

As even Arthur Schlesinger, Jr., observed, "Now we launch a sneak attack on a pathetic island of 110,000 people with no army, no navy or air force, and claim a glorious victory."[9]

A group of men and women mend the road ahead of us with hoes and rock hammers, wheelbarrows, and other hand tools. They step to one side as we pass by. One woman wipes her face with the end of her headcloth, leaning upon the handle of her scythe. Another woman is barefooted, young, but when she smiles I see all of her front teeth are missing. The PRG brought free medical care to Grenada, and no more school fees. Most estate workers and peasants in the small villages saw a dentist for the first time in their lives. Literacy was raised by teacher education and a planned each-one-teach-one program throughout the countryside.

Revolution. A nation decides for itself what it needs. How best to get it. Food. Dentists. Doctors. Roads. When I first visited Grenada in 1978, one-third of the farmable land in the country lay idle, owned by absentee landlords who did not work it. The PRG required that plans be filed either for farming that land, turning it over to those who would, or deeding it to the state. The World Bank notes the health of the Grenadian economy, surpassing all other Caribbean economies in the rate of its growth and stability despite the opposition of the U.S. Unemployment dips from 40 percent to 14 percent. Now there is no work again.

Four years ago, the U.S. acted through the International Monetary Fund to assure that there would be no western money available for the Grenadian economy, much less for protecting her shores from an invasion threatened by Gairy operating out of San Diego, California, where he had sought asylum. When the PRG sought economic aid from the the U.S. in 1979 to help rebuild the infrastructure of a country fallen into disrepair during the twenty-nine years of Gairy's regime, the U.S. response was to offer the insult of $5,000 from an ambassador's discretionary fund! Now it is 1983, post-invasion, and the conquerors are promising Grenadians welfare, their second main exportable drug. Three million dollars thus far, administered under U.S. guns, so long as the heads that take it are bowed.

5. S. Taylor, *New York Times,* October 26, 1983, p. A19.
6. A. Lewis, *New York Times,* November 3, 1983, and A. Cockburn, *Village Voice,* November 8, 1983, p. 10.
7. S. Mydans, *New York Times,* Januiary 15, 1984, p. 9.
8. *Christian Science Monitor,* November 7, 1983.
9. A. Schlesinger, Jr., *Wall Street Journal,* October 26, 1983.

Had the amount this invasion cost each one of us in taxes been lent to the PRG when it requested economic aid from the U.S. five years ago, the gratitude of Grenadians would have been real, and hundreds of lives could have been saved. But then Grenada would have been self-defined, independent; and, of course, that could not be allowed. What a bad example, a dangerous precedent, an independent Grenada would be for the peoples of Color in the Caribbean, in Central America, for those of us here in the United States.

The ready acceptance by the majority of Americans of the Grenadian invasion and of the shady U.S. involvement in the events leading up to the assassination of Prime Minister Maurice Bishop both happen in an America whose moral and ethical fiber is weakened by racism as thoroughly as wood is weakened by dry rot. White America has been well-schooled in the dehumanization of Black people. A Black island nation? Why, don't be ridiculous! If they weren't all so uppity, we'd have enough jobs and no recession. The lynching of Black youth and shooting down of Black women, 60 percent of Black teenagers unemployed and rapidly becoming unemployable, the presidential dismantling of the Civil Rights Commission, and more Black families below the poverty line than twenty years ago—if these facts of American life and racism can be passed over as unremarkable, then why not the rape and annexation of tiny Black Grenada?

The Pentagon has been spoiling for a fight it could win for a long time; the last one was the battle for Inchon in the 1950s. How better to wipe out the bitter memories of Vietnam defeats by Yellow people than with a restoration of power in the eyes of the American public—the image of American Marines splashing through a little Black blood? ". . . to keep our honor clean" the Marine anthem says. So the American public was diverted from recession, unemployment, the debacle in Beirut, from nuclear madness and dying oceans and a growing national depression and despair, by the bombing of a mental hospital where fifty people were killed. Even that piece of proud news was withheld for over a week while various cosmetic stories were constructed. Bread and circuses.

If the United Stats is even remotely interested in seeing democracy flourish in the Caribbean, why does it continue to support Haiti and the Dominican Republic, two of the most corrupt and repressive governments in the Americas? The racism that coats the U.S. government lies about Grenada is the same racism that blinded American eyes to the Black faces of 131 Haitians washed up on shore in Miami, drowned fleeing the Duvalier regime. It is the same racism that keeps American eyes turned aside from the corrosive apartheid eating like acid into the face of White South Africa and the Reagan government which shares her bed under the guise of "constructive engagement." White South Africa has the highest standard of living of any nation in the world, and 50 percent of Black South Africa's children die before they are five. A statistic. The infant mortality rate for Black Americans is almost twice that of White

Americans—in the most highly industrialized country in the world. White America has been well-schooled in the acceptance of Black destruction. So, what is Black Grenada and its 110,000 Black lives?

Unemployment in Grenada dropped 26 percent in four years.[10] On October 25, 1983, American Corsair missiles and naval shells and mortars pounded into the hills behind Grenville, St. Georges, Gouyave. American Marines tore through homes and hotels searching for "Cubans." Now the ministries are silent. The state farms are at a standstill. The cooperatives are suspended. The cannery plant in True Blue is a shambles, shelled to silence. On the day after the invasion, unemployment was back up to 35 percent. A cheap, acquiescent labor pool is the delight of supply-side economics. One month later, the U.S. Agency for International Development visits Grenada. They report upon the role of the private sector in Grenada's future, recommending the revision of tax codes to favor private enterprise (usually foreign), the development of a labor code that will ensure a compliant labor movement, and the selling off of public sector enterprises to private interests.[11] How soon will it be Grenadian women who were going blind from assembling microcomputer chips at $.80 an hour for international industrial corporations? "I used to work at the radio station," says a young woman on the beach, shrugging. "But that ended in the war."

This short, undeclared, and cynical war against Grenada is not a new direction for American foreign policy. It is merely a blatant example of a 160-year-old course of action called the Monroe Doctrine. In its name America has invaded small Caribbean and Central American countries over and over since 1823, cloaking these invasions under a variety of names. Thirty-eight such invasions occurred prior to 1917 before the Soviet Union even existed. For example, in 1897 U.S. Marines landed in Puerto Rico to fight the Spanish-American War. They never left.

Beginning in 1981, the United States rehearsed the invasion of Grenada openly. It practiced the war game *Ocean Venture* in which it bombed the Puerto Rican island of Vieques, calling it "Amber of the Amberines" (Grenada of the Grenadines). In this grisly make-believe, a situation is supposed to occur where Americans are held hostage. As we know, this was the first excuse used to justify the invasion of Grenada. As for Americans really being in danger, there were still over 500 resident American citizens who chose to remain in Grenada during and after the invasion. But since *Ocean Venture* appears to be the script, we must remember that it also calls for the assassination of the Prime Minister of Amber. Are we now to believe that the U.S./CIA was not involved directly or indirectly with Prime Minister Maurice Bishop's death? Was the coup which served as the opening for *Ocean Venture* to become a reality merely an

10. C. Sunshine, ed., *Grenada—The Peaceful Revolution* E.P.I.C.A., Washington, D.C., 1982).
11. C. Sunshine, *The Guardian,* December 28, 1983.

unhappy coincidence of personal intrigue, or was it an event lengthily orchestrated by clever manipulators.

The Pentagon has admitted in secret Congressional briefings that it knew of the coup against Bishop two weeks before it happened.[12] The Ranger unit participating in the invasion had spent six days between September 23 and October 2, 1983, practicing the takeover of an airport and the liberation of hostages, a maneuver about which the Pentagon had requested no publicity.[13] One Senator disclosed that there were CIA agents accompanying the seventy students flown out of Grenada on October 26, the day after the invasion.[14]

There will be a long and painstaking search for answers to these questions.

P.S.Y.O.P.S., the psychological operations unit of the U.S. occupation forces—a new development heard from in combat here for the first time—was quick to plaster St. Georges and the rest of Grenada with posters of Bernard Coard and General Hudson Austin, stripped naked and blind folded holding them up to ridicule and scorn as the slayers of the Grenadian people's beloved Maurice Bishop. It is well known that had Bishop lived, Grenada would have fought any invasion down to the last child. So scapegoats for his death were essential. The details of the power struggles which occurred within the New Jewel Movement Party—if such they were—are yet to be known and assuredly complex. Yet months later, these men are still being held incommunicado in Richmond Hill prison, St. Georges, by "security forces," non-Grenadian. They have not been charged nor brought to trial as of this writing, nor have the forty-odd other Grenadians still detained with them.

Nothing is now heard of the two Americans known to have been involved in the last days of the Bishop regime, one of whom was wanted on a weapons charge here in the U.S., and one of whom holds passports in two countries.[15] Who were they working for and on what side? Their identities have never been divulged—a favorite tactic to cover destabilization operatives—and their existence attested to only by one line in the back pages of the *New York Times*. So, too, was the assertion by Ambassador to France Evan Galbraith on public TV that the U.S. was involved in Grenada "weeks before Bishop's death."[16]

A West German nurse working in Grenada, Regina Fuchs, reports she was jailed and relentlessly interrogated after being falsely accused of harboring fugitives by two Americans, one of whom, Frank Gonzales, identified himself to her as CIA.[17]

The action in Grenada served many purposes for the United States, provided the ground for many tests. A major one was addressed to the concern

12. E. Ray and B. Schaap, "U.S. Crushes Caribbean Jewel," *Covert Action Bulletin* #20, Winter 1984, p. 11.
13. Ibid., p. 13.
14. Ibid., p. 5.
15. S. Taylor, *New York Times,* November 6, 1983, p. 20.
16. Ibid.
17. *Washington Post,* November 21, 1983.

long expressed by the Pentagon as to whether or not Black American soldiers could be gotten to fire upon other Black people. This becomes a vital question as the U.S. military-industrial complex executes increasingly military solutions to this country's precarious position in the Third World, where the U.S. either ignores or stands upon the wrong side of virtually every single struggle for liberation by oppressed peoples. Of course, there were also lesser tests. In addition to trying out new armaments, there was the question of whether the Marines liked their new Nazi-style helmets.

Listen to the language that came from the Pentagon, orchestrated by the psychological warfare experts operating in Grenada.

—*We got there just in time.*

—*Not an invasion, a rescue mission.*

Mopping up.

—*It was our turf.* We had every right.

—*Armed thugs* (the Grenadian militia).

—*An Idi Amin—type character, capable of taking hostages* (General Austin). Imprisoned for spreading ill will among the people.

This language is calculated to reduce a Black nation's aspirations in the eyes and ears of White Americans already secretly terrified by the Black Menace, enraged by myths of Black Progress, at the same time encouraged by government action never to take the life of a Black person seriously.

Even many Black Americans, threatened by some specter of a socialism that is mythic and undefined at best, have bought the government line of "them" against "us." But; which one of us as a Black American has ever taken the time to examine this threat of socialism for any reality nearly as destructive as racism is within all of our lives? With the constant manipulation of the media, many Black Americans are honestly confused, defending "our" invasion of Black Grenada under a mistaken mirage of patriotism.

Nineteen eighty-four is upon us, and doublethink has come home to scramble our brains and blanket our protest.

In addition to being a demonstration to the Caribbean community of what will happen to any country that dares to assume responsibility for its own destiny, the invasion of Grenada also serves as a naked warning to thirty million African-Americans. Watch your step. We did it to them down there and we will not hesitate to do it to you. Internment camps. Interrogation booths. Isolation cells hastily built by U.S. occupation forces. Blindfolded stripped prisoners. House-to-house searches for phantom Cubans. Neighbors pressured to inform against each other. No strange gods before us. U.S. soldiers at roadblocks and airports, assisted by former members of Gairy's infamous Mongoose Gang, U.S. soldiers at roadblocks and airports carrying notebooks with lists of Bishop and PRG sympathizers.[19] The tactics for quelling a conquered people. No courts, no

19. *The London Guardian,* November 4, 1983.

charges, no legal process. Welfare, but no reparation for damaged businesses, destroyed homes and lives. Street passes: Imprisonment of "trouble-makers." The new radio station blaring The Beach Boys rock group music hour after hour.

Whose country was Grenada?

Hundreds of Grenadian bodies are buried in unmarked graves, relatives missing and unaccounted for, survivors stunned and frightened into silence by fear of being jailed and accused of "spreading unrest among the people." No recognition and therefore no aid to the sisters, mothers, wives, children of the dead, families disrupted and lives vandalized by the conscious brutality of a planned undeclared war. No attention given to the Grenadian bodies shipped back and forth across the sea in plastic bodybags from Barbados to Grenada to Cuba and back again to Grenada. After all, they all look alike, and besides, maybe if they are flown around the world long enough they will simply disappear, or become invisible, or some other peoples' sacrifice.

"My brother died in Calliste when they shot up the house," Isme said, "because they thought Cubans were living there. My father lost his arm and a leg. They took him to hospital in Barbados but he passed away there. His body was brought back to Pearl's Airport but I've got to borrow some money now to bring him home for his funeral."

Weeks after the invasion, Grenadians were still smelling out and burying bodies which lay all over the island. The true casualty figures will never be known.

No civilian body count is available. Even the bodies of Maurice Bishop and his slain ministers are never positively identified, no doubt to forestall any possible enshrinement by the people who loved him, no doubt to make the task of smearing his popular memory more easily accomplished. It has already begun.

For the first time in an American war, the American press was kept out until the stage could be set. This extends by precedent the meaning of military censorship in this country. At the time, it also deflected attention from the invasion itself. Mission accomplished with "surgical precision" meant attempting to conceal the bombing and destruction of civilian homes, the destruction of a hospital and a radio station and police headquarters, attempting to conceal the American heavy transports left mangled on the side of the road by soldiers not trained to drive to the left, and the civilian cars those army vehicles collided with. It meant the appropriation, use, and destruction of homes and stores and other businesses with no compensation. When the American press was finally admitted after the cosmetic cleanup, we were treated to photographs of smiling Grenadians welcoming their conquerors (look what your tax dollars have brought). But no photos of the signs calling for information about neighbors. No photos of the signs throughout the countryside calling for an end to yankee imperialism. *NO BISHOP NO REVO.*

So what did Revolution in Grenada mean? It meant the inauguration of an agro-industry; which for the first time in the island's history processed the island's own, fruit, its own coffee, under its own brand, Spice Isle Foods. Canned products from their own soil available in stores. The beginning of a fishing and fish-processing industry. In a country rich with tropical fruit, whose waters abound with fish, why should the most common fruit juice be Florida orange juice, the most commonly used fish, imported saltfish from Canada?

It meant almost doubling the number of doctors on the island from twenty-three to forty, a health center set up in every parish for the first time, a dental clinic. It meant a public health anti-mosquito cleanup campaign implemented by the National Youth Organization that successfully protected Grenada from the wave of Dengue Fever sweeping through the rest of the Caribbean in the summer of 1981.[20]

It meant 12-year-old Lyndon Adams of L'Esterre, Carriacou, teaching a 73-year-old woman how to read and write as part of the each-one-teach-one program against functional illiteracy conducted by the Center for Popular Education. This highly successful program enlisted the aid of one of the most brilliant educators of all time, Paulo Freire, head of the World Council of Churches' literacy program. When the echos of *Ocean Venture* drifted across the Caribbean from Vieques in 1981, and the stench of the threat of U.S. invasion hung over the hills from Grand Etang to Harvey Vale, Lyndon, one of the youngest teachers in the CPE program, was quoted as saying: "Before the revolution we were not in the light. I will never give up. I rather they killed me dead than I go work for them if they come to take over we land and try to oppress we again."

The American medical student who witnessed the shooting of the first American Marine killed landing on Grenada resists the prompting of her TV interviewer. *Pockets of foreign resistance. Cubans hiding in the hills.* "Oh no, he wasn't shot by Cubans. It was an old man and his son, firing from their house." Lyndon Adams and his neighbor are not Cuban. The old man and his son defending their home were not Cubans. They were Grenadians who dared to believe that they could have a right to define themselves and the future of their nation independent of the United States.

Grenada is a highly stratified society made up of a large, extremely poor mass of estate workers and small land-holding peasants, a small but growing group of urban service workers, and a tiny well-to-do middle class, civil servants and landed, who traditionally have involved themselves with the economics of import-export rather than the economics of national production. The Bishop government was becoming a successful bridge between these different groups. Problems of colorism and classism are deep, far-reaching, and very complex legacies left from successive colonialisms. Grenadians, rightly so, are highly resistant to any external suggestions of a superficial solution. By

20. *Grenada—The Peaceful Revolution,* p. 87.

bringing the goals of these diverse groups together, the Revolution became even more threatening to the U.S.

To the average Grenadian, the United States is a large but dim presence where some dear relative lives. Until the information campaigns of the PRG, lack of international news coverage and commentary kept Grenadians largely unaware of the U.S. position in world politics and its history of institutionalized racism and classism. Ronald Reagan was seen as a fatherly movie star unconnected to policies of systematic economic and military oppression of people of Color throughout the developing countries of the world. . . .

The conflicts in the New Jewel Movement, Bishop's house arrest, the subsequent demonstration of ten thousand Grenadians, the second smaller march which resulted in Bishop's liberation and murder along with other Ministers and hundreds of Grenadians on Richmond Hill, and the four-day military curfew that followed these events left terror in the hearts of all Grenadians. Any ending seemed preferable at the time.

The U.S.-operated Spice Island Radio went into operation the afternoon of the invasion, and most Grenadians obtained whatever information they got about events from posters and handbills put up around the countryside by P.S.Y.O.P.S. Rumors have been rife among the people, attempting to explain the inexplicable. One shopgirl in St. Georges told me she had heard the reason why the army fired upon the people at Fort Rupert was because "the Russians had put the tablets into their milk would make them shoot anybody on sight."

It remains to be seen if the future plans of the U.S. for Grenada will justify the vision of many Grenadians of the United States as savior. Even now this view is not nearly as widespread as the American media would have us believe. Says a newly-unemployed 19-year-old laborer in St. Georges, "They can call it a rescue mission all they want, but I haven't been rescued yet." There is much pain beneath the veneer of gratitude: too many fathers and uncles and brothers and daughters injured and killed because "the Americans thought there were Cubans living in there." All over Grenada, I felt the deadening effect of horror and disbelief in every conversation about the war, often beneath a surface animation.

I came to Grenada my second time six weeks after the invasion, wanting to know she was still alive, wanting to examine what my legitimate position as a concerned Grenadian-American was toward the military invasion of this tiny Black nation by the mighty U.S. I looked around me, talked with Grenadians on the street, the shops, the beaches, on porches in the solstice twilight. Grenada is their country. I am only a relative. I must listen long and hard and ponder the implications of what I have heard, or be guilty of the same quick arrogance of the U.S. government in believing there are external solutions to Grenada's future.

I also came for reassurance, to see if Grenada had survived the onslaught of the most powerful nation on earth. She has. Grenada is bruised but very much alive. Grenadians are a warm and resilient people (I hear my mother's voice: "Island women make good wives. Whatever happens, they've seen worse"), and they have survived colonizations before. I am proud to be of stock from the country that mounted the first Black English-speaking People's Revolution in this hemisphere. Much has been terribly lost in Grenada, but not all—not the spirit of the people. *Forward Ever, Backward Never*[22] is more than a mere whistle in the present dark.

Source

Audre Lorde "Grenada Revisited: An Interim Report" *The Black Scholar* (January–February 1984) Vol. 15, No. 1, p. 21–29. Audre Lorde "Sisterhood and Survival" *The Black Scholar* (March–April 1986) 2: 5–7.

Selected Bibliography

Lorde, Audre. *The Black Unicorn: Poems.* New York: Norton, 1978.
—— *A Burst of Light: Essays.* Ithaca, New York: Firebrand Books, 1988.
—— *The Cancer Journals.* Argyle, New York: Spinsters, Ink, 1980.
—— *The Collected Poems of Audre Lorde.* New York: Norton, 1997.
—— *Sister Outsider: Essays and Speeches.* Trumansburg, N.Y.: Crossing Press, 1984.
—— *Zami, A New Spelling of My Name.* Trumansburg, N.Y.: Crossing Press, 1982.
Staples, Robert. *The Black Family: Essays and Studies.* Belmont, Calif.: Wadsworth Pub. Co., 1971.

22. Slogan of the Grenadian Revolution.

eleven

"The Continuity of Struggle"

On May 2, 1973, three members of the Black Panther Party, including Assata Shakur (JoAnne Deborah Chesimard, 1947–), were stopped by state police officers on the New Jersey Turnpike. A gun battle ensued, leaving one state trooper and one Black Panther killed. According to Shakur, police officers shot her once while her hands were in the air and once in her back as she lay on the ground. She was then taken to a hospital, chained to a bed, and arrested. Shakur was then beaten, tortured, kept incommunicado for four to five days, and denied the right to see a lawyer.[1] An all-white jury found Shakur guilty of murder, sentencing her to life plus an additional thirty years and thirty days. After spending a total of six years in prison (including two years of solitary confinement in a men's prison), Shakur escaped and eventually found political asylum in Cuba.

Assata Shakur's case made U.S. headlines again in 1998 when New Jersey Republican governor Christine Todd Whitman launched a campaign to "capture" Shakur and bring her back to prison. Outraging hundreds of African American leaders and activists, Whitman argued that the United States should refuse to "normalize" relations with Cuba so long as Shakur remained there. The state of New Jersey subsequently offered $50,000 to anyone who would secure her return.

The following interview was recorded in 1997 during a Columbia University African American Studies delegation's visit to Cuba. In it, Shakur discusses the social, economic, and political conditions of the country since the Cuban revolution and the future of social change.

All Go on Survival: Race and Revolution

When I came to Cuba, at first people were very reluctant to deal or to talk about race, to talk about racism. You could talk to anybody; they would say, "Well, there is no such thing. It's been eliminated." And what I think they meant was that all laws that upheld segregation in terms of housing and neighborhoods had been virtually eliminated. That doesn't mean that some historic segregation doesn't exist. In other words, old Havana had a huge number of African people and all of them have not moved to other areas. In areas that were historically black, there are still a lot of black people living there. But I think that the nature of neighborhoods has changed completely and areas that were completely white before are now very mixed.

Two seconds after the revolution took power, all hell broke loose, and they [revolutionary leaders] were under the gun on every side of the question. So the issue was unity. The consciousness that existed at that time was the consciousness that pretty well existed all around the world, the U.S. included. In terms of socialist theory at that time, you [would] give everybody the right health care, education, etc., [and] the conditions were going to make racism automatically disappear. Also, what was considered racism at that time was "White Only" signs [or] being forbidden from work in certain places. So, those things having been eliminated, there was this perception of "all Cubans." The national character of Cuba was never considered unmixed; it was considered that there's no Cuban that's all European and there's no Cuban that's all African. It was a popular saying here, the saying that there were no pure whites in Cuba.

Of course Cuba inherited a racist mentality of white supremacy that existed for hundreds of years. This was one of the last places were slavery was abolished, in 1886. All the racist ideas that upheld slavery, that justified slavery, were present here. There was a systematic whitening process that was institutionalized in the Spanish form of colonialism. You could buy, for [a] certain amount of [money], a paper that declared you white. If you wanted to be a don or a doña, someone who had power in the society, all you had to do was get a white father to say you didn't know who your mother was and you could buy a paper that purified your blood. Also, in order to work in certain areas if you were a so-called freed slave, you could work in [certain] areas if you had a paper that said you were white. And people bought those papers for their children so that their children could have a future.

Those attitudes did not disappear after the revolution. In fact, I think that many people felt that the revolution gave them more of a possibility. To many people, especially those who had college degrees, a white partner made them even much more of a contributor to the struggle against racism. I think that there was a whole sense of "Everything is going to be fine with Cubans together, white and black." [There was a feeling that] there were no differences until the Third Congress of the Cuban Communist Party, when Raúl and Fidel said that "Look, number one, the power structures in the country have got to reflect the ratio of the composition of the country." They talked about race, they talked about gender, and they also talked about young people. And there were changes made in terms of people being promoted to vice ministers. There were a lot of black vice ministers—and when I say that I'm not saying it in a sarcastic way. I'm saying that the old guard, those who fought in the mountains, you don't get rid of those people easy. So it was a big shift, moving [black] people into positions [of power].

That movement, or that effort, was short-lived. It was short-lived in the sense that shortly thereafter the socialist camp in Europe started to crumble and the revolution was looking at basic, bare survival. It was life or death and they were up shit's creek without paddle, between a rock and a hard place. That was the reality. [Cubans] lost like 80-something percent of their ability to import and their ability to export. There was not enough of anything. The price of sugar was in the pits and controlled completely by capitalist markets. The socialist camp did not honor trade agreements with Cuba. Not only did they not honor agreements, but diplomatically, economically, they became hostile toward Cuba. And every other place said, "We don't owe you anything. And those papers that we signed? That's your problem." And that's the position that Cuba found itself in. All of the focus of the revolution for three, four, five years at the beginning of the Special Period was on survival. The [official] position was: "We don't have time to argue about anything else. One percent of nothing is nothing. One hundred percent of nothing is nothing. So right now we've got to preserve our revolution." And the perception of black people in Cuba was the same. It was, like: All go on survival.

A Boxing Ring, 24-7: Tourism and Cuba in the Global Economy

I don't think that any place in the history of the planet has ever built as many hotels, as many tourist installations, in the six years that we're talking about than Cuba has. Everything goes back on tourism. At the same time the focus on women, the focus on black people was, like, "That's not our problem. The problem is food, shelter, clothing." There was some discussion of affirmative action in the sense of "How do you have a policy of affirmative action when you don't have [anything]?" My position is that you can't. You cannot. If you do not have enough stuff for all the population, if you don't have enough food for the whole population, you cannot have an economic affirmative action program. But you can do things that make a difference. You can deal with the educational system. You can deal with the cultural aspects—what is on television, on radio. You can deal with how teachers, how professionals, are trained. There are things I believe that can be done.

As the tourist industry began to grow and prosper and as the joint ventures, the joint business ventures, began to become more and more common in Cuba, what I began to see was blondes in bikinis on all the travel brochures. The African people, when they were presented, were presented in the folklore mode, dressed up like Changó with a knife between their teeth. There was a commercialization of the African religions. There was, and still is, a generalized perception by the public that corporations tend to have a preference for light-skinned Cubans. Tourism has brought all of these Europeans and South Americans and Mexicans with their racist ideas and the racist attitudes about the natives. And they come here, many of them, condoms in hand, looking for black pussy.

The Cuban government has really made an effort to try to promote what they call sane and healthy family tourism. Easier said than done. They have either tried to make regulations for the hotels where Cubans had prostitutes [so that prostitutes] would have difficulty going into hotels. They tried to have health tourism, ecology tourism, political tourism, healing tourism—all kinds of tourism to try to evade the money tourism. People come down here with big money, with big money attitudes, and no respect for the people, no respect for the revolution. They're coming down here for sun, sand, women and men, or whatever. And so the change is evident. It is evident in my opinion not only [in that] the tourism is there [but in] attitudes. You will find young women who are proud of going out with an Italian, Spaniard, whatever. [You find] people who want to know them, befriend them, who want to rediscover their Spanish roots: the resurrection of the Galician Association, the Catalonian Association, the Spanish Club. Because people say, "I may get some money in this. Let me reestablish my connections." So the tourism industry makes a kind of attitude that does not do anything but reinforce white supremacist values, mentality, relations, and power relations. You don't see a lot of black tourists come into Cuba. It's economic, so that power is associated with white people. Those that speed around Havana in fast cars are white people. [Cubans] look at television, they look at U.S. films, and they are affected by all this. You can't see all this around you and be unaffected by it. So there is the tendency for people to feel. "Well, maybe Europe isn't so bad. Maybe the States aren't so bad."

I think it is a mistake to think that the attitudes around race are totally separated from the attitudes around class, around gender. The resurgence of the woman as a sex object is more and more easy to see. When I came to Cuba, there was a national pride that was: "We're Socialists." I'm not saying that that national pride has disappeared or evaporated, but what I am saying is that the contradictions that are in the society are more evident. And you cannot have contradictions in how people live, what people see, without people having ideological problems, ideological questions. And the real bottom line is that when there are less crumbs on the table, the fight gets a little raunchy. The middle-management administrators in many cases tended to be white and not completely beyond helping each other at the expense of African people. I mean, they aren't going to come out and say that they're doing it. They try to hide it. They try to be slick about it. But there is in my opinion a group of white folks that look out for their own. Black folks are again observing, making sharper criticisms—and also in certain places dealing and saying, "Wait a minute. Hold on. There need to be changes. There need to be things that are addressed."

I believe that it would be historically impossible for this situation that I'm looking at now not to have occurred. I think it is historically inevitable because I think that when a country happens to put all its efforts on bare survival, they don't have time to rest. I mean, it's not like they're sitting there saying, "Oh my God, what do we talk about today?" This is basic survival with the raunchiest, most vicious enemy blockading you, trying to accelerate the blockade. You're trying to get a hand in but also at the same time trying to get an economic handle [and] that undermines the ideological, philosophical aspect of the revolution. Practically not one of the people investing in Cuba is doing so because they want to benefit and uphold the revolution. In a situation where [Cuba's] allies are the kind of allies that hang out with wolves and can barely make it to the UN to vote no on the blockade, it's been hard. This is no joke here. I mean, the U.S. has battered and bullied and knocked people down to the point that you got these whole little countries shaking in their boots. [These countries] will not even come out to make a [UN] vote unless everybody else has decided on it. In terms of economic integration, the English-speaking Caribbean is still running after the queen, and French Caribbeans think they're French men and women, so we have a real sick situation in terms of the worldwide vision. So Cuba has had to really be in a boxing ring 24-7. When you're in a boxing ring, it doesn't give you a lot of space and time to sit and concentrate on your internal problems and solve them.

Our Communities Are Sick: Healing Alienation

I hope that the revolution at this moment will pay more attention to not just serving the health system, the education system, but [to] dealing with the democratic functions in the country and relating that to what is going on in terms of race, in terms of gender, in terms of class. Saturday night in Cuba they see movies, and usually the movies come from the States. You have to put on whatever films you can put on. And 99 percent of what comes out of the States or out of Brazil is ideological poison. People think that this is how life is. Someone thirty years ago said, "Wow, I want a nice house and I want a house to have a bedroom, a bathroom." Now they want a kitchen with a little island in it, a sunken tub, a house with a deck. This is the image of what, materially, people should aspire to. And so [you find] the problems of ideological struggle in terms of just changing the whole focus of Eurocentrist fuckers that are part of every education system.

If you were to take every book you ever read and put them in piles and put the European pile on one hand and the Latin American, the Asian piles, you know what a distorted picture you would have. So can you imagine that even though socialism has been able to do something to reduce the Eurocentrism, it has not been able to accomplish that much? The Soviets claimed they knew everything. [They claimed] they had everything under control and had solved everything. Therefore, their line was "the line." And all this discussion about race was: You got a doctor, a free education and [racism] would evaporate. The Cubans got it from the West and they got it from the East. So that [now] they are faced with the task that every single country in the world with people of color [is] faced with: How can we de-Eurocentrize our system? Struggling against racism is I think very much connected to struggling to end Eurocentrism, [to end] the strict view that we can just take Marx and Engels and Lenin and have what they said become a coloring book—and we just color in the colors. I think that vision of social change is no longer applicable, if it ever was.

If we don't change the lifestyle that we are living right now—what we do in the morning to what we do at night, how we relate to other people, how our families are structured—I don't think we will be able to deal social justice. Because there's no way that this planet can offer a chicken in every pot, a computer in every den, a Mercedes-Benz in every garage. I don't think that the material reality exists on this planet for that. Our values and what we are fighting for have to change, and how we live and relate to each other has to change. The Cubans are looking at all this stuff. Anybody that is dealing with social change now better start looking at it. Because people are in a tremendous amount of pain, the pain is not just from not having enough food, not just [from not] having access to medical care. It is also because we have to live in [a] state of almost universal alienation. We do not have community. Our communities are sick. Our families are sick, and healing is needed in order for us to live in a society where we're not afraid to look somebody in the eyes and say good morning. We've got to change some real things other than material struggle. And so I think the world revolutionary movement, those who are struggling to make social justice on this planet, have got to rethink a lot of things about where we're going to go in the next millennium. I think we have to rethink our material focus. I think we have to think about how we see ourselves and what vision is our vision of liberation.

Monsterism: Youth and the Culture of Violence

One of the problems I have with young people, they do not understand what we mean when we say we were fighting for freedom. A lot of times we cannot articulate what our vision of freedom is, so how can we expect them to continue something that we can't express? They're talking about the youth culture, the violence, and some people say that, "Well, rap creates violence." I think our consciousness creates what comes out of our mouths and what comes out of our mouths reflects our consciousness. Big business uses what comes out of young African people's mouths to pollute other young African people with ideas that are very capitalist. Most [rappers] are saying. "We want the shit, we want the sneakers, we want the gold, we want everything. You told us we can't have shit, so we're going to be gangsters." [They're] illegitimate capitalists. That is the only difference. They say, "You told us we could be capitalists, we could go to school. I can't get into school. I could barely make it in school, but I could sell these rocks out here and I could make it." You look at all the videos and you see models making $50 a day shaking their butts around a swimming pool in a big old house, somebody with their pants hanging down and drawers sticking out, and people think that's keeping it real. That is selling the capitalist dream to people who cannot even sniff at it. They're going to jail and can't even make commissary money. I spent big time in jail and I know what's in there. There ain't no Rockefellers or gangsters up there. But there is a dream that's being sold just like *The Godfather.*

We watch it on TV; we can't escape from it. Nor can we escape from monsterism. My daughter laughs at me because I'm scared. I look at some monster pictures and I get upset. I feel that these people who kill everybody just take over my consciousness for an hour and a half. And I'm, like, "Damn, how many monsters are these people going to create?" They got a human monster, animal monster, plant monster, mineral monster. It is a society that is innovative with monsters but is creating real live monsters. You know how little kids have baseball cards—you know, back in the old days, my day? Now they have mass murderer cards that kids trade. So the violence of the society is big business. And they're exporting it so that the Cubas of the world and any other process that wants to build a revolution has got not only to deal with the material—how you build a health clinic, how you do this—but: How do you build new values? How do you build new human relationships?

They talk about black women being with the families and stuff like that. And all I can think of is: If every guy walked off a video, if one day all these guys came talking, "Bitch, come get the money, ho, hood rat," etc., if all these guys walked off the videos and tried to marry somebody, can you imagine what the relationship would be like? Can you imagine that this is some way for human beings to live in and raise a family? I saw Snoop Doggy Dog, he was on video, and he had his little baby saying, "Hey, little motherfucker, pimp motherfucker." If we consider political change in more than a structural way, in more than a power way, I don't see how we're going to get social justice, 'cause who is going to live in the society of Snoop Doggy Dog?

Are You Part Whatever? The Limits of Multiculturalism

I think social change can't be limited to the way that we have approached things in the past. I think it's got to be related to a lot of healing, 'cause we got people out there that are just too crazy to struggle. I'm serious. We got a lot of crazy people out there, people out of their minds. And dysfunctional families. I'm not talking about dysfunctional families in terms of African families. I'm talking about a dysfunctional world and how you raise a sane family in a dysfunctional world. The racism in the United States right now, everything is a code word. It is a racist agenda. It's saying to you, "Segregation for another hundred years. We [gave you] some affirmative action that was never very active or very affirmative, we gave you some rights that weren't too civil or too right, so what you got to complain about? You better get a job even though there aren't any." I mean, our future is a serious one. I mean, they got African people in England and in Holland, they represent a small percentage of the population, and they've become the number one enemy. They have a country like Denmark where they have two Africans, and one of them has got a suitcase on the way out—and you got people there convinced that those two Africans are the problem!

So in the States what's happening now with the multiculturalism, everybody's talking about, "I'm part Egyptian and part whatever." And I appreciate people discovering that about themselves and discovering aspects of who they are. But that is not political activity. The police are not going to ask you as they shoot you down, "Oh, are you part whatever?" The census is not going to change the district 'cause you are one-fifth Cherokee or whatever.

I think that we have to take a new look at what globalization means in terms of gender issues, in terms of race issues, and to rethink very seriously the kinds of not only structures that we deal with in terms of building social justice but the kinds of lives we live and the kinds of examples we're setting for those people who follow us. Because unless we make our lives as people who are dedicated to social change attractive so people are attracted to it, they feel good, they feel warm, they feel a sense of community, we're going to lose a majority of our youth. Because I think that in our style of political work, political activism has left a lot to be desired. I think a lot of people struggled for a lot of years without forming some kind of family or creating warm relationships. I think this has meaning. [Without this], I think we haven't discovered a new way of humanity.

Relating Politically and Personally: Toward a New Style of Politics

It's almost impossible for us not to have a double consciousness in terms of class, in terms of gender, our vision of family. Most of us go for what we know, and what we know is some historical model that is not applicable today. But we haven't been able to substitute all of it. We've substituted part of it. I mean,

I can read whoever—Marx, this, that, and the other—then say, "Damn, I wish I was near a swimming pool." There is a bourgeois side to our consciousness because we were raised in a bourgeois society. I remember in the Seventies after we finished dissing everyone, we started talking about humanism and unity and democracy. Not only were we imitating Europeans—that's one thing—but we were unaware completely about our double consciousness, our internal contradictions, and of the pact we had individually of fighting against those things. Because you cannot fight against something that you don't talk about and you don't admit. [Back then], everybody was more revolutionary than everybody else and everybody's mind was more correct than everybody else's. I think that this time if we talk about the things that shaped us, our values, etc., and they are full of contradiction, then we can start to go somewhere else and move to somewhere else. But the arrogance, the dishonesty that so many of us have had . . .

I don't mean we're bad people because of it, because I think it was a political style that we inherited. I thought being a good revolutionary was being like that or trying to be a talking head or . . . I had millions of powerful images of what being active in a movement for social change meant. Now I'm in another place in my life—and maybe this is a touchy-feely stage that I'm going through—but I like the idea of people relating politically and relating personally, of communion, coming together, having picnics, of people talking about themselves as human beings and not just about social change in the abstract. Because I think that what happens when you talk about social change in the abstract, what happens is that you see the social being in the theoretical phase as one type of being. [But] the diversity of the social being is almost infinite. And in order to take into consideration those small people who had different visions, who have different needs, who have different whatever from the big picture, we have to stop and sympathize in terms of the social relationships we're trying to create. Because I don't think that the general is enough.

Change Is a Way of Life: Looking to the Future

I also feel very optimistic. I think a lot of dead weight has been removed from the back of social change. Creativity is part of the struggle—it is one of the most important parts. When people talk about sacrifice—you know, sacrifices that people made in the Sixties—I feel almost very weird. Had I not become involved in the struggle, I would be tagging along with some kind of needle stuck somewhere or some fate worse than that. So I think that the movement has done much more for me than I'll ever be able to do for the movement. [Even] with all of the boring, terrible, miserable experiences I've had, this has been a lifesaving experience intellectually, spiritually, socially. I don't think I would've met the kind of beautiful people I've been lucky enough to have met in life. So I feel very fortunate to have not *chosen* this path—but to have stumbled, fallen, into it.

I think the continuity of struggle is something we pay a lot more attention to in terms of being aware of people that struggled before. I think we have sometimes forgotten the continuity, thought that the struggle was going to be five minutes and, after, we could all go to the movies. I think that when we understand the world is not going to change in five minutes, we can be part of that change, and being part of that change is a way of life. It is something that I like. I look at the Clintons and, I mean, these are grotesque people. They really are. I just don't like them.

I'm one of those people who had to piece my life together with Band-Aids. And I mean that physically, mentally, and every other way. So I don't look at the U.S. as being my country. Maybe my daughter or my grand-something will look at it another way. I'm one of those people that has been alienated. I am a victim. I feel like Malcolm. And until there is another "Savior," my attitude is going to be the same. But I understand that this is a process, and what's going on with us has to become connected with what's going on in Africa, what's going on in the Caribbean. Because I do see us winning, not by ourselves and not with just looking at the United States as this isolated place, but looking at our African ancestors—whether they are in Cuba, whether they are here—and our spiritual ancestors, whoever they may be.

Note

1. Assata Shakur, "The Continuity of Struggle," *Souls: A Critical Journal of Black Politics, Culture and Society* 1 (spring 1999): 93.

Source

Assata Shakur, "The Continuity of Struggle," *Souls: A Critical Journal of Black Politics, Culture and Society* 1 (spring 1999): 93–100.

Selected Bibliography

Bin Wahad, Dhoruba, Mumia Abu-Jamal, Assata Shakur, et al. *Still Black, Still Strong: Survivors of the U.S. War Against Black Revolutionaries.* New York: Semiotext(e), 1993.

Shakur, Assata. *Assata: An Autobiography.* Westport, Conn: L. Hill, 1987.

—— *Assata Shakur Speaks: Message to the New Afrikan Nation.* Stone Mountain, Ga.: Universal Truth, 1990.

—— *Black Human Rights Statement from Assata Shakur.* Los Angeles: National Black Human Rights Coalition, Los Angeles Chapter, 1979.

part 2

Political, Economic, and Social Justice

chapter four

Political Leadership and Social Protest

one

Petitions

Enslaved Africans actually found countless ways to protest their condition and sometimes they sought redress through formal petitions. The following documents are notable because they are some of the earliest known petitions. Although the first letter is signed by a slave named Felix, it is more than a mere request for his own freedom; rather, Felix wrote on behalf of "many SLAVES, living in the Town of BOSTON, and other Towns in the Province."

Despite the necessity of having to be deferential and obsequious, Felix captured the harsh reality of slavery and suggested some of the ways that religion was used by African Americans as a kind of buffer, offering salvation in an afterworld, and helping to shield slaves from the worst aspects of their condition. The second document was written by an anonymous slave who appealed to William, Earl of Dartmouth, through a prose poem. The third letter, from four fugitive slaves to the United States Congress of 1797, is the first petition to the United States Congress that is still extant.

Petition of the Africans, Living in Boston

PROVINCE OF THE MASSACHUSETTS-BAY.
To his Excellancy THOMAS HUTCHINSON,[1] Esq; Governor;
To the Honorable His Majesty's Council, and
To the Honorable House of REPRESENTATIVES in
General Court
assembled at BOSTON, the 6th Day of January, 1773.

The humble PETITION of many SLAVES, living in the Town of BOSTON, and other Towns in the Province, is this, namely,

That your Excellency and Honors, and the Honorable the Representatives would be pleased to take their unhappy State and Condition under your wise and just Consideration.

We desire to bless GOD, who loves Mankind, who sent his Son to die for their Salvation, and who is no Respector of Persons; that he hath lately put it into the Hearts of Multitudes on both Sides of the Water, to bear our Burthens, some of whom are Men of great Note and Influence; who have pleaded our Cause with Arguments which we hope will have their weight with this Honorable Court.

We presume not to dictate to your EXCELLENCY and Honors, being willing to rest our Cause on your Humanity and Justice; yet would beg leave to say a Word or two on the Subject.

Although some of the Negroes are vicious, (who doubtless may be punished and restrained by the same Laws which are in Force against other of the King's Subjects) there are many others of a quite different Character, and who if made free, would soon be able as well as willing to bear a Part in the Public Charges; many of them good natural Parts, are discreet, sober, honest, and industrious; and may it not be said of many, that they are virtuous and religious, although their Condition is in itself so unfriendly to Religion, and every moral Virtue except *Patience.* How many of that Number have there been, and now are in this Province, who have had every Day of their Lives imbittered with this most intolerable Reflection, That, let their Behaviour be what it will, neither they, nor their Children to all Generations, shall ever be able to do, or to possess and enjoy any Thing, no, not even *Life itself,* but in a Manner as the *Beasts that perish.*

We have no Property? We have no Wives! No Children! We have no City! No Country! But we have a Father in Heaven, and we are determined as far as his Grace shall enable us, and as far as our degraded contemptuous Life will admit, to keep all his Commandments: Especially will we be obedient to our Masters, so long as GOD in his sovereign Providence shall *suffer* us to be holden in Bondage.

It would be impudent, if not presumptuous in us, to suggest to your Excellency and Honors any Law or Laws proper to be made in relation to our unhappy State, which, although our greatest Unhappiness, is not our *Fault;* and this gives us great Encouragement to pray and hope for such Relief as is consistent with your Wisdom, Justice, and Goodness.

We think ourselves very happy that we may thus address the Great and General Court of this Province, which great and good Court is to us, the best judge, under GOD, of what is wise, just, and good.

We humbly beg leave to add but this one Thing more: We pray for such Relief only, which by no Possibility can ever be productive of the least Wrong or Injury to our Masters; but to us will be as Life from the dead.

Signed, FELIX
1773

To the Right Honourable WILLIAM, Earl of DARTMOUTH, His Majesty's Principal Secretary of State for North America

Hail, happy day, when, smiling like the morn,
Fair *Freedom* rose *New-England* to adorn:
The northern clime beneath her genial ray,
Dartmouth, congratulates thy blissful sway:
Elate with hope her race no longer mourns,
Each soul expands, each grateful bosom burns,
While in thine hand with pleasure we behold
The silken reins, and *Freedom*'s charms unfold.
Long lost to realms beneath the northern skies
She shines supreme, while hated *faction* dies:
Soon as appear'd the *Goddess* long desir'd,
Sick at the view, she languished and expir'd;
Thus from the splendors of the morning light
The owl in sadness seeks the caves of night.

No more *America,* in mournful strain
Of wrongs, and grievance unredress'd complain,
No longer shall thou dread the iron chain,
Which wanton *Tyranny* with lawless hand
Had made, and with it meant t'enslave the land.

Should you, my lord, while you peruse my song,
Wonder from whence my love of *Freedom* sprung,
Whence flow these wishes for the common good,

By feeling hearts alone best understood,
I, young in life, by seeming cruel Fate
Was snatch'd from *Afric's* fancy'd happy seat:
What pangs excruciating must molest,
What sorrows labour in my parent's breast?
Steel'd was that soul and by no misery mov'd
That from a father seiz'd his babe belov'd:
Such, such my case. And can I then but pray
Others may never feel tyrannic sway?

For favours past, great Sir, our thanks are due,
And thee we ask favours to renew,
Since in thy pow'r, as in thy will before,
To sooth the griefs, which thou did'st once deplore.
May heav'nly grace the sacred sanction give
To all thy works, and thou for ever live
Not only on the wings of fleeting *Fame,*
Though praise immortal crowns the patriot's name,
But to conduct to heav'ns refulgent fane,
May fiery coursers sweep th'ethereal plain,
And bear thee upwards to that blest abode,
Where, like the prophet, thou shalt find thy God.

1773

The Earliest Extant Negro Petition to Congress, 1797

In 1775 the revolutionary state of North Carolina passed a law forbidding the manumission of slaves: except for meritorious services as judged and approved by a county court. Nevertheless, as the preamble to a law of 1778 declared, "divers evil-minded persons, intending to disturb the public peace, did liberate and set free their slaves," and this provoked the courts of Perquimans and Pasquotank to order these Negroes captured and sold to the highest bidder. The act of 1778 approved this, but warned that no Negro who had gained his liberty by faithful service in the Revolutionary Army was to be re-enslaved.

Ten years later the North Carolina legislature passed another act on this question because, despite the law of 1775, "divers persons from religious motives [mostly Quakers—ed.], in violation of the said law, continue to liberate their slaves, who are now going at large to the terror of the people of this State." This act of 1788 provided for the apprehension of all illegally manumitted Negroes, with twenty percent of the sale price going to the informer. Something like a reign of terror descended upon many free Negroes and quite a few fled the State. On January 23, 1797, four of these Negroes, named Jacob Nicholson, Jupiter Nicholson, Joe Albert and Thomas Pritchet, residing in Philadelphia, petitioned Congress through Representative John Swanwick of Pennsylvania for a redress of their grievance. On January 30, 1797, the question as to whether or not to accept a petition from fugitive slaves was debated in Congress and rejected by a vote of fifty to thirty-three. In the course of the debate, Representative William Smith, of South Carolina, declared: "The practice of a former time, in a similar case, was that the petition was sealed up and sent back to the petitioners." This petition of 1797 appears to be the first from Negroes to Congress, however, that is still extant.

To the President, Senate, and House of Representatives. The Petition and Representation of the under-named Freemen, respectfully showeth:—

That, being of African descent, late inhabitants and natives of North Carolina, to you only, under God, can we apply with any hope of effect, for redress of our grievances, having been compelled to leave the State wherein we had a right of residence, as freemen liberated under the hand and seal of humane and conscientious masters, the validity of which act of justice, in restoring us to our native right of freedom, was confirmed by judgment of the Superior Court of North Carolina, wherein it was brought to trial: yet, not long after this decision, a law of that State was enacted, under which men of cruel disposition, and void of just principle received countenance and authority in violently seizing, imprisoning, and selling into slavery, such as had been so emancipated: whereby we were reduced to the necessity of separating from some of our nearest and most tender connexions, and of seeking refuge in such parts of the Union where more regard is paid to the public declaration in favor of liberty and the common right of man, several hundreds, under our circumstances, having in consequence of the said law, been hunted day and night, like beasts of the forest, by armed men with dogs, and made a prey of as free and lawful plunder. Among others thus exposed, I, Jupiter Nicholson, of Perquimans county, N.C., after being set free by my master, Thomas Nicholson, and having been about two years employed as a seaman in the service of Zachary Nickson, on coming on shore, was pursued by men with dogs and arms; but was favored to escape by night to Virginia, with my wife, who was manumitted by Gabriel Cosand, where I resided about four years in the town of Portsmouth, chiefly employed in sawing boards and scantling; from thence I removed with my wife to Philadelphia, where I have been employed, at times, by water, working along shore, or sawing wood. I left behind me a father and mother, who were manumitted by Thomas Nicholson and Zachary Dickson; they have since been taken up, with a beloved brother, and sold into cruel bondage.

I, Jacob Nicholson, also of North Carolina, being set free by my master, Joseph Nicholson, but continuing to live with him till, being pursued night and day, I was obliged to leave my abode, sleep in the woods, and stacks in the fields, &c, to escape the hands of violent men who, induced by the profit afforded them by law, followed this course as a business: at length, by night, I made my escape, leaving a mother, one child, and two brothers, to see whom I dare not return.

I, Joe Albert, manumitted by Benjamin Albertson, who was my careful guardian to protect me from being afterwards taken and sold, providing me with a house to accommodate me and my wife, who was liberated by William Robertson: but we were night and day hunted by men armed with guns, swords, and pistols, accompanied with mastiff dogs: from whose violence, being one night apprehensive of immediate danger, I left my dwelling, locked and barred, and fastened with a chain, being at some distance from it, while my wife was by my kind master locked up under his roof. I heard them break into my house, where, not finding their prey, they got but a small booty, a handkerchief of about a dollar value, and some provisions; but, not long after, I was discovered and seized by Alexander Stafford, William Stafford, and Thomas Creesy, who were armed with guns and clubs. After binding me with my hands behind me, and a rope around my arms and body, they took me about four miles to Hartford prison, where I lay four weeks, suffering much from want of provision; from thence, with the assistance of a fellow-prisoner, (a white man) I made my escape and for three dollars was conveyed, with my wife, by a humane person, in a covered wagon by night, to Virginia, where, in the neighborhood of Portsmouth, I continued unmolested about four years, being chiefly engaged in sawing boards and plank. On being advised to move northward, I came with my wife to Philadelphia, where I have labored for a livelihood upwards of two years, in Summer mostly, along shore in vessels and stores, and sawing wood in the Winter. My mother was set free by Phineas Nickson, my sister by John Trueblood, and both taken up and sold into slavery, myself deprived of the consolation of seeing them, without being exposed to the like grievous oppression.

I, Thomas Pritchet, was set free by my master Thomas Pritchet, who furnished me with land to raise provisions for my use, where I built myself a house, cleared a sufficient spot of woodland to produce ten bushels of corn; the second year about fifteen, and the third, had as much planted as I suppose would have produced thirty bushels; this I was obliged to leave about one month before it was fit for gathering, being threatened by Holland Lockwood, who married my said master's widow, that if I would not come and serve him, he would apprehend me, and send me to the West Indies; Enoch Ralph also threatening to send me to jail, and sell me for the good of the country: being thus in jeopardy, I left my little farm, with my small stock and utensils, and my corn standing, and escaped by night into Virginia, where shipping myself for Boston, I was, through stress of weather landed in New York, where I served as a waiter for seventeen months; but my mind being distressed on account of the situation of my wife and children, I returned to Norfolk in Virginia, with a hope of at least seeing them, if I could not obtain their freedom; but finding I was advertised in the newspaper, twenty dollars the reward for apprehending me, my dangerous situation obliged me to leave Virginia, disappointed of seeing my wife and children, coming to Philadelphia, where I resided in the employment of a waiter upward of two years.

In addition to the hardship of our own case, as above set forth, we believe ourselves warranted, on the present occasion, in offering to your consideration the singular case of a fellow-black now confined in the jail of this city, under sanction of the act of General Government, called the Fugitive Law, as it appears to us a flagrant proof how far human beings, merely on account of color and complexion, are, through prevailing prejudice, outlawed and excluded from common justice and common humanity, by the operation of such partial laws in support of habits and customs cruelly oppressive. This man, having been many years past manumitted by his master in North Carolina, was under the authority of the aforementioned law of that State, sold again into slavery, and, after serving his purchaser upwards of six years, made his escape to Philadelphia, where he has resided eleven years, having a wife and [f]our children: and, by an agent of the Carolina claimer, has been lately apprehended and committed to prison, his said claimer, soon after the man's escaping from him, having advertised him, offering a reward of ten silver dollars to any person that would bring him back, or five times that sum to any person that would make due proof of his being killed, and no questions asked by whom.

We beseech your impartial attention to our hard condition, not only with respect to our personal sufferings, as freemen, but as a class of that people who, distinguished by color, are therefore with a degrading partiality, considered by many, even of those in eminent stations, as unentitled to that public justice and protection which is the great object of Government. We indulge not a hope, or presume to ask for the interposition of your honorable body, beyond the extent of your constitutional power or influence, yet are willing to believe your serious, disinterested, and candid consideration of the premises, under the benign impressions of equity and mercy, producing upright exertion of what is in your power, may not be without some salutary effect, both for our relief as a people, and toward the removal of obstructions to public order and well-being.

If, notwithstanding all that has been publicly avowed as essential principles respecting the extent of human right to freedom; notwithstanding we have had that right restored to us, so far as was in the power of those by whom we were held as slaves, we cannot claim the privilege of representation in your councils, yet we trust we may address you as fellow-men, who, under God, the sovereign Ruler of the Universe, are intrusted with the distribution of justice, for the terror of evil-doers, the encouragement and protection of the innocent, not doubting that you are men of liberal minds, susceptible of benevolent feelings and clear conception of rectitude to a catholic extent, who can admit that black people (servile as their condition generally is throughout this Continent) have natural affections, social and domestic attachments and sensibilities; and that, therefore, we may hope for a share in your sympathetic attention while we represent that the unconstitutional bondage in which multitudes of our fellows in complexion are held, is to us a subject sorrowfully affecting; for we cannot conceive this condition (more especially those who have been emancipated and tasted the sweets of liberty, and again reduced to slavery by kidnappers and man-stealers) to be less afflicting or deplorable than the situation of citizens of the United States, captured and enslaved through the unrighteous policy prevalent in Algiers. We are far from considering all those who retain slaves as wilful oppressors, being well assured that numbers in the State from whence we are exiles, hold their slaves in bondage, not of choice, but possessing them by inheritance, feel their minds burdened under the slavish restraint of legal impediments to doing justice which they are convinced is due to fellow-rationals. May we not be allowed to consider this stretch of power, morally and politically, a Governmental defect, if not a direct violation of the declared fundamental principles of the Constitution; and finally, is not some remedy for an evil of such magnitude highly worthy of the deep inquiry and unfeigned zeal of the supreme Legislative body of a free and enlightened people? Submitting our cause to God, and humbly craving your best aid and influence, as you may be favored and directed by that wisdom which is from above, wherewith that you may be eminently dignified and rendered conspicuously, in the view of nations, a blessing to the people you represent, is the sincere prayer of your petitioners.

Note

1. Thomas Hutchinson (1711–1780), colonial governor of Massachusetts.

Source

[Felix?], "Petition to Thomas Hutchinson," and anonymous, addressed to "Honourable William, Earl of Dartmouth," in Dierdre Mullane, ed., *Crossing the Danger Water: Three Hundred Years of African-American Writing,* 44–45 (New York: Anchor Books, 1993); and "Earliest Extant Petition to Congress, 1797" (1849; reprinted in Herbert Aptheker, ed., *A Documentary History of the Negro People in the United States,* 39–44 [New York: Citadel Press, 1951]).

Selected Bibliography

Berlin, Ira. *Many Thousands Gone: The First Two Centuries of Slavery in North America.* Cambridge, Mass.: Harvard University Press, 1988.

Blackburn, Robin. *The Overthrow of Colonial Slavery, 1776–1848.* New York: Verso, 1989.

Quarles, Benjamin. *Black Abolitionists*. New York: Da Capo, 1991.
Stewart, James Brewer. *Holy Warriors: Abolitionists and American Slavery.* New York: Hill and Wang, 1997.
Wood, Peter. *Strange New Land: African-Americans, 1617–1776.* New York: Oxford University Press, 1996.

two

Letter to Thomas Jefferson

Often called the first African American man of science, Benjamin Banneker (1731–1806) was a mathematician, astronomer, craftsman, and surveyor who produced the first almanac written by a black man. Banneker's letter to Thomas Jefferson,[1] originally appeared in the 1793 version of Banneker's almanac. Banneker politely but convincingly challenged the common belief that African Americans were intellectually inferior to whites, and in the process, he offered fuel for white abolitionists. In this light, Banneker's almanac was one of the most influential publications of its time.

Banneker was born near Baltimore, Maryland, and he was taught to read by his grandmother. In 1753 he demonstrated his precocity by building an impressive wooden clock, based solely on his study of a small pocket watch. In 1763 he purchased his first book, the Bible, and in 1792 he published the first version of his almanac, which showcased his ability to make difficult astronomical calculations. He died in 1806, and the site of his burial was rediscovered and marked in 1990. In 1980 Banneker was honored by appearing on a U.S. postage stamp.

Maryland, Baltimore County,

Near Ellicotts' Lower Mills, August 19th, 1791.

THOMAS JEFFERSON, Secretary of State.

Sir:—I am fully sensible of the greatness of that freedom, which I take with you on the present occasion, a liberty which seemed to me scarcely allowable, when I reflected on that distinguished and dignified station in which you stand, and the almost general prejudice and prepossession which is so prevalent in the world against those of my complexion.

I suppose it is a truth too well attested to you, to need a proof here, that we are a race of beings who have long laboured under the abuse and censure of the world, that we have long been considered rather as brutish than human, and scarcely capable of mental endowments.

Sir, I hope I may safely admit, in consequence of that report which hath reached me, that you are a man far less inflexible in sentiments of this nature than many others, that you are measureably friendly and well disposed towards us, and that you are ready and willing to lend your aid and assistance to our relief, from those many distressed and numerous calamities, to which we are reduced.

Now, sir, if this is founded in truth, I apprehend you will readily embrace every opportunity to eradicate that train of absurd and false ideas and opinions, which so generally prevails with respect to us, and that your sentimemts are concurrent with mine, which are that one universal father hath given being to us all, and that he hath not only made us all of one flesh, but that he hath also without partiality afforded us all the same sensations, and endued us all with the same faculties, and that however variable we may be in society or religion, however diversified in situation or colour, we are all of the same family, and stand in the same relation to him.

Sir, if these are sentiments of which you are fully persuaded, I hope you cannot but acknowledge, that it is the indispensable duty of those who maintain for themselves the rights of human nature, and who profess the obligations of christianity, to extend their power and influence to the relief of every part of the human race, from whatever burthen or oppression they may unjustly labour under, and this I apprehend a full conviction of the truth and obligation of these principles should lead all to.

Sir, I have long been convinced, that if your love for yourselves and for those inestimable laws, which preserve to you the rights of human nature, was founded on sincerity, you could not but be solicitous that every individual of whatever rank or distinction, might with you equally enjoy the blessings thereof, neither could you rest satisfied, short of the most active diffusion of your exertions, in order, to their promotion from any state of degradation, to which the unjustifiable cruelty and barbarism of men may have reduced them.

Sir, I freely and cheerfully acknowledge that I am of the African race, and in that colour which is natural to them of the deepest dye, and it is under a sense of the most profound gratitude to the supreme ruler of the Universe, that I now confess to you, that I am not under that state of tyrannical thraldom, and inhuman captivity, to which too many of my brethren are doomed, but that I have abundantly tasted of the fruition of those blessings, which proceed from that free and unequalled liberty, with which you are favored, and which, I hope you will willingly allow, you have received from the immediate hand of that being, from whom proceedeth every good and perfect gift.

Sir, suffer me to recall to your mind that time in which the arms and tyranny of the British crown were exerted with every powerful effort in order to reduce you to a state of servitude; look back, I entreat you, on the variety of dangers to which you were exposed; reflect on that time in which every human aid appeared unavailable, and in which even hope and fortitude wore the aspect of inability to the conflict, and you cannot but be led to a serious and grateful sense of your miraculous and providential preservation; you cannot but acknowledge, that the present freedom and tranquility which you enjoy, you have mercifully received, and that is the peculiar blessing of heaven.

This, sir, was a time in which you clearly saw into the injustice of a state of slavery, and in which you had just apprehension of the horrors of its condition, it was now, sir, that your abhorrence thereof was so excited, that you publicly held forth this true and invaluable doctrine, which is worthy to be recorded and remembered in all succeeding ages. "We hold these truths to be self-evident, that all men are created equal, and that they are endowed by their creator with certain inalienable rights, that among these are life, liberty and the pursuit of happiness."[2]

Here, sir, was a time in which your tender feelings for yourselves had engaged you thus to declare, you were then impressed with proper ideas of the great valuation of liberty, and the free possession of those blessings to which you were entitled by nature; but, sir, how pitiable is it to reflect that although you were so fully convinced of the benevolence of the Father of mankind, and of his equal and impartial distribution of those rights and privileges which he had conferred upon them, that you should at the same time counteract his mercies, in detaining by fraud and violence so numerous a part of my brethren, under groaning captivity and cruel oppression, that you should at the same time be found guilty of that most criminal act, which you professedly detested in others with respect to yourselves.

Sir, I suppose that your knowledge of the situation of my brethren, is too extensive to need recital here; neither shall I presume to prescribe methods by which they may be relieved, otherwise than by recommending to you and all others, to wean yourselves from those narrow prejudices which you have imbibed with respect to them, and as Job proposed to his friends, "put your souls in their souls stead",[3] thus shall your hearts be enlarged with kindness and benevolence towards them, and thus shall you need neither the direction of myself nor others, in what manner to proceed herein.

And now, sir, although my sympathy and affection for my brethren hath cause my enlargement thus far, I ardently hope that your candour and generosity, will plead with you in my behalf, when I make known to you, that it was not orginally my design; but that having taken up my pen, in order to direct to you as a present, a copy of an almanac, which I have calculated for the succeeding year, I was unexpectedly and unavoidably led thereto.

This calculation, sir, is the production of my arduous study in this my advanced stage of life; for having long had unbounded desires to become acquainted with the secrets of nature, I have had to gratify my curiosity herein through my own assiduous application to astronomical study, in which I need not to recount to you the many difficulties and disadvantages which I have had to encounter.

And although I had almost declined to make my calculation for the ensuing year, in consequence of that time which I had allotted therefor, being taken up at the Federal Territory, by the request of Mr. Andrew Ellicott, yet finding myself under several engagements to printers of this State, to whom I had communicated my design, on my return to my place to residence, I industriously applied myself thereto, which I hope I have accomplished with correctness and accuracy, a copy of which I have taken the liberty to direct to you, and which I humbly request you will favorably receive, and although you may have the opportunity of perusing it after its publication, yet I chose to send it to you in manuscript previous thereto, that thereby you might not only have an earlier inspection; but that you might also view it in my own hand-writing.

And now, sir, I shall conclude and subscribe myself, with the most profound respect, your most obedient humble servant,

B. BANNEKER.

THOMAS JEFFERSON, Secretary of State, Philadelphia.

N.B. Any communication to me, may be had by a direction to Mr. Elias Ellicott, merchant, in Baltimore Town.

Notes

1. Thomas Jefferson (1743–1826), third president of the United States (1801–1809).
2. From the Declaration of Independence, adopted July 4, 1776, by delegates of the thirteen colonies, announcing their separation from Great Britain and the creation of the United States. Primarily written by Thomas Jefferson.
3. Job 16:4.

Source

Benjamin Banneker, "Letter to Thomas Jefferson, 8/19/1791," in Carter G. Woodson, ed., *The Mind of the Negro As Reflected in His Letters Written During the Crisis, 1800–1860,* xiv–xxvii (New York: Negro Universities Press, 1926).

Selected Bibliography

Allen, Will. *Banneker: The Afro-American Astronomer.* Salem, N.H.: Ayer, 1971.

Bedini, Silvio. *The Life of Benjamin Banneker.* Baltimore: Maryland Historical Society, 1998.

Litwin, Laura B. *Benjamin Banneker: Astronomer and Mathematician.* Berkeley Heights, N.J.: Enslow, 1999.

Logan, Rayford W. and Michael R. Winston. *Dictionary of American Negro Biography.* New York: Norton, 1982.

three

Oration on the Abolition of the Slave Trade

Historians know little about Peter Williams Jr. (??–1849), but Carter G. Woodson characterized him as "a hospitable and generous man, well trained and interested in the education of the Negroes."[1] He was the son of one of the founders of the African Methodist Episcopal Zion church in New York City, and later he became a pastor at St. Phillips Church, also in New York City. In this oration, Williams traces the history of slavery, implores his listeners to put themselves in the position of captive Africans, and celebrates the abolition of the slave trade. Yet at the same time, Williams also asks that blacks employ "a steady and upright deportment," in order to win the respect of the white majority, and he predicts the "luxuriant growth of knowledge and virtue" among African Americans.

Fathers, Brethren, and Fellow Citizens: At this auspicious moment I felicitate you on the abolition of the Salve Trade. This inhuman branch of commerce which, for some centuries past, has been carried on to a considerable extent, is, by the singular interposition of Divine Providence, this day extinguished. An event so important, so pregnant with happy consequences, must be extremely consonant to every philanthropic heart.

But to us, Africans and descendants of Africans, this period is deeply interesting. We have felt, sensibly felt, the sad effects of this abominable traffic. It has made, if not ourselves, our forefathers and kinsmen its unhappy victims; and pronounced on them, and their posterity, the sentence of perpetual slavery. But benevolent men have voluntarily stepped forward to obviate the consequences of this injustice and barbarity. They have striven, assiduously, to restore our natural rights; to guaranty them from fresh innovations; to furnish us with necessary information; and to stop the source from whence our evils have flowed.

The fruits of these laudable endeavors have long been visible; each moment they appear more conspicuous; and this day has produced an event which shall ever be memorable and glorious in the annals of history. We are now assembled to celebrate this momentous era; to recognize the beneficial influences of humane exertions; and by suitable demonstrations of joy, thanksgiving, and gratitude, to return to our heavenly Father, and to our earthly benefactors, our sincere acknowledgments.

Review, for a moment, my brethren, the history of the Slave Trade. Engendered in the foul recesses of the sordid mind, the unnatural monster inflicted gross evils on the human race. Its baneful footsteps are marked with blood; its infectious breath spreads war and desolation; and its train is composed of the complicated miseries of cruel and unceasing bondage.

Before the enterprising spirit of European genius explored the western coast of Africa, the state of our forefathers was a state of simplicity, innocence, and contentment. Unskilled in the arts of dissimulation, their bosoms were the seats of confidence; and their lips were the organs of truth. Strangers to the refinements of civilized society, they followed with implicit obedience the (simple) dictates of nature. Peculiarly observant of hospitality, they offered a place of refreshment to the weary, and an asylum to the unfortunate. Ardent in their affections, their minds were susceptible of the warmest emotions of love, friendship, and gratitude.

Although unacquainted with the diversified luxuries and amusements of civilized nations, they enjoyed some singular advantages from the bountiful hand of nature and from their own innocent and amiable manners, which rendered them a happy people. But, alas! this delightful picture has long since vanished; the angel of bliss has deserted their dwelling; and the demon of indescribable misery has rioted, uncontrolled, on the fair fields of our ancestors. After Columbus unfolded to civilized man the vast treasures of this western world, the desire of gain, which had chiefly induced the first colonists of America to cross the waters of the Atlantic, surpassing the bounds of reasonable acquisition, violated the sacred injunctions of the gospel, frustrated the designs of the pious and humane, and, enslaving the harmless aborigines, compelled them to drudge in the mines.

The severities of this employment was so insupportable to men who were unaccustomed to fatigue that, according to Robertson's "History of America," upwards of nine hundred thousand were destroyed in the space of fifteen years on the island of Hispaniola. A consumption so rapid must, in a short period, have deprived them of the instruments of labor, had not the same genius which first produced it found out another method to obtain them. This was no other than the importation of slaves from the coast of Africa.

The Genoese made the first regular importation, in the year 1517, by virtue of a patent granted by Charles of Austria to a Flemish favorite; since which, this commerce has increased to an astonishing and almost incredible degree.

After the manner of ancient piracy, descents were first made on the African coast; the towns bordering on the ocean were surprised, and a number of the inhabitants carried into slavery.

Alarmed at these depredations, the natives fled to the interior, and there united to secure themselves from the common foe. But the subtle invaders were not easily deterred from their purpose. Their experience, corroborated by historical testimony, convinced them that this spirit of unity would baffle every violent attempt; and that the most powerful method to dissolve it would be to diffuse in them the same avaricious disposition which they themselves possessed; and to afford them the means of gratifying it, by ruining each other. Fatal engine: fatal thou hast proved to man in all ages: where the greatest violence has proved ineffectual, their undermining principles have wrought destruction. By thy deadly power, the strong Grecian arm, which bid the world defiance, fell nerveless; by thy potent attacks, the solid pillars of Roman grandeur shook to their base; and, oh! Africans! by this parent of the Slave Trade, this grandsire of misery, the mortal blow was struck which crushed the peace and happiness of our country. Affairs now assumed a different aspect; the appearances of war were changed into the most amicable pretensions; presents apparently inestimable were made; and all the bewitching and alluring wiles of the seducer were practiced. The harmless African, taught to believe a friendly countenance, the sure token of a corresponding heart, soon disbanded his fears and evinced a favorable disposition towards his flattering enemies.

Thus the foe, obtaining an intercourse by a dazzling display of European finery, bewildered their simple understandings and corrupted their morals. Mutual agreements were then made; the Europeans were to supply the Africans with those gaudy trifles which so strongly affected them; and the Africans in return were to grant the Europeans their prisoners of war and convicts as slaves. These stipulations, naturally tending to delude the mind, answered the twofold purpose of enlarging their criminal code and of exciting incessant war at the same time that it furnished a specious pretext for the prosecution of this inhuman traffic. Bad as this may appear, had it prescribed the bounds of injustice, millions of unhappy victims might have still been spared. But, extending widely beyond measure and without control, large additions of slaves were made by kidnaping and the most unpalliated seizures.

Trace the past scenes of Africa and you will manifestly perceive these flagrant violations of human rights. The prince who once delighted in the happiness of his people, who felt himself bound by a sacred contract to defend their persons and property, was turned into their tyrant and scourge: he, who once strove to preserve peace and good understanding with the different nations, who never unsheathed his sword but in the cause of justice, at the signal of a slave ship assembled his warriors and rushed furiously upon his unsuspecting friends. What a scene does that town now present, which a few moments past was the abode of tranquillity. At the approach of the foe, alarm and confusion pervade every part; horror and dismay are depicted on every countenance; the aged chief, starting from his couch, calls forth his men to repulse the hostile invader: all ages obey the summons; feeble youth and decrepit age join the standard; while the foe, to effect his purpose, fires the town.

Now, with unimaginable terror the battle commences: hear now the shrieks of the women, the cries of the children, the shouts of the warriors, and the groans of the dying. See with what desperation the inhabitants fight in defense of their darling joys. But, alas! overpowered by a superior foe, their force is broken; their ablest warriors fall; and the wretched remnant are taken captives.

Where are now those pleasant dwellings, where peace and harmony reigned incessant? where those beautiful fields, whose smiling crops and enchanting verdure enlivened the heart of every beholder? Alas! those tenements are now enveloped in destructive flames; those fair fields are now bedewed with blood and covered with mangled carcasses. Where are now those sounds of mirth and gladness, which loudly rang throughout the village? where those darling youth, those venerable aged, who mutually animated the festive throng? Alas! those exhilarating peals are now changed into the dismal groans of inconceivable distress; the survivors of those happy people are now carried into cruel captivity. Ah! driven from their native soil, they cast their languishing eyes behind, and with aching hearts bid adieu to every prospect of joy and comfort.

A spectacle so truly distressing is sufficient to blow into a blaze the most latent spark of humanity; but, the adamantine heart of avarice, dead to every sensation of pity, regards not the voice of the sufferers, but hastily drives them to market for sale.

Oh, Africa, Africa! to what horrid inhumanities have thy shores been witness; thy shores, which were once the garden of the world, the seal of almost paradisaical joys, have been transformed into regions of woe; thy sons, who were once the happiest of mortals, are reduced to slavery, and bound in weighty shackles, now fill the trader's ship. But, though defeated in the contest for liberty, their magnanimous souls scorn the gross indignity, and choose death in preference to slavery. Painful; ah! painful, must be that existence which the rational mind can deliberately doom to self-destruction. Thus the poor Africans, robbed of every joy, while they see not the saddened hearts, sink into the abyss of consummate misery. Their lives, embittered by reflection, anticipation, and present sorrows, they feel burthensome; and death (whose dreary mansions appal the stoutest hearts) they view as their only shelter.

You, my brethren, beloved Africans, who had passed the days of infancy when you left your country, you best can tell the aggravated sufferings of our unfortunate race; your memories can bring to view these scenes of bitter grief. What, my brethren, when dragged from your native land on board the slave ship, what was the anguish which you saw, which you felt? what the pain, what the dreadful forebodings which filled your throbbing bosoms?

But you, my brethren, descendants of African forefathers, I call upon you to view a scene of unfathomable distress. Let your imagination carry you back to former days. Behold a vessel, bearing our forefathers and brethren from the place of their nativity to a distant and inhospitable clime; behold their dejected countenances, their streaming eyes, their fettered limbs; hear them, with piercing cries, and pitiful moans, deploring their wretched fate. After their arrival in port, see them separated without regard to the ties of blood or friendship: husband from wife; parent from child; brother from sister; friend from friend. See the parting tear rolling down their fallen cheeks; hear the parting sigh die on their quivering lips.

But let us no longer pursue a theme of boundless affliction. An enchanting sound now demands your attention. Hail! hail! glorious day, whose resplendent rising disperseth the clouds which have hovered with destruction over the land of Africa, and illumines it by the most brilliant rays of future prosperity. Rejoice, oh! Africans! No longer shall tyranny, war, and injustice, with irresistible sway, desolate your native country; no longer shall torrents of human blood deluge its delightful plains; no longer shall it witness your countrymen wielding among each other the instruments of death; nor the insidious kidnapper, darting from his midnight haunt, on the feeble and unprotected; no longer shall its shores resound with the awful howlings of infatuated warriors, the deathlike groans of vanquished innocents, nor the clanking fetters of woe-doomed captives. Rejoice, oh, ye descendants of Africans! No longer shall the United States of America, nor the extensive colonies of Great Britain, admit the degrading commerce of the human species; no longer shall they swell the tide of African misery by the importation of slaves. Rejoice, my brethren, that the channels are obstructed through which slavery, and its direful concomitants, have been entailed on the African race. But let incessant strains of gratitude be mingled with your expressions of joy. Through the infinite mercy of the great Jehovah, this day announces the abolition of the Slave Trade. Let, therefore, the heart that is warmed by the smallest drop of African blood glow in grateful transports, and cause the lofty arches of the sky to reverberate eternal praise to his boundless goodness.

Oh, God! we thank Thee, that thou didst condescend to listen to the cries of African's wretched sons, and that Thou didst interfere in their behalf. At Thy call humanity sprang forth and espoused the cause of the oppressed; one hand she employed in drawing from their vitals the deadly arrows of injustice; and the other in holding a shield, to defend them from fresh assaults; and at that illustrious moment, when the sons of '76 pronounced these United States free and independent; when the spirit of patriotism erected a temple sacred to liberty; when the inspired voice of Americans first uttered those noble sentiments, "We hold these truths to be self-evident, that all men are created equal; that they are endowed by their Creator with certain unalienable rights; among which are life, liberty, and the pursuit of happiness"; and when the bleeding African, lifting his fetters, exclaimed, "Am I not a man and a brother"; then, with redoubled efforts, the angel of humanity strove to restore to the African race the inherent rights of man.

To the instruments of divine goodness, those benovolent men who voluntarily obeyed the dictates of humanity, we owe much. Surrounded with innumerable difficulties, their undaunted spirits dared to oppose a powerful host of interested men. Heedless to the voice of fame, their independent souls dared to oppose the strong gales of popular prejudice. Actuated by principles of genuine philanthropy, they dared to despise the emoluments of ill-gotten wealth, and to sacrifice much of their temporal interests at the shrine of benevolence.

As an American, I glory in informing you that Columbia boasts the first men who distinguished themselves eminently in the vindication of our rights and the improvement of our state.

Conscious that slavery was unfavorable to the benign influences of Christianity, the pious Woolman loudly declaimed against it; and, although destitute of fortune, he resolved to spare neither time not pains to check its progress. With this view he traveled over several parts of North America on foot and exhorted his brethren, of the denomination of Friends, to abjure the iniquitous custom. These, convinced by the cogency of his arguments, denied the privileges of their society to the slaveholder, and zealously engaged in destroying the aggravated evil. Thus, through the beneficial labors of this pattern of piety and brotherly kindness, commenced a work which has since been promoted by the humane of every denomination. His memory ought therefore to be deeply engraven on the tablets of our hearts; and ought ever to inspire us with the most ardent esteem.

Nor less to be prized are the useful exertions of Anthony Benezet. This inestimable person, sensible of the equality of mankind, rose superior to the illiberal opinions of the age; and, disallowing an inferiority in the African genius, established the first school to cultivate our understandings and to better our condition.

Thus, by enlightening the mind and implanting the seeds of virtue, he banished, in a degree, the mists of prejudice, and laid the foundations of our future happiness. Let, therefore, a due sense of his meritorious actions ever create in us a deep reverence of his beloved name. Justice to the occasion, as well as his merits, forbid me to pass in silence over the name of the honorable William Wilberforce. Possessing talents capable of adorning the greatest subjects, his comprehensive mind found none more worthy his constant attention than the abolition of the Slave Trade. For this he soared to the zenith of his towering eloquence, and for this he struggled with perpetual ardor. Thus, anxious in defense of our rights, he pledged himself never to desert the cause; and, by his repeated and strenuous exertions, he finally obtained the desirable end. His extensive services have, therefore, entitled him to a large share of our affection, and to a lasting tribute of our unfeigned thanks.

But think not, my brethren, that I pretend to enumerate the persons who have proved our strenuous advocates, or that I have portrayed the merits of those I have mentioned. No, I have given but a few specimens of a countless number, and no more than the rude outlines of the beneficence of these. Perhaps there never existed a human institution which has displayed more intrinsic merit than the societies for the abolition of slavery.

Reared on the pure basis of philanthropy, they extend to different quarters of the globe, and comprise a considerable number of humane and respectable men. These, greatly impressed with the importance of the work, entered into it with such disinterestedness, engagedness, and prudence, as does honor to their wisdom and virtue. To effect the purposes of these societies no legal means were left untried which afforded the smallest prospects of success. Books were disseminated, and discoursed delivered, wherein every argument was employed which the penetrating mind could adduce from religion, justice or reason, to prove the turpitude of slavery, and numerous instances related calculated to awaken sentiments of compassion. To further their charitable intentions, applications were constantly made to different bodies of legislature, and every concession improved to our best possible advantage. Taught by preceding occurrences, that the waves of oppression are ever ready to overwhelm the defenseless, they became the vigilant guardians of all our reinstated joys. Sensible that the inexperienced mind is greatly exposed to the allurements of vice, they cautioned us, by the most salutary precepts and virtuous examples against its fatal encroachments; and the better to establish us in the paths of rectitude they instituted schools to instruct us in the knowledge of letters and the principles of virtue.

By these and similar methods, with divine assistance they assailed the dark dungeon of slavery; shattered its rugged wall, and enlarging thousands of the captives, bestowed on them the blessings of civil society. Yes, my brethren, through their efficiency, numbers of us now enjoy the invaluable gem of liberty; numbers have been secured from a relapse into bondage, and numbers have attained a useful education.

I need not, my brethren, take a further view of our present circumstances, to convince you of the providential benefits which we have derived from our patrons; for if you take a retrospect of the past situation of Africans, and descendants of Africans, in this and other countries, to your observation our advancements must be obvious. From these considerations, added to the happy event which we now celebrate, let us ever entertain the profoundest veneration for our munificent benefactors, and return to them from the altars of our hearts the fragrant incense of incessant gratitude. But let not, my brethren, our demonstrations of gratitude be confined to the mere expressions of our lips.

The active part which the friends of humanity have taken to ameliorate our sufferings has rendered them, in a measure, the pledges of our integrity. Your must be well aware that notwithstanding their endeavors, they have yet remaining, from interest, and prejudice, a number of opposers. These, carefully watching for every opportunity to injure the cause, will not fail to augment the smallest defects in our lives and conversation; and reproach our benefactors with them as the fruits of their actions.

Let us, therefore, by a steady and upright deportment, by a strict obedience and respect to the laws of the land, form an invulnerable bulwark against the shafts of malice. Thus, evincing to the world that our garments are unpolluted by the stains of ingratitude, we shall reap increasing advantages from the favours conferred; the spirits of our departed ancestors shall smile with complacency on the change of our state; and posterity shall exult in the pleasing remembrance.

May the time speedily commence when Ethiopia shall stretch forth her hands; when the sun of liberty shall beam resplendent on the whole African race; and its genial influences promote the luxuriant growth of knowledge and virtue.

Note

1. Carter G. Woodson, ed, *Negro Orators and Their Orations* (Washington, D.C.: Associated Publishers, 1925), 32.

Source

Peter Williams Jr., "Oration on the Abolition of the Slave Trade, delivered in the African Church in the City of New York, January 1, 1808," in Carter G. Woodson, ed, *Negro Orators and Their Orations,* 32–41 (Washington, D.C.: Associated Publishers, 1925).

Selected Bibliography

Eltis, David. *The Abolition of the Atlantic Slave Trade: Origins and Effects in Europe, Africa, and the Americas*. Madison: University of Wisconsin Press, 1981.

Horton, James O. *In Hope of Liberty: Culture, Community, and Protest Among Northern Free Blacks, 1700–1860.* New York: Oxford University Press, 1998.

Klein, Herbert S. *The Atlantic Slave Trade.* New York: Cambridge University Press, 1999.

Pease, Jane H. and William B. Pease. *They Who Would Be Free: Blacks' Search for Freedom, 1830–1861.* Urbana: University of Illinois Press, 1990.

four

Editorial from the First Edition of *Freedom's Journal*

Freedom's Journal, the first black newspaper in the United States, began publication in 1827. It brought black consciousness and organization to unprecedented heights. Originally edited jointly in New York by Rev. Samuel Cornish and John Russwurm, Cornish resigned shortly after the paper was launched. In the following document, Cornish and Russwurm set forth their editorial mission. Insisting that "[for] too long have others spoken for us," the essay offers insight into the agenda of black abolitionists in the antebellum period. Among those influenced by *Freedom's Journal* was William Lloyd Garrison, the premier white abolitionist of his day.

In addition to polemics, historical essays, condemnations of racism, and examples of black achievement, *Freedom's Journal* also touted a moralistic, self-improvement ethic, arguing that in order for African Americans to advance in society, they must work hard and practice thrift, temperance, and good manners. Its most significant achievement, however, may have been that it articulated opposition to colonization in ways that were often ignored in the white press, marshalling black opinion not simply in New York but also in Philadelphia, Boston, and Baltimore. However, when Russwurm reversed his position and came out in favor of colonization, he was roundly denounced in the black community. This backlash contributed to the decline of *Freedom's Journal,* which ran its last issue on March 28, 1829.

To Our Patrons

In presenting our first number to our patrons, we feel all the diffidence of persons entering upon a new and untried line of business. But a moment's reflection upon the noble objects, which we have in view by the publication of this Journal: the expediency of its appearance at this time, when so many schemes are in action concerning our people—encourage us to come boldly before an enlightented publick. For we believe, that a paper devoted to the dissemination of useful knowledge among our brethren, and to their moral and religious improvement, must meet with the cordial approbation of every friend to humanity.

The peculiarities of this Journal, renders it important that we should advertise to the world our motives by which we are actuated, and the objects which we contemplate.

We wish to plead our own cause. Too long have others spoken for us. Too long has the publick been deceived by misrepresentations, in things which concern us dearly, though in the estimation of some mere trifles; for though there are many in society who exercise towards us benevolent feelings; still (with sorrow we confess it) there are others who make it their business to enlarge upon the least trifle, which tends to the discredit of any person of colour; and pronounce anathemas and denounce our whole body for the misconduct of this guilty one. We are aware that there are many instances of vice among us, but we avow that it is because no one has taught its subjects to be virtuous; many instances of poverty, because no sufficient efforts accommodated to minds contracted by slavery, and deprived of early education have been made, to teach them how to husband their hard earnings, and to secure to themselves comfort.

Education being an object of the highest importance to the welfare of society, we shall endeavour to present just and adequate views of it, and to urge upon our brethren the necessity and expediency of training their children, while young, to habits of industry, and thus forming them for becoming useful members of society. It is surely time that we should awake from this lethargy of years, and make a concentrated effort for the education of our youth. We form a spoke in the human wheel and it is necessary that we should understand our pendence on the different parts, and theirs on us; in order to perform our part with propriety.

Though not desiring of dictating, we shall feel it our incumbent duty to dwell occasionally upon the general principles and rules of economy. The world has grown too enlightened, to estimate any man's character by his personal appearance. Though all men acknowledge the excellency of Franklin's maxims,[1] yet comparatively few practise upon them. We may deplore when it is too late, the neglect of these self-evident truths, but it avails little to mourn. Ours will be the task of admonishing our brethren on these points.

The civil rights of a people being of the greatest value, it shall ever be our duty to vindicate our brethren, when oppressed; and to lay the case before the publick. We shall also urge upon our brethren, (who are qualified by the laws of the different states) the expediency of using their elective franchise; and of making an independent use of the same. We wish them not to become the tools of party.

And as much time is frequently lost, and wrong principles instilled, by the perusal of works of trivial importance, we shall consider it a part of our duty to recommend to our young readers, such authors as will not only enlarge their stock of useful knowledge, but such as will also serve to stimulate them to higher attainments in science.

We trust also, that through the columns of the *Freedom's Journal*, many practical pieces, having for their bases, the improvement of our brethren, will be presented to them, from the pens of many of our respected friends, who have kindly promised their assistance.

It is our earnest wish to make our Journal a medium of intercourse between our brethren in the different states of this great confederacy: that through its columns an expression of our sentiments, on many interesting subjects which concern us, may be offered to the publick: that plans which apparently are beneficial may be candidly discussed and properly weighed; if worth, receive our cordial approbation; if not, our marked disapprobation.

Useful knowledge of every kind, and everything that relates to Africa, shall find a ready admission into our columns; and as that vast continent becomes daily more known, we trust that many things will come to light, proving that the natives of it are neither so ignorant nor stupid as they have generally been supposed to be.

And while these important subjects shall occupy the columns of the *Freedom's Journal,* we would not be unmindful of our brethren who are still in the iron fetters of bondage. They are our kindred by all the times of nature; and though but little can be effected by us, still let our sympathies be poured forth, and our prayers in their behalf, ascend to Him who is able to succour them.

From the press and the pulpit we have suffered much by being incorrectly represented. Men whom we equally love and admire have not hesitated to represent us disadvantageously, without becoming personally acquainted with the true state of things, nor discerning between virtue and vice among us. The virtuous part of our people feel themselves sorely aggrieved under the existing state of things—they are not appreciated.

Our vices and our degradation are ever arrayed against us, but our virtues are passed by unnoticed. And what is still more lamentable, our friends, to whom we concede all the principles of humanity and religion, from these very causes seem to have fallen into the current of popular feeling and are imperceptibly floating on the stream—actually living in the practice of prejudice, while they abjure it in theory, and feel it not in their hearts. Is it not very desirable that such should know more of our actual condition; and of our efforts and feelings, that in forming or advocating plans for our amelioration, they may do it more understandingly? In the spirit of candor and humility we intend by a simple representation of facts to lay our case before the public, with a view to arrest the progress of prejudice, and to shield ourselves against the consequent evils. We wish to conciliate all and to irritate none, yet we must be firm and unwavering in our principles, and persevering in our efforts.

If ignorance, poverty and degradation have hitherto been our unhappy lot; has the Eternal decree gone forth, that our race alone are to remain in this state, while knowledge and civilization are shedding their enlivening rays over the rest of the human family? The recent travels of Denham and Clapperton in the interior of Africa, and the interesting narrative which they have published;[2] the establishment of the republic of Hayti after years of sanguinary warfare;[3] its subsequent progress in all the arts of civilization; and the advancement of liberal ideas in South America, where despotism has given place to free governments, and where many of our brethren now fill important civil and military stations, prove the contrary.

The interesting fact that there are FIVE HUNDRED THOUSAND free persons of colour, one half of whom might peruse, and the whole be benefitted by the publication of the Journal; that no publication, as yet, has been devoted exclusively to their improvement—that many selections from approved standard authors, which are within the reach of few, may occasionally be made—and more important still, that this large body of our citizens have no public channel—all serve to prove the real necessity, at present, for the appearance of the *Freedom's Journal.*

It shall ever be our desire so to conduct the editorial department of our paper as to give offence to none of our patrons; as nothing is farther from us than to make it the advocate of any partial views, either in politics or religion. What few days we can number, have been devoted to the improvement of our brethren; and it is our earnest wish that the remainder may be spent in the same delightful service.

In conclusion, whatever concerns us as a people, will ever find a ready admission into the *Freedom's Journal,* interwoven with all the principal news of the day.

And while every thing in our power shall be performed to support the character of our Journal, we would respectfully invite our numerous friends to assist by their communications, and our coloured brethren to strengthen our hands by their subscriptions, as our labour is one of common cause, and worthy of their consideration and support. And we most earnestly solicit the latter, that if at any time we should seem to be zealous, or too pointed in the inculcation of any important lesson, they will remember, that they are equally interested in the cause in which we are engaged, and attribute our zeal to the peculiarities of our situation; and our earnest engagedness in their well-being.

Freedom's Journal, *New York, March 16, 1827*

Notes

1. Refers to the teachings of Benjamin Franklin (1706–1790), printer, scientist, and writer who promoted thrift, industry, and capitalist moralism.
2. Hugh Clapperton (1788–1827), British explorer who published, posthumously, *Journal of a Second Expedition into the Interior of Africa* (1829).
3. Haiti, independent republic, founded in 1804.

Source

Samuel Cornish and John Russwurm, "Editorial from the First Edition of *Freedom's Journal,* March 16, 1827," in Deirdre Mullane, ed., *Crossing the Danger Water: Three Hundred Years of African-American Writing,* 63–66 (New York: Anchor Books, 1993).

Selected Bibliography

Goodman, Paul. *Of One Blood: Abolitionism and the Origins of Racial Equality.* Berkeley: University of California Press, 1998.

Horton, James O. *In Hope of Liberty: Culture, Community, and Protest Among Northern Free Blacks, 1700–1860.* New York: Oxford University Press, 1998.

Jacobs, Donald M. *Antebellum to Black Newspapers: Indices to New York Freedom's Journal (1827–1829), Rights of All (1829), The Weekly Advocate (1837) and The Colored American (1837–1841).* Westport, Conn.: Greenwood Press, 1976.

—— *Courage and Conscience: Black and White Abolitionists in Boston.* Bloomington: University of Indiana Press for the Boston Athenaeum, 1993.

Penn, I. Garland. *The Afro-American Press and Its Editors.* Springfield, Mass.: Wiley & Co., 1891.

five

Men of Color, To Arms!

Frederick Douglass (1817–1895) was the preeminent black abolitionist of his day and is often called the "father of the civil rights movement." During the Civil War, he was foremost among the black abolitionists who called for African American participation in the Civil War, saying he had "little hope of the freedom of the slave by peaceful means."[1] Though initially ignored by the president, Douglass asked the Lincoln administration to recruit African Americans into the Union Army and free slaves as a war measure. Eventually, on January 1, 1863 President Lincoln issued the Emancipation Proclamation, which declared slaves in states of rebellion free and allowed them into armies.

After Massachusetts became the first state to allow blacks to fight in the war, Douglass urgently called on African Americans to enlist in the Northern cause, writing the classic editorial "Men of Color, To Arms!" on March 2, 1863. "A war undertaken and brazenly carried on for the perpetual enslavement of colored men," Douglass reasoned, "calls logically and loudly for colored men to help suppress it." Approximately 180,000 blacks fought in the Civil War, and 38,000 were killed.

1. Benjamin Quarles, "Frederick Douglass," in Rayford W. Logan and Michael R. Winston, eds., *Dictionary of American Negro Biography* (New York: W. W. Norton & Co., 1982), 184.

When first the rebel cannon shattered the walls of Sumter[1] and drove away its starving garrison, I predicted that the war then and there inaugurated would not be fought out entirely by white men. Every month's experience during these dreary years has confirmed that opinion. A war undertaken and brazenly carried on for the perpetual enslavement of colored men, calls logically and loudly for colored men to help suppress it. Only a moderate share of sagacity was needed to see that the arm of the slave was the best defense against the arm of the slaveholder. Hence with every reverse to the national arms, with every exulting shout of victory raised by the slaveholding rebels, I have implored the imperiled nation to unchain against her foes, her powerful black hand.

Slowly and reluctantly that appeal is beginning to be heeded. Stop not now to complain that it was not heeded sooner. It may or it may not have been best that it should not. This is not the time to discuss that question. Leave it to the future. When the war is over, the country is saved, peace is established, and the black man's rights are secured, as they will be, history with an impartial hand will dispose of that and sundry other questions. Action! Action! not criticism, is the plain duty of this hour. Words are now useful only as they stimulate to blows. The office of speech now is only to point out when, where, and how to strike to the best advantage.

There is no time to delay. The tide is at its flood that leads on to fortune. From East to West, from North to South, the sky is written all over, "Now or never." Liberty won by white men would lose half its luster. "Who would be free themselves must strike the blow." "Better even die free, than to live slaves." This is the sentiment of every brave colored man amongst us.

There are weak and cowardly men in all nations. We have them amongst us. They tell you this is the "white man's war"; that you will be no "better off after than before the war;" that the getting of you into the army is to "sacrifice you on the first opportunity." Believe them not; cowards themselves, they do not wish to have their cowardice shamed by your brave example. Leave them to their timidity, or to whatever motive may hold them back.

I have not thought lightly of the words. I am now addressing you. The counsel I give comes of close observation of the great struggle now in progress, and of the deep conviction that this is your hour and mine. In good earnest then, and after the best deliberation. I now for the first time during this war feel at liberty to call and counsel you to arms.

By every consideration which binds you to your enslaved fellow-countrymen, and the peace and welfare of your country; by every aspiration which you cherish for the freedom and equality of yourselves and your children; by all the ties of blood and identity which make us one with the brave black men now fighting our battles in Louisiana and in South Carolina, I urge you to fly to arms, and smite with death the power that would bury the government and your liberty in the same hopeless grave.

I wish I could tell you that the State of New York calls you to this high honor. For the moment her constituted authorities are silent on the subject. They will speak by and by, and doubtless on the right side; but we are not compelled to wait for her. We can get at the throat of treason and slavery through the State of Massachusetts. She was first in the War of Independence; first to break the chains of her slaves; first to make the black man equal before the law; first to admit colored children to her common schools, and she was first to answer with her blood the alarm cry of the nation, when its capital was menaced by rebels. You know her patriotic governor, and you know Charles Sumner.[2] I need not add more.

Massachusetts now welcomes you to arms as soldiers. She has but a small colored population from which to recruit. She has full leave of the general government to send one regiment to the war, and she has undertaken to do it. Go quickly and help fill up the first colored regiment from the North. I am authorized to assure you that you will receive the same wages, the same rations, the same equipments, the same protection, the same treatment, and the same bounty, secured to the white soldiers. You will be led by able and skillful officers, men who will take especial pride in your efficiency and success. They will be quick to accord to you all the honor you shall merit by your valor, and see that your rights and feelings are respected by other soldiers. I have assured myself on these points, and can speak with authority.

More than twenty years of unswerving devotion to our common cause may give me some humble claim to be trusted at this momentous crisis. I will not argue. To do so implies hesitation and doubt, and you do not hesitate. You do not doubt. The day dawns; the morning star is bright upon the horizon! The iron gate of our prison stands half open. One gallant rush from the North will fling it wide open, while four millions of our brothers and sisters shall march out into liberty. The chance is now given you to end in a day the bondage of centuries, and to rise in one bound from social degradation to the plane of common equality with all other varieties of men.

Remember Denmark Vesey[3] of Charleston; remember Nathaniel Turner[4] of Southampton; remember Shields Green and Copeland, who followed noble John Brown, and fell as glorious martyrs for the cause of the slave.[5] Remember that in a contest with oppression, the Almighty has no attribute which can take sides with oppressors.

The case is before you. This is our golden opportunity. Let us accept it, and forever wipe out the dark reproaches unsparingly hurled against us by our enemies. Let us win for ourselves the gratitude of our country, and the best blessings of our posterity through all time. The nucleus of this first regiment is now in camp at Readville, a short distance from Boston. I will undertake to forward to Boston all persons adjudged fit to be mustered into the regiment, who shall apply to me at any time within the next two weeks.

Frederick Douglass, March 2, 1863

Notes

1. On April 12, 1861, Fort Sumter—a fortification in Charleston Harbor, South Carolina—was the site of the first clash of the Civil War.
2. Charles Sumner (1811–1874), U.S. senator from Massachusetts (1851–1874) and abolitionist.
3. Denmark Vesey (1767–1822), slave, carpenter, and insurrectionist.
4. Nathaniel Turner (1800–1831), slave, liberation theologian, and insurrectionist.
5. Refers to John Brown's raid on the federal arsenal at Harper's Ferry, Virginia, on October 16, 1859.

Source

Frederick Douglass, "Men of Color, To Arms!" in *The Life and Times of Frederick Douglass,* 344–46 (Rochester, 1863).

Selected Bibliography

Blight, David W. *Frederick Douglass' Civil War: Keeping Faith in Jubilee.* Baton Rouge: Louisiana State University Press, 1989.

Chesebrough, David B. *Frederick Douglass: Oratory from Slavery.* Westport, Conn.: Greenwood Press, 1998.

Douglass, Frederick. *Narrative of the Life of Fredrick Douglass, an American Slave.* Edited by David W. Blight. Boston: Bedford Books of St. Martin's Press, 1993.

Lawson, Bill E., ed. *Frederick Douglass: A Critical Reader.* Malden: Blackwell, 1998.

Levine, Robert S. *Martin Delany, Frederick Douglass, and the Politics of Representative Identity.* Chapel Hill: University of North Carolina Press, 1997.

Martin, Waldo. *The Mind of Frederick Douglass.* Chapel Hill: University of North Carolina Press, 1986.

McFeely, William S. *Frederick Douglass.* New York: Simon & Schuster, 1992.

six

Speech to the Georgia Legislature

Henry McNeal Turner (1834–1915) was a clergyman, activist, and author who advocated black migration as a solution to race discrimination in the United States. After serving as a chaplain for black troops in the Civil War, Turner became active in Reconstruction politics between 1867 and 1871, briefly serving in the Georgia state legislature.

Believing that racial alliances between blacks and whites would bring racial reform, Turner adopted more conciliatory politics, seeking the favor of his white Republican colleagues. This tactic, however, was met with great hostility. In September 1868, responding to both Turner's actions and a resurgence in white supremacy, Georgia's white legislators expelled him by making it illegal for all blacks to hold public office. Black members of the legislature were forbidden to vote on the measure, which passed by a margin of 83 to 23.

The decision enraged Turner, compelling him to write the angry speech reprinted here. He delivered the three-hour address on September 3, 1868. The whites in the legislative chamber who heard Turner's speech were struck by his audacity, and immediately after he finished speaking, Turner stormed out of the capitol building with a delegation of African American representatives behind him.

Soon after the legislature restored black seats, Turner sought a legislative seat once again. He appeared to have won election to the legislature in 1870 by a margin of seventeen votes, but the pronouncement was rescinded after a fraudulent recount. The antiblack hostilities Turner encountered led him to change his stance on interracial unity and espouse racial separation and black emigration as means of black empowerment.

Mr. Speaker:

Before proceeding to argue this question upon its intrinsic merits, I wish the members of this House to understand the position that I take. I hold that I am a member of this body. Therefore, sir, I shall neither fawn or cringe before any party, nor stoop to beg them for my rights. Some of my colored fellow members, in the course of their remarks, took occasion to appeal to the sympathies of Members on the opposite side, and to eulogize their character for magnanimity. It reminds me very much, sir, of slaves begging under the lash. I am here to demand my rights, and to hurl thunderbolts at the men who would dare to cross the threshold of my manhood. There is an old aphorism which says, "Fight the Devil with fire," and if I should observe the rule in this instance, I wish gentlemen to understand that it is but fighting them with their own weapon.

The scene presented in this House, today, is one unparalleled in the history of the world. From this day, back to the day when God breathed the breath of life into Adam, no analogy for it can be found. Never, in the history of the world, has a man been arraigned before a body clothed with legislative, judicial or executive functions, charged with the offence of being of a darker hue than his fellowmen. I know that questions have been before the Courts of this country, and of other countries, involving topics not altogether dissimilar to that which is being discussed here today. But, sir, never in all the history of the great nations of this world—never before—has a man been arraigned, charged with an offence committed by the God of Heaven Himself. Cases may be found where men have been deprived of their rights for crimes and misdemeanors; but it has remained for the State of Georgia, in the very heart of the nineteenth century, to call a man before the bar, and there charge him with an act for which he is no more responsible than for the head which he carries upon his shoulders. The Anglo-Saxon race, sir, is a most surprising one. No man has ever been more deceived in that race than I have been for the last three weeks. I was not aware that there was in the character of that race so much cowardice, or so much pusillanimity. The treachery which has been exhibited in it by gentlemen belonging to that race has shaken my confidence in it more than anything that has come under my observation from the day of my birth.

What is the question at issue? Why, sir, this Assembly, today, is discussing and deliberating on a judgment; there is not a Cherubim that sits around God's eternal Throne, today, that would not tremble—even were an order issued by the Supreme God Himself—to come down here and sit in judgment on my manhood. Gentlemen may look at this question in whatever light they choose, and with just as much indifference as they may think proper to assume, but I tell you, sir, that this is a question which will not die today. This event shall be remembered by posterity for ages yet to come, and while the sun shall continue to climb the hills of heaven.

Whose Legislature is this? Is it a white man's Legislature, or is it a black man's Legislature? Who voted for a Constitutional Convention, in obedience to the mandate of the Congress of the United States? Who first rallied around the standard of Reconstruction? Who set the ball of loyalty rolling in the State of Georgia? And whose voice was heard on the hills and in the valleys of this State? It was the voice of the brawny-armed Negro, with the few humanitarian-hearted white men who came to our assistance. I claim the honor, sir, of having been the instrument of convincing hundreds—yea, thousands—of white men, that to reconstruct under the measures of the United States Congress was the safest and the best course for the interest of the State.

Let us look at some facts in connection with this matter. Did half the white men of Georgia vote for this Legislature? Did not the great bulk of them fight, with all their strength, the Constitution under which we are acting? And did they not fight against the organization of this Legislature? And further, sir, did they not vote against it? Yes, sir! And there are persons in this Legislature today, who are ready to spit their poison in my face, while they themselves opposed, with all their power, the ratification of this Constitution. They question my right to a seat in this body, to represent the people whose legal votes elected me. This objection, sir, is an unheard of monopoly of power. No analogy can be found for it, except it be the case of a man who should go into my house, take possession of my wife and children, and then tell me to walk out. I stand very much in the position of a criminal before your bar, because I dare to be the exponent of the views of those who sent me here. Or, in other words, we are told that if black men want to speak, they must speak through white trumpets; if black men want their sentiments expressed, they must be adulterated and sent through white messengers, who will quibble, and equivocate, and evade, as rapidly as the pendulum of a clock. If this be not done, then the black men have committed an outrage, and their Representatives must be denied the right to represent their constituents.

The great question, sir, is this: Am I a man? If I am such, I claim the rights of a man. Am I not a man because I happen to be of a darker hue than honorable gentlemen around me? . . .

But Mr. Speaker, I do not regard this movement as a thrust at me, it is a thrust at the Bible—a thrust at the God of the Universe, for making a man and not finishing him; it is simply calling the Great Jehovah a fool. Why, sir, though we are not white, we have accomplished much. We have pioneered civilization here; we have built up your country; we have worked in your fields, and garnered your harvests, for two hundred and fifty years! And what do we ask of you in return? Do we ask you for compensation for the sweat our fathers bore for you—for the tears you have caused, and the hearts you have broken, and the lives you have curtailed, and the blood you have spilled? Do we ask retaliation? We ask it not. We are willing to let the dead past bury its dead; but we ask you now for our RIGHTS. You have all the elements of superiority upon your side; you have our money and your own; you have our education and your own; and you have your land and our own, too. We, who number hundreds of thousands in Georgia, including our wives and families, with not a foot of land to call our own—strangers in the land of our birth; without money, without education, without aid, without a roof to cover us while we live, not sufficient clay to cover us when we die! It is extraordinary that a race such as yours, professing gallantry, and chivalry, and education, and superiority, living in a land where ringing chimes call child and sire to the Church of God—a land where Bibles are read and Gospels truths are spoken, and where courts of justice are presumed to exist; it is extraordinary to say, that, with all these advantages on your side, you can make war upon the poor defenseless black man. . . .

You may expel us, gentlemen, but I firmly believe that you will someday repent it. The black man cannot protect a country, if the country doesn't protect him; and if, tomorrow, a war should arise, I would not raise a musket to defend a country where my manhood is denied. The fashionable way in Georgia when hard work is to be done, is, for the white man to sit at his ease, while the black man does the work; but, sir, I will say this much to the colored men of Georgia, as if I should be killed in this campaign, I may have no opportunity of telling them at any other time: Never lift a finger nor raise a hand in defense of Georgia, unless Georgia acknowledges that you are men, and invests you with the rights pertaining to manhood. Pay your taxes, however, obey all orders from your employers, take good counsel from friends, work faithfully, earn an honest living, and show, by your conduct, that you can be good citizens. . . .

You may expel us, gentlemen, by your votes, today; but, while you do it, remember that there is a just God in Heaven, whose All-Seeing Eye beholds alike the acts of the oppressor and the oppressed, and who, despite the machinations of the wicked, never fails to vindicate the cause of Justice, and the sanctity of His own handiwork.

September 3, 1868

Source

Henry M. Turner, "Speech to the Georgia Legislature, September 3, 1863," in Edmund L. Drago, ed., *Respect Black: The Writings and Speeches of Henry McNeal Turner,* 14–16, 25, 27–28 (New York: Arno Press and the New York Times, 1971).

Selected Bibliography

Angell, Stephen W. *Bishop Henry McNeal Turner and African-American Religion in the South*. Knoxville: University of Tennessee Press, 1992.

Drago, Edmund L. *Black Politicians and Reconstruction in Georgia: A Splendid Failure*. Baton Rouge: Louisiana State University Press, 1982.

Wilmore, Gayraud S. *Black Religion and Black Radicalism: An Interpretation of the Religious History of Afro-American People*. Maryknoll, N.Y.: Orbis Books, 1983.

seven

Nimrod Rowley to Abraham Lincoln, August 1864

In 1863, President Abraham Lincoln called on African Americans to fight in the Civil War. Lincoln made his decision primarily as a result of wartime exigencies, but he was also influenced by black abolitionists. Although black troops proved to be courageous and capable soldiers, this letter from a black soldier illustrates that the "colored troops" suffered from mistreatment even as they fought on behalf of the Union. It also reflects the sacrifice that African Americans made to the war effort.

Black Soldier Protests "Weak and Starving Condition"

"New Orleans Camp Parpit Louisiana [August] 1864

My Dear Friend and x Pre

I thake up my Pen to Address you a fiew simpels And facts. We so called the 20th u.s. Colored troops we was got up in the state of New York so said By A grant of the President. we Dont think he know wether we are white or Black we have not Bin Organized yet And A grate meney Brought Away without Being Musterd in, and we are treated in a Different maner to what others Rigiments is Both Northern men or southern Raised Rigiment. Instead of the musket It is the spad and the Whelbarrow and the Axe cuting in one of the most horable swamps in Louisiana stinking and misery. Men are Call to go on thes fatiuges wen sum of them are scarc Able to get Along the Day Before on the sick List And Perhaps weeks to And By this treatment meney are thowen Back in sickness wich thay very soldom get over. we had when we Left New York over A thousand strong now we scarce rise Nine hundred the total is said to Be. we lost 1.60 men who have Left thire homes friends and Relation And Come Down hear to lose thire Lives in For the Country thy Dwll in or stayd in the Colored man is like A lost sheep. Meney of them old and young was Brave And Active. But has Bin hurrided By and ignominious Death into Eternity. But I hope God will Presearve the Rest Now in existance to Get Justice and Rights. we have to Do our Duty or Die and no help for us. It is true the Country is in A hard strugle. But we All must Remember Mercy and Justice Grate and small. it is Devine. we All Listed for so much Bounty Clothing and Ration And 13 Dollars A month. And the most has fallen short in all thes Things. we havent Recived A cent of Pay Since we Bin in the field. Instead of them Coming to us Like men with our 13 Dollars thay come with only seven Dollars A month wich only A fiew tuck it. we stand in Need of Money very much indeed And think it is no more than Just an Right we should have it. And Another thing we are Cut short of our Ration in A most Shocking maner. I wont Relate All now But we Are Nerly Deprived of All Comforts of Life. Hardly have Anough Bread to Keep us From starving six or 8 ounces of it to Do A Soldier 24 hours on Gaurd or eney other Labor and About the Same in Meat and Coffee. sum times No meat for 2 Days. soup meat Licqour with very Little seazing the Boys calls hot water or n eat tea for Diner. It is A hard thing to be Keept in such a state of misery Continuly. It is spoken Dont musel the ox that treads out the corn. Remember we are men standing in Readiness to face thous vile traitors an Rebeles who are trying to Bring your Peaceable homes to Destruction. And how can we stand them in A weak and starving Condition.

Note

The letter is unsigned but was discovered in the Colored Troops Files of the National Archives in the same folder as another letter, in the same hand, by one Nimrod Rowley.

Source

"Nimrod Rowley to Abraham Lincoln, August, 1864," in Harold Holzer, ed., *The Lincoln Mailbag: America Writes to the President, 1861–1865,* 166–67 (Carbondale and Edwardsville: Southern Illinois University Press, 1998).

Selected Bibliography

Blackbery, Hubert C. *Blacks in Blue and Gray: Afro-American Service in the Civil War.* New Orleans: Portals Press, 1979.

Frankel, Noralee. *Break Those Chains at Last: African-Americans, 1860–1880.* New York: Oxford University Press, 1996.

Gertis, Louis S. *From Contraband to Freedom: Federal Policy Toward Southern Blacks, 1861–1865.* Westport, Conn.: Greenwood Press, 1973.

McPherson, James. *Battle Cry of Freedom: The Era of the Civil War.* New York: Oxford University Press, 1998.

—— *The Negro's Civil War: How American Blacks Felt and Acted During the War for the Union.* New York: Ballantine, 1991.

eight

An Address Delivered at the Centennial Anniversary of the Pennsylvania Society for Promoting the Abolition of Slavery

Poet, writer, and political leader, Frances Ellen Watkins Harper was born to free parents in Baltimore, Maryland, on September 24, 1825. An aunt and uncle adopted Harper at the age of three after both her parents had died. She soon attended her uncle's school for free blacks. Though highly educated and relatively privileged, she could find work only as a housekeeper, seamstress and babysitter for a family who owned a bookstore. This, however, allowed her to study in her free time.

In 1850 Harper moved to Ohio and became the first female faculty member of the African Methodist Episcopal's (AME) Union Seminary (later a part of Wilberforce University) near Columbus. She took up the antislavery cause in 1853 after being forced into exile. Her home state of Maryland passed a law forbidding free slaves from entering the state; returning black people were imprisoned and even enslaved. Deeply stirred, Harper involved herself in Pennsylvania's Underground Railroad and soon began her speaking career as a lecturer for the Anti-Slavery Society. She spoke out against slavery and supported racial and women's equality, once stating "a free people could be a moral people only when the women were respected."[1] Her speaking and writing would consume most of her career; she stopped briefly to marry and have a child in the early 1860s.

Harper delivered her Pennsylvania Society address on Wednesday, April 14, 1875. Also that year, Harper began a seven-year role as superintendent of the Colored Branch of both the Philadelphia and Pennsylvania chapters of the Women's Christian Temperance Union. She then directed the Northern United States Temperance Union (1883–1890). In 1896, she cofounded and led the National Association of Colored Women and served as vice president and consultant for several years. Throughout her career, Harper appeared before countless organizations and was one of only four black women to address the Women's Congress at the Columbian Exposition of 1892. Shortly after her daughter's death, Harper died of a heart ailment on February 20, 1911; she was eighty-seven years old.

Ladies and Gentlemen:

THE GREAT problem to be solved by the American people, if I understand it, is this: Whether or not there is strength enough in democracy, virtue enough in our civilization, and power enough in our religion to have mercy and deal justly with four millions of people but lately translated from the old oligarchy of slavery to the new commonwealth of freedom; and upon the right solution of this question depends in a large measure the future strength, progress, and durability of our nation. The most important question before us colored people is not simply what the Democratic party may do against us or the Republican party do for us; but what are we going to do for ourselves? What shall we do towards developing our character, adding our quota to the civilization and strength of the country, diversifying our industry, and practising those lordly virtues that conquer success, and turn the world's dread laugh into admiring recognition? The white race has yet work to do in making practical the political axiom of equal rights, and the Christian idea of human brotherhood; but while I lift mine eyes to the future I would not ungratefully ignore the past. One hundred years ago and Africa was the privileged hunting-ground of Europe and America, and the flag of different nations hung a sign of death on the coasts of Congo and Guinea, and for years unbroken silence had hung around the horrors of the African slave-trade. Since then Great Britain and other nations have wiped the bloody traffic from their hands, and shaken the gory merchandise from their fingers, and the brand of piracy has been placed upon the African slave-trade. Less than fifty years ago mob violence belched out its wrath against the men who dared to arraign the slaveholder before the bar of conscience and Christendom. Instead of golden showers upon his head, he who garrisoned the front had a halter around his neck. Since, if I may borrow the idea, the nation has caught the old inspiration from his lips and written it in the new organic world. Less than twenty-five years ago slavery clasped hands with King Cotton, and said slavery fights and cotton conquers for American slavery. Since then slavery is dead, the colored man has exchanged the fetters on his wrist for the ballot in his hand. Freedom is king, and Cotton a subject.

It may not seem to be a gracious thing to mingle complaint in a season of general rejoicing. It may appear like the ancient Egyptians seating a corpse at their festal board to avenge the Americans for their shortcomings when so much has been accomplished. And yet with all the victories and triumphs which freedom and justice have won in this country, I do not believe there is another civilized nation under Heaven where there are half so many people who have been brutally and shamefully murdered, with or without impunity, as in this Republic within the last ten years. And who cares? Where is the public opinion that has scorched with red-hot indignation the cowardly murderers of Vicksburg and Louisiana? Sheridan lifts up the vail from Southern society, and behind it is the smell of blood, and our bones scattered at the grave's mouth; murdered people; a White League with its "covenant of death and agreement with hell." And who cares? What city pauses one hour to drop a pitying tear over these mangled corpses, or has forged against the perpetrator one thunderbolt of furious protest? But let there be a supposed or real invasion of Southern rights by our soldiers, and our great commercial emporium will rally its forces from the old man in his classic shades, to clasp hands with "dead rabbits" and "plug-uglies" in protesting against military interference. What we need to-day in the onward march of humanity is a public sentiment in favor of common justice and simple mercy. We have a civilization which has produced grand and magnificent results, diffused knowledge, overthrown slavery, made constant conquests over nature, and built up a wonderful material prosperity. But two things are wanting in American civilization—a keener and deeper, broader and tenderer sense of justice—a sense of humanity, which shall crystallize into the life of the nation the sentiment that justice, simple justice, is the right, not simply of the strong and powerful, but of the weakest and feeblest of all God's children; a deeper and broader humanity, which will teach men to look upon their feeble brethren not as vermin to be crushed out, or beasts of burden to be bridled and bitted, but as the children of the living God; of that God whom we may earnestly hope is in perfect wisdom and in perfect love working for the best good of all. Ethnologists may differ about the origin of the human race. Huxley may search for it in protoplasms, and Darwin send for the missing links, but there is one thing of which we may rest assured,—that we all come from the living God and that He is the common Father. The nation that has no reverence for man is also lacking in reverence for God and needs to be instructed.

As fellow citizens, leaving out all humanitarian views—as a mere matter of political economy it is better to have the colored race a living force animated and strengthened by self-reliance and self-respect, than a stagnant mass, degraded and self-condemned. Instead of the North relaxing its efforts to diffuse education in the South, it behooves us for our national life, to throw into the South all the healthful reconstructing influences we can command. Our work in this country is grandly constructive. Some races have come into this world and overthrown and destroyed. But if it is glory to destroy, it is happiness to save; and Oh! what a noble work there is before our nation! Where is there a young man who would consent to lead an aimless life when there are such glorious opportunities before him? Before our young men is another battle—not a battle of flashing swords and clashing steel—but a moral warfare, a battle against ignorance, poverty, and low social condition. In physical warfare the keenest swords may be blunted and the loudest batteries hushed; but in the great conflict of moral and spiritual progress your weapons shall be brighter for their service and better for their use. In fighting truly and nobly for others you win the victory for yourselves.

Give power and significance to your own life, and in the great work of upbuilding there is room for woman's work and woman's heart. Oh, that our hearts were alive and our vision quickened, to see the grandeur of the work that lies before. We have some culture among us, but I think our culture lacks enthusiasm. We need a deep earnestness and a lofty unselfishness to round out our lives. It is the inner life that develops the outer, and if we are in earnest the precious things lie all around our feet, and we need not waste our strength in striving after the dim and unattainable. Women, in your golden youth; mother, binding around your heart all the precious ties of life,—let no magnificence of culture, or amplitude of fortune, or refinement of sensibilities, repel you from helping the weaker and less favored. If you have ampler gifts, hold them as larger opportunities with which you can benefit others. Oh, it is better to feel that the weaker and feebler our race the closer we will cling to them, than it is to isolate ourselves from them in selfish, or careless unconcern, saying there is a lion without. Inviting you to this work I do not promise you fair sailing and unclouded skies. You may meet with coolness where you expect sympathy; disappointment where you feel sure of success; isolation and loneliness instead of heart-support and cooperation. But if your lives are based and built upon these divine certitudes, which are the only enduring strength of humanity, then whatever defeat and discomfiture may overshadow your plans or frustrate your schemes, for a life that is in harmony with God and sympathy for man there is no such word as fail. And in conclusion, permit me to say, let no misfortunes crush you; no hostility of enemies or failure of friends discourage you. Apparent failure may hold in its rough shell the germs of a success that will blossom in time, and bear fruit throughout eternity. What seemed to be a failure around the Cross of Calvary and in the garden has been the grandest recorded success.

Note

1. Larsen Scruggs, in *Black American Literature Forum,* mentioned in Harper's biography from the Biography Resource Center, http://www.galenet.com/servlet/BioRC/, accessed July 22, 2002.

Source

Frances Ellen Watkins Harper, "An Address Delivered at the Centennial Anniversary of the Pennsylvania Society for Promoting the Abolition of Slavery," in Alice Dunbar Nelson, ed., *Masterpieces of Negro Eloquence 1818–1913,* 64–68 (New York: Dover Publications, 2000).

Selected Bibliography

Harper, Frances Ellen Watkins. *A Brighter Coming Day: A Frances Ellen Watkins Harper Reader.* New York: Feminist Press at the City University of New York, distributed by Talman Co., 1990.

—— *Iola Leroy, or Shadows Uplifted.* New York: Oxford University Press, 1988.

—— *Minnie's Sacrifice; Sowing and Reaping; Trial and Triumph: Three Rediscovered Novels.* Boston: Beacon Press, 1994.

—— *Poems.* Freeport, N.Y.: Books for Libraries Press, 1970.

nine

A Letter to the Editor of the *Birmingham Age-Herald*

An activist, educator, and writer, Booker T. Washington (1856–1915) was the most powerful and influential African American of his day. After Washington's death, historians found correspondence proving that Washington secretly funded court challenges to Jim Crow laws of segregation and black disfranchisement. Moreover, he was not entirely averse to social protest. As this editorial suggests, Washington took an unequivocal stand against lynching, which emerged as a major issue for African Americans around the turn of the century.

Born a slave in Virginia, Washington enrolled at the Hampton Institute in the fall of 1872 and graduated in 1875. In 1881, Washington launched the Tuskegee Institute, a famous school for African Americans that preached the virtues of industrial education. He rose to national stature in 1895 when he delivered an address at the Cotton States and International Exposition in Atlanta, Georgia, which helped to shape postbellum racial politics. Washington urged Southern blacks to stay in the South and humbly suggested that blacks and

PDSr Con. 1107 BTW Papers DLG. The statement originally appeared as a letter to the editor in the *Birmingham Age-Herald,* Feb. 29, 1904, and the Associated Press sent it to many other newspapers. The *New York Times,* Feb. 29, 1904, printed part of the letter.

whites could cooperate economically while at the same time occupying separate social spheres. In return for providing a program that most whites found palatable, philanthropists gave large donations to Tuskegee, and Washington became an advisor on racial issues to President Theodore Roosevelt. However, Washington's doctrine of accommodation drew sharp criticism from more militant African American leaders, such as W. E. B. Du Bois and William Monroe Trotter, who—in the age of lynching, race riots, and terrorism at the hands of the Ku Klux Klan—were less sanguine over the alleged benevolence of Southern whites. Washington further enraged his critics through his heavy-handed efforts to consolidate his own power. He died in 1915.

A Protest Against Lynching

Tuskegee, Ala., February 22, 1901

Within the last fortnight three members of my race have been burned at the stake; of these one was a woman. Not one of the three was charged with any crime even remotely connected with the abuse of a white woman. In every case murder was the sole accusation. All of these burnings took place in broad daylight and two of them occurred on Sunday afternoon in sight of a Christian church.

In the midst of the nation's busy and prosperous life few, I fear, take time to consider where these brutal and inhuman crimes are leading us. The custom of burning human beings has become so common as scarcely to excite interest or attract unusual attention.

I have always been among those who condemned in the strongest terms crimes of whatever character committed by members of my race, and I condemn them now with equal severity; but I maintain that the only protection of our civilization is a fair and calm trial of all people charged with crime and in their legal punishment if proved guilty.

There is no shadow of excuse for departure from legal methods in the cases of individuals accused of murder. The laws are as a rule made by the white people and their execution is in the hands of the white people; so that there is little probability of any guilty colored man escaping.

These burnings without a trial are in the deepest sense unjust to my race; but it is not this injustice alone which stirs my heart. These barbarous scenes followed, as they are, by publication of the shocking details are more disgraceful and degrading to the people who inflict the punishment than those who receive it.

If the law is disregarded when a Negro is concerned, it will soon be disregarded when a white man is concerned; and besides, the rule of the mob destroys the friendly relations which should exist between the races and injures and interferes with the material prosperity of the communities concerned.

Worst of all these outrages take place in communities where there are Christian churches; in the midst of people who have their Sunday school, their Christian Endeavor Societies and Young Men's Christian Associations, where collections are taken up for sending missionaries to Africa and China and the rest of the so-called heathen world.

Is it not possible for pulpit and press to speak out against these burnings in a manner that shall arouse a public sentiment that will compel the mob to cease insulting our courts, our Governors and legal authority; cease bringing shame and ridicule upon our Christian civilization?

Booker T. Washington

Source

Booker T. Washington, "A Protest Against Lynching," *Birmingham Age-Herald,* February 29, 1904, and the *New York Times,* February 29, 1904, 6; reprinted in Louis R. Harlan and Raymond W. Smock, eds., *1903–1904,* vol. 7 of *The Booker T. Washington Papers* (Urbana, Chicago, and London: University of Illinois Press, 1974), 447–48.

Selected Bibliography

Harlan, Louis R. *Booker T. Washington: The Making of a Black Leader, 1865–1901.* New York: Oxford University Press, 1972.

—— *Booker T. Washington: The Wizard of Tuskegee, 1901–1915.* New York: Oxford University Press, 1986.

Meier, August. *Negro Thought in America, 1880–1915: Racial Ideologies in the Age of Booker T. Washington.* Ann Arbor: University of Michigan Press, 1963.

ten

Of Mr. Booker T. Washington and Others

W.E.B. Du Bois's (1868–1963) *The Souls of Black Folk* has been regarded as one of the most prophetic and fundamental works of African American scholarship. When it was published in 1903, however, his social criticisms were not well received among whites and even some blacks. The chapter entitled "Of Booker T. Washington and Others" marked Du Bois's opposition to the man who was the most popular black leader at that time. In the chapter Du Bois challenges Washington's conciliatory and gradualist social plans for black people, frequently summarized by Washington's declaration "In all things that are purely social we can be as separate as the five fingers, yet one as the hand in all things essential to mutual progress."[1] Du Bois concluded that black people should support the positive aspects of Washington's plans but to "unceasingly and firmly oppose" those that stunt black peoples' potential for growth and power.

Prior to the printing of *Souls,* Du Bois and Washington maintained a cordial political relationship; in the 1890s Du Bois had been accepting of Washington's programs, which included vocational training for blacks. After the arrest of William Monroe Trotter, a more steadfast Washington critic, Du Bois came to see that Washington would not tolerate his disapproval. This drove Du Bois to create the Niagara Movement (1905–1909), a collective of intellectuals committed to racial equality and also opposed to Washington's "Tuskeegee machine." The Niagara Movement supported issues such as voting rights, higher education, freedom of the press and speech, and first-class citizenship for African Americans. The Niagara Movement became the predecessor to the National Association for the Advancement of Colored People, established in 1909. Though Du Bois and Washington often differed with one another ideologically, they made several appearances together and remained in close contact until Washington's death in 1915. After his death, many looked to Du Bois as the leading black figure in the United States.

Easily the most striking thing in the history of the American Negro since 1876 is the ascendancy of Mr. Booker T. Washington. It began at the time when war memories and ideals were rapidly passing; a day of astonishing commercial development was dawning; a sense of doubt and hesitation overtook the freedmen's sons,—then it was that his leading began. Mr. Washington came, with a simple definite programme, at the psychological moment when the nation was a little ashamed of having bestowed so much sentiment on Negroes, and was concentrating its energies on Dollars. His programme of industrial education, conciliation of the South, and submission and silence as to civil and political rights, was not wholly original; the Free Negroes from 1830 up to wartime had striven to build industrial schools, and the American Missionary Association had from the first taught various trades; and Price and others had sought a way of honorable alliance with the best of the Southerners. But Mr. Washington first indissolubly linked these things; he put enthusiasm, unlimited energy, and perfect faith into this programme, and changed it from a by-path into a veritable Way of Life. And the tale of the methods by which he did this is a fascinating study of human life.

It startled the nation to hear a Negro advocating such a programme after many decades of bitter complaint; it startled and won the applause of the South, it interested and won the admiration of the North; and after a confused murmur of protest, it silenced if it did not convert the Negroes themselves.

To gain the sympathy and coöperation of the various elements comprising the white South was Mr. Washington's first task; and this, at the time Tuskegee was founded, seemed, for a black man, well-nigh impossible. And yet ten years later it was done in the word spoken at Atlanta: "In all things purely social we can be as separate as the five fingers, and yet one as the hand in all things essential to mutual progress." This "Atlanta Compromise" is by all odds the most notable thing in Mr. Washington's career. The South interpreted it in different ways: the radicals received it as a complete surrender of the demand for civil and political equality; the conservatives, as a generously conceived working basis for mutual understanding. So both approved it, and to-day its author is certainly the most distinguished Southerner since Jefferson Davis, and the one with the largest personal following.

Next to this achievement comes Mr. Washington's work in gaining place and consideration in the North. Others less shrewd and tactful had formerly essayed to sit on these two stools and had fallen between them; but as Mr. Washington knew the heart of the South from birth and training, so by singular insight he intuitively grasped the spirit of the age which was dominating the North. And so thoroughly did he learn the speech and thought of triumphant commercialism, and the ideals of material prosperity, that the picture of a lone black boy poring over a French grammar amid the weeds and dirt of a neglected home soon seemed to him the acme of absurdities. One wonders what Socrates and St. Francis of Assisi would say to this.

And yet this very singleness of vision and thorough oneness with his age is a mark of the successful man. It is as though Nature must needs make men narrow in order to give them force. So Mr. Washington's cult has gained unquestioning followers, his work has wonderfully prospered, his friends are legion, and his enemies are confounded. To-day he stands as the one recognized spokesman of his ten million fellows, and one of the most notable figures in a nation of seventy millions. One hesitates, therefore, to criticise a life which, beginning with so little, has done so much. And yet the time is come when one may speak in all sincerity and utter courtesy of the mistakes and shortcomings of Mr. Washington's career, as well as of his triumphs, without being thought captious or envious, and without forgetting that it is easier to do ill than well in the world.

The criticism that has hitherto met Mr. Washington has not always been of this broad character. In the South especially has he had to walk warily to avoid the harshest judgments,—and naturally so, for he is dealing with the one subject of deepest sensitiveness to that section. Twice—once when at the Chicago celebration of the Spanish-American War he alluded to the color-prejudice that is "eating away the vitals of the South," and once when he dined with President Roosevelt—has the resulting Southern criticism been violent enough to threaten seriously his popularity. In the North the feeling has several times forced itself into words, that Mr. Washington's counsels of submission overlooked certain elements of true manhood, and that his educational programme was unnecessarily narrow. Usually, however, such criticism has not found open expression, although, too, the spiritual sons of the Abolitionists have not been prepared to acknowledge that the schools founded before Tuskegee, by men of broad ideals and self-sacrificing spirit, were wholly failures or worthy of ridicule. While, then, criticism has not failed to follow Mr. Washington, yet the prevailing public opinion of the land has been but too willing to deliver the solution of a wearisome problem into his hands, and say, "If that is all you and your race ask, take it."

Among his own people, however, Mr. Washington has encountered the strongest and most lasting opposition, amounting at times to bitterness, and even to-day continuing strong and insistent even though largely silenced in outward expression by the public opinion of the nation. Some of this opposition is, of course, mere envy; the disappointment of displaced demagogues and the spite of narrow minds. But aside from this, there is among educated and thoughtful colored men in all parts of the land a feeling of deep regret, sorrow, and apprehension at the wide currency and ascendancy which some of Mr. Washington's theories have gained. These same men admire his sincerity of purpose, and are willing to forgive much to honest endeavor which is doing something worth the doing. They coöperate with Mr. Washington as far as they conscientiously can; and, indeed, it is no ordinary tribute to this man's tact and power that, steering as he must between so many diverse interests and opinions, he so largely retains the respect of all.

But the hushing of the criticism of honest opponents is a dangerous thing. It leads some of the best of the critics to unfortunate silence and paralysis of effort, and others to burst into speech so passionately and intemperately as to lose listeners. Honest and earnest criticism from those whose interests are most nearly touched,—criticism of writers by readers, of government by those governed, of leaders by those led,—this is the soul of democracy and the safeguard of modern society. If the best of the American Negroes receive by outer pressure a leader whom they had not recognized before, manifestly there is here a certain palpable gain. Yet there is also irreparable loss,—a loss of that peculiarly valuable education which a group receives when by search and criticism it finds and commissions its own leaders. The way in which this is done is at once the most elementary and the nicest problem of social growth. History is but the record of such group-leadership; and yet how infinitely changeful is its type and character! And of all types and kinds, what can be more instructive than the leadership of a group within a group?—that curious double movement where real progress may be negative and actual advance be relative retrogression. All this is the social student's inspiration and despair.

Now in the past the American Negro has had instructive experience in the choosing of group leaders, founding thus a peculiar dynasty which in the light of present conditions is worth while studying. When sticks and stones and beasts form the sole environment of a people, their attitude is largely one of determined opposition to and conquest of natural forces. But when to earth and brute is added an environment of men and ideas, then the attitude of the imprisoned group may take three main forms,—a feeling of revolt and revenge; an attempt to adjust all thought and action to the will of the greater group; or, finally, a determined effort at self-realization and self-development despite environing opinion. The influence of all of these attitudes at various times can be traced in the history of the American Negro, and in the evolution of his successive leaders.

Before 1750, while the fire of African freedom still burned in the veins of the slaves, there was in all leadership or attempted leadership but the one motive of revolt and revenge,—typified in the terrible Maroons, the Danish blacks, and Cato of Stono, and veiling all the Americas in fear of insurrection. The liberalizing tendencies of the latter half of the eighteenth century brought, along with kindlier relations between black and white, thoughts of ultimate adjustment and assimilation. Such aspiration was especially voiced in the earnest songs of Phyllis, in the martyrdom of Attucks, the fighting of Salem and Poor, the intellectual accomplishments of Banneker and Derham, and the political demands of the Cuffes.

Stern financial and social stress after the war cooled much of the previous humanitarian ardor. The disappointment and impatience of the Negroes at the persistence of slavery and serfdom voiced itself in two movements. The slaves in the South, aroused undoubtedly by vague rumors of the Haytian revolt, made three fierce attempts at insurrection,—in 1800 under Gabriel in Virginia, in 1822 under Vesey in Carolina, and in 1831 again in Virginia under the terrible Nat Turner. In the Free States, on the other hand, a new and curious attempt at self-development was made. In Philadelphia and New York color-prescription led to a withdrawal of Negro communicants from white churches and the formation of a peculiar socio-religious institution among the Negroes known as the African Church,—an organization still living and controlling in its various branches over a million of men.

Walker's wild appeal against the trend of the times showed how the world was changing after the coming of the cotton-gin. By 1830 slavery seemed hopelessly fastened on the South, and the slaves thoroughly cowed into submission. The free Negroes of the North, inspired by the mulatto immigrants from the West Indies, began to change the basis of their demands; they recognized the slavery of slaves, but insisted that they themselves were freemen, and sought assimilation and amalgamation with the nation on the same terms with other men. Thus, Forten and Purvis of Philadelphia, Shad of Wilmington, Du Bois of New Haven, Barbadoes of Boston, and others, strove singly and together as men, they said, not as slaves; as "people of color," not as "Negroes." The trend of the times, however, refused them recognition save in individual and exceptional cases, considered them as one with all the despised blacks, and they soon found themselves striving to keep even the rights they formerly had of voting and working and moving as freemen. Schemes of migration and colonization arose among them; but these they refused to entertain, and they eventually turned to the Abolition movement as a final refuge.

Here, led by Remond, Nell, Wells-Brown, and Douglass, a new period of self-assertion and self-development dawned. To be sure, ultimate freedom and assimilation was the ideal before the leaders, but the assertion of the manhood rights of the Negro by himself was the main reliance, and John Brown's raid was the extreme of its logic. After the war and emancipation, the great form of Frederick Douglass, the greatest of American Negro leaders, still led the host.

Self-assertion, especially in political lines, was the main programme, and behind Douglass came Elliot, Bruce, and Langston, and the Reconstruction politicians, and, less conspicuous but of greater social significance Alexander Crummell and Bishop Daniel Payne.

Then came the Revolution of 1876, the suppression of the Negro votes, the changing and shifting of ideals, and the seeking of new lights in the great night. Douglass, in his old age, still bravely stood for the ideals of his early manhood,—ultimate assimilation *through* self-assertion, and on no other terms. For a time Price arose as a new leader, destined, it seemed, not to give up, but to re-state the old ideals in a form less repugnant to the white South. But he passed away in his prime. Then came the new leader. Nearly all the former ones had become leaders by the silent suffrage of their fellows, had sought to lead their own people alone, and were usually, save Douglass, little known outside their race. But Booker T. Washington arose as essentially the leader not of one race but of two,—a compromiser between the South, the North, and the Negro. Naturally the Negroes resented, at first signs of compromise which surrendered their civil and political rights, even though this was to be exchanged for larger chances of economic development. The rich and dominating North, however, was not only weary of the race problem, but was investing largely in Southern enterprises, and welcomed any method of peaceful coöperation. Thus, by national opinion, the Negroes began to recognize Mr. Washington's leadership; and the voice of criticism was hushed.

Mr. Washington represents in Negro thought the old attitude of adjustment and submission; but adjustment at such a peculiar time as to make his programme unique. This is an age of unusual economic development, and Mr. Washington's programme naturally takes an economic cast, becoming a gospel of Work and Money to such an extent as apparently almost completely to overshadow the higher aims of life. Moreover, this is an age when the more advanced races are coming in closer contact with the less developed races, and the race-feeling is therefore intensified; and Mr. Washington's programme practically accepts the alleged inferiority of the Negro races. Again, in our own land, the reaction from the sentiment of war time given impetus to race-prejudice against Negroes, and Mr. Washington withdraws many of the high demands of Negroes as men and American citizens. In other periods of intensified prejudice all the Negro's tendency to self-assertion has been called forth; at this period a policy of submission is advocated. In the history of nearly all other races and peoples the doctrine preached at such crises has been that manly self-respect is worth more than lands and houses, and that a people who voluntarily surrender such respect, or cease striving for it, are not worth civilizing.

In answer to this, it has been claimed that the Negro can survive only through submission. Mr. Washington distinctly asks that black people give up, at least for the present, three things,—

First, political power,
Second, insistence on civil rights,
Third, higher education of Negro youth,—

and concentrate all their energies on industrial education, the accumulation of wealth, and the conciliation of the South. This policy has been courageously and insistently advocated for over fifteen years, and has been triumphant for perhaps ten years. As a result of this tender of the palm-branch, what has been the return? In these years there have occurred:

1. The disfranchisement of the Negro.
2. The legal creation of a distinct status of civil inferiority for the Negro.
3. The steady withdrawal of aid from institutions for the higher training of the Negro.

These movements are not, to be sure, direct results of Mr. Washington's teachings; but his propaganda has, without a shadow of doubt, helped their speedier accomplishment. The question then comes: Is it possible, and probable, that nine millions of men can make effective progress in economic lines if they are deprived of political rights, made a servile caste, and allowed only the most meagre chance for developing their exceptional men? If history and reason give any distinct answer to these questions, it is an emphatic *No*. And Mr. Washington thus faces the triple paradox of his career:

1. He is striving nobly to make Negro artisans business men and property-owners; but it is utterly impossible, under modern competitive methods, for workingmen and property-owners to defend their rights and exist without the right of suffrage.
2. He insists on thrift and self-respect, but at the same time counsels a silent submission to civic inferiority such as is bound to sap the manhood of any race in the long run.
3. He advocates common-school and industrial training, and depreciates institutions of higher learning; but neither the Negro common-schools, nor Tuskegee itself, could remain open a day were it not for teachers trained in Negro colleges, or trained by their graduates.

This triple paradox in Mr. Washington's position is the object of criticism by two classes of colored Americans. One class is spiritually descended from Toussaint the Savior, through Gabriel, Vesey, and Turner, and they represent the attitude of revolt and revenge; they hate the white South blindly and distrust the white race and so far as they agree on definite action, think that the Negro's only hope lies in emigration beyond the borders of the United States. And yet, by the irony of fate, nothing has more effectually made this programme seem hopeless than the recent course of the United States toward weaker and darker peoples in the West Indies, Hawaii, and the Philippines,—for where in the world may we go and be safe from lying and brute force?

The other class of Negroes who cannot agree with Mr. Washington has hitherto said little aloud. They deprecate the sight of scattered counsels, of internal disagreement; and especially they dislike making their just criticism of a useful and earnest man an excuse for a general discharge of venom from small-minded opponents. Nevertheless, the questions involved are so fundamental and serious that it is difficult to see how men like the Grimkes, Kelly Miller, J. W. E. Bowen, and other representatives of this group, can much longer be silent. Such men feel in conscience bound to ask of this nation three things:

1. The right to vote.
2. Civic equality.
3. The education of youth according to ability.

They acknowledge Mr. Washington's invaluable service in counselling patience and courtesy in such demands; they do not ask that ignorant black men vote when ignorant whites are debarred, or that any reasonable restrictions in the suffrage should not be applied; they know that the low social level of the mass of the race is responsible for much discrimination against it, but they also know, and the nation knows, that relentless color-prejudice is more often a cause than a result of the Negro's degradation; they seek the abatement of this relic of barbarism, and not its systematic encouragement and pampering by all agencies of social power from the Associated Press to the Church of Christ. They advocate, with Mr. Washington, a broad system of Negro common schools supplemented by thorough industrial training; but they are surprised that a man of Mr. Washington's insight cannot see that no such educational system ever has rested or can rest on any other basis than that of the well-equipped college and university, and they insist that there is a demand for a few such institutions throughout the South to train the best of the Negro youth as teachers, professional men, and leaders.

This group of men honor Mr. Washington for his attitude of conciliation toward the white South; they accept the "Atlanta Compromise" in its broadest interpretation; they recognize, with him, many signs of promise, many men of high purpose and fair judgment, in this section; they know that no easy task has been laid upon a region already tottering under heavy burdens. But, nevertheless, they insist that the way to truth and right lies in straightforward honesty, not in indiscriminate flattery; in praising those of the South who do well and criticising uncompromisingly those who do ill; in taking advantage of the opportunities at hand and urging their fellows to do the same, but at the same time in remembering that only a firm adherence to their higher ideals and aspirations will ever keep those ideals within the realm of possibility. They do not expect that the free right to vote, to enjoy civic rights, and to be educated, will come in a moment; they do not expect to see the bias and prejudices of years disappear at the blast of a trumpet; but they are absolutely certain that the way for a people to gain their reasonable rights is not by voluntarily throwing them away and insisting that they do not want them; that the way for a people to gain respect is not by continually belittling and ridiculing themselves; that, on the contrary, Negroes must insist continually, in season and out of season, that voting is necessary to modern manhood, that color discrimination is barbarism, and that black boys need education as well as white boys.

In failing thus to state plainly and unequivocally the legitimate demands of their people, even at the cost of opposing an honored leader, the thinking classes of American Negroes would shirk a heavy responsibility,—a responsibility to themselves, a responsibility to the struggling masses, a responsibility to the darker races of men whose future depends so largely on this American experiment, but especially a responsibility to this nation,—this common Fatherland. It is wrong to encourage a man or a people in evil-doing; it is wrong to aid and abet a national crime simply because it is unpopular not to do so. The growing spirit of kindliness and reconciliation between the North and South after the frightful differences of a generation ago ought to be a source of deep congratulation to all, and especially to those whose mistreatment caused the war; but if that reconciliation is to be marked by the industrial slavery and civic death of those same black men, with permanent legislation into a position of inferiority, then those black men, if they are really men, are called upon by every consideration of patriotism and loyalty to oppose such a course by all civilized methods, even though such opposition involves disagreement with Mr. Booker T. Washington. We have no right to sit silently by while the inevitable seeds are sown for a harvest of disaster to our children, black and white.

First, it is the duty of black men to judge the South discriminatingly. The present generation of Southerners are not responsible for the past, and they should not be blindly hated or blamed for it. Furthermore, to no class is the indiscriminate endorsement of the recent course of the South toward Negroes more nauseating than to the best thought of the South. The South is not "solid"; it is a land in the ferment of social change, wherein forces of all kinds are fighting for supremacy; and to praise the ill the South is to-day perpetrating is just as wrong as to condemn the good. Discriminating and broad-minded criticism is what the South needs,—needs it for the sake of her own white sons and daughters, and for the insurance of robust, healthy mental and moral development.

To-day even the attitude of the Southern whites toward the blacks is not, as so many assume, in all cases the same; the ignorant Southerner hates the Negro, the workingmen fear his competition, the money-makers wish to use him as a laborer, some of the educated see a menace in his upward development, while others—usually the sons of the masters—wish to help him to rise. National opinion has enabled this last class to maintain the Negro common schools, and to protect the Negro partially in property, life, and limb. Through the pressure of the money-makers, the Negro is in danger of being reduced to semi-slavery, especially in the country districts; the workingmen, and those of the educated who fear the Negro, have united to disfranchise him, and some have urged his deportation; while the passions of the ignorant are easily aroused to lynch and abuse any black man. To praise this intricate whirl of thought and prejudice is nonsense; to inveigh indiscriminately against "the South" is unjust; but to use the same breath in praising Governor Aycock, exposing Senator Morgan, arguing with Mr. Thomas Nelson Page, and denouncing Senator Ben Tillman, is not only sane, but the imperative duty of thinking black men.

It would be unjust to Mr. Washington not to acknowledge that in several instances he has opposed movements in the South which were unjust to the Negro; he sent memorials to the Louisiana and Alabama constitutional conventions, he has spoken against lynching, and in other ways has openly or silently set his influence against sinister schemes and unfortunate happenings. Notwithstanding this, it is equally true to assert that on the whole the distinct impression left by Mr. Washington's propaganda is, first, that the South is justified in its present attitude toward the Negro because of the Negro's degradation; secondly, that the prime cause of the Negro's failure to rise more quickly is his wrong education in the past; and, thirdly, that his future rise depends primarily on his own efforts. Each of these propositions is a dangerous half-truth. The supplementary truths must never be lost sight of: first, slavery and race-prejudice are potent if not sufficient causes of the Negro's position; second, industrial and common-school training were necessarily slow in planting because they had to await the black teachers trained by higher institutions,—it being extremely doubtful if any essentially different development was possible, and certainly a Tuskegee was unthinkable before 1880; and, third, while it is a great truth to say that the Negro must strive and strive mightily to help himself, it is equally true that unless his striving be not simply seconded, but rather aroused and encouraged, by the initiative of the richer and wiser environing group, he cannot hope for great success.

In his failure to realize and impress this last point, Mr. Washington is especially to be criticised. His doctrine has tended to make the whites, North and South, shift the burden of the Negro problem to the Negro's shoulders and stand aside as critical and rather pessimistic spectators; when in fact the burden belongs to the nation, and the hands of none of us are clean if we bend not our energies to righting these great wrongs.

The South ought to be led, by candid and honest criticism, to assert her better self and do her full duty to the race she has cruelly wronged and is still wronging. The North—her co-partner in guilt—cannot salve her conscience by plastering it with gold. We cannot settle this problem by diplomacy and suaveness, by "policy" alone. If worse come to worst, can the moral fibre of this country survive the slow throttling and murder of nine millions of men?

The black men of America have a duty to perform, a duty stern and delicate,—a forward movement to oppose a part of the work of their greatest leader. So far as Mr. Washington preaches Thrift, Patience, and Industrial Training for the masses, we must hold up his hands and strive with him, rejoicing in his honors and glorying in the strength of this Joshua called of God and of man to lead the headless host. But so far as Mr. Washington apologizes for injustice, North or South, does not rightly value the privilege and duty of voting, belittles the emasculating effects of caste distinctions, and opposes the higher training and ambition of our brighter minds,—so far as he, the South, or the Nation, does this,—we must unceasingly and firmly oppose them. By every civilized and peaceful method we must strive for the rights which the world accords to men, clinging unwaveringly to those great words which the sons of the Fathers would fain forget: "We hold these truths to be self-evident: That all men are created equal; that they are endowed by their Creator with certain unalienable rights; that among these are life, liberty, and the pursuit of happiness."

Note

1. From the Atlanta Exposition in 1895.

Source

W.E.B. Du Bois, *The Souls of Black Folk* (Chicago: A.C. McClurg & Co., 1903).

Select Bibliography

Du Bois, W. E. B. *Against Racism: Unpublished Essays, Papers, Addresses, 1887–1961.* Amherst: University of Massachusetts Press, 1985.

—— *The Autobiography of W. E. B. DuBois; A Soliloguy on Viewing My Life from the Last Decade of Its First Century.* New York: International Publishers 1968.

—— *Darkwater; Voices from Within the Veil.* New York: Schocken Books, 1969.

—— *Dusk of Dawn; An Essay Toward an Autobiography of a Race Concept.* New York: Schocken Books 1968.

Du Bois, W. E. B. and Herbert Aptheker. *The Correspondence of W. E. B. Du Bois.* Amherst: University of Massachusetts Press, 1973.

eleven

Selected Poems by Claude McKay

Poet and novelist Claude McKay (Festus Claudius McKay) is noted for his contributions to the Harlem Renaissance in the 1920s. He was born in Sunny Ville, Jamaica, around 1889 (numerous sources dispute his birth date) and was the youngest of eleven children. As a youth he was exposed to a number of religious and educational influences.

The following poems were written during the former part of McKay's career. McKay left Jamaica for the United States in 1912 and traveled extensively thereafter. He studied agriculture at the Tuskegee Institute for a short period and moved to Harlem in 1914. He wrote "In Memoriam: Booker T. Washington" shortly after the leader's death in 1915. McKay's "To the White Fiends," published in the September 1919 issue of the *Liberator*, was one his most popular works during this period. Like his acclaimed poem "If We Must Die," also from that year, it reflected McKay's disillusionment with America. He was disturbed by the treatment of African Americans during the First World War and by the racial riots that soon followed in cities throughout the United States. By the end of 1919, whites had lynched seventy-six black people.

During the Red Scare of 1919 and after harsh criticism by the U.S. government, McKay moved to London, England, where he studied Marxism and wrote for the Communist publication *The Worker's Dead-*

nought. He published *Spring in New Hampshire* in 1920. He returned to the United States to continue his work with *The Liberator* in 1921 and published "Enslaved" in its July edition. He also became involved in the Universal Negro Improvement Association during this time and wrote several articles for its publication, *Negro World.* Soon after he traveled to Russia, where he attended the Fourth Congress of the Communist Party. He then moved to France and spent over a decade touring Europe.

In 1928 McKay published his most popular novel, *Home to Harlem,* which Marcus Garvey and W.E.B. Du Bois condemned for its exploitation of black stereotypes. His novels would later become more racially sensitive yet less commercially successful as exemplified in *Banana Bottom* (1933). In 1938 McKay grew interested in Catholicism and joined the Roman Catholic Church in 1944. He died of heart failure in Chicago in 1948. After a funeral there his body was transported to Harlem for a second funeral and laid to rest in Queens, New York.

IN MEMORIAM: BOOKER T. WASHINGTON

I vividly recall the noon-day hour
    You walked into the wide and well-filled hall:
    We rose and sang, at the conductor's call,
Dunbar's Tuskegee hymn. A splendid tower
of strength, as would a gardener on the flower
    Nursed tenderly, you gazed upon us all
    Assembled there, a serried, sable wall
Fast mortared by your subtle tact and power.
O how I loved, adored your furrowed face!
    And fondly hoped, before your days were done,
You would look in mine too with paternal grace.
    But vain are hopes and dreams!—gone: you are gone,
Death's hand has torn you from your trusting race,
    And O! We feel so utterly alone.

ENSLAVED

Oh when I think of my long-suffering race,
For weary centuries, despised, oppressed
Enslaved and lynched, denied a human place
In the great life line of the Christian West;
And in the Black Land disinherited,
Robbed in the ancient country of its birth,

My heart grows sick with hate, becomes as lead,
For this my race that has no home on earth.
Then from the dark depth of my soul I cry
To the avenging angel to consume
The white man's world of wonders utterly:
Let it be swallowed up in the earth's vast womb,
Or upward roll as sacrificial smoke
To liberate my people from its yoke!

TO THE WHITE FIENDS

Think you I am not fiend and savage too?
Think you I could not arm me with a gun
And shoot down ten of you for every one
Of my black brothers murdered, burnt by you?
Be not deceived, for every deed you do
I could match—out-match: am I not Afric's son,
Black of that black land where black deeds are done?
But the Almighty from the darkness drew
My soul and said: Even thou shalt be a light
Awhile to burn on the benighted earth,
Thy dusky face I set among the white
For thee to prove thyself of higher worth;
Before the world is swallowed up in night,
To show thy little lamp: go forth, go forth!

MULATTO

Because I am the white man's son—his own,
Bearing his bastard birth-mark on my face,
I will dispute his title to his throne,
Forever fight him for my rightful place.
There is a searing hate within my soul,
A hate that only kin can feel for kin,
A hate that makes me vigorous and whole,
And spurs me on increasingly to win.
Because I am my cruel father's child,
My love of justice stirs me up to hate,
A warring Ishmaelite, unreconciled,
When falls the hour I shall not hesitate
Into my father's heart to plunge the knife
To gain the utmost freedom that is life.

Source

Claude McKay, "In Memorium: Booker T. Washington," "Enslaved," "To the White Fiends," and "Mulatto," in Wayne F. Cooper, ed., *The Passion of Claude Mckay,* 116–26 (New York: Schocken Books, 1973).

Selected Bibliography

James, Winston. *A Fierce Hatred of Injustice: Claude McKay's Jamaica and His Poetry of Rebellion.* New York: Verso, 2000.

McKay, Claude. *Banana Bottom.* Chatham, N.J.: Chatham Bookseller, 1970.

—— *Banjo: A Story Without a Plot.* New York: Harcourt, Brace, Jovanovich, 1970.

—— *Home to Harlem.* Boston, Northeastern University Press, 1987.

—— *A Long Way from Home.* New York: Arno Press, 1969.

—— *The Negroes in America.* Port Washington, N.Y.: Kennikat Press, 1979.

twelve

Letter from a Birmingham Jail

Martin Luther King Jr. (1929–1968) is probably the most revered African American leader in history. King was born to a middle-class family in Atlanta, Georgia, where his father was a prominent minister. He entered Morehouse College in 1944, at the age of fifteen. He later attended Crozer Theological Seminary, where he graduated valedictorian in 1951, and Boston University, where he finished his Ph.D. in 1955. In this year he also emerged as leader of the Montgomery Bus Boycott, which began after Rosa Parks famously refused to give up her seat near the front of a Montgomery bus.

Throughout his career, King advocated nonviolent civil disobedience and argued that black victims must learn to love (and thereby transform) their racist oppressors. In 1958 King was elected president of the Southern Christian Leadership Conference (SCLC), a group that soon emerged at the forefront of civil rights protest. On August 28, 1963, King gave his famous "I Have a Dream" speech from the steps of the Lincoln Memorial, before a crowd of over 200,000. In 1964 King won the Nobel Peace Prize, and *Time* magazine named him "Man of the Year." But as the 1960s progressed, King grew more pessimistic about the possibility for harmonious race relations in the United States. In 1968, he traveled to Memphis, Tennessee to support striking sanitation workers, where he was assassinated on April 4, 1968. In 1986, King's birthday became a national holiday.

Martin Luther King Jr.'s "Letter from a Birmingham Jail" is a classic document of American protest writing and one of King's finest expositions on nonviolent civil disobedience. King wrote the twenty-page letter in the spring of 1963, after he was arrested and incarcerated for nine days in Birmingham, Alabama, for challenging that city's segregation laws. The letter was originally written on toilet paper that had been smuggled into King's jail cell, and it was intended as a response to an open letter, signed by eight white clergymen, who denounced the anti–Jim Crow demonstrations in Birmingham. This document is notable as the single best source for understanding the backbone of King's philosophy.

My Dear Fellow Clergymen:

While confined here in the Birmingham city jail, I came across your recent statement calling my present activities "unwise and untimely." Seldom do I pause to answer criticism of my work and ideas. If I sought to answer all the criticisms that cross my desk, my secretaries would have little time for anything other than such correspondence in the course of the day, and I would have no time for constructive work. But since I feel that you are men of genuine good will and that your criticisms are sincerely set forth, I want to try to answer your statement in what I hope will be patient and reasonable terms.

I think I should indicate why I am here in Birmingham, since you have been influenced by the view which argues against "outsiders coming in." I have the honor of serving as president of the Southern Christian Leadership Conference, an organization operating in every southern state, with headquarters in Atlanta, Georgia. We have some eighty-five affiliated organizations across the South, and one of them is the Alabama Christian Movement for Human Rights. Frequently we share staff, educational, and financial resources with our affiliates. Several months ago the affiliate here in Birmingham asked us to be on call to engage in a nonviolent direct-action program if such were deemed necessary. We readily consented, and when the hour came we lived up to our promise. So I, along with several members of my staff, am here because I was invited here, I am here because I have organizational ties here.

But more basically, I am in Birmingham because injustice is here. Just as the prophets of the eighth century B.C. left their villages and carried their "thus saith the Lord" far beyond the boundaries of their home towns, and just as the Apostle Paul left his village of Tarsus and carried the gospel of Jesus Christ to the far corners of the Greco-Roman world, so am I compelled to carry the gospel of freedom beyond my own home town. Like Paul, I must constantly respond to the Macedonian call for aid.

Moreover, I am cognizant of the interrelatedness of all communities and states. I cannot sit idly by in Atlanta and not be concerned about what happens in Birmingham. Injustice anywhere is a threat to justice everywhere. We are caught in an inescapable network of mutuality, tied in a single garment of destiny. Whatever affects one directly, affects all indirectly. Never again can we afford to live with the narrow, provincial "outside agitator" idea. Anyone who lives inside the United States can never be considered an outsider anywhere within its bounds.

You deplore the demonstrations taking place in Birmingham. But your statement, I am sorry to say, fails to express a similar concern for the conditions that brought about the demonstrations. I am sure that none of you would want to rest content with the superficial kind of social analysis that deals merely with effects and does not grapple with underlying causes. It is unfortunate that demonstrations are taking place in Birmingham, but it is even more unfortunate that the city's white power structure left the Negro community with no alternative.

In any nonviolent campaign there are four basic steps: collection of the facts to determine whether injustices exist; negotiation; self-purification; and direct action. We have gone through all these steps in Birmingham. There can be no gainsaying the fact that racial injustice engulfs this community. Birmingham is probably the most thoroughly segregated city in the United States. Its ugly record of brutality is widely known. Negroes have experienced grossly unjust treatment in the courts. There have been more unsolved bombings of Negro homes and churches in Birmingham than in any other city in the nation. These are the hard, brutal facts of the case. On the basis of these conditions, Negro leaders sought to negotiate with the city fathers. But the latter consistently refused to engage in good-faith negotiation.

Then, last September, came the opportunity to talk with leaders of Birmingham's economic community. In the course of the negotiations, certain promises were made by the merchants—for example, to remove the stores' humiliating racial signs. On the basis of these promises, the Reverend Fred Shuttlesworth[1] and the leaders of the Alabama Christian Movement for Human Rights agreed to a moratorium on all demonstrations. As the weeks and months went by, we realized that we were the victims of a broken promise. A few signs, briefly removed, returned; the others remained.

As in so many past experiences, our hopes had been blasted, and the shadow of deep disappointment settled upon us. We had no alternative except to prepare for direct action, whereby we would present our very bodies as a means of laying our case before the conscience of the local and the national community. Mindful of the difficulties involved, we decided to undertake a process of self-purification. We began a series of workshops on nonviolence, and we repeatedly asked ourselves: "Are you able to accept blows without retaliating?" "Are you able to endure the ordeal of jail?" We decided to schedule our direct-action program for the Easter season, realizing that except for Christmas, this is the main shopping period of the year. Knowing that a strong economic-withdrawal program would be the byproduct of direct action, we felt that this would be the best time to bring pressure to bear on the merchants for the needed change.

Then it occurred to us that Birmingham's mayoral election was coming up in March, and we speedily decided to postpone action until after election day, When we discovered that the Commissioner of Public Safety, Eugene "Bull" Connor,[2] had piled up enough votes to be in the run-off, we decided again to postpone action until the day after the run-off so that the demonstrations could not be used to cloud the issues. Like many others, we wanted to see Mr. Connor defeated, and to this end we endured postponement after postponement. Having aided in this community need, we felt that our direct-action program could be delayed no longer.

You may well ask, "Why direct action? Why sit-ins, marches, and so forth? Isn't negotiation a better path?" You are quite right in calling for negotiation. Indeed, this is the very purpose of direct action. Nonviolent direct action seeks to create such a crisis and foster such a tension that a community which has constantly refused to negotiate is forced to confront the issue. It seeks so to dramatize the issue that it can no longer be ignored. My citing the creation of tension as part of the work of the nonviolent-resister may sound rather shocking. But I must confess that I am not afraid of the word "tension." I have earnestly opposed violent tension, but there is a type of constructive, nonviolent tension which is necessary for growth. Just as Socrates[3] felt that it was necessary to create a tension in the mind so that individuals could rise from the bondage of myths and half-truths to the unfettered realm of creative analysis and objective appraisal, so must we see the need for nonviolent gadflies to create the kind of tension in society that will help men rise from the dark depths of prejudice and racism, to the majestic heights of understanding and brotherhood.

The purpose of our direct-action program is to create a situation so crisis-packed that it will inevitably open the door to negotiation. I therefore concur with you in your call for negotiation. Too long has our beloved Southland been bogged down in a tragic effort to live in monologue rather than dialogue.

One of the basic points in your statement is that the action that I and my associates have taken in Birmingham is untimely. Some have asked: "Why didn't you give the new city administration time to act?" The only answer that I can give to this query is that the new Birmingham administration must be prodded about as much as the outgoing one, before it will act. We are sadly mistaken if we feel that the election of Albert Boutwell as mayor will bring the millennium to Birmingham. While Mr. Boutwell is a much more gentle person than Mr. Connor, they are both segregationists, dedicated to maintenance of the status quo. I have hoped that Mr. Boutwell will be reasonable enough to see the futility of massive resistance to desegregation. But he will not see this without pressure from devotees of civil rights. My friends, I must say to you that we have not made a single gain in civil rights without determined legal and nonviolent pressure. Lamentably, it is an historical fact that privileged groups seldom give up their privileges voluntarily. Individuals may see the moral light and voluntarily give up their unjust posture; but, as Reinhold Niebuhr[4] has reminded us, groups tend to be more immoral than individuals.

We know through painful experience that freedom is never voluntarily given by the oppressor; it must be demanded by the oppressed. Frankly, I have yet to engage in a direct-action campaign that was "well timed" in the view of those who have not suffered unduly from the disease of segregation. For years now I have heard the word "Wait!" It rings in the ear of every Negro with piercing familiarity. This "Wait" has almost always meant "Never." We must come to see, with one of our distinguished jurists, that "justice too long delayed is justice denied."

We have waited for more than 340 years for our constitutional and God-given rights. The nations of Asia and Africa are moving with jetlike speed toward gaining political independence, but we still creep at horse-and-buggy pace toward gaining a cup of coffee at a lunch counter. Perhaps it is easy for those who have never felt the stinging darts of segregation to say, "Wait." But when you have seen vicious mobs lynch your mothers and fathers at will and drown your sisters and brothers at whim; when you have seen hate-filled policemen curse, kick, and even kill your black brothers and sisters; when you see the vast majority of your twenty million Negro brothers smothering in an airtight cage of poverty in the midst of an affluent society; when you suddenly find your tongue twisted and your speech stammering as you seek to explain to your six-year-old daughter why she can't go to the public amusement park that has just been advertised on television, and see tears welling up in her eyes when she is told that Fun-town is closed to colored children, and see ominous clouds of inferiority beginning to form in her little mental sky, and see her beginning to distort her personality by developing an unconscious bitterness toward white people; when you have to concoct an answer for a five-year-old son who is asking. "Daddy, why do white people treat colored people so mean?"; when you take a cross-country drive and find it necessary to sleep night after night in the uncomfortable corners of your automobile because no motel will accept you; when you are humiliated day in and day out by nagging signs reading "white" and "colored"; when your first name becomes "nigger," your middle name becomes "boy" (however old you are) and your last name becomes "John," and your wife and mother are never given the respected title "Mrs."; when you are harried by day and haunted by night by the fact that you are a Negro, living constantly at tiptoe stance, never quite knowing what to expect next, and are plagued with inner fears and outer resentments; when you are forever fighting a degenerating sense of "nobodiness"—then you will understand why we find it difficult to wait. There comes a time when the cup of endurance runs over, and men are no longer willing to be plunged into the abyss of despair. I hope, sirs, you can understand our legitimate and unavoidable impatience.

You express a great deal of anxiety over our willingness to break laws. This is certainly a legitimate concern. Since we so diligently urge people to obey the Supreme Court's decision of 1954 outlawing segregation in the public schools, at first glance it may seem rather paradoxical for us consciously to break laws. One may well ask: "How can you advocate breaking some laws and obeying others?" The answer lies in the fact that there are two types of laws: just and unjust. I would be the first to advocate obeying just laws. One has not only a legal but a moral responsibility to obey just laws. Conversely, one has a moral responsibility to disobey unjust laws. I would agree with St. Augustine[5] that "an unjust law is no law at all."

Now, what is the difference between the two? How does one determine whether a law is just or unjust? A just law is a man-made code that squares with the moral law or the law of God. An unjust law is a code that is out of harmony with the moral law. To put it in the terms of St. Thomas Aquinas:[6] An unjust law is a human law that is not rooted in eternal law and natural law, Any law that uplifts human personality is just. Any law that degrades human personality is unjust. All segregation statutes are unjust because segregation distorts the soul and damages the personality. It gives the segregator a false sense of superiority and the segregated a false sense of inferiority. Segregation, to use the terminology of the Jewish philosopher Martin Buber,[7] substitutes an "I-it" relationship for an "I-thou" relationship and ends up relegating persons to the status of things. Hence segregation is not only politically, economically, and sociologically unsound, it is morally wrong and sinful. Paul Tillich[8] has said that sin is separation. Is not segregation an existential expression of man's tragic separation, his awful estrangement, his terrible sinfulness? Thus it is that I can urge men to obey the 1954 decision of the Supreme Court, for it is morally right; and I can urge them to disobey segregation ordinances, for they are morally wrong.

Let us consider a more concrete example of just and unjust laws. An unjust law is a code that a numerical or power majority group compels a minority group to obey but does not make binding on itself. This is *difference* made legal. By the same token, a just law is a code that a majority compels a minority to follow and that it is willing to follow and that it is willing to follow itself. This is *sameness* made legal.

Let me give another explanation. A law is unjust if it is inflicted on a minority that, as a result of being denied the right to vote, had no part in enacting or devising the law. Who can say that the legislature of Alabama which set up that state's segregation laws was democratically elected? Throughout Alabama all sorts of devious methods are used to prevent Negroes from becoming registered voters, and there are some counties in which, even though Negroes constitute a majority of the population, not a single Negro is registered. Can any law enacted under such circumstances be considered democratically structured?

Sometimes a law is just on its face and unjust in its application. For instance, I have been arrested on a charge of parading without a permit. Now, there is nothing wrong in having an ordinance which requires a permit for a parade. But such an ordinance becomes unjust when it is used to maintain segregation and to deny citizens the First-Amendment privilege of peaceful assembly and protest.

I hope you are able to see the distinction I am trying to point out. In no sense do I advocate evading or defying the law, as would the rabid segregationist. That would lead to anarchy. One who breaks an unjust law must do so openly, lovingly, and with a willingness to accept the penalty. I submit that an individual who breaks a law that conscience tells him is unjust, and who willingly, accepts the penalty of imprisonment in order to arouse the conscience of the community over its injustice, is in reality expressing the highest respect for law.

Of course, there is nothing new about this kind of civil disobedience. It was evidenced sublimely in the refusal of Shadrach, Meshach, and Abednego to obey the laws of Nebuchadnezzar, on the ground that a higher moral law was at stake. It was practiced superbly by the early Christians, who were willing to face hungry lions and the excruciating pain of chopping blocks rather than submit to certain unjust laws of the Roman Empire. To a degree, academic freedom is a reality today because Socrates practiced civil disobedience. In our own nation, the Boston Tea Party represented a massive act of civil disobedience.

We should never forget that everything Adolf Hitler[9] did in Germany was "legal" and everything the Hungarian freedom fighters did in Hungary was "illegal." It was "illegal" to aid and comfort a Jew in Hitler's Germany. Even so, I am sure that, had I lived in Germany at the time, I would have aided and comforted my Jewish brothers. If today I lived in a Communist country where certain principles dear to the Christian faith are suppressed, I would openly advocate disobeying that country's anti-religious laws.

I must make two honest confessions to you, my Christian and Jewish brothers. First, I must confess that over the past few years I have been gravely disappointed with the white moderate. I have almost reached the regrettable conclusion that the Negro's great stumbling block in his stride toward freedom is not the White Citizen's Counciler[10] or the Ku Klux Klanner, but the white moderate, who is more devoted to "order" than to justice; who prefers a negative peace which is the absence of tension to a positive peace which is the presence of justice; who constantly says, "I agree with you in the goal you seek, but I cannot agree with your methods of direct action"; who paternalistically believes he can set the timetable for another man's freedom; who lives by a mythical concept of time and who constantly advises the Negro to wait for a "more convenient season." Shallow understanding from people of good will is more frustrating than absolute misunderstanding from people of ill will. Lukewarm acceptance is much more bewildering than outright rejection.

I had hoped that the while moderate would understand that law and order exist for the purpose of establishing justice and that when they fail in this purpose they become the dangerously structured dams that block the flow of social progress. I had hoped that the white moderate would understand that the present tension in the South is a necessary phase of the transition from an obnoxious negative peace, in which the Negro passively accepted his unjust plight, to a substantive and positive peace, in which all men will respect the dignity and worth of human personality. Actually, we who engage in nonviolent direct action are not the creators of tension. We merely bring to the surface the hidden tension that is already alive. We bring it out in the open, where it can be seen and dealt with. Like a boil that can never be cured so long as it is covered up but must be opened with all its ugliness to the natural medicines of air and light, injustice must be exposed, with all the tension its exposure creates, to the light of human conscience and the air of national opinion, before it can be cured.

In your statement you assert that our actions, even though peaceful, must be condemned because they precipitate violence. But is this a logical assertion? Isn't this like condemning a robbed man because his possession of money precipitated the evil act of robbery? Isn't this like condemning Socrates because his unswerving commitment to truth and his philosophical inquiries precipitated the act by the misguided populace in which they made him drink hemlock? Isn't this like condemning Jesus because his unique God-consciousness and never-ceasing devotion to God's will precipitated the evil act of crucifixion? We must come to see that, as the federal courts have consistently affirmed, it is wrong to urge an individual to cease his efforts to gain his basic constitutional rights because the quest may precipitate violence. Society must protect the robbed and punish the robber.

I had also hoped that the white moderate would reject the myth concerning time in relation to the struggle for freedom. I have just received a letter from a white brother in Texas. He writes: "All Christians know that the colored people will receive equal rights eventually, but it is possible that you are in too great a religious hurry. It has taken Christianity almost two thousand years to accomplish what it has. The teachings of Christ take time to come to earth." Such an attitude stems from a tragic misconception of time, from the strangely irrational notion that there is something in the very flow of time that will inevitably cure all ills. Actually, time itself is neutral; it can be used either destructively or constructively. More and more I feel that the people of ill will have used time much more effectively than have the people of good will. We will have to repent in this generation not merely for the hateful words and actions of the bad people, but for the appalling silence of the good people. Human progress never rolls in on wheels of inevitability; it comes through the fireless efforts of men willing to be co-workers with God, and without this hard work, time itself becomes an ally of the forces of social stagnation. We must use time creatively, in the knowledge that the time is always ripe to do right. Now is the time to make real the promise of democracy and transform our pending national elegy into a creative psalm of brotherhood. Now is the time to lift our national policy from the quicksand of racial injustice to the solid rock of human dignity.

You speak of our activity in Birmingham as extreme. At first I was rather disappointed that fellow clergymen would see my nonviolent efforts as those of an extremist. I began thinking about the fact that I stand in the middle of two opposing forces in the negro community. One is a force of complacency, made up in part of Negroes who, as a result of long years of oppression, are so drained of self-respect and a sense of "somebodiness" that they have adjusted to segregation; and in part of a few middle-class Negroes who, because of a degree of academic and economic security and because in some ways they profit by segregation, have become insensitive to the problems of the masses. The other force is one of bitterness and hatred, and it comes perilously close to advocating violence. It is expressed in the various black nationalist groups that are springing up across the nation, the largest and best-known being Elijah Muhammad's Muslim movement. Nourished by the Negro's frustration over the continued existence of racial discrimination, this movement is made up of people who have lost faith in America, who have absolutely repudiated Christianity and who have concluded that the white man is an incorrigible "devil."

I have tried to stand between these two forces, saying that we need emulate neither the "do-nothingism" of the complacent nor the hatred and despair of the black nationalist. For there is the more excellent way of love and non violent protest. I am grateful to God that, through the influence of the Negro church, the way of nonviolence became an integral part of our struggle.

If this philosophy had not emerged, by now many streets of the South would, I am convinced, be flowing with blood. And I am further convinced that if our white brothers dismiss as "rabblerousers" and "outside agitators" those of us who employ nonviolent direct action, and if they refuse to support our nonviolent efforts, millions of Negroes will, out of frustration and despair, seek solace and security in black-nationalist ideologies—a development that would inevitably lead to a frightening racial nightmare.

Oppressed people cannot remain oppressed forever. The yearning for freedom eventually manifests itself, and that is what has happened to the American Negro. Something within has reminded him of his birthright of freedom, and something without has reminded him that it can be gained. Consciously or unconsciously, he has been caught up by the *Zeitgeist,* and with his black brothers of Africa and his brown and yellow brothers of Asia, South America, and the Caribbean, the United States Negro is moving with a sense of great urgency toward the promised land of racial justice. If one recognizes this vital urge that has engulfed the Negro community, one should readily understand why public demonstrations are taking place. The Negro has many pent-up resentments and latent frustrations, and he must release them. So let him march; let him make prayer pilgrimages to the city hall; let him go on freedom rides—and try to understand why he must do so. If his repressed emotions are not released in nonviolent ways, they will seek expression through violence; this is not a threat but a fact of history. So I have not said to my people, "Get rid of your discontent." Rather, I have tried to say that this normal and healthy discontent can be channeled into the creative outlet of nonviolent direct action. And now this approach is being termed extremist.

But though I was initially disappointed at being categorized as an extremist, as I continued to think about the matter I gradually grained a measure of satisfaction from the label. Was not Jesus an extremist for love: "Love your enemies, bless them that curse you, do good to them that hate you, and pray for them which despitefully use you, and persecute you."[11] Was not Amos[12] an extremist for justice: "Let justice roll down like waters and righteousness like an ever-flowing stream." Was not Paul[13] an extremist for the Christian gospel: "I bear in my body the marks of the Lord Jesus." Was not Martin Luther[14] an extremist: "Here I stand: I cannot do otherwise, so help me God." And John Bunyan:[15] " I will stay in jail to the end of my days before I make a butchery of my conscience." And Abraham Lincoln: "This nation cannot survive half slave and half free." And Thomas Jefferson[16]: "We hold these truths to be self-evident, that all men are created equal. . . ." So the question is not whether we will be extremists, but what kind of extremists we will be. Will we be extremists for hate or for love? Will we be extremists for the preservation of injustice or for the extension of justice? In that dramatic scene on Calvary's hill[17] three men were crucified. We must never forget that all three were crucified for the same crime-the crime of extremism. Two were extremists for immorality, and thus fell below their environment. The other, Jesus Christ, was an extremist for love, truth, and goodness, and thereby rose above his environment. Perhaps the South, the nation, and the world are in dire need of creative extremists.

I had hoped that the white moderate would see this need. Perhaps I was too optimistic: perhaps I expected too much. I suppose I should have realized that few members of the oppressor race can understand the deep groans and passionate yearnings of the oppressed race, and still fewer have the vision to see that injustice must be rooted out by strong, persistent, and determined action. I am thankful, however, that some of our white brothers in the South have grasped the meaning of this social revolution and committed themselves to it. They are still all too few in quantity, but they are big in quality. Some—such as Ralph McGill, Lillian Smith, Harry Golden, James McBridge Dabbs, Ann Braden, and Sarah Patton Boyle—have written about our struggle in eloquent and prophetic terms. Others have marched with us down nameless streets of the South. They have languished in filthy, roach-infested jails, suffering the abuse and brutality of policemen who view them as "dirty nigger-lovers." Unlike so many of their moderate brothers and sisters, they have recognized the urgency of the moment and sensed the need for powerful "action" antidotes to combat the disease of segregation.

Let me take note of my other major disappointment. I have been so greatly disappointed with the white church and its leadership. Of course, there are some notable exceptions. I am not unmindful of the fact that each of you has taken some significant stands on this issue. I commend you, Reverend Stallings, for your Christian stand on this past Sunday, in welcoming Negroes to your worship service on a nonsegregated basis. I commend the Catholic leaders of this state for integrating Spring Hill College several years ago.

But despite these notable exceptions, I must honestly reiterate that I have been disappointed with the church. I do not say this as one of those negative critics who can always find something wrong with the church. I say this as a minister of the gospel, who loves the church; who was nurtured in its bosom; who has been sustained by its spiritual blessings and who will remain true to it as long as the cord of life shall lengthen.

When I was suddenly catapulted into the leadership of the bus protest in Montgomery, Alabama, a few years ago, I felt we would be supported by the white church. I felt that the white ministers, priests, and rabbis of the South would be among our strongest allies. Instead, some have been outright, opponents, refusing to understand the freedom movement and misrepresenting its leaders; all too many others have been more cautious than courageous and have remained silent behind the anesthetizing security of stainedglass windows.

In spite of my shattered dreams, I came to Birmingham with the hope that the white religious leadership of this community would see the justice of our cause and, with deep moral concern, would serve as the channel through which our just grievances could reach the power structure. I had hoped that each of you would understand. But again I have been disappointed.

I have heard numerous southern religious leaders admonish their worshippers to comply with a desegregation decision because it is the law, but I have longed to hear white ministers declare: "Follow this decree because integration is morally right and because the Negro is your brother." In the midst of a blatant injustices inflicted upon the Negro, I have watched white churchmen stand on the sideline and mouth pious irrelevancies and sanctimonious trivialities. In the midst of a mighty struggle to rid our nation of racial and economic injustice. I have heard many ministers say: "Those are social issues, with which the gospel has no real concern." And I have watched many churches commit themselves to a completely otherworldly religion which makes a strange, un-Biblical distinction between body and soul, between the sacred and the secular.

I have traveled the length and breadth of Alabama, Mississippi, and all the other southern states. On sweltering summer days and crisp autumn mornings I have looked at the South's beautiful churches with their lofty spires pointing heavenward. I have beheld the impressive outlines of her massive religious-education buildings. Over and over I have found myself asking: "What kind of people worship here? Who is their God? Where were their voices when the lips of Governor Barnett[18] dripped with words of interposition and nullification? Where were they when Governor Wallace[19] gave a clarion call for defiance and hatred? Where were their voices of support when bruised and weary Negro men and women decided to rise from the dark dungeons of complacency to the bright hills of creative protest?"

Yes, these questions are still in my mind. In deep disappointment I have wept over the laxity of the church. But be assured that my tears have been tears of love. There can be no deep disappointment where their is not deep love. Yes, I love the church. How could I do otherwise? I am in the rather unique position of being the son, the grandson, and the great-grandson of preachers. Yes, I see the church as the body of Christ. But, oh! How we have blemished and scarred that body through social neglect and through fear of being nonconformists.

There was a time when the church was very powerful—in the time when the early Christians rejoiced at being deemed worthy to suffer for what they believed. In those days the church was not merely a thermometer that recorded the ideas and principles of popular opinion; it was a thermostat that transformed the mores of society. Whenever the early Christians entered a town, the people in power became disturbed and immediately sought to convict the Christians for being "disturbers of the peace" and "outside agitators." But the Christians pressed on, in the conviction that they were "a colony of heaven," called to obey God rather than man. Small in number, they were big in commitment. They were too God-intoxicated to be "astronomically intimidated." By their effort and example they brought an end to such ancient evils as infanticide and gladiatorial contests.

Things are different now. So often the contemporary church is a weak, ineffectual voice with an uncertain sound. So often it is an arch-defender of the status quo. Far from being disturbed by the presence of the church, the power structure of the average community is consoled by the church's silent—and often even vocal—sanction of things as they are.

But the judgment of God is upon the church as never before. If today's church does not recapture the sacrificial spirit of the early church, it will lose its authenticity, forfeit the loyalty of millions, and be dismissed as an irrelevant social club with no meaning for the twentieth century. Every day I meet young people whose disappointment with the church has turned into outright disgust.

Perhaps I have once again been too optimistic. Is organized religion too inextricably bound to the status quo to save our nation and the world? Perhaps I must turn my faith to the inner spiritual church, the church within the church, as the true *ekklesia* and the hope of the world. But again I am thankful to God that some noble souls from the ranks of organized religion have broken loose from the paralyzing chains of conformity and joined us as active partners in the struggle for freedom. They have left their secure congregations and walked the streets of Albany, Georgia, with us. They have gone down the highways of the South on tortuous rides for freedom. Yes, they have gone to jail with us. Some have been dismissed from their churches, have lost the support of their bishops and fellow ministers. But they have acted in the faith that right defeated is stronger than evil triumphant. Their witness has been the spiritual salt that has preserved the true meaning of the gospel in these troubled times. They have carved a tunnel of hope through the dark mountain of disappointment.

I hope the church as a whole will meet the challenge of this decisive hour. But even if the church does not come to the aid of justice, I have no despair about the future. I have no fear about the outcome of our struggle in Birmingham, even if our motives are at present misunderstood. We will reach the goal of freedom in Birmingham and all over the nation, because the goal of America is freedom. Abused and scorned though we may be, our destiny is tied up with America's destiny. Before the pilgrims landed at Plymouth, we were here. Before the pen of Jefferson etched the majestic words of the Declaration of Independence across the pages of history, we were here. For more than two centuries our forebears labored in this country without wages; they made cotton king: they built the homes of their masters while suffering gross injustice and shameful humiliation—and yet out of a bottomless vitality they continued to thrive and develop. If the inexpressible cruelties of slavery could not stop us, the opposition we now face will surely fail. We will win our freedom because the sacred heritage of our nation and the eternal will of God are embodied in our echoing demands.

Before closing I feel impelled to mention one other point in your statement that has troubled me profoundly. You warmly commended the Birmingham police force for keeping "order" and "preventing violence." I doubt that you would have so warmly commended the police force if you had seen its dogs sinking their teeth into unarmed, nonviolent Negroes. I doubt that you would so quickly commend the policemen if you were to observe their ugly and inhumane treatment of Negroes here in the city jail: if you were to watch them push and curse old Negro women and young Negro girls; if you were to see them slap and kick old Negro men and young boys; if you were to observe them, as they did on two occasions refuse to give us food because we wanted to sing our grace together I cannot join you in your praise of the Birmingham police department.

It is true that the police have exercised a degree of discipline in handling the demonstrators. In this sense they have conducted themselves rather "nonviolently" in public. But for what purpose? To preserve the evil system of segregation. Over the past few years I have consistently preached that nonviolence demands that the means we use must be as pure as the ends we seek. I have tried to make clear that it is wrong to use immoral means to attain moral ends. But now I must affirm that it is just as wrong or perhaps even more so, to use moral means to preserve immoral ends. Perhaps Mr. Connor and his policemen have been rather nonviolent in public, as was Chief Pritchett in Albany, Georgia, but they have used the moral means of nonviolence to maintain the immoral end of racial injustice. As T. S. Eliot has said, "The last temptation is the greatest treason: To do the right deed for the wrong reason."[20]

I wish you had commended the Negro sit-inners and demonstrators of Birmingham for their sublime courage, their willingness to suffer and their amazing discipline in the midst of great provocation. One day the South will recognize its real heroes. They will be the James Merediths,[21] with the noble sense of purpose that enables them to face jeering and hostile mobs, and with the agonizing loneliness that characterizes the life of the pioneer. They will be old, oppressed, battered Negro women, symbolized in a seventy-two-year-old woman in Montgomery, Alabama, who rose up with a sense of dignity and with her people decided not to ride segregated buses, and who responded with ungrammatical profundity to one who inquired about her weariness: "My feets is tired, but my soul is at rest." They will be the young high school and college students, the young ministers of the gospel and a host of their elders, courageously and nonviolently sitting in at lunch counters and willingly going to jail for conscience sake. One day the South will know that when these disinherited children of God sat down at lunch counters, they were in reality standing up for what is best in the American dream and for the most sacred values in our Judaeo-Christian heritage, thereby bringing our nation back to those great wells of democracy which were dug deep by the founding fathers in their formulation of the Constitution and the Declaration of Independence.

Never before have I written so long a letter. I'm afraid it is much too long to take your precious time. I can assure you that it would have been much shorter if I had been writing from a comfortable desk, but what else can one do when he is alone in a narrow jail cell, other than write long letters, think long thoughts, and pray long prayers?

If I have said anything in this letter that overstates the truth and indicates an unreasonable impatience, I beg you to forgive me. If I have said anything that understates the truth and indicates my having a patience that allows me to settle for anything less than brotherhood, I beg God to forgive me.

I hope this letter finds you strong in the faith. I also hope that circumstances will soon make it possible for me to meet each of you, not as an integrationist or a civil-rights leader but as a fellow clergyman and a Christian brother. Let us all hope that the dark clouds of racial prejudice will soon pass away and the deep fog of misunderstanding will be lifted from our fear-drenched communities, and in some not too distant tomorrow the radiant stars of love and brotherhood will shine over our great nation with all their scintillating beauty.

Yours for the cause of Peace and Brotherhood,

Martin Luther King, Jr. 1964

Notes

1. Fred Shuttlesworth (1922–), civil rights activist and minister.
2. Theophilus Eugene "Bull" Connor (1897–1973), Birmingham, Alabama, politician; during the civil rights movement, the name "Bull Connor" came to symbolize hard-core Southern racism.
3. Socrates, ancient Greek philosopher.
4. Reinhold Niebuhr (1892–1971), American theologian.
5. St. Augustine (354–430), early Christian church father.
6. St. Thomas Aquinas (1225–1274), Christian philosopher and theologian.
7. Martin Buber (1878–1965), German-born Israeli intellectual.
8. Paul Tillich (1886–1965), American theologian.
9. Adolf Hitler (1889–1945), German dictator, founder, and leader of Nazism.
10. Southern white supremacist group that tried to combat integration.
11. Matthew 5:44.
12. Amos, Old Testament prophet.
13. Paul, New Testament apostle.
14. Martin Luther (1483–1546), German-born philosopher.
15. John Bunyan (1628–1688), English preacher and author.
16. Thomas Jefferson (1743–1826), third president of the United States.
17. In the Gospels, the place where Jesus was crucified, outside what was then the wall of Jerusalem.
18. Ross Barnett (1898–1988), segregationist governor of Mississippi.
19. George Wallace (1919–1988), segregationist governor of Alabama.
20. From T. S. Eliot's verse play *Murder in the Cathedral* (1935).
21. James Meredith (1933–), the first African American to enroll at the University of Mississippi.

Source

Henry Louis Gates Jr. and Nellie Y. McKay, eds., *The Norton Anthology* of African American Literature (New York: W. W. Norton & Company, 1997), 1854–66.

Selected Bibliography

Branch, Taylor. *Parting the Waters: America in the King Years, 1954–1963*. New York: Simon & Schuster, 1988.

—— *Pillar of Fire: America in the King Years, 1963–1965*. New York: Simon & Schuster, 1998.

Garrow, David. *Bearing the Cross: Martin Luther King, Jr., and the Southern Christian Leadership Conference*. New York: W. Morrow, 1986.

King, Martin Luther, Jr. *Why We Can't Wait*. New York: New American Library, 1964.

Miller, Keith D. *Voice of Deliverance: The Language of Martin Luther King, Jr., and Its Sources*. Athens: University of Georgia Press, 1998.

thirteen

From Protest to Politics

Bayard Rustin (1910–1987) was an important pacifist and civil rights activist who was also a confidant of Martin Luther King Jr. In the following landmark essay, "From Protest to Politics," Rustin argued that although African Americans had won de jure citizenship rights by 1965, many blacks still faced economic discrimination, unemployment, and poverty. Demonstrating his faith in white liberal allies, Rustin held that the black/white coalition that was built during the early civil rights movement needed to be maintained, but that a new wave of activism should shift its focus toward electoral politics.

Rustin was born in Pennsylvania, where he was raised by his Quaker grandparents. After high school, he joined the Young Communist League (YCL), which was one of the few mostly-white organizations that tried to improve the racial climate of the South. In 1941 he became a field secretary for A. J. Muste's Fellowship of Reconciliation (FOR), the premier pacifist organization of its day. Rustin was also an active proponent of Gandhism, but in the McCarthy era his reputation suffered as a result of his former association with the Communist Party and because of his known homosexuality. Nevertheless, in 1955 he began working with Martin Luther King Jr., and he went on to become one of his most trusted advisors. He died in 1987.

The decade spanned by the 1954 Supreme Court decision on school desegregation[1] and the Civil Rights Act of 1964[2] will undoubtedly be recorded as the period in which the legal foundations of racism in America were destroyed. To be sure, pockets of resistance remain; but it would be hard to quarrel with the assertion that the elaborate legal structure of segregation and discrimination, particularly in relation to public accommodation, has virtually collapsed. On the other hand, without making light of the human sacrifices involved in the direct-action tactics (sit-ins, freedom rides, and the rest) that were so instrumental to this achievement, we must recognize that in desegregating public accommodations, we affected institutions which are relatively peripheral both to the American socio-economic order and to the fundamental conditions of life of the Negro people. In a highly industrialized, 20th-century civilization, we hit Jim Crow precisely where it was most anachronistic, dispensable, and vulnerable—in hotels, lunch counters. . . . For in these forms, Jim Crow does impede the flow of commerce . . . it is a nuisance in a society on the move (and on the make). Not surprisingly, therefore, it was the most mobility-conscious and relatively liberated groups in the Negro community—lower middle class college students—who launched the attack that brought down the imposing but hollow structure.

The term "classical" appears especially apt for this phase of the civil rights movement. But in the few years that have passed since the first flash of sit-ins, several developments have taken place that have complicated matters enormously. One is the shifting focus of the movement in the South, symbolized by Birmingham; another is the spread of the revolution to the North; and the third, common to the two, is the expansion of the movement's base in the Negro community. . . .

Thus, the movement in the South began to attack areas of discrimination which were not so remote from the Northern experience as were Jim Crow lunch counters. At the same time, the interrelationship of these apparently distinct areas became increasingly evident. What is the value of winning access to public accommodations for those who lack money to use them? The minute the movement faced this question, it was compelled to expand its vision beyond race relations to economic relations, including the role of education in modern society. And what also became clear is that all these interrelated problems, by their very nature, are not soluble by private, voluntary efforts but require government action—or politics. . . .

The very decade which has witnessed the decline of legal Jim Crow has also seen the rise of *de facto* segregation in our most fundamental socio-economic institutions. . . . And behind this is the continuing growth of racial slums, spreading over our central cities and trapping Negro youth in a milieu which, whatever its legal definition, sows an unimaginable demoralization. Again, legal niceties aside, a resident of a racial ghetto lives in segregated housing, and more Negroes fall into this category than ever before.

These are the facts of life which generate frustration in the Negro community and challenge the civil rights movement. At issue, after all, is not *civil rights,* strictly speaking, but social and economic conditions. Last summer's riots[3] were not race riots; they were outbursts of class aggression in a society where class and color definitions are converging disastrously. . . .

It is precisely this sense of isolation . . . the tendency within the civil rights movement which, despite its militancy, pursues what I call a "no-win" policy. Sharing with many moderates a recognition of the magnitude of the obstacles to freedom, spokesmen for this tendency survey the American scene and find no forces prepared to move toward radical solutions. From this they conclude that the only viable strategy is shock; above all, the hypocrisy of white liberals must be exposed. These spokesmen are often described as the radicals of the movement, but they are really its moralists. They seek to change the white hearts—by traumatizing them. Frequently abetted by white self-flagellants, they may gleefully applaud (though not really agreeing with) Malcolm X because, while they admit he has no program, they think he can frighten white people into doing the right thing. To believe this, of course, you must be convinced, even if unconsciously, that at the core of the white man's heart lies a buried affection for Negroes—a proposition one may be permitted to doubt. But in any case, hearts are not relevant to the issue; neither racial affinities nor racial hostilities are rooted there. It is institutions—social, political, and economic institutions—which are the ultimate molders of collective sentiments. Let these institutions be reconstructed today, and let the ineluctable gradualism of history govern the formation of new psychology.

My quarrel with the "no win" tendency in the civil rights movement . . . parallels my quarrel with the moderates outside the movement. As the latter lack the vision or will for fundamental change, the former lack a realistic strategy for achieving it. For such a strategy they substitute militancy. But militancy is a matter of posture and volume and not effect.

A handful of Negroes, acting alone, could integrate a lunch counter by strategically locating their bodies so as *directly* to interrupt the operation of the proprietor's will; their numbers were relatively unimportant. In politics, however, such a confrontation is difficult because the interests involved are merely *represented.* In the execution of a political decision a direct confrontation, may ensue. . . . But in arriving at a political decision, numbers and organizations are crucial, especially for the economically disenfranchised. . . .

Neither that movement [civil rights] nor the country's twenty million black people can win political power alone. We need allies. The future of the Negro struggle depends on whether the contradictions of this society can be resolved by a coalition of progressive forces which becomes the *effective* political majority in the United States. I speak of the coalition which staged the March on Washington,[4] passed the Civil Rights Act, and laid the basis for the Johnson landslide[5]—Negroes, trade unionists, liberals, and religious groups. . . .

The task of molding a political movement . . . is not simple, but no alternatives have been advanced. We need to choose our allies on the basis of common political objectives. It has become fashionable in some no-win Negro circles to decry the white liberal as the main enemy. . . . But the objective fact is that *Eastland and Goldwater*[6] are the main enemies—they are the opponents of civil rights, of the war on poverty, of medicare, of social security, of federal aid to education, of unions, and so forth. The labor movement, despite its obvious faults, has been the largest single organized force in this country. . . . And where the Negro-labor-liberal axis is weak, as in the farm belt, it was the religious groups that were most influential in rallying support for the Civil Rights Bill.

The durability of the coalition was interestingly tested during the election. I do not believe that the Johnson landslide proved the "white backlash" to be a myth. It proved, rather, that economic interests are more fundamental than prejudice. . . . This was a valuable first step in re-educating such people, and it must be kept alive, for the civil rights movement will be advanced only to the degree that social and economic welfare gets to be inextricably entangled with civil rights. . . .

Notes

1. In 1954, the U.S. Supreme Court decided in *Brown v. Board of Education of Topeka, Kansas,* that de jure segregation in public schools was a violation of the equal protection clause of the Fourteenth Amendment of the United States Constitution.
2. Outlawed segregation in public facilities and racial discrimination in employment and education. In addition to African Americans, women and other victims of discrimination benefited from the act.
3. In the summer of 1964, major domestic uprisings broke out in Harlem, Philadelphia, and other major cities.
4. On August 28, 1963, 250,000 people attended a protest "March on Washington for Jobs and Freedom" in order to urge support for pending civil rights legislation. The event was highlighted by Martin Luther King Jr.'s "I Have a Dream" speech before a crowd of over 200,000.
5. Lyndon Baines Johnson (1908–1973) was elected for a full presidential term in November 1964 after a landslide victory over his Republican opponent, Barry Goldwater.
6. James Oliver Eastland (1904–1986), U.S. senator from Mississippi (1943–1979), repeatedly opposed civil rights bills. Barry Morris Goldwater (1909–1998), conservative U.S. senator from Arizona (1953–1965, 1969–1987), ran unsuccessfully for president of the United States in 1964 on the Republican ticket.

Source

Peter B. Levy, *Documentary History of the Modern Civil Rights Movement* (New York: Greenwood Press, 1992), 165–68.

Selected Bibliography

Anderson, Jervis. *Bayard Rustin: Troubles I've Seen.* New York: HarperCollins, 1997.

Branch, Taylor. *Parting the Waters: America in the King Years, 1954–1963.* New York: Simon & Schuster, 1988.

Rustin, Bayard. *Down the Line: The Collected Writings of Bayard Rustin.* New York: Holt, Rinehart, and Winston, 1969.

—— *Strategies for Freedom: The Changing Patterns of Black Protest.* New York: Columbia University Press, 1976.

Young, Andrew. *An Easy Burden: The Civil Rights Movement and the Transformation of America.* New York: HarperCollins, 1996.

fourteen

The Business of America Is War, and It Is Time for a Change

Shirley Chisholm (1924–) was the first African American woman ever to sit in the U.S. Congress. In her 1969 speech to the House of Representatives, reprinted here, Chisholm displayed some of the liberal iconoclasm that earned her the moniker "Fighting Shirley Chisholm." Along with many other African Americans of the late 1960s, Chisholm believed it was profane for the United States government to spend nearly two billion dollars per month on the Vietnam War when these same resources could be used for economic and civil rights programs at home.

Chisholm was born Shirley Anita St. Hill in Brooklyn, New York, in 1924. She graduated cum laude from Brooklyn College and earned an M.A. degree from Columbia University. In 1964, Chisholm was elected to the New York State Assembly, and in 1968 she won a seat in the House of Representatives. She was originally assigned to the House Agricultural Subcommittee on Forestry and Rural Villages, but after protesting that this was foreign to her interests and experience, she was reassigned to the Veterans Affairs Committee. A vocal critic of the Vietnam War and a staunch opponent of racism, Chisholm ran for the Democratic presidential nomination in 1972. Though her campaign did not fare well, she won some support from women and from the poor, and she achieved her objective of keeping the presidential race from remaining the province of white males.

MR. SPEAKER, on the same day President Nixon[1] announced he had decided the United States will not be safe unless we start to build a defense system against missiles, the Headstart program in the District of Columbia was cut back for the lack of money.

As a teacher, and as a woman, I do not think I will ever understand what kind of values can be involved in spending nine billion dollars—and more, I am sure—on elaborate, unnecessary and impractical weapons when several thousand disadvantaged children in the nation's capital get nothing.

When the new administration took office, I was one of the many Americans who hoped it would mean that our country would benefit from the fresh perspectives, the new ideas, the different priorities of a leader who had no part in the mistakes of the past. Mr. Nixon had said things like this:

"If our cities are to be livable for the next generation, we can delay no longer in launching new approaches to the problems that beset them and to the tensions that tear them apart."

And he said, "When you cut expenditures for education, what you are doing is shortchanging the American future."

But frankly, I have never cared too much what people say. What I am interested in is what they do. We have waited to see what the new administration is going to do. The pattern now is becoming clear.

Apparently launching those new programs can be delayed for a while, after all. It seems we have to get some missiles launched first. . . .

The new Secretary of Health, Education and Welfare, Robert Finch, came to the Hill to tell the House Education and Labor Committee that he thinks we should spend more on education, particularly in city schools. But, he said, unfortunately we cannot "afford" to, until we have reached some kind of honorable solution to the Vietnam war. I was glad to read that the distinguished Member from Oregon asked Mr. Finch this:

"With the crisis we have in education, and the crisis in our cities, can we wait to settle the war? Shouldn't it be the other way around? Unless we can meet the crisis in education, we really can't afford the war."

Secretary of Defense Melvin Laird came to Capitol Hill, too. His mission was to sell the antiballistic-missile insanity to the Senate. . . . Mr. Laird talked of being prepared to spend at least two more years in Vietnam.

Two more years, two more years of hunger for Americans, of death for our best young men, of children here at home suffering the lifelong handicap of not having a good education when they are young. Two more years of high taxes, collected to feed the cancerous growth of a Defense Department budget that now consumes two thirds of our federal income.

Two more years of too little being done to fight our greatest enemies, poverty, prejudice and neglect, here in our own country. Two more years of fantastic waste in the Defense Department and of penny pinching on social programs. Our country cannot survive two more years, or four, of these kinds of policies. It must stop—this year—now.

Now, I am not a pacifist. I am deeply, unalterably opposed to this war in Vietnam. Apart from all the other considerations—and they are many—the main fact is that we cannot squander there the lives, the money, the energy that we need desperately here, in our cities, in our schools.

I wonder whether we cannot reverse our whole approach to spending. For years, we have given the military, the defense industry, a blank check. New weapons systems are dreamed up, billions are spent, and many times they are found to be impractical, inefficient, unsatisfactory, even worthless. What do we do then? We spend more money on them. But with social programs, what do we do? Take the Job Corps. Its failure has been mercilessly exposed and criticized. If it had been a military research and development project, they would have been covered up or explained away, and Congress would have been ready to pour more billions after those that had been wasted on it.

The case of Pride, Inc., is interesting. This vigorous, successful black organization, here in Washington, conceived and built by young inner-city men, has been ruthlessly attacked by its enemies in the government, in this Congress. At least six auditors from the General Accounting Office were put to work investigating Pride. They worked seven months and spent more than $100,000. They uncovered a fraud. It was something less than $2,100. Meanwhile, millions of dollars—billions of dollars, in fact—were being spent by the Department of Defense, and how many auditors and investigators were checking into their negotiated contracts? Five.

We Americans have come to feel that it is our mission to make the world free. We believe that we are the good guys, everywhere—in Vietnam, in Latin America, wherever we go. We believe we are the good guys at home, too. When the Kerner Commission[2] told white America what black America had always known, that prejudice and hatred built the nation's slums, maintain them and profit by them, white America would not believe it. But it is true. Unless we start to fight and defeat the enemies of poverty and racism in our own country and make our talk of equality and opportunity ring true, we are exposed as hypocrites in the eyes of the world when we talk about making other people free.

I am deeply disappointed at the clear evidence that the number-one priority of the new administration is to buy more and more weapons of war, to return to the era of the cold war, to ignore the war we must fight here—the war that is not optional. There is only one way, I believe, to turn these policies around. The Congress can respond to the mandate that the American people have clearly expressed. They have said, "End this war. Stop the waste. Stop the killing. Do something for your own people first." We must find the money to "launch the new approaches," as Mr. Nixon said. We must force the administration to rethink its distorted, unreal scale of priorities. Our children, our jobless men, our deprived, rejected and starving fellow citizens must come first.

For this reason, I intend to vote "No" on every money bill that comes to the floor of this House that provides any funds for the Department of Defense. Any bill whatsoever, until the time comes when our values and priorities have been turned right side up again, until the monstrous waste and the shocking profits in the defense budget have been eliminated and our country starts to use its strength, its tremendous resources, for people and peace, not for profits and war.

It was Calvin Coolidge,[3] I believe, who made the comment that "the Business of America is Business." We are now spending eighty billion dollars a year on defense—that is two thirds of every tax dollar. At this time, gentlemen, the business of America is war, and it is time for a change.

Notes

1. Richard Milhous Nixon (1913–1994), thirty-seventh president of the United States.
2. Formally, "the National Advisory Commission on Civil Disorders," headed by Governor Otto Kerner of Illinois. The commission's 1968 report famously warned that the nation was moving toward "two societies, one black, one white, separate and unequal."
3. Thirtieth president of the United States (1923–1929).

Source

Shirley Chisholm, "The Business of America Is War, and It Is Time for a Change," in Warren J. Halliburton, *Historic Speeches of African Americans* (New York: F. Watts, 1993), 140–43.

Selected Bibliography

Chisholm, Shirley. *Unbought and Unbossed: An Autobiography.* Boston: Houghton Mifflin, 1970.

Duffy, Susan, ed. *Shirley Chisholm: A Bibliography of Writings by and About Her.* Metuchen, N.J.: Scarecrow Press, 1988.

Ragsdale, Bruce A. *Black Americans in Congress, 1870–1989.* Upland: DIANE, 1996.

fifteen

The Struggle Continues

A powerful orator, activist, and minister, Jesse Jackson (1941–) is one of the most visible African American leaders of our time. In 1984, Jackson ran a celebrated campaign for the Democratic presidential nomination, gaining some three and one-half million votes. In 1988 he made a second bid for the presidency. Although he lost to Michael Dukakis, he once again demonstrated his potency as a candidate. His stirring speeches were well received by party faithful, and he galvanized many new voters and finished first in fourteen primaries. Once again Jackson demonstrated his potency as a candidate. Speaking in Atlanta, Georgia, Jackson presented the speech below on July 22, 1988.

Born in Greenville, South Carolina, Jackson moved to Chicago in 1965, where he studied at the Chicago Theological Seminary, worked locally on various civil rights issues, and became a confidant of Martin Luther King Jr. In 1966 he joined the Southern Christian Leadership Conference (SCLC), and from 1967 to 1971 he was the national director of the SCLC's Operation Breadbasket. Though he has never held elective office, Jackson remains a player in Democratic party politics, and he continues to crusade on behalf of human rights and the causes of poor black Americans.

I greet you this morning with a sense of joy, a sense that because we've come this way we've maintained faith in the legacy of our forefathers and our foremothers. We're moving on up and have every reason to be hopeful, to be excited, knowing that we are close to where we are going, a long way from where we started, and in our lifetime—you and I—we'll be in the White House.

We must always put these struggles for change in historical context. I looked around last night and I thought about Atlantic City just 24 years ago—Fannie Lou Hamer[1] and Aaron Henry on the outside, trying to get a seat in the Mississippi delegation. Last night the state chairman of the Regular Democratic Party in Mississippi was Ed Cole, an African American man. Black and white sat together, lion and lamb voted together, and none was afraid because we've progressed.

If you think there is some agony or hurt here today, you try Atlantic City in 1964 when the Democratic Party would not unseat the Regular Democratic delegation from Mississippi. But life moves on. From 1964 to 1968 Julian Bond[2] and Channing Phillips and others took us a step higher and took the seats that were rightfully ours. Willie Brown[3] rightfully got his delegates in Florida. Our Illinois delegation unseated Mayor Daley in 1972. The victory for Jimmy Carter[4] in 1976 clearly represented the rise of the New South because of our votes and a new coalition.

Then we had the deluge of Reaganism and all of the diversion it has represented. But the fantasy is ending, the foolishness is ending and the air is coming out of the balloon. The struggle continues.

I told you on Sunday, let's measure where we are. Don't make Friday morning decisions on Sunday night. What were our objectives? Expand the party. The Democratic National Committee was opened up this morning—there will be an additional vice-chair and 18 new positions, all of which we recommended. Expansion. Inclusion.

Look at our legislative agenda. This is so basic to the growth process of this country. The Conyers bill calling for universal on-site, same-day voter registration. It will save many millions of dollars in voter registration drives and put millions more people on the books.

I was down in Savannah, Georgia, a few months ago, where at 7 P.M. 9,000 people were gathered, many of whom wanted to register to vote. The registrar's office closed at 6:30, and we were not even allowed to pay the registrar overtime to keep the office open, or to have him come to the auditorium, which was exactly one and a half blocks down the street, to register people. The Conyers bill will end that. And that's progress.

The support of, without equivocation, the Dellums Bill on South Africa. The word went out that South Africa had been declared a terrorist state. All of Africa rejoiced. Because what does that mean? It means that either you declare there are no terrorist states, or South Africa is a terrorist state. And if it is a terrorist state, it then means anti-terrorist policy applies to it. It means that we do not trade with terrorist states, and we're not going to sell arms to countries that sell arms to terrorist states, and that we'll pull all American companies out of a terrorist state. That position alone shook the foundation of the whole apartheid system. And that's progress.

A commitment to economic set-asides, with the ability and will to enforce them. Economic set-asides by law are five to ten percent. Should it be ten percent across the board? What is five or ten percent of a $1 trillion budget? That's $50 to $100 billion a year set aside by law. It's a law, but it's like the Emancipation Proclamation—we got the proclamation without the emancipation. We have economic set-asides, but we have no apparatus to have them set aside, so the motion dies for lack of a second. We will implement that. It is urban reinvestment. It is business development. And that's progress.

The commitment to the ABC child-care legislation and to statehood for the District of Columbia, which means two U.S. Senators from Washington, D.C.—and a governor.

We've gotten Jim Wright, Speaker of the House, to commit himself to taking the Conyers bill and the Dellums bill to the floor. A Democratic majority means we can pass the Conyers voter registration bill. It means we can pass the Dellums South African sanctions bill. It means economic set-asides, ABC childcare legislation and statehood for the District of Columbia. Those are some of the commitments we've received. And that's progress.

A commitment to end the abandonment of the homeless. A commitment to end the abandonment of our children. A commitment to end the abandonment of women, infants and children. A commitment to reach out across lines of race, and sex, and religion, and affirm everybody's Americanness. It's time for a fundamental change in direction.

I said earlier in the week, the media came looking for a show, and found people serious. They said, "But where are the fireworks?" That was their business. We came looking for noble works, not fireworks. Not show business, but serious business.

The victory lies not in what Governor Dukakis and Lloyd Bentsen can do for us. That's not the victory. The victory lies in the fact that our minds have changed about ourselves, and our reasonable expectations have been expanded.

Mickey Leland can walk around, organizing a move to run for U.S. Senate in Texas, and not be looked down upon as being absurd. Lou Stokes can contemplate running for the U.S. Senate in Ohio, and not be dismissed as absurd. Andy Young can walk around here thinking about running for governor of Georgia, and not be dismissed as absurd. And David Dinkins can think about running for mayor of New York, and not be dismissed as absurd.

There's big business at stake here. Affordable housing. The stakes are high. Education for our children. The stakes are high. Stopping the dealing with dealers who are giving drugs to our children. The stakes are high.

I've had to learn the science of politics. I've watched it from its many angles. I'm often asked, what does the Lloyd Bentsen wing of the ticket mean to me? I tell you what it means. It represents a wing. We represent a wing. It takes two wings to fly. When all is said and done, hawks and doves are just birds. As long as they fly the same air, they cannot afford to have that air poisoned by pollution.

What does Bentsen being on the ticket mean to me in practical terms? It means that the contras have lost a vote. It means D.C. statehood has gained a vote. It means Mandela has gained an ally. And so, my friends, in this process we're transformed. We've become bigger people, and better people.

I am convinced we have reason to be hopeful, reason to build a coalition, reason to leave here and work, reason to have a record turnout, reason to keep this progressive campaign alive and building: in 1988 it's the White House; in 1990 it's the census; in 1991 it's reapportionment. We have reason to work.

We'll be blending Dukakis and Jackson supporters at the national, state and congressional district levels. We'll have access to where policies are made and priorities are set. Expansion, inclusion, relationships. Those have been the operative words for the week: expansion, inclusion, relationships, future, and the struggle continues.

I feel hopeful this morning. I feel delighted. I feel secure. I feel comfort that you will be protected in your role in the campaign, in the DNC, and I feel comfortable in the role I chose. That's why I don't want a job or a title. I want to be free to serve at my own pace. Free to support, and free to challenge. We have a role—to support, and to get respect according to our support. We have never had those two things before, a role and respect. And from that, everything else grows.

Throughout, this campaign has been about expansion, it's been about inclusion and about relationships. This morning, our enemies are sad and our friends rejoice because we've kept this campaign above the temptation of demagoguery, of racial divisions, and on a high and principled level. And friends, we're well on our way. The long-distance race doesn't go to the swift but to the strong—to those who can hold out. I don't feel tired. Even Reagan ran three times.

These last seven years have been especially painful. While our sons and daughters have died in Grenada and Lebanon and Europe, this President has not met with the Congressional Black Caucus one time. Denial of access. In these last seven years, this man suggested that those in South Africa who were shot in the back had provoked the shootings. In these last seven years, our complicity with South Africa, in Angola, in Namibia and inside South Africa, continues. In these last seven years, Reagan opened up his presidential campaign in Philadelphia, Mississippi, sending a signal that was missed by too many people. There's not even a railroad in Philadelphia, Mississippi, not even a small airport. The only thing it is known for is that it is where the civil rights activists Schwerner, Goodman and Chaney[5] were found murdered. On that day of Reagan's announcement, even the Klan were there in their paraphernalia. I tell you from Philadelphia, Mississippi, to Bitburg, Germany, to Johannesburg, South Africa, it's been an unbroken line by Reagan, unchallenged by Bush.

My friends, I'm going to keep on arguing a preferable case to you about our live options. We might think now that in 1960 John Kennedy[6] won unanimously. But he won by 112,000 votes—less than one vote per precinct. Kennedy won against Nixon with less than one vote per precinct difference in the American mind.

In 1960, we won by the margin of our hope, because Kennedy took the risks to relate to us publicly and to reach out to Dr. King.[7]

In 1968, the psychology shifted. Dr. King was killed on April 4. Robert Kennedy[8] was killed on June 5. There were riots at the Chicago Democratic Convention. With all of that death, all of that despair, all of those broken hearts, all of that lost blood, Nixon beat Humphrey by 550,000 votes.

The difference between Nixon and Humphrey was tremendous. But we could not make a distinction between the Great Society and the lost society. We lost by the margin of our despair what we had won eight years before by the margin of our hope.

Now we come forth in 1988, with much more strength and much greater capability. We've had to knock down doors in the DNC. It's not unusual. We give thanks that we have the ability to knock them down, and open them up. We can do that. We've always had the paradoxical burden of fighting to save the nation just to save ourselves.

If you're in the back seat of a truck, and you don't like the driver and the car's going over the cliff, don't take solace in the fact that he's going over the cliff, because he isn't going to push a button and eject you. You'll have to save the driver just to save yourself. And so here we are today, still knocking on doors. We're still winning every day and winning in every way.

Many things have changed this week in Atlanta—among other things, relationships. There have been serious meetings this week with Paul Kirk and the DNC leadership, and there will be serious changes in the DNC as of this morning because of you—not because those doors voluntarily opened up and certainly not because you stopped knocking. Some combination of your knocking and determination to get in has changed things.

I'm clear about it. John Kennedy supported the civil rights movement but the children in Birmingham wrote it. Lyndon Johnson[9] didn't get the Voting Rights Act passed. Folks in Selma got it passed. And then Johnson wrote in ink what they had written in blood.

He had the will but not the capacity because there are checks and balances in this government. He told Dr. King, "I'm for it, but we can't get it because the Congress is too conservative. I just can't get it passed." But "street heat" in

Selma gave him a new alternative. He then could say, "I'm for some change, now we shall overcome."

I'll tell you one reason I want to be close enough to serve and far enough away to challenge—because change requires a combination of new leadership and "street heat." John Kennedy and Robert Kennedy could not go to Birmingham and say, I feel ashamed, therefore I will enact a Public Accommodations bill. It took a combination of their leadership and our "street heat."

We've got to keep up the "street heat." My friends, if we put on two to three million new voters between now and October 8, there will be enough heat to cook our meat, and enough heat for George Bush[10] to get out of the kitchen.

You do understand that the contra vote that comes up again next week—they can't get that vote now. You do understand that when Mayor Marion Barry and Rep. Walter Fauntroy try to get the D.C. statehood bill passed, that the wing of the party that's been holding it back—they have to deliver now. That's the art and science of politics. It takes different temperatures to cook different kinds of meat. That's "street heat."

I'm excited. There's going to be a change. Why are Republicans already talking about "They're running a three-man ticket-Dukakis, Bentsen and Jackson"? Well, they're trying to create some mess. That's a trick to drive us away, but we're not leaving.

There isn't a three-man ticket. Psychologically, I don't require it. A political ticket doesn't need it. We're more grown than that. We got this commitment on the Dellums Bill, and Mandela can rejoice, and on the Conyers Bill, and unregistered voters can rejoice, and on two senators and a governor in D.C., which could completely change the balance in the U.S. Senate, and we can all rejoice.

Let's look at a few more things here. I suppose the first victory for us is that we're together. People who didn't support us in 1984 supported us in 1988. There are those who didn't support us in 1988 who are going to support us from now on because it's clear what time of day it is.

We're also in major league politics now. This isn't softball. The next step is to go back to your states—to every state we won, every district we won—and see how your congressperson voted, see how your senator voted, and see how your DNC member voted. That's the basis for new politics right where you live.

That's the first thing you've got to do. In Mississippi they got themselves lawyers, organized over the long haul and now they are the leaders of the state Democratic Party. Our Mississippi delegation ran a ticket and won the leadership positions in the state party. We must do this in every state we won—from Maine to Delaware to Virginia to South Carolina to Georgia to Alabama to Louisiana—in every one of those states where we the people were humiliated on Wednesday night because we won the popular vote but the superdelegates imposed their will on us.

Some people say what did we get? Well, we got new rules and the party can't run over us again in 1992.

When you win Michigan two-to-one, and then come out 80-80 at the convention, it's time to go back home and do some work.

If you decide to go back home and not work, you're doing your enemy a favor. The threat is not that we might leave, the threat is we might stay. We're just an attitude away from winning. Just an attitude away.

When you go back to your states, remember that we are trying to put together a campaign state-by-state not just for Dukakis and Bentsen, but for ourselves. If you went to the grocery store and folks at your house were hungry, and you came back home with an empty grocery bag and a pocket full of money, they would say, "What's wrong with you?" You'd say, "Well, I went to the grocery store and they didn't have any steak." But they would rightfully ask about pork chops, sausage and the other stuff you can get there. When you go shopping in a presidential election, you're not just shopping for the top of the ticket. There's also city council races, school board elections and lots of other seats at stake. There's a whole grocery bag of elections.

Now we're going to do something else too. We must follow Michigan's lead and get your state legislature to pass same-day, on-site voter registration. It's a central civil rights issue.

Why did we win Michigan? I know why we won Michigan. Because my sons Jesse Jr. and Jonathan, and the actress Kim Fields, went into the high schools speaking to students and registering them to vote. They turned out to vote—about 150 high school senior classes with 300 to 400 seniors per school. These high school seniors weren't in anybody's computers.

The same youth that now are using their power against themselves have the power to completely change this nation. Change never does come about until our youth come alive. We've got to stop them from using their power in self-destructive ways.

The next thing is to run for office. Run for governor, run for U.S. senator, run for a local judgeship, run for everything that's open. Integrate slates—black, brown and white, male and female. If you don't win, you will at least create a new equation. And, if you get nothing out of it but learning how to run, you learn.

You know most African Americans who live in Chicago don't know Illinois. They know Chicago. They don't relate to folk in East St. Louis or Springfield or Peoria—they have Chicago on the brain.

The fact is we are putting too much focus on the city council people and not enough on state legislators, because city council folks by and large are there where the daily newspaper is and the television cameras are. They put city council issues on TV at night because the city council has got the day-to-day burden. But it's the state legislatures that have the budget.

I understand the psychology of it. Once you get to Chicago, you do not want to go to Springfield. You've paid your Springfield dues. You've left Springfield to get to Chicago. The fact is, my friends, the power is in Springfield, not in city hall.

New York—once you get to the bright lights! Big deal—the power's in Albany not in New York City. Once you get to Philadelphia—right on! But the power is in Harrisburg, because that's where the budget is. Go to your state legislatures.

When should the Rainbow Convention meet in your state? Go find out from your state legislature when budget time is. Have your convention at budget time. Then you can lobby about the budget. They cut up a multibillion dollar budget in those little towns called Springfield, Harrisburg, Albany; but you can't get thirty people there. The city council will have a meeting on dog mess, and it's city council here I come. The TV cameras will be rolling, people will be jumping up and down for and against the dog. But in state capitals, when it's time to discuss the budget reforms or education and everything else, you can't get thirty people there. The lights are too dim in state legislatures. We've got big mayors on the brain. But the best of mayors can't spend money they don't have—that's the business of state legislatures.

I want us to become more politically sophisticated. We should have thousands marching and meeting at budget time. The budget's the real issue with the Dukakis ticket.[11] We must keep "street heat" on the budget because it is fundamental.

We must continue to build our own political organizations at the state level. We must meet and work together with their campaign people. Don't just be picked off one by one—let's relate in a disciplined fashion and keep our organization together. Learn from the campaign, don't disintegrate. Don't go away. We've got some big elections in 1989, the census in 1990 and reapportionment in 1991.

We will leave here with a bigger, better, stronger Rainbow Coalition. We've proven it can happen. It wasn't easy, but look around this room. There are white farmers in here, African Americans and Hispanics, Arabs and Jews, peace activists—this is our dream.

You look at the Democratic platform—most of the policies are our language—that's Jackson action. That stuff about South Africa being declared a terrorist state—that's Jackson action. That stuff about reinvest in America—that's Jackson action. You put 13 minority reports on the table and you win on nine of them—that's winning.

The fact that we were able to raise the issue of U.S. policy in the Middle East so the whole party could discuss it and think about it—that's profound change.

Now, if we have come this far—half asleep and half walking—you know what's next. We got 1,200 delegates and didn't even hardly believe it ourselves.

I have to keep looking on the bright side. On the day that we were in Oregon, they locked up two folks that threatened to assassinate me. We got 40 percent of the white vote in Oregon on that day. Do you know what that means? In Oregon? On that day?

And so our strategy was simple—expand our options without tearing up the party, because it's the key vehicle we've got for the fight. We cannot fight by walking away from it. That will not win. I know better than that. We've got better judgment than that. We're long-distance runners.

The media keeps on wanting to project us as being an emotional, irrational, irascible, enigmatic kind of movement. But we stayed on Wednesday night and Willie Brown went up to the podium and, with grace, supported Michael Dukakis by acclamation. That's good judgment. And Mickey Leland, from Texas, went up there last night and by acclamation supported Lloyd Bentsen[12] for vice president. That's good judgment.

And do you realize what we did this week in this town? Do you know the impact we've had? The whole world has been watching us all week, because we never stopped campaigning and we're not going to stop.

I want some of the party's resources to register more of us to vote. I want a record turnout. We cannot be bypassed. We can't be locked out. And, when you're too tough and mature to cry when you're hurting, I'll suffer for you. I'll die for you, I want you to suffer with me, and together our suffering will not be in vain. We're going to win. We're winning every day. Winning every day. Every day. Every day! Every day!

Notes

1. Civil rights activist.
2. Civil rights activist, politician, and organization president.
3. Civil rights activist and mayor of San Francisco.
4. Thirty-ninth president of the United States.
5. Three civil rights workers, Michael Schwerener, Andrew Goodman, and James Chaney, were killed while traveling through Philadelphia, Mississippi, August 4, 1961.
6. Thirty-fifth president of the United States.
7. Civil rights leader and minister.
8. U.S. attorney general (1961–1964), candidate for the Democratic presidential nomination in 1968.
9. Lyndon Baines Johnson (1908–1973), thirty-sixth president of the United States.
10. George Herbert Walker Bush (1924–), forty-first president of the United States.
11. Michael Dukakis (1933–), U.S. politician; in 1988, he ran unsuccessfully as the Democratic candidate for president of the United States.
12. U.S. politician; in 1988, he ran unsuccessfully on the Democratic ticket for vice president of the United States.

Source

Jesse Jackson, "The Struggle Continues," in *Keep Hope Alive: Jesse Jackson's 1988 Presidential Campaign: A Collection of Major Speeches, Issue Papers, Photographs, and Campaign Analysis,* 213–18 (Keep Hope Alive PAC and South End Press, 1989).

Selected Bibliography

Coulton, Elizabeth O. *The Jesse Jackson Phenomenon: The Man, the Power, and the Message.* New York: Doubleday, 1989.

Frady, Marshall. *Jesse: The Life and Pilgrimage of Jesse Jackson.* New York: Random House, 1996.

House, Ernest R. *Jesse Jackson and the Politics of Charisma: The Rise and Fall of the PUSH-Excel Program.* Boston: Westview Press, 1988.

Marable, Manning. *Black American Politics: From the Washington Marches to Jesse Jackson.* New York: Verso, 1992.

—— *Black Leadership.* New York: Columbia University Press, 1999.

Reed, Adolph. *The Jesse Jackson Phenomenon: The Crisis of Purpose in Afro-American Politics.* New Haven, Conn.: Yale University Press, 1986.

chapter five

In Pursuit of Justice

one

Speech on the Fugitive Slave Bill

Samuel Rinngold Ward (1817–c. 1866) was a prominent abolitionist, orator, minister, and journalist. Although proslavery advocates surely expected the Fugitive Slave Act of 1850 to bolster the institution of slavery, the outrageous injustice of the law and the backlash it caused actually helped to strengthen the abolitionist movement. Many black leaders urged ex-slaves to make their way to Canada; Ward's "Speech on the Fugitive Slave Bill" represented a growing trend in the abolitionist movement toward militancy and defiance.

Ward was born a slave, but when he was a small child, his parents carried him away to New Jersey, where the family went to escape slavery. In 1839 Ward earned his license to preach, and he became a travelling agent for the American Anti-Slavery Society and the New York Anti-Slavery Society, where he quickly earned his reputation as a vigorous, sharp-tongued orator. Ward campaigned for the Liberty Party; pastored a church in Cortland Village, New York; and edited a paper that was published in Syracuse, New York, *The Impartial Citizen.* In October 1851 he helped to orchestrate the dramatic rescue of Jerry McHenry, a fugitive slave who was being held in a Syracuse jail. In the aftermath, however, over two dozen activists were indicted for their involvement in the plot, and Ward fled to Canada. Later he moved to England, where he was well received by British abolitionists. In 1855 he published his *Autobiography of a Fugitive Negro.* Ward lived out his last days in obscurity and poverty in Jamaica.

I am here to-night simply as a guest. You have met here to speak of the sentiments of a Senator of your State whose remarks you have the honor to repudiate. In the course of the remarks of the gentleman who preceded me, he has done us the favor to make honorable mention of a Senator of my own State—Wm. H. Seward.[1] [Three hearty cheers were given for Senator Seward.]

I thank you for this manifestation of approbation of man who has always stood head and shoulders above his party, and who has never receded from his position on the question of slavery. It was my happiness to receive a letter from him a few days since, in which he said he never would swerve from his position as the friend of freedom. [Applause.]

To be sure, I agree not with Senator Seward in politics, but when an individual stands up for the rights of men against slaveholders, I care not for party distinctions. He is my brother [Loud cheers.]

We have here much of common cause and interest in this matter. That infamous bill of Mr. Mason,[2] of Virginia, proves itself to be like all other propositions presented by Southern men. It finds just enough of Northern doughfaces who are willing to pledge themselves, if you will pardon the uncouth language of a backwoodsman, to lick up the spittle of the slavocrats, and swear it is delicious. [Applause.]

You of the old Bay State[3]—a State to which many of us are accustomed to look as to our fatherland, just as well look back to England as our mother country—you have a Daniel who has deserted the cause of freedom.[4] We, too, in New York, have a "Daniel who has come to judgment," only he don't come quite fast enough to the right kind of judgment. [Tremendous enthusiasm.] Daniel S. Dickinson[5] represents some one, I suppose, in the State of New York; God knows, he doesn't represent me. I can pledge you that our Daniel will stand cheek by jowl with your Daniel. [Cheers.] He was never known to surrender slavery, but always to surrender liberty.

The bill of which you most justly complain, concerning the surrender of fugitive slaves, is to apply alike to your State and to our State, if it shall ever apply at all. But we have come here to make a common oath upon a common altar, that that bill shall never take effect. [Applause.] Honorable Senators may record their names in its behalf, and it may have the sanction of the House of Representatives; but we, the people, who are superior to both Houses and the Executive, too [hear! hear!], we, the people will never be human bipeds, to howl upon the track of the fugitive slave, even though led by the corrupt Daniel of your State, or the degraded one of ours. [Cheers.]

Though there are many attempts to get up compromises—and there is no term which I detest more than this, it is always the term which makes right yield to wrong; it has always been accursed since Eve made the first compromise with the devil. [Repeated rounds of applause.] I was saying, sir, that it is somewhat singular, and yet historically true, that whensoever these compromises are proposed, there are men of the North who seem to foresee that Northern men, who think their constituency will not look into these matters, will seek to do more than the South demands. They seek to prove to Northern men that all is right and all is fair; and this is the game Webster is attempting to play.

"Oh." says Webster, "the will of God has fixed that matter, we will not re-enact the will of God." Sir, you remember the time in 1841, '42, '43 and '44, when it was said that Texas could never be annexed. The design of such dealing was that you should believe it, and then, when you thought yourselves secure, they would spring the trap upon you. And now it is their wish to seduce you into the belief that slavery never will go there, and then the slaveholders will drive slavery there as fast as possible. I think that this is the most contemptible proposition of the whole, except the support of that bill which would attempt to make the whole North the slave-catchers of the South.

You will remember that that bill of Mr. Mason says nothing about color. Mr. Phillips,[6] a man whom I always loved [applause], a man who taught me my horn-book on this subject of slavery, when I was a poor boy, has referred to Marshfield. There is a man who sometimes lives in Marshfield, and who has the reputation of having an honorable dark skin. Who knows but that some postmaster may have to sit upon the very gentleman whose character you have been discussing to-night? [Hear! hear!] "What is sauce for the goose is sauce for the gander." [Laughter.] If this bill is to relieve grievances, why not make an application to the immortal Daniel of Marshfield? [Applause.] There is no such thing as complexion mentioned. It is not only true that the colored man of Massachusetts—it is not only true that the fifty thousand colored men of New York may be taken—though I pledge you there is one, whose name is Sam Ward, who will never be taken alive. [Tremendous applause.] Not only is it true that the fifty thousand black men in New York man be taken, but any one else also can be captured. My friend Theodore Parker[7] alluded to Ellen Crafts.[8] I had the pleasure of taking tea with her, and accompanied her here to-night. She is far whiter than many who come here slave-catching. This line of distinction is so nice that you cannot tell who is white or black. As Alexander Pope[9] used to say, "White and black soften and blend in so many thousand ways, that it is neither white nor black." [Loud plaudits.]

This is the question, Whether a man has a right to himself and his children, his hopes and his happiness, for this world and the world to come. That is a question which, according to this bill, may be decided by any backwoods postmaster in this State or any other. Oh, this is a monstrous proposition; and I do thank God that if the Slave Power has such demands to make on us, that the proposition has come now—now, that the people know what is being done—now that the public mind is turned toward this subject—now that they are trying to find what is the truth on this subject.

Sir, what must be the moral influence of this speech of Mr. Webster on the minds of young men, lawyers and others, here in the North? They turn their eyes towards Daniel Webster as towards a superior mind, and a legal and constitutional oracle. If they shall catch the spirit of this speech, its influence upon them and upon following generations will be so deeply corrupting that it never can be wiped out or purged.

I am thankful that this, my first entrance into Boston, and my first introduction to Faneuil Hall, gives me the pleasure and privilege of uniting with you in uttering my humble voice against the two Daniels, and of declaring, in behalf of our people, that if the fugitive slave is traced to our part of New York State, he shall have the law of Almighty God to protect him, the law which says, "Thou shalt not return to the master the servant that is escaped unto thee, but he shall dwell with thee in thy gates, where it liketh him best."[10] And if our postmasters cannot maintain their constitutional oaths, and cannot live without playing the pander to the slave-hunter, they need not live at all. Such crises as these leave us to the right of Revolution, and if need be, that right we will, at whatever cost, most sacredly maintain.

Notes

1. William Henry Seward (1801–1872), American statesman.
2. James Murray Mason (1798–1871), U.S. senator from Virginia, author of the Fugitive Slave Law of 1850.
3. Massachusetts.
4. Refers to Daniel Webster (1782–1852), U.S. senator from Massachusetts.
5. Daniel Stevens Dickinson (1800–1866), U.S. senator from New York.
6. Wendell Phillips (1811–1884), American reformer, orator, and abolitionist.
7. Theodore Parker (1810–1866), American reformer.
8. Ellen Crafts (1826–1891), abolitionist.
9. Alexander Pope (1688–1744), English poet.
10. Deut. 23:15.

Source

Samuel Rinngold Ward, "Speech on the Fugitive Slave Bill," *Liberator* 20, no. 14 (April 1850): 53.

Selected Bibliography

Pease, Jane H. and William B. Pease. *They Who Would Be Free: Blacks' Search for Freedom, 1830–1861*. Urbana: University of Illinois Press, 1990.

Ripley, Peter C. *The Black Abolitionist Papers.* 5 vols. Chapel Hill: University of North Carolina, 1985–92.

Ward, Samuel Ringgold. *Autobiography of a Fugitive Negro.* Chicago: Johnson Publishing House, 1970.

Winks, Robin W. *The Blacks in Canada.* Montreal: McGill Queens University Press; New Haven: Yale University Press, 1971.

two

Hannah Johnson to Abraham Lincoln, July 31, 1863

Although the "colored troops" who fought for the North in the Civil War faced inequitable pay, treatment, and medical care from their own commanding officers, black soldiers who had the misfortune of being captured by the Confederates fared even worse. Many were reenslaved, and in other instances, Confederate troops gave no quarter to captured black soldiers. Most infamously, at Fort Pillow, Tennessee, in April 1964, Confederates massacred some two hundred helpless black prisoners under the orders of General Nathan Bedford Forrest.

In a letter to Abraham Lincoln, Hannah Johnson, the mother of a black soldier, asked Lincoln to take measures of retaliation against Southern war prisoners in order to compel Confederate forces to give better treatment to African Americans captives. "I know a colored man ought to run no greater risques than a white," she argued, "so why should not our enemies be compelled to treat him the same." Lincoln did not reply to the letter, but by some coincidence, the very day that Johnson wrote him, he issued a public order that vowed to enslave a Confederate prisoner for every black Union soldier who was enslaved by the enemy.

Buffalo [New York] July 31 1863

Excellent Sir

My good friend says I must write to you and she will send it. My son went in the 54th regiment. I am a colored woman and my son was strong and able to fight for his country and the colored people have as much to fight for as any. My father was a Slave and escaped from Louisiana before I was born morn forty years agone I have but poor education but. I never went to schol, but I know just as well as any what is right between man and man. Now I know it is right that a colored man should go and fight for his country, and so ought to a white man. I know that a colored man ought to run no greater risques than a white, his pay is no greater his obligation to fight is the same. So why should not our enemies be compelled to treat him the same, Made to do it.

My son fought at Fort Wagoner but thank God he was not taken prisoner, as many were I thought of this thing before I let my boy go but then they said Mr. Lincoln will never let them sell our colored soldiers for slaves, if they do he will get them back quck he will rettalliate and stop it. Now Mr. Lincoln dont you think you oght to stop this thing and make them do the same by the colored men they have lived in idleness all their lives on stolen labor and made savages of the colored people, but they now are so furious because they are proving themselves to be men, such as have come away and got some edication. It must not be so. You must put the rebels to work in State prisons to making shoes and things, if they sell our colored soldiers, till they let them all go. And give their wounded the same treatment, it would seem cruel, but their no other way, and a just man must do hard things sometimes, that shew him to be a great man. They tell me some do you will take back the proclamation, don't do it. When you are dead and in Heaven, in a thousand years that action of yours will make the Angels sing your praises I know it. Ought one man to own another, law for or not, who made the law, surely the poor slave did not. so it is wicked, and a horrible Outrage, there is no sense in it, because a man has lived by robbing all his life and his father before him, should he complain because the stolen things found on him are taken. Robbing the colored people of their labor is but a small part of the robbery their souls are almost taken, they are made bruits of often. You know all about this

Will you see that the colored men fighting now, are fairly treated. You ought to do this, and do it at once, Not let the thing run along meet it quickly and manfully, and stop this, mean cowardly cruelty. We poor oppressed ones, appeal to you, and ask fair play.

Yours for Christs sake

Hannah Johnson

Source

"Hannah Johnson to Abraham Lincoln, July 31, 1863," in Harold Holzer, ed., *The Lincoln Mailbag: America Writes to the President, 1860–1865,* 97–98 (Carbondale and Edwardsville: Southern Illinois University Press, 1998).

Selected Bibliography

Berlin, Ira, et al., eds. *The Black Military Experience.* Series 2 of *Freedom: A Documentary History of Emancipation, 1861–1867.* New York: Cambridge University Press, 1983.

Gertis, Louis S. *From Contraband to Freedom: Federal Policy Toward Southern Blacks, 1861–1865.* Westport, Conn.: Greenwood Press, 1973.

McPherson, James. *Battle Cry of Freedom: The Era of the Civil War.* New York: Oxford University Press, 1998.

—— *The Negro's Civil War: How American Blacks Felt and Acted During the War for the Union.* New York: Ballantine, 1991.

Trudeau, Noah Andre. *Like Men of War: Black Troops in the Civil War, 1862–1865.* Boston: Little Brown, 1998.

three

Sojourner Truth: Extracts from Her Lecture on Capital Punishment

Sojourner Truth (c. 1799–1883) worked and traveled until the end of her life. In 1878 she was one of three Michigan delegates to the thirtieth anniversary meeting of the first Woman's Rights Convention in Rochester, New York. Also at this time, Southern blacks began migrating to Kansas. To ensure that they were properly settled, Truth left her home in Battle Creek, Michigan, to assist them. Before leaving, she told a local reporter, "There will be, child, a great glory come out of that. I don't expect I will live to see it. But before this generation has passed away, there will be a grand change. This colored people is going to be a people. Do you think God has had them robbed and scourged all the days of their life for nothing?"[1] She urged the newcomers not to settle in cities but to utilize the Homestead Law and apply for land of their own.

Some of the last issues on which Sojourner Truth lectured included prison reform, working men's rights, and capital punishment. On June 3, 1881, two years before her death, she addressed members of the state legislature of Michigan, which was considering a measure to institute capital punishment in the state. Her lecture was printed on the front page of the June 8 issue of the Battle Creek *Nightly Moon*.

She closed the speech speaking of the progress of temporal inventions such as the telegraph, telephone, and locomotive. She also shared her regret that no one had written a bible that discarded laws such as "an eye for an eye and a tooth for a tooth." When told that the Wyckoff hanging bill had been defeated, Truth shouted for joy, declaring Michigan the most blessed state in the union. Truth later died in her home in Battle Creek on November 26, 1883.

I have come here to-night to see about a thing that fairly shocked me. It shocked me worse than slavery. I've heard that you are going to have hanging again in this state. Before God only think of it. When I had thought for so many years that I lived in the most blessed state in the union, and then to think of its being made the awful scene of hanging people by the neck until they are dead. Where is the man or woman who can sanction such a thing as that? We are the makers of murderers if we do it. Where do we get this stupid spirit from? Years ago I found out that the religion of Jesus was forgiveness. When I prayed "Father, forgive me as I forgive those who trespass against me." I found that was against hanging. When a man kills another in cold blood, and you hang him, then you murder in cold blood also. When a prisoner is put into jail to be hung the ministers go to convert him, and they pray that God will forgive him. When he is converted they put a rope around his neck and swing him off; but that is not Jesus' law. But they tell me that we must abide by the public laws. I won't sanction any law in my heart that upholds murder. I am against it! I am against it! In olden times it was "an eye for an eye and a tooth for a tooth," but the Savior taught us better things than these, and commanded us to love one another. I talk to a great many people, but none older than myself. I hate to see these younger people, who have every advantage to learn, keep traveling the road of life and filling their minds with nonsense and foolishness. When I was a child, and heard about Jesus Christ, I thought he was some big man like Napoleon Bonaparte, or George Washington living off in some part of the country; but as I grew up the truth came to me, and I found out there was a Jesus who was to go between me and God.

See the progression that has been made in temporal things. When I was growing up all the way that we could travel was with oxen, horses, and sloops. These things have all come for our benefit, but don't give God any glory, or you would not want to go back to the awful system of hanging. The advocates of such a barbarous thing have murder in their hearts.

Remember, the things I am saying to you in this capitol to-night will never die. He who sanctions the crime of hanging will have to answer for it. I believe that God has spared me to do good to this white population which has done so much good to the black race. How wonderful God turns things.

I should like to see you make a law that would hang whisky out of the United States, for I believe that it is at the bottom of a great many crimes. In a great many cases it is not the man that murders, but whisky. There is one trouble about this temperance work. You get a man to sign the pledge and that is all there is of it, when you ought to get him to work, and carry food and clothing to his poor starving wife and children. Treat them as human beings should be treated, and fewer temperance converts would backslide.

The newspapers of my childhood used to have pictures of hell. I bought one once in New York, and there was one whole side covered with such a picture. On one side was a narrow stair leading to heaven, and the rest of the picture was a terrible abyss, the smoke rolling up out of it, and numberless human beings swimming around in the flames. Then there was the old Evil One, with a long snout and tail, stirring the others up with a pitchfork, and when I gazed upon that picture I said, "My God, dat is hell, sure nuff." There are probably persons here who can remember these things. As I got older I found out there wasn't no such thing as hell, and that the narrow stairs only showed the narrowness of the mind that conceived the picture. I have found out and know that God's brightness and goodness and glory is hot enough to scorch all the sinners in the world.

Note

1. Jacqueline Bernard, *Journey Toward Freedom, The Story of Sojourner Truth* (New York: Norton & Company, 1967), 248.

Source

Suzanne Pullon Fitch and Roseann M. Mandziuk, *Sojourner Truth as Orator* (Westport, Conn.: Greenwood Press, 1997), 135–36.

Selected Bibliography

Bernard, Jacqueline. *Journey Toward Freedom, The Story of Sojourner Truth.* New York: Norton & Company, 1967.

Mabee, Carleton. *Sojourner Truth: Slave, Prophet, Legend.* New York: New York University Press, 1993.

Ortiz, Victoria. *Sojourner Truth, A Self-Made Woman.* Philadelphia: Lippincot, 1974.

Painter, Nell Irvin. *Sojourner Truth, A Life, A Symbol.* New York: W. W. Norton, 1996.

Yellin, Jean Fagan. *Women and Sisters: The Antislavery Feminists in American Culture.* New Haven: Yale University Press, 1989.

f o u r

Lynch Law in All Its Phases

The great wave of lynchings throughout the South near the turn of the century, and then again after World War I and beyond, proved that even with the Fourteenth Amendment, the federal government failed to extend equal protection of the law to African Americans. Ida B. Wells-Barnett (1862–1931) was a journalist, lecturer, social activist, feminist, and antilynching activist. In an oration delivered in Boston in 1893, Barnett described an 1892 lynching that led her to pursue her career as an aggressive antilynching crusader.

Wells-Barnett was born a slave in Holly Springs, Mississippi. In 1878, after both of her parents died during a yellow fever epidemic, the sixteen-year-old Wells-Barnett became the primary caretaker for the rest of the family, earning a meager income as a schoolteacher. She was elected secretary of the Colored Press Association in 1889 and became an editor and part owner of a militant, Memphis-based journal, *Free Speech and Headlight.* In 1892 she alleged that lynchings often arose out of the private insecurities of white males. Aroused into a furor, the white community around Memphis destroyed the offices of the *Free Speech and Headlight,* and Wells-Barnett was exiled from the South. In the North, however, she won praise as an eloquent and effective lecturer, and she soon resumed her career as a journalist and "crusader for justice." In 1913 she founded the Alpha Suffrage Club of Chicago, the first black suffrage organization, and she ran unsuccessfully for state senator in 1930. In 1990 the federal government honored Wells-Barnett by issuing a postage stamp in her honor.

I am before the American people to-day through no inclination of my own, but because of a deep-seated conviction that the country at large does not know the extent to which lynch law prevails in parts of the Republic, nor the conditions which force into exile those who speak the truth. I cannot believe that the apathy and indifference which so largely obtains regarding mob rule is other than the result of ignorance of the true situation. And yet, the observing and thoughtful must know that in one section, at least, of our common country, a government of the people, by the people, and for the people, means a government by the mob; where the land of the free and home of the brave means a land of lawlessness, murder and outrage; and where liberty of speech means the license of might to destroy the business and drive from home those who exercise this privilege contrary to the will of the mob. Repeated attacks on the life, liberty and happiness of any citizen or class of citizens are attacks on distinctive American institutions; such attacks imperiling as they do the foundation of government, law and order, merit the thoughtful consideration of far-sighted Americans; not from a standpoint of sentiment, not even so much from a standpoint of justice to a weak race, as from a desire to preserve our institutions.

The race problem or negro question, as it has been called, has been omnipresent and all-pervading since long before the Afro-American was raised from the degradation of the slave to the dignity of the citizen. It has never been settled because the right methods have not been employed in the solution. It is the Banquo's ghost of politics, religion, and sociology which will not down at the bidding of those who are tormented with its ubiquitous appearance on every occasion. Times without number, since invested with citizenship, the race has been indicted for ignorance, immorality and general worthlessness—declared guilty and executed by its self-constituted judges. The operations of law do not dispose of negroes fast enough, and lynching bees have become the favorite pastime of the South. As excuse for the same, a new cry, as false as it is foul, is raised in an effort to blast race character, a cry which has proclaimed to the world that virtue and innocence are violated by Afro-Americans who must be killed like wild beasts to protect womanhood and childhood.

Born and reared in the South, I had never expected to live elsewhere. Until this past year I was one among those who believed the condition of the masses gave large excuse for the humiliations and proscriptions under which we labored; that when wealth, education and character became more general among us—the cause being removed—the effect would cease, and justice be accorded to all alike. I shared the general belief that good newspapers entering regularly the homes of our people in every state could do more to bring about this result than any agency. Preaching the doctrine of self-help, thrift and economy every week, they would be the teachers to those who had been deprived of school advantages, yet were making history every day—and train to think for themselves our mental children of a larger growth. And so, three years ago last June, I became editor and part owner of the *Memphis Free Speech.* As editor, I had occasion to criticize the city School Board's employment of inefficient teachers and poor school-buildings for Afro-American children. I was in the employ of that board at the time, and at the close of that school-term one year ago, was not re-elected to a position I had held in the city schools for seven years. Accepting the decision of the Board of Education, I set out to make a race newspaper pay—a thing which older and wiser heads said could not be done. But there were enough of our people in Memphis and surrounding territory to support a paper, and I believed they would do so. With nine months' hard work the circulation increased from 1,500 to 3,500; in twelve months it was on a good paying basis. Throughout the Mississippi Valley in Arkansas, Tennessee and Mississippi—on plantations and in towns, the demand for and interest in the paper increased among the masses. The newsboys who would not sell it on the trains, voluntarily testified that they had never known colored people to demand a paper so eagerly.

To make the paper a paying business I became advertising agent, solicitor, as well as editor, and was continually on the go. Wherever I went among the people, I gave them in church, school, public gatherings, and home, the benefit of my honest conviction that maintenance of character, money getting and education would finally solve our problem and that it depended on us to say how soon this would be brought about. This sentiment bore good fruit in Memphis. We had nice homes, representatives in almost every branch of business and profession, and refined society. We had learned that helping each other helped all, and every well-conducted business by Afro-Americans prospered. With all our proscription in theatres, hotels and on railroads, we had never had a lynching and did not believe we could have one. There had been lynchings and brutal outrages of all sorts in our own state and those adjoining us, but we had confidence and pride in our city and the majesty of its laws. So far in advance of other Southern cities was ours, we were content to endure the evils we had, to labor and to wait.

But there was a rude awakening. On the morning of March 9 [1892], the bodies of three of our best young men were found in an old field horribly shot to pieces. These young men had owned and operated the "People's Grocery," situated at what was known as the Curve—a suburb made up almost entirely of colored people—about a mile from city limits. Thomas Moss, one of the oldest letter-carriers in the city, was president of the company, Calvin McDowell was manager and Will Stewart was a clerk. There were about ten other stockholders, all colored men. The young men were well known and popular and their business flourished, and that of Barrett, a white grocer who kept store there before the "People's Grocery" was established, went down. One day an officer came to the "People's Grocery" and inquired for a colored man who lived in the neighborhood, and for whom the officer had a warrant. Barrett was with him and when McDowell said he knew nothing as to the whereabouts of the man for whom they were searching. Barrett, not the officer, then accused McDowell of harboring the man, and McDowell gave the lie. Barrett drew his pistol and struck McDowell with it; thereupon McDowell, who was a tall, fine-looking six-footer, took Barrett's pistol from him, knocked him down and gave him a good thrashing, while Will Stewart, the clerk, kept the special officer at bay. Barrett went to town, swore out a warrant for their arrest on a charge of assault and battery. McDowell went before the Criminal Court, immediately gave bond and returned to his store. Barrett then threatened (to use his own words) that he was going to clean out the whole store. Knowing how anxious he was to destroy their business, these young men consulted a lawyer who told them they were justified in defending themselves if attacked, as they were a mile beyond city limits and police protection. They accordingly armed several of their friends—not to assail, but to resist the threatened Saturday night attack.

When they saw Barrett enter the front door and a half dozen men at the rear door at 11 o'clock that night, they supposed the attack was on and immediately fired into the crowd, wounding three men. These men, dressed in citizen's clothes, turned out to be deputies who claimed to be hunting another man for whom they had a warrant, and whom any one of them could have arrested without trouble. When these men found they had fired upon officers of the law, they threw away their firearms and submitted to arrest, confident they should establish their innocence of intent to fire upon officers of the law. The daily papers in flaming headlines roused the evil passions of the whites, denounced these poor boys in unmeasured terms, nor permitted them a word in their own defense.

The neighborhood of the Curve was searched next day, and about thirty persons were thrown into jail, charged with conspiracy. No communication was to be had with friends any of the three days these men were in jail; bail was refused and Thomas Moss was not allowed to eat the food his wife prepared for him. The judge is reported to have said, "Any one can see them after three days." They were seen after three days, but they were no longer able to respond to the greetings of friends. On Tuesday following the shooting at the grocery, the papers which had made much of the sufferings of the wounded deputies, and promised it would go hard with those who did the shooting, if they died, announced that the officers were all out of danger, and would recover. The friends of the prisoners breathed more easily and relaxed their vigilance. They felt that as the officers would not die, there was no danger that in the heat of passion the prisoners would meet violent death at the hands of the mob. Besides, we had such confidence in the law. But the law did not provide capital punishment for shooting which did not kill. So the mob did what the law could not be made to do, as a lesson to the Afro-American that he must not shoot a white man,—no matter what the provocation. The same night after the announcement was made in the papers that the officers would get well, the mob, in obedience to a plan known to every prominent white man in the city, went to the jail between two and three o'clock in the morning, dragged out these young men, hatless and shoeless, put them on the yard engine of the railroad which was in waiting just behind the jail, carried them a mile north of city limits and horribly shot them to death while the locomotive at a given signal let off steam and blew the whistle to deaden the sound of the firing.

"It was done by unknown men," said the jury, yet the *Appeal-Avalanche,* which goes to press at 3 a.m., had a two-column account of the lynching. The papers also told how McDowell got hold of the guns of the mob, and as his grasp could not be loosened, his hand was shattered with a pistol ball and all the lower part of his face was torn away. There were four pools of blood found and only three bodies. It was whispered that he, McDowell, killed one of the lynchers with his gun, and it is well known that a policeman who was seen on the street a few days previous to the lynching, died very suddenly the next day after.

"It was done by unknown parties," said the jury, yet the papers told how Tom Moss begged for his life, for the sake of his wife, his little daughter and his unborn infant. They also told us that his last words were, "If you will kill us, turn our faces to the West."

All this we learned too late to save these men, even if the law had not been in the hands of their murderers. When the colored people realized that the flower of our young manhood had been stolen away at night and murdered, there was a rush for firearms to avenge the wrong, but no house would sell a colored man a gun; the armory of the Tennessee Rifles, our only colored military company, and of which McDowell was a member, was broken into by order of the Criminal Court judge, and its guns taken. One hundred men and irresponsible boys from fifteen years and up were armed by order of the authorities and rushed out to the Curve, where it was reported that the colored people were massing, and at point of the bayonet dispersed these men who could do nothing but talk. The cigars, wines, etc., of the grocery stock were freely used by the mob, who possessed the place on pretence of dispersing the conspiracy. The money drawer was broken into and contents taken. The trunk of Calvin McDowell, who had a room in the store, was broken open, and his clothing, which was not good enough to take away, was thrown out and trampled on the floor.

These men were murdered, their stock was attached by creditors and sold for less than one-eighth of its cost to that same man Barrett, who is to-day running his grocery in the same place. He had indeed kept his word, and by aid of the authorities destroyed the People's Grocery Company root and branch. The relatives of Will Stewart and Calvin McDowell are bereft of their protectors. The baby daughter of Tom Moss, too young to express how she misses her father, toddles to the wardrobe, seizes the legs of the trousers of his letter-carrier uniform, hugs and kisses them with evident delight and stretches up her little hands to be taken up into the arms which will nevermore clasp his daughter's form. His wife holds Thomas Moss. Jr., in her arms, upon whose unconscious baby face the tears fall thick and fast when she is thinking of the sad fate of the father he will never see, and of the two helpless children who cling to her for the support she cannot give. Although these men were peaceable, law-abiding citizens of this country, we are told there can be no punishment for their murderers nor indemnity for their relatives.

I have no power to describe the feeling of horror that possessed every member of the race in Memphis when the truth dawned upon us that the protection of the law which we had so long enjoyed was no longer ours; all this had been destroyed in a night, and the barriers of the law had been thrown down, and the guardians of the public peace and confidence scoffed away into the shadows, and all authority given into the hands of the mob, and innocent men cut down as if they were brutes—the first feeling was one of utter dismay, then intense indignation. Vengeance was whispered from ear to ear, but sober reflection brought the conviction that it would be extreme folly to seek vengeance when such action meant certain death for the men, and horrible slaughter for the women and children, as one of the evening papers took care to remind us. The power of the State, country and city, the civil authorities and the strong arm of the military power were all on the side of the mob and of lawlessness. Few of our men possessed firearms, our only company's guns were confiscated, and the only white man who would sell a colored man a gun, was himself jailed, and his store closed. We were helpless in our great strength. It was our first object lesson in the doctrine of white supremacy; an illustration of the South's cardinal principle that no matter what the attainments, character or standing of an Afro-American, the laws of the South will not protect him against a white man.

There was only one thing we could do, and a great determination seized upon the people to follow the advice of the martyred Moss, and "turn our faces to the West," whose laws protect all alike. The *Free Speech* supported by our ministers and leading business men advised the people to leave a community whose laws did not protect them. Hundreds left on foot to walk four hundred miles between Memphis and Oklahoma. A Baptist minister went to the territory, built a church, and took his entire congregation out in less than a month. Another minister sold his church and took his flock to California, and still another has settled in Kansas. In two months, six thousand persons had left the city and every branch of business began to feel this silent resentment of the outrage, and failure of the authorities to punish the lynchers. There were a number of business failures and blocks of houses were for rent. The superintendent and treasurer of the street railway company called at the office of the *Free Speech,* to have us urge the colored people to ride again on the street cars. A real estate dealer said to a colored man who returned some property he had been buying on the installment plan: "I don't see what you 'niggers' are cutting up about. You got off light. We first intended to kill every one of those thirty-one 'niggers' in jail, but concluded to let all go but the 'leaders.'" They did let all go to the penitentiary. These so-called rioters have since been tried in the Criminal Court for the conspiracy of defending their property, and are now serving terms of three, eight, and fifteen years each in the Tennessee State prison.

To restore the equilibrium and put a stop to the great financial loss, the next move was to get rid of the *Free Speech*—the disturbing element which kept the waters troubled; which would not let the people forget, and in obedience to whose advice nearly six thousand persons had left the city. In casting about for an excuse, the mob found it in the following editorial which appeared in the Memphis *Free Speech*—May 21, 1892: "Eight negroes lynched in one week. Since last issue of the *Free Speech* one was lynched at Little Rock, Ark., where the citizens broke into the penitentiary and got their man: three near Anniston, Ala., and one in New Orleans, all on the same charge, the new alarm of assaulting white women—and three near Clarksville, Ga., for killing a white man. The same program of hanging—then shooting bullets into the lifeless bodies—was carried out to the letter. Nobody in this section of the country believes the old threadbare lie that negro men rape white women. If Southern white men are not careful they will overreach themselves, and public sentiment will have a reaction. A conclusion will then be reached which will be very damaging to the moral reputation of their women." Commenting on this, *The Daily Commercial* of Wednesday following said: "Those negroes who are attempting to make lynching of individuals of their race a means for arousing the worst passions of their kind, are playing with a dangerous sentiment. The negroes may as well understand that there is no mercy for the negro rapist, and little patience with his defenders. A negro organ printed in this city in a recent issue published the following atrocious paragraph: 'Nobody in this section believes the old threadbare lie that negro men rape white women. If Southern white men are not careful they will overreach themselves and public sentiment will have a reaction. A conclusion will be reached which will be very damaging to the moral reputation of their women.' The fact that a black scoundrel is allowed to live and utter such loathsome and repulsive calumnies is a volume of evidence as to the wonderful patience of Southern whites. There are some things the Southern white man will not tolerate, and the obscene intimidation of the foregoing has brought the writer to the very uttermost limit of public patience. We hope we have said enough."

The Evening *Scimitar* of the same day copied this leading editorial and added this comment: "Patience under such circumstances is not a virtue. If the negroes themselves do not apply the remedy without delay, it will be the duty of those he has attacked, to tie the wretch who utters these calumnies to a stake at the intersection of Main and Madison streets, brand him in the forehead with a hot iron and—"

Such open suggestions by the leading daily papers of the progressive city of Memphis were acted upon by the leading citizens and a meeting was held at the Cotton Exchange that evening. *The Commercial* two days later had the following account of it:

ATROCIOUS BLACKGUARDISM

There will be no Lynching and no Repetition of the Offense.

> In its issue of Wednesday *The Commercial* reproduced and commented upon an editorial which appeared a day or two before in a negro organ known as the *Free Speech.* The article was so insufferably and indecently slanderous that the whole city awoke to a feeling of intense resentment which came within an ace of culminating in one of those occurrences whose details are so eagerly seized and so prominently published by Northern newspapers. Conservative counsels, however, prevailed, and no extreme measures were resorted to. On Wednesday afternoon a meeting of citizens was held. It was not an assemblage of hoodlums or irresponsible fire-eaters, but solid, substantial business men who knew exactly what they were doing and who were far more indignant at the villanous insult to the women of the South than they would have been at any injury done themselves. This meeting appointed a committee to seek the author of the infamous editorial and warn him quietly that upon repetition of the offense he would find some other part of the country a good deal safer and pleasanter place of residence than this. The committee called a negro preacher named Nightingale, but he disclaimed responsibility and convinced the gentlemen that he had really sold out his paper to a woman named Wells. This woman is not in Memphis at present. It was finally learned that one Fleming, a negro who was driven out of Crittenden Co. during the trouble there a few years ago, wrote the paragraph. He had, however, heard of the meeting, and fled from a fate which he feared was in store for him, and which he knew he deserved. His whereabouts could not be ascertained, and the committee so reported. Later on, a communication from Fleming to a prominent Republican politician, and that politician's reply were shown to one or two gentlemen. The former was an inquiry as to whether the writer

might safely return to Memphis, the latter was an emphatic answer in the negative, and Fleming is still in hiding. Nothing further will be done in the matter. There will be no lynching, and it is very certain there will be no repetition of the outrage. If there should be—Friday, May 25 [sic].

The only reason there was no lynching of Mr. Fleming who was business manager and half owner of the *Free Speech,* and who did not write the editorial, was because this same white Republican told him the committee was coming, and warned him not to trust them, but get out of the way. The committee scoured the city hunting him, and had to be content with Mr. Nightingale who was dragged to the meeting, shamefully abused (although it was known he had sold out his interest in the paper six months before). He was struck in the face and forced at the pistol's point to sign a letter which was written by them, in which he denied all knowledge of the editorial, denounced and condemned it as slander on white women. I do not censure Mr. Nightingale for his action because, having never been at the pistol's point myself, I do not feel that I am competent to sit in judgment on him, or say what I would do under such circumstances.

I had written that editorial with other matter for the week's paper before leaving home the Friday previous for the General Conference of the A.M.E. Church in Philadelphia. Conference adjourned Tuesday, and Thursday, May 25[sic]. at 3 p.m. I landed in New York City for a few days' stay before returning home, and there learned from the papers that my business manager had been driven away and the paper suspended. Telegraphing for news, I received telegrams and letters in return informing me that the trains were being watched, that I was to be dumped into the river and beaten, if not killed: it had been learned that I wrote the editorial and I was to be hanged in front of the court-house and my face bled if I returned, and I was implored by my friends to remain away. The creditors attached the office in the meantime and the outfit was sold without more ado, thus destroying effectually that which it had taken years to build. One prominent insurance agent publicly declares he will make it his business to shoot me down on sight if I return to Memphis in twenty years, while a leading white lady had remarked that she was opposed to the lynching of those three men in March, but she did wish there was some way by which I could be gotten back and lynched.

I have been censured for writing that editorial, but when I think of the five men who were lynched that week for assault on white women and that not a week passes but some poor soul is violently ushered into eternity on this trumped-up charge, knowing the many things I do, and part of which I tried to tell in the *New York Age* of June 25 (and in the pamphlets I have with me) seeing that the whole race in the South was injured in the estimation of the world because of these false reports, I could no longer hold my peace, and I feel, yes, I am sure, that if it had to be done over again (provided no one else was the loser save myself) I would do and say the very same again.

The lawlessness here described is not confined to one locality. In the past ten years over a thousand colored men, women and children have been butchered, murdered and burnt in all parts of the South. The details of these horrible outrages seldom reach beyond the narrow world where they occur. Those who commit the murders write the reports, and hence these lasting blots upon the honor of a nation cause but a faint ripple on the outside world. They arouse no great indignation and call forth no adequate demand for justice. The victims were black, and the reports are so written as to make it appear that the helpless creatures deserved the fate which overtook them.

Not so with the Italian lynching of 1891. They were not black men, and three of them were not citizens of the Republic, but subjects of the King of Italy. The chief of police of New Orleans was shot and eleven Italians were arrested charged with the murder; they were tried and the jury disagreed; the good, law-abiding citizens of New Orleans thereupon took them from the jail and lynched them at high noon. A feeling of horror ran through the nation at this outrage. All Europe was amazed. The Italian government demanded thorough investigation and redress, and the Federal Government promised to give the matter the consideration which was its due. The diplomatic relations between the two countries became very much strained and for a while war talk was freely indulged. Here was a case where the power of the Federal Government to protect its own citizens and redeem its pledges to a friendly power was put to the test. When our State Department called upon the authorities of Louisiana for investigation of the crime and punishment of the criminals, the United States government was told that the crime was strictly within the authority of the State of Louisiana, and Louisiana would attend to it. After a farcical investigation, the usual verdict in such cases was rendered: "Death at the hand of parties unknown to the jury," the same verdict which has been pronounced over the bodies of over 1,000 colored persons! Our general government has thus admitted that it has no jurisdiction over the crimes committed at New Orleans upon citizens of the country, nor upon those citizens of a friendly power to whom the general government and not the State government has pledged protection. Not only has our general government made the confession that one of the states is greater than the Union, but the general government has paid $25,000 of the people's money to the King of Italy for the lynching of those three subjects, the evil-doing of one State, over which it has no control, but for whose lawlessness of the whole country must pay. The principle involved in the treaty power of the government has not yet been settled to the satisfaction of foreign powers: but the principle involved in the right of State jurisdiction in such matters, was settled long ago by the decision of the United States Supreme Court.

I beg your patience while we look at another phase of the lynching mania. We have turned heretofore to the pages of ancient and medieval history, to Roman tyranny, the Jesuitical Inquisition of Spain for the spectacle of a human being burnt to death. In the past ten years three instances, at least, have been furnished where men have literally been roasted to death to appease the fury of Southern mobs. The Texarkana instance of last year and the Paris, Texas, case of this month are the most recent as they are the most shocking and repulsive. Both were charged with crimes for which the laws provide adequate punishment. The Texarkana man, Ed Coy, was charged with assaulting a white woman. A mob pronounced him guilty, strapped him to a tree, chipped the flesh from his body, poured coal oil over him and the woman in the case set fire to him. The country looked on and in many cases applauded, because it was published that this man had violated the honor of the white woman, although he protested his innocence to the last. Judge Tourjee in the Chicago *Inter-Ocean* of recent date says investigation has shown that Ed Coy had supported this woman (who was known to be of bad character) and her drunken husband for over a year previous to the burning.

The Paris, Texas, burning of Henry Smith, February 1st, has exceeded all the others in its horrible details. The man was drawn through the streets on a float, as the Roman generals used to parade their trophies of war, while the scaffold ten feet high, was being built, and irons were heated in the fire. He was bound on it, and red-hot irons began at his feet and slowly branded his body, while the mob howled with delight at his shrieks. Red-hot irons were run down his throat and cooked his tongue: his eyes were burned out, and when he was at last unconscious, cotton seed hulls were placed under him, coal oil poured all over him, and a torch applied to the mass. When the flames burned away the ropes which bound Smith and scorched his flesh, he was brought back to sensibility—and burned and maimed and sightless as he was, he rolled off the platform and away from the fire. His half-cooked body was seized and trampled and thrown back into the flames while a mob of twenty thousand persons who came from all over the country howled with delight, and gathered up some buttons and ashes after all was over to preserve for relics. This man was charged with outraging and murdering a four-year-old white child, covering her body with brush, sleeping beside her through the night, then making his escape. If true, it was the deed of a madman, and should have been clearly proven so. The fact that no time for verification of the newspaper reports was given, is suspicious, especially when I remember that a negro was lynched in Indianola, Sharkey Co., Miss., last summer. The dispatches said it was because he had assaulted the sheriff's eight-year-old daughter. The girl was more than eighteen years old and was found by her father in this man's room, who was a servant on the place.

These incidents have been made the basis of this terrible story because they overshadow all others of a like nature in cruelty and represent the legal phases of the whole question. They could be multiplied without number—and each outrival the other in the fiendish cruelty exercised, and the frequent awful lawlessness exhibited. The following table shows the number of black men lynched from January 1, 1882, to January 1, 1892: In 1882, 52; 1883, 39; 1884, 53; 1885, 77; 1886, 73; 1887, 70; 1888, 72; 1889, 95; 1890, 100; 1891, 169. Of these 728 black men who were murdered, 269 were charged with rape, 253 with murder, 44 with robbery, 37 with incendiarism, 32 with reasons unstated (it was not necessary to have a reason), 27 with race prejudice, 13 with quarreling with white men, 10 with making threats, 7 with rioting, 5 with miscegenation, 4 with burglary. One of the men lynched in 1891 was Will Lewis, who was lynched because "he was drunk and saucy to white folks." A woman who was one of the 73 victims in 1886, was hung in Jackson, Tenn., because the white woman for whom she cooked, died suddenly of poisoning. An examination showed arsenical poisoning. A search in the cook's room found rat poison. She was thrown into jail, and when the mob had worked itself up to the lynching pitch, she was dragged out, every stitch of clothing torn from her body, and was hung in the public court house square in sight of everybody. That white woman's husband has since died, in the insane asylum, a raving maniac, and his ravings have led to the conclusion that he and not the cook, was the poisoner of his wife. A fifteen-year-old colored girl was lynched last spring, at Rayville, La., on the same charge of poisoning. A woman was also lynched at Hollendale. Miss., last spring, charged with being an accomplice in the murder of her white paramour who had abused her. These were only two of the 159 persons lynched in the South from January 1, 1892, to January 1, 1893. Over a dozen black men have been lynched already since this new year set in, and the year is not yet two months old.

It will thus be seen that neither age, sex nor decency are spared. Although the impression has gone abroad that most of the lynchings take place because of assaults on white women only one-third of the number lynched in the past ten years have been charged with that offense, to say nothing of those who were not guilty of the charge. And according to law none of them were guilty until proven so. But the unsupported word of any white person for any cause is sufficient to cause a lynching. So bold have the lynchers become, masks are laid aside, the temples of justice and strongholds of law are invaded in broad daylight and prisoners taken out and lynched, while governors of states and officers of law stand by and see the work well done.

And yet this Christian nation, the flower of the nineteenth century civilization, says it can do nothing to stop this inhuman slaughter. The general government is willingly powerless to send troops to protect the lives of its black citizens, but the state governments are free to use state troops to shoot them down like cattle, when in desperation the black men attempt to defend themselves, and then tell the world that it was necessary to put down a "race war."

Persons unfamiliar with the condition of affairs in the Southern States do not credit the truth when it is told them. They cannot conceive how such a condition of affairs prevails so near them with steam power, telegraph wires and printing presses in daily and hourly touch with the localities where such disorder reigns. In a former generation the ancestors of these same people refused to believe that slavery was the "league with death and the covenant with hell." Wm. Lloyd Garrison declared it to be, until he was thrown into a dungeon in Baltimore, until the signal lights of Nat Turner lit the dull skies of Northampton County, and until sturdy old John Brown made his attack on Harpers Ferry. When Freedom of speech was martyred in the person of Elijah Lovejoy at Alton, when the liberty of free-discussion in Senate of the Nation's Congress was struck down in the person of the fearless Charles Summer, the Nation was at last convinced that slavery was not only a monster but a tyrant. That same tyrant is at work under a new name and guise. The lawlessness which has been here described is like unto that which prevailed under slavery. *The very same forces are at work now as then.* The attempt is being made to subject to a condition of civil and industrial dependence, those whom the Constitution declares to be free men. The events which have led up to the present wide-spread lawlessness in the South can be traced to the very first year Lee's conquered veterans marched from Appomattox to their homes in the Southland. They were conquered in war, but not in spirit. They believed as firmly as ever that it was their right to rule black men and dictate to the National Government. The knights of White Liners, and the Ku Klux Klans were composed of veterans of the Confederate army who were determined to destroy the effect of all the slave had gained by the war. They finally accomplished their purpose in 1876. The right of the Afro-American to vote and hold office remains in the Federal Constitution, but is destroyed in the constitution of the Southern states. Having destroyed the citizenship of the man, they are now trying to destroy the manhood of the citizen. All their laws are shaped to this end,—school laws, railroad car regulations, those governing labor liens on crops,—every device is adopted to make slaves of free men and rob them of their wages. Whenever a malicious law is violated in any of its parts, any farmer, any railroad conductor, or merchant can call together a posse of his neighbors and punish even with death the black man who resists and the legal authorities sanction what is doen by failing to prosecute and punish the murders. The Repeal of the Civil Rights Law removed their last barrier and the black man's last bulwark and refuge. The rule of the mob is absolute.

Those who know this recital to be true, say there is nothing they can do—they cannot interfere and vainly hope by further concession to placate the imperious and dominating part of our country in which this lawlessness prevails. Because this country has been almost rent in twain by internal dissension, the other sections seem virtually to have agreed that the best way to heal the breach is to permit the taking away to civil, political, and even human rights, to stand by in silence and utter indifference while the South continues to wreak fiendish vengeance on the irresponsible cause. They pretend to believe that with all the machinery of law and government in its hands; with the jails and penitentiaries and convict farms filled with petty race criminals; with the well-known fact that no negro has ever been known to escape conviction and punishment for any crime in the South—still there are those who try to justify and condone the lynching of over a thousand black men in less than ten years—an average of one hundred a year. The public sentiment of the country, by its silence in press, pulpit and in public meetings has encouraged this state of affairs, and public sentiment is stronger than law. With all the country's disposition to condone and temporize with the South and its methods; with its many instances of sacrificing principle to prejudice for the sake of making friends and healing the breach made by the late war; of going into the lawless country with capital to build up its waste places and remaining silent in the presence of outrage and wrong—the South is as vindictive and bitter as ever. She is willing to make friends as long as she is permitted to pursue unmolested and uncensured, her course of proscription, injustice, outrage and vituperation. The malignant misrepresentation of General Butler, the uniformly indecent and abusive assault of this dead man whose only crime was a defence of his country, is a recent proof that the South has lost none of its bitterness. The *Nashville American,* one of the leading papers of one of the leading southern cities, gleefully announced editorially that "'The Beast is dead.' Early yesterday morning, acting under the devil's orders, the angel of Death took Ben Butler and landed him in the lowest depths of hell, and we pity even the devil the possession he has secured." The men who wrote these editorials are without exception young men who know nothing of slavery and scarcely anything of the war. The bitterness and hatred have been instilled in and taught them by their parents, and they are men who make and reflect the sentiment of their section. The South spares nobody else's feelings, and it seems a queer logic that when it comes to a question of right, involving lives of citizens and the honor of the government, the South's feelings must be respected and spared.

Do you ask the remedy? A public sentiment strong against lawlessness must be aroused. Every individual can contribute to this awakening. When a sentiment against lynch law as strong, deep and mighty as that roused against slavery prevails, I have no fear of the result. It should be already established as a fact and not as a theory, that every human being must have a fair trial for his life and liberty, no matter what the charge against him. When a demand goes up from fearless and persistent reformers from press and pulpit, from industrial and moral associations that this shall be so from Maine to Texas and from ocean to ocean, a way will be found to make it so.

In deference to the few words of condemnation uttered at the M.E. General Conference last year, and by other organizations, Governors Hogg of Texas, Northern of Georgia, and Tillman of South Carolina, have issued proclamations offering rewards for the apprehension of lynchers. These rewards have never been claimed, and these governors knew they would not be when offered. In many cases they knew the ringleaders of the mobs. The prosecuting attorney of Shelby County, Tenn., wrote Governor Buchanan to offer a reward for the arrest of the lynchers of three young men murdered in Memphis. Everybody in that city and state knew well that the letter was written for the sake of effect and the governor did not even offer the reward. But the country at large deluded itself with the belief that the officials of the South and the leading citizens condemned lynching. The lynchings go on in spite of offered rewards, and in face of Governor Hogg's vigorous talk, the second man was burnt alive in his state with the utmost deliberation and publicity. Since he sent a message to the legislature the mob found and hung Henry Smith's stepson, because he refused to tell where Smith was when they were hunting for him. Public sentiment which shall denounce these crimes in season and out; public sentiment which turns capital and immigration from a section given over to lawlessness; public sentiment which insists on the punishment of criminals and lynchers by law must be aroused.

It is no wonder in my mind that the party which stood for thirty years as the champion of human liberty and human rights, the party of great moral ideas, should suffer overwhelming defeat when it has proven recreant to its professions and abandoned a position it created; when although its followers were being outraged in every sense, it was afraid to stand for the right, and appeal to the American people to sustain them in it. It put aside the question of a free ballot and fair count of every citizen and gave its voice and influence for the protection of the coat instead of the man who wore it, for the product of labor instead of the laborer; for the seal of citizenship rather than the citizen, and insisted upon the evils of free trade instead of the sacredness of free speech. I am no politician but I believe if the Republican party had met the issues squarely for human rights instead of the tariff it would have occupied a different position to-day. The voice of the people is the voice of God, and I long with all the intensity of my soul for the Garrison, Douglas, Sumner, Wittier, and Phillips who shall rouse this nation to a demand that from Greenland's icy mountains to the coral reefs of the Southern seas, mob rule shall be put down and equal and exact justice be accorded to every citizen of whatever race, who finds a home within the borders of the land of the free and the home of the brave.

Then no longer will our national hymn be sounding brass and a tinkling cymbal, but every member of this great composite nation will be a living, harmonious illustration of the words, and all can honestly and gladly join in singing:

My country! 'tis of thee,
Sweet land of liberty
    Of thee I sing.
Land where our fathers died,
Land of the Pilgrim's pride,

From every mountain side
Freedom does ring.

Source

Ida B. Wells-Barnett, "Lynch Law in All Its Phases" (1893; reprinted in Melvin Donaldson, ed., *Cornerstones: An Anthology of African-American Literature*, 35–47 [New York: St. Martin's Press, 1996]).

Selected Bibliography

Cartwright, Joseph H. *The Triumph of Jim Crow: Race Relations in the 1880s*. Knoxville: University of Tennessee Press, 1976.

Duster, Alfreda M., ed. *Crusader for Justice, the Autobiography of Ida B. Wells*. Chicago: University of Chicago Press, 1970.

Holt, Thomas C. "The Lonely Warrior: Ida B. Wells-Barnett and the Struggle for Black Leadership," in John Hope Franklin and August Meier, eds., *Black Leaders of the Twentieth Century*. Urbana: University of Illinois Press, 1982.

Lerner, Gerda. "Early Community Work of Black Club Women," *Journal of Negro History* 59 (April 1954): 158–67.

Neverdon-Morton, Cynthia. *Afro-American Women of the South and the Advancement of Race, 1895–1925*. Knoxville: University of Tennessee Press, 1989.

Sterling, Dorothy. *Black Foremothers: Three Lives*. Old Westbury, N.Y.: Feminist Press, 1979.

five

Songs of the Prison Plantation

Just as slaves fostered community bonds and affirmed their religious beliefs through traditional work songs, black convicts sang songs of the prison plantation to commiserate with one another, to slow the pace of work, and to sustain their faith, even in the face of chain gangs, the convict lease system, and the prison farms. Though traditional slave songs sometimes morphed into prison songs, others—such as "Go Down, Old Hannah" and "Midnight Special"—almost certainly had their origins inside the prison walls and barbed wire fences of the Jim Crow penitentiary. Many of these haunting songs used terms that now seem antiquated or that have left our vocabulary altogether: for example, the "Hannah" in "Go Down, Old Hannah," refers to the sun, a "Midnight Special" was black argot for a pardon, and the "Rider" in "Easy Rider" refers to a prison guard on horseback. These songs represent a distinctive folk art and they continue to be sung, with varied lyrics and styles, even today.

Chorus

> But never will I pick a bale a cotton,
> How in the world can I pick a bale a day.

Like the three complete songs reprinted here, those lines were recorded in the Texas prison system between 1964 and 1966 by Bruce

Jackson and reproduced in his marvelous book, *Wake Up Dead Man: Afro-American Worksongs from Texas Prisons*.

Besides amassing a rich and deep book-length collection of songs from one prison system, Jackson also gathered from the prisoners themselves descriptions of the functions served by this poetry and music. In addition to timing the work so they could endure from sunup to sundown, the prisoners also used the songs to prevent any individual from being singled out for punishment for working too slowly, since they are all working to the same beat. One "long-time" man told him:

You get worked to death or beat to death. That's why we sang so many of these songs. We would work together and help ourselves as well as help out our fellow man. Try to keep the officials we was workin' under pacified and we'd make it possible to make a day.[1]

No verbal description of these convict work songs can do more than hint of their beauty and enormous power. Fortunately, many of them have now been preserved on records; each of the following gives a sample of their range and scope: *Negro Prison Camp Work Songs* (Folkways FE-4475), *Negro Prison Songs from the Mississippi State Penitentiary* (Tradition TLP-1020), *Prison Worksongs* (Folk-Lyric LFS A-5), and *Negro Work Songs and Calls* (Library of Congress Archive of American Folk Song L-8). A more immediate experience of the songs comes through in a 1966 film, *Afro-American Worksongs in a Texas Prison* (Folklore Research Films), by Dan and Toshi Seeger, with audio work by Pete Seeger and Bruce Jackson.

Though some of the slave songs migrated into prison while others were metamorphosed as they were modified by the particulars of penal imprisonment, still other songs seem to have originated directly in the prison experience. "Go Down, Old Hannah," the first song reprinted here, is almost certainly the special creation of African American convicts, as attested to by Leadbelly, who does a magnificent version on his *Last Sessions* (Folkways FA 1941):

> They called the sun Old Hannah because it was hot and they just give it a name. That's what the boys called it when I was in prison. I didn't hear it before I went down there. The boys were talking about Old Hannah—I kept looking and I didn't see no Hannah, but they looked up and said, "That's the sun."[2]

Dozens of versions of "Go Down, Old Hannah" have been recorded in prison or by ex-convict singers, and the song has picked up stanzas referring to historical events as early as 1910.

"Midnight Special" also seems to have had its genesis in prison. Although "Easy Rider" may possibly have originated outside prison, it transmuted into a widely diffused prison work song, as shown in the version reprinted here, which is all about the problem of survival on the prison plantation (a "rider" is a guard on horseback). Both these songs later took on other identities as they were commodified.

Prisoner work songs recapitulate and expand the historic cultural role of the slave song. Like their enslaved forebears, the prisoners are allowed to own only one thing of any importance: the collective property embodied in their poetry and music. But that property, ironically enough, eventually transforms into a major commodity of American culture.

Go Down, Old Hannah

Well you ought to been down on this old river, WELL, WELL, WELL,
Nineteen forty-four, NINETEEN FORTY-FOUR,
Oughta been down on this old river,
Nineteen forty-FOUR.
Well you could find a dead man, WELL, WELL, WELL,
On every turn row, ON EVERY TURN ROW,
You could find a DEAD MAN,
On every TURN ROW.

I say get up dead man, WELL, WELL, WELL,
Help me carry my row, HELP ME CARRY MY ROW,
I say get up DEAD MAN
Help me carry MY ROW.
Well my row so grassy, WELL, WELL, WELL,
I can't hardly go, CAN'T HARDLY GO.
Well my row so GRASSY,
I can't HARDLY GO.

I say go down old Hannah . . . (*burden and repetition continue as above*)
Don't rise no more . . .
If you rise in the mornin' . . .
Bring judgment sure . . .

SOLO SINGER:
Well I ain't tired a livin' . . .
Man, but I got so long . . .
Well they got some on the highway . . .
Little boy, they got some goin' home . . .

Well I looked at old Hannah . . .
And old Hannah looked red . . .
Well I looked at my poor partner . . .
Little boy was half mos' dead . . .

Well my partner said, "Help me, . . .
Help me if you can" . . .
I said, "Partner who fooled you . . .
Down on this long old line" . . . (*repeat is* "on this river line")

"Who told you you could make it . . .
On this river line?" . . .
He say, "I'm not tired a workin' . . .
Pardner I got so long" . . .

I said, "Write your mama . . .
Tell her the shape you in . . .
Tell her I say write the governor . . .
That your time has come" . . .

"Ask the governor for a pardon . . .
And he may grant you a reprieve" . . .

SOLO SINGER:
Well I see Bud Russell . . .
Little boy, with his ball and chain . . .
Little boys he gonna take you . . .
Back to Sugarland . . .

Little boys you get worried . . .
Little boy, don't try to run away . . .
Little boy you'll get to see you mama . . .
On some lonesome day . . .

And who fooled you on the river . . .
With the great long time . . .

Midnight Special

Let the Midnight Special shine her light on me,
Let the Midnight Special shine her ever-lovin' light on me.

"Here come Bud Russel." "How in the world do you know?"
Well he know him by his wagon and the chains he wo'.

Big pistol on his shoulder, big knife in his hand:
He's comin' to carry you back to Sugarland.

Let the Midnight Special shine her light on me,
Let the Midnight Special shine her ever-lovin' light on me.

Oh, yonder come Rosie. "How'n the world do you know?"
I know her by her apron and the dress she wore.

Umbrella on her shoulder, piece a paper in her hand,
She hollerin' and cryin', "Won't you free my man?"

Well she cause me to worry, whoopin', hollerin', and a-cryin',
Well she cause me to worry, 'bout my great long time.

Well let the Midnight Special shine her light on me,
Oh let the Midnight Special shine her ever-lovin' light on me.

If you ever go to Paris, man, you better walk right,
And you better not stumble, and you better not fight.

Po-lice he'll 'rest you, and 'll drag you down,
The judge he'll find you, you'll be penitentiary bound.

Let the Midnight Special shine the light on me,
Let the Midnight Special shine her ever-lovin' light on me.

Easy Rider

Oh, easy rider, what make you so mean,
You not the meanest man in the world, but the meanest one I've seen.

Say, oh, easy rider, what make you so mean,
I yell for water, partner, give me gasoline.

Waterboy, won't you bring the water 'round,
If you don't like your job, boy, set your bucket down.

I hate to see the rider, when he rides so near.
He so cruel and cold-hearted, boy, these twenty year.

I ask him for mercy, he don't give me none,
He ask me my trouble, and I didn't have none.

Notes

1. Bruce Jackson, *Wake Up Dead Man: Afro-American Worksongs from Texas Prisons* (Cambridge, Mass.: Harvard University Press, 1972), 2.
2. *The Leadbelly Songbook,* ed. Moses Asch and Alan Lomax (New York: Oak Publications, 1962), 50.

Source

"Songs of the Prison Plantation: "Go Down, Old Hannah," "Midnight Special," and "Easy Rider" recorded in the Texas Prison system between 1964 and 1966. Originally published by Bruce Jackson in *Wake Up Dead Man: Afro-American Worksongs from Texas Prisons,* 2 (Cambridge, Mass.: Harvard University Press, 1972).

Selected Bibliography

Asch, Moses and Alan Lomax, eds. *The Leadbelly Songbook.* New York: Oak Publications, 1962.

Hindus, Michael Stephen. *Prison and Plantation: Crime, Justice, and Authority in Massachusetts and South Carolina, 1767–1978.* Chapel Hill: University of North Carolina Press, 1980.

Jackson, Bruce. *Wake Up Dead Man: Afro-American Worksongs from Texas Prisons.* Cambridge, Mass: Harvard University Press, 1972.

Oshinsky, David M., *Worse Than Slavery: Parchman Farm and the Ordeal of Jim Crow Justice* (New York: Free Press, 1996).

six

The Lynching

Jamaican-born poet and novelist Claude McKay (1890–1948) is known for the pioneering role he played in the Harlem Renaissance. With his 1920 poem "The Lynching," McKay tried to address the horrific proliferation of "Lynch Law" that emerged in the postbellum period as a token feature of white supremacy. Depicting a mutilated black corpse as a Christ figure, the poem comments on the "fiendish glee" with which white mobs "danced round" their victims. Yet some critics argued that white violence toward Southern blacks was so pervasive and grotesque that even this vivid description failed to capture the true horror of lynching.

The year "The Lynching" was published, McKay had returned to the United States from England and attempted (rather ineffectively) to align himself with militant African American intellectuals. There, McKay published a collection of poetry entitled *Spring in New Hampshire,* which contained the noted poem "Harlem Shadows" about the predicament of black prostitutes. A metaphor for the state of all black people, "Harlem Shadows" was later used as a title of his 1922 collection, his first publication in the United States. A successful piece overall, *Harlem Shadows* included his most renowned poem, "If We Must Die."

His Spirit in smoke ascended to high heaven.
His father, by the cruelest way of pain,
Had bidden him to his bosom once again;
The awful sin remained still unforgiven.
All night a bright and solitary star
(Perchance the one that ever guided him,
Yet gave him up at last to Fate's wild whim)
Hung pitifully o'er the swinging char.
Day dawned, and soon the mixed crowds came to view
The ghastly body swaying in the sun.
The women thronged to look, but never a one
Showed sorrow in her eyes of steely blue.

And little lads, lynchers that were to be,
Danced round the dreadful thing in fiendish glee.

Source

Claude McKay, "The Lynching," *Cambridge Magazine* 10 (summer 1920): 56; reprinted in *The Selected Poems of Claude McKay,* 37 (New York: Bookman Associates, 1953). 8

Selected Bibliography

Cooper, Wayne F. *Claude McKay: Rebel Sojourner in the Harlem Renaissance; A Biography.* Baton Rouge: Louisiana State University Press, 1987.

Gayle, Addison. *Claude McKay: Black Poet at War.* Detroit: Broadside Press, 1972.

James, Winston. *Holding Aloft the Banner of Ethiopia: Caribbean Radicalism in America.* New York: Verso, 1998.

Lewis, David Levering. *When Harlem Was in Vogue.* New York: Oxford University Press, 1981.

McKay, Claude. *Selected Poems of Claude McKay.* San Diego: Harcourt Brace, 1969.

Tillary, Tyrone. *Claude McKay: A Black Poet's Struggle for Identity.* Amherst: University of Massachusetts Press, 1992.

s e v e n

Freedom Songs

Just as other genres of the African American music tradition have served various social functions, the freedom songs of the civil rights movement spurred both black and white Americans into political action and provided a rich source of inspiration, courage, and communication to those who were immersed in the black freedom struggle. Yet the freedom songs are also valuable to scholars, for even today they capture much of the civil rights movement's animating spirit. These three songs are some of the best known anthems of the era.

Guide My Feet While I Run This Race

Never turn back, while I run this race (3 times)
'Cause I don't want to run this race in vain.

Guide my feet while I run this race (3 times)
'Cause I don't want to run this race in vain.

Guide my heart. . . . .

Guide my tongue. . . . .

Guide my vote. . . . .

Guide my mind. . . . .

Woke Up This Morning with My Mind on Freedom

Woke up this morning with my mind (my mind it was) stayed on freedom,
(Oh well I) woke up this morning with my mind stayed on freedom,
(Oh well I) woke up this morning with my mind (my mind it was) stayed on freedom,
Hallelu, hallelu, hallelu, hallelu, hallelujah!

Ain't no harm to keep your mind stayed on freedom,
Ain't no harm to keep your mind stayed on freedom,
Ain't no harm to keep your mind stayed on freedom,
Hallelu, hallelu, hallelu, hallelu, hallelujah!

Walkin' and talkin' with my mind stayed on freedom . . .

Singin' and prayin' with my mind stayed on freedom . . .

Doin' the twist with my mind stayed on freedom . . .

Keep Your Eyes on the Prize

Paul and Silas, bound in jail,
had no money for to go their bail,
Keep your eyes on the prize, hold on.

CHORUS
Hold on, hold on,
Keep your eyes on the prize,
Hold on, hold on.

Paul and Silas begin to shout,
the jail door opened and they walked on out.
Keep your eyes on the prize, hold on.

Freedom's name is mighty sweet,
soon one day we're gonna meet.

Got my hand on the Gospel plow,
I wouldn't take nothing for my journey now.

The only chain that a man can stand,
is that chain of hand in hand.

The only thing we did wrong,
stayed in the wilderness a day too long.

But the one thing we did right,
was the day we started to fight.

We're gonna board that big Greyhound,
carryin' love from town to town.

We're gonna ride for civil rights,
we're gonna ride both black and white.

We've met jail and violence too,
but God's love has seen us through.

Haven't been to heaven but I've been told,
streets up there are paved with gold.

Source

"Guide My Feet While I Run This Race," "Woke Up This Morning with My Mind on Freedom," and "Keep Your Eyes on the Prize," adapted from traditional spirituals; reprinted in Guy Carawan and Candie Carawan, eds., *Sing for Freedom: The Story of the Civil Rights Movement Through Its Songs,* 83, 102, 111 (Bethlehem, Pa.: A Sing Out Publication, 1990).

Selected Bibliography

Carawan, Guy, and Candie, eds. *Sing for Freedom: The Story of the Civil Rights Movement Through Its Songs*. Bethlehem: A Sing Out Publication, 1990.

Sanger, Kerran L. *"When the Spirit Says Sing!": The Role of Freedom Songs in the Civil Rights Movement.* New York: Garland, 1995.

Seeger, Pete and Robert Reiser. *Everybody Says Freedom.* New York: W. W. Norton, 1990.

eight

To Praise Our Bridges

Fannie Lou Hamer (1917–1977) epitomized the bottom-up, grassroots nature of the black freedom struggle. In this excerpt from Hamer's oral history, she briefly described her childhood as a sharecropper, how she was fired from her job on the Marlow plantation because of her organizing efforts, and her beating at the hands of two sadistic white police officers.

Hamer was born into oppressive poverty in rural Mississippi, the youngest of twenty children. In 1962 she attended her first Student Nonviolent Coordinating Committee (SNCC) meeting; soon afterward she made the first of several attempts to try to register to vote. Later she began working for SNCC on voter registration. Hamer came to national attention in 1964 when she traveled to Atlantic City, New Jersey, along with delegates from the SNCC-organized Mississippi Freedom Democratic Party, to demand that they be seated at the Democratic National Convention. However, the party only offered them two token seats. In response, Hamer capably articulated the anger and frustration of the young activists, telling a national television audience that she was "sick and tired of being sick and tired" and that if the black delegates could not be seated, "I question America." Her 1977 funeral was crowded with luminaries from the civil rights movement, including Andrew Young, Stokely Carmichael, and Ella Baker.

I was born October sixth, nineteen and seventeen in Montgomery County, Mississippi. My parents moved to Sunflower County when I was two years old, to a plantation about four and a half miles from here, Mr. E. W. Brandon's plantation.

. . . My Parents were sharecroppers and they had a big family. Twenty children. Fourteen boys and six girls. I'm the twentieth child. All of us worked in the fields, of course, but we never did get anything out of sharecropping.

My life has been almost like my mother's was, because I married a man who sharecropped. We didn't have it easy and the only way we could ever make it through the winter was because Pap had a little juke joint and we made liquor. That was the only way we made it. I married in 1944 and stayed on the plantation until 1962 when I went down to the courthouse in Indianola to register to vote. That happened because I went to a mass meeting one night.

Until then I'd never heard of no mass meeting and I didn't know that a Negro could register and vote. Bob Moses.[1] Reggie Robinson,[2] Jim Bevel[3] and James Forman[4] were some of the SNCC[5] workers who ran that meeting. When they asked for those to raise their hands who'd go down to the courthouse the next day, I raised mine. Had it up as high as I could get it. I guess if I'd had any sense I'd a-been a little scared, but what was the point of being scared? The only thing they could do to me was kill me and it seemed like they'd been trying to do that a little bit at a time ever since I could remember.

Well, there was eighteen of us who went down to the courthouse that day and all of us were arrested. Police said the bus was painted the wrong color—said it was too yellow. After I got bailed out I went back to the plantation where Pap and I had lived for eighteen years. My oldest girl met me and told me that Mr. Marlow, the plantation owner, was mad and raising sand. He had heard that I had tried to register. That night he called on us and said. "We're not going to have this in Mississippi and you will have to withdraw. I am looking for your answer, yea or nay?" I just looked. He said, "I will give you until tomorrow morning. And if you don't withdraw you will have to leave. If you do go withdraw, it's only how I feel, you might still have to leave." So I left that same night. Pap had to stay on till work on the plantation was through. Ten days later they fired into Mrs. Tucker's house where I was staying. They also shot two girls at Mr. Sissel's.

That was a rough winter. I hadn't a chance to do any canning before I got kicked off, so didn't have hardly anything. I always can more than my family can use 'cause there's always people who don't have enough. That winter was bad, though. Pap couldn't get a job nowhere 'cause everybody knew he was my husband. We made it on through, though, and since then I just been trying to work and get our people organized.

I reckon the most horrible experience I've had was in June of 1963. I was arrested along with several others in Winona, Mississippi. That's in Montgomery County, the county where I was born. I was carried to a cell and locked up with Euvester Simpson. I began to hear the sound of licks, and I could hear people screaming. . . .

After then, the State Highway patrolmen came and carried me out of the cell into another cell where there were two Negro prisoners. The patrolman gave the first Negro a long blackjack that was heavy. It was loaded with something and they had me lay down on the bunk with my face down, and I was beat. I was beat by the first Negro till he gave out. Then the patrolman ordered the other man to take the blackjack and he began to beat. . . .

. . . After I got out of jail, half dead, I found out that Medgar Evers had been shot down in his own yard.

I've worked on voter registration here ever since I went to that first mass meeting. In 1964 we registered 63,000 black people from Mississippi into the Freedom Democratic Party. We formed our own party because the whites wouldn't even let us register. We decided to challenge the white Mississippi Democratic Party at the National Convention. We followed all the laws that the white people themselves made. We tried to attend the precinct meetings and they locked the doors on us or moved the meetings and that's against the laws they made for their ownselves. So we were the ones that held the real precinct meetings. At all these meetings across the state we elected our representatives to go to the National Democratic Convention in Atlantic City. But we learned the hard way that even though we had all the law and all the righteousness on our side—that white man is not going to give up his power to us.

We have to build our own power. We have to win every single political office we can, where we have a majority of black people.

The question for black people is not, when is the white man going to give us our rights, or when is he going to give us good education for our children, or when is he going to give us jobs—if the white man gives you anything—just remember when he gets ready he will take it right back. We have to take for ourselves.

Notes

1. Robert Moses (1935–), civil rights activist, educator.
2. Reggie Robinson, civil rights activist.
3. James Bevel, civil rights activist.
4. James Foreman (1928–), civil rights activist who is credited with giving the Student Nonviolent Coordinating Committee a firm organizational base.
5. Student Nonviolent Coordinating Committee, U.S. civil rights organization founded as a student companion to the Southern Christian Leadership Conference (SCLC). However, SNCC grew decidedly more militant than the SCLC in the late 1960s.

Source

Fannie Lou Hamer, "To Praise Our Bridges," in *To Praise Our Bridges: An Autobiography of Mrs. Fanny* reprinted in Clayborne Carson et al., eds., *Eyes on the Prize Civil Rights Reader: Documents, Speeches, and Firsthand Accounts from the Black Freedom Struggle, 1954–1990,* 176–79 (New York: Penguin Books, 1991). Used by permission of Arybie Rose, Fannie Lou Hamer Living Memorial Charitable Trust Fund, and the Hamer family.

Selected Bibliography

Crawford, Vicki L., Jacqueline Anne Rouse, and Barbara Woods, eds. *Women in the Civil Rights Movement: Trailblazers and Torchbearers, 1941–1965.* Brooklyn: Carlson, 1990.

Mills, Kay. *This Little Light of Mine: The Life of Fannie Lou Hamer.* New York: Dutton, 1993.

Rubel, David. *Fannie Lou Hamer: From Sharecropping to Politics.* Silver Burdett Press, 190.

nine

The Resistant Spirit

In this editorial reprinted from his newsletter *The Crusader*, Robert Williams (1925–1996) made the case that African Americans should be armed and willing to defend themselves in response to terrorist attacks from white supremacist groups such as the Ku Klux Klan. This was a cornerstone of Williams's strategy for advancing the black freedoms struggle. (He also helped to organize a self-defense network and debated nonviolence with Martin Luther King Jr. in *Liberation* magazine.) As editor, writer, grassroots leader, and radio disc jockey, Robert Williams was a legendary figure among many African American activists for his uncompromising militancy and his dramatic confrontations with white supremacy.

Williams was born in "Newtown," a poor, segregated neighborhood in Monroe, North Carolina. In 1955 he became president of the Monroe branch of the NAACP. He fled to Cuba in 1961 to avoid a bloody confrontation with a white mob, where he was befriended by Che Guevera and Fidel Castro. From there, he broadcast *Radio Free Dixie,* a weekly radio program that could be heard as far away as New York and Los Angeles. In 1962 he published *Negroes with Guns,* a book that was an important influence on Huey Newton and the Black Panther Party. Later he lived in China before finally returning to the

United States and working at the Center for Chinese Studies at the University of Michigan. Williams died in 1996.

The Resistant Spirit

Why do I speak from exile?

Because a Negro community in the South took up guns in self-defense against racist violence—and used them. I am held responsible for this action, that for the first time in history American Negroes have armed themselves as a group, to defend their homes, their wives, their children, in a situation where law and order had broken down, where the authorities could not, or rather would not, enforce their duty to protect Americans from a lawless mob. I accept this responsibility and am proud of it. I have asserted the right of Negroes to meet the violence of the Ku Klux Klan by armed self-defense—and have acted on it. It has always been an accepted right of Americans, as the history of our Western states proves, that where the law is unable, or unwilling, to enforce order, the citizens can, and must, act in self-defense against lawless violence. I believe this right holds for black Americans as well as whites.

Many people will remember that in the summer of 1957 the Ku Klux Klan made an armed raid on an Indian community in the South and were met with determined rifle fire from the Indians acting in self-defense. The nation approved of the action and there were widespread expressions of pleasure at the defeat of the Kluxers, who showed their courage by running away despite their armed superiority. What the nation doesn't know, because it has never been told, is that the Negro community in Monroe, North Carolina, had set the example two weeks before when we shot up an armed motorcade of the Ku Klux Klan, including two police cars, which had come to attack the home of Dr. Albert E. Perry, vice president of the Monroe chapter of the National Association for the Advancement of Colored People. The stand taken by our chapter resulted in the official re-affirmation by the NAACP of the right of self-defence. The Preamble to the resolution of the 50th Convention of the NAACP, New York City, July 1959, states: . . . "we do not deny, but reaffirm, the right of an individual and collective self-defense against unlawful assaults."

Because there has been much distortion of my position, I wish to make it clear that I do not advocate violence for its own sake, or for the sake of reprisals against whites. Nor am I against the passive resistance advocated by the Reverend Martin Luther King[1] and others. My only difference with Dr. King is that I believe in flexibility in the freedom struggle. This means that I believe in non-violent tactics where feasible and the mere fact that I have a Sit-In case pending before the U.S. Supreme Court bears this out.

Massive civil disobedience is a powerful weapon under civilized conditions, where the law safeguards the citizens' right of peaceful demonstrations. In civilized society the law serves as a deterrent against lawless forces that would destroy the democratic process. But where there is a breakdown of the law, the individual citizen has a right to protect his person, his family, his home and his property. To me this is so simple and proper that it is self-evident.

When an oppressed people show a willingness to defend themselves, the enemy, who is a moral weakling and coward is more willing to grant concessions and work for a respectable compromise. Psychologically, moreover, racists consider themselves superior beings and they are not willing to exchange their superior lives for our inferior ones. They are most vicious and violent when they can practice violence with impunity. This we have shown in Monroe. Moreover, when because of our self-defense there is a danger that the blood of whites may be spilled, the local authorities in the South suddenly enforce law and order when previously they had been complaisant toward lawless, racist violence. This too we have proven in Monroe. It is remarkable how easily and quickly state and local police control and disperse lawless mobs when the Negro is ready to defend himself with arms.

Furthermore, because of the international situation, the Federal Government does not want racial incidents which draw the attention of the world to the situation in the South. Negro self-defense draws such attention, and the Federal Government will be more willing to enforce law and order if the local authorities don't. When our people become fighters, our leaders will be able to sit at the conference table as equals, not dependent on the whim and the generosity of the oppressors. It will be to the best interests of both sides to negotiate just, honorable and lasting settlements.

The majority of white people in the United States have literally no idea of the violence with which Negroes in the South are treated daily—nay, hourly. This violence is deliberate, conscious, condoned by the authorities. It has gone on for centuries and is going on today, every day, unceasing and unremitting. It is our way of life. Negro existence in the South has been one long travail, steeped in terror and blood—our blood. The incidents which took place in Monroe, which I witnessed and which I suffered, will give some idea of the conditions in the South, such conditions that can no longer be borne.

Note

1. Martin Luther King Jr. (1929–1968), civil rights leader, minister.

Source

Robert F. Williams, "The Resistant Spirit: Why Do I Speak From Exile?" in the *Crusader,* a weekly newsletter published and edited by Robert F. Williams.

Selected Bibliography

Barksdale, Marcellus C. "Robert F. Williams and the Indigenous Civil Rights Movement in Monroe, North Carolina, 1961." *Journal of Negro History* 69 (spring 1984): 73–89.

Tyson, Timothy. *Radio Free Dixie: Robert F. Williams and the Roots of Black Power.* Chapel Hill: University of North Carolina Press, 1999.

ten

Life in Prison

In a letter written in April 1970 to his lawyer, George Jackson (1941–1971) offered a harrowing, behind-the-scenes account of Soledad Prison. Of particular interest is Jackson's analysis of the ways that prisoners in state penitentiaries continue to be brutalized, degraded, and deeply affected by their experience long after they have been released. A leading member of the Black Panther Party, Jackson was a celebrated author who died a martyr's death in San Quentin prison when he was shot by a prison guard.

Jackson was born in Chicago, Illinois. In 1960, after two prior convictions as a juvenile, he was handed a one-year-to-life prison sentence for robbing a gas station of seventy-one dollars. While in prison, Jackson avidly studied Marxism, political economy, philosophy, and race relations history. He also recruited black prisoners to the Black Panther Party from inside prison walls at Soledad and San Quentin. In 1970 he was charged with murdering a prison guard; his case quickly grew into a cause célèbre when black activists argued that the case was a political frame-up. Later that year, a collection of Jackson's prison letters, *Soledad Brother,* was published to great acclaim. In 1971 Jackson was gunned down by a tower guard during a prison riot, allegedly while making a mad dash to escape. However, Jackson's family and supporters have argued that the state's account is inconsistent and implausible.

April, 1970

Dear Fay,[1]

On the occasion of your and Senator Dymally's[2] tour and investigation into the affairs here at Soledad, I detected in the questions posed by your team a desire to isolate some rationale that would explain why racism exists at the prison with "particular prominence." Of course the subject was really too large to be dealt with in one tour and in the short time they allowed you, but it was a brave scene. My small but mighty mouthpiece, and the black establishment senator and his team, invading the state's maximum security row in the worst of its concentration camps. I think you are the first woman to be allowed to inspect these facilities. Thanks from all. The question was too large, however. It's tied into the question of why all these California prisons vary in character and flavor in general. It's tied into the larger question of why racism exists in this whole society with "particular prominence," tied into history. Out of it comes another question. Why do California joints produce more Bunchy Carters[3] and Eldridge Cleavers[4] than those over the rest of the country?

I understand your attempt to isolate the set of localized circumstances that give to this particular prison's problems of race is based on a desire to aid us right now, in the present crisis. There are some changes that could be made right now that would alleviate some of the pressures inside this and other prisons. But to get at the causes, you know, one would be forced to deal with questions at the very center of Amerikan political and economic life, at the core of the Amerikan historical experience. This prison didn't come to exist where it does just by happenstance. Those who inhabit it and feed off its existence are historical products. The great majority of Soledad pigs are southern migrants who do not want to work in the fields and farms of the area, who couldn't sell cars or insurance, and who couldn't tolerate the discipline of the army. And of course prisons attract sadists. After one concedes that racism is stamped unalterably into the present nature of Amerikan sociopolitical and economic life in general (the definition of fascism is: a police state wherein the political ascendancy is tied into the protects the interests of the upper class—characterized by militarism, racism, and imperialism), and concedes further that criminals and crime arise from material, economic, sociopolitical causes, we can then burn *all* of the criminology and penology libraries and direct our attention where it will do some good.

The logical place to begin any investigation into the problems of California prisons is with our "pigs are beautiful" Governor Reagan, radical reformer turned reactionary. For a real understanding of the failure of prison policies, it is senseless to continue to study the criminal. All of those who can afford to be honest know that the real victim, that poor, uneducated, disorganized man who finds himself a convicted criminal, is simply the end result of a long chain of corruption and mismanagement that starts with people like Reagan and his political appointees in Sacramento. After one investigates Reagan's character (what makes a turncoat) the next logical step in the inquiry would be a look into the biggest political prize of the state—the directorship of the Department of Corrections.

All other lines of inquiry would be like walking backward. You'll never see where you're going. You must begin with directors, assistant directors, adult authority boards, roving boards, supervisors, wardens, captains, and guards. You have to examine these people from director down to guard before you can logically examine their product. Add to this some concrete and steel, barbed wire, rifles, pistols, clubs, the tear gas that killed Brother Billingslea in San Quentin in February 1970, while he was locked in his cell, and the pick handles of Folsom, San Quentin, and Soledad.

To determine how men will behave once they enter the prison it is of first importance to know that prison. Men are brutalized by their environment—not the reverse.

I gave you a good example of this when I saw you last. Where I am presently being held, they never allow us to leave our cell without first handcuffing us and belting or chaining the cuffs to our waists. This is preceded always by a very thorough skin search. A force of a dozen or more pigs can be expected to invade the row at any time searching and destroying personal effects. The attitude of the staff toward the convicts is both defensive and hostile. Until the convict gives in completely it will continue to be so. By giving in, I mean prostrating oneself at their feet. Only then does their attitude alter itself to one of paternalistic condescension. Most convicts don't dig this kind of relationship (though there are some who do love it) with a group of individuals demonstrably inferior to the rest of the society in regard to education, culture, and sensitivity. Our cells are so far from the regular dining area that our food is always cold before we get it. Some days there is only one meal that can be called cooked. We *never* get anything but cold-cut sandwiches for lunch. There is no variety to the menu. The same things week after week. One is confined to his cell 23 1/2 hours a day. Overt racism exists unchecked. It is not a case of the pigs trying to stop the many racist attacks; they actively encourage them.

They are fighting upstairs right now. It's 11:10 A.M., June 11. No black is supposed to be on the tier upstairs with anyone but other blacks but—mistakes take place—and one or two blacks end up on the tier with 9 or 10 white convicts frustrated by the living conditions or openly working with the pigs. The whole ceiling is trembling. In hand-to-hand combat we always win; we lose sometimes if the pigs give them knives or zip guns. Lunch will be delayed today, the tear gas or whatever it is drifts down to sting my nose and eyes. Someone is hurt bad. I hear the meat wagon from the hospital being brought up. Pigs probably gave them some weapons. But I must be fair. Sometimes (not more often than necessary) they'll set up one of the Mexican or white convicts. He'll be one who has not been sufficiently racist in his attitudes. After the brothers (enraged by previous attacks) kick on this white convict whom the officials have set up, he'll fall right into line with the rest.

I was saying that the great majority of the people who live in this area of the state and seek their employment from this institution have overt racism as a *traditional* aspect of their characters. The only stops that regulate how far they will carry this thing come from the fear of losing employment here as a result of the outside pressures to control the violence. That is O Wing, Max (Maximum Security) Row Soledad—in part anyway.

Take an individual who has been in the general prison population for a time. Picture him as an average convict with the average twelve-year-old mentality, the nation's norm. He wants out, he wants a woman and a beer. Let's say this average convict is white and has just been caught attempting to escape. They may put him on Max Row. This is the worst thing that will ever happen to him. In the general population facility there are no chains and cuffs. TVs, radios, record players, civilian sweaters, keys to his own cell for daytime use, serve to keep his mind off his real problems. There is also a recreation yard with all sorts of balls and instruments to strike or thrust at. There is a gym. There are movies and a library well stocked with light fiction. And of course there is work, where for 2 or 3 cents an hour convicts here at Soledad make paper products, furniture, and clothing. Some people actually like this work since it does provide some money for the small things and helps them to get through their day—*without thinking* about their real problems.

Take an innocent con out of this general population setting (because a pig "thought" he may have seen him attempting a lock). Bring him to any part of O Wing (the worst part of the adjustment center of which Max Row is a part). He will be cuffed, chained, belted, pressured by the police who think that every convict should be an informer. He will be pressured by the white cons to join their racist brand of politics (they *all* go under the nickname "Hitler's Helpers"). If he is predisposed to help black he will be pushed away—by black. Three weeks is enough. The strongest hold out no more than a couple of weeks. There has been one white man only to go through this O Wing experience without losing his balance, without allowing himself to succumb to the madness of ribald, protrusive racism.

It destroys the logical processes of the mind, a man's thoughts become completely disorganized. The noise, madness streaming from every throat, frustrated sounds from the bars, metallic sounds from the walls, the steel trays, the iron beds bolted to the wall, the hollow sounds from a cast-iron sink or toilet.

The smells, the human waste thrown at us, unwashed bodies, the rotten food. When a white con leaves here he's ruined for life. No black leaves Max Row walking. Either he leaves on the meat wagon or he leaves crawling licking at the pig's feet.

Ironic, because one cannot get a parole to the outside prison directly from O Wing, Max Row. It's positively not done. The parole board won't even consider the Max Row case. So a man licks at the feet of the pig not for a release to the outside world but for the privilege of going upstairs to O Wing adjustment center. There the licking process must continue if a parole is the object. You can count on one hand the number of people who have been paroled to the streets from O Wing proper in all the years that the prison has existed. No one goes from O Wing, Max Row straight to the general prison population. To go from here to the outside world is unthinkable. A man *must* go from Max Row to the regular adjustment center facility upstairs. Then from there to the general prison population. Only then can he entertain thoughts of eventual release to the outside world.

One can understand the depression felt by an inmate on Max Row. He's fallen as far as he can into the social trap, relief is so distant that it is very easy for him to lose his holds. In two weeks that little average man who may have ended up on Max Row for *suspicion* of *attempted* escape is so brutalized, so completely without holds, that he will never heal again. It's worse than Vietnam.

He's dodging lead. He may be forced to fight a duel to the death with knives. If he doesn't sound and act more zealous than everyone else he will be challenged for not being loyal to his race and its politics, fascism. Some of these cons support the pigs' racism without shame, the others support it inadvertently by their own racism. The former are white, the latter black. But in here as on the street black racism is a forced *reaction*. A survival adaptation.

The picture that I have painted of Soledad's general population facility may have made it sound not too bad at all. That mistaken impression would result from the absence in my description of one more very important feature of the main line—terrorism. A frightening, petrifying diffusion of violence and intimidation is emitted from the offices of the warden and captain. How else could a small group of armed men be expected to hold and rule another much larger group except through *fear?*

We have a gym (inducement to throw away our energies with a ball instead of revolution). But if you walk into this gym with a cigarette burning, you're probably in trouble. There is a pig waiting to trap you. There's a sign "No Smoking." If you miss the sign, trouble. If you drop the cigarette to comply, trouble. The floor is regarded as something of a fire hazard (I'm not certain what the pretext is). There are no receptacles. The pig will pounce. You'll be told in no uncertain terms to scrape the cigarette from the floor with your hands. It builds from there. You have a gym but only certain things may be done and in specified ways. Since the rules change with the pigs' mood, it is really safer for a man to stay in his cell.

You have work with emoluments that range from nothing to three cents an hour! But once you accept the pay job in the prison's industrial sector you cannot get out without going through the bad conduct process. When workers are needed, it isn't a case of accepting a job in this area. You take the job or you're automatically refusing to work, even if you clearly stated that you would cooperate in other employment. The same atmosphere prevails on the recreation yard where any type of minor mistake could result not in merely a bad conduct report and placement in adjustment center, but death. A fistfight, a temporary, trivial loss of temper will bring a fusillade of bullets down on the darker of the two men fighting.

You can't begin to measure the bad feeling caused by the existence of one TV set shared by 140 men. Think! One TV, 140 men. If there is more than one channel, what's going to occur? In Soledad's TV rooms there has been murder, mayhem, and destruction of many TV sets.

The blacks occupy one side of the room and the whites and Mexicans the other. (Isn't it significant in some way that our numbers in prison are sufficient to justify the claiming of half of all these facilities?)

We have a side, they have a side. What does your imagination envisage out of a hypothetical situation where Nina Simone sings, Angela Davis speaks, and Jim Brown "splits" on one channel, while Merle Haggard yodels and begs for an ass kicking on another. The fight will follow immediately after some brother, who is less democratic than he is starved for beauty (we did vote but they're 60 to our 40), turns the station to see Angela Davis. What lines do you think the fighting will be along? Won't it be Angela and me against Merle Haggard?

But this situation is tolerable at least up to a point. It was worse. When I entered the joint on this offense, they had half and we had half, but our half was in the back.

In a case like the one just mentioned, the white convicts will start passing the word among themselves that all whites should be in the TV room to vote in the "Cadillac cowboy." The two groups polarize out of a situation created by whom? It's just like the outside. Nothing at all complicated about it. When people walk on each other, when disharmony is the norm, when organisms start falling apart it is the fault of those whose responsibility it is to govern. They're doing something wrong. They shouldn't have been trusted with the responsibility. And long-range political activity isn't going to help that man who will die tomorrow or tonight. The apologists recognize that these places are controlled by absolute terror, but they justify the pig's excesses with the argument that we exist outside the practice of any civilized codes of conduct. Since we are convicts rather than men, a bullet through the heart, summary execution for fistfighting or stepping across a line is not extreme or unsound at all. An official is allowed full range in violent means because a convict can be handled no other way.

Fay, have you ever considered what type of man is capable of handling absolute power. I mean how many would not abuse it? Is there any way of isolating or classifying generally who can be trusted with a gun and *absolute* discretion as to who he will kill? I've already mentioned that most of them are KKK types. The rest, all the rest, in general, are so stupid that they shouldn't be allowed to run their own bath. A *responsible* state government would have found a means of weeding out most of the savage types that are drawn to gunslinger jobs long ago. How did all these pigs get through?! Men who can barely read, write, or reason. How did they get through!!? You may as well give a baboon a gun and set him loose on us!! It's the same in here as on the streets out there. *Who* has loosed this thing on an already suffering people? The Reagans, Nixons, the men who have, who own. Investigate them!! There are no qualifications asked, no experience necessary. Any fool who falls in here and can sign his name might shoot me tomorrow from a position 30 feet above my head with an automatic military rifle!! He could be dead drunk. It could really be an accident (a million to one it won't be, however), but he'll be protected still. He won't even miss a day's wages.

The textbooks on criminology like to advance the idea that prisoners are mentally defective. There is only the merest suggestion that the system itself is at fault. Penologists regard prisons as asylums. Most policy is formulated in a bureau that operates under the heading Department of Corrections. But what can we say about these asylums since *none* of the inmates are ever cured. Since in every instance they are sent out of the prison more damaged physically and mentally than when they entered. Because that is the reality. Do you continue to investigate the inmate? Where does administrative responsibility begin? Perhaps the administration of the prison cannot be held accountable for every individual act of their charges, but when things fly apart along racial lines, when the breakdown can be traced so clearly to circumstances even beyond the control of the guards and administration, investigation of anything outside the tenets of the fascist system itself is futile.

Nothing has improved, nothing has changed in the weeks since your team was here. We're on the same course, the blacks are fast losing the last of their restraints. Growing numbers of blacks are openly passed over when paroles are considered. They have become aware that their only hope lies in resistance. They have learned that resistance is actually possible. The holds are beginning to slip away. Very few men imprisoned for economic crimes or even crimes of passion against the oppressor feel that they are really guilty. Most of today's black convicts have come to understand that they are the most abused victims of an unrighteous order. Up until now, the prospect of parole has kept us from confronting our captors with any real determination. But now with the living conditions of these places deteriorating, and with the sure knowledge that we are slated for destruction, we have been transformed into an implacable army of liberation. The shift to the revolutionary antiestablishment position that

Huey Newton, Eldridge Cleaver, and Bobby Seale projected as a solution to the problems of Amerika's black colonies has taken firm hold of these brothers' minds. They are now showing great interest in the thoughts of Mao Tse-tung, Nkrumah, Lenin, Marx, and the achievements of men like Che Guevara, Giap, and Uncle Ho.

Some people are going to get killed out of this situation that is growing. That is not a warning (or wishful thinking). I see it as an "unavoidable consequence" of placing and leaving control of our lives in the hands of men like Reagan.

These prisons have always borne a certain resemblance to Dachau and Buchenwald, places for the bad niggers, Mexicans, and poor whites. But the last ten years have brought an increase in the percentage of blacks for crimes that can *clearly* be traced to political-economic causes. There are still some blacks here who consider themselves criminals—but not many. Believe me, my friend, with the time and incentive that these brothers have to read, study, and think, you will find no class or category more aware, more embittered, desperate, or dedicated to the ultimate remedy—revolution. The most dedicated, the best of our kind—you'll find them in the Folsoms, San Quentins, and Soledads. They live like there was no tomorrow. And for most of them there isn't. Somewhere along the line they sensed this. Life on the installment plan, three years of prison, three months on parole; then back to start all over again, sometimes in the same cell. Parole officers have sent brothers back to the joint for selling newspapers (the Black Panther paper). Their official reason is "Failure to Maintain Gainful Employment," etc.

We're something like 40 to 42 percent of the prison population. Perhaps more, since I'm relying on material published by the media. The leadership of the black prison population now definitely identifies with Huey, Bobby, Angela, Eldridge, and antifascism. The savage repression of blacks which can be estimated by reading the obituary columns of the nation's dailies, Fred Hampton, etc., has not failed to register on the black inmates. The holds are fast being broken. Men who read Lenin, Fanon, and Che don't riot, "they mass," "they rage," they dig graves.

When John Clutchette was first accused of this murder he was proud, conscious, aware of his own worth but uncommitted to any specific remedial action. Review the process that they are sending this beautiful brother through now. It comes at the end of a long train of similar incidents in his prison life. Add to this all of the things he has witnessed happening to others of our group here. Comrade Fleeta spent eleven months here in O Wing for possessing photography taken from a newsweekly. It is such things that explain why California prisons produce more than their share of Bunchy Carters and Eldridge Cleavers.

Fay, there are only two types of blacks ever released from these places, the Carters and the broken men.

The broken men are so damaged that they will never again be suitable members of any sort of social unit. Everything that was still good when they entered the joint, anything inside of them that may have escaped the ruinous effects of black colonial existence, anything that may have been redeemable when they first entered the joint—is gone when they leave.

This camp[5] brings out the very best in brothers or destroys them entirely. But none are unaffected. None who leave here are normal. If I leave here alive, I'll leave nothing behind. They'll never count me among the broken men, but I can't say that I am normal either. I've been hungry too long. I've gotten angry too often. I've been lied to and insulted too many times. They've pushed me over the line from which there can be no retreat. I *know* that they will not be satisfied until they've pushed me out of this existence altogether. I've been the victim of so many racist attacks that I could never relax again. My reflexes will never be normal again. I'm like a dog that has gone through the K-9 process.

This is not the first attempt the institution (camp) has made to murder me. It is the most determined attempt, but not the first.

I look into myself at the close of every one of these pretrial days for any changes that may have taken place. I can still smile now, after ten years of blocking knife thrusts and pick handles, of faceless sadistic pigs, of anticipating and reacting for ten years, seven of them in Solitary. I can still smile sometimes, but by the time this thing is over I may not be a nice person. And I just lit my seventy-seventh cigarette of this 21-hour day. I'm going to lay down for two or three hours, perhaps I'll sleep . . .

Seize the Time.

Notes

1. Fay Stender, George Jackson's lawyer.
2. Mervyn Dymally (1926–), California state senator (1967–1973).
3. Alprentice "Bunchy" Carter (1942–1969), Black Panther leader shot on UCLA campus, January 17, 1969.
4. Eldridge Cleaver (1935–1998), Black Power militant, writer.
5. Jackson is using the imagery of a Nazi concentration camp and equating it with prisons operating in the United States.

Source

George Jackson, "Life in Prison," in *Soledad Brother: The Prison Letters of George Jackson,* 251–66 (New York: Coward-McCann, 1970).

Selected Bibliography

Davis, Angela. *If They Come in the Morning: Voices of Resistance.* New York: Third Press, 1971.

Jackson, George. *Blood in My Eye.* New York: Random House, 1972.

—— *Soledad Brother: The Prison Letters of George Jackson.* New York: Coward-McCann, 1970.

eleven

The Legacy of George Jackson

A prominent activist, writer, and public intellectual, Angela Davis (1944–) began teaching philosophy at University of California, Los Angeles, in 1969. Months later, UCLA learned of Davis's affiliation with the Communist party and fired her. She soon infuriated the UCLA board of regents with her support for the "Soledad Brothers," George Jackson and W. L. Nolen, inmates at Soledad prison who advocated Marxist, Fanonist revolution.

On August 7, 1970, George Jackson's younger brother attempted a prison rescue at a Marin County courtroom. Armed with Davis's firearms, Jonathan Jackson held up the courtroom, took hostages, and fled to an escape van. A police shootout ensured, leaving young Jonathan, a judge, and two inmates dead. Though never at the scene of the crime, Davis was charged with aiding a criminal conspiracy, placed on the FBI's "Ten Most Wanted List," and later imprisoned. The case spurred the international "Free Angela" movement.

On August 21, 1971, George Jackson was shot and killed by prison guards during an alleged escape. From her own prison cell, Davis issued a tribute to Jackson to be read at his memorial service at a West Oakland church. The letter was printed in the *Daily World*, August 25, 1971. Contending that Jackson was deliberately murdered by a prison guard for his revolutionary political commitments, Davis urged African Americans to pay tribute to Jackson's memory by redoubling their efforts and strengthening "the mass movement which alone is capable of freeing all our brothers and sisters in prisons."

Though California governor Ronald Reagan once vowed Davis would never teach in California again, Davis has held a number of teaching positions throughout the state. She is currently the professor of the history of consciousness at University of California, Santa Barbara.

An enemy bullet has once more brought grief and sadness to black people and to all who oppose racism and injustice and who love and fight for freedom. On Saturday, August 21, a San Quentin guard's sniper bullet executed George Jackson[1] and wiped out that last modicum of freedom with which he had persevered and resisted so fiercely for eleven years.

Though deprived so long of the freedom of movement enjoyed by his oppressors, even as he died, George was far more free than they. Like he lived, he died resisting. A field marshal of the Black Panther Party, George belongs to a very special breed of fallen black leaders, for his struggle was the most perilous.

He was recognized as a leader of the movement which sought to deepen the political consciousness of black and brown prisoners who constitute 30 to 40 percent of California's prison population. His impact on the community outside was and continues to be boundless. George's example of courage in the face of the specter of summary execution, his insights honed in the torment of seven years of solitary confinement, his perseverance in the face of overwhelming odds will continue to be a source of inspiration to all our sisters and brothers inside prison walls and outside.

His book, *Soledad Brother,*[2] a stirring chronicle of the development of the highest form of revolutionary fortitude and resistance, serves as a primer to captured brothers and sisters across the world. Equally important, his volume, perhaps more than any other, has given impetus to, and shaped the direction of, the growing support movement outside the prisons.

George, from behind seemingly impenetrable walls, has placed the issue of the prison struggle squarely on the agenda of the people's movement for revolutionary change. His book reveals the indivisible nature of the struggle on the outside of the prison system with the one inside.

Whether in prison or not, black and third-world people are the victims and targets of a common system of oppression and exploitation. Only the methods used are different.

The prevailing conditions of race and class exploitation invariably result in the captivity of a disproportionate number of black and third-world people. Our brothers and sisters are usually locked up for crimes they did not commit, or for crimes against property—crimes for which white youths receive prosecutorial, judicial, and penal leniency.

George himself was an eighteen-year-old man-child when he was sentenced to serve from one to life for a robbery involving seventy dollars—one to life—or eleven years' enslavement and sudden death. Through George's life and the lives of thousands of other brothers and sisters, the absolute necessity for extending the struggle of black and third-world people into the prison system itself becomes unmistakably clear.

The legacy left us by George and his dead brother, Jon, means that we must strengthen the mass movement which alone is capable of freeing all of our brothers and sisters in prisons. We know that the road to freedom has always been stalked by death. George knew that the price of his intense revolutionary commitment was having to live each day fighting off potential death blows. He had repeatedly seen death used as a standard reprisal for blacks who "stepped out of line." In January of 1970, he had seen his brother prisoners, Nolan, Miller and Edwards, warrantlessly and viciously murdered in the Soledad Prison yard. In *Soledad Brother,* George graphically told of the manner in which he had learned to thwart the many past attempts to murder him.

The dimensions of the task which lies ahead of us are clearer now, but the price of our new vision has been the death of two brilliant and brave revolutionaries, brothers in blood.

Associate Warden James Park promises us that the new wave of repression which has been unleashed within San Quentin will not halt with George's death. Rather, he has ushered in new terrorism by openly inviting guards to make a show of force and fully exhaust their vengeance on the prisoners themselves. Efforts to squelch revolutionary prison activity will not stop with one murder, Park tells us, but will continue until San Quentin is purged of all revolutionaries and every revolutionary thought.

The newspaper of George's party, the Black Panther Party, is hereafter forbidden within San Quentin's walls. "Old-fashioned prison methods," namely raw brutality, without its cosmetic dressings, is officially the new regime. Brothers Ruchell Magee, Fleeta Drumgo, and John Clutchette are identified targets; others in the so-called Adjustment Center who have taken sides are equally in danger.

Our responsibility extends to all these brothers upon whom war has been declared. The people must secure their safety and ultimately their freedom. Prison authorities seek only to cover up their own murderous crimes by attempting to initiate new frame-ups. These efforts must be swiftly and forcefully countered.

The Jackson family must be saluted. Their grief is deep. In little more than a year, two of their sons, George and Jonathan, were felled by fascist bullets. I express my love to Georgia and Robert Jackson, Penny, Frances and Delora.

For me, George's death has meant the loss of a comrade and revolutionary leader, but also the loss of an irretrievable love. This love is so agonizingly personal as to be indescribable. I can only say that in continuing to love him, I will try my best to express that love in the way he would have wanted—by reaffirming my determination to fight for the cause George died defending. With his example before me, my tears and grief are rage at the system responsible for his murder. He wrote his epitaph when he said:

"Hurl me into the next existence, the descent into hell won't turn me. I'll crawl back to dog his trail forever. They won't defeat my revenge, never, never. I'm part of a righteous people who anger slowly, but rage undammed. We'll gather at his door in such a number that the rumbling of our feet will make the earth tremble."

Notes

1. George Jackson (1941–1971), Black Panther, prisoner.
2. A collection of George Jackson's letters from prison, published as a book in 1970.

Source

Angela Davis, "The Legacy of George Jackson," *Daily World,* August 25, 1971; reprinted in Philip S. Foner, ed., *The Voice of Black America: Major Speeches by Negroes in the United States, 1797–1971,* 1191–94 (New York: Simon and Schuster, 1972).

Selected Bibliography

Aptheker, Bettina. *The Morning Breaks: The Trial of Angela Davis.* New York: International Publishers, 1975.

Davis, Angela. *Angela Davis: An Autobiography.* New York: International Publishers, 1988.

—— *The Angela Y. Davis Reader.* Edited by James Joy. Malden, Mass.: Blackwell, 1998.

—— ed. *If They Come in the Morning: Voices of Resistance.* New York: Third Press, 1971.

Jackson, George. *Blood In My Eye.* New York: Random House, 1972.

—— *Soledad Brother: The Prison Letters of George Jackson.* New York: Coward-McCann, 1970.

twelve

B-Block Days and Nightmares

A journalist and former Black Panther who was convicted of killing a police officer, Mumia Abu-Jamal (1954–) presently sits on death row in Pennsylvania. In his 1990 essay "B-Block Days and Nightmares," Abu-Jamal discussed the growing trend of prison riots in Pennsylvania prisons and argued that this was predictable behavior given the dramatic failure of officials to provide prisoners with even minimal standards of decency.

Born Wesley Cook on April 24, 1954, Abu-Jamal helped found the Philadelphia chapter of the Black Panther Party when he was only fifteen years old. On December 9, 1981, while he was moonlighting as a taxi driver, Abu-Jamal had an altercation with Daniel Faulkner, a Philadelphia police officer. When it was over, Abu Jamal lay bleeding from a gunshot wound to the chest, and Faulkner was dead. Although we will never know the full truth of what happened that night, it is clear that Abu-Jamal did not have a fair trial. Albert Sabo, the judge in the case, was a notorious racist, and in addition to several judicial irregularities that cast grave doubts over the prosecution's version of events, new witnesses have come forward to say that they saw another, unidentified man fleeing the scene of the crime. After Abu-Jamal was sentenced to death, a core of dedicated, grassroots activists have argued that his trial was a miscarriage of justice, and many human and civil rights organizations, such as Human Rights Watch, Amnesty International, and the NAACP Legal Defense Fund, have called for him to be given a new trial.

For whence did Dante take the materials of his hell but from our actual world? And yet he made a very proper hell of it.

—Arthur Schopenhauer, "Homo homini lupus"[1]

A shove, a slur, a flurry of punches, and an inmate is cuffed and hustled to the restricted housing unit (RHU), where a beating commences. Wrapped in the sweet, false escape of dreams, I hear the unmistakable sounds of meat being beaten by blackjack, of bootfalls, yells, curses; and it merges into the mind's moviemaking machine, evoking distant memories of some of the Philadelphia Police Department's greatest hits—on me.

"Get off that man, you fat, greasy, racist, redneck pig bitch muthafucka!"

My tired eyes snap open; the cracks, thuds, "oofs!" come in all too clear. Damn. No dream.

Anger simmers at this abrupt intrusion into one of life's last pleasures on B block—"home" of the state's largest death row—the all-too-brief respite of dreams.

Another dawn, another beating, another shackled inmate pummeled into the concrete by a squadron of guards.

This was late October 1989, the beginning of furious days and nights when prisoners throughout the state erupted in rage. The scene had been replayed a thousand gruesome times, leading to the modest demand that Huntingdon's administrators put an end to beatings of handcuffed prisoners in B block. The conflict it prompted was ultimately crushed by club and boot, by fire hose and taser electric stun gun.

As walls fall in the Eastern bloc, and as demonstrators rejoice over an end to state police brutality, walls climb ever higher in the West. Prisons in America jeer at the rhetoric of liberty espoused by those who now applaud Eastern Europe's glasnost. The U.S. Supreme Court has welded prison doors shut. It has cut off the rights of free press, religion, or civil rights. (See *Shabazz v. O'Lone*[2] and *Thronburgh v. Abbott*[3] for examples.) Indeed, in the late 1980s the term "prisoners' rights" became oxymoronic.

---

1. From *The World as Will and Representation* by Arthur Schopenhauer, translated by E. F. Payne; Dover Press, 1966.
2. *Estate of Shabazz v. O'Lone* 482 U.S. 342, 107, S.Ct. 2400 (1987).
3. *Thornburgh v. Abbott* 490 U.S. 401, 109,0 S.Ct. 1874 (1989).

The riots that rocked Pennsylvania prisons were flickering reminders of this reality: they were not riots of aggression but of desperation, of men pushed beyond fear, beyond reason, by the clang not only of prison gates but of the slamming of doors to the courthouse, their only legal recourse.

At Huntingdon's A block, fistfights between guard and prisoner evolved into a full-scale riot.

"Walk, you fuckin' nigger! I'm not gonna carry your black ass!"

"You black nigger motherfucker!" Grunts, thuds, groans, and curses assailed the ear as a bloody promenade of cuffed prisoners, many of them the A-block rebels, were dragged, flogged, and flayed down the dirty gray corridors of B block's death row en route to outdoor cages, man-sized dog pens of chain-link fence.

"Officer," a visiting guard barked to a Huntingdon regular, "stop dragging that man!"

"Captain," the local guard answered, her voice pitched higher by rage, "this fuckin' nigger don't wanna walk!"

The prisoners were herded into cages—most bloody, some in underwear, all wet, all exposed to the night air for hours.

Days later, Camp Hill in central Pennsylvania erupted, with prisoners taking hostages, assaulting some, and putting much of the forty-eight-year-old facility to the torch. For two nights the state's most overcrowded prison stole the public's attention. It took a battery of guards and state troopers to wrest back some semblance of control.

"Say 'I'm a nigger!' Say it!" the baton-wielders taunted black prisoners, beating those who refused, according to MOVE political prisoner and eyewitness Chuck Africa, who, although not a participant in the rebellion, was nonetheless beaten by guards.

Days after the fires of Camp Hill cooled, while convicts stood shackled together in the soot-covered yard, Philadelphia's Holmesburg burst into its worst riot in almost twenty years. At its peak, prisoners yelled, "Camp Hill! Camp Hill!"

Now, as costs for "Camp Hell"'s reconstruction soar (latest estimate: $21 million), and bills are introduced to cover county costs for riot prosecutions (to the tune of $1.25 million), one must question the predictably conventional wisdom attributing the days and nights of rage to simple overcrowding. To be sure, the system's "jam and cram" policy was a factor, but only one among many.

In 1987 the Governor's Interdepartmental Task Force on Corrections, composed of eight cabinet-level secretaries, issued a comprehensive report calling for changes in the state's prisons: reform of the misconduct system, institution of earnest (known as "good") time, liberalization of visiting procedures, release of death row prisoners from the RHU, and introduction of substantial education programs. The report, despite its pedigree, died a pauper's death, its biggest promises unfulfilled.

The naming of David Owens, Jr., as prison commissioner in 1987, the first black in the top post, may have heightened expectations, especially among blacks, who make up 56 percent of the prison population, but it also deepened frustrations. Prisoners saw no change in rule by predominantly rural whites over predominantly urban Afros and Latinos. Was it mere coincidence that rebellion burned hottest at Camp Hill, within sight of the commissioner's office?

Owens's tenure proved as short-lived as it was historic. Politicians protested when he proposed nominal compensation for prisoners who lost their property in the state's shakedown after the riots. Mindful of looming gubernatorial elections and of politicians angling to make Owens and the prisons an issue, Pennsylvania's first-term, socially conservative governor, Robert Casey, accepted Owens's resignation. With the state's captive population breaking twenty-one thousand, prisons overcrowded by 50 percent, and more than seven hundred convicts in the federal system, it's not surprising that there are now no takers for Owens's politically sensitive job.

Perhaps there is a certain symmetry in the circumstance of a prison system in crisis in the very state where the world's first true penitentiary arose, under Quaker influence. Two hundred years after initiation of this grim experiment, it is clear that it has failed.

One state representative (since criticized by her colleagues for making "irresponsible" statements) boldly told United Press International the simple hidden truth. Unless serious change is forthcoming, she predicted, "we are going to continue to have riots."

Repression is not change; it's the same old stuff.

Source

Mumia Abu-Jamal, "B-Block Days and Nightmares," *The Nation,* April 23, 1990, 559–60.

Selected Bibliography

Abu-Jamal, Mumia. *Death Blossoms.* Farmington, Penn.: Plough, 1997.

—— *Live from Death Row.* Reading, Mass.: Addison-Wesley, 1995.

Weinglass, Leonard. *Race for Justice.* Monroe, Maine: Common Courage, 1995.

chapter six

Work, Labor, and Economic Development

one

Work Songs

Historians and anthropologists alike have noted the important role that work songs played in the lives of slaves. Often times, the lyrics to work songs concealed religious messages or themes of resistance. In other instances, slaves accompanied their work songs with hand clapping and stomping, call and response, and improvisation in order to soften the impact of the harsh work routines that slaves were usually forced to submit to. Long after the end of slavery, many of these songs continued to be passed on and revised by sharecroppers and black prisoners. The selections reprinted here—"Pick a Bale of Cotton," "Go Down, Old Hannah," and "Can't You Line It—are three such songs.

Pick a Bale of Cotton

Jump down, turn around to pick a bale of cotton.
Jump down, turn around, pick a bale a day.

Jump down, turn around to pick a bale of cotton.
Jump down, turn around, pick a bale a day.

Oh, Lordy, pick a bale of cotton!
Oh, Lordy, pick a bale a day!

Me and my gal can pick a bale of cotton.
Me and my gal can pick a bale a day. . . .
Me and my wife can pick a bale of cotton,
Me and my wife can pick a bale a day. . . .

Me and my friend can pick a bale of cotton,
Me and my friend can pick a bale a day. . . .

Me and my poppa can pick a bale of cotton,
Me and my poppa can pick a bale a day.
Oh, Lordy, pick a bale of cotton!
Oh, Lordy, pick a bale a day!

Go Down, Old Hannah[1]

Go down, old Hannah,
Won't you rise no more?
Go down, old Hannah,
Won't you rise no more?

Lawd, if you rise,
Bring judgment on.
Lawd, if you rise,
Bring judgment on.

Oh, did you hear
What the captain said?
Oh, did you hear
What the captain said?

That if you work
He'll treat you well,

1. The sun.

And if you don't
He'll give you hell.

Oh, go down, old Hannah,
Won't you rise no more?
Won't you go down, old Hannah,
Won't you rise no more?

Oh, long-time man,
Hold up your head.
Well, you may get a pardon
And you may drop dead.

Lawdy, nobody feels sorry
For the life-time man.
Nobody feels sorry
For the life-time man.

Can't You Line It?[2]

1. When I get in Illinois
I'm going to spread the news about the Florida boys.

CHORUS:
(All men straining at rail in concert.)
Shove it over! Hey, hey, can't you line it?
(Shaking rail.) Ah, shack-a-lack-a-lack-a-lack-a-lack-a-lack.
(Grunt as they move rail.) Can't you move it? Hey, hey, can't you try.

2. Tell what the hobo told the bum,
If you get any corn-bread save me some.

CHORUS

3. A nickle's worth of bacon, and a dime's worth of lard,
I would buy more but the time's too hard.

2. This song is common to the railroad camps. It is suited to the "lining" rhythm. That is, it fits the straining of the men at the lining bars as the rail is placed in position to be spiked down [Zora Neale Hurston's note].

CHORUS

4. Wonder what's the matter with the walking boss,
It's done five-thirty and he won't knock off.

CHORUS

5. I ast my Cap'n what's the time of day,
He got mad and throwed his watch away.

CHORUS

6. Cap'n got a pistol and he try to play bad,
But I'm going to take it if he make me mad.

CHORUS

7. Cap'n got a burner[3] I'd like to have,
A 32:20 with a shiny barrel.

CHORUS

8. De Cap'n can't read, de Cap'n can't write,
How do he know that the time is right?

CHORUS

9. Me and my buddy and two three more,
Going to ramshack Georgy everywhere we go.

CHORUS

10. Here come a woman walking 'cross the field,
Her mouth exhausting like an automobile.

Source

"Pick a Bale of Cotton" and "Go Down, Old Hannah," traditional; reprinted in Henry Louis Gates and Nellie McKay, eds., *The Norton Anthology of African-American Literature,* 52–53 (New York: W. W. Norton, 1997).

---

3. Gun [Hurston's note].

Selected Bibliography

Floyd, Samuel A. *The Power of Black Music: Interpreting Its History from Africa to the United States*. New York: Oxford University Press, 1995.

Joyner, Charles W. *Shared Traditions: Southern History and Folk Culture*. Urbana: University of Illinois Press, 1999.

Oliver, Paul. *The Story of the Blues*. Boston: Northeastern University Press, 1998.

two

Industrial Education for the Negro

In the essay reprinted here, Thomas McCants Stewart (1854–1923) described a visit he made to the Hampton Institute in 1883. Founded in 1868 by Samuel Chapman Armstrong, the Hampton Institute, located in Hampton, Virginia, was one of the first black colleges to promote the kind of industrial education and vocational training that was later favored by liberal philanthropists and championed by Booker T. Washington.

A lawyer, minister, and political activist, Stewart was born a free person in Charleston, South Carolina. He studied at Howard University and Princeton Theological Seminary before moving to Liberia in 1883, where he was on the faculty at Liberia (West Africa) College. However, Stewart continued to study African American educational institutions in the United States and wrote articles for T. Thomas Fortune's *New York Age*. Stewart later lived in Honolulu and England, where he founded the Pan-Africanist African Progress Union in 1906.

The day after my arrival, I was put into the hands of an excellent New England gentleman, who was to show me through the Institute. He took me first to the barn, a large and substantial building in which are stored the products of the farm, and in which the stock have their shelter. We ascended a winding staircase, reached the top, and looked down upon the Institute grounds with their wide shell-paved walls, grassplots, flower-beds, orchards, groves and many buildings—the whole full of life, and giving evidence of abundant prosperity, and surrounded by a beautiful and charming country.

We went into the shoe-making department. It is in the upper part of a two-story brick building. On the first floor the harness-making department is located. We were told that Frederick Douglass[1] has his harness made here. One certainly gets good material and honest work; and reasonable prices are charged. In the shoe department several Indian boys and youths were at work. There were also three or four colored boys. They make annually for the United States government two thousand pairs of shoes for the Indians. They also look after outside orders, and do all the repairing, etc., of boots and shoes for the faculty, officers, and students—making fully five thousand pairs of shoes a year, if we include the repairing in this estimate. At the head of this department is a practical shoemaker from Boston. Each department has a practical man at its head. We visited, not all the first day, the blacksmith, wheelwright and tin shops, and looked through the printing office, and the knitting-room, in which young men are engaged manufacturing thousands of mittens annually for a firm in Boston. These two departments are in a commodious brick edifice, called the "Stone Building." It is the gift of Mrs. Valeria Stone.

One of the most interesting departments is located also in the "Stone Building"—the sewing-room. In it are nearly a score, perhaps more, of cheerful, busy girls. The rapid ticking of the machine is heard, and the merry laugh followed by gentle whispers gives life to the room. These young girls are the future wives and mothers; and the large majority of them will be married to poor men. In the kitchen, the laundry, and the sewing-room, they are acquiring a knowledge and habits of industry that will save their husbands' pennies, and thus keep them from living from hand to mouth, making an everlasting struggle to save their nose from the grindstone. In the schoolroom, they are gathering up those intellectual treasures, which will make them in a double sense helpmeets unto their husbands.

Standing in the carpenter and paint shops, and in the saw mill, and seeing Negro youths engaged in the most delicate kind of work, learning valuable and useful trades, I could not help from feeling that this is an excellent institution, and that I would like to have my boys spend three years here, from fourteen to seventeen, grow strong in the love for work, and educated to feel the dignity of labor, and get a trade: then if they have the capacity and desire to qualify for a "top round in the ladder," for leadership in the "world's broad field of battle," it will be time enough to think of Harvard and Yale and Edinburgh, or perhaps similar African institutions.

Mr. George H. Corliss, of Rhode Island, presented to the school in 1879 a sixty-horse power Corliss engine. Soon after Mr. C.P. Huntington, of the Missouri & Pacific R.R., gave a saw mill, and as a result of these gifts large industrial operations were begun. The saw mill is certainly an extensive enterprise. Logs are brought up from the Carolinas, and boards are sawn out, and in the turning department fancy fixtures are made for houses, piazzas, etc.

There are two farms. The Normal School farm, and the Hemenway farm, which is four miles from the Institute. On the former seventy tons of hay and about one hundred and twenty tons of ensilaged fodder-corn were raised last year, besides potatoes, corn, rye, oats, asparagus, and early vegetables. Five hundred thousand bricks were also made. The Hemenway farm, of five hundred acres, is in charge of a graduate and his wife. Its receipts reach nearly three thousand dollars a year, and the farm promises to do invaluable service in time towards sustaining this gigantic work. All of the industries do not pay. For example, the deficit in the printing office last year was about seven hundred dollars. This is due to the employment and training of student labor. The primary aim is not the making of money but the advancement of the student. After they learn, they are good, profitable workmen; but they then leave the Institute to engage in the outside world in the battle of life. On the farm is a large number of stock, milch cows and calves, beef cattle, horses and colts, mules, oxen, sheep and hogs—in all nearly five hundred heads.

In these various industries, the farm, saw mill, machine shop, knitting, carpentering, harness making, tinsmithing, blacksmithing, shoe-making, wheelwrighting, tailoring, sewing, printing, etc., over five hundred students are engaged in 1883. They earned over thirty thousand dollars—an average of seventy dollars each. There is no question about the fact that this is a "beehive" into which a bee can enter, if accepted, with nothing but his soul and his muscle, and get a good education!

Note

1. Frederick Douglass (1817–1895), prominent African American abolitionist.

Source

Stewart, Thomas McCants, "Industrial Education for the Negro" (1884; reprinted in Leslie H. Fischel Jr. and Benjamin Quarles, eds., *The Negro American: A Documentary History,* 319–21 [New York: William & Morrow, 1967]).

Selected Bibliography

Broussard, Albert S. *African-American Odyssey: The Stewarts, 1853–1963.* Lawrence, Kans.: University Press of Kansas, 1998.

Peabody, Francis Greenwood. *Education For Life: The Story of Hampton Institute, Told in Connection with the Fiftieth Anniversary of the Foundation of the School.* College Park, Md.: McGrath, 1969.

Schall, Keith L., ed. *Stony the Road: Chapters in the History of Hampton Institute.* Charlottesville: University Press of Virginia, 1977.

Spivey, Donald. *Schooling for the New Slavery: Black Industrial Education, 1868–1915.* Westport, Conn.: Greenwood Press, 1978.

three

Harvest Song

Jean Toomer (1894–1967) was among the most celebrated writers of his day. The poem "Harvest Song" is a lyrical and abstract piece that first appeared in *Cane* (1923)—a book that is sometimes used to signify the advent of the literary movement known as the Harlem Renaissance. In this poem, Toomer appropriated the voice of a black farmer, forced to confront the pain and hardships of his life.

Born in Washington, D.C., Toomer attended five schools of higher education without graduating from any of them. He then labored through a variety of odd jobs before finally taking a position as principal of Sparta Agriculture and Industrial Institute, a small school in rural Georgia. His experiences in several different racial climates deeply influenced his finest work, *Cane*—a collection of lyrical short stories, poems, vignettes, and a play that combine to portray the black folk heritage in the South. Although *Cane* received an enormous amount of critical acclaim, none of his other writings reached the same stature. Many believe that this was a fallout of Toomer's change in topics, from a preoccupation with racial issues to his quest for spiritual enlightenment and his conversion to doctrines of the Russian mystic Georgi Gurdjieff. Whatever the case, Toomer continued to write until his death in 1967.

I am a reaper whose muscles set at sundown. All my oats are cradled.
But I am too chilled, and too fatigued to bind them. And I hunger.

I crack a grain between my teeth. I do not taste it.
I have been in the fields all day. My throat is dry. I hunger.

My eyes are caked with dust of oatfields at harvest-time.
I am a blind man who stares across the hills, seeking stack'd fields of other harvesters.

It would be good to see them . . . crook'd, split, and iron-ring'd handles of the scythes. It would be good to see them, dust-caked and blind. I hunger.

(Dusk is a strange fear'd sheath their blades are dull'd in.)
My throat is dry. And should I call, a cracked grain like the oats . . . eoho—

I fear to call. What should they hear me, and offer me their grain, oats, or wheat, or corn? I have been in the fields all day. I fear I could not taste it. I fear knowledge of my hunger.

My ears are caked with dust of oatfields at harvest-time.
I am a deaf man who strains to hear the calls of other harvesters whose throats are also dry.

It would be good to hear their songs . . . reapers of the sweet-stalk'd cane, cutters of the corn . . . even though their throats cracked and the strangeness of their voices deafened me.

I hunger. My throat is dry. Now that the sun has set and I am chilled, I fear to call. (Eoho, my brothers!)

I am a reaper. (Eoho!) All my oats are cradled. But I am too fatigued to bind them. And I hunger. I crack a grain. It has no taste to it. My throat is dry . . .

O my brothers, I beat my palms, still soft, against the stubble of my harvesting. (You beat your soft palms, too.) My pain is sweet. Sweeter than the oats or wheat or corn. It will not bring me knowledge of my hunger.

Source

Jean Toomer, "Harvest Song," in *Cane* (New York: Liveright, 1923), 69.

Selected Bibliography

Benson, Brian and Mabel M. Dillard. *Jean Toomer.* Boston: Twayne Publishers, 1980.

Byrd, Rudolph P. *Jean Toomer and the Writers of the Harlem Renaissance: Was He There with Them?* New York: Garland, 1989.

McKay, Nellie Y. *Jean Toomer, Artist: A Study of His Literary Life and Work, 1894–1936.* Chapel Hill: University of North Carolina Press, 1984.

O'Daniel, Therman B., ed. *Jean Toomer: A Critical Evaluation.* Washington, D.C.: Howard University Press, 1988.

four

Song to a Negro Wash-woman

A leading light of the Harlem Renaissance, Langston Hughes (1902–1967) was black America's most popular poet, and today he is often remembered as "the Shakespeare of Harlem." In his 1925 poem "Song to a Negro Wash-woman," Hughes uplifted the ideal of the black worker and foreshadowed his interest in socialism, which accelerated during the Great Depression.

Hughes studied writing at Columbia University, and although he was never very happy there, the experience helped him to sharpen his mastery of black working-class vernacular and African American musical forms (mainly blues and jazz). He rose to prominence with his first collection of poetry, *Weary Blues* (1926), although he also wrote short stories, novels, a weekly newspaper column for the *Chicago Defender,* and an autobiography. It is often pointed out that early in his career, Hughes's work primarily centered on the daily lives of African Americans, whereas in the wake of the Great Depression, his writing became more overtly political.

Oh, wash-woman,
Arms elbow-deep in white suds,
Soul washed clean,
Clothes washed clean,
I have many songs to sing you
Could I but find the words.

Was it four o'clock or six o'clock on a winter afternoon, I saw you wringing out the last shirt in Miss White Lady's kitchen? Was it four o'clock or six o'clock? I don't remember.

But I know, at seven one spring morning you were on Vermont Street with a bundle in your arms going to wash clothes.

And I know I've seen you in the New York subway in the late afternoon coming home from washing clothes.

Yes, I know you, wash-woman.

I know how you send your children to school, and high-school, and even college.
I know how you work to help your man when times are hard.
I know how you build your house up from the washtub and call it home.
And how you raise your churches from white suds for the service of the Holy God.

I've seen you singing, wash-woman. Out in the backyard garden under the apple trees, singing, hanging white clothes on long lines in the sunshine.
And I've seen you in church on Sunday morning singing, praising your Jesus because some day you're going to sit on the right hand side of the Son of God and forget you ever were a wash-woman.
And the aching back and the bundles of clothes will be unremembered then.

Yes, I've seen you singing.

So for you,
O singing wash-woman,
For you, singing little brown woman,
Singing strong black woman,

Singing tall yellow woman,
Arms deep in white suds,
Soul washed clean,
Clothes washed clean,
For you I have
Many songs to sing
Could I but find the words.

Source

Langston Hughes, "Song to a Negro Wash-Woman," in Richard A. Long and Eugenia W. Collier, eds., *Afro-American Writing: An Anthology of Prose and Poetry*, 371–72 (New York: New York University Press, 1972).

Selected Bibliography

Dickinson, Donald C. *A Bio-Bibliography of Langston Hughes, 1902–1967*. Hamden, Conn.: Archon Books, 1967.

Gates, Henry Louis and K. A. Appiah, eds. *Langston Hughes: Critical Perspectives Past and Present*. New York: Amistad (distributed by Penguin, USA), 1998.

Huggins, Nathan I. *Harlem Renaissance*. New York: Oxford University Press, 1971.

Lewis, David Levering. *When Harlem Was in Vogue*. New York: Knopf, 1981.

Trotman, James C., ed. *Langston Hughes: The Man, His Art, and His Continuing Influence*. New York: Garland, 1995.

five

Why Should We March?

A. Philip Randolph (1889–1979) was a controversial civil rights activist for most of his life. He wrote the spirited essay "Why Should We March" in 1942, as he was attempting to organize a march on Washington in response to antiblack discrimination in defense industries. After large numbers of African Americans demonstrated their enthusiasm for a massive march that would have proved embarrassing to white officials in Washington, President Franklin D. Roosevelt established a Fair Employment Practice Committee, and the march was called off.

Born in Florida and educated in New York, Randolph earned his first radical credentials when he helped found the Brotherhood of Sleeping Car Porters in 1925. Later, he immersed himself in trade union politics and advocated the type of nonviolent, direct action protests that were commonly used by civil rights demonstrators in the 1950s. In 1940 he became a member of the NAACP board of directors, and in 1946 he became the NAACP's vice president. In 1955 he was elected vice president of the AFL-CIO.

Though I have found no Negroes who want to see the United Nations lose this war, I have found many who, before the war ends, want to see the stuffing knocked out of white supremacy and of empire over subject peoples. American Negroes, involved as we are in the general issues of the conflict, are confronted not with a choice but with the challenge both to win democracy for ourselves at home and to help win the war for democracy the world over.

There is no escape from the horns of this dilemma. There ought not to be escape. For if the war for democracy is not won abroad, the fight for democracy cannot be won at home. If this war cannot be won for the white peoples, it will not be won for the darker races.

Conversely, if freedom and equality are not vouchsafed the peoples of color, the war for democracy will not be won. Unless this doublebarreled thesis is accepted and applied, the darker races will never wholeheartedly fight for the victory of the United Nations. That is why those familiar with the thinking of the American Negro have sensed his lack of enthusiasm, whether among the educated or uneducated, rich or poor, professional or non-professional, religious or secular, rural or urban, north, south, east or west.

That is why questions are being raised by Negroes in church, labor union and fraternal society; in poolroom, barbershop, schoolroom, hospital, hairdressing parlor; on college campus, railroad, and bus. One can hear such questions asked as these: What have Negroes to fight for? What's the difference between Hitler[1] and that "cracker" Talmadge[2] of Georgia? Why has a man got to be Jim-Crowed[3] to die for democracy? If you haven't got democracy yourself, how can you carry it to somebody else?

What are the reasons for this state of mind? The answer is: discrimination, segregation, Jim Crow. Witness the navy, the army, the air corps; and also government services at Washington. In many parts of the South, Negroes in Uncle Sam's uniform are being put upon, mobbed, sometimes even shot down by civilian and military police, and on occasion lynched. Vested political interests in race prejudice are so deeply entrenched that to them winning the war against Hitler is secondary to preventing Negroes from winning democracy for themselves. This is worth many divisions to Hitler and Hirohito.[4] While labor, business, and farm are subjected to ceilings and floors and not allowed to carry on as usual, these interests trade in the dangerous business of race hate as usual.

When the defense program began and billions of the taxpayers' money were appropriated for guns, ships, tanks and bombs, Negroes presented themselves for work only to be given the cold shoulder. North as well as South, and despite their qualifications, Negroes were denied skilled employment. Not until their wrath and indignation took the form of a proposed protest march on Washington, scheduled for July 1, 1941, did things begin to move in the form of defense jobs for Negroes. The march was postponed by the timely issuance (June 25, 1941) of the famous Executive Order No. 8802[5] by President Roosevelt. But this order and the President's Committee on Fair Employment Practice, established thereunder, have as yet only scratched the surface by way of eliminating discriminations on account of race or color in war industry.

Both management and labor unions in too many places and in too many ways are still drawing the color line.

It is to meet this situation squarely with direct action that the March on Washington Movement launched its present program of protest mass meetings. Twenty thousand were in attendance at Madison Square Garden, June 16; sixteen thousand in the Coliseum in Chicago, June 26; nine thousand in the City Auditorium of St. Louis, August 14. Meetings of such magnitude were unprecedented among Negroes. The vast throngs were drawn from all walks and levels of Negro life—businessmen, teachers, laundry workers, Pullman porters, waiters, and red caps; preachers, crapshooters, and social workers; jitterbugs, and Ph.D.'s. They came and sat in silence, thinking, applauding only when they considered the truth was told, when they felt strongly that something was going to be done about it.

The March on Washington Movement is essentially a movement of the people. It is all Negro and pro-Negro, but not for that reason anti-white or anti-semitic, or anti-Catholic, or anti-foreign, or anti-labor. Its major weapon is the non-violent demonstration of Negro mass power. Negro leadership has united back of its drive for jobs and justice. "Whether Negroes should march on Washington, and if so, when?" will be the focus of a forthcoming national conference. For the plan of a protest march has not been abandoned. Its purpose would be to demonstrate that American Negroes are in deadly earnest, and all out for their full rights. No power on earth can cause them today to abandon their fight to wipe out every vestige of second class citizenship and the dual standards that plague them.

A community is democratic only when the humblest and weakest person can enjoy the highest civil, economic, and social rights that the biggest and most powerful possess. To trample on these rights of both Negroes and poor whites is such a commonplace in the South that it takes readily to anti-social, anti-labor, anti-Semitic and anti-Catholic propaganda. It was because of laxness in enforcing the Weimar constitution in republican Germany that Nazism[6] made headway. Oppression of the Negroes in the United States, like suppression of the Jews in Germany, may open the way for a fascist dictatorship.

By fighting for their rights now, American Negroes are helping to make America a moral and spiritual arsenal of democracy. Their fight against the poll tax, against lynch law, segregation, and Jim Crow, their fight for economic, political, and social equality, thus becomes part of the global war for freedom.

Program of the March on Washington Movement

1. We demand, in the interest of national unity, the abrogation of every law which makes a distinction in treatment between citizens based on religion, creed, color, or national origin. This means an end to Jim Crow in education, in housing, in transportation and in every other social, economic, and

political privilege; and especially, we demand, in the capital of the nation, an end to all segregation in public places and in public institutions.

2. We demand legislation to enforce the Fifth and Fourteenth Amendments guaranteeing that no person shall be deprived of life, liberty or property without due process of law, so that the full weight of the national government may be used for the protection of life and thereby may end the disgrace of lynching.

3. We demand the enforcement of the Fourteenth and Fifteenth Amendments and the enactment of the Pepper Poll Tax bill so that all barriers in the exercise of the suffrage are eliminated.

4. We demand the abolition of segregation and discrimination in the army, navy, marine corps, air corps, and all other branches of national defense.

5. We demand an end to discrimination in jobs and job training. Further, we demand that the F.E.P.C.[7] be made a permanent administrative agency of the U.S. Government and that it be given power to enforce its decisions based on its findings.

6. We demand that federal funds be withheld from any agency which practices discrimination in the use of such funds.

7. We demand colored and minority group representation on all administrative agencies so that these groups may have recognition of their democratic right to participate in formulating policies.

8. We demand representation for the colored and minority racial groups on all missions, political and technical, which will be sent to the peace conference so that the interests of all people everywhere may be fully recognized and justly provided for in the post-war settlement.

Notes

1. Adolf Hitler (1889–1945), founder and leader of the Nazi Party in Germany, who murdered millions of Jews in the name of white supremacy.
2. Eugene Talmadge (1884–1946), governor of Georgia.
3. Jim Crow laws, named for an antebellum minstrel character, were statutes that emerged in Southern states in the late nineteenth century and that created a racial caste system.
4. Emperor Hirohito (1901–1989), emperor of Japan (1926–1989).
5. Outlawed racially discriminatory hiring policies in defense plants.
6. Racist ideology of the National Socialist and German Workers Party, which governed in Germany under Adolf Hitler from 1933 to 1945.
7. Fair Employment Practices Commission, established in 1941 by President Franklin D. Roosevelt to redress discrimination in the federal government's employment practices.

Source

A. Philip Randolph, "Why Should We March?" *Survey Graphic* 31 (November 1942): 488–89.

Selected Bibliography

Anderson, Jervis. *A. Philip Randolph: A Biographical Portrait.* New York: Harcourt Brace Jovanovich, 1973.

Harris, William Hamilton. *Keeping the Faith: A Philip Randolph, Milton P. Webster, and the Brotherhood of Sleeping Car Porters, 1925–1937.* Urbana: University of Illinois Press, 1977.

Pfeffer, Paula F. *A. Philip Randolph, Pioneer of the Civil Rights Movement.* Baton Rouge: Louisiana State University Press, 1990.

Santino, Jack. *Miles of Smiles, Years of Struggle: Stories of Black Pullman Porters.* Urbana: University of Illinois Press, 1989.

Wintz, Cary D., ed. *African American Political Thought, 1890–1930: Washington, DuBois, Garvey, and Randolph.* Armonk, N.Y.: M. E. Sharpe, 1996.

six

Black Boy: A Record of Childhood and Youth

Richard Wright (1908–1960) was an internationally known writer. This excerpt from *Black Boy,* Wright's celebrated and harrowing autobiography, reveals the cruel and vindictive treatment that African Americans sometimes received when they fell into competition with white workers in the deep South.

Born on a plantation in Roxie, Mississippi, Wright suffered through a difficult childhood and moved frequently. Still, he was a topflight student and a devoted reader, and he published his first story in a local newspaper when he was in ninth grade. After living in Memphis, Tennessee, and in Chicago, Wright published *Uncle Tom's Children* (1938) and *Native Son* (1940), a famous sociological novel based on the character Bigger Thomas, a young black man who was turned into a hardened, nihilistic criminal through his experiences with racism and poverty. Bitterly disappointed with continued racism in the United States and an antiradical backlash, Wright exiled himself to Paris in 1947. While in France, he became increasingly involved in existential writings and in the Pan-Africanist and anticolonial political movements. He died of a heart attack in 1960.

My life now depended upon my finding work, and I was so anxious that I accepted the first offer, a job as a porter in a clothing store selling cheap goods to

Negroes on credit. The shop was always crowded with black men and women pawing over cheap suits and dresses. And they paid whatever price the white man asked. The boss, his son, and the clerk treated the Negroes with open contempt, pushing, kicking, or slapping them. No matter how often I witnessed it, I could not get used to it. How can they accept it? I asked myself. I kept on edge, trying to stifle my feelings and never quite succeeding, a prey to guilt and fear because I felt that the boss suspected that I resented what I saw.

One morning, while I was polishing brass our front, the boss and his son drove up in their car. A frightened black woman sat between them. They got out and half dragged and half kicked the woman into the store. White people passed and looked on without expression. A white policeman watched from the corner, twirling his night stick, but he made no move. I watched out of the corner of my eyes, but I never slackened the strokes of my chamois upon the brass. After a moment or two I heard shrill screams coming from the rear room of the store; later the woman stumbled out, bleeding, crying holding her stomach, her clothing torn. When she reached the sidewalk, the policeman met her, grabbed her, accused her of being drunk, called a patrol wagon and carted her away.

When I went to the rear of the store, the boss and his son were washing their hands at the sink. They looked at me and laughed uneasily. The floor was bloody, strewn with wisps of hair and clothing. My face must have reflected my shock, for the boss slapped me reassuringly on the back.

"Boy, that's what we do to niggers when they don't pay their bills," he said.

His son looked at me and grinned.

"Here, hava cigarette." he said.

Not knowing what to do, I took it. He lit his and held the match for me. This was a gesture of kindness, indicating that, even if they had beaten the black woman, they would not beat me if I knew enough to keep my mouth shut.

"Yes, sir," I said.

After they had gone, I sat on the edge of a packing box and stared at the bloody floor until the cigarette went out.

The store owned a bicycle which I used in delivering purchases. One day while returning from the suburbs, my bicycle tire was punctured. I walked along the hot, dusty road, sweating and leading the bicycle by the handle bars.

A car slowed at my side.

"What's the matter there, boy?" a white man called.

I told him that my bicycle was broken and that I was walking back to town.

That's too bad." he said. "Hop on the running board."

He stopped the car. I clutched hard at my bicycle with one hand and clung to the side of the car with the other.

All set?"

"Yes, sir."

The car started. It was full of young white men. They were drinking. I watched the flask pass from mouth to mouth.

"Wanna drink, boy?" one asked.

The memory of my six-year-old drinking came back and filled me with caution. But I laughed, the wind whipping my face.

"Oh, no!" I said.

The words were barely out of my mouth before I felt something hard and cold smash me between the eyes. It was an empty whisky bottle. I saw stars, and fell backwards from the speeding car into the dust of the road, my feet becoming entangled in the steel spokes of the bicycle. The car stopped and the white men piled out and stood over me.

"Nigger, ain't you learned no better sense'n that yet?" asked the man who hit me. "Ain't you learned to say sir to a white man yet?"

Dazed, I pulled to my feet. My elbows and legs were bleeding. Fists doubled, the white man advanced, kicking the bicycle out of the way.

"Aw, leave the bastard alone. He's got enough," said one.

They stood looking at me. I rubbed my shins, trying to stop the flow of blood. No doubt they felt a sort of contemptuous pity, for one asked:

"You wanna ride to town now, nigger? You reckon you know enough to ride now?"

"I wanna walk," I said simply.

Maybe I sounded funny. They laughed.

"Well, walk, you black sonofabitch!"

Before they got back into their car, they comforted me with: "Nigger, you sure ought to be glad it was us you talked to that way. You're a lucky bastard, 'cause if you'd said that to some other white man, you might've been a dead nigger now."

I was learning rapidly how to watch white people, to observe their every move, every fleeting expression, how to interpret what was said and what left unsaid.

Late one Saturday night I made some deliveries in a white neighborhood. I was pedaling my bicycle back to the store as fast as I could when a police car, swerving toward me, jammed me into the curbing.

"Get down, nigger, and put up your hands!" they ordered.

I did. They climbed out of the car, guns drawn, faces set and advanced slowly.

"Keep still!" they ordered.

I reached, my hands higher. They searched my pockets and packages. They seemed dissatisfied when they could find nothing incriminating. Finally, one of them said:

"Boy, tell your boss not to send you out in white neighborhoods at this time of night."

"Yes, sir." I said.

I rode off, feeling that they might shoot at me, feeling that the pavement might disappear. It was like living in a dream, the reality of which might change at any moment.

Each day in the store I watched the brutality with growing hate, yet trying to keep my feelings from registering in my face. When the boss looked at me I would avoid his eyes. Finally the boss's son cornered me one morning.

"Say, nigger, look here," he began.

"Yes, sir."

"What's on your mind?"

"Nothing, sir," I said, trying to look amazed, trying to fool him.

"Why don't you laugh and talk like the other niggers?" he asked.

"Well, sir, there's nothing much to say or smile about," I said, smiling.

His face was hard, baffled; I knew that I had not convinced him. He whirled from me and went to the front of the store; he came back a moment later, his face red. He tossed a few green bills at me.

"I don't like your looks, nigger. Now, get!" he snapped.

I picked up the money and did not count it. I grabbed my hat and left.

I held a series of petty jobs for short periods, quitting some to work elsewhere, being driven off others because of my attitude, my speech, the look in my eyes. I was no nearer than ever to my goal of saving enough money to leave. At times I doubted if I could ever do it.

One jobless morning I went to my old classmate, Griggs, who worked for a Capitol Street jeweler. He was washing the windows of the store when I came upon him.

"Do you know where I can find a job?" I asked.

He looked at me with scorn.

"Yes, I know where you can find a job," he said, laughing.

"Where?"

"But I wonder if you can hold it." he said.

"What do you mean?" I asked. "Where's the job?"

"Take your time," he said. "You know, Dick, I know you. You've been trying to hold a job all summer, and you can't. Why? Because you're impatient. That's your big fault."

I said nothing, because he was repeating what I had already heard him say. He lit a cigarette and blew out smoke leisurely.

"Well," I said, egging him on to speak.

"I wish to hell I could talk to you," he said.

"I think I know what you want to tell me," I said.

He clapped me on the shoulder; his face was full of fear, hate, concern for me.

"Do you want to get killed?" he asked me.

"Hell, no!"

"Then, for God's sake, learn how to live in the South!"

"What do you mean?" I demanded. "Let white people tell me that. Why should you?"

"See?" he said triumphantly, pointing his finger at me, "There it is, *now!* It's in your face. You won't let people tell you things. You rush too much. I'm trying to help you and you won't let me." He paused and looked about; the streets were filled with white people. He spoke to me in a low, full tone. "Dick, look, you're black, black, *black,* see? Can't you understand that?"

"Sure, I understand it," I said.

"You don't act a damn bit like it," he spat.

He then reeled off an account of my actions on every job I had held that summer.

"How did you know that?" I asked.

"White people make it their business to watch niggers," he explained. "And they pass the word around. Now, my boss is a Yankee and he tells me things. You're marked already."

Could I believe him? Was it true? How could I ever learn this strange world of white people?

"Then tell me how must I act." I asked humbly. "I just want to make enough money to leave."

"Wait and I'll tell you," he said.

At that moment a woman and two men stepped from the jewelry store; I moved to one side to let them pass, my mind intent upon Griggs's words. Suddenly Griggs reached for my arm and jerked me violently, sending me stumbling three or four feet across the pavement. I whirled.

"What's the matter with you?" I asked.

Griggs glared at me, then laughed.

"I'm teaching you how to get out of white people's way," he said.

I looked at the people who come out of the store; yes, they were *white,* but I had not noticed it.

"Do you see what I mean?" he asked. "White people want you out of their way." He pronounced the words slowly so that they would sink into my mind.

"I know what you mean," I breathed.

"Dick, I'm treating you like a brother," he said. "You act around white people as if you didn't know that they were white. And they see it."

"Oh, Christ, I can't be a slave," I said hopelessly.

"But you've got to eat," he said.

"Yes, I got to eat."

"Then start acting like it," he hammered at me, pounding his fist in his palm. "When you're in front of white people, *think* before you act, *think* before you speak. Your way of doing things is all right among *our* people, but not for *white* people. They won't stand for it."

I stared bleakly into the morning sun. I was nearing my seventeenth birthday and I was wondering if I would ever be free of this plague. What Griggs was saying was true, but it was simply utterly impossible for me to calculate, to scheme, to act, to plot all the time. I would remember to dissemble for short periods, then I would forget and act straight and human again, not with the desire to harm anybody, but merely forgetting the artificial status of race and class. It was the same with whites as with blacks; it was my way with everybody. I sighed, looking at the glittering diamonds in the store window, the rings and the neat rows of golden watches.

"I guess you're right," I said at last. "I've got to watch myself, break myself . . ."

"No," he said quickly, feeling guilty now. Someone—a white man—went into the store and we paused in our talk. "You know, Dick, you may think I'm an Uncle Tom, but I'm not. I hate these white people, hate 'em with all my heart. But I can't show it; if I did, they'd kill me." He paused and looked around to *see* if there were any white people within hearing distance. "Once I heard an old drunk nigger say:

All these white folks dressed so fine
Their ass-holes smell just like mine . . . "

I laughed uneasily, looking at the white faces that passed me. But Griggs, when he laughed, covered his mouth with his hand and bent at the knees, a gesture which was unconsciously meant to conceal his excessive joy in the presence of whites.

"That's how I feel about 'em," he said proudly after he had finished his spasm of glee. He grew sober. "There's an optical company upstairs and the boss is a Yankee from Illinois. Now, he wants a boy to work all day in summer, mornings and evenings in winter. He wants to break a colored boy into the optical trade. You know algebra and you're just cut out for the work. I'll tell Mr. Crane about you and I'll get in touch with you."

"Do you suppose I could see him now?" I asked.

"For God's sake, take your *time!*" he thundered at me.

"Maybe that's what's wrong with Negroes," I said, "They take too much time."

I laughed, but he was disturbed. I thanked him and left. For a week I did not hear from him and I gave up hope. Then one afternoon Griggs came to my house.

"It looks like you've got a job," he said. "You're going to have a chance to learn a trade. But remember to keep your head. Remember you're black. You start tomorrow."

"What will I get?"

"Five dollars a week to start with; they'll raise you if they like you," he explained.

My hopes soared. Things were not quite so bad, after all. I would have a chance to learn a trade. And I need not give up school. I told him that I would take the job, that I would be humble.

"You'll be working for a Yankee and you ought to get along," he said.

The next morning I was outside the office of the optical company long before it opened. I was reminding myself that I must be polite, must think before I spoke, must think before I acted, must say "yes sir, no sir," that I must so conduct myself that white people would not think that I thought I was as good as they. Suddenly a white man came up to me.

"What do you want?" he asked me.

"I'm reporting for a job, sir," I said.

"O.K. Come on."

I followed him up a flight of steps and he unlocked the door of the office. I was a little tense, but the young white man's manner put me at ease and I sat and held my hat in my hand. A white girl came and began punching the typewriter. Soon another white man, thin and gray, entered and went into the rear room. Finally a tall, red-faced white man arrived, shot me a quick glance and sat at his desk.

His brisk manner branded him a Yankee.

"You're the new boy, eh?

"Yes, sir."

"Let me get my mail out of the way and I'll talk with you," he said pleasantly.

"Yes, sir."

I even pitched my voice to a low plane, trying to rob it of any suggestion or overtone of aggressiveness.

Half an hour later Mr. Crane called me to his desk and questioned me closely about my schooling, about how much mathematics I had had. He seemed pleased when I told him that I had had two years of algebra.

"How would you like to learn this trade?" he asked.

"I'd like it fine, sir. I'd like nothing better," I said.

He told me that he wanted to train a Negro boy in the optical trade: he wanted to help him, guide him. I tried to answer in a way that would let him know that I would try to be worthy of what he was doing. He took me to the stenographer and said:

"This is Richard. He's going to be with us."

He then led me into the rear room of the office, which turned out to be a tiny factory filled with many strange machines smeared with red dust.

"Reynolds," he said to a young white man, "this is Richard."

"What you saying there, boy!" Reynolds grinned and boomed at me.

Mr. Crane took me to the older man.

"Pease, this is Richard, who'll work with us."

Pease looked at me and nodded. Mr. Crane then held forth to the two white men about my duties; he told them to break me in gradually to the workings of the shop, to instruct me in the mechanics of grinding and polishing lenses. They nodded their assent.

"Now, boy, let's see how clean you can get this place," Mr. Crane said.

"Yes, sir."

I swept, mopped, dusted, and soon had the office and the shop clean. In the afternoons, when I had caught up with my work, I ran errands. In an idle moment I would stand and watch the two white men grinding lenses on the machines. They said nothing to me and I said nothing to them. The first day passed, the second, the third, a week passed and I received my five dollars. A month passed. But I was not learning anything and nobody had volunteered to help me. One afternoon I walked up to Reynolds and asked him to tell me about the work.

"What are you trying to do, get smart, nigger?" he asked me.

"No sir," I said.

I was baffled. Perhaps he just did not want to help me. I went to Pease, reminding him that the boss had said that I was to be given a chance to learn the trade.

"Nigger, you think you're white, don't you?"

"No, sir."

"You're acting mighty like it," he said.

"I was only doing what the boss told me to do," I said.

Pease shook his fist in my face.

"This is a *white* man's work around here," he said.

From then on they changed toward me; they said good morning no more. When I was just a bit slow in performing some duty, I was called a lazy black sonofabitch. I kept silent, striving to offer no excuse for worsening of relations. But one day Reynolds called me to his machine.

"Nigger, you think you'll ever amount to anything?" he asked in a slow, sadistic voice.

"I don't know, sir," I answered, turning my head away.

"What do niggers think about?" he asked.

"I don't know, sir." I said, my head still averted.

"If I was a nigger, I'd kill myself," he said

I said nothing. I was angry.

"You know why?" he asked.

I still said nothing.

"But I don't reckon niggers mind being niggers," he said suddenly and laughed.

I ignored him. Mr. Pease was watching me closely; then I saw them exchange glances. My job was not leading to what Mr. Crane had said it would. I had been humble, and now I was reaping the wages of humility.

"Come here, boy." Pease said.

I walked to his bench.

"You didn't like what Reynolds just said, did you?" he asked.

"Oh, it's all right." I said smiling.

"You didn't like it. I could see it on your face," he said.

I stared at him and backed away.

"Did you ever get into any trouble?" he asked.

"No, sir."

"What would you do if you got into trouble?"

"I don't know, sir."

"Well, watch yourself and don't get into trouble," he warned.

I wanted to report these clashes to Mr. Crane, but the thought of what Pease or Reynolds would do to me if they learned that I had "snitched" stopped me. I worked through the days and tried to hide my resentment under a nervous, cryptic smile.

The climax came at noon one summer day. Pease called me to his workbench; to get to him I had to go between two narrow benches and stand with my back against a wall.

"Richard, I want to ask you something." Pease began pleasantly, not looking up from his work.

"Yes, sir."

Reynolds came over and stood blocking the narrow passage between the benches; he folded his arms and stared at me solemnly. I looked from one to the other, sensing trouble. Pease looked up and spoke slowly, so there would be no possibility of my not understanding.

"Richard, Reynolds here tells me that you called me Pease," he said.

I stiffened. A void opened up in me. I knew that this was the showdown.

He meant that I had failed to call him Mr. Pease. I looked at Reynolds; he was gripping a steel bar in his hand. I opened my mouth to speak, to protest, to assure Pease that I had never called him simply *Pease,* and that I had never had any intention of doing so, when Reynolds grabbed me by the collar, ramming my head against a wall.

"Now, be careful, nigger," snarled Reynolds, baring his teeth. "I heard you call 'im *Pease*. And if you say you didn't, you're calling me a liar, see?" He waved the steel bar threateningly.

If I had said: No, sir, Mr. Pease, I never called you *Pease,* I would by inference having been calling Reynolds a liar; and if I had said: Yes, sir, Mr. Pease, I called you *Pease,* I would have been pleading guilty to the worst insult that a Negro can offer to a southern white man. I stood trying to think of a neutral course that would resolve this quickly risen nightmare, but my tongue would not move.

"Richard, I asked you a question!" Pease said. Anger was creeping into his voice.

"I don't remember calling you *Pease,* Mr. Pease," I said cautiously. "And if I did, I sure didn't mean . . ."

"You black sonofabitch! You called me *Pease,* then!" he spat, rising and slapping me till I bent sideways over a bench.

Reynolds was up on top of me demanding:

"Didn't you call him *Pease?* If you say you didn't, I'll rip your gut string loose with this f–k–g bar, you black granny dodger! You can't call a white man a liar and get away with it!"

I wilted, I begged them not to hit me. I knew what they wanted. They wanted me to leave the job.

"I'll leave," I promised. "I'll leave right now!"

They gave me a minute to get out of the factory, and warned me not to show up again or tell the boss. Reynolds loosened his hand on my collar and I ducked out of the room. I did not see Mr. Crane or the stenographer in the office. Pease and Reynolds had so timed it that Mr. Crane and the stenographer would be out when they turned on the terror. I went to the street and waited for the boss to return. I saw Griggs wiping glass shelves in the jewelry store and I beckoned to him. He came out and I told him what had happened.

"Then what are you standing there like a fool for?" he demanded "Won't you ever learn? Get home! They might come down!"

I walked down Capitol Street feeling that the sidewalk was unreal, that I was unreal, that the people were unreal, yet expecting somebody to demand to know what right I had to be on the streets. My wound went deep; I felt that I had been slapped out of the human race. When I reached home. I did not tell the family what had happened; I merely told them that I had quit, that I was not making enough money, that I was seeking another job.

That night Griggs came to my house; we went for a walk.

"You got a goddamn tough break," he said.

"Can you say it was my fault?" I asked.

He shook his head.

"Well, what about your goddamn philosophy of meekness?" I asked him bitterly.

"These things just happen." he said, shrugging.

"They owe me money," I said.

"That's what I came about," he said. "Mr. Crane wants you to come in at ten in the morning. Ten sharp, now mind you, because he'll be there and those guys won't gang up on you again."

The next morning at ten I crept up the stairs and peered into the office of the optical shop to make sure that Mr. Crane was in. He was at his desk. Pease and Reynolds were at their machines in the rear.

"Come in, Richard," Mr. Crane said.

I pulled off my hat and walked into the office. I stood before him.

"Sit down," he said.

I sat. He stared at me and shook his head.

"Tell me, what happened?"

An impulse to speak rose in me and died with the realization that I was facing a wall that I would never breach. I tried to speak several times and could make no sounds. I grew tense and tears burnt my cheeks.

"Now, just keep control of yourself," Mr. Crane said.

I clenched my fists and managed to talk.

"I tried to do my best here," I said.

"I believe you," he said. "But I want to know what happened. Which one bothered you?"

"Both of 'em," I said.

Reynolds came running to the door and I rose. Mr. Crane jumped to his feet.

"Get back in there," he told Reynolds.

"That nigger's lying!" Reynolds said. 'I'll kill 'im if he lies on me!"

"Get back in there or get out," Mr. Crane said.

Reynolds backed away, keeping his eyes on me.

"Go ahead," Mr. Crane said. "Tell me what happened."

Then again I could not speak. What could I accomplish by telling him. I was black: I lived in the South. I would never learn to operate those machines as long as those two white men in there stood by them. Anger and fear welled in me as I felt what I had missed; I leaned forward and clapped my hands to my face.

"No, no, now," Mr. Crane said. "Keep control of yourself. No matter what happens, keep control . . ."

"I know," I said in a voice not my own. "There's no use of my saying anything."

"Do you want to work here?" he asked me.

I looked at the white faces of Pease and Reynolds; I imagined their waylaying me, killing me. I was remembering what had happened to Ned's brother.

"No, sir," I breathed.

"Why?"

"I'm scared," I said. "They would kill me."

Mr. Crane turned and called Pease and Reynolds into the office.

"Now, tell me which one bothered you. Don't be afraid. Nobody's going to hurt you." Mr. Crane said.

I stared ahead of me and did not answer. He waved the men inside. The white stenographer looked at me with wide eyes and I felt drenched in shame, naked to my soul. The whole of my being felt violated, and I knew that my own fear had helped to violate it. I was breathing hard and struggling to master my feelings.

"Can I get my money, sir?" I asked at last.

"Just sit a minute and take hold of yourself," he said.

I waited and my roused senses grew slowly calm.

"I'm awfully sorry about this," he said.

"I had hoped for a lot from this job," I said. "I'd wanted to go to school, to college . . ."

"I know," he said. "But what are you going to do now?"

My eyes traveled over the office, but I was not seeing.

"I'm going away," I said.

"What do you mean?"

"I'm going to get out of the South," I breathed.

"Maybe that's best," he said. "I'm from Illinois. Even for me, it's hard here. I can do just so much."

He handed me my money, more than I had earned for the week. I thanked him and rose to leave. He rose. I went into the hallway and he followed me. He reached out his hand.

"It's tough for you down here," he said.

I barely touched his hand. I walked swiftly down the hall, fighting against crying again. I ran down the steps, then paused and looked back up. He was standing at the head of the stairs, shaking his head. I went into the sunshine and walked home like a blind man.

Source

Richard Wright, *Black Boy: A Record of Childhood and Youth* (New York: Harper and Brothers, 1945), 160–69.

Selected Bibliography

Butler, Robert. J. *Critical Responses to Richard Wright.* Westport, Conn.: Greenwood Press, 1995.

Gayle, Addison. *Richard Wright: Ordeal of a Native Son.* Glouscester, Mass.: P. Smith, 1983.

Kinnamon, Kenneth. *Emergence of Richard Wright: A Study in Literature and Society.* Urbana: University of Illinois Press, 1972.

Rampersad, Arnold, ed. *Richard Wright: A Collection of Critical Essays.* Englewood Cliffs, N.J.: Prentice Hall, 1995.

Walker, Margaret. *Richard Wright, Daemonic Genius: A Portrait of the Man, a Critical Look at His Work.* New York: Warner Books, 1988.

seven

A Giant Step Toward Unity

William H. Simons is a retired member of the Steering Committee of the Coalition of Black Trade Unionists, which was formed in September 1973. He was also president of Local 6 of the Washington Teachers Union and a member of the National Urban League and the NAACP. In 1994, Simons proudly served as an AFL-CIO observer in the first democratic elections in South Africa. In a 1973 interview with Jacoby Sims for the left-wing *Daily World,* Simons gave a behind-the-scenes analysis of a September 1972 conference that drew twelve hundred participants and led to the founding of the Coalition of Black Trade Unionists—a militant labor organization that responded to the failure of the white-dominated AFL-CIO to address the concerns of its black members.

During two cool days in Chicago last September, 1,200 African-American trade unionists gathered to form the Coalition of Black Trade Unionists. The attendance far surpassed the initiators' dreams. One unionist said, "The sleeping giant is awakening."

There are some three million African-American trade unionists in the U.S. This is one-third of the total Black labor force. If they were all organized, their influence would be sizeable, both in the labor movement and in government.

Members of the Coalition feel that the demands of Afro-American labor must be felt in those two areas.

Rank-and-filers and union officials from 37 union throughout the nation attended the conference. Prior to a national constitutional convention planned for this spring, there will be regional conferences in New York, Chicago, Detroit, Washington, D.C., Cleveland and, possibly, San Francisco or Los Angeles.

On January 19, I interviewed William Simons, a member of the Coalition's steering committee and president of Local 6 of the Washington Teacher's Union, AFT, in the offices of his union.

Mr. Simons, besides his organized labor activities, has been involved in the struggle for equal rights with such groups as the National Urban League and the NAACP. He has also been active in the movement against U.S. intervention in the affairs of people of the "Third World."

Q: Mr. Simons, what is the Coalition of Black Trade Unionists?

A: The Coalition of Black Trade Unionists is a group that was organized this past summer. The purpose of organizing at that time was to express our displeasure to the position taken by George Meany and the executive council (of the AFL-CIO) on the elections, that of neutrality.

The group was also concerned about the fact that much needs to be done in the labor movement to eradicate the racist practices, the discriminatory practices, which still exist within certain union.

And we felt if we could organize, we would then be able to demonstrate that there are real concerns to which the labor movement is not addressing itself. We want the labor movement to address itself not only to the concerns of Black trade unionists but to those of all trade unionists.

Q: Who participated in the conference?

A: In the formation of the group there was Bill Lucy, Secretary-Treasurer of the American Federation of State, County and Municipal Employees, Nelson Jack Edwards from the United Auto Workers, Charlie Hayes from the Amalgamated Meatcutters, myself and there were one or two others.

There were members from both the AFL-CIO unions and from non-AFL-CIO unions. We had our initial meeting in Miami in August and we had additional meeting in Washington and we laid plans for the September conference.

Since that conference there have been three meetings. Their purpose was to try to put together a constitution and a structure in order to mobilize trade unionists around the country.

While the name of the organization is the Coalition of Black Trade Unionists, we do not by any means intend to limit it to Black Trade unionists.

At our last meeting, we discussed taking our positions to the Secretary of Labor designee, Peter Brennan. We sought to have a conference with him simply to raise certain issues, to get his feeling about how he is going to use his position to further the growth of labor in the United States. Unfortunately Mr. Brennan did not see fit to meet with us.

Today we testified before the Senate Subcommittee holding hearing on the confirmation of Mr. Brennan. We raised these questions with the sub-committee. The sub-committee agreed it would place these questions before Mr. Brennan and elicit responses from him concerning the issues we raised. We did not take a position for or against Mr. Brennan, we simply indicated there were some concerns that we would like the sub-committee to investigate thoroughly before they arrive at any decision with respect to his confirmation.

Q: Who testified for the Coalition?

A: Bill Lucy read the main statement. Dick Parrish, representing the New York Distributive Workers of America, made some comments and I also made a few comments.

Q: You just stated that the Coalition is not limited to just Black workers and Black trade unionists. Who else can participate?

A: We have not drawn up our constitution as yet. But we envision that any trade unionist who is concerned with the same problems as the Coalition will be eligible for membership. I might point out that out of the 1,200 delegates in Chicago, there were at least 200–300 non black, and other minority delegates. And they had full participation in the deliberations of the conference.

Q: When will the constitutional conference take place?

A: We are shooting for a date some time this spring, possibly in April. That has not been finalized.

Q: Is there a preliminary constitution?

A: No, we only have working papers, documents not in finalized form. We are working on a structure and quite frankly we intend to just about parallel the same kind of structure that the AFL-CIO has. That is, with the central body or executive committee or whatever name we give to it—with state federations and local bodies with each body being autonomous—within the framework of being bound by only the constitutional guidelines that are going to be established.

Q: How will rank-and-file participation be encouraged?

A: Rank-and-file participation will be encouraged at the local and state levels. Each local jurisdiction can organize—have membership. And then each local jurisdiction would send delegates to the state federation. And then of course the governing body would be elected by the entire membership at the convention.

Q: Will you be working with the same unions involved in the original conference and will the group be expanded?

A: It's going to expand. Hopefully, we will get a broad-based participation from the whole spectrum of the labor movement, from those unions which are in the AFL-CIO and those which are not.

Q: What is the purpose of the Coalition?

A: The purpose is to identify the problem that exists in the labor movement as a whose. And to bring whatever pressures we can to try to get these situations corrected, so that all workers can get a fair share of the pie in the labor movement. We are not going to be a watchdog, in terms of practices that exist in individual unions. In other words, a member cannot bring a grievance to the Coalition and expect the Coalition to take action. That is not our purpose at all.

We are looking at the overall trends and, for example, we are trying to influence the decisions made by the executive council of the AFL-CIO. We will try to influence broad policy decisions of internationals.

Also, we intend to concentrate not only on problems in the labor movement per se, but also problems in the community and country.

Q: Could you specify some of the problems which U.S. workers face?

A: For example, I think we had a clear indication just yesterday, when we learned that the American Telephone and Telegraph Company has been ordered to pay some 38 million dollars to upgrade the salaries of women and other non-white workers against whom they were discriminating.

This is the kind of thing we would call attention to in other companies. This practice has been condoned by the Communication Workers (of America) over the years. They represent the majority of the employees in the telephone system. There are also some workers organized by the IBEW (International Brotherhood of Electrical Workers). Condoning discrimination has been the policy of the union leadership. These are the kind of things we would call attention to.

Q: In the September conference, rank-and-file workers are particularly concerned with methods whereby they could get more Black elected officials in their locals. Could the Coalition lend support here?

A: Yes, in terms of working with groups of workers and acquainting them with their union structure and how officials are elected. And if a structure is democratic enough—and many unions do have a democratic process—we will tell the Black workers they have to begin organizing on a political basis and be able to mobilize their voting strength at conventions or meetings or wherever voting takes place.

Q: Are there any qualifications for membership in the Coalition? Is it open to trade unionists regardless of political affiliation?

A: The only qualification will be that the person is a member of a qualified union.

Q: What about President Nixon? Since he is a lame duck President, what might he unleash on the Black worker, and workers in general?

A: Of course we have already seen how the wage-price guidelines have affected workers. I suspect there will probably be some efforts on the part of the administration to try to curb the bargaining power of unions.

I do not expect that we are going to get very much in the way of positive action by the President to lift up the workers in this country. It has not been the pattern in the past and I can see nothing that will project that in the future.

Q: Will the Coalition continue to stress independent political action, such as trade unionists running for elected offices?

A: Very definitely we would stress that kind of action. It is absolutely essential that there should be representatives of the workers in legislative bodies in order to try to help shape the legislation that will benefit the workers.

And also we would support those candidates in state legislatures as well as Congress who have a sympathetic viewpoint toward the problems which the working man faces.

Source

William H. Simons, "A Giant Step Toward Unity," *Daily World,* February 10, 1973; reprinted in Philip S. Foner, and Ronald Lewis, eds., *Black Workers: A Documentary History from Colonial Times to the Present,* 662–66 (Philadelphia: Temple University Press, 1989).

Selected Bibliography

Foner, Philip S. *Organized Labor and the Black Worker, 1619–1981.* New York: International Publishers, 1982.

Robinson, Archie. *George Meany and His Times: A Biography.* New York: Simon & Schuster, 1981.

Tillman, Ray M. and Michael S. Cummings. *The Transformation of U.S. Unions: Voices, Visions, and Strategies for the Grassroots.* Boulder: Lynne Rienner Publishing, 1999.

eight

All God's Dangers

Best known under the pseudonym "Nate Shaw," Ned Cobb (1885–1973) was active in the Alabama Sharecroppers Union (which was linked to the Communist Party). Cobb's autobiography, *All God's Dangers* (as told to Theodore Rosengarten), won the National Book Award in 1975. In the following excerpt, Cobb described how a white landowner named Mr. Tucker cheated him in a sharecropping agreement.

Cobb was an illiterate black tenant farmer born in Alabama during the postbellum period. Although many African American sharecroppers moved north in the early twentieth century, Cobb remained in Alabama his entire life, determined to forge a living despite harrowing ordeals with race oppression and economic peonage in the Jim Crow South. Following the abolition of slavery, sharecropping arose in large segments of the South, which remained heavily dependent on its agricultural economy. In return for land, seed, and credit that landlords provided, sharecroppers cultivated crops and received a share of their value, minus their debt to the landlord. In many instances, landlords resorted to high interest rates and fraud as a means for increasing their own profits and maintaining a stable labor force.

I wanted to stretch out where I could get more land to work, and Miss Hattie Lu and Mr. Reeve—they had a little girl child but he weren't the father of it. Miss Hattie Lu had the chap before they married. And this girl had married and moved up there on the place with her husband. So I couldn't get more land than I had. They wanted to keep me there but on the amount of land they wanted, and it was too little for me. Then, too, me and Mrs. Reeve's son-in-law didn't agree much with each other. When he moved up on the place he wanted to take it over and boss me too. Well, you know blood's thicker than water, and Miss Hattie Lu was goin to let him have his way. I decided I'd pull out and I was pullin out in time, too.

I looked ahead and figured my best route. Moved down on Sitimachas Creek on the old Bannister place. And there, regardless to my dealins with Mr. Tucker, I begin to prosper good and heavy. I had learned a rule for my life workin with Mr. Reeve—I could make it anywhere by workin and tendin my own business. I was able to advance myself because I never made under five bales of cotton—made five bales the first year I rented from the Reeves; next year I made six; next year I made eight—with one mule and no help to speak of. Cotton picked up the second and third years to between fifteen and twenty cents, along in there. It was a big difference in the price since I started farmin for myself. I was under the impression that the government was takin hold of the market—1912, 1913. The second year I quit workin halves and took my business in my own hands, cotton floated up to a higher level.

But things went bad the year I moved down on the creek. Cotton fell to a nickel a pound, 1914. A man couldn't pay nothin much on his old debts and nothin at all on his new ones. I disremember just exactly what I paid Mr. Reeve on the money he furnished me that year—he stuck by me, furnished me cash money the first year I dealt with Mr. Tucker—but I didn't pay him off. And I owed him a little over two hundred dollars after I sold my cotton and paid him what I could. And in addition to that, I owed Mr. Harry Black a hundred and thirty dollars for fertilizer that I'd used the last year I worked on Mrs. Reeve's place. He was a guano salesman, lived out in the country above Tuskegee; and every year I lived with Mr. Reeve I bought my guano from him. 1913, I carried my guano debt over to my next crop; it weren't unusual to do that in this country and he agreed. But when cotton fell to a nickel I couldn't pay nothin hardly. And, to tell the truth, I didn't make the cotton I had been makin on the Reeve place. So I owed money for fertilizer that applied to a bigger crop than I was makin now.

That was boll weevil time, the boll weevil was in circulation. He had just come in a year or two before then—these white folks down here told the colored people if you don't pick them cotton squares off the ground and destroy them boll weevils, we'll quit furnishin you. Told em that—puttin the blame on the colored man for the boll weevil comin in this country. Well, that was a shame. Couldn't nobody pay on his debts when the weevil et up his crop. The boll weevil cut in my cotton to a certain extent, but at that time it was mainly the low price that injured my chances. If I had got the price, I could have paid a heap more on my debts although I was makin less cotton.

I was runnin two plows—myself and my brother-in-law, little Waldo Ramsey, my wife's brother. But when cotton fell to the bottom both our crops combined couldn't pay what I owed. I did manage to pay Mr. Black thirty dollars; owed him a hundred and thirty dollars and I paid him thirty and that hundred runned over for five years before I could pay it.

That first year I moved on the Bannister place, Mr. Reeve died—died that fall, while I was gatherin my crop. What did Miss Hattie Lu do when he died? She come to me and told me, "Nate, Mr. Reeve's gone now; he aint with us no more. We want to arrange to get in all of his estate, get it all together."

I agreed with her.

She said, "Now what you owed Mr. Reeve"—I couldn't pay him on account of cotton goin down, and then too that was my first year on that rocky place, my crop weren't quite what it had been; boll weevil seed to that also—"and whoever else owes him; like you do"—everybody doin business with the man owed hims you know—"we will, if it suits you, name somebody to take up your debt with Mr. Reeve."

And she named Mr. Tucker as the man to take up my debt, at ninety percent on the dollar. They knocked off ten percent to get Mr. Reeve's business closed in. Miss Hattie Lu told me, "Nate, Cousin Lemuel Tucker"—Miss Hattie Lu and Mr. Tucker was cousins someway—"he'll take up your debt, what you owe Mr. Reeve. And you only entitled to pay Cousin Lemuel ninety cents on the dollar. That ten cents, we knocked it off, that's our laws. You just pay ninety cents on the dollar to Mr. Reeve's estate; pay it to Cousin Lemuel, he taken up your debt."

I didn't know nothin against Mr. Tucker to make me contrary to the idea, so I told her, "Let him take it up." But the amount that I owed Mr. Reeve, I couldn't pay Mr. Tucker nothin on it that year. And I had that guano debt besides. Mr. Reeve transacted his business like this: he'd furnish you money to buy groceries and anything else you needed except fertilize; he wouldn't give you a penny for fertilize. You could buy fertilize from whoever you pleased but you had to arrange to pay the dealer out of your crop. I got along well under Mr. Reeve's system as long as cotton was bringin anything. But when cotton fell, that's when the trouble come.

So Miss Hattie Lu consulted with Mr. Tucker and he took my debt over. And he come down to my house on the creek one day, told me, "Nate, I took over your debt and paid Miss Hattie Lu the money you owed her dear husband's estate. I settled your account in full. Now you just pay me what you owed Mr. Reeve."

I said, "Mr. Tucker, you didn't have to pay the whole debt, you only had to pay ninety percent on the balance. The knock-off wasn't given to you."

He jumped up when I told him that. "Did she tell you that? She's mighty dam smart to tell you all that."

Right there was where I caught him. Miss Hattie Lu had put me in the light.

He said, "The thing for you to do is pay me what you owed Mr. Reeve."

She told me to pay ninety cents on the dollar and he wanted the whole thing, what he didn't have to pay.

I said, "Mr. Tucker, she told me that ten cents weren't given to you; it's their loss, just their loss. Yes sir, she told me in a straight way; I'm entitled to pay you only ninety cents on the dollar and the dime goes loose."

He said, "The thing for you to do is pay me what you owed Mr. Reeve; that's the thing for you to do."

I said, "Do you think it's right to charge me for somethin you didn't have to pay?"

He said nothin. But I had no political pull; that was my flaw. I said, "All right, Mr. Tucker, go ahead. I'll see you later."

Well, he took up Mr. Reeve's debt and made himself ten cents on the other man's dollar. I had the brains to see how that transaction was runnin over me, but I had no voice on account of my color—and never had any with most men, only had a voice with some.

I had bargained to buy the old place, the Bannister place, but I got so deep in debt by Tucker takin up what I owed Mr. Reeve at his death, havin to reach back and pay off the whole claim—I couldn't make the payments on the place and it fell back into Mr. Tucker's hands. I stayed on there, rentin, and Mr. Tucker kept the title to the place.

That barn I built on the premises, it didn't cost him a penny, not one penny. I put four stables to the barn. In fact of the business, the old barn was there but at the present time that I took a hold of the place, there wasn't but two stables in it. And I went ahead and tore the old barn out practically, braced it and sturdied it up and took out the old log supports—it was a old log barn—and built it up in a frame way. I bought lumber to make the change and when I quit workin on the barn I had four good stables when there weren't but two when I started. My brother helped me some but mostly I done it by myself, and well done it too. I nailed two by fours to the upright logs, braced em, then sawed out doors and even covered that barn. In other words, I rebuilt that barn to meet my standards. I had went in the name of buyin the property so the expenses come on me—he didn't allow me nothin on improvements. And when I become so deep I couldn't buy the place, he inherited my labor in that barn.

I had just bought a horse at that time and I had that pair of mules and I prepared that barn to hold all them stock. Every place I wanted a stable I cut out and done it with planks—them old logs been decayed. And when I wound up I had four stables, needed em. Mr. Reeve furnished me money to build that barn and Mr. Tucker got that out of me on top of the barn.

So I decided, I was owin Tucker, I didn't know really what I was goin to do, at one time it struck my mind to just sell what I had and pay Tucker up. And I took a notion I'd sell my Mattie mule—everybody wanted her and I had another mule and a horse at that time. But Tucker had done mortgaged that mule and all of my personal property at that time and all the property of all his hands; he runned us up all together on a joint note. So I let Mr. Tucker know that I was intendin to sell that mule. I didn't mean to take just any kind of deal for her. She was one of the lightest mules, in weight, that I ever owned but she weighed right at a thousand pounds. She was a thoroughgoin mule, just right for a plow mule, single or double. And when it come around to sellin her, I hung up, of course, to an extent.

Tucker wanted to sell the mule hisself, claimed he had a right to sell her on account of that mortgage he held. So he brought a white man to my house one day to look at the mule. I led em out to the pasture—didn't know the white man on sight. Drove the mule up, let him look at her. We was out there in the pasture at the edge of a big pine thicket, big enough pines to saw for lumber. White man looked the mule over. I didn't say a word. When he asked about the mule he asked just like he was askin Tucker—but I done the answerin.

He said, "Well, she's a nice mule all right, but she's too light for what I want her for."

He'd done asked what I'd take for the mule, had I made up my mind if I was goin to sell her and what did I want for her. Well, I gived a hundred and eighty-five dollars and then done broke her and she become quiet. My wife just thought the world of that mule and she named her Mattie.

"Take two hundred dollars to move her."

He looked and he looked; he decided she was too light for that much money—and she was just as pretty as a peeled onion.

They begin to walk away, him and Tucker, after he made his excuse. Tucker didn't care—I knowed his theory—he didn't want to see the man turn the mule down, just so it didn't undercut *his* price. I knowed he had a opinion of it but his opinion was too light. So as they started walkin off I just throwed it into em like this: "Well, you think she's too light for you?"

"Yes, too light for that much money."

I'd a raised the devil if Tucker had went on and tried to sell that mule to him anyhow, cut my price. I said, "You needn't go on off over the hill somewhere and come back, it won't do you no good. It'll take two hundred dollars to move her; I won't take a penny less. If you don't want her, just go on, don't come back."

That white man never did come back. He went on out of there, Mr. Tucker tellin him, "Uh-uh-uh-uh, O yes, that's a dandy good mule, worth all of two hundred dollars."

Mr. Tucker had a special place he sent his hands to trade; weren't his store, just some of his friend people there in Apafalya that sold groceries. All the hands that Tucker had out in the country here, right in between Two Forks and Pottstown—some of these people was on *his* places and some of em was on places he had rented for em. He'd rent places from other white men and sub-rent em to his niggers or let em work on halves, and he stood for em.

Weren't no use to kick against his orders, we, all of us on his places, was forced to trade where he sent us. I don't mean that he'd drive a man like a dog or a hog, but if the poor fellow wanted a home and he fit him up, that man traded where he was sent. It was just a way of controllin the nigger, his money and hisself. Sometime a colored man would kick against the proposition but very seldom.

Prices weren't no higher at the store he'd send us than the average other places in town. But, you understand, this was a friend to him, he goes in there and gives him all of his trade, makes arrangements with him for his hands to come there and get groceries, monthly or anytime they wanted em. And he'd go to the bank, draw money—he had every bit of our stuff mortgaged by his own rulins; he knowed what all we had and mortgaged it to stand a security for the money he was gettin. And he'd take that mortgage money and traipse around the stores—kept a doin that every year. That's how he'd run his business. We'd trade where he told us to trade and he'd pay it up once a month with the money he got from mortgagin our stuff.

But there weren't no great sight of groceries got at a store by me because at that time I raised my meat and lard, corn, vegetables—we was a family of people that all we bought at the store was coffee, flour, sugar, salt. So it weren't no burden on me to trade at Tucker's choice of a store because I didn't trade much.

I'd be askin all along for five long years and every fall I'd come up just a little deeper—1914, 1915, 1916, 1917, 1918—I'd go to Mr. Tucker for a settlement and he'd tell me, "Well, you lackin so much and so much of comin out—" For five long years I was fallin behind dealin with that man. Up until the fifth year I dropped into town to pay him: "Well, what are you holdin against me now, Mr. Tucker?"

"You owe me five hundred dollars, Nate."

Done got all of my crops for five years and I still owed him five hundred dollars. That was his tune. Five hundred dollars and one penny. I labored under that debt—I'm tellin what God's pleased with—lingered five long years and he was gettin every string I had to give.

So, the fifth year I lived with him, he left his plantations up here and went down below Montgomery to boss a big farm business for some rich folks. And he traveled back up here every week to see what his men was doin. Get on his car and get out from down there and come up here every weekend. In them days he didn't have nothin but a little old Ford car—hadn't got up to buyin

Chevrolets, Buicks, and so on. He come up here every weekend on that little old Ford; lookin around, seein how we was gettin along, men that he was standin for—me, Wilson Rowe, Leroy Roberts, Silas Todd. Come to see if we had anything he could get any money out of.

He was travelin around amongst his hands one day in the fall and he come to my house. He had already told me I owed him five hundred dollars and one cent. So he come down there one evenin in the mist and rain. He lived out here in the piney woods between Pottstown and Apafalya and I lived back close to Sitimachas Creek, somethin like two miles from him. And I was in the house with my family when he come.

I had done ginned and baled and hauled back home and throwed in the yard three bales of cotton. He come up there and he seed that. Whoooooo—he had a knack of scratchin his leg and spittin when he talked; that was his way of doin. So he come in my house and he got to scratchin his leg and cryin bout how he needed money: "Uh-uh-uh-uh, by George, Nate, I see you got three bales of cotton in the yard and I'm up here for some money, I need it for my business affairs. And I see you got this cotton ginned off and layin out here."

I said, "Yes sir."

"Uh-uh-uh-uh, by George, I'm just in bad shape for money, I can't tell you how bad I need it. Load your cotton up and bring it out to Apafalya and sell it and get me up some money."

I loaded that cotton, went on out there that evenin and sold it. Well, many people say it, "A good thing follows a bad one, a bad thing follows a good one." Any trap set somewhere goin to break loose after a while.

Well, the government had done jumped back into the cotton business at that time—I knowed I owed him, I just loaded up them three bales of cotton. My little boys was big enough to push some so I set skids alongside the wagon and rolled them three bales up there on the flat-body, hitched my mules to the wagon and pulled it into Apafalya. Them three bales of cotton knocked the bark off the whole tree: I collected, I got a check for five hundred and sixty dollars out of them three bales of cotton—if I'm not tellin the truth, I'm the biggest liar ever spoke. Cotton was up around forty cents or a little better—that was in wartime; hit the war and cotton brought a little over forty cents a pound. Five years before that, I moved onto the Tucker place and made my first crop, cotton was down to five cents. Now it was bringin forty on account of that war.

Had that check in my hand from the man that bought my cotton, I walked on to the bank. Mr. Tucker was there waitin on me. I said, "Mr. Tucker, what was that you told me that I owed you?"

"Uh-uh-uh-uh, let me figure—"

Whirled around there and went through a little alley to where generally there was a little old table of some kind—you go into a bank, they got nice fixins there for you to write on. Well, he run over there to that little old table and he figured. Whirled around to me again and he come out with this: five hundred dollars and one penny. "If you pay me the five hundred I'll knock the penny off."

Mr. Grace standin right there, C.D. Grace, the banker, president of the bank. He standin there listenin at us. I just issued my check to him; it called for five hundred and sixty-nine dollars and somethin cents. I said, "Take out that five hundred dollars, Mr. Grace, and give me the balance."

Got out of them bales of cotton, five hundred and sixty-nine dollars, some-odd cents. Mr. Tucker got five hundred of it, Mr. Grace gived me the balance. I just stuck that money in my inside coat pocket. I happened to have on my coat that day—it was cold and rainy.

I said, "Now, Mr. Grace, I want my note."

I was payin Mr. Tucker all I owed him, but that weren't killin the bird, understand. Mr. Tucker went to scratchin his leg, "Uh-uh-uh-uh, Nate, I don't know whether you can get your note or not until I pay my bills."

There was a fraud in that but Mr. Grace overruled.

"I-I-I don't know whether you can get your note or not."

That was killin to me. Because if he didn't pay what he owed, they'd come to me for it. We were under that joint note business, all of his hands and the man himself. He was the only one that could draw money on it but we were all responsible for what he owed. He took a joint note on everything we had—Leroy Roberts, Wilson Rowe, Silas Todd, and me. I signed the note but I didn't know what I was signin when I signed; he didn't tell us what it was but a note. I've always heard that it was illegal to force a man to sign a note without readin it to him, tellin him what he's signin—I've heard that. Just fooled us to do it. Had us come in to the bank there one at a time to sign and had a different paper for each of us, but it was all for the same note.

A joint note is a bad note; you might say it's a clearin-house note. I caught how it could damage a man—if that note messes me up it's goin to mess you up too, goin to mess up everyone that's signed to it. And if you didn't understand it, they just took advantage of your ignorance. What man would freely of himself sign such a note? If you and I both sign this note and you can't make your payment, they goin to take it out of me. My stuff is subject to your transaction, your stuff is subject to my transaction—that's a bad note. Some of my color and some of the white people too talked to me bout it afterwards. Told me, "Nate, didn't you know no better than that? That's a joint note. They goin to work you until they get everything you got."

I said, "I didn't know it at the time I signed. Mr. Tucker pulled the blinds over my eyes and I believe it's illegal."

But illegal or legal, don't make no difference—any way we fix it goes for the nigger.

So I kept a lookin at Mr. Grace. And he was lookin at me and lookin at Mr. Tucker and he acted undecided for a minute. Then he said, "Yes, Lemuel, he can get his note. He done paid you all he owed you; he can get it."

"Uh-uh-uh-uh, by George, give it to him." O, he scratched his leg, "Give it to him."

Mr. Grace marked that note up and handed it to me. I put it in my inside coat pocket along with the balance of the money I got from my cotton. Right there and then it struck my heart and mind: 'You'll never get another note on me, never under Christ's kingdom.'

Mr. Grace turned me loose from that joint note business and I walked on out the bank.

That next spring he sent me word to meet him out in Apafalya, he got word to all his other hands and one of em come to me and told me—Silas Todd, he was livin my closest neighbor. Silas got Mr. Tucker's word and he come to my house one day. He called himself a cousin to me; said, "Cousin Nate, Mr. Lemuel said for us all to meet in Apafalya Saturday and sign up for our year's supply. And we aint got nothin to do but sign our notes."

Every spring as long as that joint note was goin on—it went on five years with me—the week Mr. Tucker wanted us to sign, on a certain Saturday, he'd notify us not later than the middle of the week. That would be in February, when notes was openin up and the farmin people was gettin their business straightened out for the new crop.

So, here come Silas Todd tellin me, "Mr. Tucker said for us all to meet him at the bank Saturday."

Good God, I had just paid him up and got through with him that previous fall—high-priced cotton pulled the kinks out of me. And when Silas gived me Tucker's word, I just shooed it off, wouldn't let it take my head. I acted careless about it and short and Silas smiled; then he broke out and laughed: "You don't want to go. You aint goin, is you?"

"I don't know what I'll do. I have to study it."

I wouldn't tell Silas definitely I wasn't goin; told him, "I don't know what I'll do. I'm undecided."

I failed to go. I wouldn't go sign no note. I was ignorant out of the knowledge of knowin what a joint note meant until I paid Mr. Tucker and saw for myself everything that was on that note.

First business I had after I got the order to come out to the bank and sign that note, I went to Apafalya—that was my tradin town. One Monday I got on my buggy and drove out to Apafalya and just as I got inside the suburbs of town I seed a little old Ford car come a flyin, meetin me, comin up the road. I never had a thought it was him. And when he got close to me I could see it *was* him. Mr. Tucker looked and seed it was me. He drove by me a little piece before he checked that little old Ford up out of the road and jumped out. I looked back and I stopped too. He left that little old Ford car and come trottin back to my buggy. When he got to me he said, "Uh-uh-uh-uh"—he talked thataway—"uh-uh-uh-uh, Nate, uh-uh-uh, I see you didn't come down Saturday and sign the note. You know—uh-uh, you goin downtown now, aint you?"

I said, "Yes, I'm goin down there."

"Well, you aint got nothin to do but just go straight into the bank and sign."

Mr. Tucker was weedin a bad row for satisfaction then.

I said, "Mr. Tucker, I don't reckon I'll sign no notes this time."

He commenced a scratchin his leg. "Uh-uh, what's the trouble? What's the trouble?"

I said, "Well—" I'd sworn to God and man, in all of my thoughts, when I got that note that Mr. Grace just gived me anyhow, that was the last one. I wouldn't be tied up no suchaway as that again. Mr. Tucker gived me trouble about it but it was nothin that a colored man didn't expect. Long trouble. I had done paid him the money I owed Mr. Reeve and everything. Then I didn't owe nobody nothin but him and Mr. Harry Black. And I paid him every penny he had comin, then I went and paid Mr. Harry Black, too. All right. He couldn't get me to sign at all.

"No sir, I aint signin."

"Well, what's your objection? What's your objection? What you goin to do?"

I said, "Well—"

He said, "You know you aint able to help yourself."

I said, "I don't know that, Mr. Tucker. But it's a matter that I paid you every penny I owed you last fall down there at the bank. I got straight with you at last. I think it would really be better for me now to suffer for some things than to tie myself up in a situation such as that any more. I aint goin to sign no note. Be honest with you, I aint goin to sign. I'm goin to live the best I can, the hard way. Furthermore, I see my way clear that I can go part of the way and then very well live off the fat of my gut."

He said, "You better just go ahead and sign that note because you know you're goin to need—"

I said, "I don't doubt what I'll need but I can do without some, too."

"Uh-uh-uh-uh, by George, I see what you mean now. You goin to fool right around here until May and then you goin to cry for help."

I said, "Well, if I do, there's plenty of time to sign a note in May if it gets up in May and I need money. You can sign a note any time of year."

He seed he couldn't do nothin with me—I was set.

"And I aint signin no note this time at all; no way, shape, form, or fashion."

Jumped back, beggin me. I said, "No, Mr. Tucker, there aint no use. I aint signin no notes. I've made up my mind. I'd rather do without somethin and suffer for it than to get in your debt and be as long payin it as I was before."

Passed him up and he went on and got back in his car, went on home or somewhere and I went on down to Apafalya and done what I wanted to do, every way but sign that note.

All right. Lingered, lingered, lingered—he come back home and he told the rest of the hands, "Uh-uh-uh-uh, by George, old Nate is actin a fool this time. I can't get him to sign no note or do noway. Just actin a fool and he'll pay a fool's pay."

I said, when I seed him again, "If you want me to move, Mr. Tucker, I'll move. It's gettin mighty late in the year to move. You couldn't rent that place to nobody if I move off it. And I'll move before I'll sign any note, I'll just move, let you have your place."

He wouldn't kick at me then. I said to myself, 'Well, now I don't owe you nothin and I've set out to manage my own business.'

And I kept my word: I went several years, all through the year and nothin I had had no mortgage against it. I hauled lumber for the Graham-Pike Lumber Company after my crop was laid by. They paid me enough that I supported my family—my mules got to where they didn't want to eat no corn raised at home, they et so much sweet feed and number one timothy hay and oats; they got to where they wouldn't eat my corn and I had plenty of it.

When I got my note after a five-year run of bein in his debt and I wouldn't sign no other, Mr. Tucker run to every guano dealer there was in Apafalya—he knowed em all—and told em not to let me have no guano. I didn't know he done it until I went into Mr. Bishop's store one day that spring to buy my guano. I thought I'd recognize Mr. Bishop and get my guano where I'd been gettin it. I was my own man, doin business wherever I pleased.

That man turned me down just like I was a dog.

I said, "Mr. Bishop, I been buyin guano from you through Mr. Tucker for several years. Now I paid Mr. Tucker every penny I owed him and I don't owe nobody but what I can pay on it. I don't owe Mr. Tucker a thing. And I thought that by bein straight"—had got enough to get myself straight—"I can just buy my guano myself."

He looked at me, "I wouldn't sell you a bit. Go ahead and buy through Mr. Tucker like you been doin."

I just turned around and walked out. All those white folks there was throwin their weight for one another—I hate to speak as much as I do, in a way, I hate it; wish it hadn't a never happened—Mr. Tucker runned around there and forbidded em all of sellin to me. I couldn't get my guano from Mr. Jack Bishop and I seed I was bein headed somewhere I hadn't planned to go. I left Mr. Bishop and knowin that Mr. Russell was a guano dealer, I walked right straight up the street and went in his store. He was a big shot man, had piles of money. Laid the same larceny on me.

Told him, "I don't owe nobody anythin but what I can pay. I'm clear otherwise. If I could buy guano from you I'd appreciate it, Mr. Russell. I'd go ahead and make my crop and I could easily pay you. I don't owe nobody nothin and I'm only buyin groceries on a light scale. I know my circumstances well—the notes I've made until now I've paid. Haven't had no trouble with nobody that way."

Mr. Russell stood there and listened at me. I told him my background—he said, "Uh-uh-uh-uh-uh-uh, I wouldn't sell you a bit."

Them's the words *he* told me—he stuttered when he talked. "I wouldn't sell you a bit."

I was comin to see in my mind that Tucker had me barred; he done posted my name and guano dealers wouldn't sell to me—tryin to drive me back to him. I didn't like bein geehawsed about that way and objected to. The days I owed Mr. Tucker I labored until I paid him and then I was clear. I was supposed to be a free man to buy from whoever I pleased that would deal with me. But I was knocked clean back just like a dog; couldn't get nothin from nobody. Friendship business amongst the white folks drivin me to one man, the man I'd throwed off me. Well, I seed Mr. Tucker there in Apafalya that evenin and I walked up to him—I was aimin to talk to him bout my fertilize for that year. I said, "Mr. Tucker, it appears to me that I can't buy no guano at all this year, nobody will sell me a bit. You have a hand in that mess, surely. What I want to know is this: what are you goin to do about my fertilize?"

"Uh-uh-uh-uh, by George, you went over to the bank and signed that note?"

I said, "No sir, I aint signed it today and I aint goin to sign."

Told him again. He said, "I aint goin to let you have no guano less'n you sign that note."

I kept a tellin him, "Well, I'll just move. If I can't get no guano I'll move, I'll get off your place. I'm barred by every guano dealer I been to. Mr. Bishop denied me, Mr. Russell denied me—they are the main guano dealers in town."

Told me, "Go on over there and sign that note and you can get all the guano you want."

Told him, "No, I won't sign no note."

Well, Mr. Harry Black would come into town on Saturdays to conduct his business and I knowed where to find him. He was a guano dealer—lived out in the country; didn't have no store operation—and durin the years I lived with Mr. Reeve I bought my guano from him. I was free to buy my guano anywhere I wanted then; in fact of the business, under Mr. Reeve's administration you had to trade for guano thoroughly on your own.

I just politely walked up to Mr. Black and laid my plight to him. I said, "Mr. Black, Mr. Tucker got me barred on fertilize. Won't none of em furnish me no guano. Mr. Bishop first and then Mr. Russell, nary one of them men will sell me a bit. Turned me down straight."

He looked at me, said, "The hell they won't. Goddamnit, I'm goin to see to it—Go on back home and Monday mornin, when you get up, hitch your mules to your wagon and come on down here to Apafalya to the carbox and get all the damn guano you want. I'm goin to show em. They can't do you that way."

I knows a heap and I considers things, too. He was just a different type of man. He was a white man that recognized *all* men.

Mr. Black gived me them strong words. But he hesitated in the doin of it. He said, "Go back to Mr. Tucker *one more time*. Then if he don't let you have it—"

Told me what he'd do if Tucker didn't give me satisfaction. So I went back to Mr. Tucker and I said, "Mr. Tucker, what are you goin to do about lettin me have some guano? You goin to let me have it or not?"

I was sure of myself then. Mr. Black done told me if he objected me again, take my wagon to the carbox Monday mornin and get all the damn guano I wanted. All right. I went back to Mr. Tucker and he seed I weren't desperate no more.

I said, "Mr. Tucker, I'm not tellin you what I'll do if you don't let me have guano, but it won't leave me in no hard position."

He fell out of the box when I told him that. I was my own man; I'd found somebody that would deal with me.

"Uh-uh-uh-uh, by George, go on over there and tell Mr. Bishop I told you to tell him to sell you your guano."

It suited me better to buy my guano from Mr. Bishop and it suited Mr. Black, too. He decided—in business, people have these thoughts—he'd buck them other white men if they was stuck down definitely on me and weren't goin to let me have no guano at all. He fretted with the problem—"Go back to Mr. Tucker one more time—" and he treated me like a gentleman and got his satisfaction out of the deal, too. Mr. Tucker cleared the way for me to get my guano and Mr. Black stayed out of my business. He didn't say he was afraid to let me have it; told me, "Come and get it." But the way the thing worked out that weren't necessary. He just protected hisself and me too.

Mr. Black wasn't goin to let Mr. Tucker bar me from gettin guano after the way Mr. Tucker done treated *him*. Durin the years that joint note mess was runnin, I owed Mr. Black a hundred dollars for guano I'd used on the Reeve place. The first year Mr. Tucker had a hold of me, I met Mr. Black in Apafalya one day, right about the time I was ready to start my crop.

I said, "Mr. Black, I paid you last fall thirty dollars, all that I could pay you for guano. I know I owe you justice—one hundred dollars more. Mr. Tucker has got my business in charge now, what little I got, and I just can't pay you. Thing I'm goin to do is give you a note"—but not thinkin that Tucker would keep Mr. Black roped off like he done—"I'll give you a note that I owes you one hundred cash dollars for fertilize."

He told me, "No, Nate, a note from you wouldn't do me no good because Tucker done got your business in hand. I don't expect you'll soon have the money to pay me."

I said, "Yes sir, I don't doubt what you say, Mr. Black, but I'm goin to give you a note anyhow showin that I owe you until I can pay."

Fall of the year come, first year Mr. Tucker took me over, I couldn't pay Mr. Black a dime. Well, at planting time next spring I offered to give him another note. He told me, "Nate, you didn't pay me nothin, but I understand the matter."

I said, "Yes sir, I'm glad you do. Tucker's between us. Hit or miss, Mr. Black, I'll keep you with a note showin that I owe you."

He was a quiet man, dealt with me quiet. Said, "Your note aint worth a damn, Nate. You aint goin to be able to pay me until Tucker gets out of the way, no matter how long that is. As long as Tucker standin in the gap you aint goin to be able to pay me nothin. No, I wouldn't have a note from you."

I said, "Mr. Black, it'd show that I owes you."

He said, "Yeah, but owin me it makes no difference what it shows. If you can't pay it, you can't pay it."

Left it like that. One day I went into town, met Mr. Black again. He said, "Nate—"

I said, "Yes sir."

He said, "I got a question to ask you."

We stepped off to the side and talked. He said, "Well, my question is this, that I want to ask you." Looked right in my face. Said, "If I die before you pay me, will you pay what you owe me to my children?"

He had grown children, married children at that time. I gladly told him, "Yes sir, Mr. Black, I'll pay it because I know I justly owe you that hundred dollars. I'll pay your children if you happen to die before I pay you."

He said, "That's all, Nate, I wanted your word."

Rocked along there five years and when I did wind up with Mr. Black—he come to see me when I paid off Mr. Tucker; Mr. Tucker put him on me. Five hundred and sixty-nine dollars I got out of three bales of cotton and I paid Mr. Tucker five hundred dollars of it. That left me sixty-nine dollars and some-odd cents. Mr. Tucker jumped up then and got the word to Mr. Black that I done paid him up on all I owed him, clear. Told him—Mr. Black told me about it—told him, "Now's your time come. Nate's got more cotton in the field and he can pay you now."

One day Mr. Black drove his horse and buggy—had a big black mare that he drove to that buggy—come down to my house on Sitimachas Creek. Drove down to the edge of the yard and stopped and I went out to meet him.

He said, "Nate—"

I said, "Mr. Black, I been lookin out for you. I wanted to tell you that I paid Mr. Tucker up on everything I owed him and now you next. You goin to get your money. Ah, yes, you goin to get your money."

He said, "Nate, I didn't drive down here huntin no money; I just drove down here to show myself to you and to let you know what Lemuel done. You done paid him and soon as he got his money he reported it to me. But I didn't come here after your money. I'm goin to leave it up to you and I believe you'll pay me. And I'll just wait until you *can* pay me."

I said, "Well, Mr. Black—"

He said, "I thinks but little of Tucker the way he treated you and the way he treated me. He was the chunk in the way until now. And if he hadn't a done like he did, you woulda paid me, I believe you would."

I offered to give him the balance of the money I got out of them three bales of cotton—he wouldn't have it. Told me, "Nate, I aint worried. I believe you'll pay me and have no diddlin around about it."

I said, "Mr. Black, you just look for it. I'll be down there to your home this comin Wednesday and bring you your money."

I knowed I could take another half a bale of cotton to the gin—cotton was bringin that high wartime price—and I could pay him then. And in the wind-up of the deal I was the most deceived fellow you ever saw. I hurried up and ginned that half a bale of cotton and made a little under a hundred dollars. Went to him Wednesday to my word—Mr. Black is dead now; that's a good white man gone. I'm goin to hold em up if they done right; if they done wrong, I aint scared to tell it—Wednesday come, I told my wife, "Well, I've got to go now and give Mr. Black his money. He wouldn't have what I had here when he come a few days ago. Left that in case I'd a got in a tight, I'd a had a little money. And I promised to go down there today and take him his hundred dollars."

Hitched one of my mules to the buggy, jumped in there, and drove out to Mr. Harry Black. He lived out in the country on the west side of Apafalya on a pretty straight line between Apafalya and Tuskegee. Didn't have to go into Apafalya to get there. Got down there and I called to him. His wife come to the door. She said, "He's gone to Tuskegee and I'm lookin for him any minute."

I told her, "Yes'm. I come here to pay Mr. Black what I owe him. Miz Black, I'll just hitch my mule out here and wait till he comes."

After awhile, I looked down the road and here come Mr. Black, drivin that big black mare and she was fat as a pig. He drove up to the yard and one of his boys come out of the house and took that horse and buggy over. Mr. Black walked right up toward me and I walked part of the way up to him.

I said, "Hello, Mr. Black, I'm here with your money."

He said, "All right, Nate."

I run my hand in my pocket and counted it out to him—one hundred dollars.

He looked it over; he was satisfied. Now what did he do? Somethin I wasn't lookin for! When I counted that hundred dollars into that white man's hand he looked at me, said, "Now hold out your hand—"

I couldn't imagine hard as I tried what he meant by tellin me to hold out my hand.

He said, "Hold out your hand. Hold out your hand."

Counted fifty dollars of that money back in my hand, half of what I'd just paid him. And said, "Now, Nate, I know you've had a hard time. Take that money and go on back home and buy your wife and children some shoes and clothes, as far as it will go with that money. Nate, don't spend it for nothin else."

When I got home with that fifty dollars I gived it to my wife and told her what Mr. Black told me. And that's what it went for—shoes and clothes, clothes and shoes.

Source

Nate Shaw, *All God's Dangers: The Life of Nate Shaw,* compiled by Theodore Rosengarten (New York: Knopf, a division of Random House, 1975), 149–52.

Selected Bibliography

Davis, Ronald L. F. *Good and Faithful Labor: From Slavery to Sharecropping in the Natchez District, 1860–1890.* Westport, Conn.: Greenwood Press, 1982.

Jones, Jacqueline. *Labor of Love, Labor of Sorrow: Black Women, Work, and the Family from Slavery to the Present.* New York: Basic Books, 1985.

Nieman, Donald G., ed. *From Slavery to Sharecropping: White Land and Black Labor in the Rural South, 1865–1900.* New York: Garland, 1994.

Tolnay, Stewart Emory. *The Bottom Rung: African-American Family Life on Southern Farms.* Urbana: University of Illinois Press, 1999.

chapter seven

A Vision of Democracy

one

America

James Monroe Whitfield (1822-1871) was a poet, abolitionist, and emigrationist. In his best-known poem, "America," Whitfield exposed the hypocrisy of a nation that proclaimed its devotion to liberty—thereby articulating a theme that continues to reverberate in African American writing even today. According to one scholar, "Whitfield's poetry of protest and despair are among the . . . most convincing of his time."[1]

Scholars know little about his early life, but as a young man, Whitfield moved to Buffalo, New York, and worked as a barber. Although he never received a formal education, he contributed poems to various abolitionist papers, including Frederick Douglass's *North Star,* in the mid-1840s. In 1854 Whitfield helped to sponsor the National Emigration Convention of Colored Men, and in 1859 he explored potential emigration sites in Central America.

America, it is to thee,
Thou boasted land of liberty,—
It is to thee I raise my song,
Thou land of blood, and crime, and wrong.

It is to thee, my native land,
From which has issued many a band
To tear the black man from his soil,
And force him here to delve and toil;
Chained on your blood-bemoistened sod,
Cringing beneath a tyrant's rod,
Stripped of those rights which Nature's God
    Bequeathed to all the human race.
Bound to a petty tyrant's nod,
    Because he wears a paler face.
Was it for this that freedom's fires
Were kindled by your patriot sires?
Was it for this they shed their blood,
On hill and plain, on field and flood?
Was it for this that wealth and life
Were staked upon that desperate strife,
Which drenched this land for seven long years
With blood of men, and women's tears?
When black and white fought side by side,
    Upon the well-contested field,—
Turned back the fierce opposing tide,
    And made the proud invader yield—
When, wounded, side by side they lay,
    And heard with joy the proud hurrah
From their victorious comrades say
    That they had waged successful war.
The thought ne'er entered in their brains
That they endured those toils and pains,
To forge fresh fetters, heavier chains
For their own children, in whose veins
Should How that patriotic blood,
So freely shed on field and flood.
Oh, no: they fought, as they believed.
    For the inherent rights of man:
But mark, how they have been deceived
    By slavery's accursed plan.
They never thought, when thus they shed
    Their heart's best blood, in freedom's cause,
That their own sons would live in dread,
    Under unjust, oppressive laws:
That those who quietly enjoyed
    The rights for which they fought and fell,

Could be the framers of a code,
    That would disgrace the fiends of hell!
Could they have looked, with prophet's ken,
    Down to the present evil time,
    Seen free-born men, uncharged with crime,
Consigned unto a slaver's pen,—
Or thrust into a prison cell,
With thieves and murderers to dwell—
While that same flag whose stripes and stars
Had been their guide through freedom's wars
As proudly waved above the pen
Of dealers in the souls of men!
Or could the shades of all the dead,
    Who fell beneath that starry flag.
Visit the scenes where they once bled,
    On hill and plain, on vale and crag,
By peaceful brook, or ocean's strand,
    By inland lake, or dark green wood,
Where'er the soil of this wide land
    Was moistened by their patriot blood.—
And then survey the country o'er,
    From north to south, from east to west,
And hear the agonizing cry
Ascending up to God on high,
From western wilds to ocean's shore,
    The fervent prayer of the oppressed:
The cry of helpless infancy
    Torn from the parent's fond caress
By some base tool of tyranny,
    And doomed to woe and wretchedness;
The indignant wail of fiery youth,
    Its noble aspirations crushed,
Its generous zeal, its love of truth,
    Trampled by tyrants in the dust:
The aerial piles which fancy reared,
    And hopes too bright to be enjoyed,
Have passed and left his young heart scared,
    And all its dreams of bliss destroyed.
The shriek of virgin purity,
Doomed to some libertine's embrace,
Should rouse the strongest sympathy
    Of each one of the human race;

And weak old age, oppressed with care,
  As he reviews the scene of strife,
Puts up to God a fervent prayer,
  To close his dark and troubled life,
The cry of fathers, mothers, wives,
  Severed from all their hearts hold dear,
And doomed to spend their wretched lives
  In gloom, and doubt, and hate, and fear:
And manhood, too, with soul of fire,
And arm of strength, and smothered ire,
Stands pondering with brow of gloom,
Upon his dark unhappy doom,
Whether to plunge in battle's strife,
And buy his freedom with his life,
And with stout heart and weapon strong,
Pay back the tyrant wrong for wrong
Or wait the promised time of God,
  When his Almighty ire shall wake,
And smite the oppressor in his wrath,
And hurl red ruin in his path,
And with the terrors of his rod,
  Cause adamantine hearts to quake.
Here Christian writhes in bondage still,
  Beneath his brother Christian's rod,
And pastors trample down at will,
  The image of the living God.
While prayers go up in lofty strains.
  And pealing hymns ascend to heaven,
The captive, toiling in his chains,
  With tortured limbs and bosom riven,
Raises his fettered hand on high,
  And in the accents of despair,
To him who rules both earth and sky,
  Puts up a sad, a fervent prayer,
To free him from the awful blast
  Of slavery's bitter galling shame—
Although his portion should be cast
  With demons in eternal flame!
Almighty God! 'tis this they call
  The land of liberty and law;
Part of its sons in baser thrall
  Than Babylon or Egypt saw—

Worse scenes of rapine, lust and shame,
    Than Babylonian ever knew,
Are perpetrated in the name
    Of God, the holy, just, and true:
And darker doom than Egypt felt,
May yet repay this nation's guilt.
Almighty God! thy aid impart,
And fire anew each faltering heart,
And strengthen every patriot's hand.
Who aims to save our native land.
We do not come before thy throne,
    With carnal weapons drenched in gore,
Although our blood has freely flown,
    In adding to the tyrant's store.
Father! before thy throne we come,
    Not in the panoply of war,
With pealing trump, and rolling drum,
    And cannon booming loud and far:
Striving in blood to wash out blood,
    Through wrong to seek redress for wrong:
For while thou'rt holy, just and good,

The battle is not to the strong:
But in the sacred name of peace,
    Of justice, virtue, love and truth.
We pray, and never mean to cease,
    Till weak old age and fiery youth
In freedom's cause their voices raise,
And burst the bonds of every slave:
Till, north and south, and east and west,
The wrongs we bear shall be redressed.

Note

1. Rayford W. Logan and Michael R. Winston, *Dictionary of American Negro Biography* (New York: Norton, 1982), 650.

Source

James Monroe Whitfield, "America," in *America and Other Poems* (Buffalo, N.Y.: James S. Leavitt, 1853), 9–16.

Selected Bibliography

Brawley, Benjamin, ed. *Early American Negro Writers: Selections with Biographical and Critical Introductions*. Urbana: University of Illinois Press, 1989.

Loggins, Vernon. *The Negro Author: His Development in America to 1900*. Port Washington, N.Y.: Kennikat Press, 1964.

Sherman, Joan R. *Invisible Poets: Afro-Americans of the 19th Century*. Urbana: University of Illinois Press, 1989.

Whitfield, James Monroe. *America and Other Poems*. Alexandria, Va.: Chadwyck-Healy, 1995.

t w o

On American "Democracy" and the Negro

Robert Purvis (1810–1898) was among the most revered activists and abolitionists of his day. His speech "On American 'Democracy' and the Negro," which was delivered on the cusp of the Civil War, originally appeared in the *Liberator*—a leading abolitionist newspaper. Purvis put forth a withering indictment of the United States government, calling it to task for its failure to extend democracy to black slaves.

Born in Charleston, South Carolina, Purvis gave his first antislavery speech at the age of seventeen. He later attended Amherst College. In 1826 Purvis inherited a large sum of money, and in 1831 he married Harriet Forten, daughter of the well-known abolitionist Charles Forten. In addition to cofounding the American Anti-Slavery Society, Purvis also delivered antislavery lectures, housed runaway slaves, and was an early supporter of women's rights.

What is the attitude of your boasting, braggart republic toward the 600,000 free people of color who swell its population and add to its wealth? I have already alluded to the dictum of Judge Taney[1] in the notorious Dred Scott decision.[2] That dictum reveals the animus of the whole government; it is a fair example of the cowardly and malignant spirit that pervades the entire policy of the country. The end of that policy is, undoubtedly, to destroy the colored man, as a man, to prevent him from having any existence in the land except as a "chattel personal to all intents, constructions and purposes whatsoever." With this view, it says a colored man shall not sue and recover his lawful property; he shall not bear arms and train in the militia; he shall not be a commander of a vessel, not even of the meanest craft that creeps along the creeks and bays of your Southern coast; he shall not carry a mailbag or serve as a porter in a post-office; and he shall not even put his face in a United States court-room for any purpose, except by the sufferance of the white man.

I had occasion, a few days since, to go to the United States court-room in the city of Philadelphia. My errand was a proper one; it was to go bail for one of the noble band of colored men who had so bravely risked their lives for the rescue of a brother man on his way to eternal bondage. As I was about entering the door, I was stopped, and ordered back. I demanded the reason. "I have my orders," was the reply, What orders? "To keep out all colored people." Now, sir, who was the man that offered me this indignity? It was Deputy-Marshal Jenkins, the notorious slave-catcher. And why did he do it? Because he had his orders from pious, praying, Christian Democrats, who hold and teach the damnable doctrine that the "black man has no rights that the white man is bound to respect." It is true that Marshal Yost, to whom I indignantly appealed, reversed this man's orders, and apologized to me, assuring me that I could go in and out at my pleasure. But, sir, the apology made the matter worse; for, mark you, it was not me personally that was objected to, *but the race* with which I stand identified. Great God! who can think of such outrages, such meanness, such dastardly, cowardly cruelty, without burning with indignation, and choking for want of words with which to denounce it? And in the case of the noble little band referred to, the men who generously, heroically risked their lives to rescue the man who was about being carried back to slavery; look at their conduct; you know the circumstances. We recently had a slave trial in Philadelphia—no new thing in the city of "*Brotherly Love.*" A victim of Virginia tyranny, a fugitive from Southern injustice, had made good his escape from the land of whips and chains to Pennsylvania, and had taken up his abode near the capital of the State. The place of his retreat was discovered; the bloodhounds of the law scented him out, and caught him; they put him in chains and brought him before Judge Cadwallader—a man whose pro-slavery antecedents made him a fitting instrument for the execution of the accursed Fugitive Slave Law.[3]

The sequel can easily be imagined. Brewster, a leading Democrat—the man, who, like your O'Conor of this city, has the unblushing hardihood to defend the enslavement of the black man upon principle—advocated his return. The man was sent into life-long bondage. While the trial was going on, slaveholders, Southern students and pro-slavery Market-street salesmen were freely admitted; but the colored people, the class most interested, were carefully excluded. Prohibited from entering, they thronged around the door of the court-house. At last the prisoner was brought out, handcuffed and guarded by his captors; he was put into a carriage which started off in the direction of the South. Some ten or twelve brave black men made a rush for the carriage, in hopes of effecting a rescue; they were overpowered, beaten, put under arrest and carried to prison, there to await their trial, before this same Judge Cadwallader, for violating the Fugitive Slave law! Mark you, they may go into the court-room as *prisoners,* but not as *spectators*. They may not have an opportunity of hearing the law expounded, but they may be punished if they make themselves chargeable with violating it!

Sir, people talk of the bloody code of Draco,[4] but I venture to assert, without fear of intelligent contradiction, that, all things considered, that code was mild, that code was a law of love, compared with the hellish laws and precedents that disgrace the statute-books of this modern Democratic, Christian Republic! I said that a man of color might not be a commander of the humblest craft that sails in your American waters. There was a man in Philadelphia, the other day, who stated that he owned and sailed a schooner between that city and different ports in the State of Maryland—that his vessel had been seized in the town of Easton, (I believe it was,) or some other town on the Eastern Shore, on the allegation that, contrary to law, there was no white man on board. The vessel constituted his entire property and sole means of supporting his family. He was advised to sue for its recovery, which he did, and, after a long and expensive litigation, the case was decided in his favor. But by this time the vessel had rotted and gone to wreck, and the man found himself reduced to beggary. His business in Philadelphia was to raise $50 with which to take himself and family out of this cursed land, to a country where liberty is not a mockery, and freedom a mere idle name! . . .

But, sir, narrow and proscriptive as, in my opinion, is the spirit of what is called Native Americanism, there is another thing I regard as tenfold more base and contemptible, and that is your American Democracy—your piebald and rotten Democracy, that talks loudly about equal rights, and at the same time tramples one-sixth of the population of the country in the dust, and declares that they have "no rights which a white man is bound to respect." And, sir, while I repudiate your Native Americanism and your bogus Democracy, allow me to add, at the same time, that I am not a Republican. I could not be a member of the Republican party if I were so disposed; I am disfranchised; I have no vote; I am put out of the pale of political society. The time was in Pennsylvania, under the old Constitution, when I could go to the polls as other men do, but your modern Democracy have taken away from me that right. Your Reform Convention, your Pierce Butlers—the man who, a year ago, put up nearly four hundred human beings on the block in Georgia, and sold them to the highest bidder—your Pierce Butlers disfranchised me, and I am without any political rights whatever. I am taxed to support a government which takes my money and tramples on me. But, sir, I would not be a member of the Republican party if it were in my power. How could I, a colored man, join a party that styles itself emphatically the "white man's party!?" How could I, an Abolitionist, belong to a party that is and must of necessity be a pro-slavery party? The Republicans may be, and doubtless are, opposed to the extension of slavery, but they are sworn to support, and they *will* support, slavery where it already exists.

Notes

1. Roger Brooke Taney (1777–1864), fifth chief justice of the U.S. Supreme Court (1836–1864). Taney's most notorious decision was in the Dred Scott case.
2. The Dred Scott case, argued before the U.S. Supreme Court in 1856–57, involved the status of slavery in the federal territories. The court's ruling that slaves and their descendents had no rights as citizens and that Congress could not forbid slavery in the territories helped precipitate the Civil War.
3. Passed by Congress in 1850, the Fugitive Slave Law made the federal government responsible for tracking down and apprehending fugitive slaves in the North and mandated that suspected runaways could not ask for a jury trial or testify on their own behalf.
4. Draco (seventh century B.C.), Athenian lawyer whose harsh legal code punished both trivial and serious crimes in Athens with death—hence the continued use of the word *draconian* to describe repressive legal measures.

Source

Robert Purvis, "On American 'Democracy' and the Negro," *The Liberator*, May 18, 1860, 78.

Selected Bibliography

Boyd, Herb, ed. *Autobiography of a People: Three Centuries of African-American History Told by Those Who Lived It.* New York: Doubleday, 2000.

Purvis, Robert. *Remarks on the Life and Character of James Forten, Delivered at Bethel Church, March 20, 1982.* Philadelphia: Merrihew and Thompson, 1848.

Reed, Harry. *Platforms for Change: The Foundations of the Northern Free Black Community, 1775–1865.* East Lansing: Michigan State University Press, 1994.

Trotter, Joe William and Eric Ledell Smith. *African-Americans in Pennsylvania.* University Park: Pennsylvania Historical Museum Commission, 1997.

three

Negro Patriotism and Devotion

Kelly Miller (1863–1939) devoted his life to promoting education for African Americans, and to defusing racial tensions across the globe. In "Negro Patriotism and Devotion," Miller testified to the patriotism of most African Americans and intervened in a debate about whether blacks should serve in World War I when their basic civil liberties were being denied to them in the United States. Miller proclaimed that democracy was a force that was swiftly being extended across the globe and that by virtue of their service in a desperate time, African Americans would benefit enormously in the postwar transformation of society.

Born during the Civil War to a Confederate father and a slave mother, Miller studied at Howard University and Johns Hopkins University. He subsequently taught at Howard from 1890 to 1934, where he served as chairman of the Department of Sociology and eventually became dean of the College of Arts and Sciences. Miller also worked as a journalist and wrote a weekly column for the black press. His books include *Race Adjustment (1903),* History of the World War and the Important Part Taken by the Negro (1919), and *The Everlasting Stain (1924).*

Patriotism consists in the love of country, the love of home and of the local community. It is essentially an emotional attribute. The Negro is endowed with high emotional qualities which find outlet in outbursts of patriotic fervor. He possesses a sense of local attachment akin to that which the Jews manifested for beloved Zion. No sooner had the African captive forgotten the pang caused by violent severance from his native land than he fell in love with the land of his captivity. He early forgot the sunny clime and palmy wine of the native soil for the "cotton, corn and sweet potatoes" of Virginia. The transplanted Negro contributed the only original American music to the repertory of song. The city of Jerusalem and the region around about Jordan have become prototypes of the land of promise, merely because the humble people who lived there poured out their souls in joy and sorrow, expressing their patriotic attachment as transcending their chief joy. The Hebrew captive hung his harp upon a willow tree and refused to sing the songs of Zion in a strange land. But the transplanted African has glorified the land of his captivity by the songs of sorrow which sprang from his heart. These "spirituels" are but the expression of blind, half-conscious poetry, breaking through the aperture of sound before the intellect had time to formulate a definite cast of statement. The emotional element of patriotism is not manifested merely in epochs and episodes which produce renowned warriors and statesmen, but in the common deeds and endearments of the humble folk, which make the deepest impression upon the human memory and imagination. It is the folk song which manifests the folk soul.

The red Indian, the aboriginal owner of this country, has left no monument of enduring patriotism interpretable in terms of European thought and feeling. Anomalously enough, it was reserved to an Anglo-Saxon poet, Longfellow, to catch up the thread of the Indian's patriotic devotion in the legend of Hiawatha, and to the son of Africa, S. Coleridge Taylor, to give it musical expression. It is difficult to describe the current of feeling that flows through the soul of the speculative auditor as he listens to Negro voices in a choral rendition of Hiawatha, uttering with lyric pathos the patriotic soul of the red Indian, as portrayed by the Anglo-Saxon poet, and colored musically by the genius of the African composer.

Robert Burns, the national poet of Scotland, has seized upon the joys and sorrows, the deeds and endearments of the humblest cotters of that land, and woven them into soulful song which has made old Scotia ever dear to human memory and imagination. Who would not gladly go to the expense of a European trip in order to retrace the steps of the immortalized Tam O'Shanter, or to review the scene of Mary—poor, departed shade?

If human memory and imagination ever turn to our Southland with a passionate yearning for a manifestation of the outpouring of the human spirit, it will not be in quest of the deeds and doings of renowned warriors and statesmen, but rather in quest of the songs and sorrows and soul strivings of humble black folk embodied in plantation melodies. "Swanee River," "My Old Kentucky Home," and "Carry Me Back to Ole Virginny," spiritualize these regions beyond any other expression which they have yet evoked. Even the motif of the musical inspiration of the southern Confederacy, the world-renowned "Dixie," was but the embellishment of the expression of longing of a Negro for his homeland, where he was born "on an autumn day and a frosty morning." Which of America's patriotic songs would we not willingly exchange for "Swing Low, Sweet Chariot," or "Steal Away to Jesus"? There is no tone of bitterness in these songs. On the contrary, an undertone of love and devotion runs like a minor chord through them all. The plantation melodies which have come up from the low grounds of sorrow portray in sub-conscious form the patriotic as well as emotional capacity of this transplanted race.

They sometimes tell us that America is a white man's country. The statement is understandable in light of the fact that the white race constitutes nine-tenths of its population, and exerts the controlling influence over the various forms of material and substantial wealth and power. But this land belongs to the Negro as much as to any other, not only because he has helped redeem it from the wilderness by the energy of his arm, but because he has bathed it in his blood, watered it with his tears, and hallowed it with the yearnings of his soul.

The Negro's patriotism is vicarious and altruistic. It seems to be an anomaly of fate that the Negro, the man of all men who is held in despite, should stand out in conspicuous relief at every crisis of our national history. His blood offering is not for himself or for his race, but for his country. His blood flows like a stream through our national history, from Boston Commons to Carrizal. Crispus Attucks was the first American to give his blood as an earnest of American independence. His statue on Boston Common stands as a mute reminder of the vicarious virtues of a transplanted race. The Negro was with Washington in the dark days of Valley Forge, when the lamp of national liberty flickered almost to extinguishment. The black troops fought gallantly with Jackson behind the fleecy breastworks at New Orleans. Two hundred thousand black boys in blue responded to the call of the immortal Lincoln for the preservation of the Union. The Negro was the positive cause of the Civil War and the negative cause of the united nation with which we face the world today.

The reckless daring of Negro troops on San Juan hill marked the turning point in that struggle which drove the last vestige of Spanish power from the western world. The nation buried with grateful honor at Arlington cemetery the Negro soldiers who fell face forward while carrying the flag to the farthest point in the heart of Mexico, in quest of the bandit who dared place hostile foot on American soil. In complete harmony with this splendid patriotic record, it so happened that it was an American Negro who proved to be the first victim of ruthless submarine warfare after President Wilson had distinctly announced to Germany that the continuance of such outrage would be considered tantamount to war. In all of these ways has the Negro shown, purposely or unconsciously, his undeviating association with the glory and honor of the nation. Greater love hath no man than this, that a man lay down his life for his country.

It is related that a Negro soldier was in hot-footed pursuit of a Mexican who had crossed the border line. The captain, noticing the pursuit, called a sharp retreat as the line of demarcation was approached. Upon his return, the captain said in a commendatory tone: "You certainly gave him a hot chase, but, you know, you must not cross the international boundary line." Thereupon the powder-colored son of thunder quickly responded: "Captain, if these Mexicans keep on fooling with us, we'll take up this international boundary line and carry it down to the Panama Canal." This reply, so aptly spoken, expresses the attitude of every right minded Afro-American. Wherever the boundary line of American opportunity, privilege and prestige is to be flung, the American Negro will do his full share in pushing it thitherward.

The Negro's vicarious patriotism is but one form of manifestation of his vicarious nature. The devotion of the black mammy to the offspring of her mistress gives a new meaning and definition to that term. Out of the superabundance of her simple, unsophisticated soul she was able to satisfy the needs of the child of her heart, though not of her flesh, as nothing else could do. The man-slave, during the Civil War, in complete reversion of the law of self-interest, remained absolutely loyal to the family and fortune of his master, who at that very time was fighting to tighten the chains that bound him to lasting bondage.

Though not often proclaimed, it is a well known fact that several colored regiments enlisted under the banner of the Confederacy. Had the Richmond government carried out its tentative purpose to enlist Negro soldiers on a wholesale plan, there is little doubt but that colored soldiers would have followed the leadership of Lee as valiantly as they did that of Grant. This altruistic quality of loyalty and devotion is not destroyed by freedom and education, but translated and expressed in other terms.

Fifty years after the glorious victory at Appomattox, the lingering remnants of the boys in blue marched down Pennsylvania Avenue in the city of Washington, in semi-centennial celebration of that great event. There was not a dry eye on that Avenue, as white and black veterans, broken with the weight of years, marched with feeble tread to the reminiscent strains of friendly reunion: "Should Auld Acquaintance Be Forgot?" One year later the rapidly thinning ranks of those who followed the fortune of the Confederacy marched down the same thoroughfare in celebration of their triumphant defeat. There was a noticeable intersprinkling of Negroes in their ranks also. The Negro's participation in these two parades epitomizes and expresses both his self-interested and his altruistic patriotism.

Ethnic character is too deep-rooted to be transformed by a political program. The Christ-like quality of long-suffering, forgiveness of spirit and loving-kindness is a natural coefficient of the Negro's nature. Booker Washington merely embodied and expressed the folk sense of his race when he said: "No man could be so mean as to make me hate him." The Negro, in the issue now upon us, will not sulk in his tent, nursing his grievances, like Achilles before the walls of Troy. He has no quarrel with the Germans. But he is fighting at the behest of his country. It is not to be wondered at if the German government, supposing that the Negro holds animosity and resentment with the stubbornness of the Teuton, should judge that he might furnish a fertile field in which to sow the seed of traitorous disloyalty. But such seed falls on stony ground. There is no depth of earth in the Negro's nature for its nourishment. The Negro will not deny or belittle his just grievances. He simply holds them in abeyance until the war is ended.

If it be a political as it is a sacred principle that without the shedding of blood there is no remission of sins, when we consider the blood of the African captive making red the Atlantic Ocean on his way to cruel bondage, the blood of the slave drawn by the lash, the blood of the black soldier shed in behalf of his country, we can say with Kipling: "If blood be the price of liberty, Lord God! the Negro has paid in full."

At such a time as this, when the national life and honor are involved in the prevailing struggle, the government must make careful appraisement of all available resources of both men and material. Mind power, man power and money power are the indispensable elements of success. The Negro, constituting one-tenth of the population, may be relied upon to contribute more than his quota of man power. There need not be the slightest apprehension concerning his loyalty, soldierly efficiency or willingness to serve his country. The Negro is sometimes called the Afro-American, and classified etymologically with the hyphenated citizens. But no hyphen separates his loyalty from that of his white fellow citizens.

The Negro's patriotism is an innate and spontaneous feeling. The race is endowed with emotional qualities which find outlet in an outburst of patriotic fervor. Strains of martial music and the Stars and Stripes floating on the breeze quicken his ardor and awaken his militant spirit. He does not stop to reason why, but is willing to follow the flag even unto death. He has also an attachment for locality which is the very essence of patriotism. He has hallowed the land of his enslavement by the sorrow songs that gushed from his heart. There is no tone of bitterness, but an undertone of love and devotion runs as a minor chord through it all.

"To the victor belong the spoils" is a righteous and just motto if the spoils be liberty. Those who fight for the honor and glory of the flag are worthy of a full measure of freedom and privilege under that flag. No right-minded American will care to dispute this proposition, and none will dare refute it. The reverse of this proposition is also true. No class that refuses to defend the flag in the hour of peril has any just claim to its protection in time of peace. The present war is a struggle for democracy; for the uplifting and ennoblement of the man farthest down. Racial and religious barriers are being swept away. Christian and heathen, Catholic and Protestant, Jew and Gentile, Asiatic and European, African and Aryan are all involved in one titanic struggle for freedom and humanity.

The world is engulfed in the red ruin of war. The present conflict is not due to the inherent deviltry of one nation or the innate goodness of the other. The cumulative ethical energies of society for generations have been damned up by barriers of hatred and greed. They seek outlet through the easiest crevice. The stored-up power is now breaking through the barrier as a cataclysmic convulsion of nations. The foundations of social order are being undermined by the shocks of doom. As an outcome of the war, the re-adjustment of the social structure will be more radical than that effected by the French Revolution. The transforming effect upon the status of the Negro will be scarcely less momentous than that produced by the Emancipation Proclamation.

The democratization of the world, coined as a fitting phrase, will be translated into actuality. The Declaration of Independence, penned by a slaveholder, sounded the death knell of slavery, although three quarters of a century elapsed between promise and fulfilment. The democratization of the world is but a restatement of this doctrine in terms of the present day. Political autocracy and racial autocracy will be buried in the same grave. The divine right of kings and the divine right of race will suffer a common fate. Hereafter no nation, however strong, will be permitted to override a weaker neighbor by sheer dominance of power; and no race will be permitted to impose an unjust and ruthless *régime* upon the weaker breeds of men through assumption of race superiority.

The people of all lands who are heavy laden and overborne will be the chief beneficiaries of this war. The Negro problem is involved in the problem of humanity. The whole is greater than any of its parts. The Negro will share in the general momentum imparted to social welfare.

The Negro has been politically disfranchised in the South and industrially disfranchised in the North. Already he has been admitted to industrial opportunity in the North with manifest reflex action upon the harsh *régime* in the South. National prohibition, which is borne forward on the wave of the world war, will immensely improve his moral status.

Thousands of Negroes have been enlisted, and seven hundred Negroes have been commissioned as officers in the army of the United States. A Negro has been made assistant cabinet officer whose function is to adjust harmoniously the race's relation to the impending struggle. The improved attitude of the white race towards the Negro is apparent in two affirmative decisions rendered by the Supreme Court of the United States with unanimous concurrence.

The Negro will emerge from this war with a redoubled portion of privilege and opportunity. The Negro will be loyal and patriotic, despite injustices and discriminations which try his soul. If he prevails, these trials and tribulations will work out a more exceeding weight of advantage. But if he allows them to overcome him, woeful will be his lot indeed! To stand sulkily by in resentful aloofness would be of the same kind of folly as to refuse to help extinguish a conflagration which threatens the destruction of one's native city, because he has a complaint against the fire department. The Negro will help put out the conflagration which threatens the world, and thus make the world his lasting debtor. He will stand shoulder to shoulder with his white fellow citizens to fight for the freedom of the world outside of our own national circle, and then hold them to moral consistency of maintaining a just and equitable *régime* inside of that circle.

The tide of democracy is sweeping through the world like a mighty river. Race problems and social ills are as marshes, backwaters, stagnant pools, estuaries, which have been shut off from free circulation with the main current. But the freshet of freedom is now overflowing its bed and purifying all the stagnant waters in its onward sweep to the ocean of human liberty and brotherhood, bearing upon its beneficent bosom all those who labor and are overborne.

Source

An Appeal to Conscience, 68–86 (New York: Arno Press, Inc., 1969).

Selected Bibliography

Lutz, Tom and Susanna Ashton, eds. *These "Colored" United States: Afro-American Essays from the 1920s.* New Brunswick, N.J.: Rutgers University Press, 1996.

Miller, Kelly. *Race Adjustment (and) The Everlasting Stain.* New York: Arno Press, 1968.

—— *Radicals and Conservatives, and Other Essays on the Negro in America,* New York: Schocken Books, 1968.

four

Our Democracy and the Ballot

James Weldon Johnson (1871–1938) had a rich and varied career as a lawyer, author, diplomat, and writer and was known as one of the most eloquent speakers of his day. In this address, delivered in 1923 at a dinner for congressman F. H. LaGuardia at the Hotel Pennsylvania in New York City, Johnson revealed the duplicity of Southern politicians who espoused the tenets of democracy even as they denied African Americans access to the ballot, thereby smothering democracy's very essence.

Born in Jacksonville, Florida, and educated at Atlanta and Columbia Universities, Johnson served as U.S. consul in Venezuela from 1906 to 1909 and in Nicaragua from 1909 to 1912. In 1920 he became the first black executive secretary of the NAACP. In 1912 he anonymously published a fictional memoir, *The Autobiography of an Ex-Colored Man,* which grappled with questions of racial identity in the United States. He also penned they lyrics to the well-known song "Lift Every Voice and Sing" (widely known today as the Negro National Anthem) and compiled and arranged two books of Negro spirituals and a collection of free-verse sermons. He was killed in an auto accident 1938.

Ladies and Gentlemen:

For some time since I have had growing apprehensions about any subject—especially the subject of a speech—that contained the word "democracy." The word "democracy" carries so many awe-inspiring implications. As the key-word of the subject of an address it may be the presage of an outpour of altitudinous and platitudinous expressions regarding "the most free and glorious government of the most free and glorious people that the world has ever seen." On the other hand, it may hold up its sleeve, if you will permit such a figure, a display of abstruse and recondite theorizations or hypotheses of democracy as a system of government. In choosing between either of these evils it is difficult to decide which is the lesser.

Indeed, the wording of my subject gave me somewhat more concern than the speech. I am not sure that it contains the slightest idea of what I shall attempt to say; but if the wording of my subject is loose it only places upon me greater reason for being more specific and definite in what I shall say. This I shall endeavor to do; at the same time, however, without being so confident or so cocksure as an old preacher I used to listen to on sundry Sundays when I taught school one summer down in the backwoods of Georgia, sometimes to my edification and often to my amazement.

On one particular Sunday, after taking a rather cryptic text, he took off his spectacles and laid them on the pulpit, closed the Bible with a bang, and said, "Brothers and sisters, this morning I intend to explain the inexplainable, to find out the indefinable, to ponder over the imponderable, and to unscrew the inscrutable."

Our Democracy and the Ballot

It is one of the commonplaces of American thought that we have a democracy based upon the free will of the governed. The popular idea of the strength of this democracy is that it is founded upon the fact that every American citizen, through the ballot, is a ruler in his own right; that every citizen of age and outside of jail or the insane asylum has the undisputed right to determine through his vote by what laws he shall be governed and by whom these laws shall be enforced.

I could be cynical or flippant and illustrate in how many ways this popular idea is a fiction, but it is not my purpose to deal in *cleverisms*. I wish to bring to your attention seriously a situation, a condition, which not only runs counter to the popular conception of democracy in America but which runs counter to the fundamental law upon which that democracy rests and which, in addition, is a negation of our principles of government and a menace to our institutions.

Without any waste of words, I come directly to a condition which exists in that section of our country which we call "the South," where millions of American citizens are denied both the right to vote and the privilege of qualifying themselves to vote. I refer to the wholesale disfranchisement of Negro citizens. There is no need at this time of going minutely into the methods employed to bring about this condition or into the reasons given as justification for those methods. Neither am I called upon to give proof of my general statement that millions of Negro citizens in the South are disfranchised. It is no secret. There are the published records of state constitutional conventions in which the whole subject is set forth with brutal frankness. The purpose of these state constitutional conventions is stated over and over again, that purpose being to exclude from the right of franchise the Negro, however literate, and to include the white man, however illiterate.

The press of the South, public men in public utterances, and representatives of those states in Congress, have not only admitted these facts but have boasted of them. And so we have it as an admitted and undisputed fact that there are upwards of four million Negroes in the South who are denied the right to vote but who in any of the great northern, mid-western or western states would be allowed to vote or would at least have the privilege of qualifying themselves to vote.

Now, nothing is further from me than the intention to discuss this question either from an anti-South point of view or from a pro-Negro point of view. It is my intention to put it before you purely as an American question, a question in which is involved the political life of the whole country.

Let us first consider this situation as a violation, not merely a violation but a defiance, of the Constitution of the United States. The Fourteenth and Fifteenth Amendments[1] to the Constitution taken together express so plainly that a grammar school boy can understand it that the Negro is created a citizen of the United States and that as such he is entitled to all the rights of every other citizen and that those rights, specifically among them the right to vote, shall not be denied or abridged by the United States or by any state. This is the expressed meaning of these amendments in spite of all the sophistry and fallacious pretense which have been invoked by the courts to overcome it.

There are some, perhaps even here, who feel that it is no more serious a matter to violate or defy one amendment to the constitution than another. Such persons will have in mind the Eighteenth Amendment. This is true in a strictly legal sense, but any sort of analysis will show that violation of the two Civil War Amendments strikes deeper. As important as the Eighteenth Amendment may be, it is not fundamental; it contains no grant of rights to the citizen nor any requirement of service from him. It is rather a sort of welfare regulation for his personal conduct and for his general moral uplift.

But the two Civil War Amendments are grants of citizenship rights and a guarantee of protection in those rights, and therefore their observation is fundamental and vital not only to the citizen but to the integrity of the government.

We may next consider it as a question of political franchise equality between the states. We need not here go into a list of figures. A few examples will strike the difference:

In the elections of 1920 it took 82,492 votes in Mississippi to elect two senators and eight representatives. In Kansas it took 570,220 votes to elect exactly the same representation. Another illustration from the statistics of the same election shows that one vote in Louisiana has fifteen times the political power of one vote in Kansas.

In the Congressional elections of 1918 the total vote for the ten representatives from the State of Alabama was 62,345, while the total vote for ten representatives in Congress from Minnesota was 299,127, and the total vote in Iowa, which has ten representatives, was 316,377.

In the Presidential election of 1916 the states of Alabama, Arkansas, Georgia, Louisiana, Mississippi, North Carolina, South Carolina, Tennessee, Texas and Virginia cast a total vote for the Presidential candidates of 1,870,209. In Congress these states have a total of 104 representatives and 126 votes in the electoral college. The State of New York alone cast a total vote for Presidential candidates of 1,706,354, a vote within 170,000 of all the votes cast by the above states, and yet New York has only 43 representatives and 45 votes in the electoral college.

What becomes of our democracy when such conditions of inequality as these can be brought about through chicanery, the open violation of the law and defiance of the Constitution?

But the question naturally arises, What if there is violation of certain clauses of the Constitution; what if there is an inequality of political power among the states? All this may be justified by necessity.

In fact, the justification is constantly offered. The justification goes back and makes a long story. It is grounded in memories of the Reconstruction period. Although most of those who were actors during that period have long since died, and although there is a new South and a new Negro, the argument is still made that the Negro is ignorant, the Negro is illiterate, the Negro is venal, the Negro is inferior; and, therefore, for the preservation of civilized government in the South, he must be debarred from the polls. This argument does not take into account the fact that the restrictions are not against ignorance, illiteracy and venality, because by the very practices by which intelligent, decent Negroes are debarred, ignorant and illiterate white men are included.

Is this pronounced desire on the part of the South for an enlightened franchise sincere, and what has been the result of these practices during the past forty years? What has been the effect socially, intellectually and politically, on the South? In all three of these vital phases of life the South is, of all sections of the country, at the bottom. Socially, it is that section of the country where public opinion allows it to remain the only spot in the civilized world—no, more than that, we may count in the blackest spots of Africa and the most unfrequented islands of the sea—it is a section where public opinion allows it to remain the only spot on the earth where a human being may be publicly burned at the stake.

And what about its intellectual and political life? As to intellectual life I can do nothing better than quote from Mr. H. L. Mencken,[2] himself a Southerner. In speaking of the intellectual life of the South, Mr. Mencken says:

> "It is, indeed, amazing to contemplate so vast a vacuity. One thinks of the interstellar spaces, of the colossal reaches of the now mythical ether. One could throw into the South France, Germany and Italy, and still have room for the British Isles. And yet, for all its size and all its wealth and all the 'progress' it babbles of, it is almost as sterile, artistically, intellectually, culturally, as the Sahara Desert. . . . If the whole of the late Confederacy were to be engulfed by a tidal wave tomorrow, the effect on the civilized minority of men in the world would be but little greater than that of a flood on the Yang-tse-kiang. It would be impossible in all history to match so complete a drying-up of a civilization. In all that section there is not a single poet, not a serious historian, not a creditable composer, not a critic good or bad, not a dramatist dead or alive."

In a word, it may be said that this whole section where, at the cost of the defiance of the Constitution, the perversion of law, the stultification of men's consciousness, injustice and violence upon a weaker group, the "purity" of the ballot has been preserved and the right to vote restricted to only lineal survivors of Lothrop Stoddard's mystical Nordic supermen[3]—that intellectually it is dead and politically it is rotten.

If this experiment in super-democracy had resulted in one one-hundredth of what was promised, there might be justification for it, but the result has been to make the South a section not only in which Negroes are denied the right to vote, but one in which white men dare not express their honest political opinions. Talk about political corruption through the buying of votes, here is political corruption which makes a white man fear to express a divergent political opinion. The actual and total result of this practice has been not only the disfranchisement of the Negro but the disfranchisement of the white man. The figures which I quoted a few moments ago prove that not only Negroes are denied the right to vote but that white men fail to exercise it; and the latter condition is directly dependent upon the former.

The whole condition is intolerable and should be abolished. It has failed to justify itself even upon the grounds which it is claimed made it necessary. Its results and its tendencies make it more dangerous and more damaging than anything which might result from an ignorant and illiterate electorate. How this iniquity might be abolished is, however, another story.

I said that I did not intend to present this subject either as anti-South or pro-Negro, and I repeat that I have not wished to speak with anything that approached bitterness toward the South. Indeed, I consider the condition of the South unfortunate, more than unfortunate. The South is in a state of superstition which makes it see ghosts and bogymen, ghosts which are the creation of its own mental processes.

With a free vote in the South the specter of Negro domination would vanish into thin air. There would naturally follow a breaking up of the South into two parties. There would be political light, political discussion, the right to differences of opinion, and the Negro vote would naturally divide itself. No other procedure would be probable. The idea of a solid party, a minority party at that, is inconceivable.

But perhaps the South will not see the light. Then, I believe, in the interest of the whole country, steps should be taken to compel compliance with the Constitution, and that should be done through the enforcement of the Fourteenth Amendment, which calls for a reduction in representation in proportion to the number of citizens in any state denied the right to vote.

And now I cannot sit down after all without saying one word for the group of which I am a member.

The Negro in the matter of the ballot demands only that he should be given the right as an American citizen to vote under the identical qualifications required of other citizens. He cares not how high those qualifications are made—whether they include the ability to read and write, or the possession of five hundred dollars, or a knowledge of the Einstein Theory[4]—just so long as these qualifications are impartially demanded of white men and black men.

In this controversy over which have been waged battles of words and battles of blood, where does the Negro himself stand?

The Negro in the matter of the ballot demands only that he be given his right as an American citizen. He is justified in making this demand because of his undoubted Americanism, an Americanism which began when he first set foot on the shores of this country more than three hundred years ago, antedating even the Pilgrim Fathers; an Americanism which has woven him into the woof and warp of the country and which has impelled him to play his part in every war in which the country has been engaged, from the Revolution down to the late World War.

Through his whole history in this country he has worked with patience, and in spite of discouragement he has never turned his back on the light. Whatever may be his shortcomings, however slow may have been his progress, however disappointing may have been his achievements, he has never consciously sought the backward path. He has always kept his face to the light and continued to struggle forward and upward in spite of obstacles, making his humble contributions to the common prosperity and glory of our land. And it is his land. With conscious pride the Negro can say:

"This land is ours by right of birth,
This land is ours by right of toil;
We helped to turn its virgin earth,
Our sweat is in its fruitful soil.

"Where once the tangled forest stood,—
Where flourished once rank weed and thorn,—
Behold the path-traced, peaceful wood,
The cotton white, the yellow corn.

"To gain these fruits that have been earned,
To hold these fields that have been won,
Our arms have strained, our backs have burned
Bent bare beneath a ruthless sun.

"That banner which is now the type
Of victory on field and flood—
Remember, its first crimson stripe
Was dyed by Attucks' willing blood.

"And never yet has come the cry—
When that fair flag has been assailed—
For men to do, for men to die,
That we have faltered or have failed."

The Negro stands as the supreme test of the civilization, the Christianity and the common decency of the American people. It is upon the answer demanded of America today by the Negro that there depends the fulfillment or the failure of democracy in America. I believe that that answer will be the right and just answer. I believe that the spirit in which American democracy was founded, though often turned aside and often thwarted, can never be defeated or destroyed but that ultimately it will triumph.

If American democracy cannot stand the test of giving to any citizen who measures up to the qualifications required of others the full rights and privileges of American citizenship, then we had just as well abandon that democracy in name as in deed. If the Constitution of the United States cannot extend the arm of protection around the weakest and humblest of American citizens as around the strongest and proudest, then it is not worth the paper it is written on.

Notes

1. The Fourteenth Amendment (1868) granted African Americans "equal protection under the law"; the Fifteenth Amendment granted African Americans the right to vote.

2. H. L. Mencken (1880–1956), American author.
3. Lothrop Stoddard (1993–1950), a racist who was widely regarded as an expert on demographics and who warned against the global population growth of dark-skinned peoples.
4. The theory of relativity ($E = MC^2$), which discards the concept of absolute motion and instead treats only relative motion between two systems of reference.

Source

James Weldon Johnson, "Our Democracy and the Ballot," in Carter G. Woodson, ed., *Negro Orators and Their Orations,* 654–58 (Washington, D.C.: Associated Publishers, 1925).

Selected Bibliography

Fleming, Robert E. *James Weldon Johnson.* Boston: Twayne, 1987.

Johnson, James Weldon. *Along This Way: The Autobiography of James Weldon Johnson.* New York: Viking, 1933.

—— *The Autobiography of an Ex-Coloured Man.* Garden City, N.Y.: Garden City Publishing, 1912.

Levy, Eugene. *James Weldon Johnson: Black Leaders, Black Voice.* Chicago: University of Chicago Press, 1973.

Price, Kenneth M. and Lawrence J. Oliver. *Critical Essays on James Weldon Johnson.* New York: Prentice Hall International, 1997.

five

The Shame of America

In his speech "The Shame of America," Archibald Grimké (1849–1930) used his considerable lawyerly skills to explain, via a historical analysis, "the negro's case against the public." The speech, which was based on an earlier writing, was delivered before the American Negro Academy. Grimké pointed to the hypocrisy of the United States, which asked young black men to die in an overseas battle when their rights were so greatly circumscribed at home. The typical black soldier returning home, he presciently argued, was a "new Negro" who was ready to "challenge injustice in his own land and to fight wrong with a courage that will not fail him in the bitter and perhaps bloody years to come."

Grimké was born in South Carolina in 1849. He earned both a bachelor's and a master's degree from Lincoln University and then received a law degree from Harvard University in 1874. As he pursued his career in law, Grimké also edited the Boston newspaper *Hub,* and from 1894 to 1898 he was U.S. consul to Haiti. He was also an active member of the Republican Party, president of the Massachusetts Suffrage League, president of the Washington, D.C., chapter of the NAACP, and author of biographies of William Lloyd Garrison and Charles Sumner.

The Shame of America, or the Negro's Case Against the Republic

The author of the Declaration of Independence[1] said once that he trembled for his country when he remembered that God was just. And he did well to do so. But while he was about it he might have quaked a little for himself. For he was certainly guilty of the same crime against humanity, which had aroused in his philosophic and patriotic mind such lively sensations of anxiety and alarm in respect to the Nation. Said Jefferson on paper: "We hold these truths to be self-evident, that all men are created equal; that they are endowed by their Creator with certain unalienable rights; that among these are life, liberty and the pursuit of happiness," while on his plantation he was holding some men as slaves, and continued to hold them as such for fifty years thereafter, and died at the end of a long and brilliant life, a Virginia slaveholder.

And yet Thomas Jefferson was sincere, or fancied that he was, when he uttered those sublime sentiments about the rights of man, and when he declared that he trembled for his country when he remembered that God was just. This inconsistency between the man's magnificence in profession and his smallness in practice, between the grandeur of what he promised and the meanness of what he performed, taken in conjunction with his cool unconsciousness of the discrepancy, is essentially and emphatically an American trait, a national idiosyncrasy. For it has appeared during the last one hundred and forty-four years with singular boldness and continuity in the social, political, and religious life of the American people and their leaders. I do not recall in all history such another example of a nation appearing so well in its written words regarding human rights, and so badly when it comes to translating those fine words into corresponding action, as this Republic has uniformly exhibited from its foundation, wherever the Negro has been concerned.

Look at its conduct in the War of the Revolution, which it began with the high sounding sentiments of the Declaration of Independence. The American colonists rose in arms because they were taxed by England without their consent, a species of tyranny which bore no sort of comparison to the slavery which they themselves were imposing on the Negro. But with such inconsistency of conduct the men of the Revolution bothered not their heads for a simple, and to them, a sufficient reason. They were white and the Negro was black and was their property. Since they were fighting for a political principle in order the better to protect their pockets, they were not disposed to give up their property rights in anything, not even in human beings. They were contending for the sacred right of loosening their own purse strings, not for the sacred privilege of loosening the bonds of their slaves. Not at all. Millions they were willing to spend in defense of the former, but not a cent to effect the latter, their loud talk in the Declaration of Independence to the contrary, notwithstanding.

Their subsequent conduct in respect to the Negro was of a piece with this characteristic beginning. First they accepted the services of the blacks, both bond and free, as soldiers, and then they debated the expediency and justice of their action, not from the point of view of the slaves but from that of the masters, and later decided upon a policy of exclusion of the slaves from the Continental army. With the adoption of such a policy the chattel rights of masters in those poor men would be better conserved. Hence the policy of exclusion. But when the British evinced a disposition to enlist the slaves as soldiers, a change passed quickly over the leaders of the Revolution, with Washington[2] at their head. The danger to the master of a policy of inclusion was overriden readily enough in the greater danger to the cause of one of exclusion. Without a thought for the slave, he was put on the military chessboard, withdrawn, then put back in response to purely selfish considerations and needs.

Thus it happened that black men fought in that war shoulder to shoulder with white men for American Independence. In every colony from Massachusetts to Georgia, they were found faithful among the faithless, and brave as the bravest during those long and bitter years, fighting and dying with incomparable devotion and valor, by the side of Warren at Bunker Hill, and of Pulaski at Savannah.

The voluntary surrender of life for country has been justly held by all ages to be an act of supreme virtue. It is in the power of any man to give less; it is in the power of none, however exalted in station, to give more. For to lay down one's life at the call of Duty is to lay down one's all. And this all of the general weighs no more than the all of a common soldier. Weighed in the scales of truth this supreme gift of the beggar on foot balances exactly that of the prince on horseback. When prince or beggar, master or slave, has given his life to a cause, he has given his utmost. Beyond that absolute measure of devotion neither can add one jot or tittle to the value of his gift. Thank God there is no color line in acts of heroism and self-sacrifice, save the royal one of their blood-tinted humanity. Such was the priceless contribution which the poor, oppressed Negro made to American Independence.

What was his guerdon? In the hour of their triumph did the patriot fathers call to mind such supreme service to reward it? In the freedom which they had won by the aid of their enslaved countrymen, did they bethink them of lightening the yoke of those miserable men? History answers, no! Truth answers, no! The descendants of those black heroes answer, no! What then? What did such bright, such blazing beacons of liberty, the Washingtons, Hamiltons, Madisons and Franklins, the Rufus Kings, Roger Shermans, and Robert Morrises? They founded the Republic on slavery, rested one end of its stately arch on the prostrate neck of the Negro. They constructed a national Constitution which safeguarded the property of man in man, introducing into it for that purpose its three-fifths slave representation provision, its fugitive slave clause, and an agreement by which the African slave trade was legalized for nineteen years after the adoption of that instrument. That was the reward which the founders of the Republic meted out with one accord to a race which had shed freely its blood to make that Republic a reality among the nations of the earth. Instead of loosening and lifting his heavy yoke of oppression, they strengthened and tightened it afresh on the loyal and long suffering neck of the Negro. Notwithstanding this shameful fact, the founders of the Republic were either so coolly unconscious of its moral enormity or else so indifferent to the amazing contradiction between what they said and what they did, as to write over the gateway of the new Constitution this sonorous preamble: "We, the people of the United States, in order to form a more perfect union, establish justice, insure domestic tranquillity, provide for the common defense, promote the general welfare, and secure the blessings of liberty to ourselves and our posterity, do ordain and establish this Constitution for the United States of America."

"We the people"! From the standpoint of the Negro, what grim irony; "establish justice"! What exquisitely cruel mockery; "to insure domestic tranquillity"! What height and breadth and depth of political duplicity; "to provide for the common defense"! What cunning paltering with words in a double sense; "to promote the general welfare"! What studied ignoring of an ugly fact; "and secure the blessings of liberty to ourselves and posterity"! What masterly abuse of noble words to mask an equivocal meaning, to throw over a great national transgression an air of virtue, so subtle and illusive as to deceive the framers themselves into believing in their own sincerity. You may ransack the libraries of the world, and turn over all the documents of recorded time to match that Preamble of the Constitution as a piece of consummate political dissimulation and mental reservation, as an example of how men juggle deliberately and successfully with their moral sense, how they raise above themselves huge fabrics of falsehood, and go willingly to live and die in a make-believe world of lies. The muse of history, dipping her iron pen in the generous blood of the Negro, has written large across the page of that Preamble, and the face of the Declaration of Independence, the words, "sham, hypocrisy."

It is the rage now to sing the praises of the fathers of the Republic as a generation of singularly liberty-loving men. They were so, indeed, if judged by their fine words alone. But they were, in reality, by no means superior to their sons in this respect, if we judge them by their acts, which somehow speak louder, more convincingly to us than their words, albeit those words proceed out of the Declaration of Independence, and the Preamble of the Constitution. If the children's teeth today are set on edge on the Negro question, it is because the fathers ate the sour grapes of race-wrong, ate those miserable grapes during their whole life, and, dying, transmitted their taste for oppression, as a bitter inheritance to their children, and children's children, for God knows how many black years to come.

Take the case of Washington as an example. He was rated an abolitionist by his contemporaries. And so he was if mere words could have made him one. On paper he was one person, but on his plantation quite another. And as far as I know his history, he never made any effectual attempt to bring this second self of his into actual accord with the first. In theory he favored emancipation, while in practice he was one of the biggest, if not the biggest slaveholder in the country, who enriched himself and his family out of the unpaid toil of more than two hundred slaves. The father of his country did not manumit them during his lifetime, or of that of his wife. Not until his death, not until the death of his widow, did he, as a matter of fact, release his hold upon the labor of those people, did they escape from his dead hands. As first President, moreover, he signed the first fugitive slave law and was not ashamed to avail himself of its hateful provisions for the reclamation of one of his runaway slave-women. And yet Washington, and Jefferson also, are the two bright, particular stars of our American democracy. They had very fine words for liberty, no two men ever had finer, but when it came to translating them into action, into churning them into butter for the poor Negro's parsnips, no atom of butter did they yield, or will ever yield, churn them ever so long. *Ex pede Herculem.*

Naturally enough under the circumstances of its origin and antecedents, American democracy has never cared a fig in practice for the fine sentiments of its Declaration of Independence, or for the high sounding ones of the Preamble to its Constitution, wherever and whenever the Negro has been concerned. It used him to fight the battles for its independent political existence, and rewarded his blood and bravery with fresh stripes and heavier chains.

History repeats itself. In America, on the Negro question, it has been a series of shameful repetitions of itself. The Negro's history in the first war with England was repeated exactly in the second. In this conflict no more loyal and daring hearts bled and broke for the country than were those of its colored soldiers and sailors. On land and water in that war the Negro died as he fought, among the most faithful and heroic defenders of the American cause. But to praise him is to condemn the country, which in this instance I will leave to no less an American than General Jackson.[3] Out of his mouth shall this condemnation be spoken. Said Jackson three weeks before the battle of New Orleans to the black soldiers who had rallied at his summons to repel a formidable invasion of our national domain by a powerful foreign enemy:

> "From the shores of Mobile I called you to arms. I invited you to share in the perils and divide the glory of your white countrymen. I expected much from you, for I was not uninformed of those qualities which must render you so formidable to an invading foe. I knew you could endure hunger and thirst, and all the hardships of war. I knew that you loved the land of your nativity, and that, like ourselves, you had to defend all that is most dear to men. But you surpass my hopes. I have found in you, united to those qualities, that noble enthusiasm that impels to great deeds.

"Soldiers: The President of the United States shall be informed of your conduct on the present occasion, and the voice of the representatives of the American nation shall applaud your valor, as your General now praises your ardor. The enemy is near. His sails cover the lakes, but the brave are united, and if he finds us contending among ourselves, it will be for the prize of valor, and fame its noblest reward."

Jackson's black troops proved themselves in the actions of Mobile Bay and New Orleans entitled to every mouthful of the ringing applause which Old Hickory gave them without stint. They got fair enough words as long as the enemy was in sight and his navy covered the waters of the country. But as soon as the peril had passed those fair words were succeeded by the foulest ingratitude. On every hand Colorphobia reared its cursed head, and struck its cruel fangs into those brave breasts which had just received the swords and the bullets of a foreign foe. They were legislated against everywhere, proscribed by atrocious laws everywhere. They had given the nation in its dire need, blood and life, and measureless love, and had received as reward black codes, an unrelenting race prejudice, and bondage bitterer than death.

Strange irony of fate which reserved to Andrew Jackson, whose mouth overflowed with praise in 1814 for his black soldiers and with fair promises of what he intended to do for them—strange irony of fate, I say, which reserved to that man, as President in 1836, the elevation of Roger B. Taney[4] to the Chief-Justiceship of the United States, of Taney, the infamous slave Judge who wrote the Dred Scott Decision, which argued that black men had no rights in America which white men were bound to respect. The downright brutality of that opinion was extremely shocking to some sensitive Americans, but it was no more so than was the downright brutality of the facts, which it reflected with brutal accuracy. The fell apparition of American inhumanity, which those words conjured up from the depths of an abominable past and from that of a no less abominable present, was indeed black, but it was no blacker than the truth. The dark soul of the nation was embodied in them, all of its savage selfishness, greed among iniquity. There they glared, large and lifelike, a devil's face among the nations, seamed and intersected with the sinister lines of a century of cruelty and race hatred and oppression. Of course the fair idealism of the Declaration of Independence was wanting in the photographic naturalism of the picture, and so was the fictive beauty of the Preamble of the Constitution, because they were wanting in the terrible original, in the malignant, merciless, and murderous spirit of a democracy which the dark words of the dark judge had limned to the life.

God has made iniquitous power ultimately self-destructive. Into every combination of evil. He puts the seed of division and strife. Without this effective check wickedness would conquer and permanently possess the earth. The law of the brute would rule it forever. Where today are the empires of might and wrong, which men reared in their pride and strength, on the Nile, the Tigris, and the Euphrates, on the Tiber, the Bosporus, and the Mediterranean? They flourished for a season and seasons, and spread themselves like green bay trees. But behold they are gone, perished, burnt up by the fires of evil passions, by the evil power which consumed them to ashes. Centuries have flown over their graves, and the places once cursed by their violence, and crushed by their oppressions, shall know them and their vulture laws and trampling armies no more forever.

So it happened in the case of the American people when in order "to form a more perfect union," they ordained and established their Constitution. Within the "more perfect union" was enfolded a fruitful germ of division and discord. No bigger at first than the smallest of seeds, the germ grew apace with the growth of the new nation, drawing abundant nourishment from the dark underworld of the slave. Slender sapling in 1815, it was a fast growing tree in 1820, bearing even then its bitter apples of Gomorrah. Where its bitter fruit fell, there fell also on the spirit of the people mutual distrust, and incipient sectional hate. And no wonder, for when the North clasped hands with her Southern sister in "a more perfect union," she did so the better to conserve a set of interests and institutions peculiar to herself and inherently hostile to those of the South, and vice versa with respect to the action of the latter in the premises. The "more perfect union" had, thank God, effected a conjunction, under a single political system, of two sets of mutually invasive and destructive social ideas and industrial forces. Differences presently sprang up between the partisans of each set, and discontent and wide-spreading fear and contention. National legislation which oxidized and enriched the blood of the North, not only impoverished but actually poisoned that of the South. And so it came to pass that the compromise Constitution which was designed "to form a more perfect union," failed of its purpose, because with human slavery at the core of it, it brought face to face two warring social systems, whose unappeasable strife it had not the secret or the strength to subdue.

As in Egypt more than three thousand years ago, the Eternal spoke to the master-race at divers times and with divers signs, saying, "let my people go," so he spoke to the master-race in this land through divers omens and events, saying likewise, "let my people go." Those with ears to hear might have heard that divine voice in the Hartford Convention and the causes which led to its call; in the successive sectional conflicts over Missouri, the Tariff, and Texas; in the storm winds of the Mexican war, as in the wild uproar which followed the annexation of new national territory at its close; in the political rage and explosions of 1850 and 1854, and in the fierce patter of blood-drops over Kansas. They might have surely heard that commanding voice from the anointed lips of holy men and prophets, from the mouths of Garrison and Sumner, and Phillips, and Douglass, from the sacred gallows where John Brown heard and repeated it while his soul went marching on from city to city, and

State to State, over mountain and river, across a continent, and front the Lakes to the Gulf with rising accent saying, "let my people go." Alas! the nation hearkened not to the voice of justice, but continued to harden its heart, until thunderlike that voice broke in the deep boom of Civil War.

When masters fall out a way oftentimes opens for the escape of their slaves. In the death grapple of the sections for political supremacy, the dead weight of two centuries of oppression lifted from the neck of the Negro. The people and their leaders of both sections despised him to such a degree that neither would in the beginning enlist his aid against the other. "We the people" of the glorious union of 1789 had quarrelled like two bloody scoundrels over their ill-gotten gains, and had come to murderous blows. Yet in spite of their deadly hatred of each other, they said in their mad race-pride and prejudice, the North to the South, and the South to the North, "go to, shall we not settle our differences without the aid of him who is our slave ? Shall not we white men fight our duel to a finish; shall either of us appeal for help to that miserable being who by our laws, written and unwritten, has never possessed any rights among us which we have ever respected?" They chose to forget how in two wars this faithful man had for their sakes, received into his sad but brave breast the swords and the bullets of a foreign enemy, and all unmindful of self had helped them to achieve and maintain their liberty and independence. And thus choosing to forget his past services and to remember only their bitter race-prejudice against him, they fought on with deadly malice and violence, the one side against the other, rending their dear Union with fraternal strife, and drenching it with fraternal blood.

Perceiving the unlimited capacity of mankind for all sorts of folly, no wonder Puck exclaimed, "What fools these mortals be!" Yes, what fools, but of all the fools who have crawled to dusty death the most stupendous and bedeviled lot are those who strut their fools' feet and toss their fools' heads across their little stage of life, thanking their fools' selves that God made them different from other men—superior to other men—to rule over other men. Puffed up with their stupid race-pride and prejudice, inflated to the bursting point with their high and mighty notions, and *noli me tangero airs,* the North and the South went on for nearly two years goring and tearing each other like two infuriated bulls of nearly equal strength, before either would call on the Negro for assistance. Not until bleeding at every pore, sickened at the loss of its sordid dollar, and in despair at the threatened destruction of that to which it ascribed, as to the Almighty, all of its sectional progress, prosperity and power, viz.: the dear Union, did the North turn for help to the Negro, whom it had despised and wronged, and whom it even then, in its heart of hearts, despised and intended, upon occasion, to wrong anew.

Think of the incredible folly and selfishness of a people fighting for existence and yet begrudging freedom to an enslaved race, whom it had called upon to help defend that existence; doling out to its faithful black allies, with miserly meanness, its blood-money and its boasted democratic equality and fair play; denying to its colored soldiers equal pay and promotion with its white ones, albeit many of those white ones were mercenary aliens from Europe. Nevertheless, of such bottomless depths of folly and meanness was the National Government certainly guilty. The Fifty-fourth and the Fifty-fifth Massachusetts regiments enlisted to fight the battles of the country, with the understanding that there would be no discrimination against them on account of their color. Yet the government violated its understood pledge, and proceeded to pay, or tried to pay those men ten dollars a month where it was paying other men, because they were white, thirteen dollars a month for the same service. All honor to Massachusetts for objecting to this shameful act, and for offering to make up to her colored regiments the three dollars out of which the National government was endeavoring to cheat them. Three times three cheers for the brave and true men who had the sagacity, and the courage, and the self-respect, to resist the injustice of the government, and to refuse firmly to compromise by a cent their right to equality of pay in the army.

Take another instance of the meanness of the government's conduct toward its colored defenders. In January of 1864, Henry Wilson embodied, in a bill to promote enlistments, a clause which provided that when "any man or boy of African descent, in service or labor in any State under its laws, should be mustered into the military or naval service of the United States, he and his mother, wife and children, shall be forever free." Now will you believe that this just and moderate measure took thirteen long months before its friends could get Congress to enact it into law? "Future generations," exclaimed Charles Sumner in closing his remarks on the subject, "future generations will read with amazement, that a great people when national life was assailed, hesitated to exercise a power so simple and beneficient; and this amazement will know no bounds, as they learn that Congress higgled for months on a question, whether the wives and children of our colored soldiers should be admitted to freedom."

Need I repeat in this presence the old, grand story, how in numbers nearly two hundred thousand strong our colored boys in blue, left their blood and their bones in every State from Virginia to Louisiana? How, like heroes, they fought and died for the Union at Port Hudson, and Fort Wagner, and Petersburg, and Honey Hill, and Olustee, and Milliken's Bend? How in winter and summer, in cold and heat, in valley and on hilltop, on horse and on foot, over rivers and swamps, through woods and brakes, they rushed to meet the foe! How leaving behind them fields strown thick with their dead and wounded, they mounted the blazing sides of grim fortresses, climbing on great deeds and self-sacrifices through storms of shot and shell, to death and a place among the stars?

No, no, it is not required of me on this occasion to read afresh that glorious record. Sufficient then this: The Northern army, reinforced by the strength which it drew from that of the Negro, broke in time the back of the Rebellion, and saved the Union, so that in 1865 the flag of the nation floated again over an undivided country, and the Republic, strong and great beneath that flag, launched anew to meet the years, and to reach her fair ideals of liberty and equality which were flashing like beacon lights upon her way.

Amid widespread rejoicing on the return of peace and the restoration of the Union, the Negro rejoiced among the gladdest, for his slave fetters were broken, he was no longer a chattel. He imagined in his simple heart, in his ignorance and poverty, that he had not only won freedom, but the lasting affection and gratitude of the powerful people for whom he had entered hell to quench for them its raging fires with his blood. Yes, although black and despised, he, the slave, the hated one, had risen above his centuries of wrongs, above their bitter memories and bitterer sufferings to the love of enemies, to the forgiveness of those who had despitefully used him, ay, to those moral heights where heroes are throned and martyrs crowned. Surely, surely, he, who had been so unmindful of self in the service of country, would not be left by that country at the mercy of those who hated him then with the most terrible hatred for that very cause. He who had been mighty to save others would surely, now in his need, be saved by those whom he had saved. "Oh! Justice, thou has fled to brutish beasts, and men have lost their gratitude."

I would gladly seal forever the dark chapter of our history, which followed the close of the war. Gladly would I forget that record of national shame and selfishness. But as it is better to turn on light than to shut it off, I will, with your forbearance, turn it on for our illumination and guidance, in the lowering present.

The chapter opened with an introduction of characteristic indifference on the part of the country in respect to the fate of the Negro. With his shackles lying close beside him, he was left in the hands of his old master who, seizing the opportunity, proceeded straightway to refit them on the disenthralled limbs of the former slave. State after State did so with such promptitude and to such effect that within a few months a formidable system of Negro serfdom had actually been constructed, and cunningly substituted in place of the system of Negro slavery, which the war had destroyed. An African serf-power, Phoenix-like,[5] was rising out of the ashes of the old slave power into national politics. At sight of this truly appalling apparition, the apparition of a returning slave power in thin disguise, all the old sectional fear and hatred which had existed against it in the free States before the Rebellion, awoke suddenly and hotly in the breast of the North. Thinking mainly, if not wholly of its own safety in the emergency which confronted it, and how best to avert the fresh perils which impended in consequence over its ascendency, the North prepared to make, and did in fact make, for the time being, short shrift of this boldly retroactive scheme of the South to recover within the Union all that it had lost by its defeated attempt to land itself outside of the Union.

Having tested to its entire satisfaction the Negro's value as a soldier in its war for the preservation of the Union, the North determined at this juncture to enlist his aid as a citizen in its further conflicts with the South, for the preservation of its sectional domination in the newly restored Union. To this end the Fourteenth and the Fifteenth Amendments[6] to the Constitution were, in the progress of events, incorporated into that instrument. By these two great acts, the North had secured itself against the danger of an immediate return of the South to anything like political equality with it in the Republic. Between its supremacy and the attacks of its old rival, it had erected a solid wall of Negro votes. But immensely important as was the ballot to its black contingent, it was not enough to meet all of his tremendous needs. Nevertheless, as the North was considering mainly its own and not the Negro's necessities at this crisis, and as the elective franchise in his hands was deemed by it adequate to satisfy its own pressing needs, it gave the peculiar wants of the Negro beyond that of the ballot but scant attention.

Homeless, landless, illiterate, just emerging from the blackness of two centuries of slavery, this simple and faithful folk had surely other sacred claims on the North and the National Government than this right to the ballot. They had in truth a strong claim to unselfish friendship and statesmanship, to unfaltering care and guardianship, during the whole of their transition from slavery to citizenship. They needed the organized hands, the wise heads, the warm hearts, the piled-up wealth, the sleepless eyes, the faith, hope and charity of a Christian people and a Christian government to teach them to walk and to save them from industrial exploitation by their old masters, as well as to vote. Did they receive from the Republic what the Republic owed them by every consideration of justice, gratitude and humanity, as of enlightened self-interest? Alas? not a tithe of this immense debt has the Republic ever undertaken to pay to those who should have been, under all circumstances, its sacredly preferred creditors. On the contrary they were left to themselves by the government in the outer darkness of that social state which had been their sad lot for more than two centuries. They were left in that darkest night of moral and civil anarchy to fight not alone their own terrible battle with poverty, ignorance, and untutored appetites and passions, but also the unequal, the cruel battle for the preservation of Northern political domination in the Union. For ten awful years they fought that battle for the North, for the Republican party, in the face of persecutions and oppressions, terrors and atrocities, at the glare of which the country and the civilized world shrank aghast.

Aghast shrank the North, but not for the poor Negro, faithful unto death to it. For itself rather it shrank from the threatening shadows which such a carnival of horrors was casting athwart its vast and spreading network of trade and production. The clamor of all its million-wheeled industry and prosperity was for peace. "Let us have peace," said Grant,[7] and "let us have peace" blew forthwith and in deafening unison, all the big and little whistles of all the big and little factories and locomotives, and steamships from Maine to California. Every pen of merchant and editor scratched paper to the same mad tune. The pulpit and the platform of the land cooed their Cuckoo-song in honor of those piping times of peace. The loud noise of chinking coin pouring into vaults like coal into bins, drowned the agonized cry of the forgotten and long-suffering Negro. Deserting him in 1876, the North, stretching across the bloody chasm its two greedy, commercial hands, grasped the ensanguined ones of the South, and repeated, "let us have peace." Little did the Northern people and the government reck then or now that at the bottom of that bloody chasm lay their faithful black friends. Little did they care that the blood on those Southern hands had been wrung drop by drop from the loyal heart of the Negro. But enough.

Years of struggle and oppression follow and we come to another chapter of American history; namely, the Spanish-American War. In the Spanish-American War the Negro attracted the attention of the world by his dashing valor. He attracted the attention of his country also. His fighting quality was of the highest, unsurpassed, and perhaps unequalled in brilliancy by the rest of the American army that invaded Cuba. He elicited applause and grudging justice from his countrymen, dashed with envy and race prejudice. Still it seemed for a brief time that his conspicuous service had given his case against the Republic a little better standing in Court—a little better chance for a fair hearing at the Bar of Public Opinion. But our characteristic national emotionalism was too shallow and insincere to last. In fact, it died aborning. The national habit of a century and a half reasserted itself. There was no attempt made to square national profession and national practice, national promise and national performance. The Negro again had given his all to his country and had got in return at the hands of that country wrong and injustice. Southern propaganda presently renewed all of its vicious and relentless activity against the Negro. He was different, he was alien, he was unassimilable, he was inferior, and he must be kept so, and in the scheme of things he must be made forever subordinate to the white race. In this scheme of things white domination could best be preserved by the establishment of a caste system based on race and color. And so following the Spanish-American War the North and the South put their heads together to complete their caste system. Everywhere throughout the Republic race prejudice, color proscription grew apace. One by one rights and privileges which the Negroes had enjoyed for a brief space were withdrawn and the wall of caste rose higher and higher. He was slowly and surely being shut out from all the things which white men enjoyed by virtue of their citizenship, and shut within narrowing limits of freedom. Everywhere within his prison house he read in large and sinister letters, "Thus far and no farther." He was trapped, and about to be caged. In spite of the Emancipation Proclamation and the Three War Amendments he found that white men were becoming bolder in ignoring or violating his freedom and citizenship under them. The walls of the new bondage were closing about his right to life, liberty and the pursuit of happiness in this boasted Land of the Free and Christian Home of Democratic Hypocrisy and Cruelty.

Then Mr. Taft[8] appeared upon the scene and became famous or infamous as a builder on the walls of the Temple of the New American Jerusalem, where profession is High Priest to the God of Broken Promises. He proved himself a master workman in following the lines of caste, in putting into place a new stone in the edifice when he announced as his policy at the beginning of his administration that he would not appoint any colored man to office in the South where the whites objected. Caste had won and the Negro's status was fixed, as far as this bourgeois apostle of American Democracy was able to fix it. His adds but another illustrious name to the long list of those architects of national dishonor who sought to build the Temple of American Liberty upon a basis of caste.

Then in the fullness of time came Woodrow Wilson,[9] the ripe, consummate fruit of all this national contradiction between profession and practice, promise and performance. He can give Messrs. Washington, Jefferson, Jackson and Company odds and beat them in the subtle art of saying sonorously, grandiosely, what in action he does not hesitate to flout and spurn. When seeking the Negro's vote in 1912 he was the most profuse and generous in eloquent profession, in iridescent promises, but when he was elected he forgot straightway those fair professions and promises and began within a week after he entered the White House to put into office men filled with colorphobia, the better to finish the work of undoing in the government the citizenship of the Negro, to whom he had promised not grudging justice but the highly sympathetic article, heaping up and running over. Mr. Taft had established the principle that no Negro was to be appointed to office in the South where the whites objected—Mr. Wilson carried the principle logically one step farther, namely, no Negro was to be put to work in any department of the Government with white men and women if these white men and women objected to his presence. Segregation along the color line in Federal employment became forthwith the fixed policy of the Wilson administration.

There sprang up under the malign influence of this false prophet of the New Freedom all sorts of movements in the District of Columbia and in the Federal Government hostile to the Negro—movements to exclude him from all positions under the Civil Service above that of laborer and messenger and charwoman, to jim-crow him on the street cars, to prohibit him from intermarrying with the whites, to establish for him a residential pale in the District; in short, to fix forever his status as a permanently inferior caste in the land for which he had toiled in peace and bled and died in war. The evil influence of this false apostle of freedom spread far and wide and spurred the enemies of the Negro to unwonted activity. The movement of residential segregation and for rural segregation grew in volume and momentum in widely separated parts of the country until it was finally checked by the decision of the Supreme Court in 1917.

The condition of the Negro was at its worst and his outlook in America at its darkest when the Government declared war against Germany. Then was revived the Republic's program of false promises and hypocritical professions in order to bring this black man with his brawn and brains, with his horny hands and lion heart, with his unquenchable loyalty and enthusiasm to its aid. No class of its citizens surpassed him in the swiftness and self-forgetfulness of his response to the call of country. What he had to give he brought to the altar and laid it there—labor and wealth, wounds and death, with unsurpassed devotion and patriotism. But what he received in return was the same old treatment, evil for his good, ingratitude and treachery for his loyalty and service. He was discriminated against everywhere—was used and abused, shut out from equal recognition and promotion with white men and women. Then when he went overseas he found American colorphobia more deadly than the gun and poison gas of the Germans. In the American army there was operated a ceaseless propaganda of meanness and malice, of jealousy and detraction against him. If our Expeditionary Force had given itself with a tithe of the zeal and industry to fighting the Germans, which a large section of it devoted to fighting the black soldier, it would have come out of the war with more honor and credit, and left behind in France a keener sense of gratitude and regard than exists for them in that country today. But, alas, thousands of them were more interested in watching the Negro and his reception by the French, in concocting villainous plots to degrade him in the eyes of that people, in segregating him from all social contact with them, and in keeping him in his place, within the hard and fast lines of caste which they had laid for him in America.

But the Negro went and saw—saw the incredible meanness and malice of his own country by the side of the immense genius for Liberty and Brotherhood of France. There he found himself a man and brother regardless of his race and color. But if he has seen these things in France he has also conquered certain other things in himself, and has come back not as he went but a New Negro. He has come back to challenge injustice in his own land and to fight wrong with a courage that will not fail him in the bitter and perhaps bloody years to come. For he knows now as he has never known before that he is an American citizen with the title deeds of his citizenship written in a century and a half of labor and suffering and blood. From his brave black lips I hear the ringing challenge, "This is my right and by the Eternal I have come back to claim all that belongs to me of industrial and political equality and liberty." And let us answer his high resolve with a courage and will to match his own, and so help to redeem our country from its shame of a century and a half of broken promises and dishonored ideals.

But be not deceived, friends. Let us, like brave men and women, face the stern reality of our situation. We are where we are. We are in the midst of a bitter and hitherto an invincible race-prejudice, which beats down into the dust all of our rights, all of our attainments, all of our aspirations after freedom and excellence. The North and the South are in substantial accord in respect to us and in respect to the position which we are to occupy in this land.

We are to be forever exploited, forever treated as an alien race, allowed to live here in strict subordination and subjection to the white race. We are to hew for it wood, draw for it water, till for it the earth, drive for it coaches, wait for it at tables, black for it boots, run for it errands, receive from it crumbs and kicks, to be for it, in short, social mudsills on which shall rest the foundations of the vast fabric of its industrial democracy and civilization.

No one can save us from such a fate but God, but ourselves. You think, I know, that the North is more friendly to you than the South, that the Republican party does more for the solution of this problem than the Democratic. Friends, you are mistaken. A white man is a white man on this question, whether he lives in the North or in the South. Of course, there are splendid exceptions. Scratch the skin of Republican or Democrat, of Northern white men or Southern white men, and you will find close to the surface race prejudice, American colorphobia. The difference, did you but know it, is not even epidermal, is not skin-deep. The hair is Democratic Esau's,[10] and the voice is Republican Jacob's.[11] That is all. Make no mistake here, for a true understanding of our actual position at this point is vital.

On Boston Commons stands a masterpiece in bronze, erected to commemorate the heroism and patriotism of Col. Robert Gould Shaw[12] and his black regiment. There day and night, through summer and winter, storm and shine, are to march forever those brave men by the side of their valiant young leader. Into the unknown they are hurrying to front and to fight their enemies and the enemies of their country. They are not afraid. A high courage looks from their faces, lives in the martial motion of their bodies, flashes from the barrels of their guns. On and yet ever on they are marching, grim bolts of war, across the Commons, through State Street, past the old State House, over ground consecrated by the martyr's blood of Crispus Attucks,[13] and the martyr's feet of William Lloyd Garrison.[14] Farther and farther they are pressing forward into the unknown, into the South, to Wagner and immortal deeds, to death and an immortal crown.

Friends, we too are marching through a living and lowering present into the unknown, through an enemy's land, at the summons of duty. We are to face great labors, great dangers, to fight like men our passions and American caste-prejudice and oppression, and God helping us, to conquer them.

Notes

1. Thomas Jefferson (1743–1826), third president of the United States (1801–1809).
2. George Washington (1732–1799), first president of the United States and general of the Continental Army.
3. Andrew Jackson (1767–1845), seventh president of the United States (1829–1837).
4. Roger Brooke Taney (1777–1864), fifth chief justice of the U.S. Supreme Court.

5. The phoenix is a bird of ancient legend. When it reached five hundred years of age, it burned itself on a pyre, from whose ashes another phoenix arose. It commonly appears in literature as a symbol of death and resurrection.
6. The Fourteenth Amendment (1868) granted African Americans "equal protection under the law"; the Fifteenth Amendment (1870) granted African Americans the right to vote.
7. Ulysses S. Grant (1822–1885), commander in chief of the Union Army of the American Civil War, eighteenth president of the United States (1869–1877).
8. William Howard Taft (1857–1930), twenty-seventh president of the United States (1900–1913).
9. Woodrow Wilson (1856–1924), twenty-eighth president of the United States (1913–1921).
10. In the Hebrew Bible, Esau, the son of Isaac, sold his birthright to his younger twin Jacob.
11. In the Hebrew Bible, Jacob was ancestor to the Hebrews. By bargain and trickery, Jacob got his birthright and the blessing that was intended for his twin, Esau.
12. Robert Gould Shaw (1837–1863) raised and commanded the first regiment of black troops in the Civil War.
13. Crispus Attucks (d. 1770), African American man killed in the American Revolution.
14. William Lloyd Garrison (1805–1879), American abolitionist.

Source

Archibald Grimké, "The Shame of America," excerpted from *The Shame of America; or The Negro's Case Against the Republic* American Academy Occasional Papers no. 31, Washington, D.C., 1924; reprinted in Carter G. Woodson, ed., *Negro Orators and their Orations*, 671–89 (Association for the Study of Negro Life and History, 1925).

Selected Bibliography

Bruce, Dickson D. *Archibald Grimké: A Portrait of a Black Independent.* Baton Rouge: Louisiana State University Press, 1993.

Grimké, Archibald. *Eulogy on Wendell Phillips, Delivered in Tremont Temple, Boston, April 9, 1884.* Boston: Rockwell and Churchill, 1884.

—— *William Lloyd Garrison, the Abolitionist.* New York: Negro University Press, 1969.

six

The Kind of Democracy the Negro Race Expects

William Pickens (1881–1954) became one of the most recognized African American leaders of his time. In the following address, which he delivered on several occasions, Pickens took a broad view of the meaning of democracy and expounded on the different ways that democratic theory could be made relevant to African Americans in their daily lives.

Pickens was the sixth of ten children born to former slaves who gained their freedom after the Civil War. He grew up in Little Rock, Arkansas, and attended Talladega College and Yale University, where he earned a reputation as a topflight orator and graduated Phi Beta Kappa. He later taught at Talladega and Wiley College before he was hired as dean of Morgan College. He authored several books, including *The New Negro: His Political, Civil, and Mental Status, and Related Essays* (1916) and *Lynching and Debt Slavery* (1921). He also served as field secretary for the NAACP.

Democracy is the most used term in the world today. But some of its uses are abuses. Everybody says "Democracy"! But everybody has his own definition. By the extraordinary weight of the presidency of the United States many undemocratic people have had this word forced upon their lips but have not yet had the right ideal forced upon their hearts. I have heard of one woman who wondered with alarm whether "democracy" would mean that colored women would have the right to take any vacant seat or space on a street car, even if they had paid for it. That such a question should be asked, shows how many different meanings men may attach to the one word DEMOCRACY. This woman doubtless believes in a democracy of me-and-my-kind, which is no democracy. The most autocratic and the worst caste systems could call themselves democratic by that definition. Even the Prussian junker believes in that type of democracy: he has no doubt that he and the other junkers should be free and equal in rights and privileges.

Many have accepted the word DEMOCRACY merely as the current password to respectability in political thinking. The spirit of the times is demanding democracy; it is the tune of the age; it is the song to sing. But some are like that man who belonged to one of our greater political parties: after hearing convincing arguments by the stump-speaker of the opposite party, he exclaimed: "Wa-al, that fellow has convinced my judgment, but I'll be d—d if he can CHANGE MY VOTE!"

It is in order, therefore, for the Negro to state clearly what he means by democracy and what he is fighting for.

First. Democracy in Education. This is fundamental. No other democracy is practicable unless all of the people have equal right and opportunity to develop according to their individual endowments. There can be no real democracy between two natural groups, if one represents the extreme of ignorance and the other the best intelligence. The common public school and the state university should be the foundation stones of democracy. If men are artificially differentiated at the beginning, if we try to educate a "working class" and a "ruling class," forcing different race groups into different lines without regard to individual fitness, how can we ever hope for democracy in the other relations of these groups? Individuals will differ, but in democracy of education peoples living on the same soil should not be widely diverged in their training on mere racial lines. This would be illogical, since they are to be measured by the same standards of life. Of course, a group that is to live in Florida should be differently trained from a group that is to live in Alaska; but that is geography and general environment, and not color or caste.—The Negro believes in democracy of education as first and fundamental: that the distinction should be made between individual talents and not between colors and castes.

Second. Democracy in Industry. The right to work in any line for which the individual is best prepared, and to be paid the standard wage. This is also fundamental. In the last analysis there could be very little democracy between multi-millionaires and the abject poor. There must be a more just and fair distribution of wealth in a democracy. And certainly this is not possible unless men work at the occupations for which they are endowed and best prepared.

There should be no "colored" wages and no "white" wages; no "man's" wage and no "woman's" wage. Wages should be paid for the work done, measured as much as possible by its productiveness. No door of opportunity should be closed to a man on any other ground than that of his individual unfitness. The cruelest and most undemocratic thing in the world is to require of the individual man that his whole race be fit before he can be regarded as fit for a certain privilege or responsibility. That rule, strictly applied, would exclude any man of any race from any position. For every man to serve where he is most able to serve is public economy and is to the best interest of the state. This lamentable war that was forced upon us should make that plain to the dullest of us. Suppose that, when this war broke out, our whole country had been like Mississippi (and I refer to geography uninvidiously),—suppose our whole country had been like Mississippi, where a caste system was holding the majority of the population in the triple chains of ignorance, semi-serfdom and poverty. Our nation would be now either the unwilling prey or the golden goose for the Prussian. The long-headed thing for any state is to let every man do his best all of the time. But some people are so short-sighted that they only see what is thrust against their noses. The Negro asks American labor in the name of democracy to get rid of its color caste and industrial junkerism.

Third. Democracy in State. A political democracy in which all are equal before the laws; where there is one standard of justice, written and unwritten; where all men and women may be citizens by the same qualifications, agreed upon and specified. We believe in this as much for South Africa as for South Carolina, and we hope that our American nation will not agree with any government, ally or enemy, that is willing to make a peace that will bind the African Negro to political slavery and exploitation.

Many other evils grow out of political inequality. Discriminating laws are the mother of the mob spirit. The political philosopher in Washington, after publishing his opinion that a Negro by the fault of being a Negro is unfit to be a member of Congress, cannot expect an ignorant white man in Tennessee to believe that the same Negro is, nevertheless, fit to have a fair and impartial trial in a Tennessee court. Ignorance is too logical for that. I disagree with the premises but I agree with the reasoning of the Tennesseean: that if being a Negro unfits a man for holding a government office for which he is otherwise fit, it unfits the same man for claiming a "white man's" chance in the courts. The first move therefore against mob violence and injustice in the petty courts is to wipe out discriminating laws and practices in the higher circles of government. The ignorant man in Tennessee will not rise in ideal above the intelligent man in Washington.

Fourth. Democracy without Sex-preferment. The Negro cannot consistently oppose color discrimination and support sex discrimination in democratic government. This happened to be the opinion also of the First Man of the Negro race in America,—Frederick Douglass. The handicap is nothing more nor less than a presumption in the mind of the physically dominant element of the universal inferiority of the weaker or subject element. It is so easy to prove that the man who is down and under, deserves to be down and under. In the first place, he is down there, isn't he? And that is three-fourths of the argument to the ordinary mind; for the ordinary mind does not seek ultimate causes. The argument against the participation of colored men and of women in self-government is practically one argument. Somebody spoke to the Creator about both of these classes and learned that they were "created" for inferior roles. Enfranchisement would spoil a good field-hand,—or a good cook. Black men were once ignorant,—women were once ignorant. Negroes had no political experience,—women had no such experience. The argument forgets that people do not get experience on the outside. But the American Negro expects a democracy that will accord the right to vote to a sensible industrious woman rather than to a male tramp.

Fifth. Democracy in Church. The preachings and the practices of Jesus of Nazareth are perhaps the greatest influence in the production of modern democratic ideas. The Christian church is, therefore, no place for the caste spirit or for snobs. And the colored races the world over will have even more doubt in the future than they have had in the past of the real Christianity of any church which holds out to them the prospect of being united in heaven after being separated on earth.

Finally. The great colored races will in the future not be kinder to a sham democracy than to a "scrap-of-paper" autocracy. The private home, private right and private opinion must remain inviolate; but the commonwealth, the public places and public property must not be appropriated to the better use of any group by "Jim-Crowing" and segregating any other group. By the endowments of God and nature there are individual "spheres"; but there are no such widely different racial "spheres." Jesus' estimate of the individual soul is the taproot of democracy, and any system which discourages the men of any race from individual achievement, is no democracy. To fix the status of a human soul on earth according to the physical group in which it was born, is the gang spirit of the savage which protects its own members and outlaws all others.

For real democracy the American Negro will live and die. His loyalty is always above suspicion, but his extraordinary spirit in the present war is born of his faith that on the side of his country and her allies is the best hope for such democracy. And he welcomes, too, the opportunity to lift the "Negro question" out of the narrow confines of the Southern United States and make it a world question. Like many other questions our domestic race question, instead of being settled by Mississippi and South Carolina, will now seek its settlement largely on the battlefields of Europe.

Notes

1. Frederick Douglass (1817–1895), American abolitionist.

Source

William Pickens, "The Kind of Democracy the Negro Race Expects," in Carter G. Woodson, ed., *Negro Orators and Their Orations,* 654–58 (Washington, D.C.: Associated Publishers, 1925).

Selected Bibliography

Adler, Bill, ed. *Black Defiance; Black Profiles in Courage.* New York: Morrow, 1972.

Avery, Sheldon. *Up from Washington: William Pickens and the Negro Struggle for Equality, 1900–1954.* Newark: University of Delaware Press, 1989.

Pickens, William. *Bursting Bonds: Enlarged Edition (of) The Heir of Slaves: The Autobiography of a "New Negro."* Edited by William L. Andrews. Bloomington: Indiana University Press, 1991.

—— *Lynching and Debt Slavery.* New York: American Civil Liberties Union, 1921.

—— *The New Negro: His Political, Civil, and Mental Status, and Related Essays.* New York: Negro Universities Press, 1969.

seven

Selected Poems by Langston Hughes

The three poems reproduced here were published in 1943, one year after the United States declared war on Japan and the Axis powers. "Democracy," also entitled "Freedom," first appeared in *Jim Crow's Last Stand* (1943) and argues against gradualist reform. "Refugee in America," later titled "Words Like Freedom," first appeared in the *Saturday Evening Post* (February 6, 1943) and was later set to music by Audrey Snyder Brown. The revised and shortened version of "Freedom's Plow" was first published in *Opportunity* in April 1943. It speaks of how the dream of freedom guides people's lives, looks at freedom sought by North American colonists, and celebrates that freedom, which is owed to and sought by laborers.

Langston Hughes's work is noted for its focus on common folk, the inhabitants of Chicago's South State Street or Harlem's Lennox Avenue, those with whom Hughes was most familiar. Because he exposed less flattering aspects of black life, whites and blacks alike (some as popular as James Baldwin) criticized his work. As a newspaper columnist in 1943, Hughes created his most famous character, Jesse B. Semple (Simple), an uneducated African American city dweller.

Hughes (1902–1967) was raised by his mother and grandmother; his father left the family to become a successful businessman in Mexico. Hughes's grandmother cared for him while his mother traveled in search of work. He descended from a long line of "race people." His grandmother's first husband, Charles Howard Langston, was killed in John Brown's 1859 raid on Harpers Ferry. Hughes's great uncle, abolitionist John Mercer Langston, became the first black man to serve in the U.S. Congress.

Hughes published his first poem at the age of seventeen in W. E. B. Du Bois's *The Crisis*. In the 1920s he began writing more frequently and embarked on what would become a lifelong fascination with travel. He taught English for a year in Mexico and then moved to New York City and enrolled in Columbia University. There he spent most of his time immersed in Harlem's local culture and became a noted figure in the Harlem Renaissance. He left school in 1922 and traveled to West Africa. That same year he traveled to the Netherlands and, in 1924, lived in Paris. In 1926 he met Zora Neale Hurston and soon accompanied her on a car trip through the South collecting black folklore. In the 1930s he published some of his more radical works and spent time in Cuba, Haiti, the Soviet Union, China, Korea, and Japan.

Democracy

Democracy will not come
Today, this year
    Nor ever
Through compromise and fear.

I have as much right
As the other fellow has
    To stand
On my two feet
And own the land.

I tire so of hearing people say,
Let things take their course.
Tomorrow is another day.
I do not need my freedom when I'm dead.
I cannot live on tomorrow's bread.

    Freedom
    Is a strong seed
    Planted
    In a great need.
    I live here, too.

I want freedom
Just as you.

Refugee in America

There are words like *Freedom*
Sweet and wonderful to say.
On my heart-strings freedom sings
All day everyday.

There are words like *Liberty*
That almost make me cry.
If you had known what I knew
You would know why.

Freedom's Plow

When a man starts out with nothing,
When a man starts out with his hands
Empty, but clean,
When a man starts out to build a world,
He starts first with himself
And the faith that is in his heart—
The strength there,
The will there to build.

First in the heart is the dream.
Then the mind starts seeking a way.
His eyes look out on the world,
On the great wooded world,
On the rich soil of the world,
On the rivers of the world.

The eyes see there materials for building,
See the difficulties, too, and the obstacles.
The hand seeks tools to cut the wood,
To till the soil, and harness the power of the waters.
Then the hand seeks other hands to help,
A community of hands to help—
Thus the dream becomes not one man's dream alone,
But a community dream.
Not my dream alone, but *our dream.*
Not my world alone,

But *your world and my world,*
Belonging to all the hands who build.

A long time ago, but not too long ago,
Ships came from across the sea
Bringing Pilgrims and prayer-makers,
Adventurers and booty seekers,
Free men and indentured servants,
Slave men and slave masters, all new—
To a new world, America!

With billowing sails the galleons came
Bringing men and dreams, women and dreams.
In little bands together,
Heart reaching out to heart,
Hand reaching out to hand,
They began to build our land.
Some were free hands
Seeking a greater freedom,
Some were indentured hands
Hoping to find their freedom,
Some were slave hands
Guarding in their hearts the seed of freedom.
But the word was there always:
    FREEDOM.

Down into the earth went the plow
In the free hands and the slave hands,
In indentured hands and adventurous hands,
Turning the rich soil went the plow in many hands
That planted and harvested the food that fed
And the cotton that clothed America.
Clang against the trees went the ax in many hands
That hewed and shaped the rooftops of America.
Splash into the rivers and the seas went the boat-hulls
That moved and transported America.
Crack went the whips that drove the horses
Across the plains of America.
Free hands and slave hands,
Indentured hands, adventurous hands,
White hands and black hands
Held the plow handles,
Ax handles, hammer handles,
Launched the boats and whipped the horses

That fed and housed and moved America.
Thus together through labor,
All these hands made America.
Labor! Out of labor came the villages
And the towns that grew to cities.
Labor! Out of labor came the rowboats
And the sailboats and the steamboats,
Came the wagons, stage coaches,
Out of labor came the factories,
Came the foundries, came the railroads,
Came the marts and markets, shops and stores,
Came the mighty products moulded, manufactured,
Sold in shops, piled in warehouses,
Shipped the wide world over:
Out of labor—white hands and black hands—
Came the dream, the strength, the will,
And the way to build America.
Now it is Me here, and You there.
Now it's Manhattan, Chicago,
Seattle, New Orleans,
Boston and El Paso—
Now it is the U.S.A.

A long time ago, but not too long ago, a man said:

> ALL MEN ARE CREATED EQUAL . . .
> ENDOWED BY THEIR CREATOR
> WITH CERTAIN INALIENABLE
> RIGHTS . . .
>
> AMONG THESE LIFE, LIBERTY
> AND THE PURSUIT OF HAPPINESS.

His name was Jefferson. There were slaves then,
But in their hearts the slaves believed him, too,
And silently took for granted
That what he said was also meant for them.
It was a long time ago,
But not so long ago at that, Lincoln said:

> NO MAN IS GOOD ENOUGH
> TO GOVERN ANOTHER MAN
> WITHOUT THAT OTHER'S CONSENT.

There were slaves then, too,
But in their hearts the slaves knew
What he said must be meant for every human being—
Else it had no meaning for anyone.
Then a man said:

BETTER TO DIE FREE,
THAN TO LIVE SLAVES.

He was a colored man who had been a slave
But had run away to freedom.
And the slaves knew
What Frederick Douglass said was true.
With John Brown at Harpers Ferry, Negroes died.
John Brown was hung.
Before the Civil War, days were dark,
And nobody knew for sure
When freedom would triumph.
"Or if it would," thought some.
But others knew it had to triumph.
In those dark days of slavery,
Guarding in their hearts the seed of freedom,
The slaves made up a song:

KEEP YOUR HAND ON THE PLOW!
HOLD ON!

That song meant just what it said: *Hold on!*
Freedom will come!

KEEP YOUR HAND ON THE PLOW!
HOLD ON!

Out of war, it came, bloody and terrible!
But it came!
Some there were, as always,
Who doubted that the war would end right,
That the slaves would be free,
Or that the union would stand.
But now we know how it all came out.
Out of the darkest days for a people and a nation,
We know now how it came out.
There was light when the battle clouds rolled away.

There was a great wooded land,
And men united as a nation.

America is a dream.
The poet says it was promises.
The people say it *is promises—that will come true.*
The people do not always say things out loud,
Nor write them down on paper.
The people often hold
Great thoughts in their deepest hearts
And sometimes only blunderingly express them,
Haltingly and stumbling say them,
And faultily put them into practice.
The people do not always understand each other.
But there is, somewhere there,
Always the *trying to understand,*
And the *trying to say,*
"You are a man. Together we are building our land."

America!
Land created in common,
Dream nourished in common,
Keep your hand on the plow! Hold-on!
If the house is not yet finished,
Don't be discouraged, builder!
If the fight is not yet won,
Don't be weary, soldier!
The plan and the pattern is here,
Woven from the beginning
Into the warp and woof of America:

ALL MEN ARE CREATED EQUAL.

NO MAN IS GOOD ENOUGH
TO GOVERN ANOTHER MAN WITHOUT
THAT OTHER'S CONSENT.

BETTER DIE FREE,
THAN LIVE SLAVES.

Who said those things? Americans!
Who owns those words? America!
Who is America? You, me!

We are America!
To the enemy who would conquer us from without,
We say, NO!
To the enemy who would divide
and conquer us from within,
We say, NO!

FREEDOM!
BROTHERHOOD!
DEMOCRACY!

To all the enemies of these great words:
We say, NO!

A long time ago,
An enslaved people heading toward freedom
Made up a song:
Keep Your Hand On The Plow! Hold On!
That plow plowed a new furrow
Across the field of history.
Into that furrow the freedom seed was dropped.
From that seed a tree grew, is growing, will ever grow.
That tree is for everybody,
For all America, for all the world.
May its branches spread and its shelter grow
Until all races and all peoples know its shade.
KEEP YOUR HAND ON THE PLOW!
HOLD ON!

Source

Langston Hughes, "Democracy", "Refugee in America", and "Freedom's Plow," in *Selected Poems of Langston Hughes,* 285, 290–297 (New York: Vintage Books, 1990).

Selected Bibliography

Hughes, Langston. *The Best of Simple.* New York: Hill and Wang, 1961.
—— *Five Plays.* Bloomington: Indiana University Press, 1963.
—— *Good Morning, Revolution; Uncollected Social Protest Writings.* New York: L. Hill, 1973.
—— *The Langston Hughes Reader.* New York: G. Braziller, 1958.
—— *The Political Plays of Langston Hughes.* Carbondale: Southern Illinois University Press, 2000.

eight

I, Too, Am American

An actor, activist, singer, lawyer, and athlete, Paul Robeson (1898–1976) was for a time the most celebrated African American of his day. Robeson was an All-American football player from Rutgers University, where he graduated valedictorian. He later earned a law degree from Columbia University before pursuing his true love of singing and acting. Robeson also grew concerned about such issues as colonialism in Africa, worker's rights, and segregation in the United States. And although he was never a member of the Communist Party, he attracted a great deal of criticism when, after traveling there in the 1930s, he publicly recognized that the Soviet Union responded more favorably to people of color than the "democratic" United States.

Back in the United States Robeson sternly opposed racism and class oppression in many ways, including picketing the White House, refusing to perform for segregated audiences, and publicly supporting antilynching legislation. By 1950, due to his political activism, the U.S. revoked his passport, concert managers blacklisted him, and his name was stricken from the list of All-Americans. In the late 1940s and 1950s, despite such rejection, as his 1949 essay "I, Too, Am American" demonstrates, Robeson never renounced his identity as an American. Rather, he persistently placed his lot with progressive elements in the United States, in an effort to hold U.S. elites to their full measure of democratic accountability.

Robeson toured the U.S. upholding his political beliefs and later published his autobiography, *Here I Stand*, in 1958. That year, after the government renewed his passport, he began touring internationally where he received numerous awards and honors. After withdrawing from the public for some time, he died on January 23, 1976.

Sometimes when I go back to my home State in New Jersey, friends of my student days say to me, "Paul, what has happened to you, you used to be such a mild sort of chap and now you are so militant and political."

I think back and wonder how my attitude has changed since my student days. I realize then that I learned my militancy and my politics from your Labour Movement here in Britain.

I came to Britain for the first time some years before the war, and I thought in those days that my sole job was to be an artist. I was made a fuss of by Mayfair.

Then one day I heard one of your aristocrats talking to his chauffeur in much the same way as he would speak to his dog. I said to myself, "Paul, that is how a southerner in the United States would speak to you."

That is how I realized that the fight of my Negro people in America and the fight of the oppressed workers everywhere was the same struggle.

These were the years of depression in Britain and I went out to sing for the Welsh miners, for the dockers of Glasgow. I took my place on the platform in those great demonstrations that you organized here for the people of Republican Spain. In that great campaign I worked with Clement Attlee[1] and Stafford Cripps.[2]

I feel at home in England. Coming over on the boat a few days ago I went down to sing to the crew. When I arrived at Southampton the dockers came on board, called me by my Christian name. I said: "Yes, I am part of this England."

But I speak, too, for those progressive forces in America who are fighting with the progressive forces everywhere against the men who are seeking to spread imperialism over the world.

As a Negro American, I am one of the 15,000,000. I was born in America. I went to University in America. I am a product of the American social background.

My ancestors were among the first to people America. Men and women of my family were brought over as slaves in 1620.

Theirs was not the only slave labour that went to build up America. Other ships were sailing to the West in those days with bound labour in their holds. Maybe some of you who read this are descendants of English peasants who were sold as slaves to the planters after the defeat of the Monmouth Rebellion against your King James II. Maybe among your ancestors are men and women shipped to the plantations as indentured servants who were little better than slaves.

There you have an aspect of American history that the advocates of race persecution like to forget: while the Negroes were sent to slavery in the cotton plantations, English, Scottish, Irish, and Welsh victims of poverty and tyranny were also slaves or near slaves in both North and South.

We are the people, black and white, whose work was the source of the first great primary wealth of America.

I see my own background against the fact that from the continent of Africa 100,000,000 Africans were torn from their land to build the wealth of "Liberal capitalism."

I know that I am part of it because my own father was a slave. He was born in 1843, escaped from slavery in 1858, five years before the liberation of the slaves, and fought in the Union army. I was born in 1898, the last of seven children.

A few weeks ago, during Henry Wallace's[3] campaign for the Presidency, I stood on the very soil on which my father worked as a slave. My relatives are there still. They are poor farming Negroes, trying to eke out some kind of living from the worn-out soil. And they have no rights that the white southerner is bound to respect.

I speak for the progressive America, of which the Negro Americans are but a part, which is fighting to carry out the plain demand of the electorate for a new deal. The reason Truman is President is that he told the people he would do what Henry Wallace wanted to do.

I am part of that America today which is being persecuted for its defence of civil liberties and for the right of men and women to live as human beings.

It is important for the people of England to know that those basic rights which are part of English civilisation are under as sharp fire to-day in America as they would have been in Hitler Germany.[4]

When I think of conditions in my country I marvel that so many people here with a record of struggle in the progressive cause, fail to realize what is happening in present-day America, fail to realize that people like Forrestal,[5] Harriman[6] and Stettinius[7] are merely seeking the expansion of American imperialism.

In the Progressive Party we believe that Truman[8] is still in the hands of those people and that we have an urgent duty to see that he fulfills his pledges. It will be one of my tasks over here to give your people the background to what is happening in America.

When they stop me speaking in American Universities because I am "un-American," when they persecute the best progressives in America because they are supposed to be more concerned with other nations than their own, I ask them whether they have not yet realized that to-day no nation can live by itself. Every nation is part of the world.

We are constantly told in America that we are part of the Western world. I would note in passing that this geographical designation includes Turkey and Japan.

They tell me that my son, aged 21, as an American is part of a revived Fascist Western Germany, that as an American I am part of a nation that is beginning to filter funds to Franco,[9] that is aiding Fascist Greece and reactionary Turkey, that is about to begin another rape of Africa.

I belong to another America. I will not belong to Franco's world. I belong to the world of Republican Spain, of resistance Greece and the new democracies. I belong to the America which seeks friendship with the Soviet Union. I am a friend of Israel, not of the oil interests. I am a friend of the new China, not of a revived Fascist Japan.

I, too, am American.

Notes

1. Clemente Richard Attlee (1883–1967), British statesman, created earl in 1955.
2. Sir Stafford Cripps (1889–1952), British statesman, knighted in 1930.
3. Henry Agard Wallace (1888–1965), vice president of the United States (1941–1945), agriculturalist, editor, and Progressive Party candidate in 1948.
4. Adolf Hitler (1889–1945), German dictator, founder and leader of Nazism. The phrase "Hitler Germany" recalls the most dreadful tyranny of the modern centuries.
5. James Forrestal (1892–1949), U.S. secretary of the navy (1944–1947) and secretary of defense (1947–1949).
6. Averell Harriman (1891–1986), American businessman and public official.
7. Edward R. Stettinius (1900–1949), American statesman and industrialist.
8. Harry S. Truman (1884–1972), thirty-third president of the United States (1945–1952).
9. Francisco Franco (1892–1975), Spanish general, caudillo (leader) of Spain (1939–1975).

Source

Paul Robeson, "I, Too, Am American," *Reynold's News,* February 27, 1949; reprinted in Philip S. Foner, ed., *Paul Robeson Speaks: Writing, Speeches, and Interviews, 1918–1974,* 191–93 (Larchmont, N.Y.: Brunner/Mazel, 1978).

Selected Bibliography

Davis, Lenwood G. *A Paul Robeson Research Guide: A Selected, Annotated Bibliography.* Westport, Conn.: Greenwood Press, 1982.

Duberman, Martin. *Paul Robeson.* New York: Knopf, 1988.

Foner, Philip S. *Paul Robeson Speaks: Writings, Speeches, Interviews, 1918–1974.* Larchmont, N.Y.: Bruner/Mazel, 1978.

Robeson, Paul. *Here I Stand.* Boston: Beacon Press, 1958.

nine

The American Dream and the American Negro

James (Arthur) Baldwin (1924–1987) was a celebrated African American writer. The first of nine children from a poor family in Harlem, New York, Baldwin endured a difficult childhood impacted by an oppressive stepfather and struggles with his Christian identity and sexuality. After graduating from high school in 1942, forgoing a college education, he worked to support his family after mental illness incapacitated his father. He later died and was buried on Baldwin's nineteenth birthday.

In 1948 he began receiving awards and fellowships for his writing, although he simultaneously grew disgusted with race relations in the United States and moved to Paris, where he spent much of his life. In Paris he met Lucien Happersberger, his friend and lover of thirty-nine years. In 1953, reflecting on his youth, he completed one of his most respected novels, *Go Tell It on the Mountain.*

In 1957, a year after the completion of *Giovanni's Room,* Baldwin traveled to the southern United States to partake in the civil rights struggle. Continuing to write novels, poetry, essays, and plays, Baldwin became politically engaged, criticizing the Vietnam War and the Hoover administration. Robert Kennedy sought his advice on dealing with riots in Birmingham, Alabama. In 1962, cultivating his self-awareness, Baldwin traveled to Africa; he published *The Fire Next Time,* one of his most respected works on race, the following year. Later in his life, Baldwin commuted from France to teach at the University of Massachusetts, Amherst and Hampshire College. Baldwin died in his home in St. Paul de Vence in France on December 1, 1987.

In his 1965 essay "The American Dream and the American Negro," Baldwin wrote with characteristic elegance about the psychic burdens of being black in the United States and of the necessity of recognizing African Americans as vital elements in American life, thought, and culture.

I find myself, not for the first time, in the position of a kind of Jeremiah. It would seem to me that the question before the house is a proposition horribly loaded, that one's response to that question depends on where you find yourself in the world, what your sense of reality is. That is, it depends on assumptions we hold so deeply as to be scarcely aware of them.

The white South African or Mississippi sharecropper[1] or Alabama sheriff has at bottom a system of reality which compels them really to believe when they face the Negro that this woman, this man, this child must be insane to attack the system to which he owes his entire identity. For such a person, the proposition which we are trying to discuss here does not exist.

On the other hand, I have to speak as one of the people who have been most attacked by the western system of reality. It comes from Europe. That is how it got to America. It raises the question of whether or not civilizations can be considered equal, or whether one civilization has a right to subjugate—in fact, to destroy—another.

Now, leaving aside all the physical factors one can quote—leaving aside the rape or murder, leaving aside the bloody catalogue of oppression which we are too familiar with anyway—what the system does to the subjugated is to destroy his sense of reality. It destroys his father's authority over him. His father can no longer tell him anything because his past has disappeared.

In the case of the American Negro, from the moment you are born every stick and stone, every face, is white. Since you have not yet seen a mirror, you suppose you are too. It comes as a great shock around the age of five, six, or seven to discover that the flag to which you have pledged allegiance, along with everybody else, has not pledged allegiance to you. It comes as a great shock to see Gary Cooper[2] killing off the Indians, and, although you are rooting for Gary Cooper, that the Indians are you.

It comes as a great shock to discover that the country which is your birthplace and to which you owe your life and identity has not, in its whole system of reality, evolved any place for you. The disaffection and the gap between people, only on the basis of their skins, begins there and accelerates throughout your whole lifetime. You realize that you are thirty and you are having a terrible time. You have been through a certain kind of mill and the most serious effect is again not the catalogue of disaster—the policeman, the taxi driver, the waiters, the landlady, the banks, the insurance companies, the millions of details twenty-four hours of every day which spell out to you that you are a worthless human being. It is not that. By that time you have begun to see it happening in your daughter, your son or your niece or your nephew. You are thirty by now and nothing you have done has helped you escape the trap. But what is worse is that nothing you have done, and as far as you can tell nothing you can do, will save your son or your daughter from having the same disaster and from coming to the same end.

We speak about expense. There are several ways of addressing oneself to some attempt to find out what the word means here. From a very literal point of view, the harbors and the ports and the railroads of the country—the economy; especially in the South—could not conceivably be what they are if it had not been (and this is still so) for cheap labor. I am speaking very seriously, and this is not an overstatement: I picked cotton, I carried it to the market, I built the railroads under someone else's whip for nothing. For nothing.

The Southern oligarchy which has still today so very much power in Washington, and therefore some power in the world, was created by my labor and my sweat and the violation of my women and the murder of my children. This in the land of the free, the home of the brave. None can challenge that statement. It is a matter of historical record.

In the Deep South you are dealing with a sheriff or a landlord or a landlady or the girl at the Western Union desk. She doesn't know quite whom she is dealing with—by which I mean, if you are not part of a town and if you are a northern nigger, it shows in millions of ways. She simply knows that it is an unknown quantity and she wants nothing to do with it. You have to wait a while to get your telegram. We have all been through it. By the time you get to be a man it is fairly easy to deal with.

But what happens to the poor white man's, the poor white woman's mind? It is this: they have been raised to believe, and by now they helplessly believe, that no matter how terrible some of their lives may be and no matter what disaster overtakes them, there is one consolation like a heavenly revelation—at least they are not black. I suggest that of all the terrible things that could happen to a human being that is one of the worst. I suggest that what has happened to the white southerner is in some ways much worse than what has happened to the Negroes there.

Sheriff Clark[3] in Selma, Alabama, cannot be dismissed as a total monster; I am sure he loves his wife and children and likes to get drunk. One has to assume that he is a man like me. But he does not know what drives him to use the club, to menace with the gun and to use the cattle prod. Something awful must have happened to a human being to be able to put a cattle prod against a woman's breasts. What happens to the woman is ghastly. What happens to the man who does it is in some ways much, much worse. Their moral lives have been destroyed by the plague called color.

This is not being done one hundred years ago, but in 1965 and in a country which is pleased with what we call prosperity, with a certain amount of social coherence, which calls itself a civilized nation and which espouses the notion of freedom in the world. If it were white people being murdered, the government would find some way of doing something about it. We have a civil rights bill now. We had the Fifteenth Amendment nearly one hundred years ago. If it was not honored then, I have no reason to believe that the civil rights bill will be honored now.

The American soil is full of the corpses of my ancestors, through four hundred years and at least three wars. Why is my freedom, my citizenship, in question now? What one begs the American people to do, for all our sakes, is simply to accept our history.

It seems to me when I watch Americans in Europe that what they don't know about Europeans is what they don't know about me. They were not trying to be nasty to the French girl, rude to the French waiter. They did not know that they hurt their feelings; they didn't have any sense that this particular man and woman were human beings. They walked over them with the same sort of bland ignorance and condescension, the charm and cheerfulness, with which they had patted me on the head and which made them upset when I was upset.

When I was brought up I was taught in American history books that Africa had no history and that neither had I. I was a savage about whom the least said the better, who had been saved by Europe and who had been brought to America. Of course, I believed it. I didn't have much choice. These were the only books there were. Everyone else seemed to agree. If you went out of Harlem the whole world agreed. What you saw was much bigger, whiter, cleaner, safer. The garbage was collected, the children were happy. You would go back home and it would seem, of course, that this was an act of God. You belonged where white people put you.

It is only since World War II that there has been a counter-image in the world. That image has not come about because of any legislation by any American government, but because Africa was suddenly on the stage of the world and Africans had to be dealt with in a way they had never been dealt with before. This gave the American Negro, for the first time, a sense of himself not as a savage. It has created and will create a great many conundrums.

One of the things the white world does not know, but I think I know, is that black people are just like everybody else. We are also mercenaries, dictators, murderers, liars. We are human, too. Unless we can establish some kind of dialogue between those people who enjoy the American dream and those people who have not achieved it, we will be in terrible trouble. This is what concerns me most. We are sitting in this room and we are all civilized; we can talk to each other, at least on certain levels, so that we can walk out of here assuming that the measure of our politeness has some effect on the world.

I remember when the ex–Attorney General Mr. Robert Kennedy[4] said it was conceivable that in forty years in America we might have a Negro President. That sounded like a very emancipated statement to white people. They were not in Harlem when this statement was first heard. They did not hear the laughter and the bitterness and scorn with which this statement was greeted. From the point of view of the man in the Harlem barber shop, Bobby Kennedy only got here yesterday and now he is already on his way to the Presidency. We were here for four hundred years and now he tells us that maybe in forty years, if you are good, we may let you become President.

Perhaps I can be reasoned with, but I don't know—neither does Martin Luther King—none of us knows how to deal with people whom the white world has so long ignored, who don't believe anything the white world says and don't entirely believe anything I or Martin say. You can't blame them.

It seems to me that the City of New York has had, for example, Negroes in it for a very long time. The City of New York was able in the last fifteen years to reconstruct itself, to tear down buildings and raise great new ones, and has done nothing whatever except build housing projects, mainly in the ghettoes, for the Negroes. And of course the Negroes hate it. The children can't bear it. They want to move out of the ghettoes. If American pretensions were based on more honest assessments of life, it would not mean for Negroes that when someone says "urban renewal" some Negroes are going to be thrown out into the streets, which is what it means now.

It is a terrible thing for an entire people to surrender to the notion that one-ninth of its population is beneath them. Until the moment comes when we, the Americans, are able to accept the fact that my ancestors are both black and white, that on that continent we are trying to forge a new identity, that we need each other, that I am not a ward of America, I am not an object of missionary charity, I am one of the people who built the country—until this moment comes there is scarcely any hope for the American dream. If the people are denied participation in it, by their very presence they will wreck it. And if that happens it is a very grave moment for the West.

Notes

1. Sharecropping was a farm tenancy system once common in parts of the United States that arose from the cotton plantation system after the Civil War.
2. Gary Cooper (1901–1961), American film actor.
3. James Clark outspoken segregationist sheriff from Selma, Alabama.
4. Robert F. Kennedy (1925–1968), U.S. attorney general, U.S. senator from New York, and candidate for Democratic presidential nomination in 1968.

Source

James Baldwin, "The American Dream and the American Negro," *The New York Times Magazine,* March 7, 1965, 32–35.

Selected Bibliography

Baldwin, James. *The Price of the Ticket: Collected Nonfiction, 1948–1985.* New York: St. Martin's Press, 1985.
Campbell, James. *Talking at the Gates: A Life of James Baldwin.* Boston: Faber and Faber, 1991.
Leeming, David Adams. *James Baldwin: A Biography.* New York: Knopf, 1994.
McBride, Dwight A. *James Baldwin Now.* New York: NYU Press, 1999.
Weatherby, William J. *James Baldwin: Artist on Fire.* New York: Dell, 1989.

ten

Who Then Will Speak for the Common Good?

Barbara Jordan (1936–1996) was an African American lawyer, public official, and educator. As a member of Congress from Texas, she delivered the speech "Who Then Will Speak for the Common Good?" before the 1976 Democratic National Convention in New York. As Jordan noted there, the fact that she was chosen as a keynote speaker indicated that important changes in the American cultural landscape were underway. But at the same time, she made an unassailable case that there was still progress to be made, and she closed her speech with an admonition to open and extend the national community to all Americans.

Jordan was born in Houston, Texas, in 1936. She received her bachelor of arts degree from Texas Southern University and her law degree from Boston University Law School. In 1966 she was elected to the Texas state senate, and in 1972 she became the first black woman to serve in the U.S. House of Representatives. Soon after her arrival, Jordan rose to national prominence when she served on the judiciary committee that investigated the Watergate scandal, earning a reputation as a defender of the U.S. Constitution and a fierce critic of governmental corruption. In 1979 she became a professor of public affairs at the University of Texas, and in 1992 she was awarded the NAACP's Spingarn Medal.

One hundred and forty-four years ago, members of the Democratic Party first met in convention to select a Presidential candidate. Since that time, Democrats have continued to convene once every four years and draft a party platform and nominate a Presidential candidate. And our meeting this week is a continuation of that tradition.

But there is something different about tonight. There is something special about tonight. What is different? What is special? I, Barbara Jordan, am a keynote speaker.

A lot of years passed since 1832, and during that time it would have been most unusual for any national political party to ask that a Barbara Jordan deliver a keynote address . . . but tonight here I am. And I feel that notwithstanding the past that my presence here is one additional bit of evidence that the American Dream need not forever be deferred.

Now that I have this grand distinction what in the world am I supposed to say?

I could easily spend this time praising the accomplishments of this party and attacking the Republicans but I don't choose to do that.

I could list the many problems which Americans have. I could list the problems which cause people to feel cynical, angry, frustrated: problems which include lack of integrity in government; the feeling that the individual no longer counts; the reality of material and spiritual poverty; the feeling that the grand American experiment is falling or has failed. I could recite these problems and then I could sit down and offer no solutions. But I don't choose to do that either.

The citizens of America expect more. They deserve and they want more than a recital of problems.

We are a people in a quandary about the present. We are a people in search of our future. We are a people in search of a national community.

We are a people trying not only to solve the problems of the present: unemployment, inflation . . . but we are attempting on a larger scale to fulfill the promise of America. We are attempting to fulfill our national purpose; to create and sustain a society in which all of us are equal.

Throughout our history, when people have looked for new ways to solve their problems, and to uphold the principles of this nation, many times they have turned to political parties. They have often turned to the Democratic Party.

What is it, what is it about the Democratic Party that makes it the instrument that people use when they search for ways to shape their future? Well I believe the answer to that question lies in our concept of governing. Our concept of governing is derived from our view of people. It is a concept deeply rooted in a set of beliefs firmly etched in the national conscience, of all of us.

Now what are these beliefs?

First we believe in equality for all and privileges for none. This is a belief that each American regardless of background has equal standing in the public forum, all of us. Because we believe this idea so firmly, we are an inclusive rather than an exclusive party. Let everybody come.

I think it no accident that most of those emigrating to America in the 19th century identified with the Democratic Party. We are a heterogeneous party made up of Americans of diverse backgrounds.

We believe that the people are the source of all governmental power; that the authority of the people is to be extended, not restricted. This can be accomplished only by providing each citizen with every opportunity to participate in the management of the government. They must have that.

We believe that the government which represents the authority of all the people, not just one interest group, but all the people, has an obligation to actively underscore, actively seek to remove those obstacles which would block individual achievement . . . obstacles emanating from race, sex, economic condition. The government must seek to remove them.

We are a party of innovation. We do not reject our traditions, but we are willing to adapt to changing circumstances, when change we must. We are willing to suffer the discomfort of change in order to achieve a better future.

We have a positive vision of the future founded on the belief that the gap between the promise and reality of America can one day be finally closed. We believe that.

This my friends, is the bedrock of our concept of governing. This is a part of the reason why Americans have turned to the Democratic Party. These are the foundations upon which a national community can be built.

Let's all understand that these guiding principles cannot be discarded for short-term political gains. They represent what this country is all about. They are indigenous to the American idea. And these are principles which are not negotiable.

In other times, I could stand here and give this kind of exposition on the beliefs of the Democratic Party and that would be enough. But today that is not enough. People want more. That is not sufficient reason for the majority of the people of this country to vote Democratic. We have made mistakes. In our haste to do all things for all people, we did not foresee the full consequences of our actions. And when the people raised their voices, we didn't hear. But our deafness was only a temporary condition, and not an irreversible condition.

Even as I stand here and admit that we have made mistakes I still believe that as the people of America sit in judgment on each party, they will recognize that our mistakes were mistakes of the heart. They'll recognize that.

And now we must look to the future. Let us heed the voice of the people and recognize their common sense. If we do not, we only blaspheme our political heritage, we ignore the common ties that bind all Americans.

Many fear the future. Many are distrustful of their leaders, and believe that their voices are never heard. Many seek only to satisfy their private work wants. To satisfy private interests.

But this is the great danger America faces. That we will cease to be one nation and become instead a collection of interest groups: city against suburb, region against region, individual against individual. Each seeking to satisfy private wants.

If that happens, who then will speak for America?

Who then will speak for the common good?

This is the question which must be answered in 1976. Are we to be one people bound together by common spirit sharing in a common endeavor or will we become a divided nation?

For all of its uncertainty, we cannot flee the future. We must not become the new puritans and reject our society. We must address and master the future together. It can be done if we restore the belief that we share a sense of national community, that we share a common national endeavor. It can be done.

There is no executive order; there is no law that can require the American people to form a national community. This we must do as individuals and if we do it as individuals, there is no President of the United States who can veto that decision.

As a first step, we must restore our belief in ourselves. We are a generous people so why can't we be generous with each other? We need to take to heart the words spoken by Thomas Jefferson:

Let us restore to social intercourse that harmony and that affection without which liberty and even life are but dreary things.

A nation is formed by the willingness of each of us to share in the responsibility for upholding the common good.

A government is invigorated when each of us is willing to participate in shaping the future of this nation.

In this election year we must define the common good and begin again to shape a common good and begin again to shape a common future. Let each person do his or her part. If one citizen is unwilling to participate, all of us are going to suffer. For the American idea, though it is shared by all of us, is realized in each one of us.

And now, what are those of us who are elected public officials supposed to do? We call ourselves public servants but I'll tell you this: we as public servants must set an example for the rest of the nation. It is hypocritical for the public official to admonish and exhort the people to uphold the common good if we are derelict in upholding the common good. More is required of public officials than slogans and handshakes and press releases. More is required. We must hold ourselves strictly accountable. We must provide the people with a vision of the future.

If we promise as public officials, we must deliver. If we as public officials propose, we must produce. If we say to the American people it is time for you to be sacrificial; sacrifice. If the public official says that, we (public officials) must be the first to give. We must be. And again, if we make mistakes, we must be willing to admit them. We have to do that. What we have to do is strike a balance between the idea that government should do everything and the idea, the belief, that government ought to do nothing. Strike a balance.

Let there be no illusions about the difficulty of forming this kind of a national community. It's tough, difficult, not easy. But a spirit of harmony will survive in America only if each of us remembers that we share a common destiny. If each of us remembers when self-interest and bitterness seem to prevail, that we share a common destiny.

I have confidence that we can form this kind of national community.

I have confidence that the Democratic Party can lead the way. I have that confidence. We cannot improve on the system of government handed down to us by the founders of the Republic, there is no way to improve upon that. But what we can do is to find new ways to implement that system and realize our destiny.

Now, I began this speech by commenting to you on the uniqueness of a Barbara Jordan making the keynote address. Well I am going to close my speech by quoting a Republican President and I ask you that as you listen to these words of Abraham Lincoln,[1] relate them to the concept of a national community in which every last one of us participates: As I would not be a slave, so I would not be a master. This expresses my idea of Democracy. Whatever differs from this, to the extent of the difference is no Democracy.

Note

1. Abraham Lincoln (1809–1865), sixteenth president of the United States (1861–1865).

Source

Barbara Jordan, "Who Then Will Speak for the Common Good?" *Vital Speeches of the Day* 42 (21): 645–46.

Selected Bibliography

Bryant, Ira Babington. *Barbara Charline Jordan: From the Ghetto to Capitol Hill.* Houston: D. Armstrong, 1977.

Holmes, Barbara Ann, ed. *A Private Woman in Public Spaces: Barbara Jordan's Speeches on Ethics, Public Religion, and Law.* Harrisburg, Penn.: Trinity Press International, 2000.

Jordan, Barbara and Shelby Hearon. *Barbara Jordan: A Self-Portrait.* Garden City, N.Y.: Doubleday, 1979.

Rogers, Mary Beth. *Barbara Jordan: American Hero.* New York: Bantam Books, 1998.

part 3

Culture, Faith, and Celebration

chapter eight

Popular Culture

o n e

Folk Tales

Throughout African American history, folk tales have often served as allegories for mores and cultural traditions that have been transmitted from Africa or as subtle ways of preaching resistance to white oppression. In "trickster tales," for example, a wily brer rabbit deceived and outwitted larger, stronger, or more powerful creatures. (Other forms of tales involved the spider *anansi;* the stereotypical bad man who engaged in such illegal activities as gambling, bootlegging, and numbers running and who took pride in the evasion of law enforcement officials; and the "colored man" who turned to his own advantage Jim Crow stereotypes that African Americans were slow and lazy.) The folk tale "All God's Chillen Had Wings" represents a somewhat different tradition. Here, African Americans use magical powers carried over from Africa to fly away and escape the tyranny of a brutal overseer. (The legend that Africans were once able to fly is long-standing and is explored in Toni Morrison's prizewinning novel *Song of Solomon* [1977].)

All God's Chillen Had Wings

Once all Africans could fly like birds; but owing to their many transgressions, their wings were taken away. There remained, here and there, in the sea islands and out-of-the-way places in the low country, some who had been overlooked, and had retained the power of flight, though they looked like other men.

There was a cruel master on one of the sea islands who worked his people till they died. When they died he bought others to take their places. These also he killed with overwork in the burning summer sun, through the middle hours of the day, although this was against the law.

One day, when all the worn-out Negroes were dead of overwork, he bought, of a broker in the town, a company of native Africans just brought into the country, and put them at once to work in the cottonfield.

He drove them hard. They went to work at sunrise and did not stop until dark. They were driven with unsparing harshness all day long, men, women and children. There was no pause for rest during the unendurable heat of the midsummer noon, though trees were plenty and near. But through the hardest hours, when fair plantations gave their Negroes rest, this man's driver pushed the work along without a moment's stop for breath, until all grew weak with heat and thirst.

There was among them one young woman who had lately borne a child. It was her first; she had not fully recovered from bearing, and should not have been sent to the field until her strength had come back. She had her child with her, as the other women had, astraddle on her hip, or piggyback.

The baby cried. She spoke to quiet it. The driver could not understand her words. She took her breast with her hand and threw it over her shoulder that the child might suck and be content. Then she went back to chopping knot-grass; but being very weak, and sick with the great heat, she stumbled, slipped and fell.

The driver struck her with his lash until she rose and staggered on.

She spoke to an old man near her, the oldest man of them all, tall and strong, with a forked beard. He replied; but the driver could not understand what they said; their talk was strange to him.

She returned to work; but in a little while she fell again. Again the driver lashed her until she got to her feet. Again she spoke to the old man. But he said: "Not yet, daughter; not yet." So she went on working, though she was very ill.

Soon she stumbled and fell again. But when the driver came running with his lash to drive her on with her work, she turned to the old man and asked: "Is it time yet, daddy?" He answered: "Yes, daughter; the time has come. Go; and peace be with you!" . . . and stretched out his arms toward her . . . so.

With that she leaped straight up into the air and was gone like a bird, flying over field and wood.

The driver and overseer ran after her as far as the edge of the field; but she was gone, high over their heads, over the fence, and over the top of the woods, gone, with her baby astraddle of her hip, sucking at her breast.

Then the driver hurried the rest to make up for her loss; and the sun was very hot indeed. So hot that soon a man fell down. The overseer himself lashed him to his feet. As he got up from where he had fallen the old man called to him in an unknown tongue. My grandfather told me the words that he said; but it was a long time ago, and I have forgotten them. But when he had spoken, the man turned and laughed at the overseer, and leaped up into the air, and was gone, like a gull, flying over field and wood.

Soon another man fell. The driver lashed him. He turned to the old man. The old man cried out to him, and stretched out his arms as he had done for the other two; and he, like them, leaped up, and was gone through the air, flying like a bird over field and wood.

Then the overseer and the driver ran at the old man with lashes ready; and the master ran too, with a picket pulled from the fence, to beat the life out of the old man who had made those Negroes fly.

But the old man laughed in their faces, and said something loudly to all the Negroes in the field, the new Negroes and the old Negroes.

And as he spoke to them they all remembered what they had forgotten, and recalled the power which once had been theirs. Then all the Negroes, old and new, stood up together; the old man raised his hands; and they all leaped up into the air with a great shout; and in a moment were gone, flying, like a flock of crows, over the field, over the fence, and over the top of the wood; and behind them flew the old man.

The men went clapping their hands; and the women went singing; and those who had children gave them their breasts; and the children laughed and sucked as their mothers flew, and were not afraid.

The master, the overseer, and the driver looked after them as they flew, beyond the wood, beyond the river, miles on miles, until they passed beyond the last rim of the world and disappeared in the sky like a handful of leaves. They were never seen again.

Where they went I do not know; I never was told. Nor what it was that the old man said . . . that I have forgotten. But as he went over the last fence he made a sign in the master's face, and cried "Kuli-ba! Kuli-ba!" I don't know what that means.

But if I could only find the old wood sawyer, he could tell you more; for he was there at the time, and saw the Africans fly away with their women and children. He is an old, old man, over ninety years of age, and remembers a great many strange things.

Source

"All God's Chillen Had Wings," in Langston Hughes and Arna Bontemps, eds., *The Book of Negro Folklore* (New York: Dodd, Mead Company, 1958), 62 reprinted in Dierdre Mullane, ed., *Crossing the Danger Water: Three Hundred Years of African-American Writing,* 257–58 (New York: Anchor Books, 1993).

Selected Bibliography

Abrahams, Roger D. *African-American Folktales: Stories from Black Traditions in the New World.* New York: Pantheon Books, 1999.

Piersen, William Dillon. *Black Legacy: America's Hidden Heritage.* Amherst: University of Massachusetts Press, 1993.

Smitherman, Geneva. *Talkin' That Talk: Language, Culture, and Education in African America.* New York: Routledge, 2000.

Talley, Thomas Washington. *The Negro Tradition.* Knoxville: University of Tennessee Press, 1993.

two

The Prize Fighter

Although his career was rarely without controversy, Jack Johnson (1878–1946)—the first African American to win a heavyweight championship—was a hero to many black people of his day. The following editorial, originally printed in *Crisis* magazine in 1914, was a sarcastic response to Johnson's critics. Although whites launched vicious attacks on Johnson's character, African Americans understood these attacks as thinly veiled racism.

Johnson began his professional boxing career in 1899 and won the heavyweight title from Canadian boxer Tommy Burns in 1908. Johnson surely would have encountered racism regardless of his personal behavior, but his lavish lifestyle and his known affiliations with white women led whites to look far and wide for a "great white hope" that might defeat him in the ring and "redeem" the white race. However, Johnson held his title until 1915 and fought his last bout at age 48. Johnson has remained something of a cultural phenomenon, largely by virtue of playwright Howard Sackler's Pulitzer Prize–winning drama *The Great White Hope* (1968).

"It comes down, then, after all to this unforgivable blackness."

Boxing is an ancient sport. It is mentioned in Homer's Iliad and Virgil's Aeneid and was a recognized branch of the celebrated Olympic games. During the middle age boxing went out of style among most nations, the preference being given to various sorts of encounters with weapons. In England it was revived in the Seventeenth Century, and fighting with bare fists became a national sport in the Eighteenth Century. Boxing gloves were invented late in that century, and in the beginning of the Nineteenth Century, John Jackson (note the prophecy!) became champion and teacher of Lord Byron[1] and other great and titled personages.

Gradually the more brutal features of the sport were eliminated and the eighth Marquess of Queensberry[2] drew up a set of rules in the sixties which have since prevailed.

There is still today some brutality connected with boxing, but as compared with football and boat racing it may be seriously questioned whether boxing deserves to be put in a separate class by reason of its cruelty. Certainly it is a highly civilized pastime as compared with the international game of war which produces so many "heroes" and national monuments.

Despite all this, boxing has fallen into disfavor—into very great disfavor. To see publications like the New York *Times* roll their eyes in shivery horror at the news from Paris (to which it is compelled to give a front page) makes one realize the depths to which we have fallen.

The cause is clear: Jack Johnson, successor of the Eighteenth Century John Jackson, has out-sparred an Irishman. He did it with little brutality, the utmost fairness and great good nature. He did not "knock" his opponent senseless. Apparently he did not even try. Neither he nor his race invented prize fighting or particularly like it. Why then this thrill of national disgust? Because Johnson is black. Of course, some pretend to object to Mr. Johnson's character. But we have yet to hear, in the case of white America, that marital troubles have disqualified prize fighters or ball players or even statesmen. It comes down, then, after all to this unforgivable blackness. Wherefore we conclude that at present prize fighting is very, very immoral, and that we must rely on football and war for pastime until Mr. Johnson retires or permits himself to be "knocked out."

Notes

1. George Gordon Noel Byron, sixth Baron Byron (1788–1824), known as Lord Byron, English poet who was one of the most important and versatile writers of the Romantic movement.
2. The ancient sport of boxing was revived in England in the early eighteenth century, and modern boxing began with the code of rules introduced in 1865 by the marquess of Queensberry, calling, for example, for the use of gloves.

Source

"The Prize Fighter," *The Crisis,* August, 1914.

Selected Bibliography

Decoy, Robert H. *The Big Black Fire.* Los Angeles: Holloway House, 1969.

Gilmore, An-Tony. *Bad Nigger! The National Impact of Jack Johnson.* Port Washington, N.Y.: Kennikat Press, 1975.

Roberts, Randy. *Papa Jack: Jack Johnson and the Era of White Hopes.* New York: Free Press, 1983.

Sackler, Howard. *The Great White Hope.* New York: Dial Press, 1968.

three

The Negro Spirituals

Alain Locke (1885–1954) was a writer, literary critic, and editor. He attended Harvard University, where he was elected to Phi Beta Kappa; in 1907 he graduated magna cum laude and became the first African American Rhodes Scholar. He later became a professor of education and philosophy at Howard University and has also taught at Harvard, Fisk, The New School of Social Research, and the College of the City of New York. Locke is known for his theory of cultural pluralism, which values the unique differences of various races, culture, and religions as part of a democratic society. He sought the end of U.S. segregation and the elimination of European colonialism throughout the world. For his anthropological works, Locke traveled to Egypt, illuminating the various African contributions to Egyptian civilization.

Through *The New Negro,* a collection he edited in 1925, Locke helped establish the Harlem Renaissance. *The New Negro* was originally a special issue of *Survey Graphic* magazine; it was later expanded and published as an anthology, showcasing such writers as W. E. B. Du Bois, James Weldon Johnson, Langston Hughes, Countee Cullen, and Jean Toomer.

Locke was also a critic and collector of African American visual art and a scholar of black folk music. In "The Negro Spirituals," printed in *The New Negro,* Locke emphasized African American music's importance to music as a whole, and he uncovered some of the emotional complexities that inform black spirituals.

In 1925, the year *The New Negro* was published, Locke lost his teaching position at Howard University amidst demands that the school's predominantly white administrators establish an environment that focused on the African Americans. In 1928 after the appointment of Howard's first African American president, Howard reinstated Locke's professorship.

The Spirituals are really the most characteristic product of the race genius as yet in America. But the very elements which make them uniquely expressive of the Negro make them at the same time deeply representative of the soil that produced them. Thus, as unique spiritual products of American life, they become nationally as well as racially characteristic. It may not be readily conceded now that the song of the Negro is America's folk-song; but if the Spirituals are what we think them to be, a classic folk expression, then this is their ultimate destiny. Already they give evidence of this classic quality. Through their immediate and compelling universality of appeal, through their untarnishable beauty, they seem assured of the immortality of those great folk expressions that survive not so much through being typical of a group or representative of a period as by virtue of being fundamentally and everlastingly human. This universality of the Spirituals looms more and more as they stand the test of time. They have outlived the particular generation and the peculiar conditions which produced them; they have survived in turn the contempt of the slave owners, the conventionalizations of formal religion, the repressions of Puritanism,[1] the corruptions of sentimental balladry, and the neglect and disdain of second-generation respectability. They have escaped the lapsing conditions and the fragile vehicle of folk arts, and come firmly into the context of formal music. Only classics survive much things.

In its disingenuous simplicity, folk art is always despised and rejected at first; but generations after, it flowers again and transcends the level of its origin. The slave songs are no exception; only recently have they come to be recognized as artistically precious things. It still requires vision and courage to proclaim their ultimate value and possibilities. But while the first stage of artistic development is yet uncompleted, it appears that behind the deceptive simplicity of Negro song lie the richest undeveloped musical resources anywhere available. Thematically rich, in idiom of rhythm and harmony richer still, in potentialities of new musical forms and new technical traditions so deep as to be accessible only to genius, they have the respect of the connoisseur even while still under the sentimental and condescending patronage of the amateur. Proper understanding and full appreciation of the Spirituals, in spite of their present vogue, is still rare. And the Negro himself has shared many of the common and widespread limitations of view with regard to them. The emotional intuition which has made him cling to this folk music has lacked for the most part that convinced enlightenment that eventually will treasure the Spirituals for their true musical and technical values. And although popular opinion and the general conception have changed very materially, a true estimate of this body of music cannot be reached until many prevailing preconceptions are completely abandoned. For what general opinion regards as simple and transparent about them is in technical ways, though instinctive, very intricate and complex, and what is taken as whimsical and child-like is in truth, though naïve, very profound.

It was the great service of Dr. Du Bois[2] in his unforgettable chapter on the Sorrow Songs in *The Souls of the Black Folk* to give them a serious and proper social interpretation, just as later Mr. Krehbiel[3] in his *Afro-American Folk Songs* gave them their most serious and adequate musical analysis and interpretation. The humble origin of these sorrow songs is too indelibly stamped upon them to be ignored or overlooked. But underneath broken words, childish imagery, peasant simplicity, lies, as Dr. Du Bois pointed out, an epic intensity and a tragic profundity of emotional experience, for which the only historical analogy is the spiritual experience of the Jews and the only analogue, the Psalms. Indeed they transcend emotionally even the very experience of sorrow out of which they were born; their mood is that of religious exaltation, a degree of ecstasy indeed that makes them in spite of the crude vehicle a classic expression of the religious emotion. They lack the grand style, but never the sublime effect. Their words are colloquial, but their mood is epic. They are primitive, but their emotionally artistry is perfect. Indeed, spiritually evaluated, they are among the most genuine and outstanding expressions of Christian mood and feeling, fit musically and emotionally, if not verbally, of standing with the few Latin hymns, the handful of Gregorian tunes, and the rarest of German chorals as a not negligible element in the modicum of strictly religious music that the Christian centuries have produced.

Perhaps there is no such thing as intrinsically religious music; certainly the traceable interplay of the secular and the religious in music would scarcely warrant an arbitrary opinion in the matter. And just as certainly as secular elements can be found in all religious music are there discoverable sensuous and almost pagan elements blended into the Spirituals. But something so intensely religious and so essentially Christian dominates the blend that they are indelibly and notably of this quality. The Spirituals are spiritual. Conscious artistry and popular conception alike should never rob them of this heritage, it is unable to their tradition and to the folk genius to give them another tone. That they are susceptible of both crude and refined secularization is no excuse. Even though their own makers worked them up from the "shout" and the rhythmic elements of the sensuous dance, in their finished form and basic emotional effect all of these elements were completely sublimated in the sincere intensities of religious seriousness. To call them Spirituals and treat them otherwise is a travesty.

It was the Negro himself who first took them out of their original religious setting, but he only anticipated the inevitable by a generation—for the folk religion that produced them is rapidly vanishing. Noble as the purpose of this transplanting was, damage was done to the tradition. But we should not be ungrateful, for surely it was by this that they were saved to posterity at all. Nevertheless it was to an alien atmosphere that the missionary campaigning of the Negro schools and colleges took these songs. And the concert stage has but taken them an inevitable step further from their original setting. We should always remember that they are essentially congregational, not theatrical, just as they are essentially a choral not a solo form. In time, however, on another level, they will get back to this tradition,—for their next development will undoubtedly be, like that of the modern Russian folk music, their use in the larger choral forms of the symphonic choir, through which they will reachieve their folk atmosphere and epic spirituality.

It is a romantic story told in the *Story of the Jubilee Singers,* and retold in Professor Work's *Folk Song of the American Negro;* the tale of that group of singers who started out from Fisk University in 1871, under the resolute leadership of George L. White, to make this music the appeal of the struggling college for philanthropic support. With all the cash in the Fisk treasury, except a dollar held back by Principal Adam K. Spencer, the troupe set out to Oberlin, where, after an unsuccessful concert of current music, they instantly made an impression by a program of Negro Spirituals. Henry Ward Beecher's invitation to Brooklyn led to fame for the singers, fortune for the college, but more important than these things, recognition for the Spirituals. Other schools, Hampton, Atlanta, Calhoun, Tuskegee joined the movement, and spread the knowledge of these songs far and wide in their concert campaigns. Later they recorded and published important collections of them. They thus were saved over that critical period of disfavor in which any folk product is likely to be snuffed out by the false pride of the second generation. Professor Work rightly estimates it as a service worth more racially and nationally than the considerable sums of money brought to these struggling schools. Indeed, as he says, it saved a folk art and preserved as no other medium could the folk temperament, and by maintaining them introduced the Negro to himself. Still the predominant values of this period in estimating the Spirituals were the sentimental, degenerating often into patronizing curiosity on the one side, and hectic exhibitionism on the other. Both races condescended to meet the mind of the Negro slave, and even while his moods were taking their hearts by storm, discounted the artistry of genius therein.

It was only as the musical appreciation of the Spirituals grew that this interest changed and deepened. Musically I think the Spirituals are as far in advance of their moods as their moods are in advance of their language. It is as poetry that they are least effective. Even as folk poetry, they cannot be highly rated. But they do have their quaint symbolisms, and flashes, sometimes sustained passages of fine imagery, as in the much quoted:

> I know moonlight, I know starlight
>   I lay dis body down
> I walk in de graveyard, I walk troo de graveyard
>   To lay dis body down.
>
> I lay in de grave an' stretch out my arms,
>   I lay dis body down,
> I go to de judgment in de evenin' of de day
>   When I lay dis body down,
> An' my soul an' yo' soul will meet de day
>   I lay dis body down.

or

> Bright sparkles in de churchyard
>   Give light unto de tomb;
> Bright summer, spring's over—
>   Sweet flowers in their bloom.
>
> My mother once, my mother twice, my mother,
>   she'll rejoice,
> In the Heaven once, in the Heaven twice,
>   she'll rejoice.
> May the Lord, He will be glad of me
> In the Heaven, He'll rejoice.

or again

> My Lord is so high, you can't get over Him,
> My Lord is so low, you can't get under Him,
>   You must come in and through de Lamb.

In the latter passages, there is a naïveté, and also a faith and fervor, that are mediaeval. Indeed one has to go to the Middle Ages to find anything quite like this combination of childlike simplicity of thought with strangely consummate artistry of mood. A quaintly literal, lisping, fervent Christianity, we feel it to be the evangelical and Protestant counterpart of the naïve Catholicism of the tenth to the thirteenth centuries. And just as there we had quaint versions of Bernard of Clairvaux[4] and Saint Francis in the Virgin songs and Saints Legends, so here we have Bunyan and John Wesley percolated through a peasant mind and imagination, and concentrated into something intellectually less, but emotionally more vital and satisfying. If the analogy seems forced, remember that we see the homely colloquialism of the one through the glamorous distance of romance, and of the other, through the disillusioning nearness of social stigma and disdain. How regrettable though, that the very qualities that add charm to the one should arouse mirthful ridicule for the other.

Over-keen sensitiveness to this reaction, which will completely-pass within a half generation or so, has unfortunately caused many singers and musicians to blur the dialect and pungent colloquialisms of the Spirituals so as not to impede with irrelevant reactions their proper artistic and emotional effect. Some have gone so far as to advocate the abandonment of the dialect versions to insure their dignity and reverence. But for all their inadequacies, the words are the vital clues to the moods of these songs. If anything is to be changed, it should be the popular attitude. One thing further may be said, without verging upon apologetics, about their verbal form. In this broken dialect and grammar there is almost invariably an unerring sense of euphony. Mr. Work goes so far as to suggest—rightly, I think—that in many instances the dropped, elided, and added syllables, especially the latter, are a matter of instinctive euphonic sense following the requirements of the musical rhythm, as, for example, "The Blood came a twinklin' down" from "The Crucifixion" or "Lying there fo' to be heal" from "Blind Man at the Pool." Mr. Work calls attention to the extra beat syllable, as in "De trumpet soun's it in-a' my soul," which is obviously a singing device, a subtle phrase-molding element from a musical point of view, even if on verbal surface value, it suggests illiteracy.

Emotionally, these folks songs are far from simple. They are not only spread over the whole gamut of human moods, with the traditional religious overtone adroitly insinuated in each instance, but there is further a sudden change of mood in the single song, baffling to formal classification. Interesting and intriguing as was Dr. Du Bois's analysis of their emotional themes, modern interpretation must break with that mode of analysis, and relate these songs to the folk activities that they motivated, classifying them by their respective song-types. From this point of view we have essentially four classes, the almost ritualistic prayer songs or pure Spirituals, the freer and more unrestrained evangelical "shouts" or camp-meeting songs, the folk ballads so overlaid with the tradition of the Spirituals proper that their distinctive type quality has almost been unnoticed until lately, and the work and labor songs of strictly secular character. In choral and musical idiom closely related, these song types are gradually coming to be regarded as more and more separate, with the term Spiritual reserved almost exclusively for the songs of intensest religious significance and function. Indeed, in the pure Spirituals one can trace the broken fragments of an evangelical folk liturgy with confession, exhortation, "inourning," conversion and "love-feast" rejoicing as the general stages of a Protestant folk-mass. The instinctive feeling for these differences is almost wholly lost, and it will require the most careful study of the communal life as it still lingers in isolated spots to set the groupings even approximately straight. Perhaps after all the final appeal will have to be made to the sensitive race interpreter, but at present many a half secularized ballad is mistaken for a "spiritual," and many a camp-meeting shout for a folk hymn. It is not a question of religious content or allusion,—for the great majority of the Negro songs have this—but a more delicate question of caliber of feeling and type of folk use. From this important point of view, Negro folk song has yet to be studied.

The distinctiveness of the Spirituals after all, and their finest meaning resides in their musical elements. It is pathetic to notice how late scientific recording has come to the task of preserving this unique folk art. Of course the earlier four-part hymn harmony versions were travesties of the real folk renditions. All competent students agree in the utter distinctiveness of the melodic, harmonic and rhythmic elements in this music. However, there is a regrettable tendency, though a very natural one in view of an inevitable bias of technical interest, to over-stress as basically characteristic one or other of these elements in their notation and analysis. Weldon Johnson[5] thinks the characteristic beauty of the folk song is harmonic in distinction to the more purely rhythmic stress in the secular music of the Negro, which is the basis of "ragtime" and "jazz"; while Krehbiel, more academically balances these elements, regarding the one as the African component in them, and the other as the modifying influence of the religious hymn. "In the United States," he says, "the rhythmic element, though still dominant, has yielded measurably to the melodic, the dance having given way to religious worship sensual bodily movement to emotional utterance." But as a matter of fact, if we separate or even over-stress either element in the Spirituals the distinctive and finer effects are lost. Strain out and emphasize the melodic element *a la* Foster, and you get only the sentimental ballad; emphasize the harmonic idiom, and you get a cloying sentimental glee; over-emphasize the rhythmic idiom and instantly you secularize the product into syncopated dance elements. It is the fusion, and that only, that is finely characteristic; and so far as possible, both in musical settings and in the singing of the Negro Spirituals, this subtle balance of musical elements should be sought after and maintained. The actual mechanics of the native singing, with its syllabic quavers, the off-tones and tone glides, the improvised interpolations and, above all, the subtle rhythmic phrase balance, has much to do with the preservation of the vital qualities of these songs.

Let us take an example. There is no more careful and appreciative student of the Spirituals than David Guion; as far as is possible from a technical and outside approach, he has bent his skill to catch the idiom of these songs. But contrast his version of "God's Goin' to Set Dis Worl' on Fire" with that of Roland Hayes.[6] The subtler rhythmic pattern, the closer phrase linkage, the dramatic recitative movement, and the rhapsodic voice glides and quavers of the great Negro tenor's version are instantly apparent. It is more than a question of musicianship, it is a question of feeling instinctively qualities put there by instinct. In the process of the art development of this material the Negro musician has not only a peculiar advantage but a particular function and duty. Maintaining spiritual kinship with the best traditions of this great folk art, he must make himself the recognized vehicle of both its transmission and its further development.

At present the Spirituals are at a very difficult point in their musical career; for the moment they are caught in the transitional stage between a folk-form and an art-form. Their increasing concert use and popularity as Carl Van Vechten[7] has clearly pointed out in a recent article, has brought about a dangerous tendency toward sophisticated over-elaboration. At the same time that he calls attention to the yeoman service of Mr. Henry T. Burleigh[8] in the introduction of the Spirituals to the attention and acceptance of the concert stage. Mr. Van Vechten thinks many of his settings tincture the folk spirit with added concert furbelows and alien florid adornments. This is true. Even Negro composers have been perhaps too much influenced by formal European idioms and mannerisms in setting these songs. But in calling for the folk atmosphere, and insisting upon the folk quality, we must be careful not to confine this wonderfully potential music to the narrow confines of "simple versions" and musically primitive molds. While it is proper to set up as a standard the purity of the tradition and the maintenance of idiom, it is not proper to insist upon an arbitrary style or form. When for similar reasons, Mr. Van Vechten insists in the name of the folk spirit upon his preference for the "evangelical renderings" of Paul Robeson's[9] robust and dramatic style as over against the subdued, ecstatic and spiritually refined versions of Roland Hayes, he overlooks the fact that the folk itself has these same to styles of singing, and in most cases discriminates according to the mood, occasion and song type, between them. So long as the peculiar quality of Negro song is maintained, and the musical idiom kept unadulterated, there is and can be no set limitation. Negro folk song is not midway its artistic career as yet, and while the preservation of the original folk forms is for the moment the most pressing necessity, and inevitable art development awaits them, as in the past it has awaited all other great folk music.

The complaint to be made is not against the art development of the Spirituals, but against the somewhat hybrid treatment characteristic of the older school of musicians. One of the worst features of this period has been the predominance of solo treatment and the loss of the vital sustained background of accompanying voices. In spite of the effectiveness of the solo versions, especially when competently sung by Negro singers, it must be realized more and more that the proper idiom of Negro folk song calls for choral treatment. The young Negro musicians, Nathaniel Dett, Carl Diton, Ballanta Taylor, Edward Boatner, Hall Johnson, Lawrence Brown and others, while they are doing effective solo settings, are turning back gradually to the choral form. Musically speaking, only the superficial resources in this direction have been touched as yet; just as soon as the traditional conventions of four-part harmony and the oratorio style and form are broken through, we may expect a choral development of Negro folk song that may equal or even outstrip the phenomenal choral music of Russia. With its harmonic versatility and interchangeable voice parts, Negro music is only conventionally in the four-part style, and with its skipped measures and interpolations it is at the very least potentially polyphonic. It can therefore undergo without breaking its own boundaries, intricate and original development in directions already the line of advance in modernistic music.

Indeed one wonders why something vitally new has not already been contributed by Negro folk song to modern choral and orchestral musical development. And if it be objected that it is too far a cry from the simple folk spiritual to the larger forms and idioms of modern music, let us recall the folk song origins of the very tradition which is now classic in European music. Up to the present the resources of Negro music have been tentatively exploited in only one direction at a time,—melodically here, rhythmically there, harmonically in a third direction. A genius that would organize its distinctive elements in a formal way would be the musical giant of his age. Such a development has been hampered by a threefold tradition each aspect of which stands in the way of the original use of the best in the Negro material. The dominance of the melodic tradition has played havoc with its more original harmonic features, and the oratorio tradition has falsely stereotyped and overlaid its more orchestral choral style, with its intricate threading in and out of the voices. Just as definitely in another direction has the traditional choiring of the orchestra stood against the opening up and development of the Negro and the African idioms in the orchestral forms. Gradually these barriers are being broken through. Edgar Varese's *Integrales,* a "study for percussion instruments," presented last season by the International Composes' Guild, suggests a new orchestral technique patterned after the characteristic idiom of the African "drum orchestra." The modernistic, *From the Land of Dreams,* by Grant Still, a young Negro composer who is his student and protége, and Louis Grünberg's setting for baritone and chamber orchestra of Weldon Johnson's *The Creation: a Negro Sermon,* are experimental tappings in still other directions into the rich veins of this new musical ore. In a recent article (*The Living Age,* October, 1924), Darius Milhaud[10] sums up these characteristics traits as "the possibilities of a thorough-going novelty of instrumental technique." Thus Negro music very probably has a great contribution yet to make to the substance and style of contemporary music, both choral and instrumental. If so, its thematic and melodic contributions from Dvorák[11] to Goldmark's[12] recent *Negro Rhapsody* and the borrowings of rhythmical suggestions by Milhaud and Stravinsky[13] are only preluding experiments that have proclaimed the value of the Negro musical idioms, but have not fully developed them. When a body of folk music is really taken up into musical tradition, it is apt to do more than contribute a few new themes. For when the rhythmic and harmonic basis of music is affected, it is more than a question of superstructure, the very foundations of the art are in process of being influenced.

In view of this very imminent possibility it is in the interest of musical development itself that we insist upon a broader conception and a more serious appreciation of Negro folk song, and of the Spiritual which is the very kernel of this distinctive folk art. We cannot accept the attitude that would merely preserve this music but must cultivate that which would also develop it. Equally with treasuring and appreciating it as music of the past, we must nurture and welcome its contribution to the music of to-morrow. Mr. Work has aptly put it in saying: "While it is now assured that we shall always preserve these songs in their original forms, they can never be the last word in the development of our music. . . . They are the starting point, not our goal; the source, not the issue, of our musical traditional."

Notes

1. In the sixteenth and seventeenth centuries, a movement for reform in the Church of England that had a profound influence on the social, political, ethical, and theological ideas in England and America.
2. W. E. B. Du Bois (1868–1963), African American civil rights leader and author.
3. Henry Edward Krehbiel (1854–1923), musicologist.
4. Bernard of Clairvaux (c. 1090–1153), French churchman, doctor of the church.
5. James Weldon Johnson (1871–1938), African American author.
6. Roland Hayes (1877–1977), African American musician and composer.
7. Carl Van Vechten (1880–1964), American author, music critic.
8. Harry Thacker Burleigh (1866–1949), musicologist.
9. Paul Robeson (1898–1976), African American actor, singer, and activist.
10. Darius Milhaud (1892–1974), French composer.
11. Antonin Dvorák (1841–1904), Bohemian composer.
12. Carl Goldmark (1830–1915), Hungarian composer whose works include *A Negro-Rhapsody* (1923).
13. Igor Fyodorovich Stravinsky (1882–1971), Russian American composer.

Source

Alain Locke, "The Negro Spirituals," in *The New Negro: An Interpretation,* 199–210 (New York: Boni, 1925).

Selected Bibliography

Harris, Leonard, ed. *The Critical Pragmatism of Alaine Locke: A Reader on Value, Theory Aesthetics, Community, Culture, Race, and Education.* Lanham, Md.: Rowman and Littlefield, 1999.

—— *The Philosophy of Alaine Locke: Harlem Renaissance and Beyond.* Philadelphia: Temple University Press, 1989.

Locke, Alain. *The Negro and His Music; Negro Art: Past and Present.* New York: Charles Boni, Inc., 1925.

Posnock, Ross. *Color and Culture: Black Writers and the Making of the Modern Intellectual.* Cambridge, Mass.: Harvard University Press, 1998.

Washington, Johnny. *A Journey Into the Philosophy of Alain Locke.* Westport, Conn.: Greenwood Press, 1994.

four

The Dilemma of the Negro Author

The multitalented James Weldon Johnson (1871–1938) has had an enduring effect on African American popular culture. In his essay "The Dilemma of the Negro Author," Johnson took up a question that many writers of the Harlem Renaissance struggled with: Whom should they write for? Johnson argued that rather than writing for either blacks *or* whites, African American writers should aspire to "fuse white and black America into one interested and approving audience."

Although he worked as a lawyer, helped to found the NAACP, and was American consul in Nicaragua and Venezuela, Johnson is best known as coauthor of the anthem "Lift Every Voice and Sing" (known as the Negro National Anthem), the novel *Autobiography of an Ex-Colored Man* (1912), and the poems in *God's Trombones* (1927).

The Negro author—the creative author—has arrived. He is here. He appears in the lists of the best publishers. He even breaks into the lists of the best-sellers. To the general American public he is a novelty, but he is by no means a new thing.

The line of American Negro authors runs back for a hundred and fifty years, back to Phillis Wheatley,[1] the poet. Since Phillis Wheatley there have been several hundred Negro authors who have written books of many kinds. But in all these generations down to within the past six years only seven or eight of the hundreds have ever been heard of by the general American public or even by the specialists in American Literature. As many Negro writers have gained recognition by both in the past six years as in all the generations gone before. What has happened is that efforts which have been going on for more than a century are being noticed and appreciated at last, and that this appreciation has served as a stimulus to greater effort and output. America is aware today that there are such things as Negro authors. Several converging forces have been at work to produce this state of mind. Had these forces been at work three decades ago, it is possible that we then should have had a condition similar to the one which now exists.

Now that the Negro author has come into the range of vision of the American public eye, it seems to me only fair to point out some of the difficulties he finds in his way. But I wish to state emphatically that I have no intention of making an apology or asking any special allowances for him; such a plea would at once disqualify him and void the very recognition he has gained. But the Negro writer does face peculiar difficulties that ought to be taken into account when passing judgment upon him.

It is unnecessary to say that he faces every one of the difficulties common to all that crowd of demon-driven individuals who feel that they must write. But the Aframerican author faces a special problem which the plain American author knows nothing about—the problem of the double audience. It is more than a double audience; it is a divided audience, an audience made up of two elements with differing and often opposite and antagonistic points of view. His audience is always both white America and black America. The moment a Negro writer takes up his pen or sits down to his typewriter he is immediately called upon to solve, consciously or unconsciously, this problem of the double audience. To whom shall he address himself, to his own black group or to white America? Many a Negro writer has fallen down, as it were, between these two stools.

It may be asked why he doesn't just go ahead and write and not bother himself about audiences. That is easier said than done. It is doubtful if anything with meaning can be written unless the writer has some definite audience in mind. His audience may be as far away as the angelic host or the rulers of darkness, but an audience he must have in mind. As soon as he selects his audience he immediately falls, whether he wills it or not, under the laws which govern the influence of the audience upon the artist, laws that operate in every branch of art.

Now, it is axiomatic that the artist achieves his best when working at his best with the materials he knows best. And it goes without saying that the material which the Negro as a creative or general writer knows best comes out of the life and experience of the colored people in America. The overwhelming bulk of the best work done by Aframerican writers has some bearing on the

Negro and his relations to civilization and society in the United States. Leaving authors, white or black, writing for coteries on special and technical subjects out of the discussion, it is safe to say that the white American author, when he sits down to write, has in mind a white audience—and naturally [so]. The influence of the Negro as a group on his work in infinitesimal if not zero. Even when he talks about the Negro he talks to white people. But with the Aframerican author the case is different. When he attempts to handle his best-known material he is thrown upon two, indeed, if it is permissible to say so, upon three horns of a dilemma. He must intentionally or unintentionally choose a black audience or a white audience or a combination of the two; and each of them presents peculiar difficulties.

If the Negro author selects white America as his audience he is bound to run up against many long-standing artistic conceptions about the Negro; against numerous conventions and traditions which through age have become binding; in a word, against a whole row of hard-set stereotypes which are not easily broken up. White America has some firm opinions as to what the Negro is, and consequently some pretty well-fixed ideas as to what should be written about him, and how.

What is the Negro in the artistic conception of white America? In the brighter light, he is a simple, indolent, docile improvident peasant; a singing, dancing, laughing, weeping child; picturesque beside his log cabin and in the snowy fields of cotton; naively charming with his banjo and his songs in the moonlight and along the lazy Southern rivers; a faithful ever-smiling and genuflecting old servitor to the white folks of quality; a pathetic and pitiable figure. In a darker light, he is an impulsive, irrational, passionate savage, reluctantly wearing a thin coat of culture, sullenly hating the white man, but holding an innate and unescapable belief in the white man's superiority; an everlastingly alien and irredeemable element in the nation; a menace to Southern civilization, a threat to Nordic race purity; a figure casting a sinister shadow across the future of the country.

Ninety-nine one-hundredths of all that has been written about the Negro in the United States in three centuries and read with any degree of interest or pleasure by white America has been written in conformity to one or more of these ideas. I am not saying that they do not provide good material for literature; in fact, they make material for poetry and romance and comedy and tragedy of a high order. But I do say they have become stencils inadequate for the portrayal and interpretation of Negro life today. Moreover, when [the Negro author] does attempt to make use of them he finds himself impaled upon the second horn of his dilemma.

II

It is known that art—literature in particular, unless it be sheer fantasy—must be based on more or less well established conventions, upon ideas that have some roots in the general consciousness, that are at least somewhat familiar to the public mind. It is this that gives it verisimilitude and finality. Even revolutionary literature, if it is to have any convincing power, must start from a basis of conventions, regardless of how unconventional its objective may be. These conventions are changed by slow and gradual processes—except they be changed in a flash. The conventions held by white America regarding the Negro will be changed. Actually they are being changed, but they have not yet sufficiently changed to lessen to any great extent the dilemma of the Negro author.

It would be straining the credulity of white America beyond the breaking point for a Negro writer to put out a novel dealing with the wealthy class of colored people. The idea of Negroes of wealth living in a luxurious manner is still too unfamiliar. Such a story wold have to be written in a burlesque vein to make it at all plausible and acceptable. Before Florence Mills[2] and Josephine Baker[3] implanted a new general idea in the public mind it would have been worse than a waste of time for a Negro author to write for white America the story of a Negro girl who rose in spite of all obstacles, racial and others, to a place of world success and acclaim on the musical revue stage. It would be proof of little less than supreme genius in a Negro poet for him to take one of the tragic characters of American Negro history—say Crispus Attucks[4] or Nat Turner[5] or Denmark Vesey[6]—put heroic language in his mouth and have white America accept the work as authentic. American Negroes as heroes form no part of white America's concept of the race. Indeed, I question if three out of ten of the white Americans who will read these lines know anything of either Attucks, Turner or Vesey, although each of the three played a role in the history of the nation. The Aframerican poet might take an African chief or warrior, set him forth in heroic couplets or blank verse and present him to white America with infinitely greater chance of having his work accepted.

But these limiting conventions held by white America do not constitute the whole difficulty of the Negro author in dealing with a white audience. In addition to these conventions regarding the Negro as a race, white America has certain definite opinions regarding the Negro as an artist, regarding the scope of his efforts. White America has a strong feeling that Negro artists should refrain from making use of white subject matter. I mean by that, subject matter which it feels belongs to the white world. In plain words, white America does not welcome seeing the Negro competing with the white man on what it considers the white man's own ground.

In many white people this feeling is dormant, but brought to the test it flares up, if only faintly. During his first season in this country after his European success a most common criticism of Roland Hayes[7] was provoked by the fact that his program consisted of groups [of] English, French, German and Italian songs, closing always with a group of Negro Spirituals. A remark frequently made was, "Why doesn't he confine himself to the Spirituals?" This in face of the fact that no tenor on the American concert stage could surpass Hayes in singing French and German songs. The truth is that white America was not quite prepared to relish the sight of a black man in a dress suit singing French and German love songs, and singing them exquisitely. The first reaction was that there was something incongruous about it. It gave a jar to the old conventions and something of a shock to the Nordic superiority complex. The years have not been many since Negro players have dared to interpolate a love duet in a musical show to be witnessed by white people. The representation of romantic love-making by Negroes struck the white audience as somewhat ridiculous; Negroes were supposed to mate in a more primeval manner.

White America has for a long time been annexing and appropriating Negro territory, and is prone to think of every part of the domain it now controls as originally—and aboriginally—its own. One sometimes hears the critics in reviewing a Negro musical show lament the fact that it is so much like white musical shows. But a great deal of this similarity would be hard to avoid because of the plain fact that two of the four chief ingredients in the present day white musical show, the music and the dancing, are directly derived from the Negro. These ideas and opinions regarding the scope of artistic effort affect the Negro author, the poet in particular. So whenever an Aframerican writer addresses himself to white America and attempts to break away from or break through these conventions and limitations he makes more than an ordinary demand upon his literary skill and power.

At this point it would appear that a most natural thing for the Negro author to do would be to say, "Damn the white audience!" and devote himself to addressing his own race exclusively. But when he turns from the conventions of white America he runs afoul of the taboos of black America. He has no more absolute freedom to speak as he pleases addressing black America than he has in addressing white America. There are certain phases of life that he dare not critically discuss, certain manners of treatment that he dare not use—except at the risk of rousing bitter resentment. It is quite possible for a Negro author to do a piece of work, good from every literary point of view, and at the same time bring down on his head the wrath of the entire colored pulpit and press, and gain among the literate element of his own people the reputation of being a prostitutor of his talent and a betrayer of his race—not by any means a pleasant position to get into.

This state of mind on the part of the colored people may strike white America as stupid and intolerant, but it is not without some justification and not entirely without precedent; the white South on occasion discloses a similar sensitiveness. The colored people of the United States are anomalously situated. They are a segregated and antagonized minority in a very large nation, a minority unremittingly on the defensive. Their faults and failings are exploited to produce exaggerated effects. Consequently, they have a strong feeling against exhibiting to the world anything but their best points. They feel that other groups may afford to do otherwise but, as yet, the Negro cannot. This is not to say that they refuse to listen to criticism of themselves, for they often listen to Negro speakers excoriating the race for its faults and foibles and vices. But these criticisms are not for the printed page. They are not for the ears or eyes of White America.

A curious illustration of this defensive state of mind is found in the Negro theaters. In those wherein Negro players give Negro performances for Negro audiences all of the Negro weaknesses, real and reputed, are burlesqued and ridiculed in the most hilarious manner, and are laughed at and heartily enjoyed. But the presence of a couple of dozen white people would completely change the psychology of the audience, and the players. If some of the performances so much enjoyed by the strictly Negro audiences in Negro theaters were put on, say, in a Broadway theatre, a wave of indignation would sweep Aframerica from the avenues of Harlem to the canebrakes of Louisiana. These taboos of black America are as real and binding as the conventions of white America. Conditions may excuse if not warrant them; nevertheless, it is unfortunate that they exist, for their effect is blighting. In past years they have discouraged in Negro authors the production of everything but nice literature; they have operated to hold their work down to literature of the defensive, exculpatory sort. They have a restraining effect at present time which Negro writers are compelled to reckon with.

This division of audience takes the solid ground from under the feet of the Negro writer and leaves him suspended. Either choice carries hampering and discouraging conditions. The Negro author may please one audience and at the same time rouse the resentment of the other; or he may please the other and totally fail to rouse the interest of the one. The situation, moreover, constantly subjects him to the temptation of posing and posturing for the one audience or the other; and the sincerity and soundness of his work are vitiated whether he poses for white or black.

The dilemma is not made less puzzling by the fact that practically it is an extremely difficult thing for the Negro author in the United States to address himself solely to either of these two audiences. If he analyzes what he writes he will find that on one page black America is his whole or main audience, and on the very next page white America. In fact, a psychoanalysis of the Negro authors of the defensive and exculpatory literature, written in strict conformity to the taboos of black America, would reveal that they were unconsciously addressing themselves mainly to white America.

III

I have sometimes thought it would be a way out, that the Negro author would be on surer ground and truer to himself, if he could disregard white America; if he could say to white America, "What I have written, I have written. I hope you'll be interested and like it. If not, I can't help it." But it is impossible for a sane American Negro to write with total disregard for nine-tenths of the people of the United States. Situated as his own race is amidst and amongst them, their influence is irresistible.

I judge there is not a single Negro writer who is not, at least secondarily, impelled by the desire to make his work have some effect on the white world for the good of his race. It may be thought that the work of the Negro writer, on account of this last named condition, gains in pointedness what it loses in breadth. Be that as it may, the situation is for the time one in which he is inextricably placed. Of course, the Negro author can try the experiment of putting black America in the orchestra chairs, so to speak, and keeping white America in the gallery, but he is likely at any moment to find his audience shifting places on him, and sometimes without notice.

And now, instead of black America and white America as separate or alternating audiences, what about the combination of the two into one? That, I believe, is the only way out. However, there needs to be more than a combination, there needs to be a fusion. In time, I cannot say how much time, there will come a gradual and natural rapprochement of these two sections of the Negro author's audiences. There will come a breaking up and remodelling of most of white America's traditional stereotypes, forced by the advancement of the Negro in the various phases of our national life. Black America will abolish many of its taboos. A sufficiently large class of colored people will progress enough and become strong enough to render a constantly sensitive and defensive attitude on the part of the race unnecessary and distasteful. In the end, the Negro author will have something close to a common audience, and will be about as free from outside limitations as other writers.

Meanwhile, the making of a common audience out of white and black America presents the Negro author with enough difficulties to constitute a third horn of his dilemma. It is a task that is a very high test for all his skill and abilities, but it can be and has been accomplished. The equipped Negro author working at his best in his best-known material can achieve this end; but, standing on his racial foundation, he must fashion something that rises above race, and reaches out to the universal in truth and beauty. And so, when a Negro author does write so as to fuse white and black America into one interested and approving audience he has performed no slight feat, and has most likely done a sound piece of literary work.

Notes

1. Phillis Wheatley (1753?–1784), African American poet.
2. Florence Mills (1896–1927), African American singer, dancer.
3. Josephine Baker (1906–1975), American-born French dancer and singer.
4. Crispus Attucks (d. 1770), one of five American colonists killed when British troops fired into a crowd during the Boston Massacre, March 5, 1770.
5. Nat Turner (1800–1831), African American slave and revolutionary.

6. Denmark Vesey (1767–1822), freedman who planned a slave rebellion in Charleston, South Carolina.
7. Roland Hayes (1887–1977), African American musician and composer.

Source

James Weldon Johnson, "The Dilemma of the Negro Author," *The American Mercury* 15 (December 1928): 477–81.

Selected Bibliography

Fleming, Robert E. *James Weldon Johnson.* Boston: Twayne, 1987.

Johnson, James Weldon. *Along This Way: The Autobiography of James Weldon Johnson.* New York: The Viking Press, 1933.

Kostelanetz, Richard. *Politics in the African-American Novel: James Weldon Johnson, W. E. B. DuBois, Richard Wright, and Ralph Ellison.* New York: Greenwood Press, 1991.

Levy, Eugene D. *James Weldon Johnson: Black Leader, Black Voice.* Chicago: University of Chicago Press, 1973.

Price, Kenneth M. and Oliver, Lawrence J. *Critical Essays on James Weldon Johnson.* New York: Prentice Hall International, 1997.

five

It Don't Mean a Thing (If It Ain't Got That Swing)

Edward Kennedy Ellington, more popularly known as Duke Ellington, was a pioneering African American jazz pianist, bandleader, and composer. The song "It Don't Mean a Thing (If It Ain't Got That Swing)" is notable because it gave a motto ("The Swing Era") to the 1930s and to jazz music in general.

Ellington was born in Washington, D.C., to James Edward Ellington and Daisy Kennedy on April 29, 1899. The only male child in his mother's family and an only child of his parents for many years, Ellington received a great deal of attention and adoration from his mother; her death in 1935 would be the greatest tragedy of his life. He was given the nickname "Duke" from a schoolmate due to his aristocratic manner; since then he was noted for his impeccable taste in food, dress, and lifestyle.

Ellington formed a band in 1918 and made his career in Harlem nightclubs. Always an innovator, some of his most famous pieces focused on moods and colors including "Solitude," "Mood Indigo," and the long concert work "Black, Brown, and Beige." Of the music, Ellington said "Jazz is above all a total freedom to express oneself."[1] Ellington's popularity declined somewhat in the 1940s and 1950s, but the band continued to perform across the world. An avid reader of the Bible, particularly the Song of Solomon, Ellington later wrote compositions that were heavily influenced by gospel and spiritual hymns, known as the "sacred concerts." In 1969 he received the Presidential Medal of Freedom from Richard Nixon and received his college diploma in 1971, long after receiving numerous honorary doctorates. He died in 1974.

Wah-dah do, wah-dah do,
Wah-dah do, dah-dah do, dah-dah do.

It don't mean a thing
If it ain't got that swing!

It don't mean a thing,
All you've got to do is sing!

It makes no difference if it's sweet or hot,
Just keep that rhythm,
Give it everything you've got!

It don't mean a thing
If it ain't got that swing!

Wah-dah-dah doo!
Yah-yah-yah-yah-dah doo!

Bup be-duh be-duh be-dut,
Dat-dat-dat

Ohhh, it don't mean a thing
If it ain't got that swing!

Note

1. Quoted by Stanley Dance in Peter Gammond, *Duke Ellington: His Life and Music,* mentioned in "Edward Kennedy Ellington" in *American Decades CD-ROM* (Detroit: Gale Research, 1998).

Source

Ivie Anderson with Duke Ellington, "It Don't Mean a Thing (If It Ain't Got That Swing)," published by Famous Music Co.; reprinted in Henry Louis Gates and Nellie Y. McKay, eds., *The Norton Anthology of African-American Literature,* 58–59 (New York and London: W.W. Norton, 1997).

Selected Bibliography

Bigard, Barney. *With Louis and the Duke: The Autobiography of a Jazz Clarinetist.* New York: Oxford University Press, 1985.

Collier, James Lincoln. *Duke Ellington.* New York: Oxford University Press, 1987.

Hasse, John Edward. *Beyond Category: The Life and Genius of Duke Ellington.* New York: Simon & Schuster, 1993.

Reisner, Robert George. *Bird: The Legend of Charlie Parker.* New York: Da Capo Press, 1962.

Woideck, Carl. *The Charlie Parker Companion: Six Decades of Commentary.* New York: Schirmer Books, 1998.

six

High Tide in Harlem

Richard Wright (1908–1960) was one of the most influential writers of the twentieth century. In his essay "High Tide in Harlem," Wright examined the cultural politics behind the famous 1938 rematch of between the African American boxer Joe Louis and the German Max Schmeling. Louis won the fight with a first-round knockout, thereby avenging an earlier defeat. The match was widely celebrated among African Americans across the country.

Born in Roxie, Mississippi, Wright recounted his difficult childhood in his memoir *Black Boy* (1945). He moved to Chicago in 1927, and by the early 1930s his literary career began to show promise, as his poems appeared in *Left Front, Anvil,* and *New Masses* and he became friends with fellow writers Ralph Ellison and Margaret Walker. In 1935 Wright was hired by the Federal Writer's Project to research the history of African Americans in Chicago. With help from a Guggenheim fellowship, Wright published his classic novel *Native Son* in 1941, which quickly propelled him to international fame.

High Tide in Harlem: Joe Louis as a Symbol of Freedom

The colossal bowl of seventy thousand hazy faces, an oval, an oval-shaped tableau compounded of criss-crossed beams of light and shadow, waited almost in silence for the gong to sound that would start the Louis-Schmeling million-dollar fight. The gaze of the seventy thousand eyes was centered on the "squared circle," a single diadem-like spot of canvas lit to blinding whiteness under the intense glaze of overhead floodlights. So dwarfed was the ring by the mammoth stadium that it seemed that each man and woman was straining forward to peer at a colorful puppet show.

The Louis-Schmeling fight for the heavyweight championship of the world at the Yankee Stadium was one of the greatest dramas of make-believe ever witnessed in America, a drama which manipulated the common symbols and impulses in the minds and bodies of millions of people so effectively as to put to shame our professional playwrights, our O'Neills,[1] our Lawsons,[2] and our Caldwells.[3] Promoter Mike Jacobs, prompted purely by commercial motives, has accidentally won the rare right, whether he wants to claim it or not, of wearing the purple robes customarily reserved for Euripides[4] and Sophocles.[5]

Each of the seventy thousand who had so eagerly jammed his way into the bowl's steel tiers under the open sky had come already emotionally conditioned as to the values that would triumph if *his* puppet won. Attached to each puppet, a white puppet and a black puppet, was a configuration of social images whose intensity and clarity had been heightened through weeks of skillful and constant agitation: social images whose emotional appeal could evoke attitudes tantamount to two distinct ways of life in the world today. Whichever puppet went down the Greek route to defeat that night would leave the path clear for the imperious sway of the balked impulses of one side or the other. The puppet emerging victorious would be the symbol of a fond wish gratified, would feed the starved faith of men caught in the mesh of circumstances.

Joe Louis, the black puppet who wore black trunks, was the betting favorite; but that was no indication as to how much actual sentiment there was for him among the seventy thousand spectators, for men like to bet on winners. And, too, just how much sentiment there was for Max Schmeling, the white puppet who wore purple trunks, no one, perhaps, will ever know; for now that the violent drama is ended the backers of the loser do not want to parade their disappointment for the scorn of others. But the two puppets were dissimilar enough in "race, creed, and previous condition of servitude" as to make their partisans wax militant, hopeful.

But out beyond the walls of the stadium were twelve million Negroes to whom the black puppet symbolized the living refutation of the hatred spewed forth daily over radio, in newspapers, in movies, and in books about their lives. Day by day, since their alleged emancipation, they have watched a picture of themselves being painted as lazy, stupid, and diseased. In helpless horror they have suffered the attacks and exploitation which followed in the wake of their being branded as "inferiors." True, hundreds of thousands of these Negroes would have preferred that the refutation could have been made in some form other than pugilism; but so effectively and completely have they been isolated and restricted in vocation that they rarely have had the opportunity to participate in the meaningful processes of America's national life. Jim Crowed[6] in the army and navy, barred from many trades and professions, excluded from commerce and finance, relegated to menial positions in government, segregated residentially, denied the right of franchise for the most part; in short, forced to live a separate and impoverished life, they were glad for even the meager acceptance of their humanity implied in the championship of Joe Louis.

Visits to Joe Louis's training camp revealed throngs of Negroes standing around in a state of deep awe, waiting for just one glimpse of their champion. They were good, simple-hearted people, longing deeply for something of their own to be loyal to. When Joe appeared, a hush fell upon them and they stared. They took Joe into their hearts because he was a public idol and was respectfully enshrined in the public's imagination in a way they knew they would never be.

But because Joe's a Negro, even though he has to his credit a most enviable list of victories, there have been constant warnings issued by the Bilbos and Ellenders from south of the Mason-Dixon Line[7] as to the wisdom of allowing a Negro to defeat a white man in public. The reactionary argument ran that such spectacles tended to create in Negroes too much pride and made them "intractable."

Naturally, Max Schmeling's victory over Louis two years ago was greeted with elation in reactionary quarters. A close study of Louis's stance, which revealed that he could be hit, together with a foul blow delivered after the bell, enabled the German boxer to win. Louis's defeat came as a shock to the boxing world and provided material for countless conversations and speculations. It was taken for granted that the second-rate Schmeling's defeat of the then reigning champion, the aging Braddock, was but a matter of time. But due to squabbles among promoters, Louis, not Schmeling, fought Braddock for the championship and won the title by a knockout in a thrilling bout in Chicago. Immediately, the Nazi press, in America and in Germany, launched a campaign of slurs against Louis, dubbing him the "so-called champion," and declaring that Schmeling's prior victory over Louis was proof of "Negro inferiority." Schmeling boasted to the press that it would be easy for him to defeat the Negro again because (1) Negroes never forget beatings, (2) his mere "white" presence would be enough to throw fear into Louis's heart, and (3) he would enter the ring with a "psychological edge" over the Negro. An open friend of Hitler[8] and an avowed supporter of the Nazis,[9] Schmeling caught the fancy of many reactionary Americans, plus the leaders of Nazi Germany, fascist Italy, Japan, and even certain circles in England. To bolster the aims of the forces of fascism, Schmeling's victory was interpreted to mean the ability of the "Aryan race to outthink inferior races." The logical implication of such a line of reasoning was that all Negroes, colonial people, and small nations were inherently backward, physically cowardly, a drag upon the rest of civilization, and should be conquered and subjected for the benefit of mankind.

But when faced with this specious proposition, the common people instinctively revolted. They knew that the majority of all prizefighters came from the so-called "backward people," that is, the working class; their capacity to fight stemming from an early life of toil in steel and iron foundries, coal mines, factories, and felds. Consequently, in his fight against Schmeling, Louis carried the good wishes of even the poor whites of the Deep South, something unparalleled in the history of America.

The appearance of the white puppet sent the crowd into a frenzy. The black puppet's ovation seemed incidental. The ring was cleared and the fight was on. The entire seventy thousand rose as one man. At the beginning of the fight there was a wild shriek which gradually died as the seconds flew. What was happening was so stunning that even cheering was out of place. The black puppet, contrary to all Nazi racial laws, was punching the white puppet so rapidly that the eye could not follow the blows. It was not really a fight, it was an act of revenge, of dominance, of complete mastery. The black puppet glided from his corner and simply wiped his feet on the white puppet's face. The black puppet was contemptuous, swift; his victory was complete, unquestionable, decisive; his blows must have jarred the marrow not only in the white puppet's but in Hitler's own bones.

In Harlem, that area of a few square blocks in upper Manhattan where a quarter of a million Negroes are forced to live through an elaborate connivance among landlords, merchants, and politicians, a hundred thousand black people surged out of taprooms, flats, restaurants, and filled the streets and sidewalks, like the Mississippi River overflowing in flood-time. With their faces to the night sky, they filled their lungs with air and let out a scream of joy that it seemed would never end, and a scream that seemed to come from untold reserves of strength. They wanted to make a noise comparable to the happiness bubbling in their hearts, but they were poor and had nothing. So they went to the garbage pails and got tin cans; they went to their kitchens and got tin pots, pans, washboards, wooden boxes, and took possession of the streets. They shouted, sang, laughed, yelled, blew paper horns, clasped hands, and formed weaving snake-lines, whistled, sounded sirens, and honked auto horns. From the windows of the tall, dreary tenements torn scraps of newspaper floated down. With the reiteration that evoked a hypnotic atmosphere, they chanted with eyes half-closed, heads lilting in unison, legs and shoulders moving and touching:

"Ain't you glad? Ain't you glad?"

Knowing full well the political effect of Louis's victory on the popular mind the world over, thousands yelled:

"Heil Louis!"

It was Harlem's mocking taunt to fascist Hitler's boast of the superiority of "Aryans" over other races. And they ridiculed the Nazi salute of the outstretched palm by throwing up their own dark ones to show how little they feared and thought of the humbug of fascist ritual.

With no less than a hundred thousand participating, it was the largest and most spontaneous political demonstration ever seen in Harlem and marked the highest tide of popular political ever witnessed among American Negroes.

Negro voices called fraternally to Jewish-looking faces in passing autos:

"I bet all the Jews are happy tonight!"

Men, women, and children gathered in thick knots and did the Big Apple, the Lindy Hop, the Truck—Harlem's gesture of defiance to the high cost of food, high rent, and misery. These ghetto-dwellers, under the stress of the joy of one of their own kind having wiped out the stain of defeat and having thrown the lie of "inferiority" into the teeth of the fascist, threw off restraint and fear. Each time a downtown auto slowed, it became covered with Joe Louis rooters, and the autos looked like clusters of black ripe grapes. A bus stopped and at once became filled with laughing throngs who "forgot" to pay their fares; children clambered up its tall sides and crawled over the hoods and fenders.

It was the celebration of Louis's victory over Camera, Baer, Pastor, Farr, and Braddock all rolled into one. Ethiopian and American flags fluttered. Effigies of Schmeling chalked with the swastika were dragged through the streets.

Then nobody knows from where and nobody bothered to ask, there appeared on the surface of the sea of people white placards hurling slogans of defiance at fascist pretensions and calling upon native lovers of democracy to be true to democratic ideals. *Oust Hitler Spies and Agents; Pass the Anti-Lynching Bill; Down with Hitler and Mussolini; Alabama Produced Joe Louis, Free the Scottsboro Boys; Democracies Must Fight Fascism Everywhere.*

Carry the dream on for yourself; lift it out of the trifling guise of a prizefight celebration and supply the social and economic details and you have the secret dynamics of proletarian aspiration. The eyes of these people were bold that night. Their fear of property, of the armed police fell away. There was in their chant a hunger deeper than that for bread as they marched along. In their joy they were feeling an impulse which only the oppressed can feel to the full. They wanted to fling the heavy burden out of their hearts and embrace the world. They wanted to feel that their expanding feelings were not limited; that the earth was theirs as much as anybody else's; that they did not have to live by proscription in one corner of it; that they could go where they wanted to and do what they wanted to, eat and live where they wanted to, like others. They wanted to own things in common and do things in common. They wanted a holiday.

Notes

1. Eugene Gladstone O'Neill (1888–1953), American playwright.

2. John Howard Lawson (1894–1977), American playwright.
3. Erskine Caldwell (1903–1987), American playwright.
4. Euripides (c. 480 B.C.–406 B.C.), major Greek tragic poet.
5. Sophocles (c. 496 B.C.–406 B.C.), Greek tragic poet.
6. Jim Crow laws were statutes enacted by Southern states and cities, beginning in the 1880s, which legalized segregation between blacks and whites.
7. Boundary between Pennsylvania and Maryland. Before the Civil War it was popularly designated as the boundary between the slave states and free states, and it is still used on occasion to distinguish the South and North.
8. Adolf Hitler (1888–1945), German dictator, founder of Nazism.
9. Term for members of the fascist National Socialist German Worker's Party.

Source

Richard Wright, "High Tide in Harlem: Joe Louis as a Symbol of Freedom," *New Masses,* July 5, 1938.

Selected Bibliography

Astor, Gerald. *"And a Credit to His Race": The Hard Life and Times of Joseph Louis Barrow, a.k.a. Joe Louis.* New York: Saturday Review Press (distributed by E. P. Dutton), 1972.

Mead, Chris. *Champion: Joe Louis, Black Hero in White America.* New York: Scribner, 1985.

Nagler, Barney. *Brown Bomber.* New York: World, 1972.

seven

The Revolution Will Not Be Televised

Gil Scott-Heron is best known for his mastery of the spoken word, which he set against a background of jazz, blues, and Latin rhythms with the help of Brian Jackson. Such a marriage of rhymes and rhythms would soon become the essence of rap music; Scott-Heron called his version "bluesology." One of his earliest and most renowned pieces, "The Revolution Will Not Be Televised" (1971), illuminates the inherent incompatibility of corporate-sponsored media and social upheaval.

Performer, musician, poet, and novelist, Gil Scott-Heron (1949–) was born in Chicago and raised in Tennessee. As a teenager, Scott-Heron began writing fiction; he later wrote novels at Lincoln University in Pennsylvania. By the time he had earned an M.A. from Johns Hopkins University in 1972, he had published three books. *Small Talk at 125th and Lenox* (1970) is a collection of Scott-Heron's poetry. Like his other works, his two novels center on themes of revolutionary social change: *The Vulture* (1970) details a black revolutionary group's attempt to wrest control away from drug dealers and rebuild their neighborhood, and *The Nigger Factory* (1972) hearkens to Scott-Heron's experience at Lincoln University and centers on students' struggle to change their small black college. Scott-Heron has released over fifteen albums and continues to perform at both musical and spoken word venues.

The Revolution Will Not Be Televised

You will not be able to stay home, brother.
You will not be able to plug in, turn on and cop out.
You will not be able to lose yourself on scag and
skip out for beer during commercials because
The revolution will not be televised.

The revolution will not be televised.
The revolution will not be brought to you by Xerox in four parts without
commercial interruption.
The revolution will not show you pictures of Nixon blowing a bugle and
leading a charge by John Mitchell, General Abramson and Spiro Agnew
to eat hog maws confiscated from a Harlem sanctuary.
The revolution will not be televised.

The revolution will not be brought to you by
The Schaeffer Award Theatre and will not star
Natalie Wood and Steve McQueen or Bullwinkle and Julia.
The revolution will not give your mouth sex appeal.
The revolution will not get rid of the nubs.
The revolution will not make you look five pounds thinner.
The revolution will not be televised, brother.

There will be no pictures of you and Willie Mae
pushing that shopping cart down the block on the dead run
or trying to slide that color t.v. in a stolen ambulance.
NBC will not be able to predict the winner at 8:32 on reports from twenty-
nine districts.
The revolution will not be televised.

There will be no pictures of pigs shooting down brothers
on the instant replay.
There will be no pictures of pigs shooting down brothers
on the instant replay.
The will be no slow motion or still lifes of Roy Wilkins strolling through
Watts in a red, black and green liberation jumpsuit that he has been
saving for just the proper occasion.

Green Acres, Beverly Hillbillies and Hooterville Junction
will no longer be so damned relevant
and women will not care if Dick finally got down with Jane
on Search for Tomorrow

because black people will be in the streets looking for
A Brighter Day.
The revolution will not be televised.

There will be no highlights on the Eleven O'Clock News
and no pictures of hairy armed women liberationists
and Jackie Onassis blowing her nose.
The theme song will not be written by Jim Webb or Francis Scott Key
nor sung by Glen Campbell, Tom Jones, Johnny Cash,
Englebert Humperdink or Rare Earth.
The revolution will not be televised.

The revolution will not be right back after a
message about a white tornado, white lightning or white people.
You will not have to worry about a dove in your bedroom,
the tiger in your tank or the giant in your toilet bowl.
The revolution will not go better with coke.
The revolution will not fight germs that may cause bad breath.
The revolution *will* put you in the driver's seat.
The revolution will not be televised
                    will not be televised
                         not be televised
                              be televised
The revolution will be no re-run, brothers.
The revolution will be LIVE.

Source

Henry Louis Gates and Nellie Y. McKay, eds., *The Norton Anthology of African-American Literature* (New York: W.W. Norton, 1977), 61–62.

Selected Bibliography

Scott-Heron, Gil. *The Nigger Factory, A Novel.* New York: Dial Press, 1972.
—— *Small Talk at 125th and Lenox; a Collection of Black Poems.* New York: World, 1970.
—— *So Far So Good.* Chicago: Third World Press, 1990.
—— *The Vulture.* New York: World, 1970.

eight

Where Are the Films About Real Black Men and Women?

Since the birth of cinema, African Americans have protested the dearth of realistic black films in Hollywood. For example, although *Birth of the Nation* (1915) has often been called a masterpiece, it promoted an outlandish, racist parody of African Americans in the Reconstruction period. As a result, black organizations across the country condemned the film, and Booker T. Washington even helped to finance a counter film, *Birth of a Race*. Hollywood continued to promote popular stereotypes in such films as *Gone with the Wind* (1939).

In the 1970s, black writers issued in the era of "blaxploitation" films, such as *Sweet Sweetback's Badass Song* and *Shaft,* which featured comically overdrawn portrayals of street characters, pimps, prostitutes, gangsters, and thugs. However, the late 1980s and early 1990s witnessed a sudden increase of sensitive and serious films about the black experience, from such directors as Spike Lee, John Singleton, Robert Townsend, and others. In this 1974 essay, the actress and writer Ellen Holly decried Hollywood's tendency to reduce black characters to racist parodies and white stereotypes.

Unlike "white" films which range at will over the full spectrum of human possibility from *Deep Throat*[1] to the six-hour, hundred-million-dollar Soviet production of *War and Peace*,[2] most "Black" films have been mired in the rut of a single formula—the so-called action film which deals with marginal antisocial elements in the Northern urban ghetto. These films have been subjected to a tremendous amount of criticism.

Law-abiding, tax-paying Black citizens who are not gunslingers, dope-pushers, pimps or prostitutes have been rightly and understandably enraged that the prevailing Black image in most films has been one that is so grossly at odds with their own.

In a healthier circumstance in which the full spectrum of Black life in all its remarkable variety could be seen on film, action films would be taken more calmly in stride as the equivalent of the cheaply made, Grade B gangster movies which shared the bottom slot of a double bill in the thirties and forties. In a healthier circumstance it would not be necessary to heap upon these films more blame (and, therefore, more significance) than they deserve, or to so hunger for alternatives that films such as *Five on the Black Hand Side* and the recently released *Claudine* are heaped with more praise than *they* deserve and heralded as events that would pale the Second Coming.

To that film critic who enthusiastically described *Claudine* as a landmark film, I would suggest that, rather, it is a charming, modest step in the right direction. A pleasant, upbeat film that has some nice things going for it. Above all, Diahann Carroll.[3] Her beauty and skill, intelligence and plain old gumption, function as the keystone that holds the whole thing in place. Another plus is a delightful bunch of kids who are delightful precisely because they don't *behave* like a bunch—each one manages to leave his own quirky, individual imprint on the proceedings at hand.

Claudine is about a welfare mother with six kids—the ins and outs of her struggle to bring them up, and the ups and downs of her courtship with an engaging garbage man called Roop. It is a film with a lot of humor, but on the serious side, it has some very pertinent things to say about the Catch-22 maze of the welfare system, the tremendous energy required to pull oneself up by one's bootstraps, and the special inter-connectedness that Black people in a ghetto can feel for each other because, lacking money or power, the one certain thing they've got going for them is each other. Then there is the music. As a matter of fact, the one consistent star to emerge from "Black" movies in general is Black Music. Again and again, from one film to the next, by the beat, funk, and vitality of their music the Marvin Gayes,[4] Isaac Hayeses[5] and Curtis Mayfields[6] have pumped life-blood into what would otherwise be thoroughly mediocre footage.

As for James Earl Jones,[7] he plays Roop, the garbage man, as a big, warm-hearted, comic teddy bear. He is ingratiating, picturesque, and non-threatening. As a Black woman, I myself have problems with Black male portrayals that are so scrupulously de-fused of any masculine authority. For those who do not, this performance, too, is a skilled one that can be enjoyed as one of *Claudine*'s assets.

More than a hundred "Black" films have come and gone in recent years. In the avalanche of buffoons and superstuds that can't be taken any more seriously than Batman and Captain Marvel, plain honest-to-goodness Black men of human stature who can be taken seriously are as scarce as hen's teeth. I suspect it's because the white-controlled film industry still has tremendous difficulty dealing with Black men as peers.

There have been many real Black heroes. *Spookwaffe,* an excellent film script by Paul Leaf dealing with the brilliant exploits of the all-Black 99th Fighter Squadron in World War II, remains undone. This group shot down more German planes over Anzio than any other fighter squadron in the history of the war. The record of the Spookwaffe (the name they facetiously gave themselves) has been as closely guarded as a military secret. Fantasy Shafts go down easily. Real Black performance does *not.*

One of the penalties of being Black and having limited money is that we seldom control our own image. We seldom appear in media as who *we* say we are, but rather as who *whites* say we are.

Entirely too many "Black" films have been Black in name only. The visible tip of the iceberg, the actors whose images flash on screen, have been Black, but they have been no more than hired hands . . . shills employed as window dressing to lure the Black public to the box office. Below the waterline, hidden from public view, lies the other seven-eighths of the iceberg, the writers who create the material, the directors who shape it, and the producers and distributors who put up the money, specify and control the content, and pocket the profits.

All too often this invisible seven-eighths of the iceberg has been solid, solid white. Black creative input behind the scenes has been virtually nil. Serious writers attempting to market scripts that deal with any kind of Black reality get nowhere while company hacks, free of any burdensome sense of racial responsibility, cheerily grind out the mindless *Hell Up in Harlem*'s that actually get on.

Half the time, the material not only isn't Black it isn't even original, as white material ready for the boneyard is given a hasty blackwash and sent on one last creaking go-round. *Cool Breeze* was a remake of *Asphalt Jungle, Blacula* and the upcoming *Blaxorcist* proclaim their origins in their titles. In the March 14 issue of *Jet* magazine, Clarence Brown listed, in dismay, still others which will shortly be coming our way. *Blackenstein, The Black Frankenstein, Werewolf from Watts, Billy Black,* and *Black the Ripper.* Are these films Black? I don't know the answer, but I think it's time somebody asked the question.

The problem will begin to be solved when Blacks gain more control over the making of their own films. Some rays of hope have begun to appear on the horizon. One of the national black sororities, Delta Sigma Theta (500 chapters cross-county, 75,000 members)—repelled by the constant presentation of the Black woman as Superslut and energized by the phenomenal organizational abilities of its national president, Lillian Benbow, and its Arts and Letters commission chairman, Dr. Jeanne Noble—has moved, through its media arm, DST Telecommunications, Inc., to finance, in association with a consortium of Black African businessmen a film called *Countdown at Kusini* that calls upon the talents of such responsible Black artists as Ossie Davis,[8] Ruby Dee,[9] and Al Freeman, Jr.

A truly decent solution to the problem, however, will require something more complex than a mere sorting out along racial lines. Being Black is no guarantee that you will make a decent film and being white is no guarantee that you will make a rip-off. I have seen Black directors turn in jobs that, in my opinion, constituted a gross betrayal of Black people and I have seen white producers like Michael Tolan (co-producer with Brock Peters of *Five on the Black Hand Side*) involve themselves out of sheer love and a deep sense of personal commitment. It is also worth remembering that whites were significantly involved with two of the most loving Black films that have yet been made, *Sounder* and *Nothing But a Man.*

While I fervently hope that more Black films will be made and controlled by Black people, I suspect that it is a lot closer to the point to hope that more black films will be made and controlled by people of any color whatsoever who *care* about Black people. That, in the final analysis, is really the point.

Notes

1. *Deep Throat,* a pornographic film.
2. *War and Peace,* a film based on the novel by Russian writer Count Leo Tolstoy (1828–1910).
3. Diahann Carroll (1934–), African American actress and business entrepreneur, born Carol Diahann Johnson.
4. Marvin Gaye (1939–1984), Motown singer.
5. Isaac Hayes (1942–), Motown singer.
6. Mayfield, Curtis (1942–1999), Motown singer.
7. James Earl Jones, (1931–), African American actor.
8. Ossie Davis (1917–), African American actor and activist.
9. Rubie Dee (1924–), African American actress and social activist.
10. Albert Cornelius Freeman Jr. (1934–), African American actor.

Source

Ellen Holly, "Where Are the Films About Real Black Men and Women?" *Freedomways* 14, no. 3 (third quarter 1974): 270–73.

Selected Bibliography

Bogle, Donald. *Toms, Coons, Mulattoes, Mammies, and Bucks: An Interpretive History of Blacks in American Films.* New York: Continuum, 1994.

George, Nelson. *Blackface: Reflections on African-Americans and the Movies*. New York: HarperCollins, 1994.

hooks, bell. *Reel to Real: Race, Sex, and Class at the Movies*. New York: Routledge, 1996.

Smith, Valerie, ed. *Representing Blackness: Issues in Film and Video*. New Brunswick, N.J.: Rutgers University Press, 1997.

nine

The Signifying Monkey

Along with folk tales, work songs, and other black musical forms, the practice of signifying has been a mainstay of African-American popular culture. According to the *Norton Anthology of African-American Literature,* signifying "refers to a wide variety of African-American verbal games involving ritual insult, competition, innuendo, parody, and other forms of loaded expression."[1] As African Americans migrated from the South to the North, this rural tradition was transformed into an urban dialogue, sometimes called "jive talking." "The Signifying Monkey" is a comic tale that has appeared in various forms over the years, often in considerably more raffish versions than that reprinted here.

The Monkey and the Lion
Got to talking one day.
Monkey looked down and said, Lion,

1. Henry Louis Gates Jr. and Nellie McKay, eds., *The Norton Anthology of African American Literature* (New York: Norton & Co., 1997), 42.

I hear you's king in every way.
But I know somebody
Who do not think that is true—
He told me he could whip
The living daylights out of you.
Lion said, Who?
Monkey said, Lion,
He talked about your mama
And talked about your grandma, too,
And I'm too polite to tell you
What he said about you.
Lion said, Who said what? Who?
Monkey in the tree,
Lion on the ground.
Monkey kept on signifying
But he didn't come down.
Monkey said, His name is Elephant—
He stone sure is not your friend.
Lion said, He don't need to be
Because today will be his end,
Lion took off through the jungle
Lickity-split,
Meaning to grab Elephant
And tear him bit to bit. Period!
He come across Elephant copping a righteous nod
Under a fine cool shady tree.
Lion said, You big old no-good so-and-so,
It's either you or me.
Lion let out a solid roar
And bopped Elephant with his paw.
Elephant just took his trunk
And busted old Lion's jaw.
Lion let out another roar,
Reared up six feet tall.
Elephant just kicked him in the belly
And laughed to see him drop and fall.
Lion rolled over,
Copped Elephant by the throat.
Elephant just shook him loose
And butted him like a goat,
Then he tromped him and he stomped him
Till the Lion yelled, Oh, no!
And it was near-nigh sunset

When Elephant let Lion go.
The signifying Monkey
Was still setting in his tree
When he looked down and saw the Lion.
Said, Why, Lion, who can that there be?
Lion said, It's me.
Monkey rapped, Why, Lion,
You look more dead than alive!
Lion said, Monkey, I don't want
To hear your jive-end jive.
Monkey just kept on signifying,
Lion, you for sure caught hell—
Mister Elephant's done whipped you
To a fare-thee-well!
Why, Lion, you look like to me
You been in the precinct station
And had the third-degree,
Else you look like
You been high on gage[1]
And done got caught
In a monkey cage!
You ain't no king to me.
Facts, I don't think that you
Can even as much as roar—
And if you try I'm liable
To come down out of this tree and
Whip your tail some more.
The Monkey started laughing
And jumping up and down.
But he jumped so hard the limb broke
And he landed—*bam!*—on the ground.
When he went to run, his foot slipped
And he fell flat down.
Grrr-rrr-rr-r! The Lion was on him
With his front feet and his hind.
Monkey hollered, Ow!
I didn't mean it, Mister Lion!
Lion said, You little flea-bag you!
Why, I'll eat you up alive.
I wouldn't a-been in this fix a-tall
Wasn't for your signifying jive.
Please, said Monkey, Mister Lion,
If you'll just let me go,

I got something to tell you, *please,*
I think you ought to know.
Lion let the Monkey loose
To see what his tale could be—
And Monkey jumped right back on up
Into his tree.
What I was gonna tell you, said Monkey,
Is you square old so-and-so,
If you fool with me I'll get
Elephant to whip your head some more.
Monkey, said the Lion,
Beat to his unbooted knees,
You and all your signifying children
Better stay up in them trees.
Which is why today
Monkey does his signifying
A-way-up out of the way.

Note

1. Marijuana.

Source

"The Signifying Monkey," in Langston Hughes and Arna Bontemps, eds., *The Book of Negro Folklore* (New York: Dodd, Mead, Company, 1958), 42–45 reprinted in Henry Louis Gates and Nellie Y. McKay, eds., *The Norton Anthology of African-American Literature,* 42–45 (New York & London: W. W. Norton & Co., 1997).

Selected Bibliography

Caponi, Gena Dagel, ed. *Signifyin(g), Sanctifyin', & Slam Dunking: A Reader in African-American Expressive Culture.* Amherst: University of Massachusetts Press, 1999.

Gates, Henry Louis. *The Signifying Monkey: A Theory of African-American Literary Criticism.* New York: Oxford University Press, 1988.

Smitherman, Geneva. *Talkin That Talk: Language, Culture, and Education in African-America.* New York: Routledge, 2000.

Watkins, Mel. *On the Real Side: Laughing, Lying, and Signifying: The Underground Tradition of African-American Humor.* New York: Simon & Schuster, 1994.

ten

What America Would Be Like Without Blacks

Ralph Ellison's (1914–1994) *The Invisible Man* (1952) was one of the towering literary accomplishments of the twentieth century. Ellison's essay "What America Would Be Like Without Blacks" drew attention not simply to separate black *contributions* to American cultural life, but also to the more nuanced ways that "materially, psychologically, and culturally, part of the nation's heritage is Negro American."

Ellison was born in Oklahoma City, and he attended Tuskegee Institute from 1933 to 1936 before moving to New York City. In New York, Ellison met fellow writer Richard Wright, became associated with the Federal Writers Project, and published short stories and articles that were later collected in *Shadow and Act* (1964). But Ellison's primary reputation rests on *The Invisible Man,* which chronicled the struggles of a young, nameless narrator throughout his struggle for identity in a hostile society. Ellison spent much of the rest of his life writing a follow-up novel, but he died in 1994, before he was finished. However, his literary executor, John F. Callahan, turned Ellison's unfinished manuscript into a posthumously published novel, *Juneteenth,* in 1999.

The fantasy of an America free of blacks is at least as old as the dream of creating a truly democratic society. While we are aware that there is something inescapably tragic about the cost of achieving our democratic ideals, we keep such tragic awareness segregated to the rear of our minds. We allow it to come to the fore only during moments of great national crisis.

On the other hand, there is something so embarrassingly absurd about the notion of purging the nation of blacks that it seems hardly a product of thought at all. It is more like a primitive reflex, a throwback to the dim past of tribal experience, which we rationalize and try to make respectable by dressing it up in the gaudy and highly questionable trappings of what we call the "concept of race." Yet, despite its absurdity, the fantasy of a blackless America continues to turn up. It is a fantasy born not merely of racism but of petulance, of exasperation, of moral fatigue. It is like a boil bursting forth from impurities in the bloodstream of democracy.

In its benign manifestations, it can be outrageously comic—as in the picaresque adventures of Percival Brownlee who appears in William Faulkner's[1] story "The Bear." Exasperating to his white masters because his aspirations and talents are for preaching and conducting choirs rather than for farming, Brownlee is "freed" after much resistance and ends up as the prosperous proprietor of a New Orleans brothel. In Faulkner's hands, the uncomprehending drive of Brownlee's owners to "get shut" of him is comically instructive. Indeed, the story resonates certain abiding, tragic themes of American history with which it is interwoven, and which are causing great turbulence in the social atmosphere today. I refer to the exasperation and bemusement of the white American with the black, the black American's ceaseless (and swiftly accelerating) struggle to escape the misconceptions of whites, and the continual confusing of the black American's racial background with his individual culture. Most of all, I refer to the recurring fantasy of solving one basic problem of American democracy by "getting shut" of the blacks through various wishful schemes that would banish them for the nation's bloodstream, from its social structure, and from its conscience and historical consciousness.

This fantastic vision of a lily-white America appeared as early as 1713, with the suggestion of a white "native American," thought to be from New Jersey, that all the Negroes be given their freedom and returned to Africa. In 1777, Thomas Jefferson, while serving in the Virginia legislature, began drafting a plan for the gradual emancipation and exportation of the slaves. Nor were Negroes themselves immune to the fantasy. In 1815, Paul Cuffe,[2] a wealthy merchant, shipbuilder, and landowner from the New Bedford area, shipped and settled at his own expense thirty-eight of his fellow Negroes in Africa. It was perhaps his example that led in the following year to the creation of the American Colonization Society,[3] which was to establish in 1821 the colony of Liberia. Great amounts of cash and a perplexing mixture of motives went into the venture. The slaveowners and many Border-state politicians wanted to use it as a scheme to rid the country not of slaves but of the militant free Negroes who were agitating against the "peculiar institution." The abolitionists, until they took a lead from free Negro leaders and began attacking the scheme, also participated as a means of righting a great historical injustice. Many blacks went along with it simply because they were sick of the black and white American mess and hoped to prosper in the quiet peace of the old ancestral home.

Such conflicting motives doomed the Colonization Society to failure, but what amazes one even more than the notion that anyone could have believed in its success is the fact that it was attempted during a period when the blacks, slave and free, made up eighteen percent of the total population. When we consider how long blacks had been in the New World and had been transforming it and being Americanized by it, the scheme appears not only fantastic, but the product of a free-floating irrationality. Indeed, a national pathology.

Nevertheless, some of the noblest of Americans were bemused. Not only Jefferson[4] but later Abraham Lincoln[5] was to give the scheme credence. According to historian John Hope Franklin,[6] Negro colonization seemed as important to Lincoln as emancipation. In 1862, Franklin notes, Lincoln called a group of prominent free Negroes to the White House and urged them to support colonization, telling them. "Your race suffers greatly, many of them by living among us, while ours suffers from your presence. If this is admitted, it affords a reason why we should be separated."

In spite of his unquestioned greatness, Abraham Lincoln was a man of his times and limited by some of the less worthy thinking of his times. This is demonstrated both by his reliance upon the concept of race in his analysis of the American dilemma and by his involvement in a plan of purging the nation of blacks as a means of healing the badly shattered ideals of democratic federalism. Although benign, his motive was no less a product of fantasy. It envisaged an attempt to relieve an inevitable suffering that marked the growing pains of the youthful body politic by an operation which would have amounted to the severing of a healthy and indispensable member.

Yet, like its twin, the illusion of secession, the fantasy of a benign amputation that would rid the country of black men to the benefit of a nation's health not only persists; today, in the form of neo-Garveyism,[7] it fascinates black men no less than it once hypnotized whites. Both fantasies become operative whenever the nation grows weary of the struggle toward the ideal of American democratic equality. Both would use the black man as a scapegoat to achieve a national catharsis, and both would, by way of curing the patient, destroy him.

What is ultimately intriguing about the fantasy of "getting shut" of the Negro American is the fact that no one who entertains it seems ever to have considered what the nation would have become had Africans *not* been brought to the New World, and had their descendants not played such a complex and confounding role in the creation of American history and culture. Nor do they appear to have considered with any seriousness the effect upon the nation of having any of the schemes for exporting blacks succeed beyond settling some fifteen thousand or so in Liberia.

We are reminded that Daniel Patrick Moynihan,[8] who has recently aggravated our social confusion over the racial issue while allegedly attempting to clarify it, is co-author of a work which insists that the American melting pot didn't melt because our white ethnic groups have resisted all assimilative forces that appear to threaten their identities. The problem here is that few Americans know who and what they really are. That is why few of these groups—or at least few of the children of these groups—have been able to resist the movies, television, baseball, jazz, football, drum-majoretting, rock, comic strips, radio commercials, soap operas, book clubs, slang, or any of a thousand other expressions and carriers of our pluralistic and easily available popular culture. And it is here precisely that ethnic resistance is least effective. On this level the melting pot did indeed melt, creating such deceptive metamorphoses and blending of identities, values, and life-styles that most American whites are culturally part Negro American without even realizing it.

If we can resist for a moment the temptation to view everything having to do with Negro Americans in terms of their racially imposed status, we become aware of the fact that for all the harsh reality of the social and economic injustices visited upon them, these injustices have failed to keep Negroes clear of the cultural mainstream; Negro Americans are in fact one of its major tributaries. If we can cease approaching American social reality in terms of such false concepts as white and nonwhite, black culture and white culture, and think of these apparently unthinkable matters in the realistic manner of Western pioneers confronting the unknown prairie, perhaps we can begin to imagine what the United States would have been, or not been, had there been no blacks to give it—if I may be so bold as to say—color.

For one thing, the American nation is in a sense the product of the American language, a colloquial speech that began emerging long before the British colonials and Africans were transformed into Americans. It is a language that evolved from the king's English but, basing itself upon the realities of the American land and colonial institutions—or lack of institutions, began quite early as a vernacular revolt against the signs, symbols, manners, and authority of the mother country. It is a language that began by merging the sounds of many tongues, brought together in the struggle of diverse regions. And whether it is admitted or not, much of the sound of that language is derived from the timbre of the African voice and the listening habits of the African ear. So there is a *de'z* and *do'z* of slave speech sounding beneath our most polished Harvard accents, and if there is such a thing as a Yale accent, there is a Negro wail in it—doubtlessly introduced there by Old Yalie John C. Calhoun,[9] who probably got it from his mammy.

Whitman[10] viewed the spoken idiom of Negro Americans as a source of a native grand opera. Its flexibility, its musicality, its rhythms, freewheeling diction, and metaphors, as projected in Negro American folklore, were absorbed by the creators of our great nineteenth-century literature even when the majority of blacks were still enslaved. Mark Twain[11] celebrated it in the prose of *Huckleberry Finn;* without the presence of blacks, the book could not have been written. No Huck and Jim, no American novel as we know it. For not only is the black man a co-creator of the language that Mark Twain raised to the level of literary eloquence, but Jim's condition as American and Huck's commitment to freedom are at the moral center of the novel.

In other words, had there been no blacks, certain creative tensions arising from the cross-purposes of whites and blacks would also not have existed. Not only would there have been no Faulkner; there would have been no Stephen Crane, who found certain basic themes of his writing in the Civil War. Thus, also, there would have been no Hemingway,[12] who took Crane[13] as a source and guide. Without the presence of Negro American style, our jokes, our tall tales, even our sports would be lacking in the sudden turns, the shocks, the swift changes of pace (all jazz-shaped) that served to remind us that the world is ever unexplored, and that while a complete mastery of life is mere illusion, the real secret of the game is to make life swing. It is its ability to articulate this tragic-comic attitude toward life that explains much of the mysterious power and attractiveness of that quality of Negro American style known as "soul." An expression of American diversity within unity, of blackness with whiteness, soul announces the presence of a creative struggle against the realities of existence.

Without the presence of blacks, our political history would have been otherwise. No slave economy, no Civil War; no violent destruction of the Reconstruction;[14] no K.K.K.[15] and no Jim Crow[16] system. And without the disenfranchisement of black Americans and the manipulation of racial fears and prejudices, the disproportionate impact of white Southern politicians upon our domestic and foreign policies would have been impossible. Indeed, it is almost impossible to conceive of what our political system would have become without the snarl of forces—cultural, racial, religious—that make our nation what it is today.

Absent, too, would be the need for that tragic knowledge which we try ceaselessly to evade: that the true subject of democracy is not simply material well-being but the extension of the democratic process in the direction of perfecting itself. And that the most obvious test and clue to that perfection is the inclusion—*not* assimilation—of the black man.

Since the beginning of the nation, white Americans have suffered from a deep inner uncertainty as to who they really are. One of the ways that has been used to simplify the answer has been to seize upon the presence of black Americans and use them as a marker, a symbol of limits, a metaphor for the "outsider." Many whites could look at the social position of blacks and feel that color formed an easy and reliable gauge for determining to what extent one was or was not American. Perhaps that is why one of the first epithets that many European immigrants learned when they got off the boat was the term "nigger"—it made them feel instantly American. But this is tricky magic. Despite his racial difference and social status, something indisputably American about Negroes not only raised doubts about the white man's value system but aroused the troubling suspicion that whatever else the true American is, he is also somehow black.

Materially, psychologically, and culturally, part of the nation's heritage is Negro American, and whatever it becomes will be shaped in part by the Negro's presence. Which is fortunate, for today it is the black American who puts pressure upon the nation to live up to its ideals. It is he who gives creative tension to our struggle for justice and for the elimination of those factors, social and psychological, which make for slums and shaky suburban communities. It is he who insists that we purify the American language by demanding that there be a closer correlation between the meaning of words and reality, between ideal and conduct, our assertions and our actions. Without the black American, something irrepressibly hopeful and creative would go out of the American spirit, and the nation might well succumb to the moral slobbism that has ever threatened its existence from within.

When we look objectively at how the dry bones of the nation were hung together, it seems obvious that some one of the many groups that compose the United States had to suffer the fate of being allowed no easy escape from experiencing the harsh realities of the human condition as they were to exist under even so fortunate a democracy as ours. It would seem that some one group had to be stripped of the possibility of escaping such tragic knowledge by taking sanctuary in moral equivocation, racial chauvinism, or the advantage of superior social status. There is no point in complaining over the past or apologizing for one's fate. But for blacks, there are no hiding places down there, not in suburbia or in penthouse, neither in country nor in city. They are an American people who are geared to what *is* and who yet are driven by a sense of what it is possible for human life to be in this society. The nation could not survive being deprived of their presence because, by the irony implicit in the dynamics of American democracy, they symbolize both its most stringent testing and the possibility of its greatest human freedom.

Notes

1. William Faulkner, (1897–1962), American novelist.
2. Paul Cuffe, (1759–1816), African American merchant, sailor, and abolitionist.
3. Organization founded in 1816 to transport free African Americans from the United States and settle them in Africa. Resettled approximately 6,000 blacks between 1821 and 1867. Disbanded in 1912.
4. Thomas Jefferson, (1743–1826), third president of the United States.
5. Abraham Lincoln, (1808–1865), sixteenth president of the United States (1861–1865).
6. John Hope Franklin, (1915–), African American historian.

7. Refers to the teachings of Marcus Garvey (1887–1940), a proponent of black nationalism who rejected integration in countries where blacks were a minority and urged a "back to Africa" movement.
8. Daniel Patrick Moynihan, (1927–), American sociologist and distinguished public official.
9. John Caldwell Calhoun, (1782–1850), American statesman.
10. Walt Whitman (1819–1892), American poet.
11. Mark Twain, (1835–1910), American writer.
12. Ernest Hemingway, (1899–1961), American writer.
13. Harold Heart "Hart" Crane (1899–1932), American poet.
14. In U.S. history, the Reconstruction (1865–1877) was a period of readjustment following the Civil War.
15. Ku Klux Klan, racist secret society founded in the South in 1866 and rejuvenated in 1915.
16. Jim Crow laws were statutes enacted by Southern states and cities, beginning in the 1880s, that legalized segregation between blacks and whites.

Source

Ralph Ellison, "What America Would Be Like Without Blacks," in *Going to the Territory,* 104–112 (New York: Random House, 1986).

Selected Bibliography

Busby, Mark. *Ralph Ellison.* Boston: Twayne, 1991.

Callahan, John F. *In the African Grain: The Pursuit of Voice in 20th Century Black Fiction.* Urbana: University of Illinois Press, 1988.

Hersey, John, ed. *Ralph Ellison: A Collection of Critical Essays.* Englewood Cliffs, N.J.: Prentice Hall, 1974.

O'Meally, Robert. *The Craft of Ralph Ellison.* Cambridge, Mass.: Harvard University Press, 1980.

Watts, Jerry Gafio. *Heroism and the Black Intellectual: Ralph Ellison, Politics, and Afro-American Intellectual Life.* Chapel Hill: University of North Carolina.

eleven

O. J. Simpson and Our Trial by Fire

Although he won a Heisman Trophy and is a Hall of Fame running back and movie actor, O. J. Simpson is best known for playing the role of defendant in the real-life "Trial of the Century." In the essay excerpted here, Michael Eric Dyson, a leading cultural critic, explored the cultural politics that made the case so phenomenally captivating to much of the nation.

In 1994 Simpson was accused of murdering his wife, Nicole Brown Simpson, and her companion, Ron Goldman. The case was a national sensation; in addition to providing grist for countless pundits, analysts, and talk show hosts, his eight-month trial drew attention to such issues as racism, interracial romance, and police corruption. Although Simpson was ultimately acquitted, he has continued to face widespread accusations of his guilt, and in 1997 he lost a civil case filed by the Goldman family and was ordered to pay $8.5 million in compensatory damages. Although the Simpson case exposed some of the racial divisions that plague the United States, Dyson argued that ultimately, the case might also have taught us lessons that could lead to racial progress.

Obsessed with O. J.: Meditations on an American Tragedy

When O. J. Simpson took that long, slow ride down the L.A. freeway in A. C. Cowlings' bronco, it wasn't the first time he used a white vehicle to escape a black reality. I'm not referring to interracial marriage per se. Compatibility in love doesn't respect race, height, sex, color, age, culture, religion, or nationality. Transgression and affection often team up to knock down artificial conventions built on bias and ignorance. But sex between blacks and whites is an especially volatile instance of interracial intimacy. Every gesture of crossover and exchange between blacks and whites indexes the bitter history of American race. When many interracial couples forge ahead against social taboo, they often act courageously to undermine rigid racial beliefs.

Some blacks, though, pursue white loves and lifestyles in a way that only reinforces the rules of race. White identity signifies for them the desirable, the healthy, the stable. Black identity, by contrast, symbolizes the undesirable, the unhealthy, the unstable. Although I cannot know for sure, I imagine that O. J., however unconsciously, may subscribe to these beliefs. He apparently belongs to that fraternity of black men who "have-to-have-a-white-woman-at-all-costs." There's a difference, after all, between preference and obsession. (Of course, even preferences don't jump at us out of a cultural void; our deepest desires bear the imprint of the society that shapes them.)

And in O. J.'s case, it seems that learning to speak correctly meant learning to talk like white folk. (I'm not equating excellence in speaking or writing "standard" English with "acting white.") He wanted to get as far away from his ghetto roots as his legs, wealth, fame, and diction could carry him. Good for him. But because he appears so uncomfortable with the idea that you can be identifiably black and have all those things, he has drowned his racial identity in an ocean of whiteness.

Critics have argued bitterly about what light O. J.'s case will shed on race in America. That's not entirely clear. Unquestionably, the case has all the elements of national farce and intrigue. I'm not sure if it will affect the lives of everyday black folk. As he faces the possibility of being locked away, O. J.'s abrupt decline embodies the plight of more black men now than when he achieved heroic heights. (After all, there are hundreds of thousands more black men in prison than in the Hall of Fame.) Less than a week before his fall, O. J. appeared to be a lifetime away from the heartless siege of troubles that vex millions of black men.

His current condition has added O. J.'s name to a growing list of (in) famous black men whose personal problems have made them poster boys for the perversions of patriarchal culture. Mike Tyson and date rape. Clarence Thomas and sexual harassment. Michael Jackson and child molestation. And now, O. J. Simpson and spousal abuse. Each of these problems merits serious action, and these men, if guilty, should be held responsible and punished accordingly. But these maladies are ancient. How is it that these black men have managed to do in disrepute what most black men can't do in honest achievement: transcend race to represent America?

Make no mistake: O. J. is not Rodney King. In the racial firmament, the King case can be considered a supernova, illuminating the ground of race relations beneath its harsh but powerful light. Millions of poor black men can identify with Rodney King because police brutality is a staple of their adolescence and adulthood, a ritual of initiation into a fraternity of black male pain. Despite his working-class hustling roots, the meaning of Rodney's beating could nevertheless travel in an upwardly mobile fashion: even well-to-do black males understood King's horror because it could be directed toward any black man on any given day.

O. J.'s case, by contrast, is considerably more narrow. Most black men charged with a capital crime have little money to seek responsible representation. Most do not count the police as their friends, or even lackeys. Nor do they have the use of fame as a powerful deterrent to their conviction. If Rodney King is an exploding star, it may be that O. J. Simpson is a black hole, a collapsed star of such immense gravity that no light can escape.

Johnnie Cochran has been called a modern-day Joe Louis.[1] In part, I can see that. He has fought tough legal battles for some of our most beleaguered black brothers: Jim Brown, Todd Bridges, Michael Jackson, and now O. J. Rascals all, in their own ways. In representing them, Cochran has slugged it out with a justice system that often punishes black men with frightening consistency.

Unlike the Brown Bomber, though, Cochran's gifts spill forth from his golden throat. He is smooth and silky, an orator of great skill whose rhetoric reflects his Baptist roots and his early days as an insurance salesman. He performs the law, dramatizing its arcane rituals of argument and translating its esoteric dogmas into stirring, poetic declaration. For many blacks, Cochran is the law, masterfully taming the chaos of white contempt camouflaged in legal language and protected by obscure codes and regulations.

The pride so many blacks feel in Cochran's performance has a lot to do with an ancient injury to black self-esteem that not even Joe Louis could relieve: the white challenge to black intelligence and its skillful defense in eloquent black speech. Among his many racial functions, the black orator lends credence to claims of black rationality. When black folk in barbershops and beauty salons say of Cochran that "The brother can talk," what they mean in part is that the brother can think. Thinking and speaking are linked in many black communities. And neither are abstract reasoning and passionate discourse often diametrically opposed in such circles. Like all great black rhetoricians, Cochran makes style a vehicle for substance.

When *Time* magazine blackened O. J.'s face on its cover, it was a gesture full of irony and, yes, dark humor. *Time*'s act raises several questions. Was their artificial enhancement of O. J.'s natural hues, which forced us to be more conscious of his color, a signifying move, suggesting that O. J. needed help with his color consciousness? Was it a subversive move, motivated by *Time*'s hidden ties to skin nationalists who argue a link between pigment and personality? Were they demonizing him by darkening him, making O. J. a Darth Vader where many once believed he was a Luke(warm) Skywalker? Was *Time* trying to help a brother out by boosting his melanin count to swing public sentiment his way? Or were they vilifying O. J.'s vanilla vision of black identity? Were they extending the spookification of black public faces? Or were they simply doing with O. J. what the media have done to countless other black men: giving him the benefit of the lout?

The riveting and repulsive drama of O. J. Simpson's freakish unraveling before our very eyes contains many ironies. An athlete whose brilliant moves on the football field were marked by beauty and grace now left an international audience aghast at his ungainly flight from the law. A champion who played Prometheus to a nation of Walter Mittys now shrank in stature to a shriveled, self-defeating parody of his former strength. An icon with an ingenious talent for turning gridiron glory into Hollywood fame and fortune was now bedeviled by the media that helped make him a national figure. And a man whose face and initials were broadly familiar became in an instant a stranger with a secret history of spousal abuse that may prove to have been an unseemly rehearsal for murder.

One of the most remarkable features of the initial commentary around Simpson's sad situation is the way in which race, in its deliberate denial, was made even more present. Like Poe's purloined letter, race laid hidden in plain sight.

On the face of things, the denial of race in the Simpson case signaled a praiseworthy attempt by the media to balance its racially skewed reporting of news events. That's not easy when politicians and pundits are obsessed with negatively linking race to everything from welfare reform to crime. But in denying the role of race in the Simpson ordeal, media critics showed that you can't get beyond race by simply pretending it's not there.

The goal should not be to transcend race, but to transcend the biased meanings associated with race. Ironically, the very attempt to transcend race by denying its presence reinforces its power to influence perceptions because it gains strength in secrecy. Like a poisonous mushroom, the tangled assumptions of race grow best in darkness. For race to have a less detrimental effect, it must be brought into the light and openly engaged as a feature of the events and discussions it influences.

In the case of O. J. Simpson, the fingerprints of race are everywhere. O. J.'s spectacular rise to fame was aided not only by his extraordinary gifts, but because he fit the mold of a talented but tamed black man, what was known in his youth as a "respectable Negro." O. J. received brownie points throughout his playing career as much for who he wasn't as for how he performed. He wasn't considered, like football star-turned-actor Jim Brown, a black "buck," an "uppity nigger," an arrogant, in-your-face threat because of his volatile presence and unpredictable behavior.

From the beginning of his career, O. J. Simpson was marketed to white society as a raceless figure whose charisma drew from his sophisticated, articulate, public persona. In this light, horrified, disbelieving gasps of "not him" unleashed at O. J.'s initial public disintegration take on new weight. Let's face it. The unspoken, perhaps unconscious belief of many whites is that if he's guilty, if this could happen to O. J.—the spotless embodiment of domesticated black masculinity—it could happen to any black man. Translation: no black male can really be trusted?

At first, the fact that Nicole Brown Simpson[2] was a beautiful blonde white woman went virtually unremarked upon. Now, of course, her ubiquitous picture has made it hard not to notice. The fact that O. J. married Nicole made a lot of people mad.

When a black man marries a white woman, it irks white supremacists ("he's spoiled one of *our* women"). It grieves many black mothers ("when a black son brings home a white woman, it's an insult to his mama"). It angers many white men ("she's throwing her life away"). It disappoints many black women ("with all these single black women, why would he choose a white woman?"). It unnerves some white women ("I could never see myself with a black man"). And it raises some black men's ire ("why all these brothers, when they get successful, got to marry a white woman?"). This small sample of anecdotal responses to interracial relationships provides a glimpse of the furious passions and unresolved conflicts that continue to haunt love in black and white.

Were O. J. and Nicole completely immune to such concerns? Probably not. Does the fact that O. J. is charged with killing his *white* wife make a difference in our world? Probably so. Can we seriously doubt that if O. J. had been accused of murdering his *black* wife, and not a symbol of ideal white beauty, we wouldn't be learning of it with a similar degree of intensity, its details so gaudily omnipresent?

Many argue that Simpson's troubles have nothing to do with race, that his fall is instead an *American* tragedy. Of course it is, because all black citizens are Americans, and all of our problems, therefore, are American problems. But we don't have to embrace our American identity at the expense of our race. The two are not mutually exclusive. We simply have to overcome the limitations imposed upon race, to make sure that neither privilege nor punishment are viciously, arbitrarily assigned to racial difference. To erase race is to erase ourselves, and to obscure how race continues to shape American perceptions and lives.

O. J.'s handsomeness has played a large part in his appeal over the years. He has long been the object of the "safe" eroticization of black masculinity by white women. His pretty face is now being beamed everywhere. His facial expressions are deconstructed around the globe. Once the master of his image in a medium where he adroitly projected a cool persona, O. J. has now lost himself, at least his public self, in the infinite gaze of international television. O. J.'s every glance is now filtered through the theories of thinkers with names like Derrida, Sartre, and Foucault. What could he mean by looking up? How could his failure to regard photos of his dead ex-wife possibly signify his guilt or angst? What are the possible meanings of his intense glare at jurors?

Before his demise, O. J. spoke with authority, breaking stereotypes of black sports icons' severe inarticulateness. His precise diction rebutted the vicious subculture of parody that dogged the verbal skills of his boyhood idol Willie Mays. Now O. J. sits mute. He is forced to minstrel his meanings by bucking his eyes like Rochester or Stepenfetchit. . . .

The polls continually show that blacks and whites are divided on how they view this case. The wonder is that so many white folk are surprised. Why? Race remains the primary prism through which Americans view reality. Yet you only see the ruinous results of race when your perspective of reality is affected.

For instance, when I appeared on television and radio, commentators frequently asked me about the "race card." They were invariably referring to Mark Fuhrman's testimony and the charges that he is a bigot who might have planted evidence to frame O. J. While Fuhrman may have been the ace of all race cards, the deck had been shuffled, and many hands dealt, long before his appearance for the prosecution.

For instance, the prosecution's and defense's choice of jurors featured denials of and concessions to race. Who would be more sympathetic to the defense, to the prosecution? Who favorably viewed the L.A. police department, who thought it stunk? And so on.

The choice to field Christopher Darden on the prosecution was a clear nod to race in this case. Darden seems oblivious to the fact that he was added to blacken up the prosecution's public face. His value derives not from his lawyerly demeanor or his rhetorical skills, which remain remarkably mediocre, but from his metaphysical presence in countering the incantatory powers of blackness invoked by Johnnie Cochran. The presence of Darden is meant to show that the prosecution is not racially insensitive. That O. J. and Cochran and Carl Douglas don't exhaust the resources of authentic black identity. The race card was played from the very beginning. . . .

Why is it that some black people spend so much energy denying the impact of race on their lives, only to embrace it when their backs are against the wall? Clarence Thomas employed this ruse. He insisted that he had not relied upon race as a crutch to succeed. Still, when he was caught in the heat of battle with Anita Hill, he fell back on race. He used it in ways that only days before he would have disdained as cowardly and dishonest.

The same may be said about O. J. He always aspired to get beyond race, to be neither white nor black, to be human. That damnable equation has stumped many who have failed to understand that it sets up a false dichotomy. There is no such thing as being black and not already being a human being. The two are not diametrically opposed. Taken separately, at least for black folk, they are impossible.

When I read in O. J.'s book, *I Want To Tell You,* that as he faced racism in the past he either ignored or denied it, I am even more saddened. This sort of person is well known in many black circles. They protect themselves from racism by turning their backs on its most hateful expressions. They hide its most brutal effects in their spiritual or moral trunks. Or they cover the wounds racism inflicts with the temporary balm of diversion or avoidance. But sooner or later they must confront themselves and the choices they have made, particularly when the peace pacts they have negotiated with their psyches have disintegrated.

It used to be—or was it ever the case?—that the dead were safe, protected by their sleep beneath the ground. Nicole Brown Simpson and Ron Goldman have gained posthumous notoriety, for no other reason than their murders may have been committed by a fallen hero, a tarnished celebrity. It is the ultimate act of violation, a gesture of profound obscenity. Their deaths have been emptied of the inherently private meaning of grief to their circle of intimates and family. Their murders have given them a life beyond their bodies, but not a life respected by tabloid media or former friends looking to turn Nicole's and Ron's murders into money. The bottom line seems to be: it's not that they died, but that they were the persons that a famous man may have killed, that makes Nicole and Ron important.

It may be that football provided O. J. with a public context to wrestle the demon of violence that haunted his private life. The pure art of his movements on the field may have countered, driven, or even complemented his desperate scrambling for escape from inner turmoil. The ritualized cleansing of violent passions that brutal sports are alleged to achieve may only in the end lead to greater violence. The irony is that Nicole Brown Simpson benefited from the public face of O. J.'s acceptable aggression—a luxurious lifestyle as the wife of a sports star—but its private expression may have killed her.

Commentators have called the Simpson case the "trial of the century." What's intriguing about the case is how its major players are a virtual rainbow of color, gender, ethnicity, and class. Judge Lance Ito is Asian-American. Johnnie Cochran is African-American. Marcia Clark is a white woman. And Robert Shapiro, like Clark, is Jewish. A judicial landmark is being constructed by people who a few decades ago couldn't stand equally together in the same court. The greatest contribution this trial may make to our country—besides the justice it may deliver for the murders of Nicole Brown Simpson and Ron Goldman—is to help ensure that representing the complex diversity of our nation becomes business-as-usual.

Notes

1. Joe Louis (1914–1981), African American boxer, world heavyweight champion (1937–1949).
2. Nicole Brown Simpson (1959–1994), murder victim in O. J. Simpson case.

Source

Michael Eric Dyson, *Between God and Gangsta Rap* (New York: Oxford University Press, 1996), 25–39.

Selected Bibliography

Abramson, Jeffrey. *Postmortem: The O. J. Simpson Case.* New York: Basic Books, 1996.

Cose, Ellis. *The Darden Dilemma: 12 Black Writers on Justice, Race, and Conflicting Loyalties.* New York: Harper Perennial, 1997.

Dyson, Michael Eric. *Race Rules: Navigating the Color Line.* New York: Vintage Books, 1997.

Toobin, Jeffrey. *The Run of His Life: The People vs. O. J. Simpson.* New York: Random House, 1996.

chapter nine

Faith and Spirituality

one

Spirituals

Richly emotional and often sorrowful, spirituals were long thought to be the only form of folk music that was truly indigenous to the United States. In the 1920s, ethnomusicologists began to argue that American spirituals had their origins in the nineteenth-century religious meetings of Southern whites. However, today, spirituals are widely thought to have resulted from a mix of African musical forms and religious hymns, making them quintessentially African American. As the spirituals that are printed below suggest, these songs often had dual meanings; although slaves often sang about other-worldly salvation, they also used spirituals to express their grievances with their own oppression under slavery.

Didn't My Lord Deliver Daniel?

Didn't my Lord deliver Daniel, [1]
Deliver Daniel, deliver Daniel?
Didn't my Lord deliver Daniel?
An' why not everyman?

He delivered Daniel from de lion's den,
Jonah from de belly of de whale.[2]
And de Hebrew children from de fiery furnace,
An' why not everyman?

Didn't my Lord deliver Daniel,
Deliver Daniel, deliver Daniel?
Didn't my Lord deliver Daniel?
An' why not everyman?

De moon run down in a purple stream,
De sun forbear to shine,
And every star disappear,
King Jesus shall be mine.

Didn't my Lord deliver Daniel,
Deliver Daniel, deliver Daniel?
Didn't my Lord deliver Daniel?
An' why not everyman?

De wind blows east and de wind blows west,
It blows like de judgment day,
And every poor soul dat never did pray'll
Be glad to pray dat day.

Didn't my Lord deliver Daniel,
Deliver Daniel, deliver Daniel?
Didn't my Lord deliver Daniel?
An' why not everyman?

I set my foot on de Gospel ship,
An' de ship begin to sail.
It landed me over on Canaan's shore[3]
And I'll never come back no more.

Didn't my Lord deliver Daniel,
Deliver Daniel, deliver Daniel?
Didn't my Lord deliver Daniel?
An' why not every man?

Steal Away to Jesus

Steal away, steal away, steal away to Jesus,
Steal away, steal away home,
I ain't got long to stay here.

My Lord, He calls me,
He calls me by the thunder,
The trumpet sounds within-a my soul,
I ain't got long to stay here.

Steal away, steal away, steal away to Jesus,
Steal away, steal away home,
I ain't got long to stay here.

Green trees a-bending,
Po' sinner stands a-trembling,
The trumpet sounds within-a my soul,
I ain't got long to stay here.

Steal away, steal away, steal away to Jesus,
Steal away, steal away home,
I ain't got long to stay here.

Wade in the Water

Wade in the water, children,
Wade in the water, children,
Wade in the water, children,
God's a-gonna trouble the water.

See that host all dressed in white,
God's a-gonna trouble the water;
The leader looks like the Israelite,
God's a-gonna trouble the water.

Wade in the water, children,
Wade in the water, children,
Wade in the water, children,
God's a-gonna trouble the water.

See that host all dressed in red,
God's a-gonna trouble the water;
Looks like the band that Moses led,
God's a-gonna trouble the water.

Wade in the water, children,
Wade in the water, children,
Wade in the water, children,
God's a-gonna trouble the water.

Been in the Storm So Long

I've been in the storm so long,
You know I've been in the storm so long,
Oh Lord, give me more time to pray,
I've been in the storm so long.

I am a motherless child,
Singin' I am a motherless child
Singin' Oh Lord, give me more time to pray,
I've been in the storm so long.

This is a needy time,
This is a needy time,
Singin' Oh Lord, give me more time to pray,
I've been in the storm so long.

Lord, I need you now,
Lord, I need you now,
Singin' Oh Lord, give me more time to pray,
I've been in the storm so long.

My neighbors need you now,
My neighbors need you now,
Singin' Oh Lord, give me more time to pray,
I've been in the storm so long.

My children need you now,
My children need you now,
Singin' Oh Lord, give me more time to pray,
I've been in the storm so long.

Just look what a shape I'm in,
Just look what a shape I'm in,
Cryin' Oh Lord, give me more time to pray,
I've been in the storm so long.

Notes

1. In the Bible, God sent an angel to save Daniel after he'd been thrown into a lion's den (Daniel 6:22).
2. In the Bible, God saved Jonah after he had been swallowed by a whale (Jonah 2:7–10).
3. Literally, present-day Israel and parts of Syria; here it refers to the promised land of heaven.

Source

"Didn't My Lord Deliver Daniel?" "Steal Away to Jesus," "God's A-Gonna Trouble the Water," "Been in the Storm So Long," in Henry Louis Gates and Nellie Y. McKay, eds., *Norton Anthology of African-American Literature,* 10–16 (New York and London: W. W. Norton, 1997).

Selected Bibliography

Cone, James H. *The Spirituals and the Blues: An Interpretation.* Maryknoll, N.Y.: Orbis Books, 1991.

Cruz, Jon. *Culture on the Margins: The Black Spiritual and the Rise of American Cultural Interpretation.* Princeton, N.J.: Princeton University Press, 1999.

Jones, Arthur. *Wade in the Water: The Wisdom of the Spirituals.* Maryknoll, N.Y.: Orbis Books, 1993.

Newman, Richard. *Go Down Moses: A Celebration of the African-American Spiritual.* New York: Clarkson Potter, 1998.

Peters, Erskine, ed. *Lyrics of the Afro-American Spiritual: A Documentary Collection.* Westport, Conn.: Greenwood Press, 1993.

two

Spiritual Song

Richard Allen (1760–1831), a minister, educator, and abolitionist, founded the African Methodist Episcopal (AME) Church, a leading African American denomination of Methodism, in 1816. In the poem "Spiritual Song," Allen protested against what he judged to be the excessive emotionalism that some African Americans displayed while worshiping, which he felt was undignified in the House of God.

Allen was born a slave in Pennsylvania and grew up on a plantation in Delaware. At the age of twenty-four, he bought his freedom for $2,000 and moved to Philadelphia. In 1787, while kneeling in prayer at St. George's Methodist Episcopal Church, Allen and his associate Absalom Jones were asked to move to a segregated balcony. Allen and Jones refused, and this led them to found the Free African Society, a service group for blacks, in 1787. He later came to believe that African Americans should have their own churches, and he founded the Bethel African Methodist Church in 1794. He was ordained as a priest in 1799.

Good morning brother Pilgrim, what marching to Zion,[1]
What doubts and what dangers have you met to-day,
Have you found a blessing, are your joys increasing?
Press forward my brother and make no delay;
Is your heart a-glowing, are your comforts a-flowing,
And feel you an evidence, now bright and clear;
Feel you a desire that burns like a fire,
And longs for the hour that Christ shall appear.

I came out this morning, and now am returning,
Perhaps little better than when I first came,
Such groaning and shouting, it sets me to doubting,
I fear such religion is only a dream;
The preachers were stamping, the people were jumping,
And screaming so loud that I neither could hear,
Either praying or preaching, such horrible screaching,
Twas truly offensive to all that were there?

Perhaps my dear brother, while they pray'd together,
You sat and consider'd and prayed not at all,
Would you find a blessing, then pray without ceasing,
Obey the command that was given by Paul,[2]
For if you should reason at any such season,
No wonder if Satan should tell in your ears,
The preachers and people they are but a rabble,
And this is no place for reflection and pray'rs.

No place for reflection, I'm fill'd with distraction.
I wonder that people could bear for to stay,
The men they were bawling, the women were squaling,
I know not for my part how any could pray;
Such horrid confusion, if this be religion,
Sure 'tis something new that never was seen,
For the sacred pages that speak of all ages,
Does no where declare that such ever has been.

Don't be so soon shaken, if I'm not mistaken,
Such things have been acted by christians of old,
When the ark was a-coming, King David came running,
And dancing before it by scripture we're told,
When the Jewish nation had laid the foundation,
And rebuilt the temple at Ezra's[3] command,

Some wept and some prais'd, and such a noise there was rais'd,
It was heard afar off, perhaps all through the land.

And as for the preacher, Ezekiel[4] the teacher,
Was taught for to stamp and to smile with his hand,
To shew the transgression of that wicked nation,
That they might repent and obey the command.
For scripture quotation in the dispensation,
The blessed Redeemer had handed them out,
If these cease from praying, we hear him declaring,
The stones to reprove him would quickly cry out.

The scripture is wrested, for Paul hath protested,
That order should be kept in the houses of God,
Amidst such a clatter who knows what they're after,
Or who can attend to what is declared;
To see them behaving like drunkards a-raving,
And lying and rolling prostrate on the ground,
I really felt awful and sometimes was fearful,
That I'd be the next that would come tumbling down.

You say you felt awful, you ought to be careful,
Least you grieve the Spirit and make it depart,
For from your expressions you felt some impressions,
The sweet melting showers has tender'd your heart;
You fear persecution, and that's the delusion,
Brought in by the devil to turn you away;
Be careful my brother, for bless'd is no other,
Than creatures who are not offended in me.

When Peter[5] was preaching, and boldly was teaching,
The way of salvation in Jesus' name,
The spirit descended and some were offended,
And said of the men they were fill'd with new wine.
I never yet doubted but some of them shouted,
While others lay prostrate by power struck down,
Some weeping, some praying, while others were saying,
They are as drunk as fools, or in falsehood abound.

Our time is a flying, our moments a-dying,
We are led to improve them and quickly appear,
For the bless'd hour when Jesus in power,
In glory shall come is now drawing near,

Methinks there will be shouting, and I'm not doubting,
But crying and screaming for mercy in vain:
Therefore my dear Brother, let's now pray together,
That your precious soul may be fill'd with the flame.

Sure praying is needful, I really feel awful,
I fear that my day of repentance is past;
But I will look to the Saviour, his mercies for ever,
These storms of temptation will not always last,
I look for the blessing and pray without ceasing,
His mercy is sure unto all that believe,
My heart is a glowing, I feel his love flowing,
Peace, comfort, and pardon, I now have received.

Notes

1. Part of Jerusalem, defined in the Bible as the City of David. The name is symbolic of the Promised Land and, among Christians, heaven.
2. In the Bible, St. Paul was apostle to the gentiles.
3. In the Bible, Ezra the priest restored Jewish law.
4. In the Bible, Ezekiel (592–570 B.C.) preached to the Jews of Babylonian captivity. Ezekiel stressed individual responsibility.
5. In the Bible, St. Peter was the most prominent of the Twelve Apostles, traditionally the first bishop of Rome.

Source

Richard Allen, "Spiritual Song," in Dorothy Parker, ed., *Early Negro Writing,* 560–61 (Baltimore, Md.: Black Classic Press, 1995).

Selected Bibliography

Campbell, James T. *Songs of Zion: The African Methodist Episcopal Church in the United States and South Africa.* New York: Oxford University Press, 1995.

George, Carol V.R. *Segregated Sabbaths: Richard Allen and the Emergence of Independent Black Churches, 1760–1840.* New York: Oxford University Press, 1973.

Mathews, Marcia M. *Richard Allen.* Baltimore: Helicon, 1963.

Raboteau, Albert J. *A Fire in the Bones: Reflections of African-American Religious History.* Boston: Beacon Press, 1995.

three

A Thanksgiving Sermon

Absalom Jones (1746–1818) was a minister, teacher, and activist who believed that African Americans should have control over their own religious worship. He was known for his emphatic preaching style and his agitation against slavery. In "A Thanksgiving Sermon," Jones rejoiced over the official closing of the African slave trade in 1808, and he drew parallels between the suffering of Egyptian Jews and American slaves. He also promoted an uplift ethos that asked blacks to lead exemplary lives and become self-supporting.

Jones was born a slave in 1746, and in 1762 he moved to Philadelphia, where he clerked in his master's grocery store. In 1784 he purchased his freedom, and he soon began serving as a lay preacher at St. George's Methodist Episcopal Church. In 1787, he and Richard Allen protested a new church policy that required African Americans to sit at the rear of a balcony during services. Later that year, they founded the Free African Society, which is considered the first independent black organization in the United States. In 1794, however, the Free African Society split into two groups, and Jones led a faction that became the St. Thomas African Episcopal Church, which grew to over 500 members in its first year. In 1802, Jones was ordained as a priest.

The official closing of the slave trade was marked by great rejoicing throughout the Blackamerican community. The Reverend Jones's sermon gives thanks to God for this act of Congress in a manner that is derived from a rhetorical tradition perfected by the ministers of the seventeenth century.

When a minister of the faith prepares a sermon based on a portion of text from the Bible he has two alternatives. He may interpret the text itself, dwelling on the words, analyzing their meaning, explaining their origin, engaging his church members in a form of intellectual inquiry so that they come away with a renewed understanding of their belief. Or the minister may choose to amplify the text; he may create for each phrase a verbal tableau drawn out of some contemporaneous experience familiar to the parishioners so that they will depart with a renewed will to act in a specific manner. The minister may, in short, strive to make the text more comprehensible on the one hand, to make it more relevant on the other.

Clearly, the Reverend Jones preaches within the second tradition. He describes the sufferings of the Hebrew children in Egypt as if they were slaves on an American plantation. The God of the Hebrews was made aware of the sufferings of the oppressed, not through His mysterious omniscience but by means of His own sight and His own hearing. And as God acted on behalf of his chosen people in Egypt so did He act on behalf of the slaves in this day: He came down into the very halls of Congress to work His will; He intervened for the abolition of the slave trade.

Continuing this tack, the preacher makes a further application of the meaning of his sermon to the lives of his church members: Black citizens must lead exemplary lives so that their white friends will have no regrets at having befriended them; they must learn to read and write, learn skills, learn a trade, and become self-supporting, an exhortation to self-sufficiency that will be repeated frequently throughout the nineteenth century, culminating in the point of view of Booker T. Washington.

What remains of the discourse is conventional peroration, as generalized, as commonplace in its imagery of sunbeams and mountains as earlier the sermon had been concrete with its leeks and its onions.

Exodus 3:7–8

> And the Lord said, I have surely seen the affliction of my people which are in Egypt, and have heard their cry by reason of their task-masters; for I know their sorrows; and I am come down to deliver them out of the hand of the Egyptians.

These words, my brethren, contain a short account of some of the circumstances which preceded the deliverance of the children of Israel from their captivity and bondage in Egypt.

They mention, in the first place, their *affliction.* This consisted in their privation of liberty: they were slaves to the kings of Egypt, in common with their other subjects; and they were slaves to their fellow slaves. They were compelled to work in the open air, in one of the hottest climates in the world; and, probably, without a covering from the burning rays of the sun. Their work was of a laborious kind: it consisted of making bricks, and travelling, perhaps to a great distance, for the straw, or stubble, that was a component part of them. Their work was dealt out to them in tasks, and performed under the eye of vigilant and rigorous masters, who constantly upbraided them with idleness. The least deficiency, in the product of their labour, was punished by beating. Nor was this all. Their food was of the cheapest kind, and contained but little nourishment: it consisted only of leeks and onions, which grew almost spontaneously in the land of Egypt. Painful and distressing as these sufferings were, they constituted the smallest part of their misery. While the fields resounded with their cries in the day, their huts and hamlets were vocal at night with their lamentations over their sons; who were dragged from the arms of their mothers, and put to death by drowning, in order to prevent such an increase in their population, as to endanger the safety of the state by an insurrection. In this condition, thus degraded and oppressed, they passed nearly four hundred years. Ah! who can conceive of the measure of their sufferings, during that time? What tongue, or pen, can compute the number of their sorrows? To them no morning or evening sun ever disclosed a single charm: to them, the beauties of spring, and the plenty of autumn had no attractions: even domestick endearments were scarcely known to them: all was misery; all was grief; all was despair.

Our text mentions, in the second place, that, in this situation, they were not forgotten by the God of their fathers, and the Father of the human race. Though, for wise reasons, he delayed to appear in their behalf for several hundred years; yet he was not indifferent to their sufferings. Our text tells us, that he saw their affliction, and heard their cry: his eye and his ear were constantly open to their complaint: every tear they shed, was preserved, and every groan they uttered, was recorded; in order to testify, at a future day, against the authors of their oppressions. But our text goes further: it describes the Judge of the world to be so much moved, with what he saw and what he heard, that he rises from his throne—not to issue a command to the armies of angels that surrounded him to fly to the relief of his suffering children—but to come down from heaven, in his own person, in order to deliver them out of the hands of the Egyptians. Glory to God for this precious record of his power and goodness: let all the nations of the earth praise him. *Clouds and darkness are round about him, but righteousness and judgment are the habitation of his throne. O sing unto the Lord a new song, for he hath done marvellous things: his right hand and his holy arm hath gotten him the victory. He hath remembered his mercy and truth toward the house of Israel, and all the ends of the earth shall see the salvation of God.*

The history of the world shows us, that the deliverance of the children of Israel from their bondage, is not the only instance, in which it has pleased God to appear in behalf of oppressed and distressed nations, as the deliverer of the innocent, and of those who call upon his name. He is as unchangeable in his nature and character, as he is in his wisdom and power. The great and blessed event, which we have this day met to celebrate, is a striking proof, that the God of heaven and earth is *the same, yesterday, and to-day, and for ever.* Yes, my brethren, the nations from which most of us have descended, and the country in which some of us were born, have been visited by the tender mercy of the Common Father of the human race. He has seen the affliction of our countrymen, with an eye of pity. He has seen the wicked arts, by which wars have been fomented among the different tribes of the Africans, in order to procure captives, for the purpose of selling them for slaves. He has seen ships fitted out from different ports in Europe and America, and freighted with trinkets to be exchanged for the bodies and souls of men. He has seen the anguish which has taken place, when parents have been torn from their children, and children from their parents, and conveyed, with their hands and feet bound in fetters, on board of ships prepared to receive them. He has seen them thrust in crowds into the holds of those ships, where many of them have perished from the want of air. He has seen such of them as have escaped from that noxious place of confinement, leap into the ocean; with a faint hope of swimming back to their native shore, or a determination to seek an early retreat from their impending misery, in a watery grave. He has seen them exposed for sale, like horses and cattle, upon the wharves; or, like bales of goods, in warehouses of West India and American sea ports. He has seen the pangs of separation between members of the same family. He has seen them driven into the sugar, the rice, and the tobacco fields, and compelled to work—in spite of the habits of ease which they derived from the natural fertility of their own country—in the open air, beneath a burning sun, with scarcely as much clothing upon them as modesty required. He has seen them faint beneath the pressure of their labours. He has seen them return to their smoky huts in the evening, with nothing to satisfy their hunger but a scanty allowance of roots; and these, cultivated for themselves, on that day only, which God ordained as a day of rest for man and beast. He has seen the neglect with which their masters have treated their immortal souls; not only in withholding religious instruction from them, but, in some instances, depriving them of access to the means of obtaining it. He has seen all the different modes of torture, by means of the whip, the screw, the pincers, and the red hot iron, which have been exercised upon their bodies, by inhuman overseers: overseers, did I say? Yes: but not by these only. Our God has seen masters and mistresses, educated in fashionable life, sometimes take the instruments of torture into their own hands, and, deaf to the cries and shrieks of their agonizing slaves, exceed even their overseers in cruelty. Inhuman wretches! though You have been deaf to their cries and shrieks, they have been heard in Heaven. The ears of Jehovah have been constantly open to them: He has heard the prayers that have ascended from the hearts of his people; and he has, as in the case of his ancient and chosen people the Jews, *come down to deliver* our suffering countrymen from the hands of their oppressors. He *came down* into the United States, when they declared, in the constitution which they framed in 1788, that the trade in our African fellow-men, should cease in the year 1808: He *came down* into the British Parliament, when they passed a law to put an end to the same iniquitous trade in May, 1807: He *came down* into the Congress of the United States, the last winter, when they passed a similar law, the operation of which commences on this happy day. Dear land of our ancestors! thou shalt no more be stained with the blood of the children, shed by British and American hands: the ocean shall no more afford a refuge to their bodies, from impending slavery: nor shall the shores of the British West India islands, and of the United States, any more witness the anguish of families, parted for ever by a public sale. For this signal interposition of the God of mercies, in behalf of our brethren, it becomes us this day to offer up our united thanks. Let the song of angels, which was first heard in the air at the birth of our Saviour, be heard this day in our assembly: *Glory to God in the highest,* for these first fruits of *peace upon earth, and good-will to man:* O! let us *give thanks unto the Lord: let us call upon his name, and make known his deeds among the people. Let us sing psalms unto him and talk of all his wondrous works.*

Having enumerated the mercies of God to our nation, it becomes us to ask, What shall we render unto the Lord for them? Sacrifices and burnt offerings are no longer pleasing to him: the pomp of public worship, and the ceremonies of a festive day, will find no acceptance with him, unless they are accompanied with actions that correspond with them. The duties which are inculcated upon us, by the event we are now celebrating, divide themselves into five heads.

In the first place, Let not our expressions of gratitude to God for his late goodness and mercy to our countrymen, be confined to this day, nor to this house: let us carry grateful hearts with us to our places of abode, and to our daily occupations; and let praise and thanksgivings ascend daily to the throne of grace, in our families, and in our closets, for what God has done for our African brethren. Let us not forget to praise him for his mercies to such of our colour as are inhabitants of this country; particularly, for disposing the hearts of the rulers of many of the states to pass laws for the abolition of slavery; for the number and zeal of the friends he has raised up to plead our cause; and for the privileges, we enjoy, of worshipping God, agreeably to our consciences, in churches of our own. This comely building, erected chiefly by the generosity of our friends, is a monument of God's goodness to us, and calls for our gratitude with all the other blessings that have been mentioned.

Secondly, Let us unite, with our thanksgiving, prayer to Almighty God, for the completion of his begun goodness to our brethren in Africa. Let us beseech him to extend to all the nations in Europe, the same humane and just spirit towards them, which he has imparted to the British and American nations. Let us, further, implore the influence of his divine and holy Spirit, to dispose the hearts of our legislatures to pass laws, to ameliorate the condition of our brethren who are still in bondage; also, to dispose their masters to treat them with kindness and humanity; and, above all things, to favour them with the means of acquiring such parts of human knowledge, as will enable them to read the holy scriptures, and understand the doctrines of the Christian religion, whereby they may become, even while they are the slaves of men, the freemen of the Lord.

Thirdly, Let us conduct ourselves in such a manner as to furnish no cause of regret to the deliverers of our nation, for their kindness to us. Let us constantly *remember the rock whence we were hewn, and the pit whence we were digged. Pride was not made for man,* in any situation; and, still less, for persons who have recently emerged from bondage. The Jews, after they entered the promised land, were commanded, when they offered sacrifices to the Lord, never to forget their humble origin; and hence, part of the worship that accompanied their sacrifices consisted in acknowledging, *that a Syrian, ready to perish, was their father:* in like manner, it becomes us, publickly and privately, to acknowledge, that an African slave, ready to perish, was our father or our grandfather. Let our conduct be regulated by the precepts of the gospel; let us be sober minded, humble, peaceable, temperate in our meats and drinks, frugal in our apparel and in the furniture of our houses, industrious in our occupations, just in all our dealings, and ever ready to honour all men. Let us teach our children the rudiments of the English language, in order to enable them to acquire a knowledge of useful trades; and, above all things, let us instruct them in the principles of the gospel of Jesus Christ, whereby they may become *wise unto salvation.* It has always been a mystery, Why the impartial Father of the human race should have permitted the transportation of so many millions of our fellow creatures to this country, to endure all the miseries of slavery. Perhaps his design was, that a knowledge of the gospel might be acquired by some of their descendants, in order that they might become qualified to be the messengers of it, to the land of their fathers. Let this thought animate us, when we are teaching our children to love and adore the name of our Redeemer. Who knows but that a Joseph may rise up among them, who shall be the instrument of feeding the African nations with the bread of life, and of saving them, not from earthly bondage, but from the more galling yoke of sin and Satan.

Fourthly, Let us be graceful to our benefactors, who, by enlightening the minds of the rulers of the earth, by means of their publications and remonstrances against the trade in our countrymen, have produced the great event we are this day celebrating. Abolition societies and individuals have equal claims to our gratitude. It would be difficult to mention the names of any of our benefactors, without offending many whom we do not know. Some of them are gone to heaven, to receive the rewards of their labours of love towards us; and the kindness and benevolence of the survivors, we hope, are recorded in the book of life, to be mentioned with honour when our Lord shall come to reward his faithful servants before an assembled world.

Fifthly, and lastly, Let the first of January, the day of the abolition of the slave trade in our country, be set apart in every year, as a day of publick thanksgiving for that mercy. Let the history of the sufferings of our brethren, and of their deliverance, descend by this means to our children, to the remotest generations, and when they shall ask, in time to come, saying, What means the lessons, the psalms, the prayers and the praises in the worship of this day? let us answer them, by saying, the Lord, on the day of which this is the anniversary, abolished the trade which dragged your fathers from their native country, and sold them as bondmen in the United States of America.

Oh thou God of all the nations upon the earth we thank thee, that thou art *no respecter of persons,* and that thou *hast made of one blood all nations of men.* We thank thee, that thou hast appeared, in the fulness of time, in behalf of the nation from which most of the worshipping people, now before thee, are descended. We thank thee, that the sun of righteousness has at last shed his morning beams upon them. *Rend* thy *heavens,* O Lord, and *come down* upon the earth; and grant that *the mountains,* which now obstruct the perfect day of thy goodness and mercy towards them, may *flow down at thy presence.* Send thy gospel, we beseech thee, among them. May the nations, which now *sit in darkness,* behold and rejoice in its *light.* May *Ethiopia soon stretch out her hands unto thee,* and lay hold of the gracious promise of thy everlasting covenant. Destroy, we beseech thee, all the false religions which now prevail among them; and grant, that they may soon *cast* their *idols, to the moles and the bats* of the wilderness. O, hasten that glorious time, when the knowledge of the gospel of Jesus Christ, shall cover the *earth, as the waters cover the sea;* when *the wolf shall dwell with the lamb, and the leopard shall lie down with the kid, and the calf and the young lion and the fatling together, and a little child shall lead them; and, when, instead of the thorn, shall come up the fir tree, and, instead of the brier, shall come up the myrtle tree: and it shall be to the Lord for a name and for an everlasting sign that shall not be cut off.* We pray, O God, for all our friends and benefactors, in Great Britain, as well as in the United States: reward them, we beseech thee, with blessings upon earth, and prepare them to enjoy the fruits of their kindness to us, in thy everlasting kingdom in heaven: and dispose us, who are assembled in thy presence, to be always thankful for thy mercies, and to act as becomes a people who owe so much to thy goodness. We implore thy blessing. O God, upon the President, and all who are in authority in the United States. Direct them by thy wisdom, in all their deliberations, and O save they people from the calamities of war. Give peace in our day, we beseech thee, O thou *God of peace!* and grant, that this highly favoured country may continue to afford a safe and peaceful retreat from the calamities of war and slavery, for ages yet to come. We implore all these blessing and mercies, only in the name of they beloved Son, Jesus Christ, our Lord. And now, O Lord, we desire, with angels and arch-angels, and all the company of heaven, ever more to praise thee, saying, *Holy, holy, holy, Lord God Almighty: the whole earth is full of thy glory.* Amen.

Note

* Preached January 1, 1808, in St. Thomas's, or The African Episcopal Church, Philadelphia: On Account of the abolition of the African Slave Trade, on that day, by the Congress of the United States. The text is from the original edition published in Philadelphia, 1808.

Source

Absalom Jones, "A Thanksgiving Sermon" (1808; reprinted in Ruth Miller, ed., *Black American Literature, 1760–Present,* 34–41 [Beverly Hills: Glencoe Press, 1971]).

Selected Bibliography

Quarles, Benjamin. *Black Abolitionists.* New York: Oxford University Press, 2000.

Reed, Harry. *Platform for Change: The Foundations of the Northern Free Black Community, 1775–1865.* East Lansing: Michigan State University Press, 1994.

Rhoden, Nancy L. and Ian K. Steele, eds. *The Human Tradition in the American Revolution.* Wilmington, Del.: Scholarly Resources, 2000.

four

Excerpt from *Clotel*

Written by William Wells Brown (1814–1884) in 1853, *Clotel* was the first novel published by an African American. Here, Brown ridiculed the way that many white slaveowners made specious use of the Bible as a way of compelling obedience from their slaves.

Born to a slave woman and a relative of her owner, Brown grew up in Lexington, Kentucky, until his escape from slavery in 1834, when he was twenty years old. He then spent two years working on a Lake Erie steamboat, where he ran fugitive slaves to Canada. In 1836 he married and moved to Buffalo, where he continued his career in the abolitionist movement by attending meetings of the Western New York Anti-Slavery Society, housing antislavery lecturers, and exploring different emigration possibilities. In 1847 he moved to Boston and took a post as a Massachusetts Anti-Slavery lecture agent. Later that year, he published his dramatic autobiography, *Narrative of William W. Brown, A Fugitive Slave.* In 1849 he moved to England. After some British abolitionists purchased his freedom, he returned to Boston, where he continued to write until his death in 1884.

> *"We hold these truths to be self-evident: that all men are created equal; that they are endowed by their Creator with certain inalienable rights, and that among these are LIFE, LIBERTY, and the PURSUIT OF HAPPINESS."*
>
> —*Declaration of American Independence.*

The Religious Teacher

> *"What! preach and enslave men?*
> *Give thanks—and rob thy own afflicted poor?*
> *Talk of thy glorious liberty, and then*
> *Bolt hard the captive's door?"*[1]
>
> —Whittier.

The Rev. John Peck[2] was a native of the state of Connecticut, where he was educated for the ministry, in the Methodist persuasion. His father was a strict follower of John Wesley,[3] and spared no pains in his son's education, with the hope that he would one day be as renowned as the great leader of his sect. John had scarcely finished his education at New Haven, when he was invited by an uncle, then on a visit to his father, to spend a few months at Natchez in the state of Mississippi, Young Peck accepted his uncle's invitation, and accompanied him to the South. Few young men, and especially clergymen, going fresh from a college to the South, but are looked upon as geniuses in a small way, and who are not invited to all the parties in the neighbourhood. Mr. Peck was not an exception to this rule. The society into which he was thrown on his arrival at Natchez was too brilliant for him not to be captivated by it; and, as might have been expected, he succeeded in captivating a plantation with seventy slaves, if not the heart of the lady to whom it belonged. Added to this, he became a popular preacher, had a large congregation with a snug salary. Like other planters, Mr. Peck confided the care of his farm to Ned Huckelby, an overseer of high reputation in his way. The Poplar Farm, as it was called, was situated in a beautiful valley nine miles from Natchez, and near the river Mississippi. The once unshorn face of nature had given way, and now the farm blossomed with a splendid harvest, the neat cottage stood in a grove where Lombardy poplars lift their tufted tops almost to prop the skies; the willow, locust, and horse-chestnut spread their branches, and flowers never cease to blossom. This was the parson's country house, where the family spent only two months during the year.

The town residence was a fine villa, seated upon the brow of a hill at the edge of the city. It was in the kitchen of this house that Currer found her new home. Mr. Peck was, every inch of him, a democrat, and early resolved that his "people," as he called his slaves, should be well fed and not overworked, and therefore laid down the law and gospel to the overseer as well as the slaves.

"It is my wish," said he to Mr. Carlton, an old school-fellow, who was spending a few days with him, "it is my wish that a new system be adopted on the plantations in this estate. I believe that the sons of Ham[4] should have the gospel, and I intend that my negroes shall. The gospel is calculated to make mankind better, and none should be without it." "What say you," replied Carlton, "about the right of man to his liberty?" "Now, Carlton, you have begun again to harp about man's rights; I really wish you could see this matter as I do. I have searched in vain for any authority for man's natural rights; if he had any, they existed before the fall. That is, Adam and Eve may have had some rights which God gave them, and which modern philosophy, in its pretended reverence for the name of God, prefers to call natural rights. I can imagine they had the right to eat of the fruit of the trees of the garden; they were restricted even in this by the prohibition of one. As far as I know without positive assertion, their liberty of action was confined to the garden. These were not 'inalienable rights,' however, for they forfeited both them and life with the first act of disobedience. Had they, after this, any rights? We cannot imagine them; they were condemned beings; they could have no rights, but by Christ's gift as king. These are the only rights man can have as an independent isolated being, if we choose to consider him in this impossible position, in which so many theorists have placed him. If he had no rights, he could suffer no wrongs. Rights and wrongs are therefore necessarily the creatures of society, such as man would establish himself in his gregarious state. They are, in this state, both artificial and voluntary. Though man has no rights, as thus considered, undoubtedly he has the power, by such arbitrary rules of right and wrong as his necessity enforces." "I regret I cannot see eye to eye with you," said Carlton. "I am a disciple of Rousseau,[5] and have for years made the rights of man my study; and I must confess to you that I can see no difference between white men and black men as it regards liberty." "Now, my dear Carlton, would you really have the negroes enjoy the same rights with ourselves?" "I would, most certainly. Look at our great Declaration of Independence; look even at the constitution of our own Connecticut, and see what is said in these about liberty." "I regard all this talk about rights as mere humbug. The Bible is older than the Declaration of Independence, and there I take my stand. The Bible furnishes to us the armour of proof, weapons of heavenly temper and mould, whereby we can maintain our ground against all attacks. But this is true only when we obey its directions, as well as employ its sanctions. Our rights are there established, but it is always in connection with our duties. If we neglect the one we cannot make good the other. Our domestic institutions can be maintained against the world, if we but allow Christianity to throw its broad shield over them. But if we so act as to array the Bible against our social economy, they must fall. Nothing ever yet stood long against Christianity. Those who say that religious instruction is inconsistent with our peculiar civil polity, are the worst enemies of that polity. They would drive religious men from its defence. Sooner or later, if these views prevail, they will separate the religious portion of our community from the rest, and thus divided we shall become an easy prey. Why, is it not better that Christian men should hold slaves than unbelievers? We know how to value the bread of life, and will not keep it from our slaves."

"Well, every one to his own way of thinking," said Carlton, as he changed his position. "I confess," added he, "that I am no great admirer of either the Bible or slavery. My heart is my guide: my conscience is my Bible. I wish for nothing further to satisfy me of my duty to man. If I act rightly to mankind, I shall fear nothing." Carlton had drunk too deeply of the bitter waters of infidelity, and had spent too many hours over the writings of Rousseau, Voltaire, and Thomas Paine,[6] to place that appreciation upon the Bible and its teachings that it demands. During this conversation there was another person in the room, seated by the window, who, although at work upon a fine piece of lace, paid every attention to what was said. This was Georgiana, the only daughter of the parson. She had just returned from Connecticut, where she had finished her education. She had had the opportunity of contrasting the spirit of Christianity and liberty in New England with that of slavery in her native state, and had learned to feel deeply for the injured negro. Georgiana was in her nineteenth year, and had been much benefited by a residence of five years at the North. Her form was tall and graceful; her features regular and well defined; and her complexion was illuminated by the freshness of youth, beauty, and health. The daughter differed from both the father and his visitor upon the subject which they had been discussing, and as soon as an opportunity offered, she gave it as her opinion, that the Bible was both the bulwark of Christianity and of liberty. With a smile she said, "Of course, papa will overlook my differing from him, for although I am a native of the South, I am by education and sympathy a Northerner." Mr. Peck laughed and appeared pleased, rather than otherwise, at the manner in which his daughter had expressed herself.

From this Georgiana took courage and said, "We must try the character of slavery, and our duty in regard to it, as we should try any other question of character and duty. To judge justly of the character of anything, we must know what it does. That which is good does good, and that which is evil does evil. And as to duty, God's designs indicate his claims. That which accomplishes the manifest design of God is right; that which counteracts it, wrong. Whatever, in its proper tendency and general effect, produces, secures, or extends human welfare, is according to the will of God, and is good; and our duty is to favour and promote, according to our power, that which God favours and promotes by the general law of his providence. On the other hand, whatever in its proper tendency and general effect destroys, abridges, or renders insecure, human welfare, is opposed to God's will, and is evil. And as whatever accords with the will of God, in any manifestation of it should be done and persisted in, so whatever opposes that will should not be done, and if done, should be abandoned. Can that then be right, be well doing—can that obey

God's behest, which makes a man a slave? which dooms him and all his posterity, in limitless generations, to bondage, to unrequited toil through life? 'Thou shalt love thy neighbour as thyself.'[7] This single passage of Scripture should cause us to have respect to the rights of the slave. True Christian love is of an enlarged, disinterested nature. It loves all who love the Lord Jesus Christ in sincerity, without regard to color or condition." "Georgiana, my dear, you are an abolitionist; your talk is fanaticism," said Mr. Peck in rather a sharp tone; but the subdued look of the girl, and the presence of Carlton, caused the father to soften his language. Mr. Peck having lost his wife by consumption, and Georgiana being his only child, he loved her too dearly to say more, even if he felt displeased. A silence followed this exhortation from the young Christian. But her remarks had done a noble work. The father's heart was touched; and the sceptic, for the first time, was viewing Christianity in its true light.

"I think I must go out to your farm," said Carlton, as if to break the silence. "I shall be pleased to have you go," returned Mr. Peck. "I am sorry I can't go myself, but Huckelby will show you every attention; and I feel confident that when you return to Connecticut, you will do me the justice to say, that I am one who looks after my people, in a moral, social, and religious point of view." "Well, what do you say to my spending next Sunday there?" "Why, I think that a good move; you will then meet with Snyder, our missionary." "Oh, you have missionaries in these parts, have you?" "Yes," replied Mr. Peck; "Snyder is from New York, and is our missionary to the poor, and preaches to our 'people' on Sunday; you will no doubt like him; he is a capital fellow." "Then I shall go," said Carlton, "but only wish I had company." This last remark was intended for Miss Peck, for whom he had the highest admiration.

It was on a warm Sunday morning, in the month of May, that Miles Carlton found himself seated beneath a fine old apple tree, whose thick leaves entirely shaded the ground for some distance round. Under similar trees and near by, were gathered together all the "people" belonging to the plantation. Hontz Snyder was a man of about forty years of age, exceedingly low in stature, but of a large frame. He had been brought up in the Mohawk Valley, in the state of New York, and claimed relationship with the oldest Dutch families in that vicinity. He had once been a sailor, and had all the roughness of character that a sea-faring man might expect to possess; together with the half-Yankee, half-German peculiarities of the people of the Mohawk Valley. It was nearly eleven o'clock when a one-horse waggon drove up in haste, and the low squatty preacher got out and took his place at the foot of one of the trees, where a sort of rough board table was placed, and took his books from his pocket and commenced.

"As it is rather late," said he, "we will leave the singing and praying for the last, and take our text, and commence immediately.[8] I shall base my remarks on the following passage of Scripture, and hope to have that attention which is due to the cause of God:—'All things whatsoever ye would that men should do unto you, do ye even so unto them;'[9] that is, do by all mankind just as you would desire they should do by you, if you were in their place and they in yours.

"Now, to suit this rule to your particular circumstances, suppose you were masters and mistresses, and had servants under you, would you not desire that your servants should do their business faithfully and honestly, as well when your back was turned as while you were looking over them? Would you not expect that they should take notice of what you said to them? that they should behave themselves with respect towards you and yours, and be as careful of every thing belonging to you as you would be yourselves? You are servants: do, therefore, as you would wish to be done by, and you will be both good servants to your masters and good servants to God, who requires this of you, and will reward you well for it, if you do it for the sake of conscience, in obedience to his commands.

"You are not to be eye-servants. Now, eye-servants are such as will work hard, and seem mighty diligent, while they think anybody is taking notice of them; but, when their masters' and mistresses' backs are turned they are idle, and neglect their business. I am afraid there are a great many such eye-servants among you, and that you do not consider how great a sin it is to be so, and how severely God will punish you for it. You may easily deceive your owners, and make them have an opinion of you that you do not deserve, and get the praise of men by it; but remember that you cannot deceive Almighty God, who sees your wickedness and deceit, and will punish you accordingly. For the rule is, that you must obey your masters in all things, and do the work they set you about with fear and trembling, in singleness of heart as unto Christ; not with eye-service, as men-pleasers, but as the servants of Christ, doing the will of God from the heart; with good-will doing service as to the Lord, and not as to men.

"Take care that you do not fret or murmur, grumble or repine at your condition; for this will not only make your life uneasy, but will greatly offend Almighty God. Consider that this is not yourselves, it is not the people that you belong to, it is not the men who have brought you to it, but *it is the will of God who hath by providence made you servants, because, no doubt, he knew that condition would be best for you in this world, and help you the better towards heaven, if you would but do your duty in it.* So that any discontent at your not being free, or rich, or great, as you see some others, is quarrelling with your heavenly Master, and finding fault with God himself, who hath made you what you are, and hath promised you as large a share in the kingdom of heaven as the greatest man alive, if you will but behave yourself aright, and do the business he hath set you about in this world honestly and cheerfully. Riches and power have proved the ruin of many an unhappy soul, by drawing away the heart and affections from God, and fixing them on mean and sinful enjoyments; so that, when God, who knows our hearts better than we know them ourselves, sees that they would be hurtful to us, and therefore keeps them from us, it is the greatest mercy and kindness he could show us.

"You may perhaps fancy that, if you had riches and freedom, you could do your duty to God and man with greater pleasure than you can now. But pray consider that, if you can but save your souls through the mercy of God, you will have spent your time to the best of purposes in this world; and he that at last can get to heaven has performed a noble journey, let the road be ever so rugged and difficult. Besides, you really have a great advantage over most white people, who have not only the care of their daily labour upon their hands, but the care of looking forward and providing necessaries for to-morrow and next day, and of clothing and bringing up their children, and of getting food and raiment[10] for as many of you as belong to their families, which often puts them to great difficulties, and distracts their minds so as to break their rest, and take off their thoughts from the affairs of another world. Whereas you are quite eased from all these cares, and have nothing but your daily labour to look after, and, when that is done, take your needful rest. Neither is it necessary for you to think of laying up anything against old age, as white people are obliged to do; for the laws of the country have provided that you shall not be turned off when you are past labour, but shall be maintained, while you live, by those you belong to, whether you are able to work or not.

"There is only one circumstance which may appear grievous, that I shall now take notice of, and that is correction.

"Now, when correction is given you, you either deserve it, or you do not deserve it. But whether you really deserve it or not, it is your duty, and Almighty God requires that you bear it patiently. You may perhaps think that this is hard doctrine; but, if you consider it right, you must needs thinks otherwise of it. Suppose, then, that you deserve correction, you cannot but say that it is just and right you should meet with it. Suppose you do not, or at least you do not deserve so much, or so severe a correction, for the fault you have committed, you perhaps have escaped a great many more and are at last paid for all. Or suppose you are quite innocent of what is laid to your charge, and suffer wrongfully in that particular thing, is it not possible you may have done some other bad thing which was never discovered, and that Almighty God who saw you doing it would not let you escape without punishment one time or another? And ought you not, in such a case, to give glory to him, and be thankful that he would rather punish you in this life for your wickedness than destroy your souls for it in the next life? But suppose even this was not the case (a case hardly to be imagined), and that you have by no means, known or unknown, deserved the correction you suffered, there is this great comfort in it, that, if you bear it patiently, and leave your cause in the hands of God, he will reward you for it in heaven, and the punishment you suffer unjustly here shall turn to your exceeding great glory hereafter.

"Lastly, you should serve your masters faithfully, because of their goodness to you. See to what trouble they have been on your account. Your fathers were poor ignorant and barbarous creatures in Africa, and the whites fitted out ships at great trouble and expense and brought you from that benighted land to Christian America, where you can sit under your own vine and fig tree and no one molest or make you afraid. Oh, my dear black brothers and sisters, you are indeed a fortunate and a blessed people. Your masters have many troubles that you know nothing about. If the banks break, your masters are sure to lose something. If the crops turn out poor, they lose by it. If one of you die, your master loses what he paid for you, while you lose nothing. Now let me exhort you once more to be faithful."

Often during the delivery of the sermon did Snyder cast an anxious look in the direction where Carlton was seated; no doubt to see if he had found favour with the stranger. Huckelby, the overseer, was also there, seated near Carlton. With all Snyder's gesticulations, sonorous voice, and occasionally bringing his fist down upon the table with the force of a sledge hammer, he could not succeed in keeping the negroes all interested: four or five were fast asleep, leaning against the trees; as many more were nodding, while not a few were stealthily cracking and eating hazelnuts. "Uncle Simon, you may strike up a hymn," said the preacher as he closed his Bible. A moment more, and the whole company (Carlton excepted) had joined in the well known hymn, commencing with

"When I can read my title clear
To mansions in the sky."[11]

After the singing, Sandy closed with prayer, and the following questions and answers read, and the meeting was brought to a close.

"Q. What command has God given to servants concerning obedience to their masters?—*A.* 'Servants, obey in all things your masters according to the flesh, not with eye-service as men-pleasers, but in singleness of heart, fearing God.'

"Q. What does God mean by masters according to the flesh?—*A.* 'Masters in this world.'

"Q. What are servants to count their masters worthy of?—*A.* 'All honour.'

"Q. How are they to do the service of their masters?—*A.* '*With good will,* doing service as unto the Lord, and not unto men.'

"Q. How are they to try to please their masters?—*A.* 'Please him well in all things, not answering again.'

"Q. Is a servant who is an eye-servant to his earthly master an eye-servant to his heavenly master?—*A.* 'Yes.'

"Q. Is it right in a servant, when commanded to do any thing, to be sullen and slow, and answer his master again?—*A.* 'No.'

"Q. If the servant professes to be a Christian, ought he not to be *as a Christian servant,* an example to all other servants of love and obedience to his master?—*A.* 'Yes.'

"Q. And, should his master be a Christian also, ought he not on that account specially to love and obey him?—*A.* 'Yes.'

"Q. But suppose the master is hard to please, and threatens and punishes more than he ought, what is the servant to do?—*A.* 'Do his best to please him.'

"Q. When the servant suffers *wrongfully* at the hands of his master, and, to please God, takes it patiently, will God reward him for it?—*A.* 'Yes.'

"Q. Is it right for the servant to *run away,* or is it right to *harbour* a runaway?—*A.* 'No.'

"Q. If a servant runs away, what should be done with him?—*A.* 'He should be caught and brought back.'

"Q. When he is brought back, what should be done with him?—*A.* 'Whip him well.'

"Q. Why may not the whites be slaves as well as the blacks?—*A.* 'Because the Lord intended the negroes for slaves.'

"Q. Are they better calculated for servants than the whites?—*A.* 'Yes, their hands are large, the skin thick and tough, and they can stand the sun better than the whites.'

"Q. Why should servants not complain when they are whipped?—*A.* 'Because the Lord has commanded that they should be whipped.'

"Q. Where has He commanded it?—*A.* 'He says, He that knoweth his master's will, and doeth it not, shall be beaten with many stripes.'

"Q. Then is the master to blame for whipping his servant?—*A.* 'Oh, no! he is only doing his duty as a Christian.' "

Snyder left the ground in company with Carlton and Huckelby, and the three dined together in the overseer's dwelling.

"Well," said Joe, after the three white men were out of hearing, "Marser Snyder bin try hesef to-day." "Yes," replied Ned; "he want to show de strange gentman how good he can preach." "Dat's a new sermon he gib us to-day," said Sandy. "Dees white fokes is de very dibble," said Dick; "and all dey whole study is to try to fool de black people." "Didn't you like de sermon?" asked Uncle Simon. "No," answered four or five voices. "He rared and pitched enough," continued Uncle Simon.

Now Uncle Simon was himself a preacher, or at least he thought so, and was rather pleased than otherwise, when he heard others spoken of in a disparaging manner. "Uncle Simon can beat dar sermon all to pieces," said Ned, as he was filling his mouth with hazelnuts. "I got no notion of dees white fokes, no how," returned Aunt Dafney. "Dey all de time tellin' dat de Lord made us for to work for dem, and I don't believe a word of it." "Marser Peck give dar sermon to Snyder, I know," said Uncle Simon. "He jest de one for dat," replied Sandy. "I think de people dat made de Bible was great fools," said Ned.

"Why?" Uncle Simon. " 'Cause dey made such a great big book and put nuttin' in it, but servants obey yer masters." "Oh," replied Uncle Simon, "thars more in de Bible den dat, only Snyder never reads any other part to us; I use to hear it read in Maryland, and that was more den what Snyder lets us hear." In the overseer's house there was another scene going on, and far indifferent from what we have here described.

Notes

1. *What! . . . captive's door?":* From Whittier, "Clerical Oppressors" (1838).
2. *Rev. John Peck:* The character was inspired by the hypocritical Reverend Peck of Rochester, whom Brown described in "The New Liberty Party"; see pp. 270–71.
3. *John Wesley:* The founder of Methodism, the English Protestant evangelical John Wesley (1703–1791) emphasized a methodical devotion to religious duties and practices; he saw good works rather than divine election as the key to salvation.
4. *sons of Ham:* In Genesis, Noah cursed his son Ham for viewing him when he lay naked in a drunken stupor; see Genesis 9:20–27. Oral traditions collected in the Talmud claimed that the curse resulted in Ham having black descendants; this interpretation was echoed by racists in the eighteenth and nineteenth centuries.
5. *Rousseau:* The influential French philosopher, writer, and social reformer Jean Jacques Rousseau (1712–1778) was best known in America for his political writings, especially *Origin of Inequality Among Men* (1753) and *Social Contract* (1761). In these works he castigated established governmental and religious institutions as sources of evil and called for social amelioration through a contractual surrendering of individual wills to a General Will.
6. *Voltaire, and Thomas Paine:* Grouped with Rousseau, the French philosopher Francoise Marie Arouet Voltaire (1694–1778), best known as the author of *Candide* (1759), and the Anglo-American political writer Thomas Paine (1737–1809), best known as the author of *Common Sense* (1776), are presented here as troubling exemplars of Enlightenment rationalism. Although they wrote powerfully in support of political freedom, they ultimately rejected Christianity as authoritarian and unreasonable.
7. *'Thou shalt love . . . as thyself.':* Leviticus 19:18.
8. *". . . . and commence immediately.":* For Snyder's sermon, Brown drew on Thomas Bacon's *Sermons Addressed to Masters and Servants* (1813); see pp. 258–62.
9. *'All . . . unto them':* Matthew 7:12.
10. *raiment:* Clothing.
11. *"When . . . the sky":* From Isaac Watts (1674–1748), *Hymns and Spiritual Songs* (1707).

Source

William Wells Brown, *Clotel, or The President's Daughter: A Narrative of Slave Life in the United States* (1853; reprint, New York: Johnson Reprint Corp., 1970), 93–100.

Selected Bibliography

Ellison, Curtis. W. *William Wells Brown and Martin R. Delany: A Reference Guide.* Boston: G. K. Hall, 1978.

Farrison, William Edward. *William Wells Brown: Author and Reformer.* Chicago: University of Chicago Press, 1969.

Heermance, J. Noel. *William Wells Brown and Clotelle; A Portrait of the Artist in the First Negro Novel.* Hamden, Conn.: Archon Books, 1969.

Osofsky, Gilbert. *Puttin' On Ole Massa: The Slave Narratives of Henry Bibb, William Wells Brown, and Solomon Northrup.* New York: Harper & Row, 1969.

Zafar, Rafia. *We Wear the Mask: African-Americans Write American Literature, 1760–1870.* New York: Columbia University Press, 1997.

five

Excerpt from *A Brand Plucked from the Fire*

Julia Foote (1823–1900) became the first woman to be made a deacon in the African Methodist Episcopal Zion (AMEZ) Church. In the following excerpt, Foote recounts how she was called to preach only to be censored by her pastor, Rev. Jeheiel C. Beman, after she engaged in the ministry in her home.

Born in Schenectady, New York, to former slaves, she joined the church at age fifteen, and in 1841 she married and moved to Boston. Foote often told of how she was called to the ministry, but her insistence that God had called her to preach put her at odds with the prevailing conventions of her day, which held that it was inappropriate for a woman to be a preacher. Nevertheless, Foote found various outlets from whence she could preach, including pulpits, camp revivals, and homes. In 1879 she published her memoir, *A Brand Plucked from Fire*. In 1894, she became the AMEZ's first woman deacon, and later she was the first woman ordained as an elder.

My Call to Preach the Gospel

For months I had been moved upon to exhort and pray with the people, in my visits from house to house; and in meetings my whole soul seemed drawn out for the salvation of souls. The love of Christ in me was not limited. Some of my mistaken friends said I was too forward, but a desire to work for the Master, and to promote the glory of his kingdom in the salvation of souls, was food to my poor soul.

When called of God, on a particular occasion, to a definite work, I said, "No, Lord, not me." Day by day I was more impressed that God would have me work in his vineyard. I thought it could not be that I was called to preach—I, so weak and ignorant. Still, I knew all things were possible with God, even to confounding the wise by the foolish things of this earth. Yet in me there was a shrinking.

I took all my doubts and fears to the Lord in prayer, when, what seemed to be an angel, made his appearance. In his hand was a scroll, on which were these words: "Thee have I chosen to preach my Gospel without delay." The moment my eyes saw it, it appeared to be printed on my heart. The angel was gone in an instant, and I, in agony, cried out, "Lord, I cannot do it!" It was eleven o'clock in the morning, yet everything grew dark as night. The darkness was so great that I feared to stir.

At last "Mam" Riley entered. As she did so, the room grew lighter, and I arose from my knees. My heart was so heavy I scarce could speak. Dear "Mam" Riley saw my distress, and soon left me.

From that day my appetite failed me and sleep fled from my eyes. I seemed as one tormented. I prayed, but felt no better. I belonged to a band of sisters whom I loved dearly, and to them I partially opened my mind. One of them seemed to understand my case at once, and advised me to do as God had bid me, or I would never be happy here or hereafter. But it seemed too hard—I could not give up and obey.

One night as I lay weeping and beseeching the dear Lord to remove this burden from me, there appeared the same angel that came to me before, and on his breast were these words: "You are lost unless you obey God's righteous commands." I saw the writing, and that was enough. I covered my head and awoke my husband, who had returned a few days before. He asked me why I trembled so, but I had not power to answer him. I remained in that condition until morning, when I tried to arise and go about my usual duties, but was too ill. Then my husband called a physician, who prescribed medicine, but it did me no good.

I had always been opposed to the preaching of women, and had spoken against it, though, I acknowledge, without foundation. This rose before me like a mountain, and when I thought of the difficulties they had to encounter, both from professors and non-professors, I shrank back and cried, "Lord, I cannot go!"

The trouble my heavenly Father has had to keep me out of the fire that is never quenched, he alone knoweth. My husband and friends said I would die or go crazy if something favorable did not take place soon. I expected to die and be lost, knowing I had been enlightened and had tasted the heavenly gift. I read again and again the sixth chapter of Hebrews.

Public Effort–Excommunication

From this time the opposition to my lifework commenced, instigated by the minister, Mr. Beman. Many in the church were anxious to have me preach in the hall, where our meetings were held at that time, and were not a little astonished at the minister's cool treatment of me. At length two of the trustees got some of the elder sisters to call on the minister and ask him to let me preach. His answer was: "No; she can't preach her holiness stuff here, and I am astonished that you should ask it of me." The sisters said he seemed to be in quite a rage, although he said he was not angry.

There being no meeting of the society on Monday evening, a brother in the church opened his house to me, that I might preach, which displeased Mr. Beman very much. He appointed a committee to wait upon the brother and sister who had opened their doors to me, to tell them they must not allow any more meetings of that kind, and that they must abide by the rules of the church, making them believe they would be excommunicated if they disobeyed him. I happened to be present at this interview, and the committee remonstrated with me for the course I had taken. I told them my business was with the Lord, and wherever I found a door opened I intended to go in and work for my Master.

There was another meeting appointed at the same place, which I, of course, attended; after which the meetings were stopped for that time, though I held many more there after these people had withdrawn from Mr. Beman's church.

I then held meetings in my own house; whereat the minister told the members that if they attended them he would deal with them, for they were breaking the rules of the church. When he found that I continued the meetings, and that the Lord was blessing my feeble efforts, he sent a committee of two to ask me if I considered myself a member of his church. I told them I did, and should continue to do so until I had done something worthy of dismembership.

At this, Mr. Beman sent another committee with a note, asking me to meet him with the committee, which I did. He asked me a number of questions, nearly all of which I have forgotten. One, however, I do remember: he asked if I was willing to comply with the rules of the discipline. To this I answered: "Not if the discipline prohibits me from doing what God has bidden me to do; I fear God more than man." Similar questions were asked and answered in the same manner. The committee said what they wished to say, and then told me I could go home. When I reached the door, I turned and said: "I now shake off the dust of my feet as a witness against you [Mark 6:11; Luke 9:5]. See to it that this meeting does not rise in judgment against you."

The next evening, one of the committee came to me and told me that I was no longer a member of the church, because I had violated the rules of the discipline by preaching.

When this action became known, the people wondered how any one could be excommunicated for trying to do good. I did not say much, and my friends simply said I had done nothing but hold meetings. Others, anxious to know the particulars, asked the minister what the trouble was. He told them he had given me the privilege of speaking or preaching as long as I chose, but that he could not give me the right to use the pulpit, and that I was not satisfied with any other place. Also, that I had appointed meeting on the evening of his meetings, which was a thing no member had a right to do. For these reasons he said he had turned me out of the church.

Now, if the people who repeated this to me told the truth—and I have no doubt but they did—Mr. Beman told an actual falsehood. I had never asked for his pulpit, but had told him and others, repeatedly, that I did not care where I stood—any corner of the hall would do. To which Mr. Beman had answered: "You cannot have any place in the hall." Then I said: "I'll preach in a private house." He answered me: "No, not in this place: I am stationed over all Boston." He was determined I should not preach in the city of Boston. To cover up his deceptive, unrighteous course toward me, he told the above falsehoods.

From his statements, many erroneous stories concerning me gained credence with a large number of people. At that time, I thought it my duty as well as privilege to address a letter to the Conference, which I took to them in person, stating all the facts. At the same time I told them it was not in the power of Mr. Beman, or any one else, to truthfully bring anything against my moral or religious character—that my only offence was in trying to preach the Gospel of Christ—and that I cherished no ill feelings toward Mr. Beman or any one else, but that I desired the Conference to give the case an impartial hearing, and then give me a written statement expressive of their opinion. I also said I considered myself a member of the Conference, and should do so until they said I was not, and gave me their reasons, that I might let the world know what my offence had been.

My letter was slightingly noticed, and then thrown under the table. Why should they notice it? It was only the grievance of a woman, and there was no justice meted out to women in those days. Even ministers of Christ did not feel that women had any rights which they were bound to respect.

Women in the Gospel

Thirty years ago there could scarcely a person be found, in the churches, to sympathize with any one who talked of Holiness. But, in my simplicity, I did think that a body of Christian ministers would understand my case and judge righteously. I was, however, disappointed.

It is no little thing to feel that every man's hand is against us, and ours against every man, as seemed to be the case with me at this time; yet how precious, if Jesus but be with us. In this severe trial I had constant access to God, and a clear consciousness that he heard me; yet I did not seem to have that plenitude of the Spirit that I had before. I realized most keenly that the closer the communion that may have existed, the keener the suffering of the slightest departure from God. Unbroken communion can only be retained by a constant application of the blood which cleanseth.

Though I did not wish to pain any one, neither could I please any one only as I was led by the Holy Spirit. I saw, as never before, that the best men were liable to err, and that the only safe way was to fall on Christ, even though censure and reproach fell upon me for obeying his voice. Man's opinion weighed nothing with me, for my commission was from heaven, and my reward was with the Most High.

I could not believe that it was a short-lived impulse or spasmodic influence that impelled me to preach. I read that on the day of Pentecost was the Scripture fulfilled as found in Joel ii. 28, 29; and it certainly will not be denied that women as well as men were at that time filled with the Holy Ghost, because it is expressly stated that women were among those who continued in prayer and supplication, waiting for the fulfillment of the promise. Women and men are classed together, and if the power to preach the Gospel is short-lived and spasmodic in the case of women, it must be equally so in that of men; and if women have lost the gift of prophecy, so have men.

We are sometimes told that if a woman pretends to a Divine call, and thereon grounds the right to plead the cause of a crucified Redeemer in public, she will be believed when she shows credentials from heaven; that is, when she works a miracle. If it be necessary to prove one's right to preach the Gospel, I ask of my brethren to show me their credentials, or I can not believe in the propriety of their ministry.

But the Bible puts an end to this strife when it says: "There is neither male nor female in Christ Jesus" [Gal. 3:28]. Philip had four daughters that prophesied, or preached. Paul called Priscilla, as well as Aquila, his "helper," or, as in the Greek, his "fellow-laborer." Rom. xv. 3; 2 Cor. viii. 23: Phil. ii. 5; 1 Thess. iii. 2. The same word, which, in our common translation, is now rendered a "servant of the church," in speaking of Phebe (Rom. xix. 1.), is rendered "minister" when applied to Tychicus. Eph. vi. 21. When Paul said, "Help those women who labor with me in the Gospel," he certainly meant that they did more than to pour out tea. In the eleventh chapter of First Corinthians Paul gives directions, to men and women, how they should appear when they prophesy or pray in public assemblies; and he defines prophesying to be speaking to edification, exhortation and comfort.

I may further remark that the conduct of holy women is recorded in Scripture as an example to others of their sex. And in the early ages of Christianity many women were happy and glorious in martyrdom. How nobly, how heroically, too, in later ages, have women suffered persecution and death for the name of the Lord Jesus.

In looking over these facts, I could see no miracle wrought for those women more than in myself.

Though opposed, I went forth laboring for God, and he owned and blessed my labors, and has done so wherever I have been until this day. And while I walk obediently, I know he will, though hell may rage and vent its spite.

Source

Julia A. Foote, *A Brand Plucked from the Fire: An Autobiographical Sketch* (1879; reprinted in William L. Andrews, ed., *Sisters of the Spirit: Three Black Women's Autobiographies of the Nineteenth Century,* 200–201, 205–9 [Bloomington: Indiana University Press, 1986]).

Selected Bibliography

Collier-Thomas, Bettye. *Daughters of Thunder: Black Women Preachers and Their Sermons, 1850–1979.* San Francisco: Jossey-Bass, 1998.

Loewenberg, Bert James and Ruth Bogin. *Black Women in Nineteenth Century American Life.* University Park: Pennsylvania State University Press, 1976.

Riggs, Marcia. *Can I Get A Witness?: Prophetic Religious Voices of African-American Women: An Anthology.* Maryknoll, N.Y.: Orbis Books, 1997.

six

An Antebellum Sermon

Paul Laurence Dunbar was the first African American to gain national eminence as a poet. Much of his poetry used African American folk material and dialects, but he was also capable of writing in the standard English of classical poets. "An Antebellum Sermon" is an example of the former style, wherein Dunbar recounts episodes from the Bible in black dialect.

The son of ex-slaves, Dunbar was born in Dayton, Ohio, in 1872. His father had escaped to Canada via the Underground Railroad, fought in the Civil War, and later died when Dunbar was twelve years old. His mother had been a plantation servant before she relocated to Dayton to live with relatives. Dunbar attended an all-white school, where he became class president and wrote and delivered the senior class poem at his high school graduation in 1891. He published his first poem in the *Dayton Herald* at the age of sixteen.

Although he lived to be only thirty-three years old, Dunbar went on to write short stories, novels, librettos, plays, songs, essays, and many more poems. His work has been characterized as "a delicate balance between accommodation and protest."[1] He published his first booklet of poetry, *Oak and Ivy*, in 1893, which he sold while working as an elevator operator. Inspired by his parents stories about their labors, *Oak and Ivy* focused on African American contributions to the

United States. One year later Dunbar worked for Frederick Douglass in the Haiti Building at the World's Columbian Exposition in Chicago. There he had met leaders such as Ida B. Wells-Barnett and Mary Church Terrell. In 1896 he published *Majors and Minors* and *Lyrics of Lowly Life*, which won national acclaim. Dunbar went on to lecture in England in 1897 where he met his wife, Alice Ruth Moore. Later that year he worked at the Library of Congress in Washington, D.C. He died in Dayton in 1906.

We is gathahed hyeah, my brothahs,
In dis howlin' wildaness,
Fu' to speak some words of comfo't
To each othah in distress.
An' we chooses fu' ouah subjic'
Dis—we'll 'splain it by an' by;
"An' de Lawd said, 'Moses, Moses,'
An' de man said, 'Hyeah am I.' "

Now ole Pher'oh, down in Egypt,
Was de wuss man evah bo'n,
An' he had de Hebrew chillun
Down dah wukin' in his co'n;
'T well de Lawd got tiahed o' his foolin,'
An' sez he: "I'll let him know—
Look hyeah, Moses, go tell Pher'oh
Fu' to let dem chillun go."

"An' ef he refuse to do it,
I will make him rue de houah,
Fu' I'll empty down on Egypt
All de vials of my powah."
Yes, he did—an' Pher'oh's ahmy
Was n't wuth a ha'f a dime;
Fu' de Lawd will he'p his chillun,
You kin trust him evah time.

An' yo' enemies may 'sail you
In de back an' in de front;
But de Lawd is all aroun' you,
Fu' to ba' de battle's brunt.
Dey kin fo'ge yo' chains an' shackles
F'om de mountains to de sea;

But de Lawd will sen' some Moses
Fu' to set his chillun free.

An' de lan' shall hyeah his thundah,
Lak a blas' f'om Gab'el's ho'n,
Fu' de Lawd of hosts is mighty
When he girds his ahmor on.
But fu' feah some one mistakes me,
I will pause right hyeah to say,
Dat I'm still a-preachin' ancient,
I ain't talkin' 'bout to-day.

But I tell you, fellah christuns,
Things 'll happen mighty strange;
Now, de Lawd done dis fu' Isrul,
An' his ways don't nevah change,
An' de love he showed to Isrul
Was n't all on Isrul spent;
Now don't run an' tell yo' mastahs
Dat I's preachin' discontent.

'Cause I is n't; I'se a-judgin'
Bible people by deir ac's;
I'se a-givin' you de Scriptuah,
I'se a-handin' you de fac's.
Cose ole Pher'oh b'lieved in slav'ry
But de Lawd he let him see,
Dat de people he put bref in,—
Evah mothah's son was free.

An' dahs othahs thinks lak Pher'oh,'
But dey calls de Scriptuah liar,
Fu' de Bible says "a servant
Is a-worthy of his hire."
An' you cain't git roun' nor thoo dat,'
An' you cain't git ovah it,'
Fu' whatevah place you git in,
Dis hyeah Bible too 'll fit.

So you see de Lawd's intention,
Evah sence de worl' began,
Was dat His almighty freedom
Should belong to evah man,

But I think it would be bettah,
Ef I'd pause agin to say,
Dat I'm talkin' 'bout ouah freedom
In a Bibleistic way.

But de Moses is a-comin',
An' he's comin', suah and fas'
We kin hyeah his feet a-trompin',
We kin hyeah his trumpit blas'.
But I want to wa'n you people,
Don't you git too briggity;
An' don't you git to braggin'
'Bout dese things, you wait an' see.

But when Moses wif his powah
Comes an' sets us chillun free,
We will praise de gracious Mastah
Dat has gin us liberty;
An' we'll shout ouah halleluyahs,
On dat mighty reck'nin' day,
When we'se reco'nised ez citiz'—
Huh uh! Chillun, let us pray!

Note

1. "Paul Laurence Dunbar," *American Decade CD-ROM* (Detroit: Gale Research, 1998). Reproduced in Biography Resource Center, http://www.galenet.com/servlet/BioRC. Accessed August 7, 2002.

Source

Paul Laurence Dunbar, "An Antebellum Sermon" (1895; reprinted in Richard A. Long and Eugenia W. Collier, eds., *African-American Writing: An Anthology of Prose and Poetry,* 220–22 [University Park and London: Pennsylvania State University Press, 1972]).

Selected Bibliography

Cunningham, Virginia. *Paul Laurence Dunbar and His Song.* New York: Dodd, Mead, 1947.

Jones, Gavin Roger. *Strange Talk: The Politics of Dialect Literature in Gilded Age America.* Berkeley: University of California Press, 1999.

Revell, Peter. *Paul Laurence Dunbar.* Boston: Twayne Publishers, 1979.

Wagner, Jean. *Black Poets of the United States: From Paul Laurence Dunbar to Langston Hughes.* Urbana: University of Illinois Press, 1973.

seven

Writings by Fenton Johnson

Although never a very popular writer, Fenton Johnson (1888–1958) has been acclaimed by critics, and his poetry is widely anthologized. As many scholars have noted, he was a transitional figure in black literature, writing after the turn of the century but before the Harlem Renaissance of the 1920s. Johnson was clearly influenced by Paul Laurence Dunbar, and he occasionally wrote in a distinctive black dialect. But Johnson was also influenced by the Romantic poets. In "Singing Hallelujia" and "My God in Heaven Said to Me," Johnson made literary use of the traditional African American spiritual.

Johnson was born in Chicago, and his first poem appeared in a local newspaper when he was only twelve years old. Later, he moved to New York City and studied at Columbia University's Journalism School. His major publications include *Visions of the Dusk* (1915), *Songs of the Soil* (1916), *For the Highest Good* (1920), and *Tales of Darkest America* (1920).

Singing Hallelujia
(A Negro Spiritual)

1

I went down to Jordan,[1]
Singing, "Hallelujia!",
I went down to Jordan
In the nighttime,
God of mine above me,
God of mine beneath me,
And the white robed angels
Singing, "Hallelujia!"

2

I looked up to Heaven,
Singing, "Hallelujia",
I looked up to Heaven
In the nighttime;
God poured down His mercy,
Christ poured down His loving,
And the choir of angels
Sang me, "Hallelujia!"

3

Threescore stood in Heaven,
Singing, "Hallelujia",
Threescore stood in Heaven
In the nighttime;
David[2] with his captains,
Jesus with His fishes,
And the white robed angels
Singing, "Hallelujia!"

4

Take me swift to Heaven,
Singing, "Hallelujia!"
Take me swift to Heaven
In the nighttime,

Seat me mid the lillies,
Crown me with the roses,
And let whiterobed angels
Sing me, "Hallelujia."

My God in Heaven Said to Me

1

My God in Heaven said to me,
"Your mansion's ready in the sky,
Come home, my weary wanderer,
And eat with Me the Bread of life,
For I have slain the fatted calf,
For I have filled the honey bowl
And thou shalt always dwell with me.
Come home, my weary wanderer,"
My God in Heaven said to me.

2

And now I board the Gospel train,
For I am going home to-night
To meet my God on Jordan's coast
My burdens to the wind I toss,
To-morrow freedom shall be mine;
A golden crown with burning stars,
And harp of David in my hand
That I may chant the Gospel tunes.

3

On God's plantation I shall dwell,
The overseer of happiness,
And dance with Israel[3] the dance
Of holiness and righteousness,
A thousand years with God to dwell
Is like a holiday below;
And Oh, my heart was glad to hear
My God in Heaven say to me,
"Your mansion's ready in the sky."

The Remnant

A Sermon

Brothers and sisters, being a duty-bound servant of God, I stand before you to-night. I am a little hoarse from a cold. But if you will bear with me a little while we will try to bring you a message of "Thus sayeth the Lord." If God is willing we will preach. The hellhounds are so swift on our trail we have to go sometime whether we feel like it or not. So we are here to-night to hear what the spirit has to say.

It always make my heart glad when I run back in my mind and see what a powerful God this is we serve. And every child . . . Pray with me a little while children—that has been borned of the spirit, I mean born until he can feel it, ought to feel proud that he is serving a captain who has never lost a battle, a God that can speak and man live, but utter his voice and man lay down and die. A God that controls play across the heaven. Oh, ain't He a powerful God? He stepped out on the scope of time one morning and declared 'I am God and there's none like me. I'm God and there is none before me. In my own appointed time I will visit the iniquities of the earth. I will cut down on the right and on the left. But a remnant I will save.' Ain't you glad, then, children that he always spares a remnant? Brothers (pray with me a little while), we must gird up our loins. We who are born of the spirit should cling close to the Master, for he has promised to be a shelter in the time of storm; a rock in a weary land. Listen at Him when He says 'behold I lay in Zion, a stone, a tried stone.' . . . What need have we to worry about earthly things. They are temporal and will fade away. But we, the born of God have laid hold on everlasting life. Every child that has had his soul delivered from death and hell (Pray with me brothers) stayed at hell's dark door until he got his orders is a traveler. His home is not in this world. He is but a sojourner in a weary land. Brothers! this being true we ought to love one another; we ought to be careful how we entertain strangers. If you neighbor mistreat you, do good for evil, for a-way by and by our God that sees all we do and hears all we say will come and woe be unto him that has offended one of these His "Little Ones." I know the way gets awful dark sometimes; and it looks like everything is against us, but listen what Job said, 'All the days of my appointed time I will wait on the Lord till my change comes! Sometimes we wake up in the dark hours of midnight, briny tears flowing down our checks (Ah, pray with me a little longer, Brothers). We cry and don't know what we are crying about. Brother, If you have been truly snatched from the greedy jaws of Hell, your feet taken out of the miry clay and placed on the rock, the sure foundation, you will shed tears sometime. You just feel like you want to run away somewhere. But listen at the Master when he says: 'Be still and know that I am God. I have heard your groans but I will not put on you a burden you cannot bear. We ought to rejoice and be glad for while some day they think, we know we have been born of God because we have felt His power, tasted His love, waited at Hell's dark door for orders, got a through ticket straight through from hell to heaven; we have seen the travel of our soul; He dressed us up, told us we were His children, sent us back into this low land of sorrows to tarry until one sweet day when He shall send the angels of death to bear our soul from this old earthly tabernacle and bear it back home to glory, I say back home because we been there once and every since that day we have been making our way back." "Brothers! A-ha! Glory to God! The Captain is on board now, Brothers. Sit still and hear the word of God, a-ha; away back, away back brothers, a-ha! Before the wind ever blowed, a-ha! Before the flying clouds, a-ha! Or before ever the earth was made, a-ha! Our god had us in mind. Ha! oh, brothers, oh brothers! Ha! ain't you glad then, a-ha! that our God, Ha! looked down through time one morning, a-ha! saw me and you, a-ha! ordained from the very beginning that we should be his children, a-ha! the work of His Almighty hand, a-ha! Old John the Revelator, a-ha! a-looking over yonder, a-ha! in bright glory, a-ha! Oh, what do you see, John! Ha! I see a number, a-ha! Who are these, a-ha! I heard the angel Gabriel when he answered, a-ha! 'These are they that come up through hard trials and great tribulations, a-ha! who washed their robes, a-ha! and made them white in the blood of the lamb, a-ha! They are now shouting around the throne of God, a-ha! Well, oh brothers! Oh, brothers! Ain't you glad that you have already been in the dressing room, had your everlasting garments fitted on and sandals on your feet. We born of God, a-ha! are shod for traveling, a-ha! Oh, Glory to God! It won't be long before some for us here, a-ha! will bid farewell, a-ha! take the wings of the morning, a-ha! where there'll be no more sin and sorrow, a-ha! no more weeping and mourning, a-ha! We can just walk around, brother, a-ha! Go over and shake hands with old Moses, a-ha! See Father Abraham, a-ha! Talk with Peter, Matthew, Luke and John, a-ha! And, Oh yes, Glory to God! we will want to see our Saviour, the Lamb that was slain, Ha! They tell me that His face outshines the sun, a-ha! but we can look on him, a-ha! because we will be like Him; and then oh brother, Oh brother, we will just fly from Cherubim to Cherubim, There with the angels we will eat off the welcome table, a-ha! Soon! Soon! we will all be gathered together over yonder. Brothers, ain't you glad you done died the sinner death and don't have to die no more. When we rise to fly that morning, we can fly with healing in our wings. . . . Now, if you don't hear my voice no more, a-ha! remember, I am a Hebrew child, a-ha! Just meet me over yonder, a-ha! on the other side of the River of Jordan, away back in the third heaven.

Notes

1. A river in Palestine. In the Bible, the Israelites crossed Jordan on their way to the Promised Land. Symbolically, Jordan is often understood as an entrance to heaven.

2. In the Bible, David was the king of the ancient Hebrews, successor of Saul, and one of the greatest Hebrew national heroes.
3. The Jewish or Hebrew people; figuratively the "chosen people" of God.

Source

Fenton Johnson, "Singing Hallelujia" and "My God in Heaven Said to Me," in Henry Louis Gates and Nellie Y. McCay, eds., *The Norton Anthology of African-American Literature,* 925–27 (New York and London: W. W. Norton, 1997).

Selected Bibliography

Johnson, Fenton. *For the Highest Good.* Chicago: The Favorite Magazine, 1920.
—— *A Little Dreaming.* College Park, Md.: McGrath, 1969.
—— *Tales of Darkest America.* Chicago: The Favorite Magazine, 1920.
Woolley, Lisa. *American Voices of the Chicago Renaissance.* DeKalb: Northern Illinois University Press, 2000.

eight

Go Down Death

Over the course of almost ten years, James Weldon Johnson (1871–1938) wrote his poetry collection *God's Trombones* (1927), which was influenced by his travels across the rural South. It consisted of seven "sermons," delivered by an African American preacher. Each of these poems make allusions to Biblical imagery, spirituals, and the rhythms and patterns of the black folk preacher.

Johnson was born in Jacksonville, Florida. He attended Atlanta University, and his first job after graduation was as a high school principal. In 1900, he wrote "Lift Every Voice and Sing,"—now known as the "Negro National Anthem"—to commemorate Abraham Lincoln's birthday. In 1906 he took a post as U.S. consul to Venezuela, and in 1912 he published the novel *Autobiography of an Ex-Colored Man* under a pseudonym. In 1920 he became the national organizer for the NAACP.

A Funeral Sermon

Weep not, weep not,
She is not dead;

She's resting in the bosom of Jesus.
Heart-broken husband—weep no more;
Grief-stricken son—weep no more;
Left-lonesome daughter—weep no more;
She's only just gone home.

Day before yesterday morning,
God was looking down from his great, high heaven,
Looking down on all his children,
And his eye fell on Sister Caroline,
Tossing on her bed of pain.
And God's big heart was touched with pity,
With the everlasting pity.

And God sat back on his throne,
And he commanded that tall, bright angel standing at his right hand:
Call me Death!
And that tall, bright angel cried in a voice
That broke like a clap of thunder:
Call Death!—Call Death!
And the echo sounded down the streets of heaven
Till it reached away back to that shadowy place,
Where Death waits with his pale, white horses.

And Death heard the summons,
And he leaped on his fastest horse,
Pale as a sheet in the moonlight.
Up the golden street Death galloped,
And the hoofs of his horse struck fire from the gold,
But they didn't make no sound.
Up Death rode to the Great White Throne,
And waited for God's command.

And God said: Go down, Death, go down,
Go down to Savannah, Georgia,
Down in Yamacraw,
And find Sister Caroline.
She's borne the burden and heat of the day,
She's labored long in my vineyard,
And she's tired—
She's weary—
Go down, Death, and bring her to me.

And Death didn't say a word,
But he loosed the reins on his pale, white horse,
And he clamped the spurs to his bloodless sides,
And out and down he rode,
Through heaven's pearly gates,
Past suns and moons and stars;
On Death rode,
And the foam from his horse was like a comet in the sky;
On Death rode,
Leaving the lightning's flash behind;
Straight on down he came.

While we were watching round her bed,
She turned her eyes and looked away,
She saw what we couldn't see:
She saw Old Death. She saw Old Death
Coming like a falling star.
But Death didn't frighten Sister Caroline;
He looked to her like a welcome friend.
And she whispered of us: I'm going home,
And she smiled and closed her eyes.

And Death took her up like a baby,
And she lay in his icy arms,
But she didn't feel no chill.
And Death began to ride again—
Up beyond the evening star,
Out beyond the morning star,
Into the glittering light of glory,
On to the Great White Throne.
And there he laid Sister Caroline
On the loving breast of Jesus.

And Jesus took his own hand and wiped away her tears,
And he smoothed the furrows from her face,
And the angels sang a little song.
And Jesus rocked her in his arms,
And kept a-saying: Take your rest,
Take your rest, take your rest.

Weep not—weep not,
She is not dead;
She's resting in the bosom of Jesus.

Source

James Weldon Johnson, "Go Down Death," in *God's Trombones,* 27–31 (New York: Viking Press, a division of Penguin-Putnam USA, 1927).

Selected Bibliography

Fleming, Robert E. *James Weldon Johnson.* Boston: Twayne, 1987.

Hubbard, Dolan. *The Sermon and the African-American Literary Imagination.* Columbia: University of Missouri Press, 1994.

Levy, Eugene D. *James Weldon Johnson, Black Leader, Black Voice.* Chicago: University of Chicago Press, 1973.

Price, Kenneth M. and Lawrence J. Oliver, eds. *Critical Essays on James Weldon Johnson.* New York: G.K. Hall; London: Prentice Hall International, 1997.

n i n e

Faith Hasn't Got No Eyes

Zora Neale Hurston's "Faith Hasn't Got No Eyes" is a widely anthologized sermon. It was delivered by the fictional character John Pearson in the climactic chapter in her novel *Jonah's Gourd Vine*. Following the sermon, Pearson stormed out of the church, arguing that churchgoers should not accept a pastor who was less than perfect: "Dey's ready fuh uh preacher tuh be uh man uhmongts men," he said, "but dey ain't ready yet fuh 'im to be uh man uhmongst women."

Hurston's birth date has been the topic of some contention; because there is no official record of her birth, dates range between 1891 and 1910. She was raised in Eatonville, Florida, which was incorporated in 1886 as the first self-governed all-black city in America. Her father had worked as a carpenter, mayor, and moderator of the South Florida Baptist Association. Her mother died when she was nine years old; Hurston left home by the age of fourteen.

Hurston attended high school at Morgan Academy; she later enrolled in Howard University in 1918, where she met her first husband, Herbert Sheen. She later became Barnard College's first black student and studied under Franz Boaz, "the father of anthropology." Today her reputation rests on her work as a collector of black folklore with such works as *Mules and Men* (1935) and *Tell My Horse* (1938) and as the author of *Jonah's Gourd Vine* (1934) and *Their Eyes Were Watching God* (1937). Some artists such as Langston Hughes have criticized her dependence on white patronage and her characterization of black people as childlike primitives; white critics typically lauded her works. At the height of her career in 1942, Hurston wrote *Dust Tracks on a Road,* her autobiography, which appeared in *Saturday Review*. By 1950 she worked as a maid in Miami, and she died in relative obscurity in Fort Pierce, Florida, in 1960.

Faith hasn't got no eyes, but she long-legged
But take de spy-glass of Faith
And look into dat upper room
When you are alone to yourself,
When yo' heart is burnt with fire, ha!
When de blood is lopin' thru yo' veins
Like de iron monasters (monsters) on de rail
Look into dat upper chamber, ha!
We notice at de supper table
As He gazed upon His friends, ha!
His eyes flowin' wid tears, ha! He said
"My soul is exceedingly sorrowful unto death, ha!
For this night, ha!
One of you shall betray me, ha!
It were not a Roman officer, ha!
It were not a centurion
But one of you
Who I have chosen my bosom friend
That sops in the dish with me shall betray me."
I want to draw a parable.
I see Jesus
Leaving heben with all of His grandeur
Dis-robin' Hisself of His matchless honor
Yielding up de scepler of revolvin' worlds
Clothing Hisself in de garment of humanity
Coming into de world to rescue His friends.
Two thousand years have went by on their rusty ankles
But with the eye of faith, I can see Him
Look down from his high tower of elevation
I can hear Him when He walks about the golden streets
I can hear'em ring under His footsteps
Sol me-e-e-, Sol do

Sol me-e-e, Sol do
I can hear Him step out upon the rim bones of nothing
Crying I am de way
De truth and de light
Ah!
God A'mighty!
I see Him grab de throttle
Of de well ordered train of mercy
I see kingdoms crush and crumble
Whilst de archangels held de winds in de corner chambers
I see Him arrive on dis earth
And walk de streets thirty and three years
Oh-h-hhh!
I see Him walking beside de sea of Galilee wid His disciples
This declaration gendered on His lips
"Let us go on to the other side."
God A'mighty!
Dey entered de boat
Wid their oarus (oars) stuck in de back
Sails unfurled to de evenin' breeze
And de ship was now sailin'
As she reached de center of de lake
Jesus was sleep on a pillow in de rear of de boat
And de dynamic powers of nature became disturbed
And de mad winds broke de heads of de Western drums
And fell down on de lake of Galilee
And buried themselves behind de gallopin' waves
And de white-caps marbilized themselves like an army

And walked out like soldiers goin' to battle
And de zig-zag lightning
Licked out her fiery tongue
And de flying clouds
Threw their wings in the channels of the deep
And bedded de waters like a road-plow
And faced de current of de chargin' billows
And de terrific bolts of thunder-they bust in de clouds
And de ship begin to reel and rock
God A'mighty!
And one of de disciples called Jesus
"Master! Carest Thou not that we perish?"
And He arose
And de storm was in its pitch

And de lightnin' played on His raiments as He stood on de prow of the boat
And placed His foot upon de neck of the storm
And spoke to the howlin' winds
And de sea fell at His feet like a marble floor
And de thunders went back in their vault
Then He set down on de rim of de ship
And took de hooks of His power
And lifted de billows in His lap
And rocked de winds to sleep on His arm
And said, "Peace, be still."
And de Bible says there was a calm.

Source

Zora Neale Hurston, *Jonah's Gourd Vine,* 274–81 (New York: Perennial Library, a division of Harper & Row, 1990).

Selected Bibliography

Cronin, Gloria L, ed. *Critical Essays on Zora Neale Hurston.* New York: G.K. Hall, 1998.

Hemenway, Robert E. *Zora Neale Hurston: A Literary Biography.* Urbana: University of Illinois Press, 1977.

Hollaway, Karla F. C. *The Character of the Word: The Texts of Zora Neale Hurston.* New York: Greenwood Press, 1987.

Hurston, Zora Neale. *Dust Tracks on a Road: An Autobiography.* New York: Harper-Perennial, 1991.

—— *Their Eyes Were Watching God.* New York: HarperPerennial, 1998.

Meisenhelder, Susan Edwards, *Hitting a Straight Lick with a Crooked Stick: Race and Gender in the Works of Zora Neale Hurston.* Tuscaloosa: University of Alabama Press, 1999.

ten

Salvation

Often called the "Shakespeare of Harlem," Langston Hughes (1902–1967) was one of the foremost figures of the Harlem Renaissance, in part because his poetry expressed the thought and language of the common, everyday residents of Harlem and because it responded to black folk music (especially jazz and the blues). In this short essay, reprinted from his autobiography *The Big Sea* (1940), Hughes described his childhood ambivalence about religion, which was made all the more difficult by his family's close connections to the church.

Hughes was born in Joplin, Missouri, and spent part of his childhood in Lawrence, Kansas. After graduating from high school, he attended Columbia University. However, Hughes was disappointed with his formal education, so he dropped out and traveled widely in Africa and Europe. His poetry appeared in the *Crisis* and the *Amsterdam News* in the early 1920s.

I was saved from sin when I was going on thirteen. But not really saved. It happened like this. There was a big revival at my Auntie Reed's church. Every night for weeks there had been much preaching, singing, praying, and shouting, and some very hardened sinners had been brought to Christ, and the membership of the church had grown by leaps and bounds. Then just before the revival ended, they held a special meeting for children, "to bring the young lambs to the fold." My aunt spoke of it for days ahead. That night I was escorted to the front row and placed on the mourners' bench with all the other young sinners, who had not yet been brought to Jesus.

My aunt told me that when you were saved you saw a light, and something happened to you inside! And Jesus came into your life! And God was with you from then on! She said you could see and hear and feel Jesus in your soul. I believed her. I had heard a great many old people say the same thing and it seemed to me they ought to know. So I sat there calmly in the hot, crowded church, waiting for Jesus to come to me.

The preacher preached a wonderful rhythmical sermon, all moans and shouts and lonely cries and dire pictures of hell, and then he sang a song about the ninety and nine safe in the fold, but one little lamb was left out in the cold. Then he said: "Won't you come? Won't you come to Jesus? Young lambs, won't you come?" And he held out his arms to all us young sinners there on the mourners' bench. And the little girls cried. And some of them jumped up and went to Jesus right away. But most of us just sat there.

A great many old people came and knelt around us and prayed, old women with jet-black faces and braided hair, old men with work-gnarled hands. And the church sang a song about the lower lights are burning, some poor sinners to be saved. And the whole building rocked with prayer and song.

Still I kept waiting to *see* Jesus.

Finally all the young people had gone to the altar and were saved, but one boy and me. He was a rounder's son named Westley. Westley and I were surrounded by sisters and deacons praying. It was very hot in the church, and getting late now. Finally Westley said to me in a whisper: "God damn! I'm tired o' sitting here. Let's get up and be saved." So he got up and was saved.

Then I was left all alone on the mourners' bench. My aunt came and knelt at my knees and cried, while prayers and songs swirled all around me in the little church. The whole congregation prayed for me alone, in a mighty wail of moans and voices. And I kept waiting serenely for Jesus, waiting, waiting—but he didn't come. I wanted to see him, but nothing happened to me. Nothing! I wanted something to happen to me, but nothing happened.

I heard the songs and the minister saying: "Why don't you come? My dear child, why don't you come to Jesus? Jesus is waiting for you. He wants you. Why don't you come? Sister Reed, what is this child's name?"

"Langston," my aunt sobbed.

"Langston, why don't you come? Why don't you come and be saved? Oh, Lamb of God! Why don't you come?"

Now it was really getting late. I began to be ashamed of myself, holding everything up so long. I began to wonder what God thought about Westley, who certainly hadn't seen Jesus either, but who was now sitting proudly on the platform, swinging his knickerbockered legs and grinning down at me, surrounded by deacons and old women on their knees praying. God had not struck Westley dead for taking his name in vain or for lying in the temple. So I decided that maybe to save further trouble, I'd better lie, too, and say that Jesus had come, and get up and be saved.

So I got up.

Suddenly the whole room broke into a sea of shouting, as they saw me rise. Waves of rejoicing swept the place. Women leaped in the air. My aunt threw her arms around me. The minister took me by the hand and led me to the platform.

When things quieted down, in a hushed silence, punctuated by a few ecstatic "Amens," all the new young lambs were blessed in the name of God. Then joyous singing filled the room.

That night, for the last time in my life but one—for I was a big boy twelve years old—I cried. I cried, in bed alone, and couldn't stop. I buried my head under the quilts, but my aunt heard me. She woke up and told my uncle I was crying because the Holy Ghost had come into my life, and because I had seen Jesus. But I really crying because I couldn't bear to tell her that I had lied, that I had deceived everybody in the church, that I hadn't seen Jesus, and that now I didn't believe there was a Jesus any more, since he didn't come to help me.

Source

Langston Hughes, "Salvation," in *The Big Sea,* 18–21 (New York: Alfred A. Knopf, 1940).

Selected Bibliography

Emanuel, James A. *Langston Hughes*. New York: Twayne, 1967.

Gates, Henry Louis and K. A. Appiah. *Langston Hughes: Critical Perspectives Past and Present.* New York: Penguin, 1993.

Hughes, Langston. *The Langston Hughes Reader.* New York: G. Braziller, 1958.

—— *Selected Poems of Langston Hughes.* New York: Vintage, 1990.

Miller, R. Baxter. *The Art and Imagination of Langston Hughes.* Lexington: University of Kentucky Press, 1989.

eleven

The Most Durable Power

Martin Luther King Jr. (1929–1968) remains one of the most revered figures of the twentieth century. The passage below is an excerpt from a sermon that King delivered in November 1956, just one week before the bus boycott won a victory in the U.S. Supreme Court. The sermon was significant because it displayed King's great ability to channel Christian religion into a secular political struggle.

King was born and raised in Atlanta, Georgia, as part of a family that had long played a prominent role in their community's religious life. At age fifteen he started attending Morehouse College, and after graduating in1948 he attended Crozer Theological Seminary and then Boston University, where he received his Ph.D. in theology in 1955. He played a leading role in the civil rights movement, beginning with the Montgomery Bus Boycott in 1955, until his death by assassination in 1968.

Always be sure that you struggle with Christian methods and Christian weapons. Never succumb to the temptation of becoming bitter. As you press on for justice, be sure to move with dignity and discipline, using only the weapon of love. Let no man pull you so low as to hate him. Always avoid violence. If you succumb to the temptation of using violence in your struggle, unborn generations will be the recipients of a long and desolate night of bitterness, and your chief legacy to the future will be an endless reign of meaningless chaos.

In your struggle for justice, let your oppressor know that you are not attempting to defeat or humiliate him, or even to pay him back for injustices that he has heaped upon you. Let him know that you are merely seeking justice for him as well as yourself. Let him know that the festering sore of segregation debilitates the white man as well as the Negro. With this attitude you will be able to keep your struggle on high Christian standards.

Many persons will realize the urgency of seeking to eradicate the evil of segregation. There will be many Negroes who will devote their lives to the cause of freedom. There will be many white persons of good will and strong moral sensitivity who will dare to take a stand for justice. Honesty impels me to admit that such a stand will require willingness to suffer and sacrifice. So don't despair if you are condemned and persecuted for righteousness' sake. Whenever you take a stand for truth and justice, you are liable to scorn. Often you will be called an impractical idealist or a dangerous radical. Sometimes it might mean going to jail. If such is the case you must honorable grace the jail with your presence. It might even mean physical death. But if physical death is the price that some must pay to free their children from a permanent life of psychological death, then nothing could be more Christian.

I still believe that standing up for the truth of God is the greatest thing in the world. This is the end of life. The end of life is not to be happy. The end of life is not to achieve pleasure and avoid pain. The end of life is to do the will of God, come what may.

I still believe that love is the most durable power in the world. Over the centuries men have sought to discover the highest good. This has been the chief quest of ethical philosophy. This was one of the big questions of Greek philosophy. The Epicureans[1] and the Stoics[2] sought to answer it; Plato[3] and Aristotle[4] sought to answer it. What is the *summum bonum* of life? I think I have discovered the highest good. It is love. This principle stands at the center of the cosmos. As John says, "God is love." He who loves is a participant in the being of God. He who hates does not know God.

Notes

1. Disciples of Epictetus (c. A.D. 50–c.138), Phrygian Stoic philosopher, once a slave.
2. Adherents of stoicism, a school of thought that held that all reality is material but is shaped by a universal working force (God) that pervades everything. Only by putting aside passion, unjust thoughts, and indulgence, and by performing one's duty with the right disposition can a person live consistently with nature and thus achieve true freedom.
3. Plato (c. 427–c.347 B.C.), Greek philosopher.
4. Aristotle (c. 382–c.322 B.C.), Greek philosopher.

Source

Martin Luther King Jr., "The Most Durable Power," *Christian Century* 74 (June 1957): 708; reprinted in James Melvin Washington, ed., *Testament of Hope: The Essential Writings and Speeches of Martin Luther King*, 10–11 (New York: HarperCollins, 1986).

Selected Bibliography

Baldwin, Lewis V. *There Is a Balm in Gilead: The Cultural Roots of Martin Luther King, Jr.* Minneapolis: Fortress Press, 1991.

Branch, Taylor. *Parting the Waters: America in the King Years, 1954–1963.* New York: Simon & Schuster, 1988.

—— *Pillar of Fire: America in the King Years, 1963–1965.* New York: Simon & Schuster, 1998.

Colaiaco, James A. *Martin Luther King, Jr.: Apostle of Militant Nonviolence.* New York: St. Martin's Press, 1993.

Garrow, David. *Bearing the Cross: Martin Luther King, Jr. and the Southern Christian Leadership Conference.* New York: W. Morrow, 1986.

Lischer, Richard. *The Preacher King: Martin Luther King, Jr. and the Word That Moved America.* New York: Oxford University Press, 1995.

twelve

Black Theology and Black Power

James H. Cone is known as the father of black theology, writing his groundbreaking work, *A Black Theology of Liberation,* in 1970. He is the Charles A. Briggs Distinguished Professor of Systematic Theology at Union Theological Seminary in New York City. In the following excerpt, Cone finds theological support for the Black Power movement in Christianity. His work has influenced Latin American liberation theology and black theology in South Africa.

Born in Fordyce, Arkansas, on August 5, 1938, Cone was strongly influenced by his father, a local activist, and his mother, a public speaker in the African Methodist Episcopal Church. He completed his undergraduate work at Philander Smith College in 1958 and enrolled in the Garrett Biblical Institute (later the Garrett Evangelical Theological Seminary) where, despite its racially biased environment, he received his B.A. in 1961. He then received M.A. and Ph.D. from Northwestern University in 1963 and 1965. He is the author of many books, including *Black Theology and Black Power* (1969) and *Martin & Malcolm & America: A Dream or a Nightmare?* (1991). In 1994 he was presented with the American Black Achievement Award in the category of religion from *Ebony* magazine.

Christ, Black Power, and Freedom

An even more radical understanding of the relationship of the gospel to Black Power is found in the concept of freedom. We have seen that freedom stands at the center of the black man's earning in America. "Freedom Now" has been and still is the echoing slogan of all civil rights groups. The same concept of freedom is presently expressed among Black Power advocates by such phrases as "self-determination" and "self-identity."

What is this freedom for which blacks have marched, boycotted, picketed, and rebelled in order to achieve? Simply stated, freedom is *not doing what I will but becoming what I should. A man is free when he sees clearly the fulfillment of his being and is thus capable of making the envisioned self a reality.* This is "Black Power!" They want the grip of white power removed what black people have in mind when they cry, "Freedom Now!" now and forever.

Is this not why God became man in Jesus Christ so that man might become what he is? Is not this at least a part of what St. Paul had in mind when he said, "For freedom, Christ has set us free" (Gal. 5:1)? As long as man is a slave to another power, he is not free to serve God with mature responsibility. He is not free to become what he is—human.

Freedom is indeed what distinguishes man from animals and plants. "In the case of animals and plants nature not only appoints the destiny but it alone carries it out.... In the case of man, however, nature provides only the destiny and leaves it to him to carry it out." Black Power means black people carrying out their own destiny.

It would seem that Black Power and Christianity have this in common: the liberation of man! If the work of Christ is that of liberating men from alien loyalties, and if racism is, as George Kelsey[1] says, an alien faith, then there must be some correlation between Black Power and Christianity. For the gospel proclaims that God is with us now, actively fighting the forces which would make man captive. And it is the task of theology and the Church to know where God is at work so that we can join him in this fight against evil. In America we know where the evil is. We know that men are shot and lynched. We know that men are crammed into ghettos. Black Power is the power to say No; it is the power of blacks to refuse to cooperate in their own dehumanization. If blacks can trust the message of Christ, if they can take him at his word, this power to say No to white power and domination is derived from him.

Looking at the New Testament, the message of the gospel is clear: Christ came into the world in order to destroy the works of Satan (I John 3:8). His whole life was a deliberate offensive against those powers which held man captive. At the beginning of his ministry there was a conflict with Satan in the wilderness (Luke 4:1-13; Mark 1:12ff.; Matt. 4:1-11), and this conflict continued throughout his ministry. In fact, every exorcism was a binding and despoiling of the evil one (Mark 3:27). It was not until Christ's death on the cross that the decisive battle was fought and won by the Son of man. In that event, the tyranny of Satan, in principle, came to an end. The Good News is that God in Christ has freed us; we need no longer be enslaved by alien forces. The battle was fought and won on Good Friday and the triumph was revealed to men at Easter.

Though the decisive battle against evil has been fought and won, the war, however, is not over. Men of the new age know that they are free, but they must never lose sight of the tension between the "now" and the "not yet" which characterizes this present age (II Tim. 1:10; Eph. 1:22; Heb. 2:8, 10:13). The crucial battle has been won already on the cross, but the campaign is not over. There is a constant battle between Christ and Satan, and it is going on now.

If we make this message contemporaneous with our own life situation, what does Christ's defeat of Satan mean for us? There is no need here to get bogged down with quaint personifications of Satan. Men are controlled by evil powers that would make them slaves. The demonic forces of racism are *real* for the black man. Theologically, Malcolm X[2] was not far wrong when he called the white man "the devil." The white structure of this American society, personified in every racist, must be at least part of what the New Testament meant by the demonic forces. According to the New Testament, these powers can get hold of a man's total being and can control his life to such a degree that he is incapable of distinguishing himself from the alien power. This seems to be what has happened to white racism in America. It is a part of the spirit of the age, the ethos of the culture, so embedded in the social, economic, and political structure that white society is incapable of knowing its destructive nature. There is only one response: Fight it!

Moreover, it seems to me that it is quite obvious who is actually engaged in the task of liberating black people from the power of white racism, even at the expense of their lives. They are men who stand unafraid of the structures of white racism. They are men who risk their lives for the inner freedom of others. They are men who embody the spirit of Black Power. And if Christ is present today actively risking all for the freedom of man, he must be acting through the most radical elements of Black Power.

Ironically, and this is what white society also fails to understand, the man who enslaves another enslaves himself. Unrestricted freedom is a form of slavery. To be "free" to do what I will in relation to another is to be in bondage to the law of least resistance. This is the bondage of racism. Racism is that bondage in which whites are free to beat, rape, or kill blacks. About thirty years ago it was quite acceptable to lynch a black man by hanging him from a tree; but today whites destroy him by crowding him into the ghetto and letting fifth and despair put the final touches on death. Whites are thus enslaved to their own egos. Therefore, when blacks assert their freedom in self-determination, whites too are liberated. They must now confront the black man as a person.

In our analysis of freedom, we should not forget what many existentialists call the burden of freedom. Authentic freedom has nothing to do with the rugged individualism of *laissez faire*,[3] the right of the businessman to pursue without restraint the profit motive or the pleasure principle which is extolled by Western capitalistic democracies. On the contrary, authentic freedom is grounded in the awareness of the universal finality of man and the agonizing responsibility of choosing between perplexing alternatives regarding his existence.

Therefore, freedom cannot be taken for granted. A life of freedom is not the easy or happy way of life. That is why Sartre[4] says man "is condemned to freedom." Freedom is not a trivial birthday remembrance but, in the words of Dostoevsky's[5] Grand Inquisitor, "a terrible gift." It is not merely an opportunity but a temptation. Whether or not we agree with the existentialists' tendency to make man totally autonomous, they are right in their emphasis on the burden of freedom.

In the New Testament, the burden of freedom is described in terms of being free from the law. To be free in Christ means that man is stripped of the law as a guarantee of salvation and is placed in a free, mature love-relationship with God and man, which is man's destiny and in which Christ is the pioneer. Christian freedom means being a slave for Christ in order to do his will. Again this is no easy life; it is a life of suffering because the world and Christ are in constant conflict. To be free in Christ is to be against the world.

With reference, then, to freedom in Christ, three assertions about Black Power can be made: First, the work of Christ is essentially a liberating work, directed toward and by the oppressed. Black Power embraces that very task. Second, Christ in liberating the wretched of the earth also liberates those responsible for the wretchedness. The oppressor is also freed of his peculiar demons. Black Power in shouting Yes to black humanness and No to white oppression is exorcising demons on both sides of the conflict. Third, mature freedom is burdensome and risky, producing anxiety and conflict for free men and for the brittle structures they challenge. The call for Black Power is precisely the call to shoulder the burden of liberty in Christ, risking everything to live not as slaves but as free men.

The Righteousness of God and Black Power

To demand freedom is to demand justice. When there is no justice in the land, a man's freedom is threatened. Freedom and justice are interdependent. When a man has no protection under the law, it is difficult for him to make others recognize him, and thus his freedom to be a "Thou" is placed in jeopardy. Therefore it is understandable that freedom and justice are probably the most often repeated words when the black man is asked, "What do you want?" The answer is simple, freedom and justice—no more and no less.

Unfortunately, many whites pretend that they do not understand what the black man is demanding. Theologians and churchmen have been of little help in this matter because much of their intellectualizing has gone into analyzing the idea of God's righteousness in a fashion far removed from the daily experiences of men. They fail to give proper emphasis to another equally if not more important concern, namely, the biblical idea of God's righteousness as the divine decision to vindicate the poor, the needy, and the helpless in society. It seems that much of this abstract theological disputation and speculation—the favorite pastime for many theological societies—serves as a substitute for relevant involvement in a world where men die for lack of political justice. A black theologian wants to know what the gospel has to say to a man who is jobless and cannot get work to support his family because the society is unjust. He wants to know what is God's Word to the countless black boys and girls who are fatherless and motherless because white society decreed that blacks have no rights. Unless there is a word from Christ to the helpless, then why should they respond to him? How do we relate the gospel of Christ to people whose daily existence is one of hunger or even worse, despair? Or do we simply refer them to the next world?

The key to the answer, in the thinking of the black theologian, is in the biblical concept of the righteousness of God. According to the Bible, God and not man is the author of justice; and since justice is a part of the Being of God, he is bound to do justly. Whatever God does must be *just* because he is justice.

It is important to note that God's righteousness refers not so much to an abstract quality related to his Being in the realm of thought—as commonly found in Greek philosophy—but to his activity in human history, in the historical events of the time and effecting his purpose despite those who oppose it. This is the biblical tradition. Israel as a people initially came to know God through the exodus. It was Yahweh who emancipated her from Egyptian bondage and subsequently established a covenant with her at Sinai, promising: "You have seen what *I did* to the Egyptians, and how I bore you on eagles' wings and brought you to myself. Now therefore, if you will obey my voice and keep my covenant, you shall be my own possession among all peoples; . . . You shall be to me a kingdom of priests and a holy nation" (Exod. 19:4–6). Divine righteousness means that God will be faithful to his promise, that his purposes for Israel will not be thwarted. Israel, therefore, need not worry about her weakness and powerlessness in a world of mighty military powers, "for all the earth is mine" (Exod. 19:5). The righteousness of God means that he will protect her from the ungodly menacing of other nations. Righteousness means God is doing justice, that he is putting right what men have made wrong.

It is significant to note the condition of the people to whom God chose to reveal his righteousness. God elected to be the Helper and Saviour to people oppressed and powerless in contrast to the proud and mighty nations. It is also equally important to notice that within Israel, his righteousness is on behalf of the poor, defenseless, and unwanted. "If God is going to see righteousness established in the land, he himself must be particularly active as the helper of the fatherless' (Ps. 10:14) to 'deliver the needy when he crieth; and the poor that hath no helper' (Ps. 72:12)." His vindication is for the poor because they are defenseless before the wicked and powerful. "For this reason," writes Barth, "in the relations and events in the life of his people, God always takes his stand unconditionally and passionately on this side alone: against the lofty and on behalf of the lowly; against those who already enjoy right and privilege and on behalf of those who are denied it and deprived of it." This is certainly the message of the eighth-century prophets—Amos, Hosea, Isaiah, and Micah. Being ethical prophets, concerned with social justice, they proclaimed Yahweh's intolerance with the rich, who, as Amos says, "trample the head of the poor into the dust of the earth" (2:7) and "sell the righteous for silver, and the needy for a pair of shoes" (2:6). God unquestionably will vindicate the poor.

And if we can trust the New Testament, God became man in Jesus Christ in order that the poor might have the gospel preached to them; that the poor might have the Kingdom of God (Luke 6:20); that those who hunger might be satisfied; that those who weep might laugh.

If God is to be true to himself, his righteousness must be directed to the helpless and the poor, those who can expect no security from this world. The rich, the secure, the suburbanite can have no part of God's righteousness because of their trust and dependence on the things of this world. "God's righteousness triumphs when man has no means of triumphing." His righteousness is reserved for those who come empty-handed, without any economic, political, or social power. That is why the prophets and Jesus were so critical of the economically secure. Their security gets in the way of absolute faith in God. "Earthly possessions dazzle our eyes and delude us into thinking that they can provide security and freedom from anxiety. Yet all the time they are the very source of all anxiety."

What, then, is God's Word of righteousness to the poor and the helpless? "I became poor in Christ in order that man may not be poor. I am in the ghetto where rats and disease threaten the very existence of my people, and they can be assured that I have not forgotten my promise to them. *My righteousness will vindicate your suffering!* Remember, I know the meaning of rejection because in Christ I was rejected; the meaning of physical pain because I was crucified; the meaning of death because I died. But my resurrection in Christ means that alien powers cannot keep you from the full meaning of life's existence as found in Christ. Even now the Kingdom is available to you. Even now I am present with you because your suffering is my suffering, and I will not let the wicked triumph." This is God's Word.

Those who wish to share in this divine righteousness must become poor without any possibility of procuring right for themselves. "The righteousness of the believer consists in the fact that God acts for him—utterly, because he cannot plead his own case and no one else can represent him." The men of faith come to God because they can go to no one else. He, and he alone, is their security.

It is within this context that men should be reminded of the awesome political responsibility which follows from justification by faith. To be made righteous through Christ places a man in the situation where he too, like Christ, must be for the poor, for God, and against the world. As Barth puts it:

> . . . there follows from this character of faith a political attitude, decisively determined by the fact that man is made responsible to all those who are poor and wretched in his eyes, that he is summoned on his part to espouse the cause of those who suffer wrong. Why? Because in them it is manifested to him what he himself is in the sight of God; because the living, gracious, merciful action of God towards him consists in the fact that God himself in his own righteousness procures right for him, the poor and wretched; because he and all men stand in the presence of God as those for whom right can be procured only by God himself. The man who lives by the faith that this is true stands under a political responsibility.

No Christian can evade this responsibility. He cannot say that the poor are in poverty because they will not work, or they suffer because they are lazy. Having come before God as nothing and being received by him into his Kingdom through grace, the Christian should know that he has been made righteous (justified) so that he can join God in the fight for justice. Therefore, whoever fights for the poor, fights for God; whoever risks his life for the helpless and unwanted, risks his life for God. God is active now in the lives of those men who feel an absolute identification with all who suffer because there is no justice in the land.

Notes

1. George Kelsey, author of *Racism and the Christian Understanding of Man* (1965).
2. Malcolm X (1925–1965), African American religious and political leader.
3. Literally, "leave alone." In economics and politics, laissez faire is a doctrine holding that an economic system functions best when there is no interference from government.
4. Jean Paul Sartre (1905–1980), French philosopher and author; a leading exponent of existentialism.
5. Fyodor Mikhailovich Dostoyevsky (1821–1881), Russian novelist; one of the towering figures of world literature.

Source

James Cone, *Black Theology and Black Power* (New York: Seabury Press, 1969), 38–43.

Selected Bibliography

Burrow, Rufus. *James H. Cone and Black Liberation Theology.* Jefferson, N.C.: McFarland, 1994.

Chapman, Mark L. *Christianity on Trial: African-American Religious Thought Before and after Black Power.* Maryknoll, N.Y.: Orbis Books, 1996.

Cone, James H. and Gayraud S. Wilmore. *Black Theology: A Documentary History.* Maryknoll, N.Y.: Orbis Books, 1993.

—— *Black Theology and Black Power.* New York: Seabury Press, 1969.

Kunnie, Julian. *Models of Black Theology: Issues in Class, Culture and Gender.* Valley Forge, Penn.: Trinity Press International, 1994.

thirteen

The Black Church and Socialist Politics

Cornel West (1953–) was born in Tulsa, Oklahoma, on June 2, 1953, the grandson of the Reverend Clifton L. West Sr., pastor of the Tulsa Metropolitan Baptist Church. West's father, Clifton L. West Jr., was a civilian Air Force administrator, whereas his mother, Irene Bias West, was an elementary school teacher and principal. West's first political experiences included marching with his family in a civil rights demonstration in Sacramento, California, and coordinating a strike with three high school friends in order to demand courses in black studies. The young West drew inspiration from Malcolm X, the Black Panther Party, and theologian James Cone.

West went on to earn his B.A. at Harvard University, where he graduated in three years at the head of his class. He then attained a graduate degree in philosophy from Princeton University. He has taught at a number of colleges and universities including Princeton Theological Seminary, Union Theological Seminary, Harvard Divinity School, and the University of Paris.

West is an academic as well as an activist. He published the following essay in 1984 while teaching at Yale. There, West participated in a demonstration to establish clerical unionism and to protest the school's investments in South African companies. He was arrested and jailed; Yale subsequently punished West by requiring him to teach full time in lieu of a planned leave to teach at the University of Paris. West decided to fulfill both of his teaching obligations and commuted between schools, teaching a total of five courses.

Notwithstanding the powerful forces of urbanization and industrialization, the vast majority of Afro-Americans remain religious. Besides the significant though marginal presence of Islam, this religious hold over Black people takes the form of an evangelical Protestant Christianity. Like all religious ideologies, this Protestant Christianity is politically ambiguous; that is, it possesses a conservative priestly pole and a progressive prophetic pole. Yet the distinctive feature of Afro-American Christianity has been its capacity to make visible and potent its progressive prophetic pole. Nat Turner, Denmark Vesey and Gabriel Prosser—Christian preachers who led slave insurrections in the 19th century—signify in dramatic fashion the crucial role of the Black Church in the Afro-American struggle for freedom. In stark contrast with other Africans in the Western Hemisphere, Black Americans have had relative control over their churches, thereby facilitating a creative fusion of religious transcendence and political opposition, belief in God and liberation themes, faith in the ultimate trustworthiness of human existence and negation of the racism in the prevailing social order. In short, the African appropriation of Christianity under conditions of slavery in the U.S.A., the land of freedom and opportunity in the eyes of many, produces a unique version of Christianity with strong prophetic tendencies.

This Afro-American Christianity serves as the major resource upon which Black people draw strength and sustenance in their encounter with the modern American capitalist order—as urban dwellers, industrial workers, bureaucratic employees and franchised citizens. It is no accident that even this modern status results, in part, from the political struggles waged by the Civil Rights Movement led by the Rev. Martin Luther King. Jr. which drew its cultural potency from the Black Church. Even the major religious rival of Afro-American Christianity, Islam, was promoted by a former Black Christian preacher turned Muslim, the late Honorable Elijah Muhammed, and Malcolm X, the son of a Black Christian minister.

The prophetic tradition of the Black Church is worth taking seriously not simply because of its important role in the Black freedom movement, but also because it may highlight some of the cultural problems now besetting the Left in the modern West. The inability of the Left, especially in the U.S.A., to deal adequately with the crucial issues of everyday life such as racism, sexism, ecology, sexual orientation, and personal despair may indeed have something to do with its refusal to grapple with the complex role and function of religion. Needless to say, since the majority of American people remain religious in some form or other, the American Left (Black or white) ignores religious and cultural issues at its own peril.

Yet the question of whether the Black Church can meet the challenges of the prevailing crisis in Black America continues to haunt prophetic Black religious leaders. And, despite the expansion of the scope of Black elites in the past few decades, Black religious leaders remain the most important leaders in Black America. Rev. Theodore Jemison's moderate National Baptist Convention, U.S.A., Inc. (the largest Black organization among Black people in the U.S.), Rev. Benjamin Hooks' liberal National Association for the Advancement of Colored People, Rev. Joseph Lowery's Left-liberal Southern Christian Leadership Conference (founded by the late Rev. Martin Luther King, Jr.), Rev. Herbert Daughtry's Leftist National Black United Front and African Peoples' Christian Organization, and Rev. Jesse Jackson's People United to Serve Humanity exemplifies the religious hegemony of Black leadership in the U.S.A.

The crisis in Black America is threefold. First, the Black community is undergoing profound economic crisis which most visibly takes the form of unprecedented unemployment, pervasive layoffs and severe cutbacks. Second, Afro-Americans are facing a political crisis that demands redefining relations to the Democratic Party. Third, Black people are experiencing a pervasive spiritual crisis as the quotient of Black distrust of one another escalates and Black suicides and homicides proliferate. In short, Black America is at the crossroads.

The economic crisis in Black America results primarily from the international crisis of the world capitalist order. The Reagan program of reconstituting global capitalism, supported by repressive cultural sensibilities and anti-democratic restructuring, has one basic domestic thrust: vicious attacks and assaults on the fragile gains of working and poor peoples. These attacks and assaults are disproportionately targeted at peoples of color, especially Black women (who head over one-half of Black households) and Black children. And as de-industrialization proceeds in the Northeast and Midwest. Black industrial workers inordinately suffer.

The political crisis in Black America is manifest in captivity to the Democratic Party. The refusal of most Black politicians to explore new forms of political empowerment outside the Democratic Party has produced paralysis and powerlessness among actual and potential Black voters. The election of Harold Washington as mayor of Chicago revealed the limitations of relying on the Democratic Party and the strengths of community mobilizing and organizing; his election is unimaginable without the support of the Black churches in Chicago. The candidacy of Rev. Jesse Jackson in presidential primaries may point in a similar direction if he is willing to seriously challenge the Democratic Party. With the election of Washington, the campaign of Mel King in Boston, and the vast voter registration drives of Rev. Hooks' NAACP, Rev. Jackson's PUSH and Rev. Jemison's vast church network, political momentum may be gaining for such a challenge.

The spiritual crisis in Black America flows from new class and strata divisions, the impact of mass culture and the invasion of drugs in the Black communities throughout the country. The slow but sure class polarization, of the growing Black petit bourgeoisie and the increasing Black underclass, creates immense problems of Black communication. These problems have spiritual consequences in that Black distrust and disrespect produces widespread frustration and cynicism among Black people. The impact of mass culture, especially radio and television, has diminished the influence of the Black Church. Among large numbers of Black youth, it is Black music which serves as the central influence for the shaping of their psyches. Since little of this music is spiritually inspiring, Black people have less and less spiritual resources to fall back on in periods of crisis. With the invasion of drugs in the Black community—with police indifference and political silence on behalf of the white power structure—a new subculture among Black youth has emerged which thrives on criminal behavior and survives on hopelessness. Hence, prison life has become an integral component of Black working class and underclass life.

There have been four basic responses to these crises by the Black Church. First, there is the conservative alternative put forward by entrepreneurial preachers like Rev. Ike who translate vast numbers of peoples' personal despair into self-serving lucrative ends. Second, the politically cautious yet open-ended perspective of moderates like Rev. Jemison and liberals like Rev. Hooks. Third, the prophetically audacious and authentically counterhegemonic praxis of Leftists like Rev. Daughtry and Left-liberals like Rev. Lowery. And lastly, the courageous electoral campaign of Rev. Jesse Jackson.

The central role of the Black Church in Black America ensures its invidious manipulation. Given its relatively loose, uncomplicated requirements for membership and its open and easy access to leadership, the Black Church is a sitting duck for charismatic con-men. And there is a long tradition of such behavior in Afro-American Christianity. This tradition is captive to American civil religion in that it is usually couched in economic terms: The American Way of Life can be yours if you would only surrender yourself, accept Jesus Christ and financially support my ministry! The present crises in Black America have made this enticing invitation attractive to many Black evangelical Christians in deep psychological and pecuniary need. It is this conservative tradition which warrants the vehement and often vociferous criticisms directed at the Black Church by insiders and outsiders.

Yet this conservative response is not that of the majority of Black Christians. Rather the latter is the viewpoint put forward by Revs. Jemison and Hooks. After a long and drawn-out battle over the leadership of the National Baptist Convention, Rev. Jemison was able to defrock the perennial Rev. J. H. Jackson. It was Rev. J. H. Jackson who forced Rev. Martin Luther King, Jr. to break away from the National Baptist Convention in 1961 and form his own Progressive National Baptist Convention, Inc. This rupture not only weakened King's movement; it also left many Black Baptists torn between King's social gospel and the old Convention's rich heritage. My own beloved grandfather,

Rev. Clifton L. West, Sr. who pastored a church in Oklahoma for forty years struggled with this dual allegiance until his death in 1979. With the replacement of Rev. J. H. Jackson in September 1982, sighs of relief and hopes for reconciliation pervaded many Black Baptists across the country. Since Rev. Jesse Jackson's support of Rev. Jemison was crucial for his election, there is real possibility for a more prophetic outlook on behalf of the leadership of the National Baptist Convention. So far Rev. Jemison is proceeding cautiously, sending out prophetic rhetorical signs yet guarding his priestly organization from discord. For example, the over twenty-year reign of Rev. J. H. Jackson has led him to promote a ten year limit on the presidency, his friendship with Rev. Jesse Jackson has prompted him to support a vast voter registration drive and his embarrassment of the Convention's treatment of King has resulted in a $100,000 donation to Morehouse College (King's alma mater) to complete its chapel and build a monument honoring King. Rev. Jemison recently made these proposals—which were ratified by the delegates—in September 1983 at the Convention's largest gathering in its history: roughly 35,000 delegates attended its deliberations in Los Angeles. So this religious body is now experiencing new life. Whether it decides to become more openly progressive and prophetic remains an open question.

Needless to say, Rev. Hooks' NAACP is explicitly political, unashamed of its old-style liberalism and reluctant to move toward a more militant progressivism. Echoing the hidden fears and anxieties of the Black middle class and stable working class, the NAACP senses that there are new currents on the move in the Black community but, in true traditionalist style, it is unwilling to allow itself to be the guinea pig. Given its deep roots in Black churches, it is no accident that it applauds the ascendancy of Rev. Jemison while it shares his cautious perspective. In his poignant speech during the recent March on Washington, Rev. Hooks declared war on Reaganism and then proceeded to invoke the Afro-American Christian God of the oppressed and downtrodden. This unusual public display of Christian piety and belief on behalf of a leader of a Black secular organization suggests that much is stirring within him. In light of the recent internal turmoil in the NAACP (e.g., his clash with his former Chairperson of the Board, Margaret Bush Wilson) and the barrage of criticisms from various groups in the Black community, Rev. Hooks may indeed be reassessing the direction and vision of the NAACP, the most distinguished Black protest organization in Afro-American history. Rev. Hooks certainly possesses the integrity and will to change courses at this crucial historical moment; whether the NAACP has the courage and wherewithal to do so awaits to be seen.

The third response to the prevailing crises in Black America by Afro-American Christian Leftists and Left-liberals is salutary yet still marginal. It is salutary in that it speaks to the great issues of our time, e.g., Third World struggles against U.S. and/or Soviet domination, maldistribution of wealth in the world, the South African apartheid regime, etc., and links these issues to the Afro-American struggle for freedom. Under the dynamic leadership of Rev. Herbert Daughtry, the National Black United Front (composed of Black Christians, Marxists, nationalists and Left-liberals) has established itself as the leading voice of Progressive Black America. Far beyond liberalism and indifferent to social democracy, this Christian-headed group is staunchly anti-U.S. imperialist and vaguely prosocialist with a Black nationalist twist. With the founding of the African Peoples' Christian Organization in March 1983, Rev. Daughtry has extended his vision by supplementing the National Black United Front with an exclusively Christian organization, especially for those prophetic Black Christians demoralized and debilitated by the secular ideological battles in NBUF: Rev. Daughtry continues to head both organizations. Rev. Lowery's Southern Christian Leadership Conference—much like the Progressive National Baptist Convention, Inc. which still upholds the legacy of King—courageously articulates the needs and interests of the Black poor, but with much less ideological fervor and international visibility. Armed with highly talented young leaders, such as Mark Ridley-Thomas in Los Angeles, Rev. Lowery's SCLC sustains the most impressive Christian ecumenical (across Black Christian denominations) progressive group in the USA. Yet it still falls short of the comprehensive Christian analysis and vision of Rev. Daughtry's progressive NBUF and prophetic APCO.

Despite their salutary presence and potential growth, these organizations remain marginal to the conscience and praxis of Black America. The hegemony of liberal political ideology still holds fast in Black America and its Christian churches. Surely the Black working poor and underclass sense that liberalism is insufficient, yet this sense is not articulated in political forms. Even Revs. Daughtry and Lowery's groups principally lie outside of the Black underclass, with deep roots in regional sections of the country among the working poor and working class. Yet even the marginality of these groups is encouraging, for they constitute an influential marginality which puts necessary pressure on the more visible liberal organizations. They also link the rich tradition of Afro-American Christianity to more sophisticated social analyses, more inclusive moral visions and more ambitious (though propitious) political praxis.

The last response of the Black Church to the present-day crises of Black America is now a major media event: the candidacy of one of the sons of the Black Church, Rev. Jesse Jackson. This is an event of utmost importance to Black Church people. Not since the appearance of King have Black Christians had a national figure who commands so much non-Black attention. In a moving interview years ago in *Ebony magazine (the leading Black American magazine). Rev. Jesse Jackson put forward the deep Christian roots of his political practice. This kind of existential candor goes far with the Black Church. The basic issue is not the extent to which the Black Church will support Rev. Jackson, but rather the way in which the Black Church views Rev. Jackson as an extension of itself: what it has produced and given to the nation. Politically, Rev. Jackson remains close to most voting Black Americans: liberal on domestic socioeconomic issues. Left-liberal on international issues and ambivalent on cultural issues. Yet, he is much more progressive than any of the white candidates vying for the nomination of the Democratic Party. His candidacy has already broadened the perimeters of public discourse in American politics, politically enlivened many dormant Black voters and brought together the prophetic forces in the Black Church; a recent breakfast meeting of local Black leaders for Rev. Jackson held in Rev. Daughtry's The House of the Lord Church in Brooklyn illustrates this possible unity.*

So despite the numerous processes of modernization occurring in Black America, the prophetic Black Church remains the major source for political leadership. But if it is to more adequately meet the present challenges, it must move toward more sophisticated social analyses of the economic depression in Black America. Such analyses should highlight the shifting international division of labor and the dominant role of U.S. corporate power. This analysis should be guided by an egalitarian vision which embraces the needs of working class and underclass Hispanics, Asians, women, whites, as well as the concerns of ecologists, feminists and peace activists. Lastly, this analysis and vision must be coupled with a spiritual awakening which combats the rapacious hedonism and narcissism in late U.S. capitalist culture, thereby enabling a more virtuous and viable Left.

Source

Cornel West, "The Black Church and Socialist Politics," *Third World Socialists: A Political Journal on the Theory and Practice of Liberation* 1 (summer 1984): 16–19.

Selected Bibliography

hooks, bell and Cornel West. *Breaking Bread: Insurgent Black Intellectual Life*. Boston: South End Press, 1991.

Lerner, Michael and Cornel West. *Jews & Blacks: A Dialogue on Race, Religion, and Culture in America*. New York: Plume, 1996.

West, Cornel. *The American Evasion of Philosophy: A Genealogy of Pragmatism*. Madison: University of Wisconsin Press, 1989.

—— *The Cornel West Reader*. New York: Basic Civitas Books, 1999.

—— *Keeping Faith: Philosophy and Race in America*. New York: Routledge, 1993.

—— *Race Matters*. Boston: Beacon Press, 1993.

fourteen

A Torchlight for America

Louis Farrakhan (1933–) is the controversial leader of the Nation of Islam (NOI), a black religious organization that combines some of the beliefs of traditional Islam with a philosophy of black nationalism, personal responsibility, and self-reliance from white racism and economic injustice. In his speech "A Torchlight for America," Farrakhan indicts white America for its failure to live up to the message of Christ and extols the Golden Rule: do unto others as you would have them do unto you, and love for your brother what you love for yourself.

Born Louis Eugene Walcott in Roxbury, Massachusetts, Farrakhan earned a reputation as a talented violinist while he was only a small child. In 1955 he joined the NOI, and following Malcolm X's death by assassination in 1965, Farrakhan emerged as one of the NOI's principal spokespersons. His national profile rose markedly in the 1980s, and he was frequently accused of black racism and anti-Semitism. In 1995, Farrakhan organized the Million Man March in Washington, D.C., which drew hundreds of thousands of black men who vowed to renew their commitments to the African American community.

Nineteen ninety-two marked the quincentennial year of the opening up of the "New World" for the purpose of Western domination. Christopher Columbus is said to have "discovered" this continent in 1492. Since 1492 the Native American people have been misused, abused and then neglected. Since 1555, the black people brought to these shores in chains have also been misused, abused and now remain neglected.

In the official History of the Seal of the United States, published by the Department of State in 1909, Gaillard Hunt wrote that late in the afternoon of July 4, 1776, The Continental Congress resolved that Dr. Benjamin Franklin, Mr. John Adams and Mr. Thomas Jefferson be a committee to prepare a device for a Seal of the United States of America. In the design proposed by the first committee, the obverse (face) of the Seal was a coat of arms in six quarters, with emblems representing England, Scotland, Ireland, France, Germany and Holland, the countries from which the new nation had been peopled. The Eye of Providence in a radiant triangle, and the motto E PLURIBUS UNUM were also proposed for the obverse.

Even though the country was populated by so-called Indians, and black slaves were brought to build the country, the official Seal of the country was never designed to reflect our presence, only that of the European immigrants. The Seal and the Constitution reflect the thinking of the founding fathers that this was to be a nation by white people and for white people. Native Americans, blacks and all other non-white people were to be the burden bearers for the "real" citizens of this nation.

For the reverse (back) of the Seal, the committee suggested a picture of Pharaoh sitting in an open chariot with a crown on his head and a sword in his hand, passing through the divided waters of the Red Sea in pursuit of the Israelites. Hovering over the sea was to be shown a pillar of fire in a cloud, expressive of the Divine presence and command. Rays from this pillar of fire were to be shown beaming on Moses, standing on the shore and extending his hand over the sea, causing it to overwhelm Pharaoh. The motto for the reverse was: REBELLION TO TYRANTS IS OBEDIENCE TO GOD.

The design reveals the spiritual blindness inherent in the genesis of the United States. The founding fathers upheld obedience to God as their symbol while practicing genocide, colonialism and slavery among the native population and our forebears.

It was Thomas Jefferson who said, "I tremble for my country when I reflect that God is just and that His justice cannot sleep forever." It was George Washington who said that he feared the slaves would become a most troublesome species of property before too many years passed over our heads.

America is faced with the political and moral dilemma of reconciling pluralism and the inclusion of non-whites with the democratic ideas espoused by the founding fathers. This is not a democracy in the fullest meaning of the word. Racism has to be overcome in order to gain a full expression of E Pluribus

Unum (out of the many, one). Is E Pluribus Unum meant to be interpreted as "out of the many white ethnic strains, one people," or "out of the many strains, white, black and other, one people?"

Within the walls of this country there are two Americas, separate and unequal, white and black (including other non-whites). In order to reconcile these two Americas, the American people must come to terms with the limited vision of the founding fathers. The founding fathers didn't envision the current population profile, where the numbers of black and Hispanic people are growing, threatening the majority status of whites. Those who desire to maintain the old vision of white rule under the name of democracy and pluralism will no longer be able to continue the subjugation of non-whites. Now is the time for freedom, justice and equality for those who have been deprived of it.

It was made easy for whites to subjugate others because they were taught to see blacks and Native Americans as heathen, savage and sub-human. This, in their minds, justified their not recognizing us as equal citizens in this country. Bearing this in mind, that the original Seal should include a picture of Pharaoh pursuing the Israelites is not without great significance. That it should include a pillar of fire in a cloud, beaming down on Moses, is not without significance for this day and time.

In my judgment, the original Seal was inspired to give America a picture of what her future could become if she did not do justice by the Native Americans and by the blacks who were brought here as her slaves.

Even though America says she wants change and renewal, she must deal with the basis of this country's woes. Either she must evolve from the limited vision of the founding fathers and repudiate that vision, or, America must say that she believes in the true vision of the founding fathers and that the darker people will never be respected as equals inside of this nation.

God has set His hand against this economy as He set His hand against the riches of Egypt. The only way to fix this economy is to deal with greed, basic immorality and the unwanted presence of 30 million or more black people and 2 million Native Americans whose cry for justice has entered the ears of God.

Integration, as it has been conceived, is not working to bring true freedom, justice and equality to America's former slaves. It is not working because it was not properly motivated and is not in harmony with the mandate of the time.

We do not want or need that kind of integration that literally results in nothing in terms of economic advancement for our people. The Honorable Elijah Muhammad[1] said that if we wanted better relations between black and white, he could show us how to achieve this. As black people, we first have to come into a knowledge of self that will help us make ourselves worthy of respect and our communities decent places in which to live. We must begin to do something for self. This act on our part will earn the respect of self as well as others. It will ultimately help us to have better relations with those who see us as an unwanted burden in this society.

The focus of black people should be on elevating self, not on trying to force ourselves into the communities of white people. Self-respecting white men do not want to see us with their women. One way to have good race relations is to leave their women and girls alone. Some of us have a false love for the white woman, and some of us have a false love for the white man. Some want the former slavemaster's woman because the former slavemaster has always had free access to our women, and some want the white man because he wields great power in the society.

In a painful recount of the position our freed forebears found themselves in after Emancipation, W. E. B. Du Bois[2] wrote:

> "For the first time he sought to analyze the burden he bore upon his back, that deadweight of social degradation partially masked behind a half-named Negro problem. He felt his poverty; without a cent, without a home, without land, tools, or savings, he had entered into competition with rich, landed, skilled neighbors. To be a poor man is hard, but to be a poor race in a land of dollars is the very bottom of hardships. He felt the weight of his ignorance, not simply of letters, but life, of business, of the humanities; the accumulated sloth and shirking and awkwardness of decades and centuries shackled his hands and feet. Nor was his burden all poverty and ignorance. The red stain of bastardy, which two centuries of systematic legal defilement of Negro women had stamped upon his race, meant not only the loss of ancient African chastity, but also the hereditary weight of a mass of corruption from white adulterers, threatening almost the obliteration of the Negro home."

At one time, white folks held up the Cadillac as the symbol of success. We who were not successful, wanted to at least have the symbol of success, so we aspired to own a Cadillac. Likewise, white men have held up white women as the best and most beautiful women on the Earth. To have a loving relationship with her—to marry her or to have sex with her—to many of our black men is the epitome of being accepted and successful.

The Honorable Elijah Muhammad taught us to take our own women and girls and respect, honor and protect them. He taught us to work hard to produce a future for our children; to rid ourselves of alcohol, tobacco, gambling, laziness and dependency; and to work to make our neighborhoods decent places for us to live. This kind of action on our part could lead to a healthier relationship between the races.

Certainly if we look at our females as that which God produced for us, then we would have to expect the white man to leave our women and girls alone. True love, however, transcends color and race. We must ask the question of those who have gone the way of having interracial relations, is the love a true love, or is it merely an acting out of a corrupted fantasy which is held by both black and white? When we, as a people, are healed of our mental, moral and spiritual sickness, then maybe we can look across racial lines and see the true value and worth of one another. However, healing of the deadly diseases of white supremacy and black inferiority has to take place first!

I have to stand and speak for the voiceless, whose leadership has often been quiet or weak in the face of an open enemy. Although I have been misrepresented by the media, here is a new opportunity to receive my message and judge it against the criterion of truth.

Am I really an anti-Semite? Am I really a hater? Can these charges really be proven? When people disagree, the intelligent and rational thing to do is to have a dialogue. Perhaps through dialogue differences can be reconciled. If anything that I have said or written is proved to be a lie, then I will retract my words and apologize before the world.

The Honorable Elijah Muhammad taught us that the way to stop backbiting and slander is to gather the parties together and allow them to present their charges and evidence to each other's face, then we will know where the truth rests and where the lie rests. We are willing to sit and meet before the world and discuss our position. We recognize the ability of the American government and business community to help the black community. The Nation of Islam, in turn, can help America solve its problems. But we cannot solve any problems by bowing down to falsehood.

The Honorable Elijah Muhammad pointed out to us that Babylon,[3] that great and wicked city, could have been healed. She was not healed because she refused to listen to guidance coming to her kings from the mouth of one of her Hebrew slaves. He pointed this out to indicate that America, though dying, can also be healed.

In the design for the original Seal for this country, the pillar of fire in a cloud, expressive of the Divine presence and command—that was also written of in the Bible as seen in a vision by Ezekiel[4]—is now a reality in America. In the Seal's design, the reason that Pharaoh[5] was depicted with a sword in his hand is to symbolize America's pursuit of world dominion by way of skilled machinations backed up by force. America has held a whole nation in captivity for over 400 years—even as Pharaoh did in the biblical history of Moses[6] and the ancient Hebrews—and she has done so by use of force and wicked machinations. The beam of light that was seen shining down on the face of Moses in the design for the original Seal of this country is a sign that the light from God is now beaming down on one from among the ex-slaves. In that light is the guidance that can heal America, the modern Babylon and the modern Egypt. Will America be healed?

A man was born in Georgia and was privileged to meet a Master Teacher, Who gave him the keys for liberating the minds of our people to form the true basis of a new world order. He laid the foundation upon which I stand today. On October 7, 1897, in a little town called Sandersville, Georgia, mother Marie

(Poole) Muhammad gave birth to a noble black man who was given a great light by his Teacher, Master Fard Muhammad, so that a light would be lifted up in the midst of gross darkness. That light is the teachings of the Honorable Elijah Muhammad, which I am sharing with America right now.

We have the torchlight. America is being challenged to take the bushel basket off the light. Let us sit down and talk about bringing real solutions before the American people, as civilized people should and are obligated to do.

The Kingdom of God is an egalitarian kingdom structured on truth, where each of us will be treated with fairness and justice. America could become the basis for the Kingdom of God. She has within her borders every nation, kindred and tongue. If they could be made peaceful, productive and mutually respecting, you would have the basis for the Kingdom of God right here on earth.

However, what America does not have is the teaching that would make one people out of the many creeds, colors and nationalities that occupy this land. That teaching cannot be the skilled wisdom from the political leadership that subordinates the language and culture of America's diverse members, while lifting the American way of life as the model—which is very racist and white supremacist in nature. The current American way of life can only produce an apparent unity among caucasians, because it negates the diversity and beauty of the non-white population. You can never achieve unity, or E Pluribus Unum, in this country under the doctrine of white supremacy.

America needs a spiritual healing. In the scriptures it reads, *"If my people, which are called by my name, shall humble themselves and pray, and seek my face, and turn from their wicked ways, then will I bear from heaven, and will forgive their sin, and will heal their land."* (II Chronicles 7:14) This is the promise of God for us, and for all of America. Moses and Aaron set two signs before the people, one of life and a blessing, and the other of death and a cursing. He said, " . . . *choose life, that both thou and thy seed may live."* (Deuteronomy 30:19) The Honorable Elijah Muhammad and Louis Farrakhan say to America the same.

We need to humble ourselves and pray to Allah, God, so that we might receive that same spiritual message that Paul refers to in his words concerning Christ. Paul said, in Christ, *"There is no Jew nor Greek, there is neither bond nor free, there is neither male nor female: for ye are all one in Christ Jesus."* (Galatians 3:28) Paul envisioned the end of nationalism, the end of classism and the end of sexism. He envisioned it through the true message of the man called Christ.

Even though America claims to be a Christian country, America, evidently, has missed the message of Christ, or has yet to receive His true message. However, once that true message is given, those who truly want righteousness, justice and peace will gravitate toward that message and they could form the basis of the Kingdom of God on earth. This can be achieved by establishing the truth that frees white people from the sickness of white supremacy and frees black people from the sickness of black inferiority, and lifts us up from an inferior condition and mentality—setting a new standard by which we all should live. The new standard is duty to God and service to our fellow man.

The Honorable Elijah Muhammad taught us that the greatest of all religious principles is to follow the Golden Rule: Do unto others as you would have them do unto you, and love for your brother what you love for yourself.

Notes

1. Elijah Muhammad (1897–1975), African American religious and political leader; headed the Nation of Islam.
2. W. E. B. Du Bois (1868–1963), African American intellectual and civil rights leader.
3. Ancient city of Mesopotamia.
4. In the Bible, Ezekiel (592–570 B.C.) preached to the Jews of Babylonian captivity.
5. King of ancient Egypt.
6. Hebrew lawgiver. In the Bible, he lived in constant touch with God.

Source

Louis Farrakhan, *A Torchlight for America,* 151–60 (Chicago: FCN, 1993).

Selected Bibliography

Alexander, Amy. *The Farrakhan Factor: African-American Writers on Leadership, Nationhood, and Minister Louis Farrakhan.* New York: Grove Press, 1997.

Magida, Arthur J. *Prophet of Rage: A Life of Louis Farrakhan and His Nation.* New York: Basic Books, 1996.

Marable, Manning. *Black Leadership.* New York: Columbia University Press, 1998.

Singh, Robert. *The Farrakhan Phenomenon: Race, Reaction, and the Paranoid Style in America.* Washington, D.C.: Georgetown University Press, 1997.

Van Deburg, William. *Modern Black Nationalism: From Marcus Garvey to Louis Farrakhan.* New York: New York University Press, 1997.

Index

Names are in bold; titles of works are in italics, and first lines of poems and songs are in roman.

Acknowledgments

Every effort has been made to trace copyright holders and give proper credit for all copyrighted material used in this book. The editor regrets if there are any oversights. The publisher will be pleased to hear from any copyright holders not acknowledged in this edition so that a correction might be made at the next available opportunity.

Chapter One

W.E.B. Du Bois, "The Damnation of Women," from *Darkwater: Voices from Within the Veil* (New York: Harcourt, Brace & Howe, 1920). Reprinted with the permission of David Graham Du Bois.

Alice Moore Dunbar-Nelson, "Women's Most Serious Problem," from *The Messenger* 9, no. 3 (February 1927): 73. Reprinted by permission of The Association for the Study of African American Life and History, Inc.

Marita Bonner, "On Being Young—a Woman—and Colored," from *Frye Street and Environs: The Collected Works of Marita Bonner*, edited by Joyce Flynn. Copyright © 1987 by Joyce Flynn and Joyce Occomy Stricklin. Reprinted with the permission of the Beacon Press, Boston.

Eldridge Cleaver, "To All Black Women, from All Black Men," in *Soul on Ice* (New York: McGraw–Hill, 1968), 205–10. Reprinted by permission of The McGraw–Hill Companies.

Frances M. Beal, "Double Jeopardy: To Be Black and Female," from *Sisterhood Is Powerful: An Anthology of Writings from the Women's Liberation Movement*, edited by Robin Morgan (New York: Random House, 1970). Reprinted with the permission of the author.

Audre Lorde, "Feminism and Black Liberation," from *The Black Scholar* 10 (May–June 1979). Copyright © 1979 by Audre Lorde. Reprinted with the permission of the Charlotte Sheedy Literary Agency.

Angela Davis, "The Approaching Obsolescence of Housework: A Working Class Perspective," from *Women, Race, and Class*. Copyright © 1981 by Angela Davis. Used by permission of Random House, Inc.

"Statement of Anita Hill to the Senate Judiciary Committee," in *African American Women Speak Out on Anita Hill–Clarence Thomas,* edited by Geneva Smitherman. Copyright © 1995 by Wayne State University Press. Reprinted with permission of the Wayne State University Press.

Barbara Smith, "Establishing Black Feminism," from *Souls: A Critical Journal of Black Politics, Culture and Society* 2 (Fall 2000). Copyright © 2000 by the Institute for Research in African-American Studies. Reprinted with permission.

Kristen Clark, "Toward a Black Feminist Liberation Agenda: Race Gender and Violence," from *Souls: A Critical Journal of Black Politics, Culture, and Society* 2, no. 4 (fall 2000): 80–88. Copyright © 2000 by the Institute for Research in African-American Studies. Reprinted with permission.

Chapter Two

Margaret Walker, "For My People," from *This Is My Century: New and Collected Poems*. Copyright © 1989 by Margaret Walker Alexander. Reprinted with the permission of The University of Georgia Press.

Ella Baker, as quoted in *Moving the Mountain: Women Working for Social Change,* edited by Ella Cantarow, copyright © 1980 by the Feminist Press, by permission of the Feminist Press at the City University of New York, www.feministpress.org.

James Baldwin, excerpt from the essay "Notes of a Native Son," from *Notes of a Native Son,* 85–98. Copyright © 1955, renewed 1983, by James Baldwin. Reprinted by permission of Beacon Press, Boston.

Henry Louis Gates Jr., "Playing Hardball," from *Colored People: A Memoir,* 78–88. Copyright © 1994 by Henry Louis Gates Jr. Used by permission of Alfred A. Knopf, a division of Random House, Inc.

Maya Angelou, "From a Black Woman to a Black Man," from *Million Man March/Day of Absence Commemorative Anthology* (Chicago: Third World Press, 1996). Copyright © 1995 by Maya Angelou. Reprinted with the permission of The Helen Brann Agency, Inc.

Manning Marable, "In My Father's House," in *Father Songs: Testimonials by African-American Sons and Daughters*, edited by Gloria Wade Gayles (Boston: Beacon Press, 1997), 177–85. Reprinted by permission of Manning Marable.

Maulana Karenga, "Kwanzaa and the Ethics of Sharing: Forging Our Future in a New Era," from www.OfficialKwanzaaWebsite.org/message99.html (accessed June 10, 2002). Reprinted with the permission of Dr. Maulana Karenga.

Chapter Three

Marcus Garvey, "Declaration of the Rights of Negro Peoples of the World," 135–43. Reprinted with the permission of Scribner, a division of Simon & Schuster Adult Publishing Group, from *Philosophy and Opinions of Marcus Garvey*, edited by Amy Jacques-Garvey. Copyright © 1923, 1925 Amy Jacques-Garvey; copyrights renewed.

Countee Cullen, "Heritage," from *Color*. Copyright © 1925 by Harper & Brothers, renewed © 1969 by Ida M. Cullen. Reprinted with the permission of Thompson and Thompson, as agents for the Estate of Countee Cullen.

Paul Robeson, "Africa Calls—Will You Help?" and "The Negro People and the Soviet Union," from *Paul Robeson Speaks: Writings, Speeches, Interviews, 1918–1974*, edited by Philip S. Foner. Copyright © 1978. Reprinted with the permission of Brunner/Mazel, Inc., a part of The Taylor & Francis Group.

El-Shabazz, El Hajj Malik [Malcolm X], "Letter from Jedda, Saudi Arabia" (April 1964) and "Letter from Accra, Ghana" (May 1964), in *Malcolm X Speaks: Selected Speeches and Statements*, edited by George Breitman (New York: Merit Publishers, 1965), 74–78. Copyright © 1965, 1989 by Betty Shabazz and Pathfinder Press. Reprinted by permission.

Audre Lorde, "Sisterhood and Survival," from *The Black Scholar* 10 (March–April 1986). Copyright © 1986 by Audre Lorde. Reprinted with the permission of the Charlotte Sheedy Literary Agency. "Grenada Revisited: An Interim Report," from *Sister Outsider*. Originally published in *The Black Scholar* 10 (January–February 1984): 21–29. Copyright © 1984 by Audre Lorde. Reprinted with the permission of The Crossing Press, a division Ten Speed Press, Berkeley, CA 94707, www.tenspeed.com.

Assata Shakur, "The Continuity of Struggle," from *Souls: A Critical Journal of Black Politics, Culture, and Society* 1 (Spring 1999): 93. Copyright © 1999 by the Institute for Research in African-American Studies. Reprinted with permission.

Chapter Four

W.E.B. Du Bois, "Of Mr. Booker T. Washington and Others," from *The Souls of Black Folk* (Chicago: A.C. McClurg, 1903). Reprinted with the permission of David Graham Du Bois.

Martin Luther King Jr., "Letter from a Birmingham Jail," from *Why We Can't Wait*. Copyright © 1963 by Dr. Martin Luther King Jr.; copyright renewed 1991 by Coretta Scott King. Reprinted by arrangement with the Estate of Martin Luther King Jr., c/o Writer's House as agent from the proprietor, New York, New York.

Bayard Rustin, "From Protest to Politics: The Future of the Civil Rights Movement," from *Commentary* (February 1965). Reprinted with the permission of *Commentary.*

Jesse Jackson, "The Struggle Continues," in *Keep Hope Alive: Jesse Jackson's 1988 Presidential Campaign: A Collection of Major Speeches, Issue Papers, Photographs, and Campaign Analysis,* (Keep Hope Alive PAC and South End Press, 1989), 213–18. Reprinted by permission of South End Press.

Chapter Five

Fannie Lou Hamer, "To Praise Our Bridges," from *To Praise Our Bridges: An Autobiography of Mrs. Fanny Lou Hamer* (Jackson, MS: KIPCO, 1967). Reprinted with the permission of Arybie Rose, Fannie Lou Hamer Living Memorial Charitable Trust Fund, and the Hamer family.

Robert F. Williams, "The Resistant Spirit: Why Do I Speak from Exile?" from *The Crusader.* Reprinted with the permission of Mabel Williams and The Robert F. Williams Memorial Fund.

George Jackson, "Letter to Fay Stender" (April 1970), from *Soledad Brother: The Prison Letters of George Jackson.* Copyright © 1970. Reprinted with the permission of IMG/Bach Literary Agency.

Angela Y. Davis, "The Legacy of George Jackson," from *Daily World* (August 25, 1971). Copyright © 1971 by Angela Y. Davis. Reprinted with the permission of the author.

Mumia Abu-Jumal, "B-Block Days and Nightmares." Reprinted with permission from the April 23, 1990, issue of *The Nation.*

Chapter Six

Jean Toomer, "Harvest Song," from *Cane.* Copyright © 1923 by Boni & Liveright, renewed 1951 by Jean Toomer. Used by permission of Liveright Publishing Corporation.

Langston Hughes, "A Song to a Negro Wash-woman," from *Collected Poems.* Copyright © 1994 by The Estate of Langston Hughes. Reprinted with the permission of Alfred A. Knopf, a division of Random House, Inc.

A. Phillip Randolph, "Why Should We March?" from *Survey Graphic* 31 (November 1942): 488–89. Reprinted by permission.

Richard Wright, "A Record of Childhood and Youth," from *Black Boy: A Record of Childhood and Youth.* Copyright © 1937, 1942, 1944, 1945 by Richard Wright. Reprinted with the permission of HarperCollins Publishers, Inc.

William H. Simons, "A Giant Step Toward Unity," from *Daily World* (February 10, 1973). Copyright © 1973 by William H. Simons. Reprinted with the permission of the author.

Nate Shaw (Ned Cobb), excerpt from *All God's Dangers: The Life of Nate Shaw,* compiled by Theodore Rosengarten. Copyright © 1974 by Theodore Rosengarten. Reprinted with the permission of Alfred A. Knopf, a division of Random House, Inc.

Chapter Seven

James Weldon Johnson, "Our Democracy and the Ballot," from *Negro Orators and Their Orations*, edited by Carter G. Woodson, 1925. Reprinted by permission of The Association for the Study of African American Life and History, Inc.

Archibald Grimké, "The Shame of America," from *The Shame of America; or, The Negroes Case Against the Republic,* 1924. Reprinted by permission of The Association for The Study of African American Life and History, Inc.

William Pickens, "The Kind of Democracy the Negro Race Expects," from *Negro Orators and Their Orations*, edited by Carter G. Woodson, 1925. Reprinted by permission of The Association for the Study of African American Life and History, Inc.

Langston Hughes, "Democracy," "Refugee in America," and "Freedom's Plow," from *Collected Poems*. Copyright © 1994 by The Estate of Langston Hughes. Reprinted with the permission of Alfred A. Knopf, a division of Random House, Inc.

Paul Robeson, "I, Too, Am American," from *Paul Robeson Speaks: Writings, Speeches, Interviews, 1918–1974*, edited by Philip S. Foner. Copyright © 1978. Reprinted with the permission of Brunner/Mazel, Inc., a part of The Taylor & Francis Group.

James Baldwin, "The American Dream and the American Negro," from *The New York Times Magazine* (March 7, 1965), 32–35. Copyright © 1965 by The New York Times Company. Reprinted with permission.

Barbara Jordan, "Who Then Will Speak for the Common Good?" (speech at the Democratic National Convention, New York, 1976). Reprinted with the permission of the Robert James Terry Library, Texas Southern University.

Chapter Eight

Alain Locke, "The Negro Spirituals," from *The New Negro: An Interpretation*. Copyright © 1925 by Albert & Charles Boni, Inc. Reprinted with the permission of Scribner, an imprint of Simon & Schuster Adult Publishing Group.

James Weldon Johnson, "The Dilemma of the Negro Author," from *The American Mercury* (December 1928). Copyright © 1928 by James Weldon Johnson. Reprinted with the permission of The Estate of James Weldon Johnson.

Duke Ellington and Ivie Anderson, "It Don't Mean a Thing (If It Ain't Got That Swing)," (Famous Music Co./ASCAP). Copyright © 1932 Famous Music Corp. Copyright renewed. All rights reserved. Reprinted by permission.

Richard Wright, "High Tide in Harlem: Joe Louis as a Symbol of Freedom," from *New Masses* (July 5, 1938). Copyright © 1938 by Richard Wright. Reprinted with the permission of John Hawkins & Associates, Inc.

Gil Scott-Heron, "The Revolution Will Not Be Televised," from *So Far, So Good*. Copyright © 1990 by Gil Scott-Heron. Reprinted with the permission of Third World Press, Inc., Chicago, Illinois.

Ellen Holly, "Where Are the Films About Real Black Men and Women?" from *Freedomways* 14, no. 3 (third quarter, 1974). Copyright © 1974 by Ellen Holly. Reprinted with the permission of the author.

Ralph Ellison, "What America Would Be Like Without Blacks," from *Going Through the Territory*. Copyright © 1986 by Ralph Ellison. Reprinted with the permission of Random House, Inc.

Michael Eric Dyson, "O. J. Simpson and Our Trial by Fire," from *Between God and Gangsta Rap*. Copyright © 1996 by Michael Eric Dyson. Reprinted with the permission of Oxford University Press, Inc.

Chapter Nine

James Weldon Johnson, "Go Down Death—A Funeral Sermon," from *God's Trombones*. Copyright © 1927 by The Viking Press, Inc., renewed © 1955 by Grace Neil Johnson. Used by permission of Viking Penguin, a division of Penguin Putnam, Inc.

Zora Neale Hurston, "Faith Hasn't Got No Eyes," from *Jonah's Gourd Vine*. Copyright © 1934 by Zora Neale Hurston, renewed © 1962 by John C. Hurston. Reprinted by permission of HarperCollins Publishers, Inc.

Langston Hughes, "Salvation," from *The Big Sea* by Langston Hughes. Copyright © 1940 by Langston Hughes. Copyright © 1968 by Arna Bontmeps and George Huston Bass. Reprinted by permission of Hill and Wang, a division of Farrar, Strauss, and Giroux, LLC.

Martin Luther King Jr., "The Most Durable Power," from *The Christian Century* (June 1957): 708. Reprinted in *Testament of Hope: The Essential Writings and Speeches of Martin Luther King, Jr.*, edited by James Melvin Washington. Copyright © 1968 by Martin Luther King Jr.; copyright renewed 1996 by Coretta Scott King. Reprinted by arrangement with the Estate of Martin Luther King, Jr., c/o Writer's House as agent from the proprietor, New York, New York.

James H. Cone, excerpt from *Black Theology and Black Power*. Copyright © 1969. Reprinted with the permission of The Crossroad Publishing Company, Inc.

Cornel West, "The Black Church and Socialist Politics," from *Prophetic Fragments*. Copyright © 1988 by Wm. B. Eerdmans Publishing Company, Grand Rapids, Michigan. Reprinted with permission.

Louis Farrakhan, excerpt from *A Torchlight for America*. Copyright © 1993. Reprinted with the permission of FCN Publishing Company.